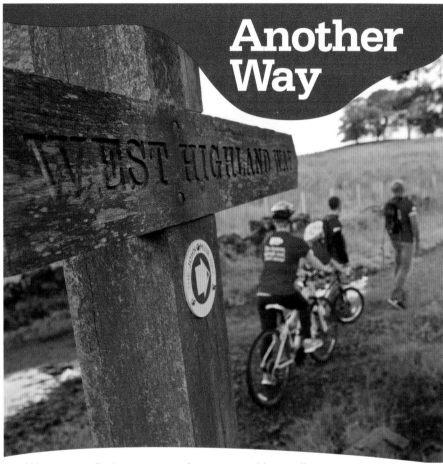

We want to find a **way** out of poverty and inequality.

We believe there is **another way** to live.

Together we can…

We invite you to join us in 2016, walking and cycling along some of Scotland's Ways to find another way for the world's poorest communities.

 **Find out more and join us:**
christianaid.org.uk/anotherway

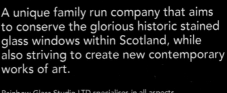

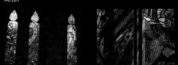

Could You Be Their Chaplain?

As an RAF chaplain you will be involved in the lives of our personnel, regardless of their rank or religious beliefs. You will provide vital religious, pastoral and ethical support to service personnel, their families and the wider RAF community. While exploring innovative ways of engaging with them, you will also fulfil the more traditional clerical roles. Partners and families are well cared for and the RAF provides excellent in-service training and education opportunities.

We have vacancies for full-time and spare-time chaplains.

Produced by Air Media Centre, HQ Air Command. 1416_14CR ©UK MOD Crown Copyright, 2015

www.raf.mod.uk/chaplains

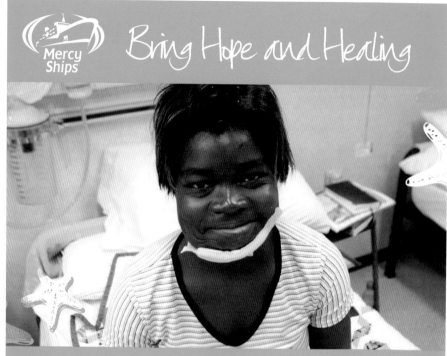

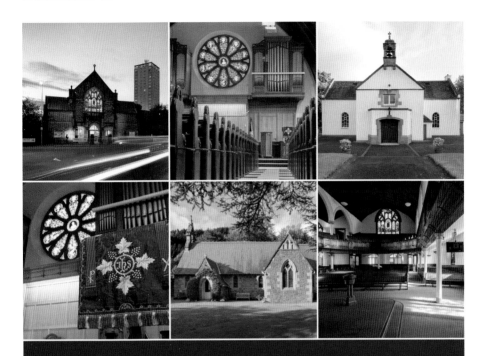

The Church of Scotland
YEAR BOOK
2015/2016

Editor
Douglas Galbraith

Published on behalf of
THE CHURCH OF SCOTLAND
by SAINT ANDREW PRESS
121 George Street, Edinburgh EH2 4YN

THE OFFICES OF THE CHURCH

121 George Street   Tel: 0131-225 5722
Edinburgh EH2 4YN   Fax: 0131-220 3113
                                          Website: www.churchofscotland.org.uk/

Office Hours: Monday–Friday 9:00am–5:00pm
Facilities Manager: Carole Tait 0131-240 2214

THE COUNCILS OF THE CHURCH
The following five Councils of the Church operate from the Church Offices, 121 George Street, Edinburgh EH2 4YN (Tel: 0131-225 5722):

- The Council of Assembly
- The Church and Society Council   E-mail: churchandsociety@churchofscotland.org.uk
- The Ministries Council   E-mail: ministries@churchofscotland.org.uk
- The Mission and Discipleship Council E-mail: mandd@churchofscotland.org.uk
- The World Mission Council   E-mail: world@churchofscotland.org.uk

The Social Care Council (CrossReach) operates from Charis House, 47 Milton Road East, Edinburgh
EH15 2SR   Tel: 0131-657 2000
                                                            Fax: 0131-657 5000
                                               E-mail: info@crossreach.org.uk
                                               Website: www.crossreach.org.uk

SCOTTISH CHARITY NUMBERS
The Church of Scotland: unincorporated Councils and Committees   SC011353
The Church of Scotland General Trustees   SC014574
The Church of Scotland Investors Trust   SC022884
The Church of Scotland Trust   SC020269
(For the Scottish Charity Numbers of congregations, see Section 7)

First published in 2015 by SAINT ANDREW PRESS, 121 George Street, Edinburgh EH2 4YN on behalf of THE CHURCH of SCOTLAND

Copyright © THE CHURCH of SCOTLAND, 2015

ISBN 978-0-86153-964-2

It is the Publisher's policy only to use papers that are natural and recyclable and that have been manufactured from timber grown in renewable, properly managed forests. All of the manufacturing processes of the papers are expected to conform to the environmental regulations of the country of origin.

Acceptance of advertisements for inclusion in the *Church of Scotland Year Book* does not imply endorsement of the goods or services or of any views expressed within the advertisements.

British Library Cataloguing in Publication Data
    A catalogue record for this book is available from the British Library.

Printed and bound by Bell and Bain Ltd, Glasgow

QUICK DIRECTORY

Action of Churches Together in Scotland (ACTS) 01259 216980
Christian Aid London 020 7620 4444
Christian Aid Scotland 0141-221 7475
Church and Society Council 0131-240 2206
Church of Scotland Insurance Co. Ltd 0131-220 4119
Conforti Institute 01236 607120
Council of Assembly 0131-240 2229
CrossReach 0131-657 2000
Eco-Congregation Scotland 0131-240 2274
Ecumenical Officer 0131-240 2208
Gartmore House 01877 382991
Glasgow Lodging House Mission 0141-552 0285
Iona Community 0141-332 6343
Media Relations Team (Press Office) 0131-240 2278
Media Relations Team (after hours) 07854 783539
Old Churches House, Dunblane (Scottish Churches House) 01786 823663
Pension Trustees (E-mail: pensions@cofscotland.org.uk) 0131-240 2255
Place for Hope 07884 580359
Principal Clerk (E-mail: pcoffice@cofscotland.org.uk) 0131-240 2240
Priority Areas Office 0141-248 2905
Safeguarding Service (item 31 in Assembly Committee list) 0131-240 2256
Scottish Churches Parliamentary Office 0131-220 0246
Scottish Storytelling Centre/John Knox House/Netherbow 0131-556 9579
Year Book Editor 01592 752403

Pulpit Supply: Fee and Expenses
See www.churchofscotland.org.uk/yearbook > Section 3F

**All correspondence regarding the *Year Book* should be sent to
The Editor, *Church of Scotland Year Book*,
Saint Andrew Press, 121 George Street, Edinburgh EH2 4YN
[E-mail: yearbookeditor@cofscotland.org.uk]
Tel: 01592 752403**

GENERAL ASSEMBLY OF 2016
The General Assembly of 2016 will convene on
Saturday, 21 May 2016

CONTENTS

FROM THE MODERATOR

Over the years, the *Church of Scotland Year Book* has been for me, as for many others, a well-nigh indispensable tool of information and communication. Here in the most accessible form can be found important facts about the Church's Councils and Committees, issues of procedure, Presbytery and other personnel lists, relevant statistics, and much else. Here too are contact details for hundreds of people in the service of the Church. Several indices make the information sought easy to locate. The *Year Book* contributes well to a sense of our being, in the Church, one large and diverse family, and it serves to make communication between us so much easier.

As a publication that seeks to reflect the breadth of this family, various movements within the Church are helpfully reflected in the *Year Book*. It gives me particular pleasure that in recent years the *Year Book* has laid some importance on making a place for the Gaelic language – both in the Moderator's preface and in the pages at the end of section two, where some discussion takes place, in both languages, about the use of Gaelic. This section highlights various ways in which the Church of Scotland seeks to continue and develop its support for the language. At a time of growing interest in Gaelic language and culture in wider society, it is my hope that further ways will be found to enable this precious part of our inheritance to bring enrichment to the Church and to contribute to its vital mission in our country.

We are deeply in the debt of the Editor and those who assist him for their extensive and valued labours in compiling this most recent edition. It gives me great pleasure to commend this valuable publication and I trust you will find it as useful in your work throughout the year as I am sure I shall continue to do.

Angus Morrison

ON MHODERATOR

Thar nam bliadhnachan, tha *Leabhar Bliadhnail Eaglais na h-Alba* air a bhith dhòmhsa, agus do dh'iomadh neach eile, na phìos-acfhainn a tha na bhunait do ar dòighean-conaltraidh agus ar modhan-fiosrachaidh. An seo, anns an dòigh as fhasa as urrainn, gheibhear fiosrachadh air leth feumail mu Chomhairlean is Comadaidhean na h-Eaglais, gnothaichean a bhuineas ri dòighean-làimhseachaidh, a' Chlèir agus liostaichean pearsanta eile, àireamhan a chuidicheas sinn, agus iomadh rud eile. An seo cuideachd, tha mion-fhiosrachadh air mar a lorgar ceudan de dhaoine a tha a' saothrachadh às leth na h-Eaglais. Tha dòrlach chlàr ann leis am faighear gu furasda am fiosrachadh a tha sinn a' sireadh. Tha an *Leabhar Bliadhnail* a' neartachadh ar dàimhean, anns an eaglais, mar aon teaghlach mòr, iomadh-fhillte, agus tha e a' dèanamh ar conaltraidh mòran nas fhasa.

Mar fhoillseachadh a tha a' feuchainn ri leud an teaghlaich seo a chur an cèill, tha deifir ghluasadan am broinn na h-eaglais air an toirt am follais gu feumail anns an *Leabhar Bhliadhnail*. Tha e a' toirt toileachadh sònraichte dhomh gun do rinn an *Leabhar Bliadhnail*, o chionn grunnan bhliadhachan, oidhirp air àite a thoirt don Ghàidhlig – an dà chuid ann an iomradh-toisich a' Mhodaràtair, agus anns na duilleagan aig deireadh an dara earrainn, far a bheil tomhas de dheasbad air cleachdadh na Gàidhlig nar measg. Tha an earrann seo a' soilleireachadh nan deifir dhòighean anns a bheil Eaglais na h-Alba a' feuchainn ri a taic don Ghàidhlig a neartachadh agus a leasachadh. Aig àm nuair a tha ùidh anns a' Ghàidhlig a' sìor fhàs nar co-chomann anns an fharsaingeachd, tha mise an dòchas gum faighear dòighean a bharrachd air an eaglais a bheairteachadh tron phàirt phrìseil seo de ar dualchas, agus a teachdaireachd bhunaiteach don dùthaich gu lèir a chur am meud. Tha sinn fada an comain an Fhir-deasachaidh agus nan daoine a tha a' toirt taic dha airson an saothrach, a tha an dà chuid farsaing is luachmhor leinn, ann a bhith a' cruinneachadh na tha anns an deasachadh as ùire seo. Tha e a' toirt toileachadh mòr da-rìribh dhòmhsa a bhith a' moladh an leabhrain fheumail seo, agus tha mi an dòchas gun dèan e uiread a dh'fheum dhuibhse nur n-obair tron bhliadhna 's a tha mi cinnteach a nì e dhòmhsa, mar a rinn e roimhe seo.

Aonghas Moireastan

USING THIS BOOK

Accessing material online
The book contains the same sections (1-10) as before and in the same sequence. The title page of each section will indicate how much, if any, is placed on line and how this may be accessed. The material will be either on the Year Book pages of the Church of Scotland website or on other pages of that site and, occasionally, on other websites.

1. In the much shortened accounts of the Councils, Committees and Departments, readers are encouraged to access these bodies' own pages. The Year Book order, haphazard through the addition over the years of new committees to fit best with the existing template, has been changed to correspond to the Church's website. Thus, the Department of the General Assembly comes first, followed by the main Councils, and then the other committees and departments in alphabetical order. Rather than offer a complex web address for each department, the **further information** pointer navigates the user through the use of arrows > which indicate which heading to select in what sequence. For example, in the Council of Assembly section:

Further information:
www.churchofscotland.org.uk > About us > Councils, committees > Councils > Council of Assembly

2. Some sections or parts of sections are now found on the Year Book's own supplementary pages on the website, for which a new direct access pathway has been provided. For example:

B. The Minister and Marriage
See www.churchofscotland.org.uk/yearbook > Section 3B

While some users may feel disadvantaged by these new arrangements, it has been possible to take advantage of the opportunities offered. For example, information can be given in a more expanded form than before, as in the case of the Prison Chaplains – which does not only include those from the Church of Scotland but those from other denominations and indeed other faiths.

The new email addresses
All Ministers, Deacons, Ministries Development Staff, and other officers and staff of the Church are now offered the address: @churchofscotland.org.uk. At the time of writing, over 700 have now activated their new addresses. In general, an address is formed by the first initial and surname of the user: e.g. aminister@churchofscotland.org.uk. However, where there are two or more people of the same initial and name, variants are used. For this reason, one can't give a 'blanket' address to all personnel. Given publishing deadlines, the editor has tried to include as many such addresses as have been intimated, but it will certainly be the case that many more will come into use in the lifetime of this book.

FROM THE EDITOR

On my desk is the first ever edition of the title, dated 1886, open at the preface. This is not mere nostalgia. That early volume bore an uncanny resemblance to the book of today. Our forebears had hit upon a winning formula.

Both advert and content suggested that the intended readership was to go far beyond the 'church professional'. A plethora of insurance companies; publishers of travel books, school books, dictionaries, histories, as well as sermons and biblical commentaries; invitations to travel steerage to London by steamer from Leith or with the Midland Railway in 'drawing room saloon' comfort (and yes, by the Waverley route); the Lightning Geyser for a hot bath in three minutes; tea by post as provided to the aristocracy; and lozenges for the Leader of the Psalmody.

And the content? Among all the statistics and committee business are elegant essays – on the mysteries of presbyterian government, the aims and outcomes of the Reformation, the history of patronage, the system of teinds (as church income), monographs on saints such as Columba and Kentigern – all clearly aimed at developing a well informed and educated church membership.

Indeed in that very first preface, Professor Charteris, one of the Church's boldest reformers in recent times, expresses hopes for 'a very large sale' for the book, assisted by its price of sixpence (two and a half of today's pence). 'In no other publication,' he writes, 'is it possible to find such trustworthy information on the constitution, history, work and duties of the Church of Scotland.' As the years unrolled, this proud claim was amply made good.

Today sixpence doesn't go so far. Costs of production and, just as important, the cost to the user, have increased uncomfortably, enough in itself to review the content of a book which has 480 pages to Charteris's 180. But there are other, more positive, pressures towards change. The medium that was born in Gutenberg's boast that 'with my twenty-six soldiers of lead I shall conquer the world' can no longer exist alone in the digital landscape of today. Thus this edition acknowledges new website bedfellows, leaping at several points from page to screen, whence we have become used these days to sourcing our information. Not only that; we expect to find it set out – and the Church of Scotland site is a prime example – colourfully and attractively, in greater detail, and through clever use of image and design.

Not that the 1886 edition was seen as standing alone. 'Year Book' for title was both to distinguish it from 'Handbook', but also, as Charteris implies, to complement it, referring to Dr James Rankin's (minister of Muthil) *Handbook to the Church of Scotland*. This gave a detailed account of the Church ranging from history and theology through property and economics to its work at home and abroad, with much on recent controversies about Establishment. The implication was that you should have both on your desk or your bedside table. For us it would be a book and a laptop, but it is worth exploring other potential developments as well.

Indeed, the earliest *Year Books* may have carried the seeds of the future even in today's terms, whether in print or in pixel. For example: from the start, they carried an annual review of the principal events and achievements of each past year – churches opened, books published, successes in home and foreign mission, a memorable speech at the Assembly, inter-church conferences, a notable departure for the mission field, a symposium towards an analysis of religion in the universities, but also the impact on church and community of the agricultural depression and the dull trade in the towns.

Further, these earliest books set out to contribute to the spiritual and devotional life of the Church, and included an 'almanac' of daily Bible texts and information about fast days in every parish. Co-incidentally, in his report to the 2015 General Assembly, the retiring Moderator, John Chalmers, referring to the increasing place of the app in social communication, remarked:

'I do not know why we are not sending … texts to every one of our members every week at least; … it's such a simple way to nourish the faith'.

Whether this calls for a reconceived *Year Book* or a slimmer book of information with sister publications (or online features) – to mark, record and celebrate the work of the Church over the previous year – needs a wider discussion, and one in which our users must be involved. Questions arise not simply around the best way to access the information and how to communicate the life and mission of the Church but also how to continue the archival function, the living record, that this succession of *Year Books* enshrines.

I recently stumbled upon the fact that the October date on or around which the *Year Book* is published is also the feast of St Dodo, an eighth-century French Benedictine abbot. Auld Alliance notwithstanding, you may scour the *Year Book* in vain for churches dedicated to this fine European saint! We trust what has been written will not be read as a memorial to a title on the way to extinction but rather as a valediction as the *Year Book* moves forward in company with younger media in the task of recording, interpreting and enabling the mission of the Church for these times.

One would like to think that perhaps Prof Charteris cheers us on.

Douglas Galbraith
July 2015

ACKNOWLEDGEMENTS

The first Year Book acknowledged some 60 contributors. Were we to include the presbytery clerks we might come near that number – and to them thanks as always for their patience with the process. The Editor would also particularly like to thank the following: our Gaelic adviser, Rev Dr Roderick MacLeod for his translations of the Moderator's preface each year (but not this year!) and his annual update 'The Church of Scotland and the Gaelic Language'; to Roy Pinkerton, elder at Greyfriars Kirk, keeper of the verbatim record at succeeding General Assemblies, who keeps the archive of discontinued parish and congregational names (Section 9) and whose encyclopaedic knowledge of the Kirk has been of great assistance to the Editor; to Sandy Gemmill, who has painstakingly assembled the statistics section (10); to the Rev. Douglas Aitken, broadcaster at the Assembly, who has willingly allowed the Editor access to his scripts; and to Dr Virginia Cano of the Communications Department and the Church of Scotland's Web Editor Jason Derr who have helped facilitate the new features of the Year Book.

SECTION 1

Assembly Councils, Committees, Departments and Agencies

The symbol > used in website information indicates the headings to be selected as they appear

THE DEPARTMENT OF THE GENERAL ASSEMBLY

The Department of the General Assembly supports the General Assembly and the Moderator, the Council of Assembly and the Ecumenical Relations Committee. In addition, Departmental staff service the following Committees (qv): Assembly Arrangements, Legal Questions, the Committee to Nominate the Moderator, the Nomination Committee, the Committee on Overtures and Cases, the Committee on Classifying Returns to Overtures and the Central Services Committee. The Clerks of Assembly are available for consultation on matters of Church Law, Practice and Procedure.

Principal Clerk:	Very Rev. John P. Chalmers BD CPS
Depute Clerk of the General Assembly:	Rev. George J. Whyte BSc BD DMin
Personal Assistant to the Principal Clerk and Depute Clerk:	Mrs Linda Jamieson Tel. 0131-240 2240
Senior Administration Officer: (Assembly Arrangements and Moderatorial Support)	Mrs Alison Murray MA 0131-225 5722 ext. 2250
Legal and Learning Resources Officer:	Ms Christine Paterson LLB DipLP Tel: 0131-225 5722 ext. 2263
Secretary to the Council of Assembly:	Mrs Pauline Weibye MA DPA Chartered FCIPD
Senior Administration Officer: (Council of Assembly, Central Services Committee and Nomination Committee)	Mrs Pauline Wilson BA Tel: 0131-240 2229
Worship Development and Mission Statistics Co-ordinator:	Rev. Fiona Tweedie BSc PhD Tel: 0131-240 3007
Ecumenical Officer:	Very Rev. Sheilagh M. Kesting BA BD DD
Senior Administrator: (Ecumenical Relations)	Miss Rosalind Milne Tel: 0131-225 5722 ext. 2370

Personnel in this department are also listed with the Councils and Committees that they serve

Contact: Tel: 0131-240 2240
Fax: 0131-240 2239
Email: pcoffice@churchofscotland.org.uk
Further information:
www.churchofscotland.org.uk > About us > Councils, committees > Departments > General Assembly

1. COUNCILS

1.1 THE COUNCIL OF ASSEMBLY

The function of the Council is to co-ordinate, support and evaluate the work of the Councils and Committees of the Church, to assist the General Assembly in determining and implementing policies, and to take necessary administrative decisions in between General Assemblies. The voting members of the Council of Assembly act as the Charity Trustees for the Unincorporated Councils and Committees of the General Assembly: Scottish Charity No. SC011353.

Convener: Rev. S. Grant Barclay LLB DipLP BD MSc PhD
Vice-Convener: Miss Catherine Coull LLB
Secretary: Mrs Pauline Weibye MA DPA Chartered FCIPD

Contact: Mrs. Pauline Wilson BA, Senior Administrative Officer
            Tel: 0131-240 2229, Email: pwilson@churchofscotland.org.uk
Further information:
www.churchofscotland.org.uk > About us > Councils, committees > Councils > Council of Assembly

---

1.2 THE CHURCH AND SOCIETY COUNCIL

The function of the Council is to facilitate the Church of Scotland's engagement with, and to comment upon, national, political and social issues through research, theological reflection, and the building of relationships with leaders in civic society, public bodies, professional associations and other networks. It also oversees the standing committee on Education; the Response to Climate Change; and Society, Religion and Technology Projects.

Convener: Rev. Sally Foster-Fulton BA BD
Vice-Convener: Rev. Richard E. Frazer BA BD DMin
Secretary: Rev. H. Martin J. Johnstone MA BD MTh PhD
                    mjohnstone@churchofscotland.org.uk

Contact: churchandsociety@churchofscotland.org.uk   Tel: 0131-240 2206
Further information:
www.churchofscotland.org.uk > About us > Councils, committees > Councils > Church and Society

---

1.3 THE MINISTRIES COUNCIL

The Council's remit is to recruit, train and support ministries in every part of Scotland, to monitor their deployment, working in partnership with ecumenical, inter-faith and statutory agencies, and giving priority to the poorest and most marginalised sections of the community.

Convener:	Rev. Neil M Glover
Vice-Conveners:	Rev. Colin M. Brough BSc BD
	Dr John Dent MB ChB MMEd
	Rev. Marjory A. MacLean LLB BD PhD RNR
	Rev. Derek H.N. Pope BD

Council Secretary:	Rev. Martin Scott DipMusEd RSAM BD PhD
	(Tel: ext. 2389; E-mail: mscott@churchofscotland.org.uk)
Depute:	Ms Catherine Skinner BA MA
Education and Support	Rev. Marjory McPherson LLB BD
Partnership Development	Rev. Angus R. Mathieson MA BD
Priority Areas:	Mr. Noel Mathias BA BTh MA (Acting Secretary)
	Tel: 0141-248 2905
Go For It:	Ms Shirley Grieve BA PGCE (Manager)
	(E-mail: goforit@churchofscotland.org.uk)
	Miss Catherine McIntosh MA (Training and Development)

Further information:
Work of Council and Ministries Support Staff:
www.churchofscotland.org.uk > About us > Councils, committeees > Councils > Ministries
Council
Vacant charges:
www.churchofscotland.org.uk > About us > Vacancies and volunteering
Recognised ministries:
www.churchofscotland.org.uk > Serve > Ministries Council > Ministries in the Church
Go for it Fund:
www.churchofscotland.org.uk > Serve > Go for it Fund
Priority Areas:
www.churchofscotland.org.uk > Serve > Ministries Council > Priority Areas
Pulpit Supply Fees:
www.churchofscotland.org.uk/yearbook > Section 3F

1.4   THE MISSION AND DISCIPLESHIP COUNCIL

The Council's remit is to stimulate and support the Church by the provision of resources nationally, regionally and locally in worship, witness, mission and discipleship. This includes the development of strategies and materials in the areas of adult education, resourcing elders, work with young adults, young people and children (including those with particular needs and disabilities), as well as in liturgy, and church art and architecture.

Convener:	Rev. Colin A.M. Sinclair BA BD
Vice-Conveners:	Rev. Daniel J.M. Carmichael MA BD
	Rev. Norman A. Smith MA BD
	Rev. Jamie Milliken BD

Council Secretary:	Rev. Dr Alister W. Bull BD (Hons) DipMin MTh

Church Without Walls: Mrs Lesley Hamilton-Messer MA
Congregational Learning: Mr Ronald H. Clarke BEng MSc PGCE
Resourcing Worship: Mr Graham Fender-Allison BA

Church Art and Architecture:
Convener: Dr J. G. Roberts MAC
Contact: bwaller@churchofscotland.org.uk

Contact: Eva Elder
               (Email: mandd@churchofscotland.org.uk)
Further information:
www.churchofscotland.org.uk > About us > Councils, committees > Mission and Discipleship
www.resourcingmission.org.uk

Church Art and Architecture www.resourcingmission.org.uk > CARTA

For The Netherbow: Scottish Storytelling Centre see below 2.24
For Life and Work see below 2.16
For Saint Andrew Press see below 2.22

1.5   THE SOCIAL CARE COUNCIL
(CrossReach)
Charis House, 47 Milton Road East, Edinburgh EH15 2SR
Tel: 0131-657 2000; Fax: 0131-657 5000
E-mail: info@crossreach.org.uk; Website: www.crossreach.org.uk

The Social Care Council, known as CrossReach, provides social-care services as part of the Christian witness of the Church to the people of Scotland, and engages with other bodies in responding to emerging areas of need. CrossReach operates 75 services across the country.

Convener: Dr Sally E. Bonnar
Vice-Conveners: Rev. Richard Begg
                 Rev. Hugh M Stewart

Chief Executive Officer: Peter Bailey (peter.bailey@crossreach.org.uk)

Director of Services to Older People: Allan Logan (allan.logan@crossreach.org.uk)
Director of Adult Care Services: Calum Murray (calum.murray@crossreach.org.uk)
Director of Children and Families: Viv Dickenson (viv.dickenson@crossreach.org.uk)
Director of Finance and Resources: Ian Wauchope (ian.wauchope@crossreach.org.uk)
Director of Human Resources and
   Organisational Development: Mari Rennie (mari.rennie@crossreach.org.uk)

Further information:
www.crossreach.org.uk

For sharing local experience and inititatives:
www.socialcareforum.scot

1.6 THE WORLD MISSION COUNCIL

The Council's remit is to enable and encourage the Church of Scotland to accompany partner churches around the world and to keep the Church informed about issues and engaged in this endeavour as together we seek to live the Christian life and offer support to each other in our witness to Christ in the world. The Council is also the principal link with Christian Aid.

Convener:	Rev. Iain D. Cunningham MA BD
Vice-Conveners:	Rev. Christine Sime BSc BD
	Mrs Valerie Brown

Council Secretary:	Rev. Ian W. Alexander BA BD STM
Secretaries:	Ms Jennie Chinembiri (Africa and Caribbean)
	Ms Carol Finlay (Twinning and Local Development)
	Mr Kenny Roger (Middle East Secretary)
	Mr Sandy Sneddon (Asia)
HIV programme:	Ms Marjorie Clark, Ms Elena Sarra, Co-ordinators
	Email: hiv@churchofscotland.org.uk
Administration:	Ms Donna Maclean

Contact: Tel: 0131-225 5722
          Email: world@churchofscotland.org.uk
Further Information:
www.churchofscotland.org.uk > About us > Councils, committees > Councils > World Mission
www.churchofscotland.org.uk > Serve > World Mission

---

2. DEPARTMENTS, COMMITTEES AND AGENCIES

2.1 ASSEMBLY ARRANGEMENTS COMMITTEE

Convener:	Rev. Derek Browning MA BD DMin
Vice-Convener:	Mrs Judith J.H. Pearson LLB LLM
Secretary:	Principal Clerk
	Tel. 0131-240 2240
	Email: pc@churchofscotland.org.uk

Further information:
www.churchofscotland.org.uk > About us > General Assembly
www.churchofscotland.org.uk > About us > Councils, committees > Committees > Assembly Arrangements

2.2 CENTRAL PROPERTIES DEPARTMENT

Remit: to provide property, facilities and health and safety services to the Councils and Departments of the central administration of the Church.

Property, Health and Safety Manager: Colin Wallace
Property, Health and Safety Officer: Jacqueline Collins
Property Officer: Eunice Hessell
Support Assistant: Joyce McMurdo

Contact: Tel: 0131-240 2254
Email: cpd@churchofscotland.org.uk

2.3 CENTRAL SERVICES COMMITTEE

The remit of this committee draws together departments which carry out the central day-to-day service work of the Church: Office Management, Central Properties, Information Technology and Human Resources Departments.

Convener: Mr Bill Steele
Vice-Convener: Mr David Brackenridge
Administrative Secretary: Mrs Pauline Wilson BA

Contact: Tel: 0131-240 2229
Email: pwilson@churchofscotland.org.uk

Further Information:
www.churchofscotland.org.uk > About us > Councils, committees > Central Services

2.4 CHURCH OF SCOTLAND TRUST

Chairman: Mr John M. Hodge WS
Vice-Chairman: Mr Christopher N. Mackay WS
Acting Treasurer: Mrs Anne F. Macintosh BA CA
Secretary and Clerk: Mrs Jennifer M. Hamilton BA
Tel: 0131-240 2222
Email: jhamilton@churchofscotland.org.uk

Further information:
www.churchofscotland.org.uk > About us > Councils, committees > Departments > Church of Scotland Trust

2.5   COMMUNICATIONS DEPARTMENT

Head of Communications: Seonag Mackinnon
Communications Manager: Rob Flett
Communications and Media Relations Team
  Senior Communications Officer: Nick Jury
  Senior Communications Officer: Helen Silvis
  Communications Officer: Cameron Brooks
Programmes Co-ordinator: Virginia Cano
Web Editor: Jason Derr
Web Developer: Alan Murray
Senior Designer: Claire Bewsey
Senior Designer: Chris Flexen

Contact Media Relations: Tels. 0131-240 2278, 0131-240 2268
        (After hours) 07854 783539
Contact department: 0131-240 2204
Further information:
www.churchofscotland.org.uk > About us > Councils, committees > Departments >
Communications

2.6   ECUMENICAL RELATIONS COMMITTEE

The Committee includes five members who are each a member of one of the five Councils, plus representatives of other denominations in Scotland, Church of Scotland representatives on British and international ecumenical bodies, with the General Secretary of ACTS as a corresponding member.

Convener: Rev. Alison P. McDonald MA BD
Vice-Convener: Rev. Peter H. Donald MA PhD BD
Secretary and Ecumenical Officer: Very Rev. Sheilagh M. Kesting BA BD DD
Senior Administrator: Miss Rosalind Milne

Contact: ecumenical@churchofscotland.org.uk
       Tel. 0131-240 2208

Further information:
www.churchofscotland.org.uk > About us > Councils, committees > Committees > Ecumenical Relations Committee
www.churchofscotland.org.uk > Connect > Ecumenism
www.churchofscotland.org.uk > Resources > Subjects > Ecumenical Resources
World Council of Churches:
www.oikumene.org
Churches Together in Britain and Ireland:
www.ctbi.org.uk

Action of Churches Together in Scotland:
www.acts-scotland.org
For other international ecumenical bodies see Committee's web pages as above
See also 'Other Churches in the United Kingdom' page 18

2.7 FORCES CHAPLAINS COMMITTEE

Convener: Rev. Gordon T. Craig BD DipMin
Vice-Convener: Rev. John A.H. Murdoch BA BD DPSS
Secretary: Mr John K. Thomson, Ministries Council
                 Tel: 0131-225 5722
                 Email: jthomson@churchofscotland.org.uk

Further information:
www.churchofscotland.org.uk > About us > Councils, committees > Forces Chaplains Committee
A list of Chaplains is found on page 264

2.8 GENERAL TRUSTEES

Chairman: Mr Iain C. Douglas RD BArch FRIAS
Vice-Chairman: Mr Roger G.G. Dodd DipBldgCons(RICS) FRICS
Secretary and Clerk: Mr David D. Robertson LLB NP
Depute Secretary and Clerk: Mr Keith S. Mason LLB NP
Assistant Secretaries: Ms Claire L. Cowell LLB (Glebes)
                              Mrs Morag J. Menneer BSc MRICS (Glebes)
                              Mr Brian D. Waller LLB (Ecclesiastical Buildings)
Energy Conservation: Mr Robert Lindores FInstPa
Acting Treasurer: Mrs Anne F. Macintosh BA CA
Assistant Treasurer: Mr Alex Semple FCCA

Buildings insurance,   Church of Scotland Insurance Co. Ltd.
all enquiries to   121 George Street, Edinburgh EH2 4YN
                              Tel: 0131-220 4119, Fax: 0131-220 4120
                              Email: enquiries@cosic.co.uk

Contact: gentrustees@churchofscotland.org.uk   0131-225 5722 ext. 2261
Further information:
www.churchofscotland.org.uk > About us > Councils, committees > Departments > General Trustees

2.9   THE GUILD

The Church of Scotland Guild is a movement within the Church of Scotland whose aim is 'to invite and encourage both women and men to commit their lives to Jesus Christ and to enable them to express their faith in worship, prayer and action'.

Convener: Linda Young
Vice-Convener: Rosemary Johnston BA
General Secretary: Iain W. Whyte BA DCE DMS

Contact: Tel: 0131-240 2217
E-mail: guild@churchofscotland.org.uk

Further information:
www.cos-guild.org.uk
www.churchofscotland.org.uk > Serve > The Guild

2.10   HOUSING AND LOAN FUND

Chairman: Mr J.G. Grahame Lees MA LLB NP
Deputy Chairman: Rev. Ian Taylor BD ThM
Secretary: Lin J. Macmillan MA
                     Tel: 0131-225 5722 ext. 2310
                     Email: lmacmillan@churchofscotland.org.uk
Property Manager: Hilary J. Hardy
Property Assistant: John Lunn

Further information:
www.churchofscotland.org.uk > About us > Councils, committees > Departments > Housing and Loan Fund

2.11   HUMAN RESOURCES DEPARTMENT

Human Resources Manager: Karen Smith Chartered CIPD
                            Tel: 0131-240 2266

Contact: hr@churchofscotland.org.uk
Further information:
www.churchofscotland.org.uk > About us > Councils, committees > Committees > Human Resources

2.12   INFORMATION TECHNOLOGY DEPARTMENT

Information Technology Manager: David Malcolm
Tel: 0131-240 2247

Contact: 0131-240 2245
Further information:
www.churchofscotland.org.uk > About us > Councils, committees > Committees > IT

2.13   INVESTORS TRUST

Chairman: Mr A.W.T. Gibb BA
Vice-Chairman: Ms C.Y. Alexander
Acting Treasurer: Mrs Anne F. Macintosh BA CA
Secretary: Mrs Nicola Robertson
                    Email: nrobertson@churchofscotland.org.uk

Further information:
www.churchofscotland.org.uk > About us > Councils, committees > Departments > Investors Trust

2.14   LAW DEPARTMENT

Solicitor of the Church
and of the General Trustees: Mrs Janette Wilson LLB NP
Depute Solicitor: Miss Mary Macleod LLB NP
Solicitors: Mrs Jennifer Hamilton BA NP
                              Mrs Elspeth Annan LLB NP
                              Miss Susan Killean LLB NP
                              Mrs Anne Steele LLB NP
                              Miss Jennifer Sharp LLB NP
                              Mr Gregor Buick LLB WS NP
                              Mrs Madelaine Sproule LLB NP

Contact: Tel: 0131-225 5722 ext. 2230; Fax: 0131-240 2246.
              Email: lawdept@churchofscotland.org.uk

Further information:
www.churchofscotland.org.uk > About us > Councils, committees > Committees > Law

2.15 LEGAL QUESTIONS COMMITTEE

The Committee's remit is to advise the General Assembly on questions of Church and Constitutional Law, assist Agencies of the Assembly in preparing and interpreting legislation, compile statistics and arrange for the care of Church Records.

Convener: Rev. George S. Cowie BSc BD
Vice-Convener: Rev. Alistair S. May LLB BD PhD
Secretary: Principal Clerk
Legal and Learning Resources Officer: Ms Christine Paterson LLB DipLP

Contact: Tel. 0131-240 2240
                        Email: pc@churchofscotland.org.uk

Further information:
www.churchofscotland.org.uk > About us > Councils, committees > Committees > Legal Questions

2.16 LIFE AND WORK
the Church of Scotland's monthly magazine

The magazine's purpose is to keep the Church informed about events in church life at home and abroad and to provide a forum for Christian opinion and debate on a variety of topics. It has an independent editorial policy. Contributions which are relevant to any aspect of the Christian faith are welcome.

Editor: Lynne McNeil
            Tel: 0131-225 5722; Fax: 0131-240 2207
            Email: magazine@lifeandwork.org

Further information:
www.lifeandwork.org
www.churchofscotland.org.uk > News and Events > Life and Work

2.17 NOMINATION COMMITTEE

Convener: Rev. Kenneth Stott MA BD
Vice-Convener: Miss Ann Lyall DCS
Secretary: Mrs Pauline Weibye MA DPA Chartered FCIPD

Contact: Mrs Pauline Wilson BA, Senior Administration Officer
                  Tel: 0131-240 2229
                  Email: pwilson@churchofscotland.org.uk

Further information:
www.churchofscotland.org.uk > About us > Councils, committees > Committees > Nomination Committee

2.18 OFFICE MANAGEMENT DEPARTMENT

Facilities Manager: Carole Tait
Tel: 0131-240 2214, Email: ctait@churchofscotland.org.uk

Further information:
www.churchofscotland.org.uk > About us > Councils, committees > Committees > Office management

2.19 PANEL ON REVIEW AND REFORM

Convener: Rev. Graham Duffin BSc BD DipEd
Vice-Convener: Rev. David C. Cameron BD CertMin
Senior Administrator: Mrs Valerie A. Cox
                        Tel: 0131-225 5722 ext. 2336
                        Email: vcox@churchofscotland.org.uk

Further information:
www.churchofscotland.org.uk > About us > Councils, committees > Committees > Panel on Review and Reform

2.20 PENSION TRUSTEES

Chairman: Mr W. John McCafferty ACII APFS TEP
Vice-Chairman: Mr Graeme R. Caughey BSc FFIA
Secretary and
Pensions Manager: Mr Steven D. Kaney BSc DipPMI Dip IEB
Pensions Administrators: Mrs Fiona McCulloch
                         Mrs Mary Mackenzie
                         Miss Marshall Paterson

Contact: Tel: 0131-240 2255
            Email: pensions@churchofscotland.org.uk

Further information:
www.churchofscotland.org.uk > About us > Councils, committees > Departments > Pension
Trustees

2.21   SAFEGUARDING SERVICE

The service ensures that the Church has robust structures and policies in place for the
prevention of harm and abuse of children and adults at risk; and to ensure a timely and appropriate response when harm or abuse is witnessed, suspected or reported.

Convener: Rev. Karen K. Campbell BD MTh DMin
Vice-Convener: Sheila Ritchie MSc DipSW MSc (Criminal Justice Social
                                   Work)
Head of Safeguarding: Richard Crosse MA (Cantab) MSW CQSW
Assistant Head of Safeguarding: Jennifer Milligan CQSW DipSW

Contact: Tel: 0131-240 2256; Fax: 0131-220 3113
             Email: safeguarding@churchofscotland.org.uk

Further Information:
www.churchofscotland.org.uk > About us > Councils, committees > Departments >
Safeguarding Service

2.22   SAINT ANDREW PRESS

Saint Andrew Press has been celebrating its 60th birthday with the publication of a new series
of highly popular resources published in the *Learn* series – a congregational learning initiative
devised by the Mission & Discipleship Council. Saint Andrew Press is managed on behalf of
the Church of Scotland by Hymns Ancient and Modern Ltd and publishes a broad range of
books and resources, ranging from the much-loved William Barclay series of New Testament
Daily Study Bible commentaries to the *Pilgrim Guide to Scotland*. The full catalogue of over
200 titles and Church of Scotland stationery as well as news of authors and special offers can
be viewed on the Saint Andrew Press website (see below).

Orders: (books and stationery): orders@norwichbooksandmusic.co.uk
Senior Commissioning Editor: Ann Crawford (anncrawford@hymnsam.co.uk)

Further information: www.standrewpress.com

2.23   SCOTTISH CHURCHES PARLIAMENTARY OFFICE
121 George Street, Edinburgh EH2 4YN

The Office exists to build fruitful relationships between the Churches and the Scottish and UK Parliaments and Governments, seeking to engage reflectively in the political process, translate their commitment to the welfare of Scotland into parliamentary debate, and contribute their experience and faith-based reflection on it to the decision-making process.

Scottish Churches Parliamentary Officer: Chloe Clemmons MA MA

Contact: Tel: 0131-220 0246
Email: chloe@actsparl.org

Further information:
www.churchofscotland.org.uk > Speak out > Politics and Government
www.actsparl.org

2.24   SCOTTISH STORYTELLING CENTRE (THE NETHERBOW)

The integrated facilities of the **Netherbow Theatre** and the **John Knox House Museum**, together with the outstanding conference and reception areas, form an important cultural and visitor centre on the Royal Mile in Edinburgh and provide advice and assistance nationally in the use of the arts in a diversity of settings. Mission and Discipleship Council are pleased to host TRACS (Traditional Arts and Culture Scotland), a grant-funded body who provide an extensive cultural and literary programme.

Contact: Tel: 0131-556 9579, Fax: 0131-557 5224
Email: reception@scottishstorytellingcentre.com

Further information:
www.scottishstorytellingcentre.co.uk

2.25   STEWARDSHIP AND FINANCE DEPARTMENT

Acting General Treasurer:	Mrs Anne F. Macintosh BA CA
Head of Stewardship:	Rev. Alan W. Gibson BA BD
Finance Managers:	
Congregational Finance	Mr Archie McDowall BA CA
General Trustees	Alex Semple FCCA
Ministries	Mrs Elaine Macadie BA CA
World Mission	Mrs Catriona M. Scrimgeour BSc ACA
Management and Pensions Accountant:	Mrs Kay C. Hastie BSc CA

Contact: Email: sfadmin@churchofscotland.org.uk
Further information and details of local consultants:
www.churchofscotland.org.uk > About us > Councils, committees > Departments > Stewardship and Budget
www.churchofscotland.org.uk > Resources > Subjects > National Stewardship Programme

2.26 THEOLOGICAL FORUM

The purpose of the Forum is to continue to develop and bring to expression doctrinal understanding of the Church with reference to Scripture and to the confessional standards of the Church of Scotland, and the implications of this for worship and witness in and beyond contemporary Scotland. It responds to requests to undertake enquiries as they arise, draws the Church's attention to particular matters requiring theological work, and promotes theological reflection throughout the Church.

Convener: Very Rev. Prof. Iain R. Torrance TD DPhil DD DTheol LHD FRSE
Vice-Convener: Rev. Frances M. Henderson BA BD PhD
Secretary (*pro tem.*): Mrs Pauline Weibye MA DPA Chartered FCIPD

Further Information:
www.churchofscotland.org.uk > About us > Councils, committees > Committees > Theological Forum

SECTION 2

General Information

(1) OTHER CHURCHES IN THE UNITED KINGDOM

THE UNITED FREE CHURCH OF SCOTLAND
General Secretary: Rev. John Fulton BSc BD, United Free Church Offices, 11 Newton Place, Glasgow G3 7PR (Tel: 0141-332 3435; E-mail: office@ufcos.org.uk).

THE FREE CHURCH OF SCOTLAND
Principal Clerk: Rev. James MacIver, 15 North Bank Street, The Mound, Edinburgh EH1 2LS (Tel: 0131-226 5286; E-mail: offices@freechurch.org).

FREE CHURCH OF SCOTLAND (CONTINUING)
Clerk of Assembly: Rev. John MacLeod, Free Church Manse, Portmahomack, Tain IV20 1YL (Tel: 01862 871467; E-mail: principalclerk@fccontinuing.org).

THE FREE PRESBYTERIAN CHURCH OF SCOTLAND
Clerk of Synod: Rev. John MacLeod, 6 Church Avenue, Sidcup, Kent DA14 6BU (E-mail: jmacl265@aol.com).

ASSOCIATED PRESBYTERIAN CHURCHES
Clerk of Presbytery: Rev. Archibald N. McPhail, APC Manse, Polvinister Road, Oban PA34 5TN (Tel: 01631 567076; E-mail: archibald.mcphail@virgin.net).

THE REFORMED PRESBYTERIAN CHURCH OF SCOTLAND
Clerk of Presbytery: Rev. Andrew Quigley, Church Offices, 48 North Bridge Street, Airdrie ML6 6NE (Tel: 01236 620107; E-mail: sandrewq@aol.com).

THE PRESBYTERIAN CHURCH IN IRELAND
Clerk of the General Assembly and General Secretary: Rev. Trevor Gribben, Church House, Fisherwick Place, Belfast BT1 6DW (Tel: 02890 322284; E-mail: clerk@presbyterianireland.org).

THE PRESBYTERIAN CHURCH OF WALES
General Secretary: Rev. Meiron Morris, Tabernacle Chapel, 81 Merthyr Road, Whitchurch, Cardiff CF14 1DD (Tel: 02920 627465; E-mail: swyddfa.office@ebcpcw.org.uk).

THE UNITED REFORMED CHURCH
General Secretary: Rev. John Proctor, 86 Tavistock Place, London WC1H 9RT (Tel: 020 7916 8646; Fax: 020 7916 2021; E-mail: john.proctor@urc.org.uk).

UNITED REFORMED CHURCH SYNOD OF SCOTLAND
Synod Clerk: Mr Patrick Smyth, 113 West Regent Street, Glasgow G1 2RU (Tel: 0141-248 5382; E-mail: psmyth@urcscotland.org.uk).

BAPTIST UNION OF SCOTLAND
General Director: Rev. Alan Donaldson, 48 Speirs Wharf, Glasgow G4 9TH (Tel: 0141-423 6169; E-mail: director@scottishbaptist.org.uk).

CONGREGATIONAL FEDERATION IN SCOTLAND
Chair: Rev. May-Kane Logan, 93 Cartside Road, Busby, Glasgow G76 8QD (Tel: 0141-237 1349; E-mail: maycita@talktalk.net).

RELIGIOUS SOCIETY OF FRIENDS (QUAKERS)
Martin Burnell, Clerk to the General Meeting for Scotland, 25 Learmonth Grove, Edinburgh EH4 1BR (Tel: 0131-343 2592; E-mail: mburnell@mbees.net).

ROMAN CATHOLIC CHURCH
Mgr Hugh Bradley, General Secretary, Bishops' Conference of Scotland, 64 Aitken Street, Airdrie ML6 6LT (Tel: 01236 764061; E-mail: gensec@bpsconfscot.com).

THE SALVATION ARMY
Lt-Col. Carol Bailey, Secretary for Scotland and Divisional Commander East Scotland Division, Headquarters and Scotland Secretariat, 12A Dryden Road, Loanhead EH20 9LZ (Tel: 0131-440 9101; E-mail: carol.bailey@salvationarmy.org.uk).

SCOTTISH EPISCOPAL CHURCH
Secretary General: Mr John F. Stuart, 21 Grosvenor Crescent, Edinburgh EH12 5EL (Tel: 0131-225 6357; E-mail: secgen@scotland.anglican.org).

THE SYNOD OF THE METHODIST CHURCH IN SCOTLAND
District Administrator: Mrs Fiona Inglis, Methodist Church Office, Old Churches House, Kirk Street, Dunblane FK15 0AJ (Tel/Fax: 01786 820295; E-mail: fiona@methodistchurchinscotland.net.

GENERAL SYNOD OF THE CHURCH OF ENGLAND
Secretary General: Mr William Fittall (until 30 November 2015), Church House, Great Smith Street, London SW1P 3NZ
(Tel: 020 7898 1360; E-mail: enquiry@churchofengland.org).

---

(2) OVERSEAS CHURCHES

See www.churchofscotland.org.uk > Serve > World Mission > Our partner churches

---

(3) HER MAJESTY'S HOUSEHOLD IN SCOTLAND
ECCLESIASTICAL

Dean of the Order of the Thistle and Dean of the Chapel Royal:	Very Rev. Prof. Iain R. Torrance TD DPhil DD DTheol LHD FRSE
Domestic Chaplains:	Rev. Kenneth I. Mackenzie DL BD CPS Rev. Neil N. Gardner MA BD
Chaplains in Ordinary:	Rev. Norman W. Drummond CBE MA BD DUniv FRSE

Rev. Alastair H. Symington MA BD
Rev. James M. Gibson TD LTh LRAM
Right Rev. Angus Morrison MA BD PhD
Very Rev. E. Lorna Hood MA BD DD
Rev. Alistair G. Bennett BSc BD
Rev. Susan M. Brown BD DipMin
Very Rev. John P. Chalmers BD CPS
Rev. Prof. David A.S. Fergusson
    MA BD DPhil DD FBA FRSE

Extra Chaplains: Rev. Kenneth MacVicar MBE DFC TD MA
Rev. Alwyn J.C. Macfarlane MA
Rev. John MacLeod MA
Very Rev. James L. Weatherhead CBE MA LLB DD
Very Rev. James A. Simpson BSc BD STM DD
Very Rev. James Harkness KCVO CB OBE MA DD
Rev. John L. Paterson MA BD STM
Rev. Charles Robertson LVO MA
Very Rev. John B. Cairns KCVO LTh LLB LLD DD
Very Rev. Gilleasbuig I. Macmillan
    KCVO MA BD Drhc DD FRSE HRSA FRCSEd
Very Rev. Finlay A.J. Macdonald MA BD PhD DD

(4) RECENT LORD HIGH COMMISSIONERS
TO THE GENERAL ASSEMBLY

1990/91	The Rt Hon. Donald MacArthur Ross FRSE
1992/93	The Rt Hon. Lord Macfarlane of Bearsden KT FRSE
1994/95	Lady Marion Fraser LT
1996	Her Royal Highness the Princess Royal LT LG GCVO
1997	The Rt Hon. Lord Macfarlane of Bearsden KT FRSE
1998/99	The Rt Hon. Lord Hogg of Cumbernauld
2000	His Royal Highness the Prince Charles, Duke of Rothesay KG KT GCB OM
2001/02	The Rt Hon. Viscount Younger of Leckie
	Her Majesty the Queen attended the opening of the General Assembly of 2002
2003/04	The Rt Hon. Lord Steel of Aikwood KT KBE
2005/06	The Rt Hon. Lord Mackay of Clashfern KT
2007	His Royal Highness the Prince Andrew, Duke of York KG KCVO
2008/09	The Rt Hon. George Reid KT MA
2010/11	Lord Wilson of Tillyorn KT GCMG PRSE
2012/13	The Rt Hon. Lord Selkirk of Douglas QC MA LLB
2014	His Royal Highness the Prince Edward, Earl of Wessex KG GCVO
2015	The Rt Hon. Lord Hope of Craighead KT PC FRSE

For Lord High Commissioners prior to this date see www.churchofscotland.org.uk/yearbook > Section 2.4

(5) RECENT MODERATORS
OF THE GENERAL ASSEMBLY

1989	William J.G. McDonald MA BD DD, Edinburgh: Mayfield
1990	Robert Davidson MA BD DD FRSE, University of Glasgow
1991	William B.R. Macmillan MA BD LLD DD, Dundee: St Mary's
1992	Hugh R. Wyllie MA DD FCIBS, Hamilton: Old Parish Church
1993	James L. Weatherhead CBE MA LLB DD, Principal Clerk of Assembly
1994	James A. Simpson BSc BD STM DD, Dornoch Cathedral
1995	James Harkness KCVO CB OBE MA DD, Chaplain General (Emeritus)
1996	John H. McIndoe MA BD STM DD, London: St Columba's linked with Newcastle: St Andrew's
1997	Alexander McDonald BA DUniv CMIWSc, General Secretary, Department of Ministry
1998	Alan Main TD MA BD STM PhD DD, University of Aberdeen
1999	John B. Cairns KCVO LTh LLB LLD DD, Dumbarton: Riverside
2000	Andrew R.C. McLellan CBE MA BD STM DD, Edinburgh: St Andrew's and St George's
2001	John D. Miller BA BD DD, Glasgow: Castlemilk East
2002	Finlay A.J. Macdonald MA BD PhD DD, Principal Clerk of Assembly
2003	Iain R. Torrance TD DPhil DD DTheol LHD FRSE, University of Aberdeen
2004	Alison Elliot OBE MA MSc PhD LLD DD FRSE, Associate Director CTPI
2005	David W. Lacy BA BD DLitt DL, Kilmarnock: Henderson
2006	Alan D. McDonald LLB BD MTh DLitt DD, Cameron linked with St Andrews: St Leonard's
2007	Sheilagh M. Kesting BA BD DD, Secretary of Ecumenical Relations Committee
2008	David W. Lunan MA BD DUniv DLitt DD, Clerk to the Presbytery of Glasgow
2009	William C. Hewitt BD DipPS, Greenock: Westburn
2010	John C. Christie BSc BD MSB CBiol, Interim Minister
2011	A. David K. Arnott MA BD, St Andrews: Hope Park with Strathkinness
2012	Albert O. Bogle BD MTh, Bo'ness: St Andrew's
2013	E. Lorna Hood MA BD DD, Renfrew: North
2014	John P. Chalmers BD CPS, Principal Clerk of Assembly
2015	Angus Morrison MA BD PhD, Orwell and Portmoak

For Moderators prior to this date see www.churchofscotland.org.uk/yearbook > Section 2.5

MATTER OF PRECEDENCE
The Lord High Commissioner to the General Assembly of the Church of Scotland (while the Assembly is sitting) ranks next to the Sovereign and the Duke of Edinburgh and before the rest of the Royal Family.

The Moderator of the General Assembly of the Church of Scotland ranks next to the Lord Chancellor of Great Britain and before the Keeper of the Great Seal of Scotland (the First Minister) and the Dukes.

(6) SCOTTISH DIVINITY FACULTIES

[* denotes a Minister of the Church of Scotland]

ABERDEEN
(School of Divinity, History and Philosophy)
50–52 College Bounds, Old Aberdeen AB24 3DS
(Tel: 01224 272366; Fax: 01224 273750; E-mail: divinity@abdn.ac.uk)

Master of Christ's College:	Rev. Prof. John Swinton* BD PhD RNM RNMD
	(E-mail: christs-college@abdn.ac.uk)
Head of School:	Prof. John Morrison MA PhD
Deputy Head of School:	Jutta Leonhardt-Balzer DipTheol PhD

For teaching staff and further information see www.abdn.ac.uk/sdhp/

ST ANDREWS
(University College of St Mary)
St Mary's College, St Andrews, Fife KY16 9JU
(Tel: 01334 462850/1; Fax: 01334 462852; E-mail: divinity@st-andrews.ac.uk)

Principal:	Very Rev. Dr Ian C. Bradley*
Head of School:	Dr Mark W. Elliott

For teaching staff and further information see www.st-andrews.ac.uk/divinity/

EDINBURGH
(School of Divinity and New College)
New College, Mound Place, Edinburgh EH1 2LX
(Tel: 0131-650 8900; Fax: 0131-650 7952; E-mail: divinity@ed.ac.uk)

Head of School:	Graham Paul Foster BD MSt PhD
Principal of New College:	Rev. Professor David A.S. Fergusson* MA BD DPhil DD FBA FRSE
Assistant Principal of New College:	Rev. Alison M. Jack* MA BD PhD

For teaching staff and further information see www.ed.ac.uk/schools-departments/divinity/

GLASGOW
School of Critical Studies
Theology and Religious Studies Subject Area
4 The Square, University of Glasgow, Glasgow G12 8QQ
(Tel: 0141-330 6526; Fax: 0141-330 4943;
Website: www.gla.ac.uk/departments/theology)

Head of Subject: Rev. Canon Dr Charlotte Methuen
Principal of Trinity College: Rev. Dr Doug Gay*

For teaching staff and further information see www.gla.ac.uk/departments/theology/

HIGHLAND THEOLOGICAL COLLEGE UHI
High Street, Dingwall IV15 9HA
(Tel: 01349 780000; Fax: 01349 780201;
E-mail: htc@uhi.ac.uk)

Principal of HTC: Rev. Hector Morrison* BSc BD MTh
Vice-Principal of HTC: Jamie Grant PhD MA LLB

For teaching staff and further information see www.htc.uhi.ac.uk

---

(7) SOCIETIES AND ASSOCIATIONS

The undernoted list shows the name of the Association, along with the name and address of the Secretary.

1. INTER-CHURCH ASSOCIATIONS

The FELLOWSHIP OF ST ANDREW: The fellowship promotes dialogue between Churches of the east and the west in Scotland. Further information available from the Secretary, Rev. John G. Pickles, 1 Annerley Road, Annan DG12 6HE (Tel: 01461 202626; E-mail: jgpickles@hotmail.com).

The FELLOWSHIP OF ST THOMAS: An ecumenical association formed to promote informed interest in and to learn from the experience of Churches in South Asia (India, Pakistan, Bangladesh, Nepal, Sri Lanka and Burma (Myanmar)). Secretary: Rev. Val Nellist, 28 Glamis Gardens, Dalgety Bay, Dunfermline KY11 5TD (Tel: 01383 824066; E-mail: valnellist@btinternet.com; Website: www.fost.org.uk).

FRONTIER YOUTH TRUST: Encourages, resources and supports churches, organisations and individuals working with young people (in particular, disadvantaged young people). Through the StreetSpace initiative, the Trust is able to help churches to explore new ways of engaging young people in the community around mission and fresh expressions of church. All correspondence to: Frontier Youth Trust, 202 Bradford Court, 123/131 Bradford Street, Birmingham B12 0NS (Tel: 0121-771 2328; E-mail: frontier@fyt.org.uk; Website: www. fyt.org.uk). For information on StreetSpace, contact Clare McCormack (E-mail: scotland@ streetspace.org.uk).

INTERSERVE SCOTLAND: We are part of Interserve, an international, evangelical and interdenominational organisation with 160 years of Christian service. The purpose of Interserve is 'to make Jesus Christ known through *wholistic* ministry in partnership with the global church, among the neediest peoples of Asia and the Arab world', and our vision is 'Lives and communities transformed through encounter with Jesus Christ'. Interserve supports over 800 people in cross-cultural ministry in a wide range of work including children and youth, the environment, evangelism, Bible training, engineering, agriculture, business development and health. We rely on supporters in Scotland and Ireland to join us. Director: Grace Penney, 4 Blairtummock Place, Panorama Business Village, Queenslie, Glasgow G33 4EN (Tel: 0141-781 1982; Fax: 0141-781 1572; E-mail: info@issi.org.uk; Website: www.interservescotlandandireland.org).

IONA COMMUNITY: An ecumenical Christian community of men and women from different walks of life and different traditions in the Church, committed to the gospel of Jesus Christ and to following where that leads, even into the unknown; engaged together, and with people of goodwill across the world, in acting, reflecting and praying for justice, peace and the integrity of creation; convinced that the inclusive community we seek must be embodied in the community we practise. The Iona Community's work with young people, Wild Goose Resource Group and Wild Goose Publications are based in the Glasgow office. The Community also runs residential centres at the Abbey and MacLeod Centre, Iona and Camas, Mull. Leader: Rev. Peter Macdonald, 4th Floor, Savoy House, 140 Sauchiehall Street, Glasgow G2 3DH (Tel: 0141-332 6343; Fax: 0141-332 1090; E-mail: admin@ iona.org.uk; Website: www.iona.org.uk). Centres Director: Rev. Rosie Magee, Iona Abbey, Isle of Iona, Argyll PA76 6SN (Tel: 01681 700404).

PLACE FOR HOPE: A body with its roots in the Church of Scotland and now an independent charity, its vision is for a world where people embrace the transformational potential of conflict and nurture the art of peacebuilding. Place for Hope accompanies and equips people and faith communities where relationships have become impaired and helps them move towards living well with difference. Through a skilled and highly trained team we aim to accompany groups navigating conflict and difficult conversations and to resource the church and wider faith communities with peacemakers. If you are aware of conflict or difficulty within your faith community and would appreciate support, or wish to encourage your church or faith group to host a community dialogue, invite us to deliver a training or workshop session to your Kirk Session or Presbytery; you may also develop your own skills through our open access training courses. (Tel: 07784 580359; E-mail: info@placeforhope. org.uk; Website: www.placeforhope.org.uk)

The ST COLM'S FELLOWSHIP: An association for all from any denomination who have trained, studied or been resident at St Colm's, either when it was a college or later as

International House. There is an annual retreat and a meeting for Commemoration; and some local groups meet on a regular basis. Hon. Secretary: Margaret Nutter, 'Kilmorich', 14 Balloch Road, Balloch G83 8SR (Tel: 01389 754505; E-mail: mnutter@blueyonder.co.uk).

SCOTTISH CHURCHES HOUSING ACTION: Unites the Scottish Churches in tackling homelessness; supports local volunteering to assist homeless people; advises on using property for affordable housing. Chief Executive: Alastair Cameron, 44 Hanover Street, Edinburgh EH2 2DR (Tel: 0131-477 4500; E-mail: info@churches-housing.org; Website: www.churches-housing.org).

SCOTTISH JOINT COMMITTEE ON RELIGIOUS AND MORAL EDUCATION: This is an interfaith body that began as a joint partnership between the Educational Institute of Scotland and the Church of Scotland to provide resources, training and support for the work of religious and moral education in schools. Rev. Ken Coulter, 121 George Street, Edinburgh EH2 4YN (Tel: 0131-225 5722; E-mail: kcoulter@churchofscotland.org.uk), and Mr Lachlan Bradley, 6 Clairmont Gardens, Glasgow G3 7LW (Tel: 0141-353 3595).

SCRIPTURE UNION SCOTLAND: 70 Milton Street, Glasgow G4 0HR (Tel: 0141-332 1162; Fax: 0141-352 7600; E-mail: info@suscotland.org.uk; Website: www.suscotland.org. uk). Scripture Union Scotland's vision is to see the children and young people of Scotland exploring the Bible and responding to the significance of Jesus. SU Scotland works in schools running Christian Focus Weeks, taking part in assemblies and supporting extra-curricular groups. It also offers 'Classroom Outdoors', an outdoor education programme for school groups that is based around Curriculum for Excellence. These events take place at its two activity centres, Lendrick Muir (Kinross) and Alltnacriche (Aviemore), which also cater for church or school groups throughout the year. During the school holidays and at weekends, it runs an extensive programme of events for school-age children – including residential holidays (some focused on disadvantaged children and young people), missions and church-based holiday clubs. In addition, it runs discipleship and training programmes for young people and is committed to promoting prayer for, and by, the young people of Scotland through a range of national prayer events and the *Pray for Schools Scotland* initiative.

STUDENT CHRISTIAN MOVEMENT: National Co-ordinator: Hilary Topp, SCM, 504F The Big Peg, 120 Vyse Street, Hockley, Birmingham B18 6NE (Tel: 0121-200 3355; E-mail: scm@movement.org.uk; Website: www.movement.org.uk). The Student Christian Movement (SCM) is a student-led community passionate about living out our faith in the real world. We have a network of groups around the country and organise national events.

UCCF: THE CHRISTIAN UNIONS: Blue Boar House, 5 Blue Boar Street, Oxford OX1 4EE (Tel: 01865 253678; E-mail: email@uccf.org.uk). UCCF is a fellowship of students, staff and supporters. Christian Unions are mission teams operating in universities and colleges, supported by the local church, and resourced by UCCF staff. This fellowship exists to proclaim the gospel of Jesus Christ in the student world.

WORLD DAY OF PRAYER: SCOTTISH COMMITTEE: Convener: Christian Williams, 61 McCallum Gardens, Strathview Estate, Bellshill ML4 2SR. Secretary: Marjorie Paton, Muldoanich, Stirling Street, Blackford, Auchterarder PH4 1QG (Tel: 07780 007022; E-mail: marjoriepaton.wdp@btinternet.com; Website: www.wdpscotland.org.uk).

YMCA SCOTLAND: Offers support, training and guidance to churches seeking to reach out to love and serve community needs. Chief Executive – National General Secretary: Ms Kerry Reilly, James Love House, 11 Rutland Street, Edinburgh EH1 2DQ (Tel: 0131-228 1464; E-mail: kerry@ymcascotland.org; Website: www.ymcascotland.org).

YOUTH FOR CHRIST INTERNATIONAL: Described as 'a movement and not an organisation, and also indigenous', every Youth for Christ programme is staffed, governed and financed locally. There are five centres in Scotland. Local Ministries Director: Liz Dumain (Tel: 0121-502 9631; E-mail: liz.dumain@yfc.co.uk; Website: www.yfc.co.uk/local-centres/ scotland).

2. CHURCH OF SCOTLAND SOCIETIES

CHURCH OF SCOTLAND ABSTAINERS' ASSOCIATION: Recognising that alcohol is a major – indeed a growing – problem within Scotland, the aim of the Church of Scotland Abstainers' Association, with its motto 'Abstinence makes sense', is to encourage more people to choose a healthy alcohol-free lifestyle. Further details are available from 'Blochairn', 17A Culduthel Road, Inverness IV24 4AG (Website: www.kirkabstainers.org.uk).

The CHURCH OF SCOTLAND CHAPLAINS' ASSOCIATION: The Association consists of serving and retired chaplains to HM Forces. It holds an annual meeting and lunch on Shrove Tuesday, and organises the annual Service of Remembrance in St Giles' Cathedral on Chaplains' Day of the General Assembly. Hon. Secretary: Rev. Neil N. Gardner MA BD RNR, The Manse of Canongate, Edinburgh EH8 8BR (Tel: 0131-556 3515; E-mail: nng22@btinternet.com).

The CHURCH OF SCOTLAND RETIRED MINISTERS' ASSOCIATION: Hon. Secretary: Rev. David Dutton, 13 Acredales, Haddington EH41 4NT (Tel: 01620 825999; E-mail: duttondw@gmail.com).

CHURCH OF SCOTLAND WORLD MISSION COUNCIL OVERSEAS ASSOCIATION (previously AROS): The WMC continues to provide information and an annual gathering for those who have served internationally. To be added to the contact list, contact the WM department (E-mail: world@churchofscotland.org.uk).

The CHURCH SERVICE SOCIETY: Founded in 1865 to study the development of Christian worship through the ages and in the Reformed tradition, and to work towards renewal in contemporary worship. Secretary: Rev. Dr Douglas Galbraith (Tel: 01592 752403; E-mail: dgalbraith@hotmail.com; Website: www.churchservicesociety.org).

FORUM OF GENERAL ASSEMBLY AND PRESBYTERY CLERKS: Secretary: Rev. David W. Clark, 3 Ritchie Avenue, Cardross, Dumbarton G82 5LL (Tel: 01389 849319; E-mail: dumbarton@cofscotland.org.uk).

COVENANT FELLOWSHIP SCOTLAND (formerly FORWARD TOGETHER): An organisation for evangelicals within the Church of Scotland. Contact the Secretary, Rev. Michael S. Goss (Tel: 01241 410194; E-mail: michaelgoss@blueyonder.co.uk), or the Chairman, Kenneth M. MacKenzie (Tel: 07836 365022; E-mail: kennethmmackenzie@ btinternet.com; Website: http://ftscotland.wordpress.com).

The FRIENDS OF TABEETHA SCHOOL, JAFFA: President: Rev. Elinor Gordon. Hon. Secretary: Rev. Iain F. Paton, Muldoanich, Stirling Street, Blackford, Auchterarder PH4 1QG (Tel: 01764 682234; E-mail: iain.f.paton@btinternet.com).

The IRISH GATHERING: Secretary: Rev. Eric G. McKimmon BA BD MTh PhD, 14 Marionfield Place, Cupar KY15 5JN (Tel: 01334 659650; E-mail: ericmckimmon@gmail.com).

SCOTTISH CHURCH SOCIETY: Founded in 1892 to 'defend and advance Catholic doctrine as set forth in the Ancient Creeds and embodied in the Standards of the Church of Scotland', the Society meets for worship and discussion at All Saints' Tide, holds a Lenten Quiet Day, an AGM in Edinburgh, and other meetings by arrangement; all are open to non members. Secretary: Rev. W. Gerald Jones MA BD MTh, The Manse, Patna Road, Kirkmichael, Maybole KA19 7PJ (Tel: 01655 750286; E-mail: revgerald@jonesg99.freeserve.co.uk).

SCOTTISH CHURCH THEOLOGY SOCIETY: Rev. Alexander Shuttleworth, 62 Toll Road, Kincardine, Alloa FK10 4QZ (Tel: 01259 731002; E-mail: revshuttleworth@aol. com). The Society encourages theological exploration and discussion of the main issues confronting the Church in the twenty-first century.

SOCIETY OF FRIENDS OF ST ANDREW'S JERUSALEM: Hon. Secretary: Major J.M.K. Erskine MBE, World Mission Council, 121 George Street, Edinburgh EH2 4YN. Membership Secretary: Walter T. Dunlop, 50 Oxgangs Road North, Edinburgh EH13 9DR (Tel: 07925 481523); E-mail: oxgangs9586@hotmail.com). Hon. Treasurer: Mrs Catriona M. Scrimgeour BSc ACA, Finance Manager, The Church of Scotland, 121 George Street, Edinburgh EH2 4YN (Tel: 0131-225 5722).

3. BIBLE SOCIETIES

The SCOTTISH BIBLE SOCIETY: Chief Executive: Elaine Duncan, 7 Hampton Terrace, Edinburgh EH12 5XU (Tel: 0131-337 9701; E-mail: info@scottishbiblesociety.org).

WEST OF SCOTLAND BIBLE SOCIETY: Secretary: Rev. Finlay Mackenzie, 6 Shaw Road, Milngavie, Glasgow G62 6LU (Tel: 07817 680011; E-mail: f.c.mack51@gmail.com; Website: www.westofscotlandbiblesociety.com).

4. GENERAL

The BOYS' BRIGADE: Scottish Headquarters, Carronvale House, Carronvale Road, Larbert FK5 3LH (Tel: 01324 562008; Fax: 01324 552323; E-mail: scottishhq@ boys-brigade.org.uk).

BROKEN RITES: Support group for divorced and separated clergy spouses (Tel: 01896 759254 or 01309 641526; E-mail: eshirleydouglas@hotmail.co.uk; Website: www.brokenrites.org).

CHRISTIAN AID SCOTLAND: Kathy Galloway, Head of Christian Aid Scotland, Sycamore House, 290 Bath Street, Glasgow G2 4JR (Tel: 0141-221 7475; E-mail: glasgow@ christian-aid.org). Edinburgh Office: Tel: 0131-220 1254. Perth Office: Tel: 01738 643982.

CHRISTIAN ENDEAVOUR IN SCOTLAND: Challenging and encouraging children and young people in the service of Christ and the Church, especially through the CE Award Scheme: 16 Queen Street, Alloa FK10 2AR (Tel: 01259 215101; E-mail: admin@cescotland.org; Website: www.cescotland.org).

DAYONE CHRISTIAN MINISTRIES (THE LORD'S DAY OBSERVANCE SOCIETY): Ryelands Road, Leominster, Herefordshire HR6 8NZ. Contact Mark Roberts for further information (Tel: 01568 613740; E-mail: info@dayone.co.uk).

ECO-CONGREGATION SCOTLAND: 121 George Street, Edinburgh EH2 4YN (Tel: 0131-240 2274; E-mail: manager@ecocongregationscotland.org; Website: www.ecocongregationscotland.org). Eco-Congregation Scotland is the largest movement of community-based environment groups in Scotland. We offer a programme to help congregations reduce their impact on climate change and live sustainably in a world of limited resources.

FEED THE MINDS: The Foundry, 17 Oval Way, London SE11 5RR (Tel: 020 3752 5800; E-mail: info@feedtheminds.org; Website: www.feedtheminds.org).

GIRLGUIDING SCOTLAND: 16 Coates Crescent, Edinburgh EH3 7AH (Tel: 0131-226 4511; Fax: 0131-220 4828; E-mail: administrator@girlguiding-scot.org.uk; Website: www. girlguidingscotland.org.uk).

The GIRLS' BRIGADE IN SCOTLAND: 11A Woodside Crescent, Glasgow G3 7UL (Tel: 0141-332 1765; E-mail: enquiries@girls-brigade-scotland.org.uk; Website: www.girls-brigade-scotland.org.uk).

The LEPROSY MISSION SCOTLAND: Suite 2, Earlsgate Lodge, Livilands Lane, Stirling FK8 2BG (Tel: 01786 449266; E-mail: contactus@tlmscotland.org.uk; Website: www.tlmscotland.org.uk). National Director: Linda Todd. Communications Manager: Stuart McAra.

RELATIONSHIPS SCOTLAND: Chief Executive: Mr Stuart Valentine, 18 York Place, Edinburgh EH1 3EP (Tel: 0845 119 2020; Fax: 0845 119 6089; E-mail: enquiries@relationships-scotland.org.uk; Website: www.relationships-scotland.org.uk).

SCOTTISH CHURCH HISTORY SOCIETY: President: Andrew T.N. Muirhead MA MLitt, Ythanglen, Copland Place, Alva FK12 5LN (Tel: 01259 760143; E-mail: andrew.muirhead1@btinternet.com).

SCOTTISH EVANGELICAL THEOLOGY SOCIETY: Secretary: Mr John Kennedy, 20 Craiglockhart Quadrant, Edinburgh EH14 1HD (Tel: 0131-444 1615; E-mail jskennedy442@gmail.com; Website: www.s-e-t-s.org.uk).

The SCOTTISH REFORMATION SOCIETY: Chairman: Rev. Dr S. James Millar. Vice-Chairman: Rev. John J. Murray. Secretary: Rev. Dr Douglas Somerset. Treasurer: Rev. Andrew W.F. Coghill, The Magdalen Chapel, 41 Cowgate, Edinburgh EH1 1JR (Tel: 0131-220 1450; E-mail: info@scottishreformationsociety.org; Website: www.scottishreformationsociety.org).

SCOUTS SCOTLAND: Scottish Headquarters, Fordell Firs, Hillend, Dunfermline KY11 7HQ (Tel: 01383 419073; E-mail: shq@scouts.scot; Website: www. scouts.scot).

The SOCIETY IN SCOTLAND FOR PROPAGATING CHRISTIAN KNOWLEDGE: Chairman: Rev. Scott McKenna; Secretary: Richard Grahame. Address: SSPCK, c/o Shepherd and Wedderburn LLP, 1 Exchange Crescent, Edinburgh EH3 8UL (Tel: 0131-228 9900; Website: www.sspck.co.uk; E-mail: SSPCK@shepwedd.co.uk).

TEARFUND: 100 Church Road, Teddington TW11 8QE (Tel: 0845 355 8355). Director: Lynne Paterson, Tearfund Scotland, Challenge House, 29 Canal Street, Glasgow G4 0AD (Tel: 0141-332 3621; E-mail: scotland@tearfund.org; Website: www.tearfund.org).

THEATRE CHAPLAINCY UK (formerly the Actor's Church Union) is an ecumenical scheme providing a Church contact and support to staff and travelling theatre groups in theatres and concert halls throughout the UK. Area Chaplain Scotland: Rev. Thomas Coupar (Tel: 07814 588904; E-mail: chaplain@robinchapel.org.uk).

The WALDENSIAN MISSIONS AID SOCIETY FOR WORK IN ITALY: David A. Lamb SSC, 36 Liberton Drive, Edinburgh EH16 6NN (Tel: 0131-664 3059; E-mail: david@ dlamb.co.uk).

YOUTH SCOTLAND: Balfour House, 19 Bonnington Grove, Edinburgh EH6 4BL (Tel: 0131-554 2561; Fax: 0131-454 3438; E-mail: office@youthscotland.org.uk; Website: www. youthscotland.org.uk).

THE YOUNG WOMEN'S MOVEMENT: Director: Jackie Scutt, Third Floor, Princes House, 5 Shandwick Place, Edinburgh EH2 4RG (Tel: 0330 121 0002; E-mail: admin@ywcascotland. org; Website: www.ywcascotland.org).

(8) TRUSTS AND FUNDS

ABERNETHY ADVENTURE CENTRES: Full board residential accommodation and adventure activities available for all Church groups, plus a range of Christian summer camps at our four centres across Scotland. Tel: 01479 818005; E-mail: marketing@abernethy.org.uk; Website: www.abernethy.org.uk).

The ARROL TRUST: The Arrol Trust gives small grants to young people between the ages of 16 and 25 for the purposes of travel which will provide education or work experience. Potential recipients would be young people with disabilities or who would for financial reasons be otherwise unable to undertake projects. It is expected that projects would be beneficial not only to applicants but also to the wider community. Application forms are available from Callum S. Kennedy WS, Lindsays WS, Caledonian Exchange, 19A Canning Street, Edinburgh EH3 8HE (Tel: 0131-229 1212).

The BAIRD TRUST: Assists in the building and repair of churches and halls, and generally assists the work of the Church of Scotland. Apply to Iain A.T. Mowat CA, 182 Bath Street,

Glasgow G2 4HG (Tel: 0141-332 0476; E-mail: info@bairdtrust.org.uk; Website: www. bairdtrust.org.uk).

The Rev. Alexander BARCLAY BEQUEST: Assists a family member of a deceased minister of the Church of Scotland who at the time of his/her death was acting as his/her housekeeper and who is in needy circumstances, and in certain circumstances assists Ministers, Deacons, Ministries Development Staff and their spouses facing financial hardship. Applications should be made to the Secretary and Clerk, The Church of Scotland Trust, 121 George Street, Edinburgh EH2 4YN (Tel: 0131-240 2222; E-mail: jhamilton@churchofscotland.org.uk) or the Pastoral Support Team, 121 George Street, Edinburgh EH2 4YN (Tel: 0131-225 5722).

BELLAHOUSTON BEQUEST FUND: Gives grants to Protestant evangelical denominations in the City of Glasgow and certain areas within five miles of the city boundary for building and repairing churches and halls and the promotion of religion. Apply to Mr Donald B. Reid, Mitchells Roberton, 36 North Hanover Street, Glasgow G1 2AD (Tel: 0141-552 3422; E-mail: info@mitchells-roberton.co.uk).

BEQUEST FUND FOR MINISTERS: Provides financial assistance to ministers in outlying districts towards the cost of manse furnishings, pastoral efficiency aids, and personal and family medical or educational (including university) costs. Apply to A. Linda Parkhill CA, 60 Wellington Street, Glasgow G2 6HJ (Tel: 0141-226 4994; E-mail: mail@parkhillmackie.co.uk).

CARNEGIE TRUST FOR THE UNIVERSITIES OF SCOTLAND: In cases of hardship, the Carnegie Trust is prepared to consider applications by students of Scottish birth or extraction (at least one parent born in Scotland), or who have had at least two years' education at a secondary school in Scotland, for financial assistance with the payment of their fees for a first degree at a Scottish university. For further details, students should apply to the Secretary, Carnegie Trust for the Universities of Scotland, Andrew Carnegie House, Pittencrieff Street, Dunfermline KY12 8AW (Tel: 01383 724990; Fax: 01383 749799; E-mail: admin@carnegie-trust.org; Website: www.carnegie-trust.org).

CHURCH OF SCOTLAND INSURANCE SERVICES LTD: Arranges Church property and liabilities insurance in its capacity of Insurance Intermediary; also arranges other classes of business including household insurance for members and adherents of the Church of Scotland and insurances for charities. It pays its distributable profits to the Church of Scotland through Gift Aid. It is authorised and regulated by the Financial Conduct Authority and the Prudential Regulation Authority. Contact at 121 George Street, Edinburgh EH2 4YN (Tel: 0131-220 4119; Fax: 0131-220 3113; E-mail: enquiries@cosic.co.uk; Website: www.cosic.co.uk).

CHURCH OF SCOTLAND MINISTRY BENEVOLENT FUND: Makes grants to retired men and women who have been ordained or commissioned for the ministry of the Church of Scotland and to widows, widowers, orphans, spouses or children of such, who are in need. Apply to Elaine Macadie BA CA, Assistant Treasurer (Ministries), 121 George Street, Edinburgh EH2 4YN (Tel: 0131-225 5722).

The CINTRA BEQUEST: See 'Tod Endowment Trust ...' entry below.

CLARK BURSARY: Awarded to accepted candidate(s) for the ministry of the Church of Scotland whose studies for the ministry are pursued at the University of Aberdeen. Applications or recommendations for the Bursary to the Clerk to the Presbytery of Aberdeen, Mastrick Church,

Greenfern Road, Aberdeen AB16 6TR by 16 October annually.

CRAIGCROOK MORTIFICATION: Pensions are paid to poor men and women over 60 years old, born in Scotland or who have resided in Scotland for not less than ten years. At present, pensions amount to £1,000–£1,500 p.a. Ministers are invited to notify the Clerk and Factor, Mrs Fiona M.M. Watson CA, Exchange Place 3, Semple Street, Edinburgh EH3 8BL (Tel: 0131-473 3500; E-mail: charity@scott-moncrieff.com) of deserving persons and should be prepared to act as a referee on the application form.

CROMBIE SCHOLARSHIP: Provides grants annually on the nomination of the Deans of Faculty of Divinity of the Universities of St Andrews, Glasgow, Aberdeen and Edinburgh, who each nominate one matriculated student who has taken a University course in Greek (Classical or Hellenistic) and Hebrew. Award by recommendation only.

The DRUMMOND TRUST: Makes grants towards the cost of publication of books of 'sound Christian doctrine and outreach'. The Trustees are also willing to receive grant requests towards the cost of audio-visual programme material, but not equipment, software but not hardware. Requests for application forms should be made to the Secretaries, Hill and Robb Limited, 3 Pitt Terrace, Stirling FK8 2EY (Tel: 01786 450985; E-mail: douglaswhyte@hillandrobb.co.uk). Manuscripts should *not* be sent.

The David DUNCAN TRUST: Makes grants annually to students for the ministry and students in training to become deacons in the Church of Scotland in the Faculties of Arts and Divinity. Preference is given to those born or educated within the bounds of the former Presbytery of Arbroath. Applications not later than 31 October to Thorntons Law LLP, Brothockbank House, Arbroath DD11 1NE (reference: G.J.M. Dunlop; Tel: 01241 872683; E-mail: gdunlop@thorntons-law.co.uk).

ERSKINE CUNNINGHAM HILL TRUST: Donates 50% of its annual income to the central funds of the Church of Scotland and 50% to other charities. Individual donations are in the region of £1,000. Priority is given to charities administered by voluntary or honorary officials, in particular charities registered and operating in Scotland and relating to the elderly, young people, ex-service personnel or seafarers. Application forms from the Secretary, Nicola Robertson, 121 George Street, Edinburgh EH2 4YN (Tel: 0131-225 5722; E-mail: nrobertson@cofscotland.org.uk).

ESDAILE TRUST: Assists the education and advancement of daughters of ministers, missionaries and widowed deaconesses of the Church of Scotland between 12 and 25 years of age. Applications are to be lodged by 31 May in each year with the Clerk and Treasurer, Mrs Fiona M.M. Watson CA, Exchange Place 3, Semple Street, Edinburgh EH3 8BL (Tel: 0131-473 3500; E-mail: charity@scott-moncrieff.com).

FERGUSON BEQUEST FUND: Assists with the building and repair of churches and halls and, more generally, with the work of the Church of Scotland. Priority is given to the Counties of Ayr, Kirkcudbright, Wigtown, Lanark, Dunbarton and Renfrew, and to Greenock, Glasgow, Falkirk and Ardrossan; applications are, however, accepted from across Scotland. Apply to Iain A.T. Mowat CA, 182 Bath Street, Glasgow G2 4HG (Tel: 0141-332 0476; E-mail: info@fergusonbequestfund.org.uk; Website: www.fergusonbequestfund.org.uk).

GEIKIE BEQUEST: Makes small grants to students for the ministry, including students studying for entry to the University, preference being given to those not eligible for SAAS awards. Apply to Elaine Macadie BA CA, Assistant Treasurer (Ministries), 121 George Street, Edinburgh EH2 4YN by September for distribution in November each year.

James GILLAN'S BURSARY FUND: Bursaries are available for male or female students for the ministry who were born or whose parents or parent have resided and had their home for not less than three years continually in the old counties of Moray or Nairn. Apply to Mr Donald Prentice, St Leonard's, Nelson Road, Forres IV36 IDR (Tel: 01309 672380).

The GLASGOW SOCIETY OF THE SONS AND DAUGHTERS OF MINISTERS OF THE CHURCH OF SCOTLAND: The Society's primary purpose is to grant financial assistance to children (no matter what age) of deceased ministers of the Church of Scotland. Applications are to be submitted by 1 February in each year. To the extent that funds are available, grants are also given for the children of ministers or retired ministers, although such grants are normally restricted to university and college students. These latter grants are considered in conjunction with the Edinburgh-based Society. Limited funds are also available for individual application for special needs or projects. Applications are to be submitted by 31 May in each year. Emergency applications can be dealt with at any time when need arises. Application forms may be obtained from the Secretary and Treasurer, Mrs Fiona M.M. Watson CA, Exchange Place 3, Semple Street, Edinburgh EH3 8BL (Tel: 0131-473 3500; E-mail: charity@scott-moncrieff.com).

HAMILTON BURSARY TRUST: Awarded, subject to the intention to serve overseas under the Church of Scotland World Mission Council or to serve with some other Overseas Mission Agency approved by the Council, to a student at the University of Aberdeen. Preference is given to a student born or residing in (1) Parish of Skene, (2) Parish of Echt, (3) the Presbytery of Aberdeen, Kincardine and Deeside, or Gordon; failing which to Accepted Candidate(s) for the Ministry of the Church of Scotland whose studies for the Ministry are pursued at Aberdeen University. Applications or recommendations for the Bursary to the Clerk to the Presbytery of Aberdeen, Mastrick Church, Greenfern Road, Aberdeen AB16 6TR by 16 October annually.

Martin HARCUS BEQUEST: Makes annual grants to candidates for the ministry resident within the City of Edinburgh. Applications to the Principal's Secretary, New College, Mound Place, Edinburgh EH1 2LX (E-mail: k.mclean@ed.ac.uk) by 15 October.

The HOPE TRUST: Gives some support to organisations involved in combating drink and drugs, and has as its main purpose the promotion of the Reformed tradition throughout the world. There is also a Scholarship programme for Postgraduate Theology Study in Scotland. Apply to Robert P. Miller SSC LLB, 31 Moray Place, Edinburgh EH3 6BY (Tel: 0131-226 5151).

KEAY THOM TRUST: The principal purposes of the Keay Thom Trust are:
1.   To benefit the widows, daughters or other dependent female relatives of deceased ministers, or wives of ministers who are now divorced or separated, all of whom have supported the minister in the fulfilment of his duties and who, by reason of death, divorce or separation, have been required to leave the manse. The Trust can assist them in the purchase of a house or by providing financial or material assistance whether it be for the provision of accommodation or not.
2.   To assist in the education or training of the above female relatives or any other children of deceased ministers.

Further information and application forms are available from Miller Hendry, Solicitors, 10 Blackfriars Street, Perth PH1 5NS (Tel: 01738 637311).

LADIES' GAELIC SCHOOLS AND HIGHLAND BURSARY ASSOCIATION: Distributes money to students, preferably with a Highland/Gaelic background, who are training to be ministers in the Church of Scotland. Apply by 15 October in each year to the Secretary, Donald J. Macdonald, 35 Durham Avenue, Edinburgh EH15 1RZ (E-mail: djandanne@btinternet.com).

The LYALL BEQUEST (Scottish Charity Number SC005542): Offers grants to ministers:
1. Grants to individual ministers and to couples for a holiday for a minimum of one week. No reapplication within a three-year period; and thereafter a 50 per cent grant to those reapplying.
2. Grants towards sickness and convalescence costs so far as not covered by the National Health Service. Applications should be made to the Secretary and Clerk, The Church of Scotland Trust, 121 George Street, Edinburgh EH2 4YN (Tel: 0131-240 2222; E-mail: jhamilton@churchofscotland.org.uk).

REV DR MACINNES AND MRS MACINNES TRUST: Provides grants to (1) retired ministers whose active ministries have been spent in the Counties of Nairn, Ross & Cromarty or Argyll and who are solely dependent upon their pensions and preaching fees and (2) widows or widowers of such ministers solely dependent on their pensions. Applications should be made to the Secretary and Clerk, The Church of Scotland Trust, 121 George Street, Edinburgh EH2 4YN (Tel: 0131-240 2222; E-mail: jhamilton@churchofscotland.org.uk).

Gillian MACLAINE BURSARY FUND: Open to candidates for the ministry of the Church of Scotland of Scottish or Canadian nationality. Preference is given to Gaelic-speakers. Application forms available from Dr Christopher T. Brett MA PhD, Clerk to the Presbytery of Argyll, Minahey Cottage, Kames, Tighnabruaich PA21 2AD (Tel: 01700 811142; E-mail: argyll@churchofscotland.org.uk). Closing date for receipt of applications is 31 October.

The E. McLAREN FUND: The persons intended to be benefited are widows and unmarried ladies, preference being given to ladies above 40 years of age in the following order:
(a) Widows and daughters of Officers in the Highland Regiment, and
(b) Widows and daughters of Scotsmen.
Further details from the Secretary, The E. McLaren Fund, Messrs BMK Wilson, Solicitors, 90 St Vincent Street, Glasgow G2 5UB (Tel: 0141-221 8004; Fax: 0141-221 8088; E-mail: rrs@bmkwilson.co.uk).

MORGAN BURSARY FUND: Makes grants to candidates for the Church of Scotland ministry studying at the University of Glasgow. Apply to the Clerk to the Presbytery of Glasgow, 260 Bath Street, Glasgow G2 4JP (Tel: 0141-332 6606).

NEW MINISTERS' FURNISHING LOAN FUND: Makes loans (of £1,000) to ministers in their first charge to assist with furnishing the manse. Apply to the Assistant Treasurer (Ministries), 121 George Street, Edinburgh EH2 4YN.

NOVUM TRUST: Provides small short-term grants – typically between £200 and £2,500 – to initiate projects in Christian action and research which cannot readily be financed from other sources. Trustees welcome applications from projects that are essentially Scottish, are distinctively new, and are focused on the welfare of young people, on the training of lay people or on new ways of communicating the Christian faith. The Trust cannot support large building projects, staff salaries or individuals applying for maintenance during courses or training. Application forms and guidance notes from novumt@cofscotland.org.uk or Mrs Susan Masterton, Blair Cadell WS, The Bond House, 5 Breadalbane Street, Edinburgh EH6 5JH (Tel: 0131-555 5800; Website: www.novum.org.uk).

PARK MEMORIAL BURSARY FUND: Provides grants for the benefit of candidates for the ministry of the Church of Scotland from the Presbytery of Glasgow under full-time training. Apply to the Clerk to the Presbytery of Glasgow, 260 Bath Street, Glasgow G2 4JP (Tel: 0141-332 6606).

PATON TRUST: Assists ministers in ill health to have a recuperative holiday outwith, and free from the cares of, their parishes. Apply to Alan S. Cunningham CA, Alexander Sloan, Chartered Accountants, 38 Cadogan Street, Glasgow G2 7HF (Tel: 0141-204 8989; Fax: 0141-248 9931; E-mail: alan.cunningham@alexandersloan.co.uk).

PRESBYTERY OF ARGYLL BURSARY FUND: Open to students who have been accepted as candidates for the ministry and the readership of the Church of Scotland. Preference is given to applicants who are natives of the bounds of the Presbytery, or are resident within the bounds of the Presbytery, or who have a strong connection with the bounds of the Presbytery. Application forms available from Dr Christopher T. Brett MA PhD, Clerk to the Presbytery of Argyll, Minahey Cottage, Kames, Tighnabruaich PA21 2AD (Tel: 01700 811142; E-mail: argyll@ churchofscotland.org.uk). Closing date for receipt of applications is 31 October.

Margaret and John ROSS TRAVELLING FUND: Offers grants to ministers and their spouses for travelling and other expenses for trips to the Holy Land where the purpose is recuperation or relaxation. Applications should be made to the Secretary and Clerk, The Church of Scotland Trust, 121 George Street, Edinburgh EH2 4YN (Tel: 0131-240 2222; E-mail: jhamilton@churchofscotland.org.uk).

SCOTLAND'S CHURCHES TRUST: Assists, through grants, with the preservation of the fabric of buildings in use for public worship by any denomination. Also supports the playing of church organs by grants for public concerts, and through tuition bursaries for suitably proficient piano or organ players wishing to improve skills or techniques. SCT promotes visitor interest in churches through the trust's Pilgrim Journeys covering Scotland. Criteria and how to apply at www.scotlandschurchestrust.org.uk. Scotland's Churches Trust, 15 North Bank Street, Edinburgh EH1 2LP (E-mail: info@scotlandschurchestrust.org.uk).

SMIETON FUND: Makes small holiday grants to ministers. Administered at the discretion of the pastoral staff, who will give priority in cases of need. Applications to the Education and Support Secretary, Ministries Council, 121 George Street, Edinburgh EH2 4YN.

Mary Davidson SMITH CLERICAL AND EDUCATIONAL FUND FOR ABERDEENSHIRE: Assists ministers who have been ordained for five years or over and are in full charge of a congregation in Aberdeen, Aberdeenshire and the north, to purchase books, or to travel for educational purposes, and assists their children with scholarships for further education or vocational training. Apply to Alan J. Innes MA LLB, 100 Union Street, Aberdeen AB10 1QR (Tel: 01224 428000).

The SOCIETY FOR THE BENEFIT OF THE SONS AND DAUGHTERS OF THE CLERGY OF THE CHURCH OF SCOTLAND: Annual grants are made to assist in the education of the children (normally between the ages of 12 and 25 years) of ministers of the Church of Scotland. The Society also gives grants to aged and infirm daughters of ministers and ministers' unmarried daughters and sisters who are in need. Applications are to be lodged by 31 May in each year with the Secretary and Treasurer, Mrs Fiona M.M. Watson CA, Exchange Place 3, Semple Street, Edinburgh EH3 8BL (Tel: 0131-473 3500; E-mail: charity@scott-moncrieff.com).

The Nan STEVENSON CHARITABLE TRUST FOR RETIRED MINISTERS: Provides houses, or loans to purchase houses, on similar terms to the Housing and Loan Fund, for any retired paid church worker with a North Ayrshire connection. Secretary and Treasurer: Mrs Ann Turner, 42 Keir Hardie Drive, Ardrossan KA22 8PA (Tel: 01294 462834; E-mail: annturner62@ btopenworld.com).

Miss M.E. SWINTON PATERSON'S CHARITABLE TRUST: The Trust can give modest grants to support smaller congregations in urban or rural areas who require to fund essential maintenance or improvement works at their buildings. Apply to Mr Callum S. Kennedy WS, Messrs Lindsays WS, Caledonian Exchange, 19A Canning Street, Edinburgh EH3 8HE (Tel: 0131-229 1212).

SYNOD OF GRAMPIAN CHILDREN OF THE CLERGY FUND: Makes annual grants to children of deceased ministers. Apply to Rev. Iain U. Thomson, Clerk and Treasurer, 4 Keirhill Gardens, Westhill AB32 6AZ (Tel: 01224 746743).

SYNOD OF GRAMPIAN WIDOWS' FUND: Makes annual grants (currently £240 p.a.) to widows or widowers of deceased ministers who have served in a charge in the former Synod. Apply to Rev. Iain U. Thomson, Clerk and Treasurer, 4 Keirhill Gardens, Westhill AB32 6AZ (Tel: 01224 746743).

TOD ENDOWMENT TRUST; CINTRA BEQUEST; TOD ENDOWMENT SCOTLAND HOLIDAY FUND: The Trustees of the Cintra Bequest and of the Tod Endowment Scotland Holiday Fund can consider an application for a grant from the Tod Endowment funds from any ordained or commissioned minister or deacon in Scotland of at least two years' standing before the date of application, to assist with the cost of the beneficiary and his or her spouse or partner and dependants obtaining rest and recuperation in Scotland. The Trustees of the Tod Endowment Scotland Holiday Fund can also consider an application from an ordained or commissioned minister or deacon who has retired. Application forms are available from Mrs J.S. Wilson, Solicitor (for the Cintra Bequest), and from Elaine Macadie BA CA, Assistant Treasurer (Ministries) (for the Tod Endowment Scotland Holiday Fund). The address in both cases is 121 George Street, Edinburgh EH2 4YN (Tel: 0131-225 5722). (Attention is drawn to the separate entry above for the Church of Scotland Ministry Benevolent Fund.)

STEPHEN WILLIAMSON & ALEX BALFOUR FUND: Offers grants to Ministers in the Presbyteries of Angus, Dunfermline, Kirkcaldy and St Andrews to assist with the cost of educational school trips for children. Applications should be made to the Secretary and Clerk, The Church of Scotland Trust, 121 George Street, Edinburgh EH2 4YN (Tel: 0131-240 2222; E-mail: jhamilton@churchofscotland.org.uk).

The undernoted hotels provide special terms as described. Fuller information may be obtained from the establishments:

CRIEFF HYDRO Ltd and MURRAYPARK HOTEL: The William Meikle Trust Fund and Paton Fund make provision whereby active ministers and their spouses and members of the Diaconate may enjoy the hotel and self-catering accommodation all year round at a supplemented rate, subject to availability and a maximum number of stays per year. Crieff Hydro offers a wide range of inclusive leisure facilities including leisure pool, gym, cinema and entertainment programme. BIG Country also provides free daily childcare for Crieff Hydro guests only. Over-60 on-site activities and five places to eat are also available at great prices. Currently, a moratorium has been placed on benefits from the Trust.

(9) LONG SERVICE CERTIFICATES

Long Service Certificates, signed by the Moderator, have to date been available for presentation to elders and others in respect of not less than thirty years of service. At the General Assembly of 2015, it was agreed that further certificates could be issued at intervals of ten years thereafter. It should be noted that the period is years of *service*, not (for example) years of ordination in the case of an elder. In the case of Sunday School teachers and Bible Class leaders, the qualifying period is twenty-one years of service. Certificates are not issued posthumously, nor is it possible to make exceptions to the rules, for example by recognising quality of service in order to reduce the qualifying period, or by reducing the qualifying period on compassionate grounds, such as serious illness. Applications for Long Service Certificates should be made in writing to the Principal Clerk at 121 George Street, Edinburgh EH2 4YN by the parish minister, or by the session clerk on behalf of the Kirk Session. Certificates are not issued from this office to the individual recipients, nor should individuals make application themselves.

(10) RECORDS OF THE CHURCH OF SCOTLAND

Church records more than fifty years old, unless still in use, should be sent or delivered to the Principal Clerk for onward transmission to the National Records of Scotland. Where ministers or session clerks are approached by a local repository seeking a transfer of their records, they should inform the Principal Clerk, who will take the matter up with the National Records of Scotland.
    Where a temporary retransmission of records is sought, it is extremely helpful if notice can be given three months in advance so that appropriate procedures can be carried out satisfactorily.

(11) ORGANIST TRAINING SCHEMES

This is a list of schemes operated by Presbyteries and other bodies to identify and train organists for Sunday services. The list is by no means exhaustive, and the Editor would be glad to know of any omissions.

1. SCOTTISH CHURCHES ORGANIST TRAINING SCHEME (SCOTS)

Established in 1997 as an initiative of the then Panel on Worship, along with the Royal School of Church Music's Scottish Committee and the Scottish Federation of Organists, this is a self-propelled scheme by which a pianist who seeks competence on the organ – and organists who wish to develop their skills – can follow a three-stage syllabus, receiving a certificate at each stage. Participants each have an Adviser whom they meet occasionally for assessment, and also take part in one of the three or four Local Organ Workshops which are held in different parts of Scotland each year. There is a regular e-newsletter, *Scots Wha Play*. Costs are kept low. SCOTS is an ecumenical scheme. Information from Douglas Galbraith (E-mail: dgalbraith@ hotmail.com).

2. PRESBYTERY SCHEMES

Hamilton: Two scholarships of £300 each to cover one year of three terms, each consisting of ten half-hour lessons (E-mail: hamilton@churchofscotland.org.uk).

Dunkeld and Meigle: Four scholarships of ten lessons (each £25) for existing or would-be organists of modest means and who are willing to be available for the accompaniment of church services (E-mail: dunkeldmeigle@churchofscotland.org.uk).

Perth: Enables up to four people with the requisite keyboard skills to have tuition for up to two years (E-mail: perth@churchofscotland.org.uk).

Dundee: Enables two persons per annum, preferably who have reached Grade 6 on keyboard or equivalent, to have organ lessons. A certificate is given on completion (E-mail: lewis_ rose48@yahoo.co.uk).

3. OTHER SCHEMES

Positif Organist: This is a year-long experience, when a group meets for an evening once a month (nine meetings) on subjects ranging from the organ and its terminology, through different traditions and periods of organ music, to playing and registering traditional and modern hymns. The cost is £150 for the year. Contact Sheila Chisholm for an application form (E-mail: coolnote@coolnote.freeserve.co.uk; more details at http://sheilachisholm.weebly. com/positif-organist.htm).

St Andrews University: The **Summer Organ School** is a week-long residential course offering expert tuition, practice time and the chance to try several fine organs. Cost: with accommodation £595, without £295. Contact Ruth Carr, Summer Organ School Co-ordinator (Tel: 01334 462226; E-mail: rac10@st-andrews.ac.uk), or download a brochure (Website: www.st-andrews.ac.uk/music/perform/shortcourses).

Royal School of Church Music (RSCM) Skills Courses: These are designed to help practising church musicians to develop the skills and understanding that they need for their role, and to equip those who want to be able to lead music in worship. The programme is based on distance learning, combining private study at home with practical experience in the student's own church. It is designed for use by students studying alone or with a teacher, and may be complemented by optional attendance at RSCM workshops, masterclasses and short residential courses. There are three levels; and participants choose one of four skills: organist, choir director, cantor, music-group leader. Registration is £135; first level £390, each subsequent level £200. Brochure downloadable (Website: www.rscm.com). There are reductions for RSCM members.

Scotland's Churches Trust: In association with the Inches Carr Trust, SCT plans to offer up to four bursaries a year of £250 for a minimum of six hours' tuition, to be used within a three-month period. SCT (see page 34) has as one of its aims the opening of church buildings to visitors and pilgrims during the week; and it is hoped that the bursaries, as well as equipping church organists, might also lead to the instruments being heard more often by the public. Information from Stuart Muir (E-mail: music@saintpaulscathedral.net), Robin Bell (E-mail: robin.bell_home@hotmail.co.uk) or Douglas Galbraith (E-mail: dgalbraith@hotmail.com).

4. OTHER RESOURCES

Different Voices: An online blog/magazine on church music which publishes articles and videos useful to organists and other church musicians (Website: www.churchofscotland.org. uk/blogs).

Scottish Federation of Organists: The national network of organists (Website: www. scotsorgan.org.uk).

Church Service Society: A Scottish society (founded in 1865) which focuses on worship, including church music (Website: www.churchservicesociety.org). See entry on page 26.

---

(12) THE CHURCH OF SCOTLAND AND THE GAELIC LANGUAGE

Duilleagan Gàidhlig
Ann an 2008, airson a' cheud turais riamh, bha earrann Ghàidhlig anns *An Leabhar Bhliadhnail.* On àm sin bha duilleagan Gàidhlig air an clò-bhualadh am measg nan duilleagan Beurla. Tha sin fhèin 'na chomharradh air an inbhe a tha Eaglais na h-Alba a' toirt do ar cànan. Tha fios againn gun do rinn mòran toileachadh gun tugadh àite don Ghàidhlig anns an leabhar seo.

Moderàtor na Bliadhna seo
Bha e 'na adhbhar toileachais nach bu bheag do na Gàidheil gur e Moderàtor le Gàidhlig a bha anns a' chathair aig Ard-sheanadh na bliadhna seo. Cha robh Moderàtor a bha fileanta anns a' Ghàidhlig anns an dreuchd seo o 1969, nuair a bha an t-Oll. Urr. Tòmas M. MacCalmain a' stiùireadh cùisean an Ard-sheanaidh. Tha Moderàtor na bliadhna seo, an t-Oll. Urr Aonghas Moireastan, air ùidh mhòr a nochdadh ann a bhith a' neartachadh suidheachadh na Gàidhlig an taobh a-staigh Eaglais na h-Alba.

Seirbheis Ghàidhlig an Ard-sheanaidh
Ann an dòigh no dhà bha seirbheis Ghàidhlig na bliadhna seo eadar-dhealaichte. Chaidh a cumail mar as àbhaist ann an Eaglais nam Manach Liath, far a bheil adhradh Gàidhlig a h-uile Didòmhnaich tron bhliadhna. Mar a thachair bho chionn grunn bhliadhnachan a-nis, ghabh Còisir Ghàidhlig Lodainn compàirt ann an seirbheis an Ard-sheanaidh. Sheinn a' chòisir cuideachd aig tè de choinneamhan an Ard-sheanaidh.

Aig aon àm bhiodh am BBC a' craobh-sgaoileadh seirbheis Ghàidhlig an Ard-sheanaidh beò air an ràdio. Ach tha corra bhliadhna a-nis bho nach do thachair sin. Ach am bliadhna bha cothrom aig Gàidheil ann an Alba agus gu dearbh air feadh an t-saoghail an t-seirbheis air fad a chluinntinn air an ràdio an dearbh latha a chaidh a cumail. Bha am Moderàtor air ceann an adhraidh agus b'esan a lìbhrig an searmon. Bha an searmon air a chlò-bhualadh anns *Na Duilleagan Gàidhlig* aig *Life and Work.* A' togail an fhuinn bha Iain MacLeòid, agus bha e 'na adhbhar misneachaidh gur e Gàidheil òga, Màiri NicRath agus Pàdraig Moireastan, a leugh na Sgriobtaran.

Co-labhairt Shònraichte
Anns a' Mhàrt am bliadhna chumadh co-chruinneachadh ann an eaglais an Tron ann an Glaschu gu bhith a' beachdachadh air staid na Gàidhlig ann an Eaglais na h-Alba agus mar a ghabhas an cànan a bhith air a neartachadh ann am beatha agus ann an adhradh na Gàidhlig. Bha làmh aig a' Mhoderàtor agus aig Rùnaire Comhairle an Ard-sheanaidh, Pauline Weibye, ann a bhith a' cur na co-labhairt seo air bhonn.

Tha a' Ghàidhlig air adhartas mòr a dhèanamh ann am foghlam agus ann an iomadh roinn eile bho bha an t-Oll. Urr. Tòmas MacCalmain 'na Mhoderàtor air an Ard-sheanadh ann an 1969. Tha Pàrlamaid na h-Eòrpa a' toirt inbhe don Ghàidhlig mar aon de mhion-chànan na Roinn Eòrpa. Ann an 2005 thug Pàrlamaid na h-Alba dhuinn Achd Gàidhlig na h-Alba. Tha Sabhal Mòr Ostaig a' dol o neart gu neart agus tha e a-nis mar phàirt de Oilthaigh na Gàidhealtachd agus nan Eilean. Tha piseach air tighinn air craobh-sgaoileadh Gàidhlig air an ràdio, agus a-nis tha seanal Gàidhlig telebhisein againn, *Alba,* air am bi mòran aig nach eil Gàidheal a' coimhead. Tha barrachd Gàidhlig anns na pàipearan-naidheachd.

Chaidh iomadh puing chudthromach a thogail aig a' cho-labhairt a chuir an luchd-èisdeachd gu rannsachadh. Mar eisimpleir, tha na mìltean de dh'òigridh air feadh Alba a' faighinn foghlaim ann an sgoiltean Gàidhlig agus ann an aonadan Gàidhlig. Ach a rèir coltais chan eil mòran ga dhèanamh airson a bhith a' frithealadh do na h-oileanaich sin ann an ainm na h-Eaglais.

Chualas mun laoidheadair ùr, *Seinneamaid Còmhla,* a dh'fhoillsich coitheanal Chille Mhoire agus Stèiseil anns an Eilean Sgitheanach, agus mar a tha seinn nan salm anns an t-seann nòs fhathast air a cumail suas anns an sgìr sin. Chualas òraidean inntinneach air craobh-sgaoileadh na Gàidhlig anns na meadhanan. agus mar a dh'fheumas sinn feum a dhèanamh de theicneòlas ùr an latha an-diugh. Bha an luchd-èisdeachd air am misneachadh ann a bhith a' cluinntinn mar a tha dòighean-adhraidh sean agus ùr air an cur air bhonn aig Sabhal Mòr Ostaig.

'S e *An Ciad Ceum* an t-ainm a thugadh air a' cho-chruinneachadh seo ann an Glaschu. Tha sinn an dòchas gum faic sinn ceumannan eile a' leantainn air a' cheum adhartach a bha seo.

In the current book, a line divides the Gaelic from the English translation
In 2008, for the first time ever, a Gaelic section was included in the *Year Book.* Since then Gaelic pages have been printed among the English pages. That in itself is an indication of the status that the Church of Scotland gives to the Gaelic language. Many people have been glad to see Gaelic receiving such recognition in this publication.

This Year's Moderator
It was a source of great pleasure to Gaels that a Gaelic-speaking Moderator was elected to occupy the chair at this year's General Assembly. Not since 1969 has a Moderator who was fluent in Gaelic held this office, when Rev. Dr. T. Murchison guided the affairs of the Assembly. This year's Moderator, Rev. Dr. Angus Morrison, has shown great enthusiasm for the strengthening of the position of Gaelic within the Church of Scotland.

General Assembly Gaelic Service

In a number of ways this year's Assembly Gaelic service was different from previous years. It was held, as always, in Greyfriars Highland and Tolbooth Kirk, where Gaelic worship takes place every Sunday throughout the year. As has happened for some years now, Lothian Gaelic Choir contributed to the Assembly service. The Choir also sang at one of the sessions of the General Assembly during the week.

At one time the BBC used to broadcast the Gaelic Assembly service live on radio. But this has not happened for some years now. But this year Gaels throughout Scotland, and indeed throughout the world, had the opportunity to hear the entire service on the radio on the same day as it took place. The Moderator conducted the service and preached the sermon. The sermon has been printed in the Gaelic Supplement of *Life and Work*. The precentor was John MacLeod, and it was encouraging that the Scriptures were read by two young Gaels, Mairi MacRae and Padruig Morrison.

A Milestone Conference

In March this year a conference was held in the Tron church in Glasgow to discuss the state of Gaelic in the Church of Scotland and to consider ways in which the language can be strengthened in the life and worship of the church. The Moderator and the Council of Assembly Secretary, Pauline Weibye, took the initiative in setting up this conference.

Gaelic has made great advances in education and in other fields in the years since Rev. Dr. Tom Murchison was Moderator of the General Assembly in 1969. The European Parliament has recognised Gaelic as one of the minority European languages. In 2005 the Scottish Parliament delivered the Gaelic (Scotland) Act, establishing Gaelic as a national language. Sabhal Mòr Ostaig continues to go from strength to strength and is now a vital part of the University of the Highlands and Islands. Gaelic broadcasting on radio has expanded, and *Alba,* the Gaelic television channel has been established, attracting thousands of viewers who do not speak Gaelic. There are more Gaelic articles in newspapers.

But it is a cause for concern that what we see is deterioration when we examine the use of Gaelic in the worship of the Church. In parishes where weekly Gaelic services used to be held, English has taken over, and Gaelic service may be held only on a monthly basis. Many important points were raised at the conference which gave those present much food for thought. For example, thousands of young people attend Gaelic medium schools and Gaelic units throughout Scotland. Yet the Church seems to be doing little in reaching out to students who are passing through the Gaelic schools.

The conference heard about *Seinneamaid Còmhla,* a new Gaelic hymnbook produced by the congregation of Kilmuir and Stenscholl in Skye, where traditional Gaelic psalm-singing is also encouraged. There was an interesting presentation on Gaelic broadcasting, and the importance of using modern means of communication was stressed. Those present were encouraged to hear about the development of contemporary and traditional Gaelic worship at Sabhal Mòr Ostaig.

This historic conference was given the title *An Ciad Ceum* (the First Step). We look forward to further important steps being taken as a follow-up to this timely first step.

SECTION 3

Church Procedure

A. THE MINISTER AND BAPTISM

See www.churchofscotland.org.uk/yearbook > Section 3A

B. THE MINISTER AND MARRIAGE

See www.churchofscotland.org.uk/yearbook > Section 3B

C. CONDUCT OF MARRIAGE SERVICES (CODE OF GOOD PRACTICE)

See www.churchofscotland.org.uk/yearbook > Section 3C

D. MARRIAGE AND CIVIL PARTNERSHIP (SCOTLAND) ACT 2014

See www.churchofscotland.org.uk/yearbook > Section 3D

E. CONDUCT OF FUNERAL SERVICES: FEES

See www.churchofscotland.org.uk/yearbook > Section 3E

F. PULPIT SUPPLY FEES AND EXPENSES

See www.churchofscotland.org.uk/yearbook > Section 3F

G. PROCEDURE IN A VACANCY

A full coverage can be found in two handbooks listed under *Interim Moderators and Nominating Committees* on the Ministries Resources pages on the Church of Scotland website: www.churchofscotland.org.uk > About us > Councils, committees > Ministries Council
Scroll down to foot of page and click on 'Ministries Resources'

SECTION 4

The
General Assembly
of 2015

(1) OFFICE-BEARERS OF THE GENERAL ASSEMBLY

The Lord High Commissioner:	The Right Honourable The Lord Hope of Craighead KT PC FRSE
Moderator:	The Right Rev. Angus Morrison MA BD PhD
Chaplains to the Moderator:	Rev. Douglas A.O. Nicol MA BD Rev. Alan D. Reid MA BD
Acting Principal Clerk:	Rev. George J. Whyte BSc BD DMin
Acting Depute Clerk:	Rev. George S. Cowie BSc BD
Procurator:	Ms Laura Dunlop QC
Law Agent:	Mrs Janette S. Wilson LLB NP
Convener of the Business Committee:	Rev. Derek Browning MA BD DMin
Vice-Convener of the Business Committee:	Ms Judith Pearson LLB LLM
Precentor:	Rev. Douglas Galbraith BD BMus PhD ARSCM
Chief Steward:	Mr. William Mearns
Assembly Officer:	Mr David McColl
Assistant Assembly Officer:	Mr Craig Marshall

(2) THE MODERATOR

The Right Reverend Angus Morrison MA BD PhD

Angus Morrison arrived in the Moderatorial Chair of the 2015 General Assembly by a unique route – one which included surgery for prostate cancer at Dundee's Ninewells Hospital – and an indication of the gracious and inclusive style of Angus came when he welcomed the surgeon who had performed the operation to the Moderator's Reception in Parliament Hall.

Angus was born in Glencoe in 1953, one of the three children of father Norman, who worked in the Northern Lighthouse Service, and mother, Mary Ann. Norman's work took the family to live in Oban, Stromness and Edinburgh, and the Christian upbringing of his childhood has influenced Angus ever since.

Following studies in Classics, Angus trained for the ministry of the Free Presbyterian Church, and it was in his first congregation in Oban that he met Marion, a teacher by profession, and they were married in Marion's home town of Fort William in 1983. Angus and Marion have four of a family, David, Judith, Robert and James.

After seven years in Oban, Angus sensed a call to the Edinburgh congregation of the Free Presbyterian Church, and here he experienced the great sadness of the excommunication from the Church of Lord Mackay of Clashfern, the Lord Chancellor, and Elder of the Edinburgh congregation, for attending a Roman Catholic funeral. The action of the Free Presbyterian Church led to the formation of the Associated Presbyterian Church with Angus as Minister of its Edinburgh congregation, one that developed over his time there – as Angus' thinking about the use of hymns and the place of women in the Church moved forward. The experience of these challenging times in Edinburgh caused Angus great dismay at the schismatic tendency of Scottish Presbyterianism, and renewed a commitment in him to work for a unity of purpose amongst Kingdom people of all denominations.

In the year 2000 Angus conducted worship as a guest of the Stornoway Associated Presbyterian congregation, and it was there that he met members of the Church of Scotland's St. Columba's congregation in the town. They called Angus to be their Minister, and Angus' acceptance as a Church of Scotland Minister opened up new doors of service for him. He has served on the Panel on Doctrine, the Church and Nation Committee, and the Special Commission on Same Sex Relationships in Ministry, and from 2005 to 2009 he served as the first Convener of the new Mission and Discipleship Council.

Angus quickly grasped the wide range of the new Council's work and that spirit of gracious inclusiveness issued in the generous support and encouragement he gave to every area. It was no easy or straightforward task to bring together the different areas of the new Council's work and, despite being based in Stornoway, Angus gave unstintingly of his time to all of the Council's concerns as he led the shaping of its developing work. For two of the General Assemblies to which he reported on the Council's work he was also Chaplain to the Lord High Commissioner, Lord Mackay of Clashfern, and he carried out these two roles to full effect.

In 2006 Angus was appointed a Chaplain in Ordinary to the Queen, and then in 2011 he was called by the congregation of Orwell and Portmoak in the Presbytery of Perth to be their Minister. His gracious and winsome manner has won many friends across the neighbouring parishes and in the wider Kinross-shire community where his nomination as Moderator-Designate of the 2014 General Assembly was greeted with genuine delight. It was with great personal (and widely-shared) disappointment that Angus had to withdraw to undergo surgery. He was deeply touched by the decision of the 2014 Assembly to open the way for his appointment as Moderator-Designate of this year's Assembly, and was delighted when fully restored health enabled him to accept the appointment. In doing so he became the first Gaelic-speaking Moderator since the Very Rev. Tom Murchison in 1969, and as his Chaplains we witnessed the joy of all who attended the Gaelic Service of the General Assembly in Greyfriars Kirk this year.

The characteristic gracious inclusiveness of Angus Morrison permeated the life and business of the 2015 General Assembly, and will without doubt be the keynote of his Moderatorial Year. All who meet him will feel at home in his company, and a life of Christian service will be reflected in all that he says and does. We pray God's blessings on both Angus and Marion and their family for this special year – and for all the years to come.

Douglas Nicol and Alan Reid
Moderator's Chaplains

Notes Footage of the Installation of the Moderator may be found on the Church of Scotland's website: www.churchofscotland.org.uk > About us > Who's who > The Moderator
Scroll down to foot of page and click on link

A diary of visits and events involving the Moderator may be also be found there: www.churchofscotland.org.uk > About us > Who's who > Moderator's Diary

(3) THE GENERAL ASSEMBLY

To capture the General Assembly in the confines of three pages of the Year Book is like trying to insert the proverbial quart into a pint pot. This is not helped by the fact that in recent years the Assembly itself has spilled over into other runnels – the outworkings and embodiment of the speech, reflection and worship that is the core work of the Assembly.

- There is that festival of tents and events in the Gardens – Heart and Soul, a note of high celebration of the endeavours and achievements of the local church.
- There is the 'Fringe', the lunches and the evening meetings which enable different groups to enthuse about what they are doing and discovering, and to make converts to the cause.
- There is the life of the Palace, where Church encounters State in ceremony and reception, while during the week the Lord High Commissioner brings the affirmation and encouragement of both to local initiatives and institutions round the country.
- More and more, there is the Assembly the world is enabled to see, streamed, packaged and interpreted through the efforts of a talented Communications team.
- People-wise, the Commissioners are augmented and infiltrated by that other, Youth, Assembly, bringing their fresh voice, while the delegates from the world church, numbering over 50, by their contributions and stories challenge the local church to a costlier discipleship.
- This year also the academy dovetailed with the Assembly as Professors Dawson and Fergusson proved that Scotland continues its role of providing scholars on the world's stage.
- And we don't forget the Cornerstone Bookshop, now an institution in the Martin Hall, counterpointing the issues and debates with a broad and inspired display of books.

One could report on reports and list deliverances, but more interesting perhaps are the strands and themes which drew all the varied work together. First, there was a strong sense of responding to the new. As the Convener of the Assembly Arrangements Committee, Dr Browning, remarked at the outset, 'we are moving through a new landscape' and had come to 'one of those exciting places in the history of God's Church'. The World Mission Council echoed this: what the church is doing in the world is different from 100 years ago because the world is different; we must become more engaged in what *God* is doing. 'Moving from maintenance to mission' was the purpose of the pilot project with 20 congregations supported by the Panel on Review and Reform, while there were examples aplenty in the imaginative forms of recruitment and deployment of a variety of ministries being proposed by the Ministries Council: 'God is calling the church to be different and that will mean that ministries will be different'. In these times, said the Mission and Discipleship Convener, we need something of the trust and imagination of those who built our cathedrals, who had the vision that they were engaged in something magnificent, but which they might never see. 'We need *cathedral thinkers*, people who can think beyond their own lifetime'.

Another theme, blazoned on the book of reports, 'Living Stones', was taken up in a number of ways. It shaped the Heart and Soul event, it was explored from several perspectives by the Moderator in his reflections at the beginning of each day, and it was a theme that was to the fore both explicitly and implicitly in several reports. The Council of Assembly – noting a new book of heartening local stories under that title, Mission and Discipleship – the title of significant new prayer material, stable mate of a wide range of resources for mission; for World Mission the phrase meant a more active engagement in what God was doing around the world and the development of mutually enriching relationships with 'living stones' across the globe.

Within all this, prompted by the election of the first native Gaelic-speaking Moderator since 1969, there was a strand of Gaelic language and culture, emerging in song, psalm and clarsach music, in the reading of Scripture, in the video link (at Heart and Soul) with a Highland congregation. The Assembly also heard of the award-winning Gaelic language project in an Inverness school in relation to its dementia care initiative on the part of CrossReach.

A single issue that dominated the discussion was the matter of 'equal marriage', although strictly speaking the Assembly was concerned only about whether individual Kirk Sessions may opt to depart from the current practice of the Church by calling and appointing ministers and deacons in civil partnerships. This had returned after Barrier Act procedure in which two out of three presbyteries had voted to proceed (although the individual vote had been much closer), and the Assembly agreed to convert the overture to law (309 to 182, with 74 Commissioners registering their dissent). Then a joint working party, set up last year to anticipate a possible decision by the Scottish Parliament to recognise in law a marriage between two people of the same gender (a decision which by now had been taken), reaffirmed the understanding of marriage as being between a man and a woman, which meant that a minister or deacon could not perform a 'same-sex' marriage and, they believed, would not be at risk in refusing to do so. Finally, the Legal Questions Committee and the Theological Forum recommended that the Assembly need not re-open the debate about Call in respect of same-gender marriage, which, to their mind, raised no new issues. This, they argued, was not endorsing such an understanding of marriage, which was a civil law only. After discussion, this, with the agreement of the Conveners, was sent to presbyteries under the Barrier Act in spite of a motion to sist the matter until the Forum could study the whole issue of same-sex marriage, a task that the Forum nevertheless promised to undertake.

As in previous debates on related and sensitive issues, the discussion was thoughtful and measured. Nevertheless, behind it lay vigorous debate and painful encounters in the Church at large. The retiring Moderator, the Very Rev John Chalmers, did not mince words in the report of his moderatorial year when he said: 'We cannot go on suffering the pain of internal attacks which are designed to undermine the work or the place of others. It's time to play for the team. And let me be very clear here – I am not speaking to one side or another of the theological spectrum. I am speaking to both ends and middle. It is time to stop calling each other names, time to shun the idea that we should define ourselves by our differences and instead define ourselves by what we hold in common – our baptism into Christ, our dependence on God's grace, our will to serve the poor and so on'.

This was only one strand in a rich speech, one which deserves to be much studied in the Church, and then studied again. It was an argument for the role of Moderator who for a year intensively engages with the whole Church – and much wider, and who may find himself or herself with urgent messages to deliver. Another strand was a warning that amidst all the good that was happening, we may be in danger of becoming just a bit too fragmented – a bit less presbyterian and a bit more congregationalist: 'In my analysis there is great strength in our Presbyterian polity and it's time to recover the best bits'. He also spoke passionately of the transformational potential of the Christian faith. Our real gift was in the nourishing of people's inner lives and we need, he said, to get down to that serious work. Yet the overarching theme was reconciliation and peace, which had permeated his year, beginning with calling for (and presiding over) 'respectful dialogue' in political change, and continuing expression in the gift he offered people as he travelled, the small glass doves made in Bethlehem by Palestinian Christians, made from glass recovered from bombsites – 'beauty from brokenness'. Fittingly, the Hall for his speech was garlanded by strings of paper doves prepared by children across the country.

Once again this year, we saw the wide embrace of the Assembly's and the Church's concern. The Guild, just when you thought they must by now have exhausted their best ideas, announced six new projects that could not fail to engage the church in mission and healing. CrossReach was said to be at the forefront of social care, particularly in the areas of dementia care, learning disabilities and children's work. The Church and Society report, as we have come to expect, embraced a wide sweep of the social and political issues that concern the people of the country; its prevailing theme was justice – social, climate, gender, criminal, international, and so on, and this was echoed in other reports, not least that of World Mission, where the global journey with others to which it called us was towards justice, peace, healing and life in all its fullness. Journey was a theme also in the report of the Ecumenical Relations Committee, whose Convener offered the story of the Samaritan woman as an image of the new discoveries about each other we are to make as we embark on what the World Council of Churches characterises as a pilgrimage of justice and peace. The presence of fellow travellers from South Sudan, Syria and Nepal, who spoke eloquently and movingly of their experiences, touched this image with reality. Perhaps the well-worn and often parroted concepts of justice and peace are another way of saying that when we enter the experience of others in the costly way of pilgrimage we share in the transformation of all things in the direction of the Kingdom.

In the speech already quoted, asking what kind of church we want to be in the 21st century and how the Assembly can serve it, Dr Browning remarked, 'The General Assembly has within its purpose the possibility of faithful imagination as well as practical outworking'. You might say that both faith and imagination were generously in play during this Assembly.

The Editor

SECTION 5

Presbytery Lists

See overleaf for an explanation of the two parts of each list; a Key to Abbreviations; and a list of the Presbyteries in their numerical order.

SECTION 5 – PRESBYTERY LISTS

In each Presbytery list, the congregations are listed in alphabetical order. In a linked charge, the names appear under the first named congregation. Under the name of the congregation will be found the name of the minister and, where applicable, that of an associate minister, ordained local minister, auxiliary minister and member of the Diaconate. The years indicated after a minister's name in the congregational section of each Presbytery list are the year of ordination (column 1) and the year of current appointment (column 2). Where only one date is given, it is both the year of ordination and the year of appointment. For an ordained local minister, the date is of ordination.

In the second part of each Presbytery list, those named are listed alphabetically. The first date is the year of ordination, and the following date is the year of appointment or retirement. If the person concerned is retired, then the appointment last held will be shown in brackets.

KEY TO ABBREVIATIONS

(E)   Indicates a Church Extension charge. New Charge Developments are separately indicated.
(GD)   Indicates a charge where it is desirable that the minister should have a knowledge of Gaelic.
(GE)   Indicates a charge where public worship must be regularly conducted in Gaelic.
(H)   Indicates that a Hearing Aid Loop system has been installed. In Linked charges, the (H) is placed beside the appropriate building as far as possible.
(L)   Indicates that a Chair Lift has been installed.
(R)   Indicates that the minister has been appointed on the basis of Reviewable Tenure.

PRESBYTERY NUMBERS

1	Edinburgh	18	Dumbarton
2	West Lothian	19	Argyll
3	Lothian	20	
4	Melrose and Peebles	21	
5	Duns	22	Falkirk
6	Jedburgh	23	Stirling
7	Annandale and Eskdale	24	Dunfermline
8	Dumfries and Kirkcudbright	25	Kirkcaldy
9	Wigtown and Stranraer	26	St Andrews
10	Ayr	27	Dunkeld and Meigle
11	Irvine and Kilmarnock	28	Perth
12	Ardrossan	29	Dundee
13	Lanark	30	Angus
14	Greenock and Paisley	31	Aberdeen
15		32	Kincardine and Deeside
16	Glasgow	33	Gordon
17	Hamilton	34	Buchan

35	Moray
36	Abernethy
37	Inverness
38	Lochaber
39	Ross
40	Sutherland
41	Caithness
42	Lochcarron – Skye
43	Uist
44	Lewis
45	Orkney
46	Shetland
47	England
48	Europe
49	Jerusalem

(1) EDINBURGH

The Presbytery meets:
- at Palmerston Place Church, Edinburgh, on 8 September, 3 November and 1 December 2015, and on 2 February, 15 March, 3 May and 28 June 2016;
- in the church of the Moderator on 6 October 2015.

Clerk:	REV. GEORGE J. WHYTE BSc BD DMin	10/1 Palmerston Place, Edinburgh EH12 5AA [E-mail: edinburgh@churchofscotland.org.uk]	0131-225 9137
Depute Clerk:	HAZEL HASTIE MA CQSW PhD AIWS	17 West Court, Edinburgh EH16 4EB [E-mail: hazel.hastie29@gmail.com]	07827 314374 (Mbl)

1 Edinburgh: Albany Deaf Church of Edinburgh (H) (0131-444 2054)

Rosemary A. Addis (Mrs) BD		2014	c/o Ministries Council, 121 George Street, Edinburgh EH2 4YN [E-mail: raddis@churchofscotland.org.uk]	07738 983393 (Mbl)

2 Edinburgh: Balerno (H)

R. Russell McLarty MA BD (Interim Minister)	1985	2015	9 Sanderson's Wynd, Tranent EH33 1DA [E-mail: russellmclarty@yahoo.co.uk]	01875 614496

3 Edinburgh: Barclay Viewforth (0131-229 6810) (E-mail: admin@barclaychurch.org.uk)

Samuel A.R. Torrens BD	1995	2005	113 Meadowspot, Edinburgh EH10 5UY [E-mail: minister@barclayviewforth.org.uk]	0131-478 2376

4 Edinburgh: Blackhall St Columba's (0131-332 4431) (E-mail: secretary@blackhallstcolumba.org.uk)

Vacant	5 Blinkbonny Crescent, Edinburgh EH4 3NB	0131-343 3708

5 Edinburgh: Bristo Memorial Craigmillar

Drausio Goncalves	2008	2013	72 Blackchapel Close, Edinburgh EH15 3SL [E-mail: drausio@bristochurch.com]	0131-657 3266

6 Edinburgh: Broughton St Mary's (H) (0131-556 4786)

Graham G. McGeoch MA BTh MTh	2009	2013	103 East Claremont Street, Edinburgh EH7 4JA [E-mail: minister@bstmchurch.org.uk]	0131-556 7313

7 Edinburgh: Canongate (H)

Neil N. Gardner MA BD	1991	2006	The Manse of Canongate, Edinburgh EH8 8BR [E-mail: nng22@btinternet.com]	0131-556 3515

8   **Edinburgh: Carrick Knowe (H) (0131-334 1505) (E-mail: ckchurch@talktalk.net)**
Fiona M. Mathieson (Mrs)   1988   2001   21 Traquair Park West, Edinburgh EH12 7AN
   BEd BD PGCommEd MTh   [E-mail: fiona.mathieson@ukgateway.net]   0131-334 9774

9   **Edinburgh: Colinton (H) (0131-441 2232) (E-mail: church.office@colinton-parish.com)**
Rolf H. Billes BD   1996   2009   The Manse, Colinton, Edinburgh EH13 0JR
                                               [E-mail: rolf.billes@colinton-parish.com]   0131-466 8384
Gayle J.A. Taylor (Mrs) MA BD   1999   2009   Colinton Parish Church, Dell Road, Edinburgh EH13 0JR
(Associate Minister)   [E-mail: gayle.taylor@colinton-parish.com]   0131-441 2232

10 **Edinburgh: Corstorphine Craigsbank (H) (0131-334 6365)**
Stewart M. McPherson BD CertMin 1991   2003   17 Craigs Bank, Edinburgh EH12 8HD   0131-467 6826
                                               [E-mail: smcpherson@blueyonder.co.uk]   07814 901429 (Mbl)

11 **Edinburgh: Corstorphine Old (H) (0131-334 7864) (E-mail: corold@aol.com)**
Moira McDonald MA BD   1997   2005   23 Manse Road, Edinburgh EH12 7SW
                                               [E-mail: moira-mc@live.co.uk]   0131-476 5893

12 **Edinburgh: Corstorphine St Anne's (0131-316 4740) (E-mail: office@stannes.corstorphine.org.uk)**
James J. Griggs BD MTh   2011   2013   1/5 Morham Gait, Edinburgh EH10 5GH
                                               [E-mail: cstannesminister@gmail.com]   0131-466 3269

13 **Edinburgh: Corstorphine St Ninian's (H) (0131-539 6204) (E-mail: office@st-ninians.co.uk)**
Alexander T. Stewart MA BD FSAScot 1975 1995 17 Templeland Road, Edinburgh EH12 8RZ
                                               [E-mail: alextstewart@blueyonder.co.uk]   0131-334 2978

14 **Edinburgh: Craigentinny St Christopher's (0131-258 2759)**
Guardianship of the Presbytery   61 Milton Crescent, Edinburgh EH15 3PQ

15 **Edinburgh: Craiglockhart (H) (E-mail: office@craiglockhartchurch.org)**
Gordon Kennedy BSc BD MTh   1993   2012   20 Craiglockhart Quadrant, Edinburgh EH14 1HD
                                               [E-mail: gordonkennedy@craiglockhartchurch.org]   0131-444 1615

16 **Edinburgh: Craigmillar Park (H) (0131-667 5862) (E-mail: cpkirk@btinternet.com)**
John C.C. Urquhart MA MA BD   2010   14 Hallhead Road, Edinburgh EH16 5QJ
                                               [E-mail: jccurquhart@gmail.com]   0131-667 1623

17 **Edinburgh: Cramond (H) (E-mail: cramond.kirk@blueyonder.co.uk)**
G. Russell Barr BA BD MTh DMin   1979   1993   Manse of Cramond, Edinburgh EH4 6NS
                                               [E-mail: rev.r.barr@blueyonder.co.uk]   0131-336 2036

18   Edinburgh: Currie (H) (0131-451 5141) (E-mail: currie_kirk@btconnect.com)
V. Easter Smart BA MDiv DMin   1996   2015   43 Lanark Road West, Currie EH14 5JX   0131-449 4719
                                                       [E-mail: esmart@churchofscotland.org.uk]

19   Edinburgh: Dalmeny linked with Edinburgh: Queensferry
David C. Cameron BD CertMin   1993   2009   1 Station Road, South Queensferry EH30 9HY   0131-331 1100
                                                       [E-mail: minister@qpcweb.org]

20   Edinburgh: Davidson's Mains (H) (0131-312 6282) (E-mail: life@dmainschurch.plus.com)
Vacant   1 Hillpark Terrace, Edinburgh EH4 7SX   0131-336 3078
                                                       [E-mail: life@dmainschurch.plus.com]

21   Edinburgh: Dean (H)
Guardianship of the Presbytery   1 Ravelston Terrace, Edinburgh EH4 3EF   0131-332 5736

22   Edinburgh: Drylaw (0131-343 6643)
Jayne E. Scott (Mrs) BA MEd MBA   1988   2015   15 House o' Hill Gardens, Edinburgh EH4 2AR   0131-531 5786
                                                       [E-mail: jayne.scott5@btinternet.com]

23   Edinburgh: Duddingston (H) (E-mail: dodinskirk@aol.com)
James A.P. Jack   1989   2001   Manse of Duddingston, Old Church Lane, Edinburgh EH15 3PX   0131-661 4240
BSc BArch BD DMin RIBA ARIAS   [E-mail: jamesjack2829@aol.com]

24   Edinburgh: Fairmilehead (H) (0131-445 2374) (E-mail: office@fhpc.org.uk)
John R. Munro BD   1976   1992   c/o Fairmilehead Parish Church, 1 Frogston Road West,   0131-446 9363
                                                         Edinburgh EH10 7AA
                                                       [E-mail: revjohnmunro@hotmail.com]
Hayley O'Connor BS MDiv   2009   19 Caiystane Terrace, Edinburgh EH10 6SR   0131-629 1610
(Assistant Minister)   [E-mail: oconnorhe@gmail.com]

25   Edinburgh: Gorgie Dalry (H) (0131-337 7936)
Peter I. Barber MA BD   1984   1995   90 Myreside Road, Edinburgh EH10 5BZ   0131-337 2284
                                                       [E-mail: pibarber@toucansurf.com]

26   Edinburgh: Granton (H) (0131-552 3033)
Norman A. Smith MA BD   1997   2005   8 Wardie Crescent, Edinburgh EH5 1AG   0131-551 2159
                                                       [E-mail: norm@familysmith.biz]

27 Edinburgh: Greenbank (H) (0131-447 9969) (E-mail: greenbankchurch@btconnect.com; Website: www.greenbankchurch.org)

Alison I. Swindells (Mrs) LLB BD	1998	2007	112 Greenbank Crescent, Edinburgh EH10 5SZ [E-mail: alisonswindells@blueyonder.co.uk]	0131-447 4032
William H. Stone BA MDiv ThM (Youth Minister)	2012		19 Caiystane Terrace, Edinburgh EH10 6SR [E-mail: billstoneii@gmail.com]	0131-629 1610 07883 815598 (Mbl)

28 Edinburgh: Greenside (H) (0131-556 5588)

Guardianship of the Presbytery	80 Pilrig Street, Edinburgh EH6 5AS	0131-554 3277 (Tel/Fax)

29 Edinburgh: Greyfriars Kirk (GE) (H) (0131-225 1900) (E-mail: enquiries@greyfriarskirk.com)

Richard E. Frazer BA BD DMin	1986	2003	12 Tantallon Place, Edinburgh EH9 1NZ [E-mail: minister@greyfriarskirk.com]	0131-667 6610
Lezley J. Stewart BD ThM MTh (Associate Minister)	2000	2014	Greyfriars Kirk, 1 Greyfriars Place, Edinburgh EH1 2QQ [E-mail: associateminister@greyfriarskirk.com]	0131-225 1900 07713 974423 (Mbl)

(New charge formed by the union of Edinburgh: Greyfriars Tolbooth and Highland Kirk and Edinburgh: Kirk o' Field)

30 Edinburgh: High (St Giles') (0131-225 4363) (E-mail: info@stgilescathedral.org.uk)

Calum I. MacLeod BA BD	1996	2014	St Giles' Cathedral, Edinburgh EH1 1RE [E-mail: cmacleod@stgilescathedral.org.uk]	0131-225 4363
Helen J.R. Alexander BD DipSW (Assist)	1981	2012	7 Polwarth Place, Edinburgh EH11 1LG [E-mail: st_giles_cathedral@btconnect.com]	0131-346 0685

31 Edinburgh: Holyrood Abbey (H) (0131-661 6002)

Vacant	100 Willowbrae Avenue, Edinburgh EH8 7HU

32 Edinburgh: Holy Trinity (H) (0131-442 3304)

Kenneth S. Borthwick MA BD	1983	2005	16 Thorburn Road, Edinburgh EH13 0BQ [E-mail: kennysamuel@aol.com]	0131-441 1403
Ian MacDonald BD MTh (Associate Minister)	2005		5 Baberton Mains Terrace, Edinburgh EH14 3DG [E-mail: ianafrica@hotmail.com]	0131-281 6153
Oliver M.H. Clegg BD (Youth Minister)	2003		4 Blinkbonny Steading, Blinkbonny Road, Currie EH14 6AE [E-mail: ollieclegg@btinternet.com]	0131-478 5341

33 Edinburgh: Inverleith St Serf's (H)

Joanne G. Foster (Mrs) DipTMus BD AdvDipCouns	1996	2012	78 Pilrig Street, Edinburgh EH6 5AS [E-mail: minister@inverleithsaintserfs.org.uk]	0131-561 1392

34	**Edinburgh: Juniper Green (H)**				
	James S. Dewar MA BD	1983	2000	476 Lanark Road, Juniper Green, Edinburgh EH14 5BQ	0131-453 3494
				[E-mail: jim.dewar@blueyonder.co.uk]	
35	**Edinburgh: Kaimes Lockhart Memorial linked with Edinburgh: Liberton**				
	John N. Young MA BD PhD	1996		7 Kirk Park, Edinburgh EH16 6HZ	0131-664 3067
				[E-mail: LLLjyoung@btinternet.com]	
36	**Edinburgh: Kirkliston**				
	Margaret R. Lane (Mrs) BA BD MTh	2009		43 Main Street, Kirkliston EH29 9AF	0131-333 3298 / 07795 481441 (Mbl)
				[E-mail: margaretlane@btinternet.com]	
37	**Edinburgh: Leith North (H) (0131-553 7378) (E-mail: nlpc-office@btinternet.com)**				
	Alexander T. McAspurren BD MTh	2002	2011	6 Craighall Gardens, Edinburgh EH6 4RJ	0131-551 5252
				[E-mail: alexander.mcaspurren@btinternet.com]	
38	**Edinburgh: Leith St Andrew's (H)**				
	Robert A. Mackenzie LLB BD	1993	2013	30 Lochend Road, Edinburgh EH6 8BS	0131-553 2122
				[E-mail: robmcknz1@gmail.com]	
39	**Edinburgh: Leith South (H) (0131-554 2578) (E-mail: slpc@dial.pipex.com)**				
	John S. (Iain) May BSc MBA BD	2012		37 Claremont Road, Edinburgh EH6 7NN	0131-554 3062
				[E-mail: johnsmay@blueyonder.co.uk]	
	Pauline Robertson (Mrs) DCS BA CertTheol			6 Ashville Terrace, Edinburgh EH6 8DD	0131-554 6564 / 07759 436303 (Mbl)
				[E-mail: pauline70@rocketmail.com]	
40	**Edinburgh: Leith Wardie (H) (0131-551 3847) (E-mail: churchoffice@wardie.org.uk)**				
	Vacant			35 Lomond Road, Edinburgh EH5 3JN	0131-552 3328
				[E-mail: minister@wardie.org.uk]	
41	**Edinburgh: Liberton (H)** See Edinburgh: Kaimes Lockhart Memorial				
42	**Edinburgh: Liberton Northfield (H) (0131-551 3847)**				
	Vacant			9 Claverhouse Drive, Edinburgh EH16 6BR	0131-658 1754
43	**Edinburgh: London Road (H) (0131-661 1149)**				
	Vacant			26 Inchview Terrace, Edinburgh EH7 6TQ	0131-669 5311

44 **Edinburgh: Marchmont St Giles' (H) (0131-447 4359)**
Karen K. Campbell BD MTh DMin   1997   2002   2 Trotter Haugh, Edinburgh EH9 2GZ   0131-447 2834
[E-mail: karen@marchmontstgiles.org.uk]

45 **Edinburgh: Mayfield Salisbury (0131-667 1522)**
Scott S. McKenna BA BD MTh MPhil   1994   2000   26 Seton Place, Edinburgh EH9 2JT   0131-667 1286
[E-mail: ScottSMcKenna@aol.com]

46 **Edinburgh: Morningside (H) (0131-447 6745) (E-mail: office@morningsideparishchurch.org.uk)**
Derek Browning MA BD DMin   1987   2001   20 Braidburn Crescent, Edinburgh EH10 6EN   0131-447 1617
[E-mail: derek.browning@churchofscotland.org.uk]

47 **Edinburgh: Morningside United (H) (0131-447 3152)**
Steven Manders   1 Midmar Avenue, Edinburgh EH10 6BS   0131-447 8724
[E-mail: stevenmanders@hotmail.com]   07808 476733 (Mbl)
    Morningside United is a Local Ecumenical Project shared with the United Reformed Church

48 **Edinburgh: Murrayfield (H) (0131-337 1091) (E-mail: mpchurch@btconnect.com)**
Keith Edwin Graham MA PGDip BD   2008   2014   45 Murrayfield Gardens, Edinburgh EH12 6DH   0131-337 1364
[E-mail: keithedwingraham@gmail.com]

49 **Edinburgh: Newhaven (H)**
Peter Bluett   2007   158 Granton Road, Edinburgh EH5 3RF   0131-476 5212
[E-mail: peterbluett@sky.com]

50 **Edinburgh: New Restalrig (H) (0131-661 5676)**
Vacant   19 Abercorn Road, Edinburgh EH8 7DP   0131-661 4045

51 **Edinburgh: Old Kirk Muirhouse (H) (0131-332 4354) (E-mail: minister.oldkirk@btinternet.com)**
Vacant   35 Silverknowes Road, Edinburgh EH4 5LL   0131-312 7773
Ann Lyall (Miss) DCS   24 Pennywell Road, Edinburgh EH4 4HD   0131-332 4354
[E-mail: ann.lyall@btinternet.com]

52 **Edinburgh: Palmerston Place (H) (0131-220 1690) (E-mail: admin@palmerstonplacechurch.com)**
Colin A.M. Sinclair BA BD   1981   1996   30B Cluny Gardens, Edinburgh EH10 6BJ   0131-447 9598
[E-mail: colins.ppc@virgin.net]   0131-225 3312 (Fax)

53 **Edinburgh: Pilrig St Paul's (0131-553 1876)**
Mark M. Foster BSc BD   1998   78 Pilrig Street, Edinburgh EH6 5AS
[E-mail: minister.psp@gmail.com]   0131-332 5736

54 **Edinburgh: Polwarth (H) (0131-346 2711) (E-mail: polwarthchurch@tiscali.co.uk)**
Jack Holt BSc BD MTh   1985   2011   88 Craiglockhart Road, Edinburgh EH14 1EP
[E-mail: jack9holt@gmail.com]   0131-441 6105

55 **Edinburgh: Portobello and Joppa (H) (0131-669 3641)**
Stewart G. Weaver BA BD PhD   2003   2014   6 St Mary's Place, Edinburgh EH15 2QF
[E-mail: stewartweaver@btinternet.com]   0131-669 2410

56 **Edinburgh: Priestfield (H) (0131-667 5644)**
Jared W. Hay BA MTh DipMin DMin   1987   2009   13 Lady Road, Edinburgh EH16 5PA
[E-mail: jared.hay@blueyonder.co.uk]   0131-468 1254

57 **Edinburgh: Queensferry (H)** See Edinburgh: Dalmeny

58 **Edinburgh: Ratho**
Ian J. Wells BD   1999   2 Freelands Road, Ratho, Newbridge EH28 8NP
[E-mail: ianjwells@btinternet.com]   0131-333 1346

59 **Edinburgh: Reid Memorial (H) (0131-662 1203) (E-mail: reid.memorial@btinternet.com)**
Vacant   20 Wilton Road, Edinburgh EH16 5NX   0131-667 3981

60 **Edinburgh: Richmond Craigmillar (H) (0131-661 6561)**
Elizabeth M. Henderson   1985   1997   Manse of Duddingston, Old Church Lane, Edinburgh EH15 3PX
MA BD MTh   [E-mail: lizhende@tiscali.co.uk]   0131-661 4240

61 **Edinburgh: St Andrew's and St George's West (H) (0131-225 3847) (E-mail: info@standrewsandstgeorges.org.uk)**
Ian Y. Gilmour BD   1985   2011   25 Comely Bank, Edinburgh EH4 1AJ
[E-mail: ianyg2@gmail.com]   0131-332 5848

62 **Edinburgh: St Andrew's Clermiston**
Alistair H. Keil BD DipMin   1989   87 Drum Brae South, Edinburgh EH12 8TD
[E-mail: ahkeil@blueyonder.co.uk]   0131-339 4149

63 Edinburgh: St Catherine's Argyle (H) (0131-667 7220)
Vacant — 5 Palmerston Road, Edinburgh EH9 1TL — 0131-667 9344

64 Edinburgh: St Cuthbert's (H) (0131-229 1142) (E-mail: office@st-cuthberts.net)
David W. Denniston BD DipMin   1981   2008 — 34A Murrayfield Road, Edinburgh EH12 6ER [E-mail: denniston.david@gmail.com] — 0131-337 6637 / 07903 926727 (Mbl)
Stark, Suzie BD — St Cuthbert's Church, 5 Lothian Road, Edinburgh EH1 2EP [Email: sstark1962@btinternet.com] — 0131-229 1142

65 Edinburgh: St David's Broomhouse (H) (0131-443 9851)
Michael J. Mair BD   2014 — 33 Traquair Park West, Edinburgh EH12 7AN [E-mail: mairmj@gmail.com] — 0131-334 1730
Liz Crocker (Mrs) DipComEd DCS — 77C Craigcrook Road, Edinburgh EH4 3PH — 0131-332 0227

66 Edinburgh: St John's Colinton Mains
Peter Nelson BSc BD   2015 — 2 Caiystane Terrace, Edinburgh EH10 6SR [E-mail: pnelson@churchofscotland.org.uk] — 07500 057889 (Mbl)

67 Edinburgh: St Margaret's (H) (0131-554 7400) (E-mail: stm.parish@virgin.net)
Carol H.M. Ford DSD RSAMD BD   2003 — 43 Moira Terrace, Edinburgh EH7 6TD [E-mail: revcford@btinternet.com] — 0131-669 7329
Pauline Robertson (Mrs) DCS BA CertTheol — 6 Ashville Terrace, Edinburgh EH6 8DD [E-mail: pauline70@rocketmail.com] — 0131-554 6564 / 07759 436303 (Mbl)

68 Edinburgh: St Martin's
Russel Moffat BD MTh PhD   1986   2008 — 5 Duddingston Crescent, Edinburgh EH15 3AS [E-mail: rbmoffat@tiscali.co.uk] — 0131-657 9894

69 Edinburgh: St Michael's (H) (E-mail: office@stmichaels-kirk.co.uk)
James D. Aitken BD   2002   2005 — 9 Merchiston Gardens, Edinburgh EH10 5DD [E-mail: james.aitken2@btinternet.com] — 0131-346 1970

70 Edinburgh: St Nicholas' Sighthill
Thomas Kisitu MTh PhD   2015 — 122 Sighthill Loan, Edinburgh EH11 4NT [E-mail: kisitu@btinternet.com] — 0131-442 3978

71 Edinburgh: St Stephen's Comely Bank (0131-315 4616)
George Vidits BD MTh   2000   2015 — 8 Blinkbonny Crescent, Edinburgh EH4 3NB [E-mail: george.vidits@gmail.com] — 0131-332 3364

72 Edinburgh: Slateford Longstone
Michael W. Frew BSc BD   1978   2005   50 Kingsknowe Road South, Edinburgh EH14 2JW   0131-466 5308
[E-mail: minister@slatefordlongstone.org.uk]

73 Edinburgh: Stenhouse St Aidan's
Vacant   65 Balgreen Road, Edinburgh EH12 5UA   0131-337 7711

74 Edinburgh: Stockbridge (H) (0131-552 8738) (E-mail: stockbridgechurch@btconnect.com)
John A. Cowie BSc BD   1983   2013   19 Eildon Street, Edinburgh EH3 5JU   0131-557 6052
[E-mail: jacowie54@gmail.com]   07506 104416 (Mbl)

75 Edinburgh: The Tron Kirk (Gilmerton and Moredun)
Cameron Mackenzie BD   1997   2010   467 Gilmerton Road, Edinburgh EH17 7JG   0131-664 7538
[E-mail: mackenz550@aol.com]

Abernethy, William LTh	1979	1993	(Glenrothes: St Margaret's)	120/1 Willowbrae Road, Edinburgh EH8 7HW	0131-661 0390
Aitken, Alexander R. MA	1965	1997	(Newhaven)	36 King's Meadow, Edinburgh EH16 5JW	0131-667 1404
Alexander, Ian W. BA BD STM	1990	2010	(World Mission Council)	121 George Street, Edinburgh EH2 4YN	0131-225 5722
				[E-mail: iwalexander@gmail.com]	
Anderson, Robert S. BD	1988	1997	(Scottish Churches World Exchange)		
Armitage, William L. BSc BD	1976	2006	(Edinburgh: London Road)	Flat 7, 4 Papermill Wynd, Edinburgh EH7 4GJ	0131-558 8534
				[E-mail: bill@billarm.plus.com]	
Baird, Kenneth S.					
MSc PhD BD MIMarEST	1998	2009	(Edinburgh: Leith North)	3 Maule Terrace, Gullane EH31 2DB	01620 843447
Barrington, Charles W.H. MA BD	1997	2007	(Associate: Edinburgh: Balerno)	502 Lanark Road, Edinburgh EH14 5DH	0131-453 4826
Beckett, David M. BA BD	1964	2002	(Edinburgh: Greyfriars, Tolbooth and	1F1, 31 Sciennes Road, Edinburgh EH9 1NT	0131-667 2672
			Highland Kirk)	[E-mail: davidbeckett3@aol.com]	
Blakey, Ronald S. MA BD MTh	1962	2000	(Assembly Council)	24 Kimmerghame Place, Edinburgh EH4 2GE	0131-343 6352
				[E-mail: kathleen.blakey@gmail.com]	07851 598101 (Mbl)
Booth, Jennifer (Mrs) BD	1996	2004	(Associate: Leith South)	39 Lilyhill Terrace, Edinburgh EH8 7DR	0131-661 3813
Boyd, Kenneth M. MA BD PhD FRCPE	1970	1996	University of Edinburgh: Medical Ethics	1 Doune Terrace, Edinburgh EH3 6DY	0131-225 6485
Brady, Ian D. BSc ARCST BD	1967	2001	(Edinburgh: Corstorphine Old)	28 Frankfield Crescent, Dalgety Bay, Dunfermline KY11 9LW	01383 825104
				[E-mail: pidb@dbay28.fsnet.co.uk]	
Brown, William D. MA	1963	1989	(Wishaw: Thornlie)	9/3 Craigend Park, Edinburgh EH16 5XY	0131-672 2936
				[E-mail: wdbrown@surefish.co.uk]	
Brown, William D. BD CQSW	1987	2013	(Edinburgh: Murrayfield)	79 Carnbee Park, Edinburgh EH16 6GG	0131-261 7297
				[E-mail: wdb@talktalk.net]	
Cameron, G. Gordon MA BD STM	1957	1997	(Juniper Green)	10 Beechwood Gardens, Stirling FK8 2AX	01786 472934
Cameron, John W.M. MA BD	1957	1996	(Liberton)	10 Plewlands Gardens, Edinburgh EH10 5JP	0131-447 1277
Chalmers, Murray MA	1965	2006	(Hospital Chaplain)	8 Easter Warriston, Edinburgh EH7 4QX	0131-552 4211

Clark, Christine M. (Mrs) BA BD MTh	2006	2013	(Aberlady with Gullane)	40 Pentland Avenue, Edinburgh EH13 0HY [E-mail: christine.clark7@aol.co.uk]	0131-312 8447
Clinkenbeard, William W. BSc BD STM	1966	2000	(Edinburgh: Carrick Knowe)	3/17 Western Harbour Breakwater, Edinburgh EH6 6PA [E-mail: bjclinks@compuserve.com]	0131-664 1358
Cook, John MA BD	1967	2005	(Edinburgh: Leith St Andrew's)	26 Silverknowes Court, Edinburgh EH4 5NR	
Curran, Elizabeth M. (Miss) BD	1995	2008	(Aberlour)	Blackford Grange, 39/2 Blackford Avenue, Edinburgh EH9 3HN [E-mail: ecurran8@aol.com]	
Cuthell, Tom C. MA BD MTh	1965	2007	(Edinburgh: St Cuthbert's)	Flat 10, 2 Kingsburgh Crescent, Waterfront, Edinburgh EH5 1JS	0131-476 3864
Davidson, D. Hugh MA	1965	2009	(Edinburgh: Inverleith)	Flat 1/2, 22 Summerside Place, Edinburgh EH6 4NZ [E-mail: hdavidson35@btinternet.com]	0131-554 8420
Davidson, Ian M.P. MBE MA BD	1954	1994	(Stirling: Allan Park South with Church of the Holy Rude)	13/8 Craigend Park, Edinburgh EH16 5XX	0131-664 0074
Dawson, Michael S. BTech BD	1979	2005	(Associate: Edinburgh: Holy Trinity)	9 The Broich, Alva FK12 5NR	01259 769309
Denniston, Jane M. MA BD MTh	2002		Ministries Council	34A Murrayfield Road, Edinburgh EH12 6ER [E-mail: mixpen.dawson@btinternet.com]	0131-337 6637
Dilbey, Mary D. (Miss) BD	1997	2002	(West Kirk of Calder)	41 Bonaly Rise, Edinburgh EH13 0QU	0131-441 9092
Donald, Alistair P. MA PhD BD	1999	2009	Chaplain: Heriot-Watt University	The Chaplaincy, Heriot-Watt University, Edinburgh EH14 4AS [E-mail: a.p.donald@hw.ac.uk]	0131-451 4508
Dougall, Elspeth G. (Mrs) MA BD	1989	2001	(Edinburgh: Marchmont St Giles')	60B Craigmillar Park, Edinburgh EH16 5PU	0131-668 1342
Douglas, Alexander B. BD	1979	2014	(Edinburgh: Blackhall St Columba's)	15 Inchview Gardens, Dalgety Bay, Dunfermline KY11 9SA [E-mail: alexandjill@douglas.net]	01383 242872
Douglas, Colin R. MA BD STM	1969	2007	(Livingston Ecumenical Parish)	34 West Pilton Gardens, Edinburgh EH4 4EQ [E-mail: colinrdouglas@btinternet.com]	0131-551 3808
Doyle, Ian B. MA BD PhD	1946	1991	(Department of National Mission)	21 Lygon Road, Edinburgh EH16 5QD	0131-667 2697
Drummond, Rhoda (Miss) DCS	1983	1998	(Deacon)	Flat K, 23 Grange Loan, Edinburgh EH9 2ER	0131-668 3631
Dunn, W. Iain C. DA LTh			(Pilrig and Dalmeny Street)	10 Fox Covert Avenue, Edinburgh EH12 6UQ	0131-334 1665
Embleton, Brian M. BD	1976	2015	(Edinburgh: Reid Memorial)	54 Edinburgh Road, Peebles EH45 8EB [E-mail: bmembleton@gmail.com]	01721 602157
Embleton, Sara R. (Mrs) BA BD MTh	1988	2010	(Edinburgh: Leith St Serf's)	54 Edinburgh Road, Peebles EH45 8EB [E-mail: srembleton@gmail.com]	01721 602157
Evans, Mark BSc MSc DCS	2006		Head of Spiritual Care NHS Fife	13 Easter Drylaw Drive, Edinburgh EH4 2QA [E-mail: mark.evans59@nhs.net]	(Home) 0131-343 3089 (Office) 01383 674136
Farquharson, Gordon MA BD DipEd	1998	2007	(Stonehaven: Dunnottar)	26 Learmonth Court, Edinburgh EH4 1PB [E-mail: gfarqu@talktalk.net]	0131-343 1047
Faulds, Norman L. MA BD FSAScot	1968	2000	(Aberlady with Gullane)	10 West Fenton Court, West Fenton, North Berwick EH39 5AE	01620 842331
Fergusson, David A.S. (Prof.) MA BD DPhil DD FBA FRSE	1984	2000	University of Edinburgh	23 Riselaw Crescent, Edinburgh EH10 6HN	
Forrester, Margaret R. (Mrs) MA BD	1974	2003	(Edinburgh: St Michael's)	25 Kingsburgh Road, Edinburgh EH12 6DZ [E-mail: margaret@rosskeen.org.uk]	0131-447 4022
Fraser, Shirley A. (Miss) MA BD	1992	2008	(Scottish Field Director: Friends International)	6/50 Roseburn Drive, Edinburgh EH12 5NS	0131-337 5646
Gardner, John V.	1997	2003	(Glamis, Inverarity and Kinnettles)	75/1 Lockharton Avenue, Edinburgh EH14 1BD [E-mail: jvgardner66@googlemail.com]	0131-347 1400 0131-443 7126

Gibson, Alan W. BA BD	2001	2012	Head of Stewardship	121 George Street, Edinburgh EH2 4YN [E-mail: agibson@churchofscotland.org.uk]	0131-225 5722
Gordon, Margaret (Mrs) DCS	1974	2009	(Edinburgh: Currie)	92 Lanark Road West, Currie EH14 5LA	0131-449 2554
Gordon, Tom MA BD	1967	2008	(Chaplain: Marie Curie Hospice, Edinburgh)	22 Gosford Road, Port Seton, Prestonpans EH32 0HF	01875 812262
Graham, W. Peter MA BD			(Presbytery Clerk)	23/6 East Comiston, Edinburgh EH10 6RZ	0131-445 5763
Hardman Moore, Susan (Prof.) BA PGCE MA PhD	2013		Ordained Local Minister	c/o New College, Mound Place, Edinburgh EH1 2LX [E-mail: s.hardmanmoore@ed.ac.uk]	0131-650 8908 (Mbl) 07811 345699
Harkness, James CB OBE QHC MA DD	1961	1995	(Chaplain General: Army)	13 Saxe Coburg Place, Edinburgh EH3 5BR	0131-343 1297
Hill, J. William BA BD	1967	2001	(Edinburgh: Corstorphine St Anne's)	33/9 Murrayfield Road, Edinburgh EH12 6EP	
Howitt, Jane M. MA BD	1996	2015	Locum, St Catherine's Argyle	5 Palmerston Road, Edinburgh EH9 1TL [E-mail: jane_m_howitt@yahoo.co.uk]	0131-667 9548
Inglis, Ann (Mrs) LLB BD	1986	2015	(Langton and Lammermuir Kirk)	34 Echline View, South Queensferry EH30 9XL [E-mail: revainglis@gmail.com]	0131-629 0233
Irving, William D. LTh	1985	2005	(Golspie)	122 Swanston Muir, Edinburgh EH10 7HY	0131-441 3384
Jeffrey, Eric W.S. JP MA	1954	1994	(Edinburgh: Bristo Memorial)	18 Gillespie Crescent, Edinburgh EH10 4HT	0131-229 7815
Kingston, David V.F. BD DipPTh	1993	2015	(Chaplain: Army)	2 Cleuch Avenue, North Middleton, Gorebridge EH23 4RP	01875 822026
Lawson, Kenneth C. MA BD	1963	1999	(Adviser in Adult Education)	56 Easter Drylaw View, Edinburgh EH4 2QP	0131-539 3311
Logan, Anne T. (Mrs) MA BD MTh DMin	1981	2012	(Edinburgh: Stockbridge)	Sunnyside Cottage, 18 Upper Broomieknowe, Lasswade EH18 1LP [E-mail: annetlogan@blueyonder.co.uk]	0131-663 9550
McCaskill, George I.L. MA BD	1953	1990	(Religious Education)	19 Tyler's Acre Road, Edinburgh EH12 7HY	0131-334 7451
Macdonald, Finlay A.J. MA BD PhD DD	1971	2010	(Principal Clerk)	8 St Ronan's Way, Innerleithen EH44 6RG [E-mail: finlay_macdonald@btinternet.com]	01896 831631
Macdonald, Peter J. BD	1986	2009	Leader of the Iona Community	63 Jim Bush Drive, Prestonpans EH32 9GB [E-mail: petermacdonald@iona.org.uk] [E-mail: petermacdonald166@btinternet.com]	(Office) 0141-332 6343 (Mbl) 07946 715166 01875 819655
Macdonald, William J. BD	1976	2002	(Board of National Mission: New Charge Development)	1/13 North Werber Park, Edinburgh EH4 1SY	0131-332 0254
MacGregor, Margaret S. (Miss) MA BD DipEd	1985	1994	(Calcutta)	16 Learmonth Court, Edinburgh EH4 1PB	0131-332 1089
McGregor, Alistair G.C. QC BD	1987	2002	(Edinburgh: Leith North)	22 Primrose Bank Road, Edinburgh EH5 3JG	0131-551 2802
McGregor, T. Stewart MBE MA BD	1957	1998	(Chaplain: Edinburgh Royal Infirmary)	19 Lonsdale Terrace, Edinburgh EH3 9HL [E-mail: cetsm@uwclub.net]	0131-229 5332
MacKay, Stewart A.	2009		Chaplain: Army	Infantry Training Battalion, Helles Barracks, Catterick Garrison DL9 4HH	
Mackenzie, James G. BA BD	1980	2005	(Jersey: St Columba's)	26 Drylaw Crescent, Edinburgh EH4 2AU [E-mail: jgmackenzie@jerseymail.co.uk]	0131-332 3720
MacLaughlan, Grant BA BD	1998	2013	Workplace Chaplain	54 Crieff Road, Perth PH1 2RS [E-mail: grm6871@gmail.com]	
Maclean, Ailsa G. (Mrs) BD DipCE	1979	1988	Chaplain: George Heriot's School	28 Swan Spring Avenue, Edinburgh EH10 6NJ	0131-445 1320
Macmillan, Gilleasbuig I. KCVO MA BD DHrc DD FRSE HRSA FRCSEd	1969	2013	(Edinburgh: High (St Giles'))	207 Dalkeith Road, Edinburgh EH16 5DS [E-mail: gmacmillan1@btinternet.com]	0131-667 5732
MacMurchie, F. Lynne LLB BD	1998	2003	Healthcare Chaplain	Edinburgh Community Mental Health Chaplaincy, 41 George IV Bridge, Edinburgh EH1 1EL	0131-220 5150

McNab, John L. MA BD	1997 2014	Ministries Council		121 George Street, Edinburgh EH2 4YN	0131-225 5722
McPake, John M. LTh	2000 2014	(Edinburgh: Liberton Northfield)		9 Claverhouse Drive, Edinburgh EH16 6BR [E-mail: john_mcpake9@yahoo.co.uk]	0131-658 1754
McPheat, Elspeth DCS		Deaconess: CrossReach		11/5 New Orchardfield, Edinburgh EH6 5ET	0131-554 4143
McPhee, Duncan C. MA BD	1953 1993	(Department of National Mission)		8 Belvedere Park, Edinburgh EH6 4LR	0131-552 6784
Macpherson, Colin C.R. MA BD	1958 1996	(Dunfermline St Margaret's)		7 Eva Place, Edinburgh EH9 3ET	0131-667 1456
McPherson, Marjory (Mrs) LLB BD MTh	1990 2012	Ministries Council		17 Craigs Bank, Edinburgh EH12 8HD [E-mail: mmcpherson@churchofscotland.org.uk]	0131-467 6826
Mathieson, Angus R. MA BD	1988 1998	Ministries Council		21 Traquair Park West, Edinburgh EH12 7AN	0131-334 9774
Moir, Ian A. MA BD	1962 2000	(Adviser for Urban Priority Areas)		28/6 Comely Bank Avenue, Edinburgh EH4 1EL	0131-332 2748
Monteith, W. Graham BD PhD	1974 1994	(Flotta and Fara with Hoy and Walls)		20/3 Grandfield, Edinburgh EH6 4TL	0131-552 2564
Morrice, William G. MA BD STM PhD	1957 1991	(St John's College Durham)		Flat 37, The Cedars, 2 Manse Road, Edinburgh EH12 7SN [E-mail: w.g.morrice@btinternet.com]	0131-316 4845
Morrison, Mary B. (Mrs) MA BD DipEd	1978 2000	(Edinburgh: Stenhouse St Aidan's)		174 Craigcrook Road, Edinburgh EH4 3PP	0131-336 4706
Morton, Andrew R. MA BD DD	1956 1994	(Board of World Mission and Unity)		7A Laverockbank Terrace, Edinburgh EH5 3DJ	0131-538 7049
Moyes, Sheila A. (Miss) DCS		(Deacon)		158 Pilton Avenue, Edinburgh EH5 2JZ [E-mail: sheilamoyes@btinternet.com]	0131-551 1731
Mulligan, Anne MA DCS		(Deacon: Hospital Chaplain)		27A Craigour Avenue, Edinburgh EH17 1NH [E-mail: mulliganne@aol.com]	0131-664 3426
Munro, George A.M.	1968 2000	(Edinburgh: Cluny)		108 Caiyside, Edinburgh EH10 7HR	0131-445 5829
Munro, John P.L. MA BD PhD	1977 2007	(Kinross)		5 Marchmont Crescent, Edinburgh EH9 1HN [E-mail: jplmunro@yahoo.co.uk]	0131-623 0198
Murrie, John BD	1953 1996	(Kirkliston)		31 Nicol Road, The Whins, Broxburn EH52 6JJ	01506 852464
Orr, Sheena BA MSc MBA BD	2011 2015	Prison Chaplain		HM Prison, Edinburgh EH11 3LN [E-mail: sheens59@gmail.com]	0131-444 3115 (Mbl) 07922 649160
Page, Ruth MA BD DPhil	1976 2000	(University of Edinburgh)		22/5 West Mill Bank, West Mill Road, Edinburgh EH13 0QT	0131-441 3740
Paterson, Douglas S. MA BD	1976 2010	(Edinburgh: St Colm's)		4 Ards Place, High Street, Aberlady EH32 0DB	01875 870192
Plate, Maria A.G. (Miss) LTh BA	1983 2000	(South Ronaldsay and Burray)		Flat 29, 77 Barnton Park View, Edinburgh EH4 6EL	0131-339 8539
Rennie, Agnes M. (Miss) DCS		(Deacon)		3/1 Craigmillar Court, Edinburgh EH16 4AD	0131-661 8475
Ridland, Alistair K. MA BD	1982 2000	Chaplain: Western General Hospital		13 Stewart Place, Kirkliston EH29 0BQ	0131-333 2711
Robertson, Charles LVO MA	1965 2005	(Edinburgh: Canongate)		3 Ross Gardens, Edinburgh EH9 3BS [E-mail: canongate1@aol.com]	0131-662 9025
Robertson, Norma P. (Miss) BD DMin MTh	1993 2002	(Kincardine O'Neil with Lumphanan)		Flat 5, 2 Burnbrae Drive, Grovewood Hill, Edinburgh EH12 8AS	0131-339 6701
Ronald, Norma A. (Miss) MBE DCS		(Deacon)		2B Saughton Road North, Edinburgh EH12 7HG	0131-334 8736
Schofield, Melville F. MA	1960 2000	(Chaplain: Western General Hospital)		25 Rowantree Grove, Currie EH14 5AT	0131-449 4745
Scott, Ian G. BSc BD STM	1965 2006	(Edinburgh: Greenbank)		50 Forthview Walk, Tranent EH33 1FE [E-mail: igscott50@btinternet.com]	01875 612907
Scott, Martin DipMusEd RSAM BD PhD	1986 2000	Ministries Council		15 House o'Hill Gardens, Edinburgh EH4 2AR [E-mail: mscott@churchofscotland.org.uk]	0131 531 5786
Shewan, Frederick D.F. MA BD	1970 2005	(Edinburgh: Muirhouse St Andrew's)		36 Glendinning Road, Kirkliston EH29 9HE	0131-333 2631
Smith, Angus MA LTh	1965 2006	(Chaplain to the Oil Industry)		3/7 West Powburn, West Savile Gait, Edinburgh EH9 3EW	0131-667 1761
Steele, Marilynn J. (Mrs) BD DCS		(Deacon)		2 Northfield Gardens, Prestonpans EH32 9LQ [E-mail: marilynnsteele@aol.com]	01875 811497

Stephen, Donald M. TD MA BD ThM	1962	2001	(Edinburgh: Marchmont St Giles')	10 Hawkhead Crescent, Edinburgh EH16 6LR [E-mail: donaldmstephen@gmail.com]	0131-658 1216
Stevenson, John MA BD PhD	1963	2001	(Department of Education)	12 Swanston Gardens, Edinburgh EH10 7DL	0131-445 3960
Stirling, A. Douglas BSc	1956	1994	(Rhu and Shandon)	162 Avontoun Park, Linlithgow EH49 6QH	01506 845021
Stitt, Ronald J. Maxwell LTh BA ThM BREd DMin FSAScot	1977	2012	(Hamilton: Gilmour and Whitehill)	413 Gilmerton Road, Edinburgh EH17 7JJ	
Tait, John M. BSc BD	1985	2012	(Edinburgh: Pilrig St Paul's)	82 Greenend Gardens, Edinburgh EH17 7QH [E-mail: johnmtait@me.com]	0131-258 9105
Taylor, William R. MA BD MTh	1983	2004	Chaplaincy Adviser (Church of Scotland): Scottish Prison Service	Calton House, 5 Redheughs Rigg, South Gyle, Edinburgh EH12 9DQ [E-mail: bill.taylor@sps.pnn.gov.uk]	0131-244 8640
Teague, Yvonne (Mrs) DCS			(Board of Ministry)	46 Craigcrook Avenue, Edinburgh EH4 3PX [E-mail: y.teague.1@blueyonder.co.uk]	0131-336 3113
Telfer, Iain J.M. BD DPS	1978	2001	Chaplain: Royal Infirmary	Royal Infirmary of Edinburgh, 51 Little France Crescent, Edinburgh EH16 4SA	0131-242 1997
Thom, Helen (Miss) BA DipEd MA DCS			(Deacon)	84 Great King Street, Edinburgh EH3 6QU	0131-556 5687
Thomson, Donald M. BD	1975	2013	(Tullibody: St Serf's)	50 Sighthill Road, Edinburgh EH11 4NY [E-mail: donniethomson@tiscali.co.uk]	
Tweedie, Fiona BSc PhD	2011		Ordained Local Minister: Mission Statistics Co-ordinator	121 George Street, Edinburgh EH2 4YN [E-mail: ftweedie@churchofscotland.org.uk]	0131-225 5722
Watson, Nigel G. MA	1998	2012	(Associate: East Kilbride: Old/Stewartfield/West)	7 St Catherine's Place, Edinburgh EH9 1NU [E-mail: nigel.g.watson@gmail.com]	0131-662 4191
Webster, Peter BD	1977	2014	(Edinburgh: Portbello St James')	51 Kempock Street, Gourock PA19 1NF [E-mail: peterwebster101@hotmail.com]	01475 321916
Whyte, George J. BSc BD DMin	1981	2008	Presbytery Clerk	4 Baberton Mains Lea, Edinburgh EH14 3HB [E-mail: edinburgh@churchofscotland.org.uk]	0131-466 1674
Whyte, Iain A. BA BD STM PhD	1968	2005	(Community Mental Health Chaplain)	14 Carlingnose Point, North Queensferry, Inverkeithing KY11 1ER [E-mail: iainisabel@whytes28.fsnet.co.uk]	01383 410732
Wigglesworth, J. Christopher MBE BSc PhD BD	1968	1999	(St Andrew's College, Selly Oak)	12 Leven Terrace, Edinburgh EH3 9LW [E-mail: wiggles@talk21.com]	0131-228 6335
Williams, Jenny M. BSc CQSW BD	1996	1997	Health, healing, spirituality	16 Blantyre Terrace, Edinburgh EH10 5AE [E-mail: butterfly.greenleaf@gmx.net]	0131-447 0050
Wilson, John M. MA	1964	1995	(Adviser in Religious Education)	27 Belfield Street, Edinburgh EH15 2BR	0131-669 5257
Wishart, William DCS			(Deacon)	1 Brunstane Road North, Edinburgh EH15 2DL [E-mail: bill@wishartfamily.co.uk]	(Mbl) 07846 555654
Wynne, Alistair T.E. BA BD	1982	2009	(Nicosia Community Church, Cyprus)	Flat 6, 14 Burnbrae Drive, Edinburgh EH12 8AS [E-mail: awynne2@googlemail.com]	0131-339 6462
Young, Alexander W. BD DipMin	1988	1999	Head of Spiritual Care: NHS Lothian	32 Lindsay Circus, The Hawthorns, Rosewell EH24 9EP [E-mail: sandy.young@nhslothian.scot.nhs.uk]	(Work) 0131-242 1997

EDINBURGH ADDRESSES

Albany	82 Montrose Terrace
Balerno	Johnsburn Road, Balerno
Barclay Viewforth	Barclay Place
Blackhall St Columba's	Queensferry Road
Bristo Memorial	Peffermill Road, Craigmillar
Broughton St Mary's	Bellevue Crescent
Canongate	
Carrick Knowe	North Saughton Road
Colinton	Dell Road
Corstorphine	
Craigsbank	Craig's Crescent
Old	Kirk Loan
St Anne's	Kaimes Road
St Ninian's	St John's Road
Craigentinny	
St Christopher's	Craigentinny Road
Craiglockhart	Craiglockhart Avenue
Craigmillar Park	Craiglockhart Park
Cramond	Cramond Glebe Road
Currie	Kirkgate, Currie
Davidson's Mains	Quality Street
Dean	Dean Path
Drylaw	Groathill Road North
Duddingston	Old Church Lane, Duddingston
Fairmilehead	Frogston Road West, Fairmilehead
Gorgie Dalry	Gorgie Road

Granton	Boswall Parkway
Greenbank	Braidburn Terrace
Greenside	Royal Terrace
Greyfriars Kirk	Greyfriars Place
High (St Giles')	High Street
Holyrood Abbey	Dalziel Place x London Road
Holy Trinity	Hailesland Place, Wester Hailes
Inverleith St Serf's	Ferry Road
Juniper Green	Lanark Road, Juniper Green
Kaimes Lockhart Memorial	Gracemount Drive
Kirkliston	The Square, Kirkliston
Leith	
North	Madeira Street off Ferry Road
St Andrew's	Easter Road
South	Kirkgate, Leith
Wardie	Primrosebank Road
Liberton	Kirkgate, Liberton
Northfield	Gilmerton Road, Liberton
London Road	London Road
Marchmont St Giles'	Kilgraston Road
Mayfield Salisbury	Mayfield Road x West Mayfield
Morningside	Cluny Gardens
Morningside United	Bruntsfield Place x Chamberlain Rd
Murrayfield	Abinger Gardens
Newhaven	Craighall Road
New Restalrig	Willowbrae Road
Old Kirk Muirhouse	Pennywell Gardens
Palmerston Place	Palmerston Place
Pilrig St Paul's	Pilrig Street

Polwarth	Polwarth Terrace x Harrison Road
Portobello	
Old	Bellfield Street
St James'	Rosefield Place
St Philip's Joppa	Abercorn Terrace
Priestfield	Dalkeith Road x Marchhall Place
Queensferry	The Loan, South Queensferry
Ratho	Baird Road, Ratho
Reid Memorial	West Savile Terrace
Richmond Craigmillar	Niddrie Mains Road
St Andrew's and	
St George's West	George Street and Shandwick Place
St Andrew's Clermiston	Clermiston View
St Catherine's Argyle	Grange Road x Chalmers Crescent
St Cuthbert's ·	Lothian Road
St David's Broomhouse	Broomhouse Crescent
St John's Colinton Mains	Oxgangs Road North
St Margaret's	Restalrig Road South
St Martin's	Magdalene Drive
St Michael's	Slateford Road
St Nicholas' Sighthill	Calder Road
St Stephen's Comely Bank	Comely Bank
Slateford Longstone	Kingsknowe Road North
Stenhouse St Aidan's	Chesser Avenue
Stockbridge	Saxe Coburg Street
The Tron Kirk	Craigour Gardens and Ravenscroft Street
(Gilmerton and Moredun)	

(2) WEST LOTHIAN

Meets in the church of the incoming Moderator on the first Tuesday of September and in St John's Church Hall, Bathgate, on the first Tuesday of every other month, except December, when the meeting is on the second Tuesday, and in January, July and August, when there is no meeting.

Clerk: REV. DUNCAN SHAW BD MTh   St John's Manse, Mid Street, Bathgate EH48 1QD   01506 653146
[E-mail: westlothian@churchofscotland.org.uk]

Abercorn (H) linked with Pardovan, Kingscavil (H) and Winchburgh (H)
A. Scott Marshall DipComm BD   1984   1998   The Manse, Winchburgh, Broxburn EH52 6TT   01506 890919
[E-mail: pkwla@aol.com]

Armadale (H)				
Julia C. Wiley (Ms) MA(CE) MDiv	1998		70 Mount Pleasant, Armadale, Bathgate EH48 3HB [E-mail: preachergrace@gmail.com]	01501 730358
Margaret Corrie (Miss) DCS	2010		44 Sunnyside Street, Camelon, Falkirk FK1 4BH [E-mail: deakcorr@virginmedia.com]	01324 670656 07955 633969 (Mbl)
Avonbridge (H) linked with Torphichen (H)				
Vacant			Manse Road, Torphichen, Bathgate EH48 4LT	01506 676803
Bathgate: Boghall (H)				
Christopher Galbraith BA LLB BD	2012		1 Manse Place, Ash Grove, Bathgate EH48 1NJ [E-mail: chrisgalbraith@phonecoop.coop]	01506 652715
Bathgate: High (H)				
Vacant			19 Hunter Grove, Bathgate EH48 1NN	01506 652654
Bathgate: St John's (H)				
Duncan Shaw BD MTh	1975	1978	St John's Manse, Mid Street, Bathgate EH48 1QD [E-mail: westlothian@churchofscotland.org.uk]	01506 653146
Blackburn and Seafield (H)				
Robert A. Anderson MA BD DPhil	1980	1998	The Manse, 5 MacDonald Gardens, Blackburn, Bathgate EH47 7RE [E-mail: robertanderson307@btinternet.com]	01506 652825
Blackridge (H) linked with Harthill: St Andrew's (H)				
Vacant			East Main Street, Harthill, Shotts ML7 5QW	01501 751239
Breich Valley (H)				
Robert J. Malloch BD	1987	2013	Breich Valley Manse, Stoneyburn, Bathgate EH47 8AU [E-mail: rojama@live.com]	01501 763142
Broxburn (H)				
Jacobus Boonzaaier BA BCom(OR) BD MDiv PhD	1995	2015	2 Church Street, Broxburn EH52 5EL [Email: jaco.boonzaaier@gmail.com]	01506 337560
Fauldhouse: St Andrew's (H)				
Vacant			7 Glebe Court, Fauldhouse, Bathgate EH47 9DX	01501 771190
Harthill: St Andrew's See Blackridge				

Kirknewton (H) and East Calder (H)				
Andre Groenewald BA BD MDiv DD	1994	2009	8 Manse Court, East Calder, Livingston EH53 0HF [E-mail: groenstes@yahoo.com]	01506 884585 / 07588 845814 (Mbl)
Brenda Robson PhD (Auxiliary Minister)	2005	2014	2 Baird Road, Ratho, Newbridge EH28 8RA [E-mail: brendarobson@hotmail.co.uk]	0131-333 2746
Kirk of Calder (H)				
John M. Povey MA BD	1981		19 Maryfield Park, Mid Calder, Livingston EH53 0SB [E-mail: revjpovey@aol.com]	01506 882495
Kay McIntosh (Mrs) DCS			4 Jacklin Green, Livingston EH54 8PZ [E-mail: kay@backedge.co.uk]	01506 440543
Linlithgow: St Michael's (H) (E-mail: info@stmichaels-parish.org.uk)				
D. Stewart Gillan BSc MDiv PhD	1985	2004	St Michael's Manse, Kirkgate, Linlithgow EH49 7AL [E-mail: stewart@stmichaels-parish.org.uk]	01506 842195
Cheryl McKellar-Young (Mrs) BA BD (Associate Minister)		2013	c/o Cross House, The Cross, Linlithgow EH49 7AL [E-mail: cheryl@stmichaels-parish.org.uk]	01506 842188
Thomas S. Riddell BSc CEng FIChemE (Auxiliary Minister)	1993	1994	4 The Maltings, Linlithgow EH49 6DS [E-mail: tsriddell@blueyonder.co.uk]	01506 843251
Linlithgow: St Ninian's Craigmailen (H)				
W. Richard Houston BSc BD	1998	2004	29 Philip Avenue, Linlithgow EH49 7BH [E-mail: wrichardhouston@blueyonder.co.uk]	01506 202246
Livingston: Old (H)				
Graham W. Smith BA BD FSAScot	1995		Manse of Livingston, Charlesfield Lane, Livingston EH54 7AJ [E-mail: gsmith2014@hotmail.com]	01506 420227
Gordon J. Pennykid BD DCS	2015		8 Glenfield, Livingston EH54 7BG [E-mail: gpennykid@churchofscotland.org.uk]	07747 652652 (Mbl)
Livingston United Parish				
Ronald G. Greig MA BD	1987	2008	2 Eastcroft Court, Livingston EH54 7ET [E-mail: rgglep@gmail.com]	01506 467426
Darren Philip BSc (Youth and Children's Worker)			72 Pinebank, Ladywell, Livingston EH54 6EX [E-mail: dphilip@churchofscotland.org.uk]	01506 797712 / 07861 455121 (Mbl)
Livingston United is a Local Ecumenical Project shared with the Scottish Episcopal, Methodist and United Reformed Churches				
Pardovan, Kingscavil and Winchburgh See Abercorn				
Polbeth Harwood linked with West Kirk of Calder (H)				
Jonanda Groenewald BA BD MTh DD	1999	2014	8 Manse Court, East Calder, Livingston EH53 0HF [E-mail: jonandagroenewald@gmail.com]	01506 884802

Strathbrock (H)
Marc B. Kenton BTh MTh | 1997 | 2009 | 1 Manse Park, Uphall, Broxburn EH52 6NX [E-mail: marc@kentonfamily.co.uk] | 01506 852550

Torphichen See Avonbridge

Uphall: South (H)
Ian D. Maxwell MA BD PhD | 1977 | 2013 | 8 Fernlea, Uphall, Broxburn EH52 6DF [E-mail: i.d.maxwell@quista.net] | 01506 239840

West Kirk of Calder (H) See Polbeth Harwood

Whitburn: Brucefield (H)
Alexander M. Roger BD PhD | 1982 | 2014 | 48 Gleneagles Court, Whitburn, Bathgate EH47 8PG [E-mail: sandy.roger@outlook.com] | 01501 229354

Whitburn: South (H)
Angus Kerr BD CertMin ThM DMin | 1983 | 2013 | 5 Mansewood Crescent, Whitburn, Bathgate EH47 8HA [E-mail: revdrkerr@gmail.com] | 01501 740333

Black, David W. BSc BD	1968	2008	(Strathbrock)	66 Bridge Street, Newbridge EH28 8SH [E-mail: dw.black666@yahoo.co.uk]	0131-333 2609
Cameron, Ian MA BD	1953	1981	(Kilbrandon and Kilchattan)	Craigellen, West George Street, Blairgowrie PH10 6DZ	01250 872087
Darroch, Richard J.G. BD MTh MA(CMS)	1993	2010	(Whitburn: Brucefield)	23 Barnes Green, Livingston EH54 8PP [E-mail: richdarr@aol.com]	01506 436648
Dundas, Thomas B.S. LTh	1969	1996	(West Kirk of Calder)	35 Coolkill, Sandyford, Dublin 18, Republic of Ireland [E-mail: deitom35@yahoo.com]	00353 12953061
Jamieson, Gordon D. MA BD	1974	2012	(Head of Stewardship)	41 Goldpark Place, Livingston EH54 6LW [E-mail: gdj1949@talktalk.net]	01506 412020
Kelly, Isobel J.M. (Miss) MA BD DipEd	1974	2010	(Greenock: St Margaret's)	76 Bankton Park East, Livingston EH54 9BN	01506 438511
Mackay, Kenneth J. MA BD	1971	2007	(Edinburgh: St Nicholas' Sighthill)	46 Chuckethall Road, Livingston EH54 8FB [E-mail: knnth_mackay@yahoo.co.uk]	01506 410884
MacRae, Norman I. LTh	1966	2003	(Inverness: Trinity)	144 Hope Park Gardens, Bathgate EH48 2QX [E-mail: normanmacrae@talktalk.com]	01506 635254
Merrilees, Ann (Miss) DCS			(Deaconess)	23 Cuthill Brae, West Calder EH55 8QE [E-mail: ann@merrilees.freeserve.co.uk]	01501 762909
Morrison, Iain C. BA BD	1990	2003	(Linlithgow: St Ninian's Craigmailen)	Whaligoe, 53 Eastcroft Drive, Polmont, Falkirk FK2 0SU [E-mail: iain@kirkweb.org]	01324 713249
Nelson, Georgina MA BD PhD DipEd	1990	1995	Hospital Chaplain	63 Hawthorn Bank, Seafield, Bathgate EH47 7EB	
Nicol, Robert M.	1984	1996	(Jersey: St Columba's)	59 Kinloch View, Blackness Road, Linlithgow EH49 7HT [E-mail: revrob.nicol@tiscali.co.uk]	01506 670391

Orr, J. McMichael MA BD PhD	1949	1986	(Aberfoyle with Port of Menteith)	
			17a St Ninians Way, Linlithgow EH49 7HL	01506 840515
			[E-mail: mikeandmargorr@googlemail.com]	
Thomson, Phyllis (Miss) DCS	2003	2010	(Deaconess)	
			63 Caroline Park, Mid Calder, Livingston EH53 0SJ	01506 883207
Trimble, Robert DCS			(Deacon)	
			5 Templar Rise, Dedridge, Livingston EH54 6PJ	01506 412504
Walker, Ian BD MEd DipMS	1973	2007	(Rutherglen: Wardlawhill)	
			92 Carseknowe, Linlithgow EH49 7LG	01506 844412
			[E-mail: walk102822@aol.com]	

(3) LOTHIAN

Meets at Musselburgh: St Andrew's High Parish Church at 7pm on the last Thursday in February, April, June and November, and in a different church on the last Thursday in September.

Clerk:	**MR JOHN D. McCULLOCH DL**		**20 Tipperwell Way, Howgate, Penicuik EH26 8QP**	**01968 676300**
			[E-mail: lothian@churchofscotland.org.uk]	

Aberlady (H) linked with Gullane (H)
Brian C. Hilsley LLB BD	1990	2015	The Manse, Hummel Road, Gullane EH31 2BG	01620 843192
			[E-mail: bhilsley@churchofscotland.org.uk]	

Athelstaneford linked with Whitekirk and Tyninghame
Joanne H.G. Evans-Boiten BD	2004	2009	The Manse, Athelstaneford, North Berwick EH39 5BE	01620 880378
			[E-mail: jevansboiten@churchofscotland.org.uk]	

Belhaven (H) linked with Spott
Laurence H. Twaddle MA BD MTh	1977	1978	The Manse, Belhaven Road, Dunbar EH42 1NH	01368 863098
			[E-mail: ltwaddle@churchofscotland.org.uk]	

Bilston linked with Glencorse (H) linked with Roslin (H)
John R. Wells BD DipMin	1991	2005	31A Manse Road, Roslin EH25 9LG	0131-440 2012
			[E-mail: wellsjr3@aol.com]	

Bonnyrigg (H)
John Mitchell LTh CertMin	1991		9 Viewbank View, Bonnyrigg EH19 2HU	0131-663 8287 (Tel/Fax)
			[E-mail: jmitchell@churchofscotland.org.uk]	

Cockenzie and Port Seton: Chalmers Memorial (H)
Kristina M. Herbold Ross (Mrs)   2008   2 Links Road, Port Seton, Prestonpans EH32 0HA   01875 819254
[E-mail: kherboldross@churchofscotland.org.uk]

Cockenzie and Port Seton: Old (H)
Guardianship of the Presbytery

Cockpen and Carrington (H) linked with Lasswade (H) and Rosewell (H)
Vacant   11 Pendreich Terrace, Bonnyrigg EH19 2DT   0131-663 6392

Dalkeith: St John's and King's Park (H)
Keith L. Mack BD MTh DPS   2002   13 Weir Crescent, Dalkeith EH22 3JN   0131-454 0206
[E-mail: kmack@churchofscotland.org.uk]

Dalkeith: St Nicholas' Buccleuch (H)
Alexander G. Horsburgh MA BD   1995   2004   16 New Street, Musselburgh EH21 6JP   0131-653 3318
[E-mail: ahorsburgh@churchofscotland.org.uk]

Dirleton (H) linked with North Berwick: Abbey (H) (Office: 01620 892800) (E-mail: abbeychurch@btconnect.com)
David J. Graham BSc BD PhD   1982   1998   Sydserff, Old Abbey Road, North Berwick EH39 4BP   01620 840878
[E-mail: dgraham@churchofscotland.org.uk]

Dunbar (H)
Gordon Stevenson BSc BD   2010   The Manse, 10 Bayswell Road, Dunbar EH42 1AB   01368 865482
[E-mail: gstev@btconnect.com]

Dunglass
Suzanne G. Fletcher (Mrs) BA MDiv MA   2001   2011   The Manse, Cockburnspath TD13 5XZ   01368 830713
[E-mail: sfletcher@churchofscotland.org.uk]

Garvald and Morham linked with Haddington: West (H)
John Vischer   1993   2011   15 West Road, Haddington EH41 3RD   01620 822213
[E-mail: jvischer@churchofscotland.org.uk]

Gladsmuir linked with Longniddry (H)
Robin E. Hill LLB BD PhD   2004   The Manse, Elcho Road, Longniddry EH32 0LB   01875 853195
[E-mail: rhill@churchofscotland.org.uk]

Glencorse (H) See Bilston

Gorebridge (H)
Mark S. Nicholas MA BD   1999   100 Hunterfield Road, Gorebridge EH23 4TT   01875 820387
[E-mail: mnicholas@churchofscotland.org.uk]

Gullane See Aberlady

Haddington: St Mary's (H)
Jennifer Macrae (Mrs) MA BD   1998   1 Nungate Gardens, Haddington EH41 4EE   01620 823109
[E-mail: jmacrae@churchofscotland.org.uk]

Haddington: West See Garvald and Morham

Howgate (H) linked with Penicuik: South (H)
Ian A. Cathcart BSc BD   1994   15 Stevenson Road, Penicuik EH26 0LU   01968 674692
[E-mail: icathcart@churchofscotland.org.uk]
Frederick Harrison   2013   33 Castle Avenue, Gorebridge EH23 4TH   01875 820908
(Ordained Local Minister)   [E-mail: fharrison@churchofscotland.org.uk]

Humbie linked with Yester, Bolton and Saltoun
Vacant   The Manse, Tweeddale Avenue, Gifford, Haddington EH41 4QN   01620 810515

Lasswade and Rosewell See Cockpen and Carrington

Loanhead
Graham L. Duffin BSc BD DipEd   1989   120 The Loan, Loanhead EH20 9AJ   0131-448 2459
[E-mail: gduffin@churchofscotland.org.uk]

Longniddry See Gladsmuir

Musselburgh: Northesk (H)
Alison P. McDonald MA BD   1991   16 New Street, Musselburgh EH21 6JP   0131-665 2128
[E-mail: alisonpmcdonald@btinternet.com]

Musselburgh: St Andrew's High (H) (0131-665 7239)
Yvonne E.S. Atkins (Mrs) BD   1997   8 Ferguson Drive, Musselburgh EH21 6XA   0131-665 1124
[E-mail: yatkins@churchofscotland.org.uk]

Musselburgh: St Clement's and St Ninian's
Guardianship of the Presbytery   The Manse, Wallyford Loan Road, Wallyford, Musselburgh EH21 8BU

Musselburgh: St Michael's Inveresk
Vacant   8 Hope Place, Musselburgh EH21 7QE   0131-665 0545

Newbattle (H) (Website: http://freespace.virgin.net/newbattle.focus)
Sean Swindells BD DipMin MTh   1996   2011   112 Greenbank Crescent, Edinburgh EH10 5SZ   0131-447 4032
    [E-mail: sswindells@churchofscotland.org.uk]   07791 755976 (Mbl)
Michael D. Watson   2013   47 Crichton Terrace, Pathhead EH37 5QZ   01875 320043
(Ordained Local Minister)   [E-mail: mwatson@churchofscotland.org.uk]

Newton
Guardianship of the Presbytery   The Manse, Newton, Dalkeith EH22 1SR   0131-663 3845
Andrew Don MBA   2006   5 Eskvale Court, Penicuik EH26 8HT   01968 675766
(Ordained Local Minister)   [E-mail: adon@churchofscotland.org.uk]

North Berwick: Abbey See Dirleton

North Berwick: St Andrew Blackadder (H) (E-mail: admin@standrewblackadder.org.uk) (Website: www.standrewblackadder.org.uk)
Neil J. Dougall BD   1991   2003   7 Marine Parade, North Berwick EH39 4LD   01620 892132
    [E-mail: ndougall@churchofscotland.org.uk]

Ormiston linked with Pencaitland
David J. Torrance BD DipMin   1993   2009   The Manse, Pencaitland, Tranent EH34 5DL   01875 340963
    [E-mail: dtorrance@churchofscotland.org.uk]

Pencaitland See Ormiston

Penicuik: North (H) (Website: www.pnk.org.uk)
Ruth D. Halley BEd BD PGCM   2012   93 John Street, Penicuik EH26 8AG   01968 675761
    [E-mail: rhalley@churchofscotland.org.uk]   07530 307413 (Mbl)

Penicuik: St Mungo's (H)
Vacant

Penicuik: South See Howgate

Prestonpans: Prestongrange

Kenneth W Donald BA BD	1982	2014	The Manse, East Loan, Prestonpans EH32 9ED [E-mail: kdonald@churchofscotland.org.uk]	01875 571579

Roslin See Bilston
Spott See Belhaven

Tranent

Erica M Wishart (Mrs) MA BD	2014	1 Toll House Gardens, Tranent EH33 2QQ [E-mail: ewishart@churchofscotland.org.uk]	01875 824604

Traprain

David D. Scott BSc BD	1981	2010	The Manse, Preston Road, East Linton EH40 3DS [E-mail: ddscott@churchofscotland.org.uk]	01620 860227 (Tel/Fax)

Tyne Valley Parish (H)

Alan R. Cobain BD	2000	2013	Cranstoun Cottage, Ford, Pathhead EH37 5RE [E-mail: acobain@churchofscotland.org.uk]	01875 320314

Whitekirk and Tyninghame See Athelstaneford
Yester See Bolton and Saltoun

Andrews, J. Edward MA BD DipCG FSAScot	1985	2005	(Armadale)	Dunnichen, 1B Cameron Road, Nairn IV12 5NS [E-mail: edward.andrews@btinternet.com]	01667 459466 (Mbl) 07808 720708
Bayne, Angus L. LTh BEd MTh	1969	2005	(Edinburgh: Bristo Memorial Craigmillar)	14 Myredale, Bonnyrigg EH19 3NW [E-mail: angus@mccookies.com]	0131-663 6871
Berry, Geoff T. BD BSc	2009	2011	Chaplain: Army	38 Muirfield Drive, Gullane EH31 2HJ [E-mail: geofftalk@yahoo.co.uk]	
Black, A. Graham MA	1964	2003	(Gladsmuir with Longniddry)	26 Hamilton Crescent, Gullane EH31 2HR [E-mail: grablack@btinternet.com]	01620 843899
Brown, Ronald H.	1974	1998	(Musselburgh: Northesk)	6 Monktonhall Farm Cottages, Musselburgh EH21 6RZ	0131-653 2531
Brown, William BD	1972	1997	(Edinburgh: Polwarth)	13 Thornyhall, Dalkeith EH22 2ND	0131-654 0929
Buchanan, John DCS			(Deacon)	19 Gillespie Crescent, Edinburgh EH10 4HZ	0131-229 0794
Burt, Thomas W. BD	1982	2013	(Carlops with Kirkurd and Newlands with West Linton: St Andrew's)	7 Arkwright Court, North Berwick EH39 4RT	01620 895494
Cairns, John B. KCVO LTh LLB LLD DD	1974	2009	(Aberlady with Gullane)	Bell House, Roxburghe Park, Dunbar EH42 1LR [E-mail: johncairns@mail.com]	01368 862501
Coltart, Ian O. CA BD	1988	2010	(Arbirlot with Carmyllie)	25 Bothwell Gardens, Dunbar EH42 1PZ	01368 860064
Dick, Andrew B. BD DipMin	1986	2015	(Musselburgh: St Michael's Inveresk)	4 Kirkhill Court, Gorebridge EH23 4TW [E-mail: dixbit@aol.com]	01875 571223
Forbes, Iain M. BSc BD	1964	2005	(Aberdeen: Beechgrove)	69 Dobbie's Road, Bonnyrigg EH19 2AY [E-mail: panama.forbes@tiscali.co.uk]	0131-454 0717

Name	Years	Position	Address	Telephone
Frail, Nicola R. BLE MBA MDiv	2000	Army Chaplain	32 Engineer Regiment, Marne Barracks, Catterick Garrison DL10 7NP [E-mail: nrfscot@hotmail.com]	
Fraser, John W. MA BD	1974 2011	(Penicuik: North)	66 Camus Avenue, Edinburgh EH10 6QX [E-mail: jjjj2005@hotmail.co.uk]	0131-623 0647
Glover, Robert L. BMus BD MTh ARCO	1971 2010	(Cockenzie and Port Seton: Chalmers Memorial)	12 Seton Wynd, Port Seton, Prestonpans EH32 0TY [E-mail: rlglover@btinternet.com]	01875 818759
Hutchison, Alan E.W.		(Deacon)	132 Lochbridge Road, North Berwick EH39 4DR	01620 894077
Johnston, June E. BSc MEd BD	2013	Ordained Local Minister	Tarmachan, Main Street, Killin FK21 8TN [E-mail: johnston330@btinternet.com]	(Mbl) 0775 444 8889
Jones, Anne M. (Mrs) BD	1998 2002	(Hospital Chaplain)	7 North Elphinstone Farm, Tranent EH33 2ND [E-mail: revamjones@aol.com]	01875 614442
Kellock, Chris N. MA BD	1998 2012	Army Chaplain	1 Plantation Road, Tidworth SP9 7SJ	01980 601070
Manson, James A. LTh	1981 2004	(Glencorse with Roslin)	31 Nursery Gardens, Kilmarnock KA1 3JA [E-mail: james.manson@virgin.net]	01563 535430
Pirie, Donald LTh	1975 2006	(Bolton and Saltoun with Humbie with Yester)	46 Caiystane Avenue, Edinburgh EH10 6SH	0131-445 2654
Ritchie, James McL. MA BD MPhil	1950 1985	(Coalsnaughton)	Flat 2/25, Croft-an-Righ, Edinburgh EH8 8EG [E-mail: jasritch_77@msn.com]	0131-557 1084
Ross, Matthew Z. LLB BD MTh FSAScot	1998 2014	General Secretary, ACTS	Braemar Villa, 2 Links Road, Port Seton, Prestonpans EH32 0HA [E-mail: matthewross@acts-scotland.org]	01875 819254 (Mbl) 07711 706950
Simpson, Robert R. BA BD	1994 2014	(Callander)	10 Bellsmains, Gorebridge EH23 4QD [E-mail: robert@pansmanse.co.uk]	01875 820843
Stein, Jock MA BD	1973 2008	(Tulliallan and Kincardine)	35 Dunbar Road, Haddington EH41 3PJ [E-mail: jstein@handselpress.org.uk]	01620 824896
Stein, Margaret E. (Mrs) DA BD DipRE	1984 2008	(Tulliallan and Kincardine)	35 Dunbar Road, Haddington EH41 3PJ [E-mail: margaretestein@hotmail.com]	01620 824896
Steven, Gordon R. BD DCS		(Deacon)	51 Nantwich Drive, Edinburgh EH7 6RB [E-mail: grsteven@btinternet.com]	0131-669 2054 (Mbl) 07904 385256
Swan, Andrew F. BD	1983 2000	(Loanhead)	Park View, 2 Park Place, Lanark ML11 9HH	
Torrance, David W. MA BD	1955 1991	(Earlston)	38 Forth Street, North Berwick EH39 4JQ [E-mail: torrance103@btinternet.com]	(Tel/Fax) 01620 895109
Underwood, Florence A. (Mrs) BD	1992 2006	(Assistant: Gladsmuir with Longniddry)	18 Covenanters Rise, Pitreavie Castle, Dunfermline KY11 8SQ [E-mail: gunderwood@tesco.net]	01383 740745
Underwood, Geoffrey H. BD DipTh FPhS	1964 1992	(Cockenzie and Port Seton: Chalmers Memorial)	18 Covenanters Rise, Pitreavie Castle, Dunfermline KY11 8SQ [E-mail: gunderwood@tesco.net]	01383 740745

(4) MELROSE AND PEEBLES

Meets at Innerleithen on the first Tuesday of February, March, May, October, November and December, and on the fourth Tuesday of June, and in places to be appointed on the first Tuesday of September.

| Clerk: | REV. VICTORIA LINFORD LLB BD | The Manse, 209 Galashiels Road, Stow, Galashiels TD1 2RE [E-mail: melrosepeebles@churchofscotland.org.uk] | 01578 730237 |

Ashkirk linked with Selkirk (H)

Minister	Ordained	Inducted	Address	Tel
Margaret D.J. Steele (Miss) BSc BD	2000	2011	1 Loanside, Selkirk TD7 4DJ [E-mail: mdjsteele@gmail.com]	01750 23308

Bowden (H) and Melrose (H)

Minister	Ordained	Inducted	Address	Tel
Alistair G. Bennett BSc BD	1978	1984	Tweedmount Road, Melrose TD6 9ST [E-mail: agbennettmelrose@aol.com]	01896 822217

Broughton, Glenholm and Kilbucho (H) linked with Skirling linked with Stobo and Drumelzier linked with Tweedsmuir (H)

Minister	Ordained	Inducted	Address	Tel
Robert B. Milne BTh	1999	2009	The Manse, Broughton, Biggar ML12 6HQ [E-mail: rbmilne@aol.com]	01899 830331

Caddonfoot (H) linked with Galashiels: Trinity (H)

Minister	Ordained	Inducted	Address	Tel
Elspeth Harley BA MTh	1991	2014	8 Mossilee Road, Galashiels TD1 1NF [E-mail: eharley@hotmail.co.uk]	01896 752420

Carlops linked with Kirkurd and Newlands (H) linked with West Linton: St Andrew's (H)

Minister	Ordained	Inducted	Address	Tel
Linda J. Dunbar BSc BA BD PhD FRHS	2000	2013	The Manse, Main Street, West Linton EH46 7EE [E-mail: revljd@gmail.com]	01968 660221 / 07939 496360 (Mbl)

Channelkirk and Lauder

Minister	Ordained	Inducted	Address	Tel
Marion (Rae) Clark MA BD		2014	The Manse, Brownsmuir Park, Lauder TD2 6QD [E-mail: raeclark@btinternet.com]	01578 718996

Earlston

Minister	Ordained	Inducted	Address	Tel
Julie M. Woods (Ms) BTh	2005	2011	The Manse, High Street, Earlston TD4 6DE [E-mail: jwoods@churchofscotland.org.uk]	01896 849236

Eddleston (H) linked with Peebles: Old (H)

Minister	Ordained	Inducted	Address	Tel
Malcolm M. Macdougall BD MTh DipCE	1981	2001	7 Clement Gunn Square, Peebles EH45 8LW [E-mail: calum.macdougall@btopenworld.com]	01721 720568
Pamela D. Strachan (Lady) MA (Cantab) (Ordained Local Minister)		2015	Glenhighton, Broughton, Biggar ML12 6JF [E-mail: pamelastrachan@btinternet.com]	01899 830423 / 07837 873688 (Mbl)

Ettrick and Yarrow

Minister	Ordained	Inducted	Address	Tel
Samuel Siroky BA MTh		2003	Yarrow Manse, Yarrow, Selkirk TD7 5LA [E-mail: sesiroky@tiscali.co.uk]	01750 82336

Galashiels: Old Parish and St Paul's (H) linked with Galashiels: St John's (H)
Leon Keller BA BD DipTheol PhD   1988   2015
Woodlea, Abbotsview Drive, Galashiels TD1 3SL   01896 753029
[E-mail: kellerleon1@gmail.com]

Galashiels: St John's See Galashiels: Old Parish and St Paul's
Galashiels: Trinity See Caddonfoot

Innerleithen (H), Traquair and Walkerburn   1991   2001
Janice M. Faris (Mrs) BSc BD
The Manse, 1 Millwell Park, Innerleithen, Peebles EH44 6JF   01896 830309
[E-mail: revjfaris@hotmail.com]

Kirkurd and Newlands See Carlops

Lyne and Manor linked with Peebles: St Andrew's Leckie (H) (01721 723121)
Malcolm S. Jefferson   2012
Mansefield, Innerleithen Road, Peebles EH45 8BE   01721 721148
[E-mail: jeffersons02@btinternet.com]

Maxton and Mertoun linked with Newtown linked with St Boswells
Sheila W. Moir (Ms) MTheol   2008
7 Strae Brigs, St Boswells, Melrose TD6 0DH   01835 822255
[E-mail: sheila377@btinternet.com]

Newtown See Maxton and Mertoun
Peebles: Old See Eddleston
Peebles: St Andrew's Leckie See Lyne and Manor
St Boswells See Maxton and Mertoun
Selkirk See Ashkirk
Skirling See Broughton, Glenholm and Kilbucho
Stobo and Drumelzier See Broughton, Glenholm and Kilbucho

Stow: St Mary of Wedale and Heriot   2010
Victoria J. Linford (Mrs) LLB BD
The Manse, 209 Galashiels Road, Stow, Galashiels TD1 2RE   01578 730237
[E-mail: victorialinford@yahoo.co.uk]

Tweedsmuir See Broughton, Glenholm and Kilbucho
West Linton: St Andrew's See Carlops

Arnott, A. David K. MA BD	1971	2010	(St Andrews: Hope Park with Strathkinness)	53 Whitehaugh Park, Peebles EH45 9DB [E-mail: adka53@btinternet.com]	01721 725979 (Mbl) 07759 709205
Bowie, Adam McC.	1976	1996	(Cavers and Kirkton with Hobkirk and Southdean)	Glenbield, Redpath, Earlston TD4 6AD	01896 848173
Cashman, P. Hamilton BSc	1985	1998	(Dirleton with North Berwick: Abbey)	38 Abbotsford Road, Galashiels TD1 3HR [E-mail: mcashman@tiscali.co.uk]	01896 752711
Cutler, James S.H. BD CEng MIStructE	1986	2011	(Black Mount with Culter with Libberton and Quothquan)	12 Kittlegairy Place, Peebles EH45 9LW [E-mail: revjc@btinternet.com]	01721 723950
Devenny, Robert P.	2002		Head of Spiritual Care, NHS Lanarkshire (Hospital Chaplain)	Blakeburn Cottage, Wester Housebyres, Melrose TD6 9BW	01896 822350
Dick, J. Ronald BD	1973	1996	(Broughton, Glenholm and Kilbucho with Skirling with Stobo and Drumelzier with Tweedsmuir)	5 Georgefield Farm Cottages, Earlston TD4 6BH	01896 848956
Dobie, Rachel J.W. (Mrs) LTh	1991	2008	(Kelso: Old and Sprouston)	20 Moss Side Crescent, Biggar ML12 6GE [E-mail: revracheldobie@talktalk.net]	01899 229244
Dodd, Marion E. (Miss) MA BD LRAM	1988	2010	(Heriot with Stow: St Mary of Wedale)	Esdaile, Tweedmount Road, Melrose TD6 9ST [E-mail: mariondodd@btinternet.com]	01896 822446
Duncan, Charles A. MA	1956	1992	(Blackridge with Harthill: St Andrew's)	10 Elm Grove, Galashiels TD1 3JA	01896 753261
Hardie, H. Warner BD	1979	2005		Keswick Cottage, Kingsmuir Drive, Peebles EH45 9AA [E-mail: hardies@bigfoot.com]	01721 724003
Hogg, Thomas M. BD	1986	2007	(Tranent)	22 Douglas Place, Galashiels TD1 3BT	01896 759381
Hughes, Barry MA	2011		Ordained Local Minister	Dunslair, Cardrona Way, Cardrona, Peebles EH45 9LD [E-mail: gill_baz@hotmail.com]	01896 831197
Kellet, John M. MA	1962	1995	(Leith: South)	4 High Cottages, Walkerburn EH43 6AZ	01896 870351
Kennon, Stanley BA BD RN	1992	2000	Chaplain: Royal Navy	HMS Raleigh, Torpoint, Cornwall PL11 2PD [E-mail: brnc-csf@fleetfost.mod.uk]	
Lawrie, Bruce B. BD	1974	2012	(Duffus, Spynie and Hopeman)	5 Thorncroft, Scotts Place, Selkirk TD7 4LN [E-mail: thorncroft54@gmail.com]	01750 725427
MacFarlane, David C. MA	1957	1997	(Eddleston with Peebles: Old) General Secretary: United Bible Societies)	Lorimer House Nursing Home, 491 Lanark Road, Edinburgh EH14 5DQ	01721 723380
Milloy, A. Miller DPE LTh DipTrMan	1979	2012	(Secretary: The Boys' Brigade)	18 Kittlegairy Crescent, Peebles EH45 9NJ [E-mail: ammilloy@aol.com]	01896 668577
Moore, W. Haisley MA	1966	1996	(Delting with Northmavine)	26 Tweedbank Avenue, Tweedbank, Galashiels TD1 3SP	01835 823375
Munson, Winnie (Ms) BD	1996	2006	(Lyne and Manor)	6 St Cuthbert's Drive, St Boswells, Melrose TD6 0DF	01721 721699
Norman, Nancy M. (Miss) BA MDiv MTh	1988	2012	(Annan: St Andrew's Greenknowe Erskine)	25 March Street, Peebles EH45 8EP [E-mail: nancy.norman1@googlemail.com]	
Rae, Andrew W.	1951	1987	(Broughton, Glenholm and Kilbucho with Skirling with Stobo and Drumelzier with Tweedsmuir)	Roseneuk, Tweedside Road, Newtown St Boswells TD6 0PQ	01835 823783
Rennie, John D. MA	1962	1996	(Jedburgh: Trinity)	29/1 Rosetta Road, Peebles EH45 8HJ [E-mail: tworennies@talktalk.net]	01721 720963
Riddell, John A. MA BD	1967	2006	(Galashiels: Old and St Paul's)	Orchid Cottage, Gingham Row, Earlston TD4 6ET	01896 848784
Steele, Leslie M. MA BD	1973	2013	(Maxton and Mertoun with St Boswells)	25 Bardfield Road, Colchester CO2 8LW [E-mail: lms@hotmail.co.uk]	01206 621939 (Mbl) 07786 797974
Taverner, Glyn R. MA BD	1957	1995	(Peebles: St Andrew's Leckie)	Woodcot Cottage, Waverley Road, Innerleithen EH44 6QW	01896 830156
Wallace, James H. MA BD	1973	2011		52 Waverley Mills, Innerleithen EH44 6RH [E-mail: jimwallace121@btinternet.com]	01896 831637

(5) DUNS

Meets at Duns, in the Parish Church hall, normally on the first Tuesday of February, March, April, May, October, November and December, on the last Tuesday in June, and in places to be appointed on the first Tuesday of September.

Clerk: DR H. DANE SHERRARD   Mount Pleasant Granary, Duns TD11 3HU   01361 882254
[E-mail: duns@churchofscotland.org.uk]   07582 468468

Ayton (H) and Burnmouth linked with Foulden and Mordington linked with Grantshouse and Houndwood and Reston
Norman R. Whyte BD MTh DipMin   1982   2006   The Manse, Beanburn, Ayton, Eyemouth TD14 5QY   01890 781333
[E-mail: burraman@msn.com]

Berwick-upon-Tweed: St Andrew's Wallace Green (H) and Lowick
Adam J.J. Hood MA BD DPhil   1989   2012   3 Meadow Grange, Berwick-upon-Tweed TD15 1NW   01289 332787
[E-mail: minister@sawg.org.uk]

Chirnside linked with Hutton and Fishwick and Paxton
Vacant   Parish Church Manse, The Glebe, Chirnside, Duns TD11 3XL   01890 819109

Coldingham and St Abbs linked with Eyemouth
Andrew Haddow BEng BD   2012   The Manse, Victoria Road, Eyemouth TD14 5JD   01890 750327
[E-mail: andy@blakkie.co.uk]

Coldstream (H) linked with Eccles
David J. Taverner MCIBS ACIS BD   1996   2011   36 Bennecourt Drive, Coldstream TD12 4BY   01890 883887
[E-mail: rahereuk@hotmail.com]

Duns and District Parishes linked with Langton and Lammermuir Kirk
Stephen A. Blakey BSc BD   1977   2012   The Manse, Castle Street, Duns TD11 3DG   01361 883755
[E-mail: stephenablakey@icloud.com]

Eccles See Coldstream
Eyemouth See Coldingham and St Abbs

Fogo and Swinton linked with Ladykirk and Whitsome linked with Leitholm (H)
Alan C.D. Cartwright BSc BD   1976   The Manse, Swinton, Duns TD11 3JJ   01890 860228
[E-mail: merse.minister@btinternet.com]

Foulden and Mordington See Ayton and Burnmouth

Gordon: St Michael's linked with Greenlaw (H) linked with Legerwood linked with Westruther
Thomas S. Nicholson BD DPS   1982   1995   The Manse, Todholes, Greenlaw, Duns TD10 6XD   01361 810316
[E-mail: nst54@hotmail.com]

Grantshouse and Houndwood and Reston See Ayton and Burnmouth
Greenlaw See Gordon: St Michael's
Hutton and Fishwick and Paxton See Chirnside
Ladykirk and Whitsome See Fogo and Swinton

Langton and Lammermuir Kirk See Duns and District Parishes

Legerwood See Gordon: St Michael's
Leitholm See Fogo and Swinton
Westruther See Gordon: St Michael's

Name	Dates	Parish	Address	Tel
Gaddes, Donald R.	1961 1994	(Kelso: North and Ednam)	2 Teindhill Green, Duns TD11 3DX [E-mail: drgaddes@btinternet.com]	01361 883172
Gale, Ronald A.A. LTh	1982 1995	(Dunoon: Old and St Cuthbert's)	55 Lennel Mount, Coldstream TD12 4NS [E-mail: rgale89@aol.com]	01890 883699
Graham, Jennifer D. (Mrs) BA MDiv PhD	2000 2011	(Eday with Stronsay: Moncur Memorial)	Lodge, Stronsay, Orkney KW17 2AN [E-mail: jdgraham67@gmail.com]	01857 616487
Higham, Robert D. BD	1985 2002	(Tiree)	36 Low Greens, Berwick-upon-Tweed TD15 1LZ	01289 302392
Hope, Geraldine H. (Mrs) MA BD	1986 2007	(Foulden and Mordington with Hutton and Fishwick and Paxton)	4 Well Court, Chirnside, Duns TD11 3UD [E-mail: geraldine.hope@virgin.net]	01890 818134
Kerr, Andrew MA BLitt	1948 1991	(Kilbarchan: West)	4 Lairds Gate, Port Glasgow Road, Kilmacolm PA13 4EX	01507 874852
Landale, William S.	2005	(Kilbarchan: West) Auxiliary Minister	Green Hope Guest House, Ellemford, Duns TD11 3SG [E-mail: bill@greenhope.co.uk]	01361 890242
Lindsay, Daniel G. BD	1978 2011	(Coldingham and St Abbs with Eyemouth)	18 Hallidown Crescent, Eyemouth TD14 5TB	01890 751389
Murray, Duncan E. BA BD	1970 2012	(Bonkyl and Preston with Chirnside with Edrom Allanton)	Beech Cottage, York Road, Knaresborough HG5 0TT [E-mail: duncanemurray@tiscali.co.uk]	01423 313287
Neill, Bruce F. MA BD	1966 2007	(Maxton and Mertoun with Newtown with St Boswells)	18 Brierydean, St Abbs, Eyemouth TD14 5PQ [E-mail: bneill@phonecoop.coop]	01890 771569
Paterson, William BD	1977 2001	(Bonkyl and Preston with Chirnside with Edrom Allanton)	Benachie, Gavinton, Duns TD11 3QT [E-mail: billdm.paterson@btinternet.com]	01361 882727
Sherrard, H. Dane BD DMin	1971 2013	(Arrochar with Luss)	The Granary, Mount Pleasant, Duns TD11 4HU [E-mail: dane@mountpleasantgranary.net]	01361 882254 (Mbl) 07801 939138

| Walker, Kenneth D.F. MA BD PhD | 1976 2008 | (Athelstaneford with Whitekirk and Tyninghame) | Allanbank Kothi, Allanton, Duns TD11 3PY [E-mail: walkerkenneth49@gmail.com] | 01890 817102 |

(6) JEDBURGH

Meets at various venues on the first Wednesday of February, March, May, September, October, November and December and on the last Wednesday of June.

| Clerk | REV. FRANK CAMPBELL | | 22 The Glebe, Ancrum, Jedburgh TD8 6UX [E-mail: jedburgh@churchofscotland.org.uk] | 01835 830318 |

Ale and Teviot United (H) (Website: www.aleandteviot.org.uk)

| Frank Campbell | 1989 1991 | 22 The Glebe, Ancrum, Jedburgh TD8 6UX [E-mail: jedburgh@churchofscotland.org.uk] | 01835 830318 |

Cavers and Kirkton linked with Hawick: Trinity (H)

| Michael D. Scouler MBE BSc BD | 1988 2009 | Trinity Manse, Howdenburn, Hawick TD9 8PH [E-mail: michaelscouler@hotmail.co.uk] | 01450 378248 |

Cheviot Churches (H) (Website: www.cheviotchurches.org)

| Robin D. McHaffie BD | 1979 1991 | The Manse, Main Street, Kirk Yetholm, Kelso TD5 8PF [E-mail: robinmchaffie@btinternet.com] | 01573 420308 |

Hawick: Burnfoot (Website: www.burnfootparishchurch.org.uk)

| Charles J. Finnie LTh DPS | 1991 1997 | 29 Wilton Hill, Hawick TD9 8BA [E-mail: charles.finnie@gmail.com] | 01450 373181 |

Hawick: St Mary's and Old (H) linked with Hawick: Teviot (H) and Roberton

| Vacant | | The Manse, Buccleuch Road, Hawick TD9 0EL | 01450 372150 |

Hawick: Teviot and Roberton See Hawick: St Mary's and Old
Hawick: Trinity See Cavers and Kirkton

Hawick: Wilton linked with Teviothead

| Lisa-Jane Rankin BD CPS | 2003 | 4 Wilton Hill Terrace, Hawick TD9 8BE [E-mail: revlj@talktalk.net] | 01450 370744 |

Hobkirk and Southdean (Website: www.hobkirkruberslaw.org) linked with Ruberslaw (Website: www.hobkirkruberslaw.org)
Douglas A.O. Nicol MA BD   1974   2009   The Manse, Denholm, Hawick TD9 8NB   01450 870268
[E-mail: daon@lineone.net]

Jedburgh: Old and Trinity (Website: www.jedburgh-parish.org.uk)
Graham D. Astles BD MSc   2007   The Manse, Honeyfield Drive, Jedburgh TD8 6LQ   01835 863417
07906 290568 (Mbl)
[E-mail: minister@jedburgh-parish.org.uk]

Kelso Country Churches linked with Kelso: Old (H) and Sprouston (Website: www.kelsolinkedchurchescofs.org)
Jenny Earl MA BD   2007   The Manse, 1 The Meadow, Stichill, Kelso TD5 7TG   01573 470607
[E-mail: jennyearl@btinternet.com]
Anna S. Rodwell (Mrs) BD DipMin   1998   2014   The Old Mill House, Hownam Howgate, Kelso TD5 8AJ   01573 440761
(Associate Minister)   [E-mail: anna.rodwell@gmail.com]

Kelso: North (H) and Ednam (H) (01573 224154) (E-mail: office@kelsonorthandednam.org.uk) (Website: www.kelsonorthandednam.org.uk)
Tom McDonald BD   1994   20 Forestfield, Kelso TD5 7BX   01573 224677
[E-mail: revtom@20thepearlygates.co.uk]

Kelso: Old and Sprouston See Kelso Country Churches

Oxnam (Website: www.oxnamkirk.co.uk)
Guardianship of the Presbytery

Ruberslaw See Hobkirk and Southdean
Teviothead See Hawick: Wilton

Auld, A. Graeme (Prof.)   1973   2008   (University of Edinburgh)   Nether Swanshiel, Hobkirk, Bonchester Bridge, Hawick TD9 8JU   01450 860636
  MA BD PhD DLitt FSAScot FRSE   [E-mail: a.g.auld@ed.ac.uk]
Combe, Neil R. BSc MSc BD   1984   2015   (Hawick: St Mary's and Old with Hawick: Teviot and Roberton)   2 Abbotsview Gardens, Galashiels TD1 3ER   01896 755869
[E-mail: neil.combe@btinternet.com]
McNicol, Bruce   1967   2006   (Jedburgh: Old and Edgerston)   42 Dounehill, Jedburgh TD8 6LJ   01835 862991
[E-mail: mcnicol1942@gmail.com]
Shields, John M. MBE LTh   1972   2007   (Channelkirk and Lauder)   12 Eden Park, Ednam, Kelso TD5 7RG   01573 229015
[E-mail: john.shields118@btinternet.com]

HAWICK ADDRESSES

Burnfoot	Fraser Avenue	St Mary's and Old	Kirk Wynd	Wilton	Princes Street
		Teviot	off Buccleuch Road		
		Trinity	Central Square		

(7) ANNANDALE AND ESKDALE

Meets on the first Tuesday of February, May, September and December, and the third Tuesday of March, June and October. The September meeting is held in the Moderator's charge. The other meetings are held in Dryfesdale Church Hall, Lockerbie, except for the June meeting, which is separately announced.

Clerk: REV. C. BRYAN HASTON LTh   The Manse, Gretna Green, Gretna **DG16 5DU**   **01461 338313**
[E-mail: annandaleeskdale@cofscotland.org.uk]
[E-mail: cbhaston@cofs.demon.co.uk]

Annan: Old (H) linked with Dornock
Vacant   12 Plumdon Park Avenue, Annan DG12 6EY   01461 201405

Annan: St Andrew's (H) linked with Brydekirk
John G. Pickles BD MTh MSc   2011   1 Annerley Road, Annan DG12 6HE   01461 202626
[E-mail: jgpickles@hotmail.com]

Applegarth, Sibbaldbie (H) and Johnstone linked with Lochmaben (H)
Paul R. Read BSc MA(Th)   2000   2013   The Manse, Barrashead, Lochmaben, Lockerbie DG11 1QF   01387 810640
[E-mail: p.read@btinternet.com]

Brydekirk   See Annan: St Andrew's

Canonbie United (H) linked with Liddesdale (H)
William Jackson BD CertMin   1994   2014   23 Langholm Street, Newcastleton TD9 0QX   01387 375242
[E-mail: wiljcksn4@aol.com]
Canonbie United is a Local Ecumenical Project shared with the United Free Church

Dalton linked with Hightae linked with St Mungo
Morag A. Dawson BD MTh   1999   2011   The Manse, Hightae, Lockerbie DG11 1JL   01387 811499
[E-mail: moragdawson@yahoo.co.uk]

Dornock See Annan: Old

Gretna: Old (H), Gretna: St Andrew's (H), Half Morton and Kirkpatrick Fleming
C. Bryan Haston LTh   1975
The Manse, Gretna Green, Gretna DG16 5DU
[E-mail: cbhaston@cofs.demon.co.uk]
[E-mail: cbhaston@gretnagreen.eu]
01461 338313

Hightae See Dalton

Hoddom, Kirtle-Eaglesfield and Middlebie
Frances M. Henderson BA BD PhD   2006   2013
The Manse, Main Road, Ecclefechan, Lockerbie DG11 3BU
[E-mail: f-henderson@hotmail.co.uk]
01576 300108

Kirkpatrick Juxta linked with Moffat: St Andrew's (H) linked with Wamphray
Adam J. Dillon BD ThM   2003   2008
The Manse, 1 Meadowbank, Moffat DG10 9LR
[E-mail: adamdillon@btinternet.com]
01683 220128

Langholm Eskdalemuir Ewes and Westerkirk
I. Scott McCarthy BD   2010
The Manse, Langholm DG13 0BL
[E-mail: iscottmccarthy@gmail.com]
01387 380252

Liddesdale See Canonbie United
Lochmaben See Applegarth, Sibbaldbie and Johnstone

Lockerbie: Dryfesdale, Hutton and Corrie
Alexander C. Stoddart BD   2001   2008
The Manse, 5 Carlisle Road, Lockerbie DG11 2DW
[E-mail: sandystoddart@supanet.com]
01576 202361

Moffat: St Andrew's See Kirkpatrick Juxta
St Mungo See Dalton

The Border Kirk (Church office: Chapel Street, Carlisle CA1 1JA; Tel: 01228 591757)
David G. Pitkeathly LLB BD   1996   2007
95 Pinecroft, Carlisle CA3 0DB
[E-mail: david.pitkeathly@btinternet.com]
01228 593243

Tundergarth
Guardianship of the Presbytery

Wamphray　See Kirkpatrick Juxta

Annand, James M. MA BD	1955	1995	(Lockerbie: Dryfesdale)	Dere Cottage, 48 Main Street, Newstead, Melrose TD6 9DX	
Beveridge, S. Edwin P. BA	1959	2004	(Brydekirk with Hoddom)	19 Rothesay Terrace, Edinburgh EH3 7RY	0131-225 3393
Brydson, Angela (Mrs) DCS			Deacon	52 Victoria Park, Lockerbie DG11 2AY	(Mbl) 07543 796820
Byers, Mairi C. (Mrs) BTh CPS	1992	1998	(Jura)	Meadowbank, Plumdon Road, Annan DG12 6SJ	01461 206512
				[E-mail: aljbyers@hotmail.com]	
Gibb, J. Daniel M. BA LTh	1994	2006	(Aberfoyle with Port of Menteith)	1 Beechfield, Newton Aycliffe DL5 7AX	
				[E-mail: dannygibb@hotmail.co.uk]	
Harvey, P. Ruth (Ms) MA BD	2009	2012	Place for Hope	Croslands, Beacon Street, Penrith CA11 7TZ	01768 840749
				[E-mail: ruth.harvey@placeforhope.org.uk]	(Mbl) 07403 638339
MacMillan, William M. LTh	1980	1998	(Kilmory with Lamlash)	Balskia, 61 Queen Street, Lochmaben, Lockerbie DG11 1PP	01387 811528
Macpherson, Duncan J. BSc BD	1993	2002	Chaplain: Army	DACG ARTD (North), Infantry Training Centre, Vimy Barracks	
				Scotton Road, Catterick DL9 3PS	
Ross, Alan C. CA BD	1988	2007	(Eskdalemuir with Hutton and Corrie with Tundergarth)	Yarra, Ettrickbridge, Selkirk TD7 5JN	01750 52324
				[E-mail: alkaross@aol.com]	
Sanders, Martyn S. BA CertEd MA	2013		Ordained Local Minister	31 Carrick Road, Dumfries DG2 9PY	(Mbl) 07814 164373
				[E-mail: rev.msanders@gmail.com]	
Seaman, Ronald S. MA	1967	2007	(Dornock)	1 Springfield Farm Court, Springfield, Gretna DG16 5EH	01461 337228
Steenbergen, Pauline (Ms) MA BD	1996	2012	Hospice Chaplain	Eden Valley Hospice, Durdar Road, Carlisle CA2 4SD	01228 817609
				[E-mail: pauline.steenbergen@edenvalleyhospice.co.uk]	
Swinburne, Norman BA	1960	1993	(Sauchie)	Dameroshay, Birch Hill Lane, Kirkbride, Wigton CA7 5HZ	01697 351497
Vivers, Katherine A.	2004		Auxiliary Minister	Blacket House, Eaglesfield, Lockerbie DG11 3AA	01461 500412
				[E-mail: katevivers@yahoo.co.uk]	(Mbl) 07748 233011
Williams, Trevor C. LTh	1990	2007	(Hoddom with Kirtle-Eaglesfield with Middlebie with Waterbeck)	c/o Presbytery Clerk	
				[E-mail: revtrev@btinternet.com]	

(8) DUMFRIES AND KIRKCUDBRIGHT

Meets at Dumfries on the last Wednesday of February, April, June, September and November.

Clerk:　REV. WILLIAM T. HOGG MA BD　　St Bride's Manse, Glasgow Road, Sanquhar DG4 6BZ　　01659 50247
　　　　　　[E-mail: dumfrieskirkcudbright@churchofscotland.org.uk]

Balmaclellan and Kells (H) linked with Carsphairn (H) linked with Dalry (H)
David S. Bartholomew BSc MSc PhD BD　　1994　　The Manse, Dalry, Castle Douglas DG7 3PJ　　01644 430380
　　　　　　[E-mail: dhbart@care4free.net]

Caerlaverock linked with Dumfries: St Mary's-Greyfriars' (H)
Vacant — 4 Georgetown Crescent, Dumfries DG1 4EQ — 01387 253877

Carsphairn See Balmaclellan and Kells

Castle Douglas (H) linked with The Bengairn Parishes
Stephen Ashley-Emery BD DPS 2006 2014 — 1 Castle View, Castle Douglas DG7 1BG [E-mail: revstephenae@gmail.com] — 01556 505983

Closeburn
Guardianship of the Presbytery

Colvend, Southwick and Kirkbean
James F. Gatherer BD 1984 2003 — The Manse, Colvend, Dalbeattie DG5 4QN [E-mail: jamesgatherer@btinternet.com] — 01556 630255

Corsock and Kirkpatrick Durham linked with Crossmichael, Parton and Balmaghie
Sally Russell BTh MTh 2006 — Knockdrocket, Clarebrand, Castle Douglas DG7 3AH [E-mail: rev.sal@btinternet.com] — 01556 503645

Crossmichael and Parton See Corsock and Kirkpatrick Durham

Cummertrees, Mouswald and Ruthwell (H)
Vacant — The Manse, Ruthwell, Dumfries DG1 4NP — 01387 870217

Dalbeattie (H) and Kirkgunzeon linked with Urr (H)
Fiona A. Wilson (Mrs) BD 2008 2014 — 36 Mill Street, Dalbeattie DG5 4HE [E-mail: weefi12b@hotmail.co.uk] — 01556 610708

Dalry See Balmaclellan and Kells

Dumfries: Maxwelltown West (H)
David A. Sutherland BD 2001 2014 — Maxwelltown West Manse, 11 Laurieknowe, Dumfries DG2 7AH [E-mail: dasrev80@gmail.com] — 01387 247538

Dumfries: Northwest
Neil G. Campbell BA BD 1988 2006 — c/o Church Office, Dumfries Northwest Church, Lochside Road, Dumfries DG2 0DZ [E-mail: ncampbell@churchofscotland.org.uk] — 01387 249964

Dumfries: St George's (H)
Donald Campbell BD — 1997 — 9 Nunholm Park, Dumfries DG1 1JP [E-mail: minister@saint-georges.org.uk] — 01387 252965

Dumfries: St Mary's-Greyfriars' See Caerlaverock

Dumfries: St Michael's and South
Maurice S. Bond MTh BA DipEd PhD — 1981 1999 — 39 Cardoness Street, Dumfries DG1 3AL [E-mail: mauricebond399@btinternet.com] — 01387 253849

Dumfries: Troqueer (H)
John R. Notman BSc BD — 1990 2015 — Troqueer Manse, Troqueer Road, Dumfries DG2 7DF [E-mail: notman@sky.com] — 01387 253043

Dunscore linked with Glencairn and Moniaive
Joachim J.H. du Plessis BA BD MTh — 1975 2013 — Wallaceton, Auldgirth, Dumfries DG2 0TJ [E-mail: jjhduplessis@gmail.com] — 01387 820245

Durisdeer linked with Penpont, Keir and Tynron linked with Thornhill (H)
J. Stuart Mill MA MBA BD — 1976 2013 — The Manse, Manse Park, Thornhill DG3 5ER [E-mail: stuartmill1@hotmail.co.uk] — 01848 331191

Gatehouse and Borgue linked with Tarff and Twynholm
Valerie J. Ott (Mrs) BA BD — 2002 — The Manse, Planetree Park, Gatehouse of Fleet, Castle Douglas DG7 2EQ [E-mail: valanddav98@btinternet.com] — 01557 814233

Glencairn and Moniaive See Dunscore

Irongray, Lochrutton and Terregles
Gary J. Peacock MA BD MTh — 2015 — The Manse, Shawhead, Dumfries DG2 9SJ [E-mail: garyjpeacock@hotmail.com] — 01387 730759

Kirkconnel (H)
Alistair J. MacKichan MA BD — 1984 2009 — The Manse, 31 Kingsway, Kirkconnel, Sanquhar DG4 6PN [E-mail: alistairjmck@btinternet.com] — 01659 67241

Kirkcudbright (H)
Douglas R. Irving LLB BD WS — 1984 1998 — 6 Bourtree Avenue, Kirkcudbright DG6 4AU [E-mail: douglasirving05@tiscali.co.uk] — 01557 330489

Kirkmahoe

David M. Almond BD	1996	2008	The Manse, Kirkmahoe, Dumfries DG1 1ST [E-mail: almond.david138@googlemail.com]	01387 710572

Kirkmichael, Tinwald and Torthorwald

Willem J. Bezuidenhout BA BD MHEd MEd	1977	2010	Manse of Tinwald, Tinwald, Dumfries DG1 3PL [E-mail: willembezuidenhout@btinternet.com]	01387 710246

Lochend and New Abbey

Maureen M. Duncan (Mrs) BD	1996	2014	New Abbey Manse, 32 Main Street, New Abbey, Dumfries DG2 8BY [E-mail: revmo@talktalk.net]	01387 850490

Penpont, Keir and Tynron See Durisdeer

Sanquhar: St Bride's (H)

William T. Hogg MA BD	1979	2000	St Bride's Manse, Glasgow Road, Sanquhar DG6 6BZ [E-mail: wthogg@yahoo.com]	01659 50247

Tarff and Twynholm See Gatehouse and Borgue
The Bengairn Parishes See Castle Douglas
Thornhill See Durisdeer
Urr See Dalbeattie and Kirkgunzeon

Bennett, David K.P. BA	1974	2000	(Kirkpatrick Irongray with Lochrutton with Terregles)	53 Anne Arundel Court, Heathhall, Dumfries DG1 3SL [E-mail:]	01387 257755
Dee, Oonagh (Mrs)		2014	Ordained Local Minister	'Kendoon', Merse Way, Kippford, Dalbeattie DG5 4LL [E-mail: oonaghdee@gmail.com]	01556 620001
Greer, A. David C. LLB DMin DipAdultEd	1956	1996	(Barra)	17 Duthac Wynd, Tain IV19 1LP [E-mail: greer2@talktalk.net]	01862 892065
Hamill, Robert BA	1956	1989	(Castle Douglas: St Ringan's)	11 St Andrew Drive, Castle Douglas DG7 1EW	01556 502962
Hammond, Richard J. BA BD	1993	2007	(Kirkmahoe)	3 Marchfield Mount, Marchfield, Dumfries DG1 1SE [E-mail: libby.hammond@virgin.net]	(Mbl) 07764 465783
Holland, William MA	1967	2009	(Lochend and New Abbey)	Ardshean, 55 Georgetown Road, Dumfries DG1 4DD [E-mail: billholland55@btinternet.com]	01387 256131 (Mbl) 07766 531732
Kelly, Ewan R. MB ChB BD PhD	1994	2014	Spiritual Care Lead (NHS)	Room 3, Logan West, Crichton Hall, Dumfries DG1 4TG [E-mail: ewan.kelly@nhs.net]	(Mbl) 07795 120965
Kelly, William W. BSc BD	1994	2014	(Dumfries: Troqueer)	c/o 7 Ripley Way, Duncraig, Perth, WA 6023, Australia [E-mail: ww.kelly@btinternet.com]	01387 246246 Ext 36601

Name	Dates	Charge	Address	Telephone
Kirk, W. Logan MA BD MTh	1988 2000	(Dalton with Hightae with St Mungo)	2 Raecroft Avenue, Collin, Dumfries DG1 4LP	01387 750489
Mack, Elizabeth A. (Miss) DipEd	1994 2011	(Auxiliary Minister)	24 Roberts Crescent, Dumfries DG2 7RS [E-mail: mackliz@btinternet.com]	01387 264847
McKay, David M. MA BD	1979 2007	(Kirkpatrick Juxta with Moffat: St Andrew's with Wamphray)	20 Auld Brig View, Auldgirth, Dumfries DG2 0XE [E-mail: davidmckay20@tiscali.co.uk]	01387 740013
McKenzie, William M. DA	1958 1993	(Dumfries: Troqueer)	41 Kingholm Road, Dumfries DG1 4SR [E-mail: mckenzie.dumfries@btinternet.com]	01387 253688
McLauchlan, Mary C. (Mrs) LTh	1997 2013	(Mochrum)	3 Ayr Street, Moniaive, Thornhill DG3 4HP [E-mail: mary@revmother.co.uk]	01848 200786
Owen, John J.C. LTh	1967 2001	(Applegarth and Sibbaldbie with Lochmaben)	5 Galla Avenue, Dalbeattie DG5 4JZ [E-mail: jj.owen@onetel.net]	01556 612125
Robertson, Ian W. MA BD	1956 1995	(Colvend, Southwick and Kirkbean)	10 Marjoriebanks, Lochmaben, Lockerbie DG11 1QH	01387 810541
Sutherland, Colin A. LTh	1995 2007	(Blantyre: Livingstone Memorial)	71 Caulstran Road, Dumfries DG2 9FJ [E-mail: colin.csutherland@btinternet.com]	01387 279954
Wallace, Mhairi (Mrs)	2013	Ordained Local Minister	5 Dee Road, Kirkcudbright DG6 4HQ [E-mail: mhairiwallace54@gmail.com]	(Mbl) 07701 375064
Wilkie, James R. MA MTh	1957 1993	(Penpont, Keir and Tynron)	31 West Morton Street, Thornhill DG3 5NF	01848 331028
Williamson, James BA BD	1986 2009	(Cummertrees with Mouswald with Ruthwell)	12 Mulberry Drive, Dunfermline KY11 8BZ [E-mail: jimwill@rcnkirk.fsnet.co.uk]	01383 734872
Wotherspoon, Robert C. LTh	1976 1998	(Corsock and Kirkpatrick Durham with Crossmichael and Parton)	7 Hillowton Drive, Castle Douglas DG7 1LL [E-mail: robert.wotherspoon@tiscali.co.uk]	01556 502267
Young, John MTh DipMin	1963 1999	(Airdrie: Broomknoll)	Craigview, North Street, Moniaive, Thornhill DG3 4HR	01848 200318

DUMFRIES ADDRESSES

Maxwelltown West	Laurieknowe
Northwest	Lochside Road
St George's	George Street
St Mary's-Greyfriars	St Mary's Street
St Michael's and South	St Michael's Street
Troqueer	Troqueer Road

(9) WIGTOWN AND STRANRAER

Meets at Glenluce, in the church hall, on the first Tuesday of March, October and December for ordinary business; on the first Tuesday of September for formal business followed by meetings of committees; on the first Tuesday of November, February and May for worship followed by meetings of committees; and at a church designated by the Moderator on the first Tuesday of June for Holy Communion followed by ordinary business.

Clerk:	MR SAM SCOBIE		40 Clenoch Parks Road, Stranraer DG9 7QT [E-mail: wigtownstranraer@cofscotland.org.uk]	01776 703975

Ervie Kirkcolm linked with Leswalt

Michael J. Sheppard BD	1997		Ervie Manse, Stranraer DG9 0QZ [E-mail: mjs@uwclub.net]	01776 854225

Glasserton and Isle of Whithorn linked with Whithorn: St Ninian's Priory

Alexander I. Currie BD CPS	1990		The Manse, Whithorn, Newton Stewart DG8 8PT	01988 500267

Inch linked with Portpatrick linked with Stranraer: Trinity (H)

John H. Burns BSc BD	1985	1988	Bayview Road, Stranraer DG9 8BE	01776 702383

Kirkcowan (H) linked with Wigtown (H)

Eric Boyle BA MTh	2006		Seaview Manse, Church Lane, Wigtown, Newton Stewart DG8 9HT [E-mail: ecthered@aol.com]	01988 402314

Kirkinner linked with Mochrum linked with Sorbie (H)

Jeffrey M. Mead BD	1978	1986	The Manse, Kirkinner, Newton Stewart DG8 9AL	01988 840643

Kirkmabreck linked with Monigaff (H)

Stuart Farmes	2011	2014	Creebridge, Newton Stewart DG8 6NR [E-mail: thefarmesfamily@tiscali.co.uk]	01671 403361

Kirkmaiden (H) linked with Stoneykirk

Vacant			Church Road, Sandhead, Stranraer DG9 9JJ	01776 830548

Leswalt See Ervie Kirkcolm

Monigaff See Kirkmabreck

New Luce (H) linked with Old Luce (H)
Thomas M. McWhirter MA MSc BD   1992 1997   Glenluce, Newton Stewart DG8 0PU   01581 300319

Old Luce See New Luce

Penninghame (H)
Edward D. Lyons BD MTh   2007   The Manse, 1A Corvisel Road, Newton Stewart DG8 6LW   01671 404425
[E-mail: edwardlyons@hotmail.com]

Portpatrick See Inch
Sorbie See Kirkinner
Stoneykirk See Kirkmaiden

Stranraer: High Kirk (H)
Ian McIlroy BSS BD   1996 2009   Stoneleigh, Whitehouse Road, Stranraer DG9 0JB   01776 700616

Stranraer: Trinity See Inch
Whithorn: St Ninian's Priory See Glasserton and Isle of Whithorn
Wigtown See Kirkcowan

Aiken, Peter W.I.	1996 2013	(Kirkmabreck with Monigaff)	Garroch, Viewhills Road, Newton Stewart DG8 6JA [E-mail: revpetevon@gmail.com]	
Baker, Carolyn M. (Mrs) BD	1997 2008	(Ochiltree with Stair)	Clanary, 1 Maxwell Drive, Newton Stewart DG8 6EL [E-mail: cncbaker@btinternet.com]	
Bellis, Pamela A. BA	2014	Ordained Local Minister	Maughold, Low Killantrae, Port William, Newton Stewart DG8 9QR [E-mail: pam@bellisconsultancy.co.uk]	01988 700590
Cairns, Alexander B. MA	1957 2009	(Turin)	Beechwood, Main Street, Sandhead, Stranraer DG9 9JG [E-mail: dorothycairns@aol.com]	01776 830389
Harvey, Joyce (Mrs)	2013	Ordained Local Minister	4A Allanfield Place, Newton Stewart DG8 6BS [E-mail: joyceharvey01@btinternet.com]	01671 403693
Munro, Mary (Mrs) BA	1993 2004	(Auxiliary Minister)	14 Auchneel Crescent, Stranraer DG9 0JH	01776 702305

(10) AYR

Meets in Alloway Church Hall on the first Tuesday of every month from September to May, excluding January and April. The June meeting takes place on the third Tuesday of the month in the newly installed Moderator's church. The October meeting is held in a venue determined by the Business Committee.

| Clerk: | REV. KENNETH C. ELLIOTT BD BA CertMin | 68 St Quivox Road, Prestwick KA9 1JF [E-mail: ayr@churchofscotland.org.uk] | 01292 478788 |
| Presbytery Office: | | Prestwick South Parish Church, 50 Main Street, Prestwick KA9 1NX [E-mail: ayroffice@churchofscotland.org.uk] | 01292 678556 |

Alloway (H)
Neil A. McNaught BD MA — 1987 — 1999 — 1A Parkview, Alloway, Ayr KA7 4QG [E-mail: nandjmcnaught@btinternet.com] — 01292 441252

Annbank (H) linked with Tarbolton
P. Jill Clancy (Mrs) BD DipMin — 2000 — 2014 — The Manse, Tarbolton, Mauchline KA5 5QL [E-mail: jgibson@totalise.co.uk] — 01292 540969

Auchinleck (H) linked with Catrine
Stephen F. Clipston MA BD — 1982 — 2006 — 28 Mauchline Road, Auchinleck KA18 2BN [E-mail: steveclipston@btinternet.com] — 01290 424776

Ayr: Auld Kirk of Ayr (St John the Baptist) (H)
David R. Gemmell MA BD — 1991 — 1999 — 58 Monument Road, Ayr KA7 2UB [E-mail: drgemmell@hotmail.com] — 01292 262580 (Tel/Fax)

Ayr: Castlehill (H)
Elizabeth A. Crumlish (Mrs) BD — 1995 — 2008 — 3 Old Hillfoot Road, Ayr KA7 3LW [E-mail: lizcrumlish@aol.com] — 01292 263001

Ayr: Newton Wallacetown (H)
Abi T. Ngunga GTh LTh MDiv MTh PhD — 2001 — 2014 — 9 Nursery Grove, Ayr KA7 3PH [E-mail: abi.t.ngunga@gmail.com] — 01292 264251

Ayr: St Andrew's (H)
Morag Garrett (Mrs) BD — 2011 — 2013 — 31 Bellevue Crescent, Ayr KA7 2DP [E-mail: morag_garrett@yahoo.co.uk] — 01292 261472

Ayr: St Columba (H)
Fraser R. Aitken MA BD   1978   1991   3 Upper Crofts, Alloway, Ayr KA7 4QX   01292 443747
[E-mail: frasercolumba@msn.com]

Ayr: St James' (H)
Vacant   1 Prestwick Road, Ayr KA8 8LD   01292 262420

Ayr: St Leonard's (H) linked with Dalrymple
Brian Hendrie BD   1992   2015   35 Roman Road, Ayr KA7 3SZ   01292 283825
[E-mail: hendrie962@btinternet.com]

Ayr: St Quivox (H)
Vacant   11 Springfield Avenue, Prestwick KA9 2HA   01292 478306

Ballantrae (H) linked with St Colmon (Arnsheen Barrhill and Colmonell)
Stephen Ogston MPhys MSc BD   2009   The Manse, 1 The Vennel, Ballantrae, Girvan KA26 0NH   01465 831252
[E-mail: ogston@macfish.com]

Barr linked with Dailly linked with Girvan: South
Ian K. McLachlan MA BD   1999   30 Henrietta Street, Girvan KA26 9AL   01465 713370
[E-mail: iankmclachlan@yetiville.freeserve.co.uk]

Catrine   See Auchinleck

Coylton linked with Drongan: The Schaw Kirk
Vacant   4 Hamilton Place, Coylton, Ayr KA6 6JQ   01292 571442
Douglas T. Moore   2003   2015   9 Midton Avenue, Prestwick KA9 1PU   01292 671352
(Auxiliary Minister)   [E-mail: douglastmoore@hotmail.com]

Craigie Symington linked with Prestwick South (H) (E-mail: office@pwksouth.plus.com)
Kenneth C. Elliott BD BA Cert Min   1989   68 St Quivox Road, Prestwick KA9 1JF   01292 478788
[E-mail: kcelliott@tiscali.co.uk]

Crosshill (H) linked with Maybole
Vacant   The Manse, 16 McAdam Way, Maybole KA19 8FD   01655 883710

Dailly   See Barr

Dalmellington linked with Patna Waterside
Eleanor J. McMahon BEd BD   1994   2015   4 Carsphairn Road, Dalmellington, Ayr KA6 7RE
(Interim Minister)   [E-mail: e.mcmahon212@btinternet.com]   01292 551503 / 07974 116539 (Mbl)

Dalrymple See Ayr: St Leonard's
Drongan: The Schaw Kirk See Coylton

Dundonald (H)
Robert Mayes BD   1982   1988   64 Main Street, Dundonald, Kilmarnock KA2 9HG
[E-mail: bobmayes@fsmail.net]   01563 850243

Fisherton (H) linked with Kirkoswald (H)
Vacant   The Manse, Kirkoswald, Maybole KA19 8HZ   01655 760210

Girvan: North (Old and St Andrew's) (H)
Richard G. Moffat BD   1994   2013   38 The Avenue, Girvan KA26 9DS
[E-mail: moffatclan@me.com]   01465 713203

Girvan: South See Barr

Kirkmichael linked with Straiton: St Cuthbert's
W. Gerald Jones MA BD MTh   1984   1985   The Manse, Patna Road, Kirkmichael, Maybole KA19 7PJ
[E-mail: revgerald@jonesg99.freeserve.co.uk]   01655 750286

Kirkoswald See Fisherton

Lugar linked with Old Cumnock: Old (H)
John W. Paterson BSc BD DipEd   1994   33 Barrhill Road, Cumnock KA18 1PJ
[E-mail: ocochurchwow@hotmail.com]   01290 420769

Mauchline (H) linked with Sorn
David A. Albon BA MCS   1991   2011   4 Westside Gardens, Mauchline KA5 5DJ
[E-mail: albon@onetel.com]   01290 518528

Maybole See Crosshill

Monkton and Prestwick: North (H)
David Clarkson BSc BA MTh   2010   40 Monkton Road, Prestwick KA9 1AR   01292 471379
[E-mail: revdavidclarkson@gmail.com]

Muirkirk (H) linked with Old Cumnock: Trinity
Scott M. Rae MBE BD CPS   1976   2008   46 Ayr Road, Cumnock KA18 1DW   01290 422145
[E-mail: scottrae1@btopenworld.com]

New Cumnock (H)
Helen E. Cuthbert MA MSc BD   2009   37 Castle, New Cumnock, Cumnock KA18 4AG   01290 338296
[E-mail: helencuthbert@mypostoffice.co.uk]

Ochiltree linked with Stair
William R. Johnston BD   1998   2009   10 Mauchline Road, Ochiltree, Cumnock KA18 2PZ   01290 700365

Old Cumnock: Old See Lugar
Old Cumnock: Trinity See Muirkirk
Patna Waterside See Dalmellington

Prestwick: Kingcase (H) (E-mail: office@kingcase.freeserve.co.uk)
Vacant   15 Bellrock Avenue, Prestwick KA9 1SQ   01292 479571

Prestwick: St Nicholas' (H)
George R. Fiddes BD   1979   1985   3 Bellevue Road, Prestwick KA9 1NW   01292 477613
[E-mail: gfiddes@stnicholasprestwick.org.uk]

Prestwick: South See Craigie Symington
St Colmon (Arnsheen Barrhill and Colmonell) See Ballantrae
Sorn See Mauchline
Stair See Ochiltree
Straiton: St Cuthbert's See Kirkmichael
Tarbolton See Annbank

Troon: Old (H)
David B. Prentice-Hyers BA MDiv   2003   2013   85 Bentinck Drive, Troon KA10 6HZ   01292 313644
[E-mail: daveph@troonold.org.uk]

Troon: Portland (H)
Jamie Milliken BD   2005   2011   89 South Beach, Troon KA10 6EQ   01292 318929
[E-mail: troonportlandchurch@gmail.com]   07929 349045 (Mbl)

Troon: St Meddan's (H) (E-mail: st.meddan@virgin.net)

| Derek Peat BA BD MTh | 2013 | | 27 Bentinck Drive, Troon KA10 6HX [E-mail: stmeddansminister@btinternet.com] | 01292 319163 |

Birse, G. Stewart CA BD BSc	1980	2013	(Ayr: Newton Wallacetown)	9 Calvinston Road, Prestwick KA9 2EL [E-mail: stewart.birse@gmail.com]	01292 864975
Black, Sandra (Mrs)	2013		Ordained Local Minister	5 Doon Place, Troon KA10 7EQ	01292 220075
Blyth, James G.S. BSc BD	1963	1986	(Glenmuick)	40 Robsland Avenue, Ayr KA7 2RW [E-mail: blacks_troon@hotmail.com]	01292 261276
Bogle, Thomas C. BD	1983	2003	(Fisherton with Maybole: West)	38 McEwan Crescent, Mossblown, Ayr KA6 5DR	01292 521215
Brown, Jack M. BSc BD	1977	2012	(Applegarth, Sibbaldbie and Johnstone with Lochmaben)	69 Berelands Road, Prestwick KA9 1ER [E-mail: jackm.brown@tiscali.co.uk]	01292 477151
Crichton, James MA BD MTh	1969	2010	(Crosshill with Dalrymple)	4B Garden Court, Ayr KA8 0AT [E-mail: crichton.james@btinternet.com]	01292 288978
Dickie, Michael M. BSc	1955	1994	(Ayr: Castlehill)	8 Noltmire Road, Ayr KA8 9ES	01292 618512
Geddes, Alexander J. MA BD	1960	1998	(Stewarton: St Columba's)	2 Gregory Street, Mauchline KA5 6BY [E-mail: sandy270736@gmail.com]	01290 518597
Glencross, William M. LTh	1968	1999	(Bellshill: Macdonald Memorial)	1 Lochay Place, Troon KA10 7HH	01292 317097
Grant, J. Gordon MA BD PhD	1957	1997	(Edinburgh: Dean)	33 Fullarton Drive, Troon KA10 6LE	01292 311852
Guthrie, James A.	1969	2005	(Corsock and Kirkpatrick Durham with Crossmichael and Parton)	2 Barrhill Road, Pinwherry, Girvan KA26 0QE [E-mail: p.h.m.guthrie@btinternet.com]	01465 841236
Hannah, William BD MCAM MIPR	1987	2001	(Muirkirk)	8 Dovecote View, Kirkintilloch, Glasgow G66 3HY [E-mail: revbillnews@btinternet.com]	0141-776 1337
Harper, David L. BSc BD	1972	2012	(Troon: St Meddan's)	19 Calder Avenue, Troon KA10 7JT [E-mail: d.l.harper@btinternet.com]	01292 312626
Harris, Samuel McC. OStJ BA BD	1974	2010	(Rothesay: Trinity)	36 Adam Wood Court, Troon KA10 6BP	01292 319603
Helon, George G. BA BD	1984	2000	(Barr linked with Dailly)	9 Park Road, Maxwelltown, Dumfries DG2 7PW	01387 259255
Jackson, Nancy	2009	2013	Auxiliary Minister	35 Auchentrae Crescent, Ayr KA7 4BD	01292 262034
Kent, Arthur F.S.	1966	1999	(Monkton and Prestwick: North)	17 St David's Drive, Evesham, Worcs WR11 2AS [E-mail: afskent@onetel.com]	01386 421562
Laing, Iain A. MA BD	1971	2009	(Bishopbriggs: Kenmuir)	9 Annfield Road, Prestwick KA9 1PP [E-mail: iandrlaing@yahoo.co.uk]	01292 471732
Lennox, Lawrie I. MA BD DipEd	1991	2006	(Cromar)	7 Carwinshoch View, Ayr KA7 4AY [E-mail: lennox127@btinternet.com]	
Lochrie, John S. BSc BD MTh PhD	1967	2008	(St Colmon)	Cosyglen, Kilkerran, Maybole KA19 8LS	01465 811262
Lynn, Robert MA BD	1984	2011	(Ayr: St Leonard's with Dalrymple)	8 Kirkbrae, Maybole KA19 7ER	(Mbl) 07771 481698
McCrorie, William	1965	1999	(Free Church Chaplain: Royal Brompton Hospital)	12 Shieling Park, Ayr KA7 2UR [E-mail: billevemccrorie@btinternet.com]	01292 288854
Macdonald, Ian U.	1960	1997	(Tarbolton)	18 Belmont Road, Ayr KA7 2PF	01292 283085

McGurk, Andrew F. BD	1983	2011	(Largs: St John's)	15 Fraser Avenue, Troon KA10 6XF [E-mail: afmcg.largs@talk21.com]	01292 676008
McLeod, Tom	2014		Ordained Local Minister	3 Martnaham Drive, Coylton KA6 6JE [E-mail: tamlin410@btinternet.com]	01292 570100
McNidder, Roderick H. BD	1987	1997	Chaplain: NHS Ayrshire and Arran Trust	6 Hollow Park, Alloway, Ayr KA7 4SR	01292 442554
McPhail, Andrew M. BA	1968	2002	(Ayr: Wallacetown)	25 Maybole Road, Ayr KA7 2QA	01292 282108
Matthews, John C. MA BD OBE	1992	2010	(Glasgow: Ruchill Kelvinside)	12 Arrol Drive, Ayr KA7 4AF [E-mail: mejohnmatthews@gmail.com]	01292 264382
Mealyea, Harry B. BArch BD	1984	2011	(Ayr: St Andrew's)	38 Rosamunde Pilcher Drive, Longforgan, Dundee DD2 5EF [E-mail: mealyeal@sky.com]	
Mitchell, Sheila M. (Miss) BD MTh	1995	2015	Healthcare Chaplaincy Director Scotland	3rd Floor, 2 Central Quay, 89 Hydepark Street, Glasgow G3 8BW [E-mail: sheila.mitchell@nes.scot.nhs.uk]	0131-656 3372
Morrison, Alistair H. BTh DipYCS	1985	2004	(Paisley: St Mark's Oldhall)	92 St Leonard's Road, Ayr KA7 2PU [E-mail: alistairmorrison@supanet.com]	01292 266021
Ness, David T. LTh	1972	2008	(Ayr: St Quivox)	17 Winston Avenue, Prestwick KA9 2EZ [E-mail: dtness@tiscali.co.uk]	
Russell, Paul R. MA BD	1984	2006	Hospital Chaplain	23 Nursery Wynd, Ayr KA7 3NZ	01292 618020
Sanderson, Alastair M. BA LTh	1971	2007	(Craigie with Symington)	26 Main Street, Monkton, Prestwick KA9 2QL [E-mail: alel@sanderson29.fsnet.co.uk]	01292 475819
Simpson, Edward V. BSc BD	1972	2009	(Glasgow: Giffnock South)	8 Paddock View, Thorntoun, Crosshouse, Kilmarnock KA2 0BH [E-mail: eddie.simpson3@talktalk.net]	01563 522841
Smith, Elizabeth (Mrs) BD	1996	2009	(Fauldhouse: St Andrew's)	16 McIntyre Road, Prestwick KA9 1BE [E-mail: smithrevb@btinternet.com]	01292 471588
Stirling, Ian R. BSc BD	1990	2002	Chaplain: The Ayrshire Hospice (Troon: Old)	Ayrshire Hospice, 35–37 Racecourse Road, Ayr KA7 2TG	01292 269200
Symington, Alastair H. MA BD	1972	2012	(Troon: Old)	1 Cavendish Place, Troon KA10 6JG [E-mail: revdahs@virginmedia.com]	01292 312556
Wilkinson, Arrick D. BSc BD	2000	2013	(Fisherton with Kirkoswald)	Dunwhinny, Main Street, Ballantrae, Girvan KA26 0NB [E-mail: arrick@dunwhinny.plus.com]	01465 831704
Young, Rona M. (Mrs) BD DipEd	1991	2015	(Ayr: St Quivox)	16 Macintyre Road, Prestwick KA9 1BE [E-mail: revronyoung@hotmail.com]	
Yorke, Kenneth B.	1982	2009	(Dalmellington with Patna Waterside)	13 Annfield Terrace, Prestwick KA9 1PS [E-mail: kenneth.yorke@googlemail.com]	(Mbl) 07766 320525

AYR ADDRESSES

Ayr

Auld Kirk	Kirkport (116 High Street)
Castlehill	Castlehill Road x Hillfoot Road
Newton Wallacetown	Main Street
St Andrew's	Park Circus
St Columba	Midton Road x Carrick Park
St James'	Prestwick Road x Falkland Park Road
St Leonard's	St Leonard's Road x Monument Road

Girvan

North	Montgomerie Street
South	Stair Park

Prestwick

Kingcase	Waterloo Road
Monkton and Prestwick North	Monkton Road
St Nicholas	Main Street
South	Main Street

Troon

Old	Ayr Street
Portland	St Meddan's Street
St Meddan's	St Meddan's Street

(11) IRVINE AND KILMARNOCK

The Presbytery meets ordinarily at 7:00pm in the Howard Centre, Portland Road, Kilmarnock, on the first Tuesday in September, December and March and on the fourth Tuesday in June for ordinary business, and at different locations on the first Tuesday in October, November, February and May for mission. The September meeting commences with the celebration of Holy Communion.

Clerk:	MR I. STEUART DEY LLB		72 Dundonald Road, Kilmarnock KA1 1RZ [E-mail: irvinekilmarnock@churchofscotland.org.uk] [E-mail: steuart.dey@btinternet.com]	01563 521686 (Home) 01563 526295 (Office)
Depute Clerk:	REV. S. GRANT BARCLAY LLB DipLP BD MSc PhD		1 Thirdpart Place, Kilmarnock KA1 1UL [E-mail: minister@stkentigern.org.uk]	01563 571280
Treasurer:	MR JAMES McINTOSH BA CA		15 Dundonald Road, Kilmarnock KA1 1RU	01563 523552

The Presbytery office is staffed each Tuesday, Wednesday and Thursday from 9am until 12:30pm. The office telephone number is 01563 526295.

Caldwell linked with Dunlop Vacant			4 Dampark, Dunlop, Kilmarnock KA3 4BZ	01560 483268
Crosshouse (H) T. Edward Marshall BD	1987	2007	27 Kilmarnock Road, Crosshouse, Kilmarnock KA2 0EZ [E-mail: marshall11654@hotmail.com]	01563 524089
Darvel (01560 322924) Charles Lines BA	2010		46 West Main Street, Darvel KA17 0AQ [E-mail: cmdlines@tiscali.co.uk]	01560 322924
Dreghorn and Springside Gary E. Horsburgh BA	1977	1983	96A Townfoot, Dreghorn, Irvine KA11 4EZ [E-mail: garyhorsburgh@hotmail.co.uk]	01294 217770
Dunlop See Caldwell				
Fenwick (H) Geoffrey Redmayne BSc BD MPhil	2000		2 Kirkton Place, Fenwick, Kilmarnock KA3 6DW [E-mail: gnredmayne@gmail.com]	01560 600217

Galston (H) (01563 820136)
Vacant
60 Brewland Street, Galston KA4 8DX

Hurlford (H)
James D. McCulloch BD MIOP MIP3 FSAScot 1996
12 Main Road, Crookedholm, Kilmarnock KA3 6JT   01563 535673
[E-mail: mccullochmanse1@btinternet.com]

Irvine: Fullarton (H) (Website: www.fullartonchurch.co.uk)
Neil Urquhart BD DipMin   1989
48 Waterside, Irvine KA12 8QJ   01294 279909
[E-mail: minister@fullartonchurch.co.uk]

Irvine: Girdle Toll (H) (Website: www.girdletoll.fsbusiness.co.uk)
Vacant
2 Littlestane Rise, Irvine KA11 2BJ   01294 213565

Irvine: Mure (H)
Vacant
9 West Road, Irvine KA12 8RE   01294 279916

Irvine: Old (H) (01294 273503)
Robert Travers BA BD   1993   1999
22 Kirk Vennel, Irvine KA12 0DQ   01294 279265
[E-mail: robert.travers@live.co.uk]

Irvine: Relief Bourtreehill (H)
Andrew R. Black BD   1987   2003
4 Kames Court, Irvine KA11 1RT   01294 216939
[E-mail: andrewblack@tiscali.co.uk]

Irvine: St Andrew's (H) (01294 276051)
Ian W. Benzie BD   1999   2008
St Andrew's Manse, 206 Bank Street, Irvine KA12 0YD   01294 216139
[E-mail: revianb@gmail.com]

Kilmarnock: Kay Park (H) (07818 550606) (Website: www.kayparkparishchurch.co.uk)
David W. Lacy BA BD DLitt DL   1976   2012
52 London Road, Kilmarnock KA3 7AJ   01563 523113 (Tel/Fax)
[E-mail: thelacys@tinyworld.co.uk]

Kilmarnock: New Laigh Kirk (H)
David S. Cameron BD   2001   2009
1 Holmes Farm Road, Kilmarnock KA1 1TP   01563 525416
[E-mail: dvdcam5@msn.com]
Barbara Urquhart (Mrs) DCS
9 Standalane, Kilmaurs, Kilmarnock KA3 2NB   01563 538289
[E-mail: barbaraurquhart1@gmail.com]

Kilmarnock: Riccarton (H) Colin A. Strong BSc BD	1989	2007	2 Jasmine Road, Kilmarnock KA1 2HD [E-mail: colinastrong@aol.com]	01563 549490
Kilmarnock: St Andrew's and St Marnock's James McNaughtan BD DipMin	1983	2008	35 South Gargieston Drive, Kilmarnock KA1 1TB [E-mail: jmcnaughtan@gmail.com]	01563 521665
Alison McBrier MA BD (Associate Minister)	2011	2015	The Howard Centre, 5 Portland Road, Kilmarnock KA1 2BT [E-mail: alison@howardcentre.org]	01563 541337 07478 937628 (Mbl)
Kilmarnock: St John's Onthank (H) Vacant			84 Wardneuk Drive, Kilmarnock KA3 2EX	01563 521815
Anne C. McAllister (Mrs) BSc DipEd CCS (Ordained Local Minister)	2013		39 Bowes Rigg, Stewarton, Kilmarnock KA3 5EN [E-mail: annecmcallister@btinternet.com]	01560 483191
Kilmarnock: St Kentigern's (Website: www.stkentigern.org.uk) S. Grant Barclay LLB DipLP BD MSc PhD	1995		1 Thirdpart Place, Kilmarnock KA1 1UL [E-mail: minister@stkentigern.org.uk]	01563 571280
Kilmarnock: South (01563 524705) H. Taylor Brown BD CertMin	1997	2012	14 McLelland Drive, Kilmarnock KA1 1SE [E-mail: kspc@live.co.uk]	01563 529920
Kilmaurs: St Maur's Glencairn (H) John A. Urquhart BD	1993		9 Standalane, Kilmaurs, Kilmarnock KA3 2NB [E-mail: john.urquhart@talktalk.net]	01563 538289
Newmilns: Loudoun (H) Vacant			Loudoun Manse, 116A Loudoun Road, Newmilns KA16 9HH	01560 320174
Stewarton: John Knox Gavin A. Niven BSc MSc BD	2010		27 Avenue Street, Stewarton, Kilmarnock KA3 5AP [E-mail: minister@johnknox.org.uk]	01560 482418
Stewarton: St Columba's (H) George K. Lind BD MCIBS	1998	2010	1 Kirk Glebe, Stewarton, Kilmarnock KA3 5BJ [E-mail: gklind@talktalk.net]	01560 485113

Ayrshire Mission to the Deaf
Richard C. Durno DSW CQSW | 1989 2013 | | 31 Springfield Road, Bishopbriggs, Glasgow G64 1PJ [E-mail: richard.durno@btinternet.com] | (Voice/Text/Fax) 0141-772 1052 (Voice/Text/Voicemail) (Mbl) 07748 607721

Name	Ord.	Ind.	Charge/Role	Address	Telephone
Brockie, Colin G.F. BSc(Eng) BD SOSc	1967	2007	(Presbytery Clerk)	36 Brachead Court, Kilmarnock KA3 7AB [E-mail: revcol@revcol.demon.co.uk]	01563 559960
Campbell, John A. JP FIEM	1984	1998	(Irvine: St Andrew's)	Flowerdale, Balmoral Road, Rattray, Blairgowrie PH10 7AF [E-mail: exrevjack@aol.com]	01250 872795
Cant, Thomas M. MA BD	1965	2004	(Paisley: Laigh Kirk)	3 Meikle Cutstraw, Stewarton, Kilmarnock KA3 5HU [E-mail: revtmcant@aol.com]	01560 480566
Christie, Robert S. MA BD ThM	1964	2001	(Kilmarnock: West High)	24 Homeroyal House, 2 Chalmers Crescent, Edinburgh EH9 1TP	01294 312515
Davidson, James BD DipAFH	1989	2002	(Wishaw: Old)	13 Redburn Place, Irvine KA12 9BQ	01563 402622
Davidson Kelly, Thomas A. MA BD FSAScot	1975	2002	(Glasgow: Govan Old)	2 Springhill Stables, Portland Road, Kilmarnock KA1 2EJ [E-mail: ktdks33@gmail.com]	
Garrity, T. Alan W. BSc BD MTh	1969	2008	(Bermuda)	17 Solomon's View, Dunlop, Kilmarnock KA3 4ES [E-mail: alangarrity@btinternet.com]	01560 486879
Gillon, C. Blair BD	1975	2007	(Glasgow: Ibrox)	East Muirshiel Farmhouse, Dunlop, Kilmarnock KA3 4EJ [E-mail: blair.gillon2@btinternet.com]	01560 483778
Godfrey, Linda BSc BD	2012	2014	(Ayr: St Leonard's with Dalrymple)	9 Taybank Drive, Ayr KA7 4RL [E-mail: godfreykayak@aol.com]	(Mbl) 07825 663866
Hall, William M. BD	1972	2010	(Kilmarnock: Old High Kirk)	33 Cairns Terrace, Kilmarnock KA1 2JG [E-mail: revwillie@talktalk.net]	01563 525080
Hare, Malcolm M.W. BA BD	1956	1994	(Kilmarnock: St Kentigern's)	Flat 5, The Courtyard, Auchlochan, Lesmahagow, Lanark ML11 0GS	
Hay, W.J.R. MA BD	1959	1995	(Buchanan with Drymen)	18 Jamieson Place, Stewarton, Kilmarnock KA3 3HX	01560 482799
Hosain Lamarti, Samuel BD MTh PhD	1979	2006	(Stewarton: John Knox)	7 Dalwhinnie Crescent, Kilmarnock KA3 1QS [E-mail: samlamar@pobroadband.co.uk]	01563 529632
Huggett, Judith A. (Miss) BA BD	1990	1998	Lead Chaplain, NHS Ayrshire and Arran	4 Westmoor Crescent, Kilmarnock KA1 1TX [E-mail: judith.huggett@aaaht.scotnhs.uk]	
Keating, Glenda K. (Mrs) MTh	1996	2015	(Craigie Symington)	8 Wardlaw Gardens, Irvine KA11 2EW [E-mail: kirkglen@btinternet.com]	
McAlpine, Richard H.M. BA FSAScot	1968	2000	(Lochgoilhead and Kilmorich)	7 Kingsford Place, Kilmaurs, Kilmarnock KA3 6FG	01563 572075
MacDonald, James M. BD ThM	1964	1987	(Kilmarnock: St John's Onthank)	29 Carmel Place, Kilmaurs, Kilmarnock KA3 2QU	01563 525254
Scott, Thomas T.	1968	1989	(Kilmarnock: St Marnock's)	6 North Hamilton Place, Kilmarnock KA1 2QN [E-mail: tomtscott@btinternet.com]	01563 531415
Shaw, Catherine A.M. MA	1998	2006	(Auxiliary Minister)	40 Merrygreen Place, Stewarton, Kilmarnock KA3 5EP [E-mail: catherine.shaw@tesco.net]	01560 483352
Welsh, Alex M. MA BD	1979	2007	Hospital Chaplain	8 Greenside Avenue, Prestwick KA9 2HB [E-mail: alexandevelyn@hotmail.com]	01292 475341

IRVINE and KILMARNOCK ADDRESSES

Irvine

Dreghorn and Springside	Townfoot x Station Brae
Fullarton	Marress Road x Church Street
Girdle Toll	Bryce Knox Court
Mure	West Road
Old	Kirkgate

Relief Bourtreehill	Crofthead, Bourtreehill
St Andrew's	Caldon Road x Oaklands Ave
Kilmarnock	
Ayrshire Mission to the Deaf	10 Clark Street
Kay Park	London Road
Kilmarnock South	Whatriggs Road

New Laigh Kirk	John Dickie Street
Riccarton	Old Street
St Andrew's and St Marnock's	St Marnock Street
St John's Onthank	84 Wardneuk Street

(12) ARDROSSAN

Meets at Saltcoats, New Trinity, on the first Tuesday of February, March, April, May, September, October, November and December, and on the second Tuesday of June.

Clerk: MR ALAN K. SAUNDERSON   17 Union Street, Largs KA30 8DG   **01475 687217**
[E-mail: ak.dj.saunderson@hotmail.co.uk]   **07866 034355** (Mbl)

Ardrossan: Park (01294 463711)
Tanya Webster BCom DipAcc BD   2011   35 Ardneil Court, Ardrossan KA22 7NQ   01294 538903
[E-mail: parkchurchminister@mail.com]

Ardrossan and Saltcoats: Kirkgate (H) (01294 472001) (Website: www.kirkgate.org.uk)
Dorothy A. Granger BA BD   2009   10 Seafield Drive, Ardrossan KA22 8NU   01294 463571
[E-mail: dorothygranger61@gmail.com]   07918 077877 (Mbl)

Beith (H) (01505 502686)
Roderick I.T. MacDonald BD CertMin   1992   2005   2 Glebe Court, Beith KA15 1ET   01505 503858
[E-mail: rodammac@btinternet.com]

Brodick linked with Corrie linked with Lochranza and Pirnmill linked with Shiskine (H)
Angus Adamson BD   2006   4 Manse Crescent, Brodick, Isle of Arran KA27 8AS   01770 302334
[E-mail: adamsonangus@btinternet.com]

Corrie See Brodick

Cumbrae linked with Largs: St John's (H) (01475 674468)
Markus Thane BTh MDiv MTh   2009   2014   1 Newhaven Grove, Largs KA30 8NS   01475 329933
                                                               [E-mail: markus.thane@yahoo.co.uk]   07445 705172 (Mbl)

Dalry: St Margaret's
James R. Teasdale BA BD   2009   33 Templand Crescent, Dalry KA24 5EZ   01294 832747
                                                               [E-mail: jamesrteasdale@hotmail.com]

Dalry: Trinity (H)
Martin Thomson BSc DipEd BD   1988   2004   Trinity Manse, West Kilbride Road, Dalry KA24 5DX   01294 832363
                                                               [E-mail: martin.thomson40@btinternet.com]

Fairlie (H) linked with Largs: St Columba's
Christian Vermeulen DipLT BTh MA   1986   2015   14 Fairlieburne Gardens, Fairlie, Largs KA29 0ER   01475 568515
                                                               [E-mail: minister@fairlieparishchurch.co.uk]

Kilbirnie: Auld Kirk (H)
David Whiteman BD   1998   2015   49 Holmhead, Kilbirnie KA25 6BS   01505 682342
                                                               [E-mail: davesoo@sky.com]

Kilbirnie: St Columba's (H) (01505 685239)
Fiona C. Ross (Miss) BD DipMin   1996   2004   Manse of St Columba's, Dipple Road, Kilbirnie KA25 7JU 01505 683342
                                                               [E-mail: fionaross@calvin78.freeserve.co.uk]

Kilmory linked with Lamlash
Lily F McKinnon (Mrs) MA BD PGCE   1993   2015   The Manse, Lamlash, Isle of Arran KA27 8LE   01770 600074
                                                               [E-mail: lily.mckinnon@yahoo.co.uk]

Kilwinning: Mansefield Trinity (01294 550746)
Vacant   47 Meadowfoot Road, West Kilbride KA23 9BU   01294 822224

Kilwinning: Old
Jeanette Whitecross BD   2002   2011   54 Dalry Road, Kilwinning KA13 7HE   01294 552606
                                                               [E-mail: jwx@hotmail.co.uk]

Lamlash See Kilmory

Largs: Clark Memorial (H) (01475 675186)
T. David Watson BSc BD — 1988 — 2014 — 31 Douglas Street, Largs KA30 8PT [E-mail: tdavidwatson@btinternet.com] — 01475 672370

Largs: St Columba's (01475 686212) See Fairlie
Largs: St John's See Cumbrae
Lochranza and Pirnmill See Brodick

Saltcoats: North (01294 464679)
Alexander B. Noble MA BD ThM — 1982 — 2003 — 25 Longfield Avenue, Saltcoats KA21 6DR — 01294 604923

Saltcoats: St Cuthbert's (H)
Arthur Sherratt BD — 1994 — 2014 — 10 Kennedy Road, Saltcoats KA21 5SF [E-mail: asherratt@sky.com] — 01294 696030

Shiskine See Brodick

Stevenston: Ardeer linked with Stevenston: Livingstone (H)
Vacant — 32 High Road, Stevenston KA20 3DR — 01294 464180

Stevenston: High (H) (Website: www.highkirk.com)
M. Scott Cameron MA BD — 2002 — Glencairn Street, Stevenston KA20 3DL [E-mail: revhighkirk@btinternet.com] — 01294 463356

Stevenston: Livingstone See Stevenston: Ardeer

West Kilbride (H) (Website: www.westkilbrideparishchurch.org.uk)
James J. McNay MA BD — 2008 — The Manse, Goldenberry Avenue, West Kilbride KA23 9LJ [E-mail: minister@westkilbrideparishchurch.org.uk] — 01294 823186
Mandy R. Hickman RGN (Ordained Local Minister) — 2013 — Lagnaleon, 4 Wilson Street, Largs KA30 9AQ [E-mail: mandyrhickman@gmail.com] — 01475 675347

Whiting Bay and Kildonan
Elizabeth R.L. Watson (Miss) BA BD — 1981 — 1982 — The Manse, Whiting Bay, Brodick, Isle of Arran KA27 8RE [E-mail: revewatson@btinternet.com] — 01770 700289

Cruickshank, Norman BA BD	(West Kilbride: Overton)	1983 2006	24D Faulds Wynd, Seamill, West Kilbride KA23 9FA	01294 822239
Currie, Ian S. MBE BD	(The United Church of Bute)	1975 2010	15 Northfield Park, Largs KA30 8NZ [E-mail: ianscurrie@tiscali.co.uk]	(Mbl) 07764 254300
Dailly, John R. BD DipPS	(Chaplain: Army)	1979 2007	2 Curtis Close, Pound Street, Warminster, Wiltshire BA12 9NN	
Drysdale, James H. LTh	(Blackbraes and Shieldhill)	1987 2006	10 John Clark Street, Largs KA30 9AH	01475 674870
Falconer, Alan D. MA BD DLitt	(Aberdeen: St Machar's Cathedral)	1972 2011	18 North Crescent Road, Ardrossan KA22 8NA [E-mail: alanfalconer@gmx.com]	01294 472991
Finlay, William P. MA BD	(Glasgow: Townhead Blochairm)	1968 2000	High Corrie, Brodick, Isle of Arran KA27 8JB	01770 810689
Ford, Alan A. BD	(Glasgow: Springburn)	1977 2013	14 Corsankell Wynd, Saltcoats KA21 6HY [E-mail: alan.andy@btinternet.com]	01294 465740
Gordon, David C.	(Gigha and Cara)	1953 1988	South Beach House, South Crescent Road, Ardrossan KA22 8DU	
Harbison, David J.H.	(Beith: High with Beith: Trinity)	1958 1998	42 Mill Park, Dalry KA24 5BB [E-mail: djh@harbi.fsnet.co.uk]	01294 834092
Hebenton, David J. MA BD	(Ayton and Burnmouth with Grantshouse and Houndwood and Reston)	1958 2002	22B Faulds Wynd, Seamill, West Kilbride KA23 9FA	01294 829228
Howie, Marion L.K. (Mrs) MA ACRS	Auxiliary Minister	1992	51 High Road, Stevenston KA20 3DY [E-mail: marion@howiefamily.net]	01294 466571
McCallum, Alexander D. BD	(Saltcoats: New Trinity)	1987 2005	59 Woodcroft Avenue, Largs KA30 9EW [E-mail: sandyandjose@madasafish.com]	01475 670133
McCance, Andrew M. BSc	(Coatbridge: Middle)	1986 1995	6A Douglas Place, Largs KA30 8PU	01475 673303
Mackay, Marjory H. (Mrs) BD DipEd CCE	(Cumbrae)	1998 2008	4 Golf Road, Millport, Isle of Cumbrae KA28 0HB [E-mail: marjory.mackay@gmail.com]	01475 530388
MacLeod, Ian L.Th BA MTh PhD	(Brodick with Corrie)	1969 2006	Cromla Cottage, Corrie, Isle of Arran KA27 8JB [E-mail: i.macleod829@btinternet.com]	01770 810237
Mitchell, D. Ross BA BD	(West Kilbride: St Andrew's)	1972 2007	11 Dunbar Gardens, Saltcoats KA21 6GJ [E-mail: ross.mitchell@virgin.net]	
Paterson, John H. BD	(Kirkintilloch: St David's Memorial Park)	1977 2000	Creag Bhan, Golf Course Road, Whiting Bay, Isle of Arran KA27 8QT	01770 700569
Roy, Iain M. MA BD	(Stevenston: Livingstone)	1960 1997	2 The Fieldings, Dunlop, Kilmarnock KA3 4AU	01560 483072
Taylor, Andrew S. BTh FPhS	(Greenock Union)	1959 1992	9 Raillies Avenue, Largs KA30 8QY [E-mail: andrew.taylor_123@btinternet.com]	01475 674709
Thomson, Margaret (Mrs)	(Saltcoats: Erskine)	1988 1993	7 Glen Farg, St Leonards, East Kilbride, Glasgow G74 2JW	01475 822224
Ward, Alan H. MA BD	(Interim Minister)	1978 2013	47 Meadowfoot Road, West Kilbride KA23 9BU	(Mbl) 07709 906130

(13) LANARK

Meets on the first Tuesday of February, March, May, September, October, November and December, and on the third Tuesday of June.

Clerk: REV. MRS HELEN E. JAMIESON BD DipEd   120 Clyde Street, Carluke ML8 5BG   01555 771218
                                                        [E-mail: lanark@churchofscotland.org.uk]
Depute Clerk: REV. BRYAN KERR BA BD   Greyfriars Manse, 3 Bellefield Way, Lanark ML11 7NW   01555 663363

Biggar (H) linked with Black Mount
Mike Fucella BD MTh   1997   2013   'Candlemas', 6C Leafield Road, Biggar ML12 6AY   01899 229291
                                               [E-mail: mike@fishwrapper.net]

Black Mount See Biggar

Cairngryffe linked with Libberton and Quothquan (H) linked with Symington (The Tinto Parishes)
George C. Shand MA BD   1981   2014   16 Abington Road, Symington, Biggar ML12 6JX   01899 309400
                                               [E-mail: georgeshand@live.co.uk]

Carluke: Kirkton (H) (Church office: 01555 750778) (Website: www.kirktonchurch.co.uk)
Iain D. Cunningham MA BD   1979   1987   9 Station Road, Carluke ML8 5AA   01555 771262
                                               [E-mail: icunningham@churchofscotland.org.uk]

Carluke: St Andrew's (H)
Helen E. Jamieson (Mrs) BD DipEd   1989   120 Clyde Street, Carluke ML8 5BG   01555 771218
                                             [E-mail: hjamieson@churchofscotland.org.uk]

Carluke: St John's (H) (Website: www.carluke-stjohns.org.uk)
Vacant   18 Old Bridgend, Carluke ML8 4HN

Carnwath (H) linked with Carstairs
Vacant   11 Range View, Kames, Carstairs, Lanark ML11 8TF

Carstairs See Carnwath

Coalburn (H) linked with Lesmahagow: Old (H) (Church office: 01555 892425)
Vacant   9 Elm Bank, Lesmahagow, Lanark ML11 0EA

Crossford (H) linked with Kirkfieldbank
Steven Reid BAcc CA BD   1989   1997   74 Lanark Road, Crossford, Carluke ML8 5RE   01555 860415
[E-mail: steven.reid@sky.com]

Forth: St Paul's (H) (Website: www.forthstpauls.com)
Vacant   22 Lea Rig, Forth, Lanark ML11 8EA   01555 812832

Kirkfieldbank See Crossford

Kirkmuirhill (H)
Vacant   The Manse, 2 Lanark Road, Kirkmuirhill, Lanark ML11 9RB   01555 892409

Lanark: Greyfriars (Church office: 01555 661510) (Website: www.lanarkgreyfriars.com)
Bryan Kerr BA BD   2002   2007   Greyfriars Manse, 3 Bellefield Way, Lanark ML11 7NW   01555 663363
[E-mail: bkerr@churchofscotland.org.uk]

Lanark: St Nicholas' (H)
Vacant   2 Kaimhill Court, Lanark ML11 9HU   01555 662600

Law
Vacant   3 Shawgill Court, Law, Carluke ML8 5SJ   01698 373180

Lesmahagow: Abbeygreen
David S. Carmichael   1982   Abbeygreen Manse, Lesmahagow, Lanark ML11 0DB   01555 893384
[E-mail: david.carmichael@abbeygreen.org.uk]

Lesmahagow: Old See Coalburn
Libberton and Quothquan See Cairngryffe
Symington See Cairngryffe

The Douglas Valley Church (Church office: 01555 850000) (Website: www.douglasvalleychurch.org)
Vacant   The Manse, Douglas, Lanark ML11 0RB   01555 851213

Upper Clyde
Nikki Macdonald BD MTh PhD   2014   31 Carlisle Road, Crawford, Biggar ML12 6TP   01864 502139
[E-mail: minister.upperclyde@gmail.com]

Name	Years	Charge	Address	Contact
Clelland, Elizabeth (Mrs) BD	2002 2012	Resident Chaplain, Divine Healing Fellowship (Scotland)	Brachead House Christian Healing and Retreat Centre, Braidwood Road, Crossford, Carluke ML8 5NQ [E-mail: liz_clelland@yahoo.co.uk]	01555 860716
Cowell, Susan G. (Miss) BA BD	1986 1998	(Budapest)	3 Gavel Lane, Regency Gardens, Lanark ML11 9FB	01555 665509
Craig, William BA LTh	1974 1997	(Cambusbarron: The Bruce Memorial)	31 Heathfield Drive, Blackwood, Lanark ML11 9SR	01555 893710
Easton, David J.C. MA BD	1965 2005	(Burnside–Blairbeth)	Rowanbank, Cormiston Road, Quothquan, Biggar ML12 6ND [E-mail: deaston@btinternet.com]	01899 308459
Findlay, Henry J.W. MA BD	1965 2005	(Wishaw: St Mark's)	2 Alba Gardens, Carluke ML8 5US	01555 759995
Houston, Graham R. BSc BD MTh PhD	1978 2011	(Cairngryffe with Symington)	3 Alder Lane, Beechtrees, Lanark ML11 9FT [E-mail: gandih6156@btinternet.com]	01555 678004
Pacitti, Stephen A. MA	1963 2003	(Black Mount with Culter with Libberton and Quothquan)	157 Nithsdale Road, Glasgow G41 5RD	0141-423 5972
Seath, Thomas J.G.	1980 1992	(Motherwell: Manse Road)	Flat 11, Wallace Court, South Vennel, Lanark ML11 7LL	01555 665399
Young, David A.	1972 2003	(Kirkmuirhill)	110 Carlisle Road, Blackwood, Lanark ML11 9RT [E-mail: david@aol.com]	01555 893357

(14) GREENOCK AND PAISLEY

Meets on the second Tuesday of September, October, November, December, February, March, April and May, and on the third Tuesday of June.

Clerk:	REV. PETER McENHILL BD PhD	The Presbytery Office as detailed below [E-mail: greenockpaisley@churchofscotland.org.uk]	
Presbytery Office:		'Homelea', Faith Avenue, Quarrier's Village, Bridge of Weir PA11 3SX	01505 615033 (Tel) 01505 615088 (Fax)

Barrhead: Bourock (H) (0141-881 9813)

Pamela Gordon BD	2006	2014	14 Maxton Avenue, Barrhead, Glasgow G78 1DY [e-mail: revpg10@gmail.com]	0141-881 8736

Barrhead: St Andrew's (H) (0141-881 8442)

James S.A. Cowan BD DipMin	1986	1998	10 Arthurlie Avenue, Barrhead, Glasgow G78 2BU [E-mail: jim_cowan@ntlworld.com]	0141-881 3457

Bishopton (H) (Office: 01505 862583)

Vacant		The Manse, Newton Road, Bishopton PA7 5JP	01505 862161

Bridge of Weir: Freeland (H) (01505 612610)
Kenneth N. Gray BA BD   1988
15 Lawmarnock Crescent, Bridge of Weir PA11 3AS
[E-mail: aandkgray@btinternet.com]
01505 690918

Bridge of Weir: St Machar's Ranfurly (01505 614364)
Suzanne Dunleavy (Miss) BD DipEd   1990 1992
9 Glen Brae, Bridge of Weir PA11 3BH
[E-mail: suzanne.dunleavy@btinternet.com]
01505 612975

Elderslie Kirk (H) (01505 323348)
Robin N. Allison BD DipMin   1994 2005
282 Main Road, Elderslie, Johnstone PA5 9EF
[E-mail: revrobin@sky.com]
01505 321767

Erskine (0141-812 4620)
Jonathan Fleming MA BD   2012
The Manse, 7 Leven Place, Linburn, Erskine PA8 6AS
[E-mail: jonathancfleming@me.com]
0141-570 8103

Gourock: Old Gourock and Ashton (H)
David W.G. Burt BD DipMin   1989 2014
331 Eldon Street, Gourock PA16 7QN
[E-mail: dwgburt@btinternet.com]
01475 633914

Gourock: St John's (H)
Glenn A. Chestnutt BA DASE MDiv ThM PhD 2009
6 Barrhill Road, Gourock PA19 1JX
[E-mail: glenn.chestnutt@gmail.com]
01475 632143

Greenock: East End linked with Greenock: Mount Kirk
Francis E. Murphy BEng DipDSE BD   2006
76 Finnart Street, Greenock PA16 8HJ
[E-mail: francis_e_murphy@hotmail.com]
01475 722338

Greenock: Lyle Kirk
Vacant
Eileen Manson (Mrs) DipCE   1994 2014
(Auxiliary Minister)
39 Fox Street, Greenock PA16 8PD
1 Cambridge Avenue, Gourock PA19 1XT
[E-mail: rev.eileen@ntlworld.com]
01475 888277
01475 632401

Greenock: Mount Kirk See Greenock: East End

Greenock: St Margaret's (R) (01475 781953)
Morris C. Coull BD   1974 2014
105 Finnart Street, Greenock PA16 8HN
[E-mail: morriscoull@mac.com]
01475 892874

Congregation / Minister	Ord.	Ind.	Address	Tel.
Greenock: St Ninian's Allan G. McIntyre BD	1985		5 Auchmead Road, Greenock PA16 0PY [E-mail: agmcintyre@lineone.net]	01475 631878
Greenock: Wellpark Mid Kirk Alan K. Sorensen BD MTh DipMin FSAScot	1983	2000	101 Brisbane Street, Greenock PA16 8PA [E-mail: alan.sorensen@ntlworld.com]	01475 721741
Greenock: Westburn Karen E. Harbison (Mrs) MA BD	1991	2014	50 Ardgowan Street, Greenock PA16 8EP [E-mail: calumkaren@yahoo.co.uk]	01475 721048
Houston and Killellan (H) Donald Campbell BD	1998	2007	The Manse of Houston, Main Street, Houston, Johnstone PA6 7EL [E-mail: houstonmanse@btinternet.com]	01505 612569
Howwood linked with Lochwinnoch Vacant			The Manse, Beith Road, Howwood, Johnstone PA9 1AS	01505 703678
Inchinnan (H) (0141-812 1263) Vacant			The Manse, Inchinnan, Renfrew PA4 9PH	0141-812 1688
Inverkip (H) linked with Skelmorlie and Wemyss Bay Archibald Speirs BD	1995	2013	3a Montgomery Terrace, Skelmorlie PA17 5DT [E-mail: archiespeirs1@aol.com]	01475 529320
Johnstone: High (H) (01505 336303) Ann C. McCool (Mrs) BD DSD IPA ALCM	1989	2001	76 North Road, Johnstone PA5 8NF [E-mail: ann.mccool@ntlworld.com]	01505 320006
Johnstone: St Andrew's Trinity Charles M. Cameron BA BD PhD	1980	2013	45 Woodlands Crescent, Johnstone PA5 0AZ [E-mail: charlescameron@hotmail.co.uk]	01505 672908
Johnstone: St Paul's (H) (01505 321632) Alistair N. Shaw MA BD MTh	1982	2003	9 Stanley Drive, Brookfield, Johnstone PA5 8UF [E-mail: ans2006@talktalk.net]	01505 320060

Kilbarchan: East
Stephen J. Smith BSc BD — 1993 — 2013 — East Manse, Church Street, Kilbarchan, Johnstone PA10 2JQ [E-mail: stephenrevsteve@aol.com] — 01505 702621

Kilbarchan: West
Vacant — West Manse, Shuttle Street, Kilbarchan, Johnstone PA10 2JR — 01505 342930

Kilmacolm: Old (H) (01505 873911)
Peter McEnhill BD PhD — 1992 — 2007 — The Old Kirk Manse, Glencairn Road, Kilmacolm PA13 4NJ [E-mail: petermcenhill@btinternet.com] — 01505 873174

Kilmacolm: St Columba (H)
R. Douglas Cranston MA BD — 1986 — 1992 — 6 Churchill Road, Kilmacolm PA13 4LH [E-mail: robert.cranston@sccmanse.plus.com] — 01505 873271

Langbank (R) linked with Port Glasgow: St Andrew's (H)
Vacant — St Andrew's Manse, Barr's Brae, Port Glasgow PA14 5QA — 01475 741486

Linwood (H) (01505 328802)
Eileen M. Ross (Mrs) BD MTh — 2005 — 2008 — 1 John Neilson Avenue, Paisley PA1 2SX [E-mail: eross@churchofscotland.org.uk] — 0141-887 2801

Lochwinnoch See Howwood

Neilston (0141-881 9445)
Fiona E. Maxwell BA BD — 2004 — 2013 — The Manse, Neilston Road, Neilston, Glasgow G78 3NP [Email: fiona.maxwell@aol.co.uk] — 0141-258 0805

Paisley: Abbey (H) (Tel: 0141-889 7654; Fax: 0141-887 3929)
Alan D. Birss MA BD — 1979 — 1988 — 15 Main Road, Castlehead, Paisley PA2 6AJ [E-mail: alan.birss@paisleyabbey.com] — 0141-889 3587

Paisley: Glenburn (0141-884 2602)
Iain M.A. Reid MA BD — 1990 — 2014 — 10 Hawick Avenue, Paisley PA2 9LD [E-mail: reviain.reid@ntlworld.com] — 0141-884 4903

Paisley: Lylesland (H) (0141-561 7139)
Alistair W. Cook BSc CA BD 2008 36 Potterhill Avenue, Paisley PA2 8BA 0141-561 9277
[E-mail: alistaircook@ntlworld.com]

Paisley: Martyrs' Sandyford (0141-889 6603)
Kenneth A.L. Mayne BA MSc CertEd 1976 2007 27 Acer Crescent, Paisley PA2 9LR 0141-884 7400

Paisley: Oakshaw Trinity (H) (Tel: 0141-889 4010; Fax: 0141-848 5139)
Gordon B. Armstrong BD FIAB BRC 1998 2012 The Manse, 16 Golf Drive, Paisley PA1 3LA 0141-887 0884
[E-mail: revgordon@ntlworld.com]
Oakshaw Trinity is a Local Ecumenical Project shared with the United Reformed Church

Paisley: St Columba Foxbar (H) (01505 812377)
Vacant 13 Corsebar Drive, Paisley PA2 9QD 0141-848 5826

Paisley: St James' (0141-889 2422)
Vacant 38 Woodland Avenue, Paisley PA2 8BH

Paisley: St Luke's (H)
D. Ritchie M. Gillon BD DipMin 1994 31 Southfield Avenue, Paisley PA2 8BX 0141-884 6215
[E-mail: revgillon@hotmail.com]

Paisley: St Mark's Oldhall (H) (0141-882 2755)
Robert G. McFarlane BD 2001 2005 36 Newtyle Road, Paisley PA1 3JX 0141-889 4279
[E-mail: robertmcf@hotmail.com]

Paisley: St Ninian's Ferguslie (New Charge Development) (0141-887 9436)
Vacant 10 Stanely Drive, Paisley PA2 6HE 0141-884 4177
Duncan Ross DCS 1 John Neilson Avenue, Paisley PA1 2SX 0141-887 2801
[E-mail: duncan@saintninians.co.uk]

Paisley: Sherwood Greenlaw (H) (0141-889 7060)
John Murning BD 1988 2014 5 Greenlaw Drive, Paisley PA1 3RX 0141-889 3057
[E-mail: revjohnmurning@hotmail.com]

Paisley: Stow Brae Kirk
Robert Craig BA BD DipRS — 2008 2012 — 25 John Neilson Avenue, Paisley PA1 2SX [E-mail: stowbraekirk@gmail.com] — 0141-328 6014

Paisley: Wallneuk North (0141-889 9265)
Peter G. Gill MA BA — 2008 — 5 Glenville Crescent, Paisley PA2 8TW [E-mail: petergill18@hotmail.com] — 0141-884 4429

Port Glasgow: Hamilton Bardrainney
Vacant — 80 Bardrainney Avenue, Port Glasgow PA14 6HD — 01475 701213

Port Glasgow: St Andrew's See Langbank

Port Glasgow: St Martin's
Vacant — Clunebraehead, Clune Brae, Port Glasgow PA14 5SL — 01475 704115

Renfrew: North (0141-885 2154)
E. Lorna Hood MA BD DD — 1978 1979 — 1 Alexandra Drive, Renfrew PA4 8UB [E-mail: revlornahood@gmail.com] — 0141-886 2074

Renfrew: Trinity (H) (0141-885 2129)
Stuart C. Steell BD CertMin — 1992 2015 — 25 Paisley Road, Renfrew PA4 8JH [E-mail: ssren@tiscali.co.uk] — 0141-387 2464

Skelmorlie and Wemyss Bay See Inverkip

Alexander, Douglas N. MA BD	1961	1999	(Bishopton)	West Morningside, Main Road, Langbank, Port Glasgow PA4 6XP	01475 540249
Armstrong, William R. BD	1979	2008	(Skelmorlie and Wemyss Bay)	25A The Lane, Skelmorlie PA17 5AR [E-mail: warmstrong17@tiscali.co.uk]	01475 520891
Bell, Ian W. LTh	1990	2011	(Erskine)	40 Brueacre Drive, Wemyss Bay PA18 6HA [E-mail: rviwbepc@ntlworld.com]	01475 529312
Bell, May (Mrs) LTh	1998	2012	(Johnstone: St Andrew's Trinity)	40 Brueacre Drive, Wemyss Bay PA18 6HA [E-mail: may.bell@ntlbusiness.com]	01475 529312
Black, Janette M.K. (Mrs) BD	1993	2006	(Assistant: Paisley: Oakshaw Trinity)	5 Craigiehall Avenue, Erskine PA8 7DB	0141-812 0794
Breingan, Mhairi	2011		Ordained Local Minister	6 Park Road, Inchinnan, Renfrew PA4 4QJ	0141-812 1425
Cameron, Margaret (Miss) DCS			(Deacon)	2 Rowans Gate, Paisley PA2 6RD	0141-840 2479
Chestnut, Alexander MBE DCS	1948	1987	(Greenock: St Mark's Greenbank)	5 Douglas Street, Largs KA30 8PS	01475 674168
Copland, Agnes M. (Mrs) MBE DCS			(Deacon)	3 Craigmuschat Road, Gourock PA19 1SE	01475 631870

Name	Years	Role / Parish	Address	Telephone
Cubie, John P. MA BD	1961 1999	(Caldwell)	36 Winram Place, St Andrews KY16 8XH	01334 474708
Easton, Lilly C. (Mrs)	1999 2012	(Renfrew: Old)	Flat 0/2, 90 Beith Street, Glasgow G11 6DG [E-mail: revlillyeaston@hotmail.co.uk]	0141-586 7628
Erskine, Morag (Miss) DCS		(Deacon)	111 Mains Drive, Park Mains, Erskine PA8 7JJ [E-mail: morag.erskine@ntlworld.com]	0141-812 6096
Forrest, Kenneth P. CBE BSc PhD	2006	Auxiliary Minister	5 Carruth Road, Bridge of Weir PA11 3HQ [E-mail: kenpforrest@hotmail.com]	01505 612651
Fraser, Ian C. BA BD	1983 2008	(Glasgow: St Luke's and St Andrew's)	62 Kingston Avenue, Neilston, Glasgow G78 3JG [E-mail: ianandlindafraser@gmail.com]	0141-563 6794
Geddes, Elizabeth (Mrs)	2013	Ordained Local Minister	9 Shillingworth Place, Bridge of Weir PA11 3DY [E-mail: geddes_liz@hotmail.com]	01505 612639
Gray, Greta (Miss) DCS		(Deacon)	67 Crags Avenue, Paisley PA3 6SG [E-mail: greta.gray@ntlworld.com]	0141-884 6178
Hamilton, W. Douglas BD	1975 2009	(Greenock: Westburn)	5 Corse Road, Penilee, Glasgow G52 4DG [E-mail: douglas.hamilton44@hotmail.co.uk]	0141-810 1194
Hetherington, Robert M. MA BD	1966 2002	(Barrhead: South and Levern)	31 Brodie Park Crescent, Paisley PA2 6EU [E-mail: r-hetherington@sky.com]	0141-848 6560
Irvine, Euphemia H.C. (Mrs) BD	1972 1988	(Milton of Campsie)	32 Baird Drive, Bargarran, Erskine PA8 6BB	0141-812 2777
Johnston, Mary (Miss) DCS		(Deacon)	19 Lounsdale Drive, Paisley PA2 9ED	0141-849 1615
Kay, David BA BD MTh	1974 2008	(Paisley: Sandyford: Thread Street)	36 Donaldswood Park, Paisley PA2 8RS [E-mail: david.kay500@o2.co.uk]	0141-884 2080
Leitch, Maureen (Mrs) BA BD	1995 2011	(Barrhead: Bourock)	Rockfield, 92 Paisley Road, Barrhead G78 1NW [E-mail: maureen.leitch@ntlworld.com]	0141-580 2927
Lodge, Bernard P. BD	1967 2004	(Glasgow: Govanhill Trinity)	6 Darluith Park, Brookfield, Johnstone PA5 8DD [E-mail: bernardlodge@yahoo.co.uk]	01505 320378
McBain, Margaret (Miss) DCS		(Deacon)	33 Quarry Road, Paisley PA2 7RD	0141-884 2920
McCarthy, David J. BSc BD	1985 2014	Mission and Discipleship Council	121 George Street, Edinburgh EH2 4YN [E-mail: dmccarthy@churchofscotland.org.uk]	0131-225 5722
McColl, James C. BSc BD	1966 2002	(Johnstone: St Andrew's Trinity)	Greenways, Winton, Kirkby Stephen, Cumbria CA17 4HL	01768 372290
McColl, John BD DipMin	1989 2001	Teacher: Religious Education	1 Birch Avenue, Johnstone PA5 0DD	01505 326506
McCully, M. Isobel (Miss) DCS		(Deacon)	10 Broadstone Avenue, Port Glasgow PA14 5BB [E-mail: mi.mccully@btinternet.com]	01475 742240
Macdonald, Alexander MA BD	1966 2006	(Neilston)	35 Lochore Avenue, Paisley PA3 4BY [E-mail: alexmacdonald42@aol.com]	0141-889 0066
McDonald, Alexander BA CMIWSC DUniv	1968 2000	(Department of Ministry)	Flat 59, Kelburne Court, 51 Glasgow Road, Paisley PA1 3PD [E-mail: amcdonald1@ntlworld.com]	0141-560 1937
McKaig, William G. BD	1979 2011	(Langbank)	54 Brisbane Street, Greenock PA16 8NT [E-mail: bill.mckaig@virgin.net]	
MacLaine, Marilyn (Mrs) LTh	1995 2009	(Inchinnan)	37 Bankton Brae, Livingston EH54 9LA	01506 400619
MacLean, Andrew T. BA BD	1980 2015	(Langbank l/w Port Glasgow St Andrew's)	Flat 1/1, 104 Brunswick Street, Glasgow G1 1TF [E-mail:standrews-pg@mac.com]	0141-564 2802

Nicol, Joyce M. (Mrs) BA DCS	1988 2003	(Deacon)	93 Brisbane Street, Greenock PA16 8NY [E-mail: joycenicol@hotmail.co.uk]	01475 723235
Page, John R. BD DipMin		(Gibraltar)	1 The Walton Building, North Street, Mere, Warminster, Wiltshire BA12 6HU	(Mbl) 07957 642709
Palmer, S.W. BD	1980 1991	(Kilbarchan: East)	4 Bream Place, Houston PA6 7ZJ	01505 615280
Prentice, George BA BTh	1964 1997	(Paisley: Martyrs')	46 Victoria Gardens, Corsebar Road, Paisley PA2 9AQ [E-mail: g.prentice04@talktalk.net]	0141-842 1585
Simpson, James H. BD LLB	1964 2004	(Greenock: Mount Kirk)	82 Harbourside, Inverkip, Greenock PA16 0BF [E-mail: jameshsimpson@yahoo.co.uk]	01475 520582
Smillie, Andrew M. LTh	1990 2005	(Langbank)	7 Turnbull Avenue, West Freeland, Erskine PA8 7DL [E-mail: andrewsmillie@talktalk.net]	0141-812 7030
Stevenson, Stuart	2011	Ordained Local Minister	143 Springfield Park, Johnstone PA5 8JT	0141-886 2131
Stewart, David MA DipEd BD MTh	1977 2013	(Howwood)	72 Glen Avenue, Largs KA30 8QQ [E-mail: revdavidst@aol.com]	
Whiteford, Alexander LTh	1996 2013	(Ardersier with Petty)	Cumbrae, 17 Netherburn Gardens, Houston, Johnstone PA6 7NG [E-mail: alex.whiteford@hotmail.co.uk]	01505 229611
Whyte, John H. MA	1946 1986	(Gourock: Ashton)	6 Castle Levan Manor, Cloch Road, Gourock PA19 1AY	01475 636788
Whyte, Margaret A. (Mrs) BA BD	1988 2011	(Glasgow: Pollokshaws)	4 Springhill Road, Barrhead G78 2AA [E-mail: tdpwhyte@tiscali.co.uk]	0141-881 4942
Young, David T. BA BD	2007 2012	Chaplain: University of Strathclyde	51 Marchfield Avenue, Paisley PA3 2QE [E-mail: david.t.young@strath.ac.uk]	0141-237 5128 (Work) 0141-553 4144

GREENOCK ADDRESSES

Gourock

Old Gourock and Ashton	41 Royal Street
St John's	Bath Street x St John's Road

Greenock

Lyle Kirk	31 Union Street; Newark Street x Bentinck Street; Esplanade x Campbell Street

(Lyle Kirk is continuing meantime to retain all three buildings)

Mount Kirk	Dempster Street at Murdieston Park
St Margaret's	Finch Road x Kestrel Crescent
St Ninian's	Warwick Square, Larkfield
Wellpark Mid Kirk	Cathcart Square
Westburn	9 Nelson Street

Port Glasgow

Hamilton Bardrainney	Bardrainney Avenue x Auchenbothie Road
St Andrew's	Princes Street
St Martin's	Mansion Avenue

PAISLEY ADDRESSES

Abbey	Town Centre
Glenburn	Nethercraigs Drive off Glenburn Road
Lylesland	Rowan Street off Neilston Road
Martyrs'	King Street
Oakshaw Trinity	Churchill
St Columba Foxbar	Amochrie Road, Foxbar
St James'	Underwood Road
St Luke's	Neilston Road
St Mark's Oldhall	Glasgow Road, Ralston
St Ninian's Ferguslie	Blackstoun Road
Sandyford (Thread St)	Montgomery Road
Sherwood Greenlaw	Glasgow Road
Stow Brae Kirk	Causeyside Street
Wallneuk North	off Renfrew Road

(16) GLASGOW

Meets at Govan and Linthouse Parish Church, Govan Cross, Glasgow (unless otherwise intimated), on the following Tuesdays: 2015: 8 September, 13 October, 10 November, 8 December; 2016: 9 February, 8 March, 12 April, 10 May, 21 June.

Clerk:	VERY REV. WILLIAM C. HEWITT BD DipPS		260 Bath Street, Glasgow G2 4JP [E-mail: glasgow@churchofscotland.org.uk] [Website: www.presbyteryofglasgow.org.uk]	0141-332 6606 0141-352 6646 (Fax)
Treasurer:	DOUGLAS BLANEY		[E-mail: treasurer@presbyteryofglasgow.org.uk]	

#				
1	**Banton linked with Twechar** Vacant			
2	**Bishopbriggs: Kenmure** James Gemmell BD MTh	1999	2010	5 Marchfield, Bishopbriggs, Glasgow G64 3PP [E-mail: revgemmell@hotmail.com]	0141-772 1468
3	**Bishopbriggs: Springfield Cambridge (0141-772 1596)** Ian Taylor BD ThM	1995	2006	64 Miller Drive, Bishopbriggs, Glasgow G64 1FB [E-mail: taylorian@btinternet.com]	0141-772 1540
4	**Broom (0141-639 3528)** James A.S. Boag BD CertMin	1992	2007	3 Laigh Road, Newton Mearns, Glasgow G77 5EX [E-mail: office@broomchurch.org.uk]	0141-639 2916 (Tel) 0141-639 3528 (Fax)
5	**Burnside Blairbeth (0141-634 4130)** William T.S. Wilson BSc BD	1999	2006	59 Blairbeth Road, Burnside, Glasgow G73 4JD [E-mail: william.wilson@burnsideblairbethchurch.org.uk]	0141-583 6470
6	**Busby (0141-644 2073)** Jeremy C. Eve BSc BD	1998		17A Carmunnock Road, Busby, Glasgow G76 8SZ [E-mail: j-eve@sky.com]	0141-644 3670
7	**Cadder (0141-772 7436)** Graham S. Finch MA BD	1977	1999	231 Kirkintilloch Road, Bishopbriggs, Glasgow G64 2JB [E-mail: gsf1957@ntlworld.com]	0141-772 1363

#	Name	Year(s)	Address	Telephone
8	**Cambuslang: Flemington Hallside** Neil M. Glover	2005	59 Hay Crescent, Cambuslang, Glasgow G72 6QA [E-mail: neilmglover@gmail.com]	0141-641 1049 07779 280074 (Mbl)
9	**Cambuslang Parish Church** A. Leslie Milton MA BD PhD	1996 2008	74 Stewarton Drive, Cambuslang, Glasgow G72 8DG [E-mail: alesliemilton.milton@gmail.com]	0141-641 2028
	Karen Hamilton (Mrs) DCS		6 Beckfield Gate, Glasgow G33 1SW [E-mail: k.hamilton6@btinternet.com]	0141-558 3195 07514 402612 (Mbl)
10	**Campsie (01360 310939)** Vacant			
11	**Chryston (H) (0141-779 4188)** Mark Malcolm MA BD	1999 2008	The Manse, 109 Main Street, Chryston, Glasgow G69 9LA [E-mail: mark.minister@btinternet.com]	0141-779 1436 07731 737377 (Mbl)
	Mark W.J. McKeown MEng MDiv (Associate Minister)	2013 2014	6 Glenapp Place, Moodiesburn, Glasgow G69 0HS [E-mail: mark.mck@chrystonparishchurch.co.uk]	01236 263406
12	**Eaglesham (01355 302047)** Vacant		The Manse, Cheapside Street, Eaglesham, Glasgow G76 0NS	01355 303495
13	**Fernhill and Cathkin** Margaret McArthur BD DipMin	1995 2002	82 Blairbeth Road, Rutherglen, Glasgow G73 4JA [E-mail: revmaggiemac@hotmail.co.uk]	0141-634 1508
14	**Gartcosh (H) (01236 873770) linked with Glenboig** David G. Slater BSc BA DipThRS	2011	26 Inchnock Avenue, Gartcosh, Glasgow G69 8EA [E-mail: minister@gartcoshchurch.co.uk] [E-mail: minister@glenboigchurch.co.uk]	01236 870331 01236 872274 (Office)
15	**Giffnock: Orchardhill (0141-638 3604)** Vacant			
16	**Giffnock: South (0141-638 2599)** Catherine J. Beattie (Mrs) BD	2008 2011	164 Ayr Road, Newton Mearns, Glasgow G77 6EE [E-mail: catherinejbeat@aol.com]	0141-258 7804

17 **Giffnock: The Park (0141-620 2204)**
Calum D. Macdonald BD   1993 2001   41 Rouken Glen Road, Thornliebank, Glasgow G46 7JD   0141-638 3023
[E-mail: parkchurch@hotmail.co.uk]

18 **Glenboig** See Gartcosh

19 **Greenbank (H) (0141-644 1841)**
Jeanne Roddick BD   2003   Greenbank Manse, 38 Eaglesham Road, Clarkston,   0141-644 1395
                                                   Glasgow G76 7DJ
                                                   [E-mail: jeanne.roddick@ntlworld.com]

20 **Kilsyth: Anderson**
Allan S. Vint BSc BD MTh   1989 2013   Anderson Manse, Kingston Road, Kilsyth, Glasgow G65 0HR   01236 822345
                                                   [E-mail: allan@vint.co.uk]   07795 483070 (Mbl)

21 **Kilsyth: Burns and Old**
Vacant

22 **Kirkintilloch: Hillhead**
Vacant

23 **Kirkintilloch: St Columba's (H) (0141-578 0016)**
David M. White BA BD DMin   1988 1992   14 Crossdykes, Kirkintilloch, Glasgow G66 3EU   0141-578 4357
                                                   [E-mail: write.to.me@ntlworld.com]

24 **Kirkintilloch: St David's Memorial Park (H) (0141-776 4989)**
Bryce Calder MA BD   1995 2001   2 Roman Road, Kirkintilloch, Glasgow G66 1EA   0141-776 1434
                                                   [E-mail: ministry100@aol.com]   07986 144834 (Mbl)

25 **Kirkintilloch: St Mary's (0141-775 1166)**
Mark E. Johnstone MA BD   1993 2001   St Mary's Manse, 60 Union Street, Kirkintilloch, Glasgow G66 1DH 0141-776 1252
                                                   [E-mail: markjohnstone@me.com]

26 **Lenzie: Old (H)**
Vacant

27 **Lenzie: Union (H) (0141-776 1046)**
Daniel JM Carmichael MA BD 1994 2003 1 Larch Avenue, Lenzix, Glasgow G66 4HX 0141-776 3831
[E-mail: minister@lupc.org]

28 **Maxwell Mearns Castle (Tel/Fax: 0141-639 5169)**
Scott R.McL. Kirkland BD MAR 1996 2011 122 Broomfield Avenue, Newton Mearns, Glasgow G77 5JR 0141-560 5603
[E-mail: scottkirkland@maxwellmearns.org.uk]

29 **Mearns (H) (0141-639 6555)**
Joseph A. Kavanagh BD DipPTh MTh MTh 1992 1998 11 Belford Grove, Newton Mearns, Glasgow G77 5FB 0141-384 2218
[E-mail: revjoe@hotmail.co.uk]

30 **Milton of Campsie (H)**
Julie H.C. Moody BA BD PGCE 2006 Dunkeld, 33 Birdston Road, Milton of Campsie, Glasgow G66 8BX 01360 310548
[E-mail: jhcwilson@msn.com] 07787 184800 (Mbl)

31 **Netherlee (H) (0141-637 2503)**
Thomas Nelson BSc BD 1992 2002 25 Ormonde Avenue, Netherlee, Glasgow G44 3QY 0141-585 7502 (Tel/Fax)
[E-mail: tomnelson@ntlworld.com]
David Maxwell 2014 248 Old Castle Road, Glasgow G44 5EZ 0141-569 6379
(Ordained Local Minister) [E-mail: david.maxwell7@ntlworld.com]

32 **Newton Mearns (H) (0141-639 7373)**
Vacant

33 **Rutherglen: Old (H)**
Vacant

34 **Rutherglen: Stonelaw (0141-647 5113)**
Alistair S. May LLB BD PhD 2002 80 Blairbeth Road, Rutherglen, Glasgow G73 4JA 0141-583 0157
[E-mail: alistair.may@ntlworld.com]

35 **Rutherglen: West and Wardlawhill (0844 736 1470) (H)**
Vacant

36 **Stamperland (0141-637 4999) (H)**
Vacant 12 Albert Drive, Rutherglen, Glasgow G73 3RT 0141-569 8547

37 Stepps (H)
Gordon MacRae BD MTh | 1985 | 2014 | 112 Jackson Drive, Crowwood Grange, Stepps, Glasgow G33 6GF | 0141-779 5742
[E-mail: ge.macrae@btopenworld.com]

38 Thornliebank (H)
Mike R. Gargrave BD | 2008 | 2014 | 19 Arthurlie Drive, Giffnock, Glasgow G46 6UR | 0141-880 5532
[E-mail: mike.gargrave@btinternet.com]

39 Torrance (R) (01360 620970)
Nigel L. Barge BSc BD | 1991 | 1 Atholl Avenue, Torrance, Glasgow G64 4JA | 01360 622379
[E-mail: nigel.barge@sky.com]

40 Twechar See Banton

41 Williamwood (0141-638 2091)
Vacant

42 Glasgow: Anderston Kelvingrove (0141-221 9408)
Vacant

43 Glasgow: Baillieston Mure Memorial (0141-773 1216) linked with Glasgow: Baillieston St Andrew's
Malcolm Cuthbertson BA BD | 1984 | 2010 | 28 Beech Avenue, Baillieston, Glasgow G69 6LF | 07740 868181 (Mbl)
[E-mail: malcuth@aol.com]
Alex P. Stuart | 2014 | 107 Baldorran Crescent, Balloch, Cumbernauld, Glasgow G68 9EX | 07901 802967 (Mbl)
(Ordained Local Minister) [E-mail: alexpstuart@btopenworld.com]

44 Glasgow: Baillieston St Andrew's See Glasgow: Baillieston Mure Memorial

45 Glasgow: Balshagray Victoria Park
Campbell Mackinnon BSc BD | 1982 | 2001 | 20 St Kilda Drive, Glasgow G14 9JN | 0141-954 9780
[E-mail: campbellbvp@live.com]

46 Glasgow: Barlanark Greyfriars (0141-771 6477)
Vacant

47 Glasgow: Blawarthill
G. Melvyn Wood MA BD | 1982 | 2009 | 46 Earlbank Avenue, Glasgow G14 9HL | 0141-579 6521
[E-mail: gmelvynwood@gmail.com]

48 Glasgow: Bridgeton St Francis in the East (H) (L) (0141-556 2830) (Church House: Tel: 0141-554 8045)
Howard R. Hudson MA BD   1982   1984   10 Albany Drive, Rutherglen, Glasgow G73 3QN   0141-587 8667
[E-mail: howard.hudson@ntlworld.com]

Margaret S. Beaton (Miss) DCS   64 Gardenside Grove, Carmyle, Glasgow G32 8EZ   0141-646 2297
(Deacon and Leader of Centre)   [E-mail: margaret@churchhouse.plus.com]   07796 642382 (Mbl)

49 Glasgow: Broomhill (0141-334 2540) linked with Glasgow: Hyndland (H) (Website: www.hyndlandparishchurch.org)
George C. MacKay   1994   2014   27 St Kilda Drive, Glasgow G14 9LN   0141-959 3204
BD CertMin CertEd DipPC   [E-mail: g.mackay3@btinternet.com]

50 Glasgow: Calton Parkhead (0141-554 3866)
Alison Davidge MA BD   1990   2008   98 Drumover Drive, Glasgow G31 5RP   07843 625059 (Mbl)
[E-mail: adavidge@sky.com]

51 Glasgow: Cardonald (0141-882 6264)
Calum MacLeod BA BD   1979   2007   133 Newtyle Road, Paisley PA1 3LB   0141-887 2726
[E-mail: pangur@sky.com]

52 Glasgow: Carmunnock (0141-644 0655)
G. Gray Fletcher BSc BD   1989   2001   The Manse, 161 Waterside Road, Carmunnock, Glasgow G76 9AJ   0141-644 1578 (Tel/Fax)
[E-mail: gray.fletcher@virgin.net]

53 Glasgow: Carmyle linked with Glasgow: Kenmuir Mount Vernon
Murdo Maclean BD CertMin   1997   1999   3 Meryon Road, Glasgow G32 9NW   0141-778 2625
[E-mail: murdo.maclean@ntlworld.com]

54 Glasgow: Carnwadric
Graeme K. Bell BA BD   1983   62 Loganswell Road, Thornliebank, Glasgow G46 8AX   0141-638 5884
[E-mail: graemekbell@googlemail.com]

Mary Gargrave (Mrs) DCS   12 Parkholm Quad, Glasgow G63 7ZH   0141-880 5532
[E-mail: mary.gargrave@btinternet.com]   07896 866618 (Mbl)

55 Glasgow: Castlemilk (H) (0141-634 1480)
Sarah Brown (Ms)   2012   156 Old Castle Road, Glasgow G44 5TW   0141-637 5451
MA BD ThM DipYW/Theol PDCCE   [E-mail: ministercastlemilk@gmail.com]   07532 457245 (Mbl)
Isobel Beck BD DCS   16 Patrick Avenue, Stevenston KA20 4AW   07919 193425 (Mbl)
[E-mail: deaconcastlemilk@aol.co.uk]

56   Glasgow: Cathcart Old (0141-637 4168)
Neil W. Galbraith BD CertMin   1987   1996   21 Courthill Avenue, Cathcart, Glasgow   G44 5AA   0141-633 5248 (Tel/Fax)
[E-mail: revneilgalbraith@hotmail.com]

57   Glasgow: Cathcart Trinity (H) (0141-637 6658)
Alasdair MacMillan   2015   82 Merrylee Road, Glasgow G43 2QZ   0141-633 3744
[E-mail: minister@cathcarttrinity.org.uk]
Wilma Pearson (Mrs) BD (Assoc)   2004   90 Newlands Road, Glasgow G43 2JR   0141-632 2491
[E-mail: wilma.pearson@ntlworld.com]

58   Glasgow: Cathedral (High or St Mungo's) (0141-552 6891)
Laurence A.B. Whitley MA BD PhD   1975   2007   41 Springfield Road, Bishopbriggs, Glasgow   G64 1PL   0141-762 2719
[E-mail: labwhitley@btinternet.com]
Ada MacLeod MA BD PGCE   2013   133 Newtyle Road, Paisley PA1 3LB   0141-887 2726
(Assistant Minister)   [E-mail: ada@uk7.net]

59   Glasgow: Clincarthill (H) (0141-632 4206)
Vacant

60   Glasgow: Colston Milton (0141-772 1922)
Christopher J. Rowe BA BD   2008   118 Birsay Road, Milton, Glasgow G22 7QP   0141-564 1138
[E-mail: ministercolstonmilton@yahoo.co.uk]

61   Glasgow: Colston Wellpark (H)
Guardianship of the Presbytery
Leslie Grieve   2014   23 Hertford Avenue, Kelvindale, Glasgow   G12 0LG   07813   255052 (Mbl)
(Ordained Local Minister)   [E-mail: leslie.grieve@gmail.com]

62   Glasgow: Cranhill (H) (0141-774 3344)
Muriel B. Pearson (Ms) MA BD PGCE   2004   31 Lethamhill Crescent, Glasgow G33 2SH   0141-770 6873
[E-mail: murielpearson@btinternet.com]   07951 888860 (Mbl)

63   Glasgow: Croftfoot (H) (0141-637 3913)
Robert M. Silver BA BD   1995   2011   4 Inchmurrin Gardens, High Burnside, Rutherglen, Glasgow   0141-258 7268
G73 5RU
[E-mail: rob.silver@talktalk.net]

64   Glasgow: Dennistoun New (H) (0141-550 2825)
Ian M.S. McInnes BD DipMin   1995   2008   31 Pencaitland Drive, Glasgow G32 8RL   0141-564 6498
[E-mail: ian.liz1@ntlworld.com]

No.	Name	Year	Year	Address	Tel.
65	**Glasgow: Drumchapel St Andrew's (0141-944 3758)**				
	John S. Purves LLB BD	1983	1984	6 Firdon Crescent, Old Drumchapel, Glasgow G15 6QQ [E-mail: john.s.purves@talk21.com]	0141-944 4566
66	**Glasgow: Drumchapel St Mark's**				
	Audrey Jamieson BD MTh	2004	2007	146 Garscadden Road, Glasgow G15 6PR [E-mail: audrey.jamieson2@btinternet.com]	0141-944 5440
67	**Glasgow: Easterhouse St George's and St Peter's (0141-771 8810)**				
	Vacant			3 Barony Gardens, Baillieston, Glasgow G69 6TS	0141-573 8200
68	**Glasgow: Eastwood**				
	Vacant				
69	**Glasgow: Gairbraid (H)**				
	Donald Michael MacInnes BD	2002	2011	4 Blackhill Gardens, Summerston, Glasgow G23 5NE [E-mail: revdmmi@gmail.com]	0141-946 0604
70	**Glasgow: Gallowgate**				
	Peter L. V. Davidge BD MTh	2003	2009	98 Drumover Drive, Glasgow G31 5RP [E-mail: rev_dav46@yahoo.co.uk]	07765 096599 (Mbl)
71	**Glasgow: Garthamlock and Craigend East**				
	Vacant				
	Marion Buchanan (Mrs) MA DCS			16 Almond Drive, East Kilbride, Glasgow G74 2HX [E-mail: marion.buchanan@btinternet.com]	01355 228776 07999 889817 (Mbl)
72	**Glasgow: Gorbals**				
	Ian F. Galloway BA BD	1976	1996	44 Riverside Road, Glasgow G43 2EF [E-mail: ianfgalloway@msn.com]	0141-649 5250
73	**Glasgow: Govan and Linthouse**				
	Moyna McGlynn (Mrs) BD PhD	1999	2008	19 Dumbreck Road, Glasgow G41 5LJ [E-mail: moyna_mcglynn@hotmail.com]	0141-419 0308
	Andrew Thomson BA (Assistant Minister)	1976	2010	3 Laurel Wynd, Drumsagard Village, Cambuslang, Glasgow G72 7BH [E-mail: thethomsons@hotmail.co.uk]	0141-641 2936 07772 502774 (Mbl)

John Paul Cathcart DCS — 9 Glen More, East Kilbride, Glasgow G74 2AP
[E-mail: paulcathcart@msn.com]
01355 243970
07708 396074 (Mbl)

74 Glasgow: High Carntyne (0141-778 4186)
Joan Ross (Miss) BSc BD PhD — 1999 2005 — 163 Lethamhill Road, Glasgow G33 2SQ
[E-mail: joan@highcarntyne.plus.com]
0141-770 9247

Patricia A. Carruth (Mrs) BD
(Associate Minister) — 1998 2014 — 38 Springhill Farm Road, Baillieston, Glasgow G69 6GW
[E-mail: patrevanne@aol.com]
0141-771 3758

75 Glasgow: Hillington Park (H)
John B. MacGregor BD — 1999 2004 — 61 Ralston Avenue, Glasgow G52 3NB
[E-mail: johnmacgregor61@hotmail.co.uk]
0141-882 7000

76 Glasgow: Hyndland See Glasgow: Broomhill

77 Glasgow: Ibrox (H) (0141-427 0896)
Elisabeth G.B. Spence (Miss) BD DipEd — 1995 2008 — 59 Langhaul Road, Glasgow G53 7SE
[E-mail: revelisabeth@spenceweb.net]
0141-883 7744

78 Glasgow: John Ross Memorial Church for Deaf People
(Voice Text: 0141-420 1391; Fax: 0141-420 3778)
Richard C. Durno DSW CQSW — 1989 1998 — 31 Springfield Road, Bishopbriggs,
Glasgow G64 1PJ (Voice/Text/Fax) (Voice/Text/Voicemail)
[E-mail: richard.durno@btinternet.com]
0141-772 1052
07748 607721 (Mbl)

79 Glasgow: Jordanhill (Tel: 0141-959 2496)
Vacant

80 Glasgow: Kelvinbridge (0141-339 1750)
Gordon Kirkwood BSc BD PGCE MTh — 1987 2013 — Flat 2/2, 94 Hyndland Road, Glasgow G12 9PZ
[E-mail: gordonkirkwood@hotmail.co.uk]
0141-334 5352

Cathie H. McLaughlin (Mrs)
(Ordained Local Minister) — 2014 — 8 Lamlash Place, Glasgow G33 3XH
[E-mail: chmclaughlin@talktalk.net]
0141-774 2483

81 Glasgow: Kelvinside Hillhead (0141-334 2788)
Vacant
Roger Sturrock (Prof.) BD MD FCRP
(Ordained Local Minister) — 2014 — 36 Thomson Drive, Bearsden, Glasgow G61 3PA
[E-mail: rogersturrock@mac.com]
0141-942 7412

82 Glasgow: Kenmuir Mount Vernon See Carmyle

83 Glasgow: King's Park (H) (0141-636 8688)
Sandra Boyd (Mrs) BEd BD   2007
1101 Aikenhead Road, Glasgow G44 5SL   0141-637 2803
[E-mail: sandraboyd.bofa@btopenworld.com]

84 Glasgow: Kinning Park (0141-427 3063)
Margaret H. Johnston BD   1988
168 Arbroath Avenue, Cardonald, Glasgow G52 3HH   0141-810 3782
[E-mail: marniejohnston7@aol.com]

85 Glasgow: Knightswood St Margaret's (H)
Alexander M. Fraser BD DipMin   1985
26 Airthrey Avenue, Glasgow G14 9LJ   0141-959 7075
[E-mail: sandyfraser2@hotmail.com]

86 Glasgow: Langside (0141-632 7520)
David N. McLachlan BD   1985
36 Madison Avenue, Glasgow G44 5AQ   0141-637 0797
[E-mail: dmclachlan77@hotmail.com]

87 Glasgow: Lochwood (H) (0141-771 2649)
Vacant

88 Glasgow: Maryhill (H) (0141-946 3512)
Stuart C. Matthews BD MA   2006
251 Milngavie Road, Bearsden, Glasgow G61 3DQ   0141-942 0804
[E-mail: stuart.maryhill@gmail.com]
James Hamilton DCS
6 Beckfield Gate, Glasgow G33 1SW   0141-558 3195
[E-mail: j.hamilton111@btinternet.com]   07584 137314 (Mbl)

89 Glasgow: Merrylea (0141-637 2009)
David P. Hood BD CertMin DipIOB(Scot)   1997
4 Pilmuir Avenue, Glasgow G44 3HX   0141-637 6700
[E-mail: dphood3@ntlworld.com]

90 Glasgow: Mosspark (H) (0141-882 2240)
Vacant

91 Glasgow: Newlands South (H) (0141-632 3055)
John D. Whiteford MA BD   1989
24 Monreith Road, Glasgow G43 2NY   0141-632 2588
[E-mail: jwhiteford@hotmail.com]

92	**Glasgow: Partick South (H)**			
	James Andrew McIntyre BD	2010	3 Branklyn Crescent, Glasgow G13 1GJ [E-mail: revparticksouth@hotmail.co.uk]	0141-959 3732
93	**Glasgow: Partick Trinity (H)**			
	Stuart J. Smith BEng BD MTh	1994	99 Balshagray Avenue, Glasgow G11 7EQ [E-mail: ssmith99@ntlworld.com]	0141-576 7149
94	**Glasgow: Pollokshaws (0141-649 1879)**			
	Roy J.M. Henderson MA BD DipMin	1987 2013	33 Mannering Road, Glasgow G41 3SW [E-mail: royhenderson1@gmail.com]	0141-632 8768
95	**Glasgow: Pollokshields (H)**			
	David R. Black MA BD	1986 1997	36 Glencairn Drive, Glasgow G41 4PW [E-mail: davidrblack@btinternet.com]	0141-423 4000
96	**Glasgow: Possilpark (0141-336 8028)**			
	Linda E. Pollock (Miss) BD ThM ThM	2001 2014	108 Erradale Street, Lambhill, Glasgow G22 6PT [E-mail: fantazomi@yahoo.co.uk]	0141-336 6909
97	**Glasgow: Queen's Park Govanhill (0141-423 3654)**			
	Elijah W. Smith BA MLitt	2015	c/o Presbytery Office [E-mail: elijah.w.smith@gmail.com]	07975 998382 (Mbl)
98	**Glasgow: Renfield St Stephen's (Tel: 0141-332 4293; Fax: 0141-332 8482)**			
	Peter M. Gardner MA BD	1988 2002	101 Hill Street, Glasgow G3 6TY [E-mail: peter@rsschurch.org.uk]	0141-353 0349
	Iain A. MacLeod (Ordained Local Minister)	2012	6 Hallydown Drive, Glasgow G13 1UF [E-mail: iainamacleod@googlemail.com]	07795 014889 (Mbl)
99	**Glasgow: Robroyston (New Charge Development) (0141-558 8414)**			
	Jonathan A. Keefe BSc BD	2009	7 Beckfield Drive, Glasgow G33 1SR [E-mail: jonathanakeefe@aol.com]	0141-558 2952
100	**Glasgow: Ruchazie (0141-774 2759)**			
	Vacant			

101 Glasgow: Ruchill Kelvinside (0141-946 0466)
Mark Lowey BD DipTh   2012   9 Kirklee Road, Glasgow G12 0RQ   0141-357 3249
[E-mail: marklowey@ymail.com]

102 Glasgow: St Andrew and St Nicholas
Lyn Peden (Mrs) BD   2010   2015   80 Tweedsmuir Road, Glasgow G52 2RX   0141-883 9873
[E-mail: lpeden@churchofscotland.org.uk]
(New charge formed by the union of Glasgow: Penilee St Andrew and Glasgow: St Nicholas' Cardonald)

103 Glasgow: St Andrew's East (0141-554 1485)
Barbara D. Quigley (Mrs)   1979   2011   43 Broompark Drive, Glasgow G31 2JB   0141-237 7982
MTheol ThM DPS
[E-mail: bdquigley@aol.com]

104 Glasgow: St Christopher's Priesthill and Nitshill (0141-881 6541)
Douglas M. Nicol BD CA   1987   1996   36 Springkell Drive, Glasgow G41 4EZ   0141-427 7877
[E-mail: dougiemnicol@aol.com]

105 Glasgow: St Columba (GE) (0141-221 3305)
Vacant

106 Glasgow: St David's Knightswood (0141-954 1081)
Graham M. Thain LLB BD   1988   1999   60 Southbrae Drive, Glasgow G13 1QD   0141-959 2904
[E-mail: graham_thain@btopenworld.com]

107 Glasgow: St Enoch's Hogganfield (H) (Tel: 0141-770 5694; Fax: 0870 284 0084) (E-mail: church@st-enoch.org.uk)
(Website: www.stenochshogganfield.org.uk)
Graham K. Blount LLB BD PhD   1976   2010   43 Smithycroft Road, Glasgow G33 2RH   0141-770 7593
[E-mail: graham.blount@yahoo.co.uk]

108 Glasgow: St George's Tron (0141-221 2141)
Alastair S. Duncan MA BD   1989   2013   29 Hertford Avenue, Glasgow G12 0LG   07968 852083 (Mbl)
(Transition Minister)
[E-mail: stgeorgestroncofs@gmail.com]

109 Glasgow: St James' (Pollok) (0141-882 4984)
John W. Mann BSc MDiv DMin   2004   30 Ralston Avenue, Glasgow G52 3NA   0141-883 7405
[E-mail: drjohnmann@hotmail.com]

110 Glasgow: St John's Renfield (0141-339 7021) (Website: www.stjohns-renfield.org.uk)
Fiona L. Lillie (Mrs) BA BD MLitt   1995   2009   26 Leicester Avenue, Glasgow G12 0LU   0141-339 4637
[E-mail: fionalillie@btinternet.com]

111 Glasgow: St Margaret's Tollcross Park
Vacant

112 Glasgow: St Paul's (0141-770 8559)
Daniel Manastireanu BA MTh   2010   2014   38 Lochview Drive, Glasgow G33 1QF   0141-770 1561
[E-mail: dmanastireanu@churchofscotland.org.uk]

113 Glasgow: St Rollox (0141-558 1809)
Vacant

114 Glasgow: Sandyford Henderson Memorial (H) (L)
Jonathan de Groot BD MTh CPS   2007   2014   66 Woodend Drive, Glasgow G13 1TG   0141-954 9013

115 Glasgow: Sandyhills (0141-778 3415)
Graham T. Atkinson MA BD MTh   2006   60 Wester Road, Glasgow G32 9JJ   0141-778 2174
[E-mail: gtatkinson75@yahoo.co.uk]

116 Glasgow: Scotstoun (R)
Richard Cameron BD DipMin   2000   15 Northland Drive, Glasgow G14 9BE   0141-959 4637
[E-mail: rev.rickycam@live.co.uk]

117 Glasgow: Shawlands (0141-649 1773) linked with Glasgow: South Shawlands (R) (0141-649 4656)
Valerie J. Duff (Miss) DMin   1993   2014   29 St Ronan's Drive, Glasgow G41 3SQ   0141-258 6782
[E-mail: valduff@tiscali.co.uk]

118 Glasgow: Sherbrooke St Gilbert's (H) (0141-427 1968)
Thomas L. Pollock   1982   2003   114 Springkell Avenue, Glasgow G41 4EW   0141-427 2094
BA BD MTh FSAScot JP   [E-mail: tompollock06@aol.com]

119 Glasgow: Shettleston New (0141-778 0857)
Ronald A.S. Craig BAcc BD   1983   2007   211 Sandyhills Road, Glasgow G32 9NB   0141-778 1286
[E-mail: rascraig@ntlworld.com]

120 Glasgow: Shettleston Old (R) (H) (0141-778 2484)
Vacant

121 Glasgow: South Carntyne (H) (0141-778 1343)
Vacant

122 Glasgow: South Shawlands See Glasgow: Shawlands

123 Glasgow: Springburn (H) (0141-557 2345)
Brian M. Casey MA BD   2014   c/o Springburn Parish Church, 180 Springburn Way, Glasgow G21 1TU [E-mail: brian.casey925@btinternet.com]   07703 166772 (Mbl)

124 Glasgow: Temple Anniesland (0141-959 1814)
Fiona Gardner (Mrs) BD MA MLitt   1997   2011   76 Victoria Park Drive North, Glasgow G14 9PJ [E-mail: fionandcolin@hotmail.com]   0141-959 5647

125 Glasgow: Toryglen (H)
Vacant

126 Glasgow: Trinity Possil and Henry Drummond
Richard G. Buckley BD MTh   1990   1995   50 Highfield Drive, Glasgow G12 0HL [E-mail: richardbuckleyis@hotmail.com]   0141-339 2870

127 Glasgow: Tron St Mary's (0141-558 1011)
Rhona E. McDonald (Miss) BA BD   2015   6 Broomfield Drive, Balornock, Glasgow G21 3HE [E-mail: revrhona@gmail.com]   0141-389 8816

128 Glasgow: Victoria Tollcross
Monica Michelin Salomon BD   1999   2007   228 Hamilton Road, Glasgow G32 9QU [E-mail: monica@michelin-salomon.freeserve.co.uk]   0141-778 2413

Fiona Blair (Miss) DCS   Mure Church Manse, 9 West Road, Irvine KA12 8RE [E-mail: fblair@churchofscotland.org.uk]   07977 235168 (Mbl)

129 Glasgow: Wallacewell (New Charge Development)
Daniel Frank BA MDiv DMin   1984   2011   8 Streamfield Gate, Glasgow G33 1SJ [E-mail: daniellouis106@gmail.com]   0141-585 0283

130 Glasgow: Wellington (H) (0141-339 0454)

David I. Sinclair BSc BD PhD DipSW	1990	2008	31 Hughenden Gardens, Glasgow G12 9YH [E-mail: davidsinclair@btinternet.com]	0141-334 2343
Roger Sturrock (Prof.) BD MD FCRP (Ordained Local Minister)		2014	36 Thomson Drive, Bearsden, Glasgow G61 3PA [E-mail: rogersturrock@mac.com]	0141-942 7412

131 Glasgow: Whiteinch (Website: www.whiteinchcofs.co.uk)

Alan McWilliam BD MTh	1993	2000	65 Victoria Park Drive South, Glasgow G14 9NX [E-mail: alan@whiteinchchurch.org]	0141-576 9020

132 Glasgow: Yoker (R)

Karen E. Hendry BSc BD		2005	15 Coldingham Avenue, Glasgow G14 0PX [E-mail: karen@hendry-k.fsnet.co.uk]	0141-952 3620

Alexander, Eric J. MA BD	1958	1997	(Glasgow: St George's Tron)	77 Norwood Park, Bearsden, Glasgow G61 2RZ	0141-942 4404
Allen, Martin A.W. MA BD ThM	1977	2007	(Chryston)	Lealenge, 85 High Barrwood Road, Kilsyth, Glasgow G65 0EE	01236 826616
Allison, May M. (Mrs) BD	1988	2012	(Glasgow: Househillwood St Christopher's)	12 Leverndale Court, Crookston, Glasgow G53 7SJ [E-mail: revmayallison@hotmail.com]	0141-810 5953
Alston, William G.	1961	2009	(Glasgow: North Kelvinside)	Flat 0/2, 5 Knightswood Court, Glasgow G13 2XN [E-mail: williamalston@hotmail.com]	0141-959 3113
Barr, Alexander C. MA BD	1950	1992	(Glasgow: St Nicholas' Cardonald)	25 Fisher Drive, Phoenix Park, Paisley PA1 2TP	0141-848 5941
Bayes, Muriel C. (Mrs) DCS			(Deacon)	Flat 6, Carlton Court, 10 Fenwick Road, Glasgow G46 6AN	0141-633 0865
Beaton, Margaret S. (Miss) DCS			Deacon	64 Gardenside Grove, Carmyle, Glasgow G32 8EZ	0141-646 2297
Bell, John L. MA BD FRSCM DUniv	1978	1988	Iona Community	Flat 2/1, 31 Lansdowne Crescent, Glasgow G20 6NH	0141-334 0688
Birch, James PgDip FRSA FIOC	2001	2007	(Auxiliary Minister)	1 Kirkhill Grove, Cambuslang, Glasgow G72 8EH	0141-583 1722
Black, William B. MA BD	1972	2011	(Stornoway: High)	33 Tankerland Road, Glasgow G44 4EN [E-mail: revwillieblack@gmail.com]	0141-637 4717
Blount, A. Sheila (Mrs) BD BA	1978	2010	(Cupar: St John's and Dairsie United)	43 Smithycroft Road, Glasgow G33 2RH [E-mail: asblount@orange.net]	0141-770 7593
Brain, Isobel J. (Mrs) MA	1987	1997	(Ballantrae)	10/11 Maxwell Street, Edinburgh EH10 5GZ	0131-466 6115
Brice, Dennis G. BSc BD	1981		(Taiwan)	8 Parkwood Close, Broxbourne, Herts EN10 7PF [E-mail: dbrice1@comcast.net]	
Bryden, William A. BD	1977	1984	(Yoker: Old with St Matthew's)	145 Bearsden Road, Glasgow G13 1BS	0141-959 5213
Bull, Alister W. BD DipMin MTh PhD	1994	2013	Mission and Discipleship Council	121 George Street, Edinburgh EH2 4YN [E-mail: abull@churchofscotland.org.uk]	0131-225 5722
Campbell, A. Iain MA DipEd	1961	1997	(Busby)	430 Clarkston Road, Glasgow G44 3QF [E-mail: bellmac@sagainternet.co.uk]	0141-637 7460
Campbell, John MA BA BSc	1973	2009	(Caldwell)	96 Boghead Road, Lenzie, Glasgow G66 4BN [E-mail: johncampbell.lenzie@gmail.com]	0141-776 0874

Cartledge, Graham R.G. MA BD STM	1977	2015	(Glasgow: Eastwood)	5 Briar Grove, Newlands, Glasgow G43 2TG	0141-637 3228
Clark, Douglas W. LTh	1993	2015	(Lenzie: Old)	1/3, 39 Saltmarsh Drive, Lenzie, Glasgow G66 3NR [E-mail: douglaswclark@hotmail.com]	0141-776 1298
Cunningham, Alexander MA BD	1961	2002	(Presbytery Clerk)	18 Lady Jane Gate, Bothwell, Glasgow G71 8BW	01698 811051
Cunningham, James S.A. MA BD BLitt PhD	1992	2000	(Glasgow: Barlanark Greyfriars)	'Kirkland', 5 Inveresk Place, Coatbridge ML5 2DA	01236 421541
Drummond, John W. MA BD	1971	2011	(Rutherglen: West and Wardlawhill)	25 Kingsburn Drive, Rutherglen, Glasgow G73 2AN	0141-571 6002
Duff, T. Malcolm F. MA BD	1985	2009	(Glasgow: Queen's Park)	54 Hawkhead Road, Paisley PA1 3NB	0141-570 0614 (Mbl) 07846 926584
Dutch, Morris M. BD BA Dip BTI	1998	2013	(Costa del Sol)	41 Baronald Drive, Glasgow G12 0HN [E-mail: mmdutch@yahoo.co.uk]	0141-357 2286
Farrington, Alexandra LTh	2003	2015	(Campsie)	'Glenburn', High Banton, Kilsyth G65 0RA [E-mail: revsfarrington@aol.co.uk]	01236 824516
Ferguson, James B. LTh	1972	2002	(Lenzie: Union)	3 Bridgeway Place, Kirkintilloch, Glasgow G66 3HW	0141-588 5868
Ferguson, William B. BA BD	1971	2012	(Glasgow: Broomhill)	20 Swift Crescent, Knightswood Gate, Glasgow G13 4QL [E-mail: revferg@btinternet.com]	0141-954 6655
Fleming, Alexander F. MA BD	1966	1995	(Strathblane)	11 Bankwood Drive, Kilsyth, Glasgow G65 0GZ	01236 821461
Forrest, Martin R. BA MA BD	1988	2012	Prison Chaplain	4/1, 7 Blochairn Place, Glasgow G21 2EB [E-mail: martinrforrest@gmail.com]	0141-552 1132
Forsyth, Sandy LLB BD DipLP PhD	2009	2013	(Associate: Kirkintilloch: St David's Memorial Park)	48 Kerr Street, Kirkintilloch, Glasgow G66 1JZ [E-mail: sandyforsyth67@hotmail.co.uk]	0141-777 8194 (Mbl) 07739 639037
Galloway, Kathy (Mrs) BD DD	1977	2002	(Leader: Iona Community)	20 Hamilton Park Avenue, Glasgow G12 8UU	0141-357 4079
Gay, Douglas C. MA BD PhD	1998	2005	University of Glasgow	1F, 16 Royal Terrace, Glasgow G3 7NY [E-mail: douggay@mac.com]	0141-332 4040 (Mbl) 07971 321452
Getliffe, Dot (Mrs) DCS BA BD DipEd	2006	2013	Families Worker, West Mearns	3 Woodview Terrace, Hamilton ML3 9DP [E-mail: dgetliffe@aol.co.uk]	01698 423504 (Mbl) 07766 910171
Gibson, H. Marshall MA BD	1957	1996	(Glasgow: St Thomas' Gallowgate)	39 Burnbroom Drive, Glasgow G69 7XG	0141-771 0749
Grant, David I.M. MA BD	1969	2003	(Dalry: Trinity)	8 Mossbank Drive, Glasgow G33 1LS	0141-770 7186
Gray, Christine M. (Mrs)			(Deacon)	11 Woodside Avenue, Thornliebank, Glasgow G46 7HR	0141-571 1008
Green, Alex H. MA BD	1986	2010	(Strathblane)	44 Laburnum Drive, Milton of Campsie, Glasgow G66 8HY [E-mail: lesvert@btinternet.com]	01360 313001
Gregson, Elizabeth M. (Mrs) BD	1996	2001	(Glasgow: Drumchapel St Andrew's)	17 Westfields, Bishopbriggs, Glasgow G64 3PL	0141-563 1918
Haley, Derek BD DPS	1960	1999	(Chaplain: Gartnavel Royal)	9 Kinnaird Crescent, Bearsden, Glasgow G61 2BN	0141-942 9281
Harvey, W. John BA BD DD	1965	2002	(Edinburgh: Corstorphine Craigsbank)	501 Shields Road, Glasgow G41 2RF	0141-429 3774
Hazlett, W. Ian P. (Prof.-Emer.) BA BD Dr theol DLitt DD	2009		University of Glasgow	587 Shields Road, Glasgow G41 2RW [E-mail: ian.hazlett@glasgow.ac.uk]	0141-423 7461 (Work) 0141-330 5155
Hewitt, William C. BD DiprS	1977	2012	Presbytery Clerk	60 Woodlands Grove, Kilmarnock KA3 1TZ [E-mail: billhewitt1@btinternet.com]	01563 533312
Hope, Evelyn P. (Miss) BA BD	1990	1998	(Wishaw: Thornlie)	Flat 0/1, 48 Moss Side Road, Glasgow G41 3UA	0141-649 1522
Houston, Thomas C. BA	1975	2004	(Glasgow: Priesthill and Nitshill)	63 Broomhouse Crescent, Uddingston, Glasgow G71 7RE	0141-771 0577
Hughes, Helen (Miss) DCS			(Deacon)	2/2, 43 Burnbank Terrace, Glasgow G20 6UQ [E-mail: helhug35@gmail.com]	0141-333 9459 (Mbl) 07752 604817
Hunter, Alastair G. MSc BD	1976	1980	(University of Glasgow)	487 Shields Road, Glasgow G41 2RG	0141-429 1687
Johnston, Robert W.M. MA BD STM	1964	1999	(Glasgow: Temple Anniesland)	13 Kilmardinny Crescent, Bearsden, Glasgow G61 3NP	0141-931 5862

Name and Qualifications	Ordained	Inducted	Position	Address	Telephone
Johnstone, H. Martin J. MA BD MTh PhD	1989	2000	Church and Society Council	3/1, 952 Pollokshaws Road, Glasgow G41 2ET [E-mail: mjohnstone@cofscotland.org.uk]	0141-636 5819
Keddie, David A. MA BD	1966	2005	(Glasgow: Linthouse St Kenneth's)	21 Ilay Road, Bearsden, Glasgow G61 1QG [E-mail: revkeddie@gmail.com]	0141-942 5173
Lang, I. Pat (Miss) BSc	1996	2003	(Dunoon: The High Kirk)	37 Crawford Drive, Glasgow G15 6TW	0141-944 2240
Levison, Chris L. MA BD	1972	1998	(Health Care Chaplaincy Training and Development Officer)	Gardenfield, Nine Mile Burn, Penicuik EH26 9LT	
Lloyd, John M. BD CertMin	1984	2009	(Glasgow: Croftfoot)	17 Acacia Way, Cambuslang, Glasgow G72 7ZY	
Love, Joanna (Ms) BSc DCS			Iona Community: Wild Goose Resource Group	92 Everard Drive, Glasgow G21 1XQ [E-mail: jo@iona.org.uk]	(Mbl) 07879 812816 / 0141-772 0149 / (Office) 0141-332 6343
Lunan, David W. MA BD DUniv DLitt DD	1970	2002	(Presbytery Clerk)	30 Mill Road, Banton, Glasgow G65 0RD	01236 824110
MacBain, Ian W. BD	1971	1993	(Coatbridge: Coatdyke)	24 Thornyburn Drive, Baillieston, Glasgow G69 7ER	0141-771 7030
McChlery, Lynn M. BA BD	2005	2015	(Eaglesham)	62 Grenville Drive, Cambuslang, Glasgow G72 8DP [E-mail: lmcchlery@btinternet.com]	0141-643 9730 / (Mbl) 0748 118008
MacDonald, Anne (Miss) BA DCS			Healthcare Chaplain: Leverndale Hospital	c/o Leverndale Hospital, Glasgow G53 7TU [E-mail: anne.macdonald2@ggc.scot.nhs.uk]	0141-211 6695 / (Mbl) 07976 786174
MacDonald, Kenneth MA BA	2001	2006	(Auxiliary Minister)	5 Henderland Road, Bearsden, Glasgow G61 1AH	0141-943 1103
McDougall, Hilary N. (Mrs) MA PGCE BD	2002	2013	Congregational Facilitator: Presbytery of Glasgow	6 Inchmurrin Gardens, High Burnside, Glasgow G73 5RU [E-mail: hilary@presbyteryofglasgow.org.uk]	0141-384 4428 / (Mbl) 07539 321832
MacFadyen, Anne M. (Mrs) BSc BD FSAScot	1995		(Auxiliary Minister)	295 Mearns Road, Glasgow G77 5LT	0141-639 3605
Mackenzie, Gordon R. BscAgr BD	1977	2014	(Chapelhall)	16 Crowhill Road, Bishopbriggs, Glasgow G64 1QY [E-mail: g.mackenzie@btopenworld.com]	0141-772 3811
MacKinnon, Charles M. BD	1989	2009	(Kilsyth: Anderson)	36 Hilton Terrace, Bishopbriggs, Glasgow G64 3HB [E-mail: cm.ccmackinnon@tiscali.co.uk]	
McLachlan, Eric BD MTh	1978	2005	(Glasgow: Cardonald)	16 Kinpurnie Road, Paisley PA1 3HH [E-mail: eric.janis@btinternet.com]	0141-810 5789
McLachlan, Fergus C. BD	1982	2009	(Hospital Chaplain)	46 Queen Square, Glasgow G41 2AZ	0141-423 3830
McLachlan, T. Alastair BSc	1972	2009	(Craignish with Kilbrandon and Kilchattan with Kilninver and Kilmelford)	9 Alder Road, Milton of Campsie, Glasgow G66 8HH [E-mail: talastair@btinternet.com]	01360 319861
McLaren, D. Muir MA BD MTh PhD	1971	2001	(Glasgow: Mosspark)	House 44, 145 Shawhill Road, Glasgow G43 1SX [E-mail: muir44@yahoo.co.uk]	(Mbl) 07931 155779
McLellan, Margaret DCS			Deacon	18 Broom Road East, Newton Mearns, Glasgow G77 5SD [E-mail: margaretmclellan@rocketmail.com]	0141-639 6853
Macleod, Donald BD LRAM DRSAM	1987	2008	(Blairgowrie)	9 Millersneuk Avenue, Lenzie G66 5HJ [E-mail: donmac2@sky.com]	0141-776 6235
MacLeod-Mair, Alisdair T. MEd DipTheol	2001	2012	(Glasgow: Baillieston St Andrew's)	2/2, 44 Leven Street, Pollokshields, Glasgow G41 2JE [E-mail: revalisdair@hotmail.com]	0141-423 9600
MacMahon, Janet P.H. (Mrs) MSc BD	1992	2010	(Kilmaronock Gartocharn)	14 Hillfoot Drive, Bearsden, Glasgow G61 3QQ [E-mail: janetmacmahon@yahoo.co.uk]	0141-942 8611
Macnaughton, J.A. MA BD	1949	1989	(Glasgow: Hyndland)	Lilyburn Care Home, 100 Birdston Road, Milton of Campsie, Glasgow G66 8BY	(Mbl) 07811 621671

MacPherson, James B. DCS	(Deacon)	1984	2001	0/1, 104 Cartside Street, Glasgow G42 9TQ	0141-616 6468
MacQuarrie, Stuart JP BD BSc MBA	Chaplain: Glasgow University	1988		The Chaplaincy Centre, University of Glasgow, Glasgow G12 8QQ	0141-330 5419
MacQuien, Duncan DCS	(Deacon)	1994	2005	35 Criffel Road, Mount Vernon, Glasgow G32 9JE	0141-575 1137
Martindale, John P.F. BD	(Glasgow: Sandyhills)	1971	2007	Flat 3/2, 25 Albert Avenue, Glasgow G42 8RB	0141-433 4367
Miller, John D. BA BD DD	(Glasgow: Castlemilk East)			98 Kirkcaldy Road, Glasgow G41 4LD [E-mail: rev.john.miller@zol.co.zw]	0141-423 0221
Moffat, Thomas BSc BD	(Culross and Torryburn)	1976	2008	Flat 8/1, 8 Cranston Street, Glasgow G3 8GG [E-mail: tom@gallus.org.uk]	0141-248 1886
Moore, William B.	(Prison Chaplain: Low Moss)	1961	1997	10 South Dumbreck Road, Kilsyth, Glasgow G65 9LX	01236 821918
Muir, Fred C. MA BD ThM ARCM	(Stepps)	1995	2011	20 Alexandra Avenue, Stepps, Glasgow G33 6BP	0141-779 2504
Murray, George M. LTh	(Glasgow: St Margaret's Tollcross Park)			6 Mayfield, Lesmahagow ML11 0FH [E-mail: george.murray7@gmail.com]	
Ninian, Esther J. (Miss) MA BD	(Newton Mearns)	1993	2015	21 St Ronan's Drive, Burnside, Rutherglen G73 3SR [E-mail: estherninian5914@btinternet.com]	0141-647 9720
Philip, George M. MA	(Glasgow: Sandyford Henderson Memorial)	1953	1996	44 Beech Avenue, Bearsden, Glasgow G61 3EX	0141-942 1327
Raeburn, Alan C. MA BD	(Glasgow: Battlefield East)	1971	2010	3 Orchard Gardens, Strathaven ML10 6UN [E-mail: acraeburn@hotmail.com] (Mbl)	07709 552161
Ramsay, W.G.	(Glasgow: Springburn)	1967	1999	53 Kelvinvale, Kirkintilloch, Glasgow G66 1RD [E-mail: billram@btopenworld.com]	0141-776 2915
Ramsden, Iain R. MStJ BTh	(Killearnan with Knockbain)	1999	2013	Flat 1/1, 15 Cardon Square, Renfrew PA4 8BY [E-mail: s4rev@sky.com] (Mbl)	07795 972560
Robertson, Archibald MA BD	(Glasgow: Eastwood)	1957	1999	19 Canberra Court, Braidpark Drive, Glasgow G46 6NS	0141-637 7572
Robertson, Blair MA BD ThM	Head of Spiritual Care	1990	1998	c/o Chaplain's Office, South Glasgow University Hospital, 1345 Govan Road, Glasgow G51 4TF	
Ross, Donald M. MA	(Industrial Mission Organiser)	1953	1994	14 Cartsbridge Road, Busby, Glasgow G76 8DH	0141-201 2357
Ross, James MA BD	(Kilsyth: Anderson)	1968	1998	53 Turnberry Gardens, Westerwood, Cumbernauld, Glasgow G68 0AY	0141-644 2220
Shackleton, Scott J.S. QCVS BA BD PhD RN	Chaplain, Royal Navy	1993	2010	Chaplaincy Team Leader, Commando Training Centre, Royal Marines Exmouth EX8 5AR [E-mail: shackletonscott@hotmail.com]	01236 730501
Shackleton, William	(Greenock: Wellpark West)	1960	1996	3 Tynwald Avenue, Burnside, Glasgow G73 4RN	0141-569 9407
Shanks, Norman J. MA BD DD	(Glasgow: Govan Old)	1983	2007	1 Marchmont Terrace, Glasgow G12 9LT [E-mail: rufuski@btinternet.com]	0141-339 4421
Simpson, Neil A. BA BD PhD	(Glasgow: Yoker Old with Yoker St Matthew's)	1992	2001	c/o Glasgow Presbytery Office	
Smeed, Alex W. MA BD	(Glasgow: Whiteinch: Associate)	2008	2013	3/1, 24 Thornwood Road, Glasgow G11 7RB [E-mail: alexsmeed@yahoo.co.uk] (Mbl)	0141-337 3878 07709 756495
Smith, G. Stewart MA BD STM	(Glasgow: King's Park)	1966	2006	33 Brent Road, Stewartfield, East Kilbride, Glasgow G74 4RA (Tel/Fax) [E-mail: stewartandmary@googlemail.com]	01355 226718
Smith, James S.A.	(Drongan: The Schaw Kirk)	1956	1991	146 Aros Drive, Glasgow G52 1TJ	0141-883 9666
Spencer, John MA BD	(Dumfries: Lincluden with Holywood)	1962	2001	10 Kinkell Gardens, Kirkintilloch, Glasgow G66 2HJ	0141-777 8935
Spiers, John M. LTh MTh	(Giffnock: Orchardhill)	1972	2004	58 Woodlands Road, Thornliebank, Glasgow G46 7JQ (Tel/Fax)	0141-638 0632
Stewart, Diane E. BD	(Milton of Campsie)	1988	2006	4 Miller Gardens, Bishopbriggs, Glasgow G64 1FG [E-mail: destewart@givemail.co.uk]	0141-762 1358

Stewart, Norma D. (Miss) MA MEd BD MTh — 1977 2000 — (Glasgow: Strathbungo Queen's Park) — 127 Nether Auldhouse Road, Glasgow G43 2YS — 0141-637 6956

Sutherland, David A. — 2001 — Auxiliary Minister — 3/1, 145 Broomhill Drive, Glasgow G11 7ND — 0141-357 2058
[E-mail: dave.a.sutherland@gmail.com]

Sutherland, Denis I. — 1963 1995 — (Glasgow: Hutchesontown) — 56 Lime Crescent, Cumbernauld, Glasgow G67 3PQ — 01236 731723

Sutherland, Elizabeth W. (Miss) BD — 1972 1996 — (Glasgow: Balornock North with Barmulloch) — 20 Kirkland Avenue, Blanefield, Glasgow G63 9BZ — 01360 770154
[E-mail: ewsutherland@aol.com]

Turner, Angus BD — 1976 1998 — (Industrial Chaplain) — 46 Keir Street, Pollokshields, Glasgow G41 2LA — 0141-424 0493

Tuton, Robert M. MA — 1957 1995 — (Glasgow: Shettleston Old) — 6 Holmwood Gardens, Uddingston, Glasgow G71 7BH — 01698 321108

Walker, Linda — 2008 2013 — Auxiliary Minister — 18 Valeview Terrace, Glasgow G42 9LA — 0141-649 1340
[E-mail: walkerlinda@hotmail.com]

Walton, Ainslie MA MEd — 1954 1995 — (University of Aberdeen) — 501 Shields Road, Glasgow G41 2RF — 0141-420 3327
[E-mail: revainslie@aol.com]

White, C. Peter BVMS BD MRCVS — 1974 2011 — (Glasgow: Sandyford Henderson Memorial) — 2 Hawthorn Place, Torrance, Glasgow G64 4EA — 01360 622680
[E-mail: revcpw@gmail.com]

Whyte, James BD — 1981 2011 — (Fairlie) — 32 Torburn Avenue, Giffnock, Glasgow G46 7RB
[E-mail: jameswhyte89@btinternet.com]

Wilson, John BD — 1985 2010 — (Glasgow: Temple Anniesland) — 4 Carron Crescent, Bearsden, Glasgow G61 1HJ — 0141-931 5609
[E-mail: revjwilson@btinternet.com]

Younger, Adah (Mrs) BD — 1978 2004 — (Glasgow: Dennistoun Central) — 7 Gartocher Terrace, Glasgow G32 0HE — 0141-774 6475

GLASGOW ADDRESSES

Banton — Kelvinhead Road, Banton

Bishopbriggs
Kenmure — Viewfield Road, Bishopbriggs
Springfield Cambridge — The Leys, off Springfield Road Mearns Road, Newton Mearns

Broom — Church Avenue, Burnside
Burnside Blairbeth — Kirkriggs Avenue, Blairbeth
Busby — Church Road, Busby
Cadder — Cadder Road, Bishopbriggs

Cambuslang
Flemington Hallside — Hutchinson Place
Parish — Arnott Way

Campsie — Main Street, Lennoxtown
Chryston — Main Street, Chryston
Eaglesham — Montgomery Street, Eaglesham
Fernhill and Cathkin — Neilvaig Drive

Gartcosh — 113 Lochend Road, Gartcosh

Giffnock
Orchardhill — Church Road
South — Eastwood Toll
The Park — Ravenscliffe Drive

Glenboig — Main Street, Glenboig
Greenbank — Eaglesham Road, Clarkston

Kilsyth
Anderson — Kingston Road, Kilsyth
Burns and Old — Church Street, Kilsyth

Kirkintilloch
Hillhead — Newdyke Road, Kirkintilloch
St Columba's — Waterside Road nr Auld Aisle Road
St David's Mem Pk — Alexandra Street
St Mary's — Cowgate

Lenzie
Old — Kirkintilloch Road x Garngaber Ave
Union — 65 Kirkintilloch Road

Maxwell
Mearns Castle — Waterfoot Road

Mearns — Mearns Road, Newton Mearns
Milton of Campsie — Antermony Road, Milton of Campsie
Netherlee — Ormonde Drive x Ormonde Avenue
Newton Mearns — Ayr Road, Newton Mearns

Rutherglen
Old — Main Street at Queen Street
Stonelaw — Stonelaw Road x Dryburgh Avenue
West and Wardlawhill — 3 Western Avenue

Stamperland — Stamperland Gardens, Clarkston
Stepps — Whitehill Avenue
Thornliebank — 61 Spiersbridge Road
Torrance — School Road, Torrance
Twechar — Main Street, Twechar
Williamwood — 4 Vardar Avenue, Clarkston

Glasgow
Anderston Kelvingrove — 759 Argyle St x Elderslie St

Baillieston	
Mure Memorial	Maxwell Drive, Garrowhill
St Andrew's	Bredisholm Road
Balshagray Victoria Pk	218–230 Broomhill Drive
Barlanark Greyfriars	Edinburgh Rd x Hallhill Rd (365)
Blawarthill	Millbrix Avenue
Bridgeton St Francis in the East	26 Queen Mary Street
Broomhill	64–66 Randolph Rd (x Marlborough Ave)
Calton Parkhead	122 Helenvale Street
Cardonald	2155 Paisley Road West
Carmunnock	Kirk Road, Carmunnock
Carmyle	155 Carmyle Avenue
Carnwadric	556 Boydstone Road, Thornliebank
Castlemilk	Carmunnock Road
Cathcart	
Old	119 Carmunnock Road
Trinity	90 Clarkston Road
Cathedral	Cathedral Square, 2 Castle Street
Clincarthill	1216 Cathcart Road
Colston Milton	Egilsay Crescent
Colston Wellpark	1378 Springburn Road
Cranhill	109 Bellrock St (at Bellrock Cr)
Croftfoot	Croftpark Ave x Crofthill Road
Dennistoun New	9 Armadale Street
Drumchapel	
St Andrew's	153 Garscadden Road
St Mark's	281 Kinfauns Drive
Easterhouse St George's and St Peter's	
Eastwood	Boydnie Street, Mansewood Road
Gairbraid	1517 Maryhill Road
Gallowgate	David Street
Garthamlock and Craigend East	46 Porchester Street
Gorbals	1 Errol Gardens
Govan and Linthouse	Govan Cross
High Carntyne	358 Carntynehall Road
Hillington Park	24 Berryknowes Road
Hyndland	79 Hyndland Rd, opp Novar Dr
Ibrox	Carillon Road x Clifford Street
John Ross Memorial	100 Norfolk Street
Jordanhill	28 Woodend Drive (x Munro Road)
Kelvinbridge	Belmont Street at Belmont Bridge
Kelvinside Hillhead	Observatory Road
Kenmuir Mount Vernon	2405 London Road, Mount Vernon
King's Park	242 Castlemilk Road
Kinning Park	Eaglesham Place
Knightswood St Margaret's	2000 Great Western Road
Langside	167–169 Ledard Road (x Lochleven Road)
Lochwood	2A Liff Place, Easterhouse
Maryhill	1990 Maryhill Road
Merrylea	78 Merrylee Road
Mosspark	167 Ashkirk Drive
Newlands South	Riverside Road x Langside Drive
Partick	
South	259 Dumbarton Road
Trinity	20 Lawrence Street x Elie Street
Pollokshaws	223 Shawbridge Street
Pollokshields	Albert Drive x Shields Road
Possilpark	124 Saracen Street
Queen's Park Govanhill	170 Queen's Drive
Renfield St Stephen's	260 Bath Street
Robroyston	34 Saughs Road
Ruchazie	4 Elibank Street (x Milncroft Road)
Ruchill Kelvinside	Shakespeare Street nr Maryhill Rd and 10 Kelbourne Street (two buildings)
St Andrew and St Nicholas	Bowfield Road x Bowfield Avenue
	224 Hartlaw Crescent
St Andrew's East	681 Alexandra Parade
St Christopher's Priesthill and Nitshill	
Priesthill building	100 Priesthill Rd (x Muirshiel Cr)
Nitshill building	36 Dove Street
St Christopher's	Meikle Road
St Columba	300 St Vincent Street
St David's Knightswood	66 Boreland Drive (nr Lincoln Avenue)
St Enoch's Hogganfield	860 Cumbernauld Road
St George's Tron	163 Buchanan Street
St James' (Pollok)	Lyoncross Road x Byrebush Road
St John's Renfield	22 Beaconsfield Road
St Margaret's Tollcross Pk	179 Braidfauld Street
St Paul's	30 Langdale St (x Greenrig St)
St Rollox	9 Fountainwell Road
Sandyford Henderson Memorial	Kelvinhaugh Street at Argyle Street
Sandyhills	28 Baillieston Rd nr Sandyhills Rd
Scotstoun	Earlbank Avenue x Ormiston Avenue
Shawlands	Shawlands Cross (1114 Pollokshaws Road)
Sherbrooke St Gilbert's	Nithsdale Rd x Sherbrooke Avenue
Shettleston New	679 Old Shettleston Road
Shettleston Old	99–111 Killin Street
South Carntyne	538 Carntyne Road
South Shawlands	Regwood Street x Deanston Drive
Springburn	180 Springburn Way
Temple Anniesland	869 Crow Road
Toryglen	Glenmore Ave nr Prospecthill Road
Trinity Possil and Henry Drummond	2 Crowhill Street (x Broadholm Street)
Tron St Mary's	128 Red Road
Victoria Tollcross	1134 Tollcross Road
Wallacewell New Charge Development	no building yet obtained
Wellington	University Ave x Southpark Avenue
Whiteinch	1a Northinch Court
Yoker	10 Hawick Street

(17) HAMILTON

Meets at Motherwell: Dalziel St Andrew's Parish Church Halls, on the first Tuesday of February, March, May, September, October, November and December, and on the third Tuesday of June.

Presbytery Office: 353 Orbiston Street, Motherwell ML1 1QW — 01698 259135
[E-mail: hamilton@churchofscotland.org.uk]
[E-mail: clerk@presbyteryofhamilton.co.uk]

Clerk: REV. GORDON A. McCRACKEN BD CertMin DMin — c/o The Presbytery Office

Depute Clerk: REV. ROBERT A. HAMILTON BA BD — c/o The Presbytery Office
Presbytery Treasurer: MR ROBERT A. ALLAN — 7 Graham Place, Ashgill, Larkhall ML9 3BA — 01698 883246
[E-mail: Fallan3246@aol.com]

1 Airdrie: Broomknoll (H) (01236 762101) linked with Calderbank
Vacant — 38 Commonhead Street, Airdrie ML6 6NS — 01236 609584

2 Airdrie: Clarkston
F. Derek Gunn BD — 1986 2009 — Clarkston Manse, Forrest Street, Airdrie ML6 7BE — 01236 603146

3 Airdrie: Flowerhill (H)
Vacant — 31 Victoria Place, Airdrie ML6 9BU — 01236 754430

4 Airdrie: High
Ian R. W. McDonald BSc BD PhD — 2007 — 17 Etive Drive, Airdrie ML6 9QL — 01236 760023
[E-mail: ian@spingetastic.freeserve.co.uk]

5 Airdrie: Jackson
Kay Gilchrist (Miss) BD — 1996 2008 — 48 Dunrobin Road, Airdrie ML6 8LR — 01236 760154
[E-mail: gilky61@yahoo.co.uk]

6 Airdrie: New Monkland (H) linked with Greengairs
Vacant — 3 Dykehead Crescent, Airdrie ML6 6PU — 01236 763554

7 Airdrie: St Columba's
Margaret F. Currie BEd BD — 1980 1987 — 52 Kennedy Drive, Airdrie ML6 9AW — 01236 763173
[E-mail: margaret_currie250@o2.co.uk]

No.	Church / Minister		Address	Telephone
8	**Airdrie: The New Wellwynd** Robert A. Hamilton BA BD	1995	20 Arthur Avenue, Airdrie ML6 9EZ [E-mail: revrob13@blueyonder.co.uk]	01236 763022
9	**Bargeddie (H)** John Fairful BD	1994 2001	The Manse, Manse Road, Bargeddie, Baillieston, Glasgow G69 6UB [E-mail: johnfairful@yahoo.co.uk]	0141-771 1322
10	**Bellshill: Central** Vacant		32 Adamson Street, Bellshill ML4 1DT	01698 849114
11	**Bellshill: West (H) (01698 747581)** Vacant		16 Croftpark Street, Bellshill ML4 1EY	01698 842877
12	**Blantyre: Livingstone Memorial** Vacant		286 Glasgow Road, Blantyre, Glasgow G72 9DB	01698 823794
13	**Blantyre: Old (H)** Sarah L. Ross (Mrs) BD MTh PGDip	2004 2013	The Manse, Craigmuir Road, High Blantyre, Glasgow G72 9UA [E-mail: revsarahlynsey@gmail.com]	01698 769046
14	**Blantyre: St Andrew's** Vacant		332 Glasgow Road, Blantyre, Glasgow G72 9LQ	01698 828633
15	**Bothwell (H)** James M. Gibson TD LTh LRAM	1978 1989	Manse Avenue, Bothwell, Glasgow G71 8PQ [E-mail: jamesmgibson@msn.com]	01698 853189 (Tel) 01698 854903 (Fax)
16	**Calderbank** See Airdrie: Broomknoll			
17	**Caldercruix and Longriggend (H)** George M. Donaldson MA BD	1984 2005	Main Street, Caldercruix, Airdrie ML6 7RF [E-mail: g.donaldson505@btinternet.com]	01236 842279
18	**Chapelhall (H)** Vacant		The Manse, Russell Street, Chapelhall, Airdrie ML6 8SG	01236 763439

19 **Chapelton linked with Strathaven: Rankin (H)** 1991
Shaw J. Paterson BSc BD MSc
15 Lethame Road, Strathaven ML10 6AD
[E-mail: s.paterson195@btinternet.com]
01357 520019 (Tel)
01357 529316 (Fax)

20 **Cleland (H) linked with Wishaw: St Mark's**
Graham Austin BD   1997   2008
The Manse, 302 Coltness Road, Wishaw ML2 7EY
[E-mail: graham.austin4@btinternet.com]
01698 384596

21 **Coatbridge: Blairhill Dundyvan (H) linked with Coatbridge: Middle**
John K. Collard MA BD   1986   2015
(Interim Minister)
1 Nelson Terrace, East Kilbride, Glasgow G74 2EY
[E-mail: jcollard@churchofscotland.org.uk]
01355 520093

22 **Coatbridge: Calder (H) linked with Coatbridge: Old Monkland**
Vacant
26 Bute Street, Coatbridge ML5 4HF
01236 421516

23 **Coatbridge: Middle** See Coatbridge: Blairhill Dundyvan

24 **Coatbridge: New St Andrew's**
Fiona Nicolson BA BD   1996   2005
77 Eglinton Street, Coatbridge ML5 3JF
01236 437271

25 **Coatbridge: Old Monkland** See Coatbridge: Calder

26 **Coatbridge: Townhead (H)**
Ecilo Selemani LTh MTh   1993   2004
Crinan Crescent, Coatbridge ML5 2LH
[E-mail: eciloselemani@msn.com]
01236 702914

27 **Dalserf**
Vacant
Manse Brae, Dalserf, Larkhall ML9 3BN
01698 882195

28 **East Kilbride: Claremont (H) (01355 238088)**
Gordon R. Palmer MA BD STM   1986   2003
17 Deveron Road, East Kilbride, Glasgow G74 2HR
[E-mail: gkrspalmer@blueyonder.co.uk]
01355 248526

29 **East Kilbride: Greenhills (E) (01355 221746)**
John Brewster MA BD DipEd   1988
21 Turnberry Place, East Kilbride, Glasgow G75 8TB
[E-mail: johnbrewster@blueyonder.co.uk]
01355 242564

No.	Charge / Minister		Address	Tel
30	**East Kilbride: Moncreiff (H) (01355 223328)** Neil Buchanan BD	1991	16 Almond Drive, East Kilbride, Glasgow G74 2HX [E-mail: neil.buchanan@talk21.com]	01355 238639
31	**East Kilbride: Mossneuk (01355 260954)** John L. McPake BA BD PhD	1987 2000	30 Eden Grove, Mossneuk, East Kilbride, Glasgow G75 8XU [E-mail: jlm1961@hotmail.co.uk]	01355 234196
32	**East Kilbride: Old (H) (01355 279004)** Anne S. Paton BA BD	2001	40 Maxwell Drive, East Kilbride, Glasgow G74 4HJ [E-mail: annepaton@fsmail.net]	01355 220732
33	**East Kilbride: South (H)** Sandra Black (Mrs) BSc BD (Interim Minister)	1988 2013	36 Glencairn Drive, Glasgow G41 4PW [E-mail: revsblack@btinternet.com]	0141-423 4000
34	**East Kilbride: Stewartfield (New Charge Development)** Douglas W. Wallace MA BD	1981 2001	8 Thistle Place, Stewartfield, East Kilbride, Glasgow G74 4RH	01355 260879
35	**East Kilbride: West (H)** Mahboob Masih BA MDiv MTh	1999 2008	4 East Milton Grove, East Kilbride, Glasgow G75 8FN [E-mail: m_masih@sky.com]	01355 224469
36	**East Kilbride: Westwood (H) (01355 245657)** Kevin Mackenzie BD DPS	1989 1996	16 Inglewood Crescent, East Kilbride, Glasgow G75 8QD [E-mail: kevin@westwoodmanse.freeserve.co.uk]	01355 223992
37	**Glassford linked with Strathaven: East** William T. Stewart BD	1980	68 Townhead Street, Strathaven ML10 6DJ	01357 521138
38	**Greengairs** See Airdrie: New Monkland			
39	**Hamilton: Cadzow (H) (01698 428695)** John Carswell BS MDiv	1996 2009	3 Carlisle Road, Hamilton ML3 7BZ [E-mail: revcarswell@gmail.com]	01698 426682
40	**Hamilton: Gilmour and Whitehill (H) linked with West** Vacant			

41	**Hamilton: Hillhouse** Vacant			66 Wellhall Road, Hamilton ML3 9BY	01698 422300
42	**Hamilton: Old (H) (01698 281905)** Vacant			1 Chateau Grove, Hamilton ML3 7DS (This congregation has united with the congregation of Hamilton: North)	01698 422511
43	**Hamilton: St John's (H) (01698 283492)** Joanne C. Hood (Miss) MA BD	2003	2012	9 Shearer Avenue, Ferniegair, Hamilton ML3 7FX [E-mail: hood137@btinternet.com]	01698 425002
44	**Hamilton: South (H) (01698 281014) linked with Quarter** Donald R. Lawrie		2012	The Manse, Limekilnburn Road, Quarter, Hamilton ML3 7XA	01698 424511
45	**Hamilton: Trinity (01698 284254)** S Lindsay A Turnbull BSc BD		2014	69 Buchan Street, Hamilton ML3 8JY [E-mail: lindsayturnbull@churchofscotland.org.uk]	01698 284919
46	**Hamilton: West (H) (01698 284670)** See Hamilton: Gilmore and Whitehill				
47	**Holytown linked with New Stevenston: Wrangholm Kirk** Caryl A.E. Kyle (Mrs) BD DipEd		2008	The Manse, 260 Edinburgh Road, Holytown, Motherwell ML1 5RU [E-mail: caryl_kyle@hotmail.com]	01698 832622
48	**Kirk o' Shotts (H)** Vacant			The Manse, Kirk o' Shotts, Salsburgh, Shotts ML7 4NS	01698 870208
49	**Larkhall: Chalmers (H)** Andrea M. Boyes		2013	Quarry Road, Larkhall ML9 1HH	01698 882238
50	**Larkhall: St Machan's (H)** Alastair McKillop BD DipMin	1995	2004	2 Orchard Gate, Larkhall ML9 1HG [E-mail: revicar@blueyonder.co.uk]	01698 321976
51	**Larkhall: Trinity** Lindsay Schluter ThE CertMin PhD		1995	13 Machan Avenue, Larkhall ML9 2HE [E-mail: lindsay.schluter@o2.co.uk]	01698 881401

52 Motherwell: Crosshill (H) linked with Motherwell: St Margaret's
Gavin W.G. Black BD — 2006 — 15 Orchard Street, Motherwell ML1 3JE — [E-mail: gavin.black12@blueyonder.co.uk] — 01698 263410

53 Motherwell: Dalziel St Andrew's (H) (01698 264097)
Derek W. Hughes BSc BD DipEd — 1990 1996 — 4 Pollock Street, Motherwell ML1 1LP — [E-mail: derekthecleric@btinternet.com] — 01698 263414

54 Motherwell: North
Derek H.N. Pope BD — 1987 1995 — 35 Birrens Road, Motherwell ML1 3NS — [E-mail: derekpopemotherwell@hotmail.com] — 01698 266716

55 Motherwell: St Margaret's See Motherwell: Crosshill

56 Motherwell: St Mary's (H)
Vacant — 19 Orchard Street, Motherwell ML1 3JE

57 Motherwell: South (H)
Vacant — 62 Manse Road, Motherwell ML1 2PT — 01698 239245

58 Newarthill and Carfin
Elaine W. McKinnon MA BD — 1988 2014 — Church Street, Newarthill, Motherwell ML1 5HS — [E-mail: elaine.mckinnon@me.com] — 01698 296850

59 Newmains: Bonkle (H) linked with Newmains: Coltness Memorial (H)
Graham Raeburn MTh — 2004 — 5 Kirkgate, Newmains, Wishaw ML2 9BT — [E-mail: grahamraeburn@tiscali.co.uk] — 01698 383858

60 Newmains: Coltness Memorial See Newmains: Bonkle

61 New Stevenston: Wrangholm Kirk See Holytown

62 Overtown
Bruce H. Sinclair BA BD — 2009 — The Manse, 146 Main Street, Overtown, Wishaw ML2 0QP — [E-mail: brucehsinclair@btinternet.com] — 01698 352090

63 Quarter See Hamilton: South

64 Shotts: Calderhead Erskine
Allan B. Brown BD MTh   1995   2010   The Manse, 9 Kirk Road, Shotts ML7 5ET   01501 823204
07578 448655 (Mbl)

65 Stonehouse: St Ninian's (H)
Paul G.R. Grant BD MTh   2003   4 Hamilton Way, Stonehouse, Larkhall ML9 3PU   01698 792587
[E-mail: minister@st-ninians-stonehouse.org.uk]
Stonehouse: St Ninian's is a Local Ecumenical Partnership shared with the United Reformed Church

66 Strathaven: Avendale Old and Drumclog (H) (01357 529748)
Alan B. Telfer BA BD   1983   2010   4 Fortrose Gardens, Strathaven ML10 6SH   01357 523031
[E-mail: minister@avendale-drumclog.com]

67 Strathaven: East See Glassford

68 Strathaven: Rankin See Chapelton

69 Uddingston: Burnhead (H)
Les Brunger BD   2010   90 Laburnum Road, Uddingston, Glasgow G71 5DB   01698 813716
[E-mail: lesbrunger@hotmail.co.uk]

70 Uddingston: Old (H) (01698 814015)
Fiona L.J. McKibbin (Mrs) MA BD   2011   1 Belmont Avenue, Uddingston, Glasgow G71 7AX   01698 814757
[E-mail: fionamckibbin@sky.com]

71 Uddingston: Viewpark (H)
Michael G. Lyall BD   1993   2001   14 Holmbrae Road, Uddingston, Glasgow G71 6AP   01698 813113
[E-mail: michaellyall@blueyonder.co.uk]

72 Wishaw: Cambusnethan North (H)
Mhorag Macdonald (Ms) MA BD   1989   350 Kirk Road, Wishaw ML2 8LH   01698 381305
[E-mail: mhoragmacdonald@btinternet.com]

73 Wishaw: Cambusnethan Old and Morningside
Iain C. Murdoch MA LLB DipEd BD   1995   22 Coronation Street, Wishaw ML2 8LF   01698 384235
[E-mail: iaincmurdoch@btopenworld.com]

74 Wishaw: Craigneuk and Belhaven (H) linked with Wishaw: Old
Vacant   130 Glen Road, Wishaw ML2 7NP   01698 375134

75 Wishaw: Old (H) (01698 376080) See Wishaw: Craigneuk and Belhaven

76 Wishaw: St Mark's See Cleland

77 Wishaw: South Wishaw (H)
Vacant
3 Walter Street, Wishaw ML2 8LQ   01698 387292

Name	Position / (Former Charge)			Address	Tel
Barrie, Arthur P. LTh	(Hamilton: Cadzow)	1973	2007	30 Airbles Crescent, Motherwell ML1 3AR [E-mail: elizabethbarrie@ymail.com]	01698 261147
Baxendale, Georgina M. (Mrs) BD	(Motherwell: South)	1981	2014	32 Meadowhead Road, Plains, Airdrie ML6 7HG [E-mail: georgiebaxendale6@tiscali.co.uk]	
Buck, Maxine	Auxiliary Minister	2007		Brownlee House, Mauldslie Road, Carluke ML8 5HW [E-mail: maxinebuck01@aol.com]	01555 759063
Colvin, Sharon E.F. (Mrs) BD LRAM LTCL	(Airdrie: Jackson)	1985	2007	25 Balblair Road, Airdrie ML6 6GQ [E-mail: dibleycol@hotmail.com]	01236 590796
Cook, J. Stanley BD Dip PSS	(Hamilton: West)	1974	2001	Mansend, 137A Old Manse Road, Netherton, Wishaw ML2 0EW [E-mail: stancook@blueyonder.co.uk]	01698 299600
Cullen, William T. BA LTh	(Kilmarnock: St John's Onthank)	1984	1996	6 Laurel Wynd, Cambuslang, Glasgow G72 7BA	0141-641 4337
Currie, David E.P. BSc BD	(Congregational Development Consultant)	1983	2012		
Currie, R. David BSc BD	(Cambuslang: Flemington Hallside)	1984	2004	69 Kethers Street, Motherwell ML1 3HN	01698 323424
Davidson, Amelia (Mrs) BD	(Coatbridge: Calder)	2004	2011	11 St Mary's Place, Saltcoats KA21 5NY	
Dick, Roddy S.	Auxiliary Minister	2010		27 Easter Crescent, Wishaw ML2 8XB [E-mail: roddy.dick@btopenworld.com]	01698 383453
Doyle, David W. MA BD	(Motherwell: St Mary's)	1977	2014	76 Kethers Street, Motherwell ML1 3HN	01698 263472
Dunn, W. Stuart LTh	(Motherwell: Crosshill)	1970	2006	10 Macrostie Gardens, Crieff PH7 4LP	01764 655178
Fraser, James P.	(Strathaven: Avendale Old and Drumclog)	1951	1988	26 Hamilton Road, Strathaven ML10 6JA	01357 522758
Gordon, Alasdair B. BD LLB EdD	(Aberdeen: Summerhill)	1970	1980	Flat 1, 13 Auchingramont Road, Hamilton ML3 6JP [E-mail: alasdairbgordon@hotmail.com]	01698 200561 (Mbl) 07768 897843
Grier, James BD	(Coatbridge: Middle)	1991	2005	14 Love Drive, Bellshill ML4 1BY	01698 742545
Hunter, James E. LTh	(Blantyre: Livingstone Memorial)	1974	1997	57 Dalwhinnie Avenue, Blantyre, Glasgow G72 9NQ	01698 826177
Jackson, John A. BD	(Cleland)	1997	2014	49 Lesmahagow Road, Boghead, Lesmahagow ML11 0JA [E-mail: johnajackson932@btinternet.com]	01555 890596
Kent, Robert M. MA BD	(Hamilton: St John's)	1973	2011	48 Fyne Crescent, Larkhall ML9 2UX [E-mail: robertmkent@talktalk.net]	01698 769244
Lusk, Alastair S. BD	(East Kilbride: Moncreiff)	1974	2010	9 MacFie Place, Stewartfield, East Kilbride, Glasgow G74 4TY	
McAlpine, John BSc	(Auxiliary Minister)	1988	2004	Braeside, 201 Bonkle Road, Newmains, Wishaw ML2 9AA	01698 384610
McCabe, George	(Airdrie: High)	1963	1996	8 Bonaly Road, Edinburgh EH13 0EA	
McCracken, Gordon A. BD CertMin DMin	Presbytery Clerk	1988	2015		
McDonald, John A. MA BD	(Cumbernauld: Condorrat)	1978	1997	17 Thomson Drive, Bellshill ML4 3ND	
McKee, Norman B. BD	(Uddingston: Old)	1987	2010	148 Station Road, Blantyre, Glasgow G72 9BW [E-mail: normanmckee946@btinternet.com]	01698 827358

Name	Years	Role / Parish	Address	Telephone
MacKenzie, Ian C. MA BD	1970 2011	(Interim Minister)	21 Wilson Street, Motherwell ML1 1NP [E-mail: iancmac@blueyonder.co.uk]	01698 301230
McKenzie, Raymond D. BD	1978 2012	(Hamilton: Burnbank with Hamilton: North)	25 Austine Drive, Hamilton ML3 7YE [E-mail: rdmackenzie@hotmail.co.uk]	
MacLeod, Norman BTh	1999 2013	(Hamilton: St Andrew's)	15 Bent Road, Hamilton ML3 6QB	01698 283264
McPherson, D. Cameron BSc BD DMin	1982 2015	(Dalserf)	6 Moa Court, Blackwood, Lanark ML11 9GF [E-mail: revcam@btinternet.com]	(Mbl) 07852 123956
Martin, James MA BD DD	1946 1987	(Glasgow: High Carntyne)	9 Magnolia Street, Wishaw ML2 7EQ	01698 385825
Melrose, J.H. Loudon MA BD MEd	1955 1996	(Gourock: Old Gourock and Ashton [Assoc])	1 Laverock Avenue, Hamilton ML3 7DD	01698 427958
Moore, Agnes A. (Miss) BD	1987 2014	(Bellshill: West)	10 Carr Quadrant, Mossend, Bellshill ML4 1HZ [E-mail: revamoore2@tiscali.co.uk]	01698 841558
Munton, James G. BA	1969 2002	(Coatbridge: Old Monkland)	2 Moorcroft Drive, Airdrie ML6 8ES [E-mail: jacjim@supanet.com]	01236 754848
Murphy, Jim	2014	Ordained Local Minister	10 Hilview Crescent, Bellshill ML4 1NX [E-mail: jim.murphy5@btopenworld.com]	01698 740189
Price, Peter O. CBE QHC BA FPhS	1960 1996	(Blantyre: Old)	22 Old Bothwell Road, Bothwell, Glasgow G71 8AW [E-mail: peteroprice@aol.com]	01698 854032
Rogerson, Stuart D. BSc BD	1980 2001	(Strathaven: West)	17 Westfield Park, Strathaven ML10 6XH [E-mail: srogerson@cnetwork.co.uk]	01357 523321
Ross, Keith W. MA BD	1984 2007	Congregational Development Officer for the Presbytery of Hamilton	Easter Bavelaw House, Pentland Hills Regional Park, Balerno EH14 7JS [E-mail: keithross.hamiltonpresbytery@googlemail.com]	(Mbl) 07855 163449
Salmond, James S. BA BD MTh ThD	1979 2003	(Holytown)	165 Torbothie Road, Shotts ML7 5NE	01698 870598
Spence, Sheila M. (Mrs) MA BD	1979 2010	(Kirk o' Shotts)	6 Drumbowie Crescent, Salsburgh, Shotts ML7 4NP	
Stevenson, John LTh	1998 2006	(Cambuslang: St Andrew's)	20 Knowehead Gardens, Uddingston, Glasgow G71 7PY [E-mail therev20@sky.com]	01698 817582
Thomson, John M.A. TD JP BD ThM	1978 2014	(Hamilton: Old)	8 Skylands Place, Hamilton ML3 8SB [E-mail: jt@john1949.plus.com]	01698 422511
Thorne, Leslie W. BA LTh	1987 2001	(Coatbridge: Clifton)	'Hatherleigh', 9 Chatton Walk, Coatbridge ML5 4FH [E-mail: lesthorne@tiscali.co.uk]	01236 432241 (Mbl) 07963 199921
Waddell, Elizabeth A. (Mrs) BD	1999 2014	(Hamilton: West)	114 Branchalfield, Wishaw ML2 8QD [E-mail: elizabethwaddell@tiscali.co.uk]	01698 382909
Wilson, James H. LTh	1970 1996	(Cleland)	21 Austine Drive, Hamilton ML3 7YE [E-mail: wilsonjh@blueyonder.co.uk]	01698 457042
Wyllie, Hugh R. MA DD FCIBS	1962 2000	(Hamilton: Old)	18 Chantinghall Road, Hamilton ML3 8NP	01698 420002
Zambonini, James LlADip	1997	Auxiliary Minister	100 Old Manse Road, Wishaw ML2 0EP	01698 350889

HAMILTON ADDRESSES

Airdrie
Broomknoll — Broomknoll Street
Clarkston — Forrest Street
Flowerhill — 89 Graham Street
High — North Bridge Street
Jackson — Glen Road
New Monkland — Glenmavis
St Columba's — Thrashbush Road
The New Wellwynd — Wellwynd

Coatbridge
Blairhill Dundyvan — Blairhill Street
Calder — Calder Street
Middle — Bank Street
New St Andrew's — Church Street
Old Monkland — Woodside Street
Townhead — Crinan Crescent

East Kilbride
Claremont — High Common Road, St Leonard's

Greenhills — Greenhills Centre
Moncreiff — Calderwood Road
Mossneuk — Eden Drive
Old — Montgomery Street
South — Baird Hill, Murray
West — Kittoch Street
Westwood — Belmont Drive, Westwood

Hamilton
Cadzow — Woodside Walk
Gilmour and — Glasgow Road, Burnbank
Whitehill — Abbotsford Road, Whitehill
Hillhouse — Clerkwell Road
Old — Leechlee Road
St John's — Duke Street
South — Strathaven Road
Trinity — Neilsland Square off Neilsland Road
West — Burnbank Road

Motherwell
Crosshill — Windmillhill Street x Airbles Street
Dalziel St Andrew's — Merry Street and Muir Street

North — Chesters Crescent
St Margaret's — Shields Road
St Mary's — Avon Street
South — Gavin Street

Uddingston
Burnhead — Laburnum Road
Old — Old Glasgow Road
Viewpark — Old Edinburgh Road

Wishaw
Cambusnethan North — Kirk Road
Old — Kirk Road
Craigneuk and Belhaven — Craigneuk Street
Old — Main Street
St Mark's — Coltness Road
South Wishaw — East Academy Street

(18) DUMBARTON

Meets at Dumbarton, in Riverside Church Halls, on the first Tuesday of February, March, April (if required), May (if required), June, September, October (if required), November and December; and on the third Tuesday of June at the incoming Moderator's church for the installation of the Moderator.

Clerk: REV. DAVID W. CLARK MA BD   3 Ritchie Avenue, Cardross, Dumbarton G82 5LL   **01389 849319**
[E-mail: dumbarton@churchofscotland.org.uk]

Alexandria
Elizabeth W. Houston MA BD DipEd   1985   1995   32 Ledrish Avenue, Balloch, Alexandria G83 8JB   01389 751933
[E-mail: cleric2@hotmail.com]

Arrochar linked with Luss
Vacant   The Manse, Luss, Alexandria G83 8NZ   01436 860240

Charge / Minister	Ord.	Ind./Adm.	Address & E-mail	Tel.
Baldernock (H) Andrew P. Lees BD	1984	2002	The Manse, Bardowie, Milngavie, Glasgow G62 6ES [E-mail: andrew.lees@yahoo.co.uk]	01360 620471
Bearsden: Baljaffray (H) Ian McEwan BSc PhD BD FRSE	2008		5 Fintry Gardens, Bearsden, Glasgow G61 4RJ [E-mail: mcewan7@btinternet.com]	0141-942 0366
Bearsden: Cross (H) Graeme R. Wilson MCIBS BD ThM	2006	2013	61 Drymen Road, Bearsden, Glasgow G61 2SU [E-mail: graeme.wilson@gmail.com]	0141-942 0507
Bearsden: Killermont (H) Alan J. Hamilton LLB BD PhD	2003		8 Clathic Avenue, Bearsden, Glasgow G61 2HF [E-mail: ajh63@sky.com]	0141-942 0021
Bearsden: New Kilpatrick (H) (0141-942 8827) (E-mail: mail@nkchurch.org.uk) Roderick G. Hamilton MA BD	1992	2011	51 Manse Road, Bearsden, Glasgow G61 3PN [E-mail: rghamilton@ntlworld.com]	0141-942 0035
Bearsden: Westerton Fairlie Memorial (H) (0141-942 6960) Christine M. Goldie LLB BD MTh DMin	1984	2008	3 Canniesburn Road, Bearsden, Glasgow G61 1PW [E-mail: christine.goldie12@btinternet.com]	0141-942 2672
Bonhill (H) (01389 756516) linked with Renton: Trinity (H) Vacant			1 Glebe Gardens, Bonhill, Alexandria G83 9NZ	
Cardross (H) (01389 841322) Vacant				
Clydebank: Abbotsford linked with Dalmuir: Barclay (0141-941 3988) Ruth Morrison MA BD	2009	2014	16 Parkhall Road, Dalmuir, Clydebank G81 3RJ [E-mail: ruthie225@hotmail.com]	0141-941 3317
Clydebank: Faifley Gregor McIntyre BSc BD	1991		Kirklea, Cochno Road, Hardgate, Clydebank G81 6PT [E-mail: mail@gregormcintyre.com]	01389 876836

Clydebank: Kilbowie St Andrew's linked with Clydebank: Radnor Park (H)
Margaret J.B. Yule BD   1992   11 Tiree Gardens, Old Kilpatrick, Glasgow G60 5AT   01389 875599
[E-mail: mjbyule@yahoo.co.uk]

Clydebank: Radnor Park See Clydebank: Kilbowie St Andrew's

Clydebank: St Cuthbert's linked with Duntocher (H)
Guardianship of the Presbytery

Craigrownie linked with Garelochhead (01436 810589) linked with Rosneath: St Modan's (H)
Christine Murdoch   1999   2015   The Manse, Argyll Road, Kilcreggan, Helensburgh G84 0JW   01436 842274
[E-mail: cmurdoch@churchofscotland.org.uk]   07973 331890 (Mbl)

Dalmuir: Barclay See Clydebank: Abbotsford

Dumbarton: Riverside (H) (01389 742551) linked with Dumbarton: West Kirk (H)
C. Ian W. Johnson MA BD   1997   2014   18 Castle Road, Dumbarton G82 1JF   01389 726685
[E-mail: ian.ciw.johnson@btinternet.com]

Dumbarton: St Andrew's (H) linked with Old Kilpatrick Bowling
Vacant   17 Mansewood Drive, Dumbarton G82 3EU   01389 726715

Dumbarton: West Kirk See Dumbarton: Riverside
Duntocher See Clydebank: St Cuthbert's
Garelochhead See Craigrownie

Helensburgh linked with Rhu and Shandon
Vacant   35 East Argyle Street, Helensburgh G84 7EL
(Helensburgh is a new charge formed by the union of Helensburgh: Park and Helensburgh: St Andrew's Kirk)

Jamestown (H)
Norma Moore MA BD   1995   2004   26 Kessog's Gardens, Balloch, Alexandria G83 8QJ   01389 756447
[E-mail: norma-moore@sky.com]

Kilmaronock Gartocharn
Guardianship of the Presbytery

Luss See Arrochar

Milngavie: Cairns (H) (0141-956 4868)
Andrew Frater BA BD MTh — 1987 1994 — 4 Cairns Drive, Milngavie, Glasgow G62 8AJ [E-mail: office@cairnschurch.org.uk] — 0141-956 1717

Milngavie: St Luke's (0141-956 4226)
Ramsay B. Shields BA BD — 1990 1997 — 70 Hunter Road, Milngavie, Glasgow G62 7BY [E-mail: rbs@minister.com] — 0141-577 9171 (Tel) / 0141-577 9181 (Fax)

Milngavie: St Paul's (H) (0141-956 4405)
Fergus C. Buchanan MA BD MTh — 1982 1988 — 8 Buchanan Street, Milngavie, Glasgow G62 8DD [E-mail: f.c.buchanan@ntlworld.com] — 0141-956 1043

Old Kilpatrick Bowling See Dumbarton: St Andrew's
Renton: Trinity See Bonhill
Rhu and Shandon See Helensburgh
Rosneath: St Modan's See Craigrownie

Booth, Frederick M. LTh	1970 2005	(Helensburgh: St Columba)	Achnashie Coach House, Clynder, Helensburgh G84 0QD [E-mail: boothef@btinternet.com]	01436 831858
Christie, John C. BSc BD MSB CBiol	1990 2014	(Interim Minister)	10 Cumberland Avenue, Helensburgh G84 8QG [E-mail: rev.jcc@btinternet.com]	01436 674078 (Mbl) 07711 336392
Clark, David W. MA BD	1975 2014	(Helensburgh: St Andrew's Kirk with Rhu and Shandon)	3 Ritchie Avenue, Cardross, Dumbarton G82 5LL [E-mail: clarkdw@talktalk.net]	01389 849319
Crombie, William D. MA BD	1947 1987	(Glasgow: Calton New with St Andrew's)	9 Fairview Court, 46 Main Street, Milngavie, Glasgow G62 6BU	0141-956 1898
Dalton, Mark BD DipMin RN	2002	Chaplain: Royal Navy	HM Naval Base Clyde, Faslane, Helensburgh G84 8HL [E-mail: mark.dalton242@mod.uk]	01436 674321 ext. 6216
Donaghy, Leslie G. BD DipMin PGCE FSAScot	1990 2004	(Dumbarton: St Andrew's)	53 Oak Avenue, East Kilbride, Glasgow G75 9ED [E-mail: leslie@donaghy.org.uk]	(Mbl) 07809 484812
Ferguson, Archibald M. MSc PhD CEng FRINA	1989 2004	(Auxiliary Minister)	The Whins, 2 Borrowfield, Station Road, Cardross, Dumbarton G82 5NL [E-mail: drarchieferguson@gmail.com]	01389 841517
Hamilton, David G. MA BD	1971 2004	(Braes of Rannoch with Foss and Rannoch)	79 Finlay Rise, Milngavie, Glasgow G62 6QL [E-mail: davidhamilton40@googlemail.com]	0141-956 4202
Harris, John W.F. MA	1967 2012	(Bearsden: Cross)	68 Mitre Road, Glasgow G14 9LL [E-mail: jwfh@sky.com]	0141-321 1061
Hudson, Eric V. LTh	1971 2007	(Bearsden: Westerton Fairlie Memorial)	2 Murrayfield Drive, Bearsden, Glasgow G61 1JE [E-mail: evhudson@hotmail.co.uk]	0141-942 6110

Kemp, Tina MA	2005		Auxiliary Minister	12 Oaktree Gardens, Dumbarton G82 1EU [E-mail: tinakemp@blueyonder.co.uk]	01389 730477
McCutcheon, John	2014		Ordained Local Minister	Flat 2/6 Parkview, Milton Brae, Milton, Dumbarton G82 2TT [E-mail: JMccuuc933@aol.com]	01389 739034
McIntyre, J. Ainslie MA BD	1963	1984	(University of Glasgow)	60 Bonnaughton Road, Bearsden, Glasgow G61 4DB [E-mail: jamcintyre@hotmail.com]	0141-942 5143 (Mbl) 07826 013266
Miller, Ian H. BA BD	1975	2012	(Bonhill)	Derand, Queen Street, Alexandria G83 0AS [E-mail: reviamiller@btinternet.com]	01389 753039
Munro, David P. MA BD STM	1953	1996	(Bearsden: North)	14 Birch Road, Killearn, Glasgow G63 9SQ [E-mail: david.munro1929@btinternet.com]	01360 550098
Nutter, Margaret	2014		Ordained Local Minister	Kilmorich, 14 Balloch Road, Balloch, Alexandria G83 8SR [E-mail: mnutter@blueyonder.co.uk]	01389 754505
O'Donnell, Barbara BD PGSE	2007		Auxiliary Minister	Ashbank, 258 Main Street, Alexandria G83 0NU	01389 752356 (Mbl) 07889 251912
Ramage, Alastair E. MA BA ADB CertEd	1996		Auxiliary Minister	16 Claremont Gardens, Milngavie, Glasgow G62 6PG [E-mail: sueandalastairramage@btinternet.com]	0141-956 2897
Robertson, Ishbel A.R. MA BD	2013		Ordained Local Minister	Oakdene, 81 Bonhill Road, Dumbarton G82 2DU [E-mail: ishbelrobertson@blueyonder.co.uk]	01389 763436
Speed, David K. LTh	1969	2004	(Glasgow: Shettleston Old)	153 West Princes Street, Helensburgh G84 8EZ [E-mail: dkspeed@btinternet.com]	01436 674493
Steven, Harold A.M. MStJ LTh FSA Scot	1970	2001	(Baldernock)	9 Cairnhill Road, Bearsden, Glasgow G61 1AT [E-mail: harold.allison.steven@gmail.com]	0141-942 1598
Stewart, Charles E. BSc BD MTh PhD	1976	2000	(Chaplain of the Fleet)	105 Sinclair Street, Helensburgh G84 9HY [E-mail: c.e.stewart@btinternet.com]	01436 678113
West, Richard B.	1994	2013	(Craigrownie with Rosneath: St Modan's)	Carriden, Shore Road, Kilcreggan, Helensburgh G84 0HG [E-mail: rickangelawest@yahoo.co.uk]	(Mbl) 07751 834832
Wright, Malcolm LTh	1970	2003	(Craigrownie with Rosneath: St Modan's)	30 Clairinsh, Drumkinnon Gate, Balloch, Alexandria G83 8SE [E-mail: malcolmcatherine@msn.com]	01389 720338

DUMBARTON ADDRESSES

Bearsden
Baljaffray — Grampian Way
Cross — Drymen Road
Killermont — Rannoch Drive
New Kilpatrick — Manse Road
Westerton — Crarae Avenue

Clydebank
Abbotsford — Town Centre

Faifley — Faifley Road
Kilbowie St Andrew's — Kilbowie Road
Radnor Park — Radnor Street
St Cuthbert's — Limnvale

Dumbarton
Riverside — High Street
St Andrew's — Arkenbar Circle
West Kirk — West Bridgend

Helensburgh — Colquhoun Square

Milngavie
Cairns — Buchanan Street
St Luke's — Kirk Street
St Paul's — Strathblane Road

(19) ARGYLL

Meets in the Village Hall, Tarbert, Loch Fyne, Argyll on the first Tuesday or Wednesday of March, June, September and December. For details, contact the Presbytery Clerk.

| Clerk: | DR CHRISTOPHER T. BRETT MA PhD | Minahey Cottage, Kames, Tighnabruaich PA21 2AD [E-mail: argyll@churchofscotland.org.uk] | 01700 811142 |
| Treasurer: | MRS PAMELA A. GIBSON | Allt Ban, Portsonachan, Dalmally PA33 1BJ [E-mail: justpam1@tesco.net] | 01866 833344 |

Appin linked with Lismore
Vacant — The Manse, Appin PA38 4DD — 01631 730143

Ardchattan (H)
Jeffrey A. McCormick BD — 1984 — Ardchattan Manse, North Connel, Oban PA37 1RG [E-mail: jeff.mcc@virgin.net] — 01631 710364

Ardrishaig (H) linked with South Knapdale
David Carruthers BD — 1998 — The Manse, Park Road, Ardrishaig, Lochgilphead PA30 8HE — 01546 603269

Barra (GD) linked with South Uist (GD)
Vacant — Cuithir, Castlebay, Isle of Barra HS9 5XD — 01871 810230

Campbeltown: Highland (H)
Vacant — Highland Church Manse, Kirk Street, Campbeltown PA28 6BN — 01586 551146

Campbeltown: Lorne and Lowland (H)
Philip D. Wallace BSc BTh DTS — 1998 — 2004 — Lorne and Lowland Manse, Castlehill, Campbeltown PA28 6AN [E-mail: pdwallace10@btinternet.com] — 01586 552468

Coll linked with Connel
George G. Cringles BD — 1981 — 2002 — St Oran's Manse, Connel, Oban PA37 1PJ [E-mail: george.cringles@btinternet.com] — (Connel) 01631 710242 / (Coll) 01879 230366

Colonsay and Oronsay (Website: www.islandchurches.org.uk)
Vacant

Connel See Coll

Craignish linked with Kilbrandon and Kilchattan linked with Kilninver and Kilmelford (Netherlorn)
Kenneth R. Ross BA BD PhD   1982   2010   The Manse, Kilmelford, Oban PA34 4XA   01852 200565
                                                    [E-mail: kenneth.ross@btinternet.com]

Cumlodden, Lochfyneside and Lochgair linked with Glenaray and Inveraray (West Lochfyneside)
Vacant   The Manse, Inveraray PA32 8XT   01499 302060

Dunoon: St John's linked with Kirn (H) linked with Sandbank (H) (Central Cowal)
Vacant   The Manse, 13 Dhailling Park, Hunter Street, Kirn, Dunoon   01369 702256
                                                    PA23 8FB
Glenda M. Wilson (Mrs) DCS   5 Allan Terrace, Sandbank, Dunoon PA23 8PR   01369 704168
                                                    [E-mail: deacglendamwilson@gmail.com]

Dunoon: The High Kirk (H) linked with Innellan (H) linked with Toward (H) (South-East Cowal)
Aileen M. Robson (Miss) BD   2003   2011   7A Mathieson Lane, Innellan, Dunoon PA23 7SH   01369 830276
                                                    [E-mail: am65robson@ymail.com]
Ruth I. Griffiths (Mrs) (Aux)   2004   Kirkwood, Mathieson Lane, Innellan, Dunoon PA23 7TA   01369 830145
                                                    [E-mail: ruthigriffiths@googlemail.com]

Gigha and Cara (H) (GD) linked with Kilcalmonell linked with Killean and Kilchenzie (H)
Vacant   The Manse, Muasdale, Tarbert, Argyll PA29 6XD   01583 421432

Glassary, Kilmartin and Ford linked with North Knapdale
Clifford R. Acklam BD MTh   1997   2010   The Manse, Kilmichael Glassary, Lochgilphead PA31 8QA   01546 606926
                                                    [E-mail: clifford.acklam@btinternet.com]

Glenaray and Inveraray See Cumlodden, Lochfyneside and Lochgair

Glenorchy and Innishael linked with Strathfillan
Vacant   The Manse, Dalmally PA33 1AA   01838 200207

Innellan See Dunoon: The High Kirk

Iona linked with Kilfinichen and Kilvickeon and the Ross of Mull
Vacant   The Manse, Bunessan, Isle of Mull PA67 6DW   01681 700227

Jura (GD) linked with Kilarrow (H) linked with Kildalton and Oa (GD) (H)
Vacant   The Manse, Bowmore, Isle of Islay PA43 7LH   01496 810271

Kilarrow See Jura
Kilbrandon and Kilchattan See Craignish
Kilcalmonell See Gigha and Cara

Kilchoman (GD) linked with Kilmeny linked with Portnahaven (GD)
Valerie G.C. Watson MA BD STM   1987   2013   The Manse, Port Charlotte, Isle of Islay PA48 7TW   01496 850241
                                                  [E-mail: vgcwatson@btinternet.com]

Kilchrenan and Dalavich linked with Muckairn
Robert E. Brookes BD   2009   Muckairn Manse, Taynuilt PA35 1HW   01866 822204
                                           [E-mail: eilanview@uwclub.net]

Kildalton and Oa See Jura

Kilfinan linked with Kilmodan and Colintraive linked with Kyles (H) (West Cowal)
David Mitchell BD DipPTheol MSc   1988   2006   West Cowal Manse, Kames, Tighnabruaich PA21 2AD   01700 811045
                                                    [E-mail: revdmitchell@icloud.com]

Kilfinichen and Kilvickeon and the Ross of Mull See Iona
Killean and Kilchenzie See Gigha and Cara
Kilmeny See Kilchoman
Kilmodan and Colintraive See Kilfinan

Kilmore (GD) and Oban (Website: www.obanchurch.com)
Dugald J.R. Cameron BD DipMin MTh   1990   2007   Kilmore and Oban Manse, Ganavan Road, Oban PA34 5TU   01631 566253
                                                      [E-mail: obancofs@btinternet.com]
Christine Fulcher BEd   2012   2014   St Blaan's Manse, Southend, Campbeltown PA28 6RQ   01586 830504
  (Ordained Local Minister)   [E-mail: chris@pcmanse.plus.com]

Kilmun (St Munn's) (H) linked with Strone (H) and Ardentinny
David Mill KJSJ MA BD   1978   2010   The Manse, Blairmore, Dunoon PA23 8TE   01369 840313
                                                     [E-mail: revandevmill@aol.com]

Kilninian and Kilmore linked with Salen (H) and Ulva linked with Tobermory (GD) (H)
linked with Torosay (H) and Kinlochspelvie (North Mull)
John H. Paton BSc BD   1983   2013   The Manse, Gruline Road, Salen, Aros, Isle of Mull PA72 6XF   01680 300001
                                                             [E-mail: jpaton160@btinternet.com]

Kilninver and Kilmelford See Craignish
Kirn See Dunoon: St John's
Kyles See Kilfinan
Lismore See Appin

Lochgilphead   1992   2005   Parish Church Manse, Manse Brae, Lochgilphead PA31 8QZ   01546 602238
Hilda C. Smith (Miss) MA BD MSc   [E-mail: hilda.smith2@btinternet.com]

Lochgoilhead (H) and Kilmorich linked with Strachur and Strathlachlan (Upper Cowal)
Robert K. Mackenzie MA BD PhD   1976   1998   The Manse, Strachur, Cairndow PA27 8DG   01369 860246
                                                             [E-mail: rkmackenzie@strachurmanse.fsnet.co.uk]

Muckairn See Kilchrenan and Dalavich
North Knapdale See Glassary, Kilmartin and Ford
Portnahaven See Kilchoman

Rothesay: Trinity (H) (Website: www.rothesaytrinity.org)
Drew Barrie BSc BD   1984   2010   12 Crichton Road, Rothesay, Isle of Bute PA20 9JR   01700 503010
                                                             [E-mail: drew.barrie@btinternet.com]

Saddell and Carradale (H) linked with Southend (H)
Stephen Fulcher BA MA   1993   2012   St Blaan's Manse, Southend, Campbeltown PA28 6RQ   01586 830504
                                                             [E-mail: steve@pcmanse.plus.com]

Salen and Ulva See Kilninian and Kilmore
Sandbank See Dunoon: St John's

Skipness
Vacant

Southend See Saddell and Carradale
South Knapdale See Ardrishaig
South Uist See Barra
Strachur and Strathlachlan See Lochgoilhead and Kilmorich
Strathfillan See Glenorchy and Innishael
Strone and Ardentinny See Kilmun

Tarbert, Loch Fyne and Kilberry (H)
Vacant   The Manse, Campbeltown Road, Tarbert, Argyll PA29 6SX   01880 821012

The United Church of Bute
John Owain Jones MA BD FSAScot   1981 2011   10 Bishop Terrace, Rothesay, Isle of Bute PA20 9HF   01700 504502
[E-mail: johnowainjones@ntlworld.com]

Tiree (GD)
Elspeth J. MacLean (Mrs) BVMS BD   2011   The Manse, Scarinish, Isle of Tiree PA77 6TN   01879 220377
[E-mail: ejmaclean@yahoo.co.uk]

Tobermory See Kilninian and Kilmore
Torosay and Kinlochspelvie See Kilninian and Kilmore
Toward See Dunoon: The High Kirk

Beautyman, Paul H. MA BD	1993	2009	Youth Adviser	130b John Street, Dunoon PA23 7BN [E-mail: paul.beautyman@argyll-bute.gov.uk]	(Mbl) 07596 164112
Bell, Douglas W. MA LLB BD	1975	1993	(Alexandria: North)	3 Cairnbaan Lea, Cairnbaan, Lochgilphead PA31 8BA	01546 606815
Bristow, W.H.G. BEd HDipRE DipSpecEd					
Crossan, William	1951	2002	(Chaplain: Army)	Choc Ban, Southend, Campbeltown PA28 6RQ	01586 830667
		2014	Ordained Local Minister	Gowanbank, Kilkerran Road, Campbeltown PA28 6JL	01586 553453
Dunlop, Alistair J. MA	1965	2004	(Saddell and Carradale)	8 Pipers Road, Cairnbaan, Lochgilphead PA31 8UF [E-mail: dunrevn@btinternet.com]	01546 600316
Forrest, Alan B. MA	1956	1993	(Uphall: South)	126 Shore Road, Innellan, Dunoon PA23 7SX	01369 830424
Gibson, Elizabeth A. (Mrs) MA MLitt BD	2003	2013	(Glenorchy and Innishael with Strathfillan)	Mo Dhachaidh, Lochdon, Isle of Mull PA64 6AP [E-mail: egibson@churchofscotland.org.uk]	01680 812541
Gibson, Frank S. BL BD STM DSWA DD	1963	1995	(Kilarrow with Kilmeny)	1/7 Joppa Station Place, Edinburgh EH15 2QU	
Goss, Alister J. BD DMin	1975	2009	(Industrial Chaplain)	24 Albert Place, Ardnadam, Sandbank, Dunoon PA23 8QF [E-mail: scimwest@hotmail.com]	01369 704495
Gray, William LTh	1971	2006	(Kilberry with Tarbert)	Lochnagar, Longsdale Road, Oban PA34 5DZ [E-mail: gray98@hotmail.com]	01631 567471
Henderson, Grahame McL. BD	1974	2008	(Kirn)	6 Gerhallow, Bullwood Road, Dunoon PA23 7QB [E-mail: ghende5884@aol.com]	01369 702433

Name	Year	Year	Charge	Address	Tel
Hood, Catriona A.	2006		Auxiliary Minister	Rose Cottage, Whitehouse, Tarbert PA29 6EP [E-mail: chood@churchofscotland.org.uk]	01880 730366
Hood, H. Stanley C. MA BD	1966	2000	(London: Crown Court)	10 Dalriada Place, Kilmichael Glassary, Lochgilphead PA31 8QA	01546 606168
Lamont, Archibald MA	1952	1994	(Kilcalmonell with Skipness)	22 Bonnyton Drive, Bearsden, Glasgow G76 0LU	
Lind, Michael J. LLB BD	1984	2012	(Campbeltown: Highland)	Maybank, Station Road, Conon Bridge, Dingwall IV7 8BJ [E-mail: mijylind@btinternet.com]	
Macfarlane, James PhD	1991	2011	(Lochgoilhead and Kilmorich)	'Lindores', 11 Bullwood Road, Dunoon PA23 7QJ [E-mail: mac.farlane@btinternet.com]	01369 710626
McIvor, Anne (Miss) SRD BD	1996	2013	(Gigha and Cara)	20 Albyn Avenue, Campbeltown PA28 6LY [E-mail: annemcivor@btinternet.com]	(Mbl) 07901 964825
MacLeod, Roderick MA BD PhD(Edin) PhD(Open)	1966	2011	(Cumlodden, Lochfyneside and Lochgair)	Creag-nam-Barnach, Furnace, Inveraray PA32 8XU [E-mail: mail@revroddy.co.uk]	01499 500629
Marshall, Freda (Mrs) BD FCII	1993	2005	(Colonsay and Oronsay with Kilbrandon and Kilchattan)	Allt Mhaluidh, Glenview, Dalmally PA33 1BE [E-mail: mail@freda.org.uk]	01838 200693
Middleton, Jeremy R.H. LLB BD	1981	2015	(Edinburgh: Davidson's Mains)	Imean Mor, Southend, Campbeltown PA28 6RF [E-mail: jmiddleton@churchofscotland.org]	01586 830439
Millar, Margaret R.M. (Miss) BTh	1977	2008	(Kilchrenan and Dalavich with Muckairn)	Fearnoch Cottage, Fearnoch, Taynuilt PA35 1JB [E-mail: macoje@aol.com]	01866 822416
Morrison, Angus W. MA BD	1959	1999	(Kildalton and Oa)	1 Livingstone Way, Port Ellen, Isle of Islay PA42 7EP	01496 300043
Park, Peter B. BD MCIBS	1997	2014	(Fraserburgh: Old)	Hillview, 24 McKelvie Road, Oban PA34 4GB [E-mail: peterpark9@btinternet.com]	01631 565849
Ritchie, Walter M.	1973	1999	(Uphall: South)	Hazel Cottage, Barr Mor View, Kilmartin, Lochgilphead PA31 8UN	01546 510343
Scott, Randolph MA BD	1991	2013	(Jersey: St Columba's)	18 Lochan Avenue, Kirn, Dunoon PA23 8HT [E-mail: rev.rs@hotmail.com]	01369 703175
Shedden, John CBE BD DipPSS	1971	2008	(Fuengirola)	Orchy Cottage, Dalmally PA33 1AX [E-mail: rev.johnshedden@gmx.com]	01838 200535
Stewart, Joseph LTh	1979	2011	(Dunoon: St John's with Sandbank)	7 Glenmorag Avenue, Dunoon PA23 7LG	01369 703438
Taylor, Alan T. BD	1980	2005	(Isle of Mull Parishes)	Erray Road, Tobermory, Isle of Mull PA75 6PS	01688 302496
Wilkinson, W. Brian MA BD	1968	2007	(Glenaray and Inveraray)	3 Achlonan, Taynuilt PA35 1JJ [E-mail: williambrian35@btinternet.com]	01866 822036

ARGYLL Communion Sundays

Parish	Communion Sundays
Ardrishaig	4th Apr, 1st Nov
Barra	2nd Mar, June, Sep, Easter, Advent
Campbeltown	
Highland	1st May, Nov
Lorne and Lowland	1st May, Nov
Craignish	1st Jun, Nov
Cumlodden, Lochfyneside and Lochgair	1st May, 3rd Nov
Dunoon	
St John's	1st Mar, Jun, Nov
The High Kirk	1st Feb, Jun, Oct
Gigha and Cara	1st May, Nov
Glassary, Kilmartin and Ford	1st Apr, Sep
Glenaray and Inveraray	1st Apr, Jul, Oct, Dec
Innellan	2nd May, Nov
Inverlussa and Bellanoch	Passion Sun., 2nd Jul, 3rd Nov
Jura	1st Mar, Jun, Sep, Dec
Kilarrow	1st Jul, 3rd Nov
Kilcalmonell	1st Jul, 2nd Dec, Easter
Kilchoman	1st Jan, Jun, Oct, Easter
Kildalton and Oa	Last Apr, Oct
Kilfinan	
Killean and Kilchenzie	1st Mar, Jul, Oct
Kilmeny	2nd May, 3rd Nov
Kilmodan and Colintraive	1st Apr, Sep
Kilmun	Last Jun, Nov
Kilninver and Kilmelford	Last Feb, Jun, Oct
Kim	2nd Jun, Oct
Kyles	1st May, Nov
Lochgair	Last Apr, Oct
Lochgilphead	2nd Oct (Gaelic)
Lochgoilhead and Kilmorich	1st Apr, Nov
	2nd Mar, Jun, Sep, Nov
	1st Aug, Easter

North Knapdale	3rd Oct, 2nd May
Portnahaven	3rd Jul
Rothesay: Trinity	1st Feb, Jun, Nov
Saddell and Carradale	2nd May, 1st Nov
Sandbank	1st Jan, May, Nov
Skipness	2nd May, Nov
Southend	1st Jun, Dec
South Knapdale	4th Apr, 1st Nov
South Uist	
Howmore	1st Jun
Daliburgh	1st Sep
Strachur and Strathlachlan	1st Mar, Jun, Nov
Strone and Ardentinny	Last Feb, Jun, Oct
Tarbert and Kilberry	1st May, Oct
Tayvallich	2nd May, Nov
The United Church of Bute	1st Feb, Jun, Nov
Toward	Last Feb, May, Aug, Nov

(22) FALKIRK

Meets at Falkirk Trinity Parish Church on the first Tuesday of September, December, March and May, on the fourth Tuesday of October and January and on the third Tuesday of June.

Clerk:	REV. ROBERT S.T. ALLAN LLB DipLP BD	9 Major's Loan, Falkirk FK1 5QF	01324 625124
		[E-mail: falkirk@churchofscotland.org.uk]	
Depute Clerk:	REV. ANDREW SARLE BSc BD	114 High Station Road, Falkirk FK1 5LN	01324 621648
		[E-mail: depclerk@falkirkpresbytery.org]	
Treasurer:	MR ARTHUR PRIESTLY	32 Broomhill Avenue, Larbert FK5 3EH	01324 557142
		[E-mail: treasurer@falkirkpresbytery.org]	

Airth (H)

| James F. Todd BD CPS | 1984 | The Manse, Airth, Falkirk FK2 8LS | 01324 831120 |

Blackbraes and Shieldhill linked with Muiravonside

| Louise J.E. McClements RGN BD | 2008 | 81 Stevenson Avenue, Polmont, Falkirk FK2 0GU | 01324 717757 |
| | | [E-mail: louise.mcclements@virgin.net] | |

Bo'ness: Old (H)

| Vacant | | 10 Dundas Street, Bo'ness EH51 0DG | 01506 204585 |

Bo'ness: St Andrew's (Website: www.standonline.org.uk) (01506 825803)

| Albert O. Bogle BD MTh | 1981 | St Andrew's Manse, 11 Erngath Road, Bo'ness EH51 9DP | 01506 822195 |
| | | [E-mail: albertbogle@mac.com] | |

Bonnybridge: St Helen's (H) (Website: www.bbshnc.com)
George MacDonald BTh   2004 2009   The Manse, 32 Reilly Gardens, High Bonnybridge FK4 2BB   01324 874807
[E-mail: georgemacdonald1@virginmedia.com]

Bothkennar and Carronshore
Andrew J. Moore BSc BD   2007   11 Hunter Place, Greenmount Park, Carronshore, Falkirk FK2 8QS   01324 570525
[E-mail: theminister@themoores.me.uk]

Brightons (H)
Murdo M. Campbell BD DipMin   1997 2007   The Manse, Maddiston Road, Brightons, Falkirk FK2 0JP   01324 712062
[E-mail: murdocampbell@hotmail.com]

Carriden (H)
Malcolm Lyon BD   2007 2014   The Spires, Foredale Terrace, Carriden, Bo'ness EH51 9LW   01506 822141
[E-mail: malcolmlyon2@hotmail.com]

Cumbernauld: Abronhill (H)
Joyce A. Keyes (Mrs) BD   1996 2003   26 Ash Road, Cumbernauld, Glasgow G67 3ED   01236 723833

Cumbernauld: Condorrat (H)
Grace Saunders BSc BTh   2007 2011   11 Rosehill Drive, Cumbernauld, Glasgow G67 4EQ   01236 452090
[E-mail: rev.grace.saunders@btinternet.com]
Marion Perry (Mrs) (Auxiliary Minister)   2009 2013   17a Tarbolton Road, Cumbernauld, Glasgow G67 2AJ   01236 898519
[E-mail: perryask@hotmail.com]   07563 180662 (Mbl)

Cumbernauld: Kildrum (H)
Vacant   64 Southfield Road, Balloch, Cumbernauld, Glasgow G68 9DZ   01236 723204
David Nicholson DCS   2D Doonside, Kildrum, Cumbernauld, Glasgow G67 2HX   01236 732260
[E-mail: deacdave@btinternet.com]

Cumbernauld: Old (H) (Website: www.cumbernauldold.org.uk)
Vacant   The Manse, 23 Baronhill, Cumbernauld, Glasgow G67 2SD   01236 721912
Valerie Cuthbertson (Miss) DCS   1999   105 Bellshill Road, Motherwell ML1 3SJ   01698 259001

Cumbernauld: St Mungo's
Vacant   18 Fergusson Road, Cumbernauld, Glasgow G67 1LS   01236 721513

Denny: Old linked with Haggs
Vacant   31 Duke Street, Denny FK6 6NR   01324 824508

Denny: Westpark (H) (Website: www.westparkchurch.org.uk)
Vacant
13 Baxter Crescent, Denny FK6 5EZ
01324 876224

Dunipace (H)
Jean W. Gallacher (Miss)   1989
BD CMin CTheol DMin
The Manse, 239 Stirling Street, Dunipace, Denny FK6 6QJ
01324 824540

Falkirk: Bainsford linked with Falkirk: St James'
Vacant
1 Valleyview Place, Newcarron Village, Falkirk FK2 7JB
01324 621087
Andrew Sarle BSc BD   2013
114 High Station Road, Falkirk FK1 5LN
01324 621648
(Ordained Local Minister)
[E-mail: asarle@churchofscotland.org.uk]

Falkirk: Camelon (Church office: 01324 870011)
Stuart Sharp MTheol DipPA   2001
30 Cotland Drive, Falkirk FK2 7GE
01324 623631
Amanda McQuarrie MA PGCE MTh   2014
5 Bethesda Grove, Maddiston, Falkirk FK2 0FR
01324 720514
[E-mail: amcquarrie@churchofscotland.org]

Falkirk: Grahamston United (H)
Ian Wilkie BD PGCE   2001   2007
16 Cromwell Road, Falkirk FK1 1SF
01324 624461
[E-mail: yanbluejeans@aol.com]
07877 803280 (Mbl)

Grahamston United is a Local Ecumenical Project shared with the Methodist and United Reformed Churches

Falkirk: Laurieston linked with Redding and Westquarter
J. Mary Henderson MA BD DipEd PhD   1990   2009
11 Polmont Road, Laurieston, Falkirk FK2 9QQ
01324 621196
[E-mail: jmary.henderson@tiscali.co.uk]

Falkirk: St Andrew's West (H)
Alastair M. Horne BSc BD   1989   1997
1 Maggiewood's Loan, Falkirk FK1 5SJ
01324 623308

Falkirk: St James'   See Falkirk: Bainsford

Falkirk: Trinity (H)
Robert S.T. Allan LLB DipLP BD   1991   2003
9 Major's Loan, Falkirk FK1 5QF
01324 625124
Kathryn Brown (Mrs)   2014
1 Callendar Park Walk, Callendar Grange, Falkirk FK1 1TA
01324 617352
(Ordained Local Minister)
[E-mail: kaybrown1cpw@talktalk.net]

Grangemouth: Abbotsgrange
Aftab Gohar MA MDiv PgDip   1995   2010
8 Naismith Court, Grangemouth FK3 9BQ
01324 482109
[E-mail: abbotsgrange@aol.com]
07528 143784 (Mbl)

Grangemouth: Kirk of the Holy Rood
David J. Smith BD DipMin — 1992 — 2003 — The Manse, Bowhouse Road, Grangemouth FK3 0EX [E-mail: davidkhrood@tiscali.co.uk] — 01324 471595

Grangemouth: Zetland (H)
Alison A. Meikle (Mrs) BD — 1999 — 2015 — Ronaldshay Crescent, Grangemouth FK3 9JH [E-mail: ameikle@churchofscotland.org.uk] — 01324 336729

Haggs (H) See Denny: Old
5 Watson Place, Dennyloanhead, Bonnybridge FK4 2BG — 01324 813786

Larbert: East
Melville D. Crosthwaite BD DipEd DipMin — 1984 — 1995 — 1 Cortachy Avenue, Carron, Falkirk FK2 8DH — 01324 562402

Larbert: Old (H)
Vacant — The Manse, 38 South Broomage Avenue, Larbert FK5 3ED — 01324 872760

Larbert: West (H)
Vacant — 11 Carronvale Road, Larbert FK5 3LZ — 01324 562878

Muiravonside See Blackbraes and Shieldhill

Polmont: Old
Deborah L. van Welie (Ms) MTheol — 2015 — 3 Orchard Grove, Polmont, Falkirk FK2 0XE [E-mail: minister@polmontold.org.uk] — 01324 713427

Redding and Westquarter See Falkirk: Laurieston

Slamannan
Guardianship of the Presbytery
Monica MacDonald (Mrs) (Ordained Local Minister) — 2014 — 32 Reilly Gardens, High Bonnybridge, Bonnybridge FK4 2BB [E-mail: monica.macdonald55@googlemail.com] — 01324 874807

Stenhouse and Carron (H)
William Thomson BD — 2001 — 2007 — The Manse, 21 Tipperary Place, Stenhousemuir, Larbert FK5 4SX — 01324 416628

Name	Ord	Ind	Charge	Address	Tel
Black, Ian W. MA BD	1976	2013	(Grangemouth: Zetland)	Flat 1R, 2 Carrickvale Court, Carrickstone, Cumbernauld, Glasgow G68 0LA [E-mail: iwblack@hotmail.com]	01236 453370
Brown, James BA BD DipHSW DipPsychol	1973	2001	(Abercorn with Dalmeny)	6 Salmon Court, Schoolbrae, Bo'ness EH51 9HF	01506 822454
Brown, T. John MA BD	1995	2006	(Tullibody: St Serf's)	1 Callendar Park Walk, Callendar Grange, Falkirk FK1 1TA [E-mail: johnbrown1cpw@talktalk.net]	01324 617352
Campbell-Jack, W.C. BD MTh PhD	1979	2011	(Glasgow: Possilpark)	35 Castle Avenue, Airth, Falkirk FK2 8GA [E-mail: c.c-j@homecall.co.uk]	01324 832011
Chalmers, George A. MA BD MLitt	1962	2002	(Catrine with Sorn)		
Christie, Helen F. (Mrs) BD	1998	2015	(Haggs)	3 Cricket Place, Brightons, Falkirk FK2 0HZ [E-mail: andychristie747@yahoo.com]	01324 712030
Hardie, Robert R. MA BD	1968	2005	(Stenhouse and Carron)	33 Palace Street, Berwick-upon-Tweed TD15 1HN	
Holland, John C.	1976	1985	(Strone and Ardentinny)	7 Polmont Park, Polmont, Falkirk FK2 0XT	01324 880109
Job, Anne J. BSc BD	1993	2010	(Kirkcaldy: Viewforth with Thornton)	5 Carse View, Airth, Falkirk FK2 8NY [E-mail: aj@aijob.co.uk]	01324 832094
Kesting, Sheilagh M. BA BD DD	1980	1993	Ecumenical Relations	12 Glenview Drive, Falkirk FK1 5JU	01324 671489
Macaulay, Glendon BD	1999	2012	(Falkirk: Erskine)	43 Gavin's Lee, Tranent EH33 2AP [E-mail: gd.macaulay@btinternet.com]	01875 615851
McCallum, John	1962	1998	(Falkirk: Irving Camelon)	11 Burnbrae Gardens, Falkirk FK1 5SB	01324 619766
McDonald, William G. MA BD	1959	1975	(Falkirk: Grahamston United)	14 Priesden Park, St Andrews KY16 8DL	01334 479770
MacDougall, Lorna I. (Miss) MA DipGC	2003		Auxiliary Minister	34 Millar Place, Carron, Falkirk FK2 8QB	01324 552739
McDowall, Ronald J. BD	1980	2001	(Falkirk: Laurieston with Redding and Westquarter)	'Kailas', Windsor Road, Falkirk FK1 5EJ	01324 871947
MacKinnon, Ronald M. DCS			(Deacon)	12 Mossywood Court, McGregor Avenue, Airdrie ML6 7DY [E-mail: ronnie@ronniemac.plus.com]	01236 763389 / 07594 427960 (Mbl)
Mathers, Daniel L. BD	1982	2001	(Grangemouth: Charing Cross and West)	10 Ercall Road, Brightons, Falkirk FK2 0RS	01324 872253
Maxton, Ronald M. MA	1955	1995	(Dollar: Associate)	5 Rulley View, Denny FK6 6QQ	01324 825441
Miller, Elsie M. (Miss) DCS	1986	1998	(Deaconess)	30 Swinton Avenue, Rowanshank, Baillieston, Glasgow G69 6JR	0141-771 0857
Ross, Evan J. LTh			(Cowdenbeath: West with Mossgreen and Crossgates)	5 Arneil Place, Brightons, Falkirk FK2 0NJ	01324 719936
Scott, Donald H. BA BD	1983	2002	Chaplain: HMYOI Polmont	14 Gibsongray Street, Falkirk FK2 0AB [E-mail: donaldhscott@hotmail.com]	01324 722241
Smith, Richard BD	1976	2002	(Denny: Old)	Easter Wayside, 46 Kennedy Way, Airth, Falkirk FK2 8GB [E-mail: richards@uklinux.net]	01324 831386
Wandrum, David	1993		Auxiliary Minister	5 Cawder View, Carrickstone Meadows, Cumbernauld, Glasgow G68 0BN	01236 723288
Wilson, Phyllis M. (Mrs) DipCom DipRE	1985	2006	(Motherwell: South Dalziel)	'Landemer', 17 Sneddon Place, Airth, Falkirk FK2 8GH [E-mail: thomas.wilson38@btinternet.com]	01324 832257

FALKIRK ADDRESSES

Blackbraes and Shieldhill	
Bo'ness: Old	Main St x Anderson Cr
St Andrew's	Panbrae Road
Carriden	Grahamsdyke Avenue
	Carriden Brae
Cumbernauld: Abronhill	Larch Road
Condorrat	Main Road
Kildrum	Clouden Road
Old	Baronhill
St Mungo's	St Mungo's Road

Denny: Old	Denny Cross
Westpark	Duke Street
Dunipace	Stirling Street
Falkirk: Bainsford	Hendry Street, Bainsford
Camelon	Dorrator Road
Grahamston United	Bute Street
Laurieston	Main Falkirk Road
St Andrew's West	Newmarket Street
St James'	Thornhill Road x Firs Street
Trinity	Kirk Wynd

Grangemouth: Abbotsgrange	Abbot's Road
Kirk of the Holy Rood	Bowhouse Road
Zetland	Ronaldshay Crescent
Haggs	Glasgow Road
Larbert: East	Kirk Avenue
Old	Denny Road x Stirling Road
West	Main Street
Muiravonside	off Vellore Road
Polmont: Old	Kirk Entry/Bo'ness Road
Redding and Westquarter	Main Street
Slamannan	Manse Place
Stenhouse and Carron	Church Street

(23) STIRLING

Meets at the Moderator's church on the second Thursday of September, and at Bridge of Allan Parish Church on the second Thursday of February, March, April, May, June, October, November and December.

Clerk: REV. ALEXANDER M. MILLAR MA BD MBA MCMI   2005 2014
St Columba's Manse, 5 Clifford Road, Stirling FK8 2AQ   01786 469979
[E-mail: alexmillar0406@gmail.com]

Depute Clerk: MR ANDREW MUIRHEAD MA MLitt
Ythanglen, Copland Place, Alva FK12 5LN   01259 760143
[E-mail: andrew.muirhead1@btinternet.com]

Treasurer: MR MARTIN DUNSMORE
60 Brookfield Place, Alva FK12 5AT   01259 762262
[E-mail: mpgduns@btinternet.com]

Presbytery Office: Bridge of Allan Parish Church, 12 Keir Street,
Bridge of Allan FK9 4NW
[E-mail: stirling@churchofscotland.org.uk]

Aberfoyle (H) linked with Port of Menteith (H) (Website: www.aberfoyleportchurches.org.uk)
Terry Ann Taylor BA MTh   2005   2014
The Manse, Lochard Road, Aberfoyle, Stirling FK8 3SZ   01877 382391
[E-mail: terryanntaylor@btinternet.com]

Alloa: Ludgate (Website: www.alloaludgatechurch.org.uk)
Carol Anne Parker (Mrs) BEd BD   2009   2014
28 Alloa Park Drive, Alloa FK10 1QY   01259 212709
[E-mail: ca.parker76@btinternet.com]

Alloa: St Mungo's (H) (Website: www.stmungosparish.org.uk)
Sang Y. Cha BD MTh   2011
37A Claremont, Alloa FK10 2DG   01259 213872
[E-mail: syc@cantab.net]

Alva (Website: www.alvaparishchurch.org.uk)
James N.R. McNeil BSc BD   1990   1997   34 Ochil Road, Alva FK12 5JT   01259 760262
[E-mail: revjim@btinternet.com]

Balfron (Website: www.balfronchurch.org.uk) linked with Fintry (H) (Website: www.fintrykirk.btck.org.uk)
Sigrid Marten   1997   2013   7 Station Road, Balfron, Glasgow G63 0SX   01360 440285
[E-mail: minister@marten.org.uk]

Balquhidder linked with Killin and Ardeonaig (H)
Vacant   The Manse, Killin FK21 8TN   01567 820247
June E. Johnston BSc MEd BD   2013   Tarmachan, Main Street, Killin FK21 8TN   0775 444 8889 (Mbl)
(Ordained Local Minister)   [E-mail: johnston330@btinternet.com]

Bannockburn: Allan (H) (Website: www.allanchurch.org.uk)
Jim Landels BD CertMin   1990   The Manse, Bogend Road, Bannockburn, Stirling FK7 8NP   01786 814692
[E-mail: revjimlandels@btinternet.com]

Bannockburn: Ladywell (H) (Website: www.ladywellchurch.co.uk)
Elizabeth M.D. Robertson (Miss) BD CertMin   1997   57 The Firs, Bannockburn FK7 0EG   01786 812467
[E-mail: lizrob@talktalk.net]

Bridge of Allan (H) (01786 834155) (Website: www.bridgeofallanparishchurch.org.uk)
Vacant   29 Keir Street, Bridge of Allan, Stirling FK9 4QJ   01786 832753

Buchanan linked with Drymen (Website: www.drymenchurch.org)
Alexander J. MacPherson BD   1986   1997   Buchanan Manse, Drymen, Glasgow G63 0AQ   01360 870212
[E-mail: revalex1@gmail.com]

Buchlyvie (H) linked with Gartmore (H)
Elaine H. MacRae (Mrs) BD   1985   2004   112 Jackson Drive, Crowwood Grange, Stepps, Glasgow G33 6GF   0141-779 5742
[E-mail: ge.macrae@btopenworld.com]   07834 269487 (Mbl)

Callander (H) (Tel/Fax: 01877 331409) (Website: www.callanderkirk.org.uk)
Vacant   3 Aveland Park Road, Callander FK17 8FD   01877 330097

Cambusbarron: The Bruce Memorial (H) (Website: www.cambusbarronchurch.org)
Graham Nash MA BD   2006   2012   14 Woodside Court, Cambusbarron, Stirling FK7 9PH   01786 442068
[E-mail: gpnash@btopenworld.com]

Clackmannan (H) (Website: www.clackmannankirk.org.uk)
Scott Raby LTh   1991   2007   The Manse, Port Street, Clackmannan FK10 4JH   01259 211255
                                                                  [E-mail: minister@clackmannankirk.org.uk]

Cowie (H) and Plean linked with Fallin (Website: www.cowiepleanandfallinchurch.com)
Alan L. Dunnett LLB BD   1994   2008   5 Fincastle Place, Cowie, Stirling FK7 7DS   01786 818413
                                                                  [E-mail: alan.dunnett@sky.com]
Linda Dunnett (Mrs) BA DCS   5 Fincastle Place, Cowie, Stirling FK7 7DS   01786 818413
                                                                  [E-mail: lindadunnett@sky.com]   07838 041683   (Mbl)

Dollar (H) linked with Glendevon linked with Muckhart (Website: www.dollarparishchurch.org.uk)
Jerome O'Brien BA LLB MTh   2001   2013   2 Princes Crescent East, Dollar FK14 7BU   01259 743593
                                                                  [E-mail: 1jeromeobrien@gmail.com]

Drymen See Buchanan

Dunblane: Cathedral (H) (Website: www.dunblanecathedral.org.uk)
Colin C. Renwick BMus BD   1989   2014   Cathedral Manse, The Cross, Dunblane FK15 0AQ   01786 822205
                                                                  [E-mail: c.renwick@btopenworld.com]
Sally Foster-Fulton (Mrs) BA BD (Assoc)   1999   2007   21 Craiglea, Causewayhead, Stirling FK9 5EE   01786 463060
                                                                  [E-mail: sallyfulton01@gmail.com]

Dunblane: St Blane's (H) linked with Lecropt (H) (Website: www.lecroptkirk.org.uk)
Gary J. Caldwell BSc BD   2007   2015   46 Kellie Wynd, Dunblane FK15 0NR   01786 825324
                                                                  [E-mail: garyjcaldwell@btinternet.com]

Fallin See Cowie and Plean
Fintry See Balfron

Gargunnock linked with Kilmadock linked with Kincardine-in-Menteith (Website: blairdrummondchurches.org.uk)
Andrew B. Campbell BD DPS MTh   1979   2011   The Manse, Manse Brae, Gargunnock, Stirling FK8 3BQ   01786 860678
                                                                  [E-mail: andycampbell53@btinternet.com]
Lynne Mack (Mrs)   2013   36 Middleton, Menstrie FK11 7HD   01259 761465
(Ordained Local Minister)   [E-mail: lynne.mack@aol.co.uk]

Gartmore See Buchlyvie

Glendevon See Dollar

Killearn (H) (Website: www.killearnkirk.org.uk)
Lee Messeder BD PgDipMin   2003   2010   2 The Oaks, Killearn, Glasgow G63 9SF   01360 550045
                                                                 [E-mail: minister@killearnkirk.org.uk]

Killin and Ardeonaig See Balquhidder
Kilmadock See Gargunnock
Kincardine-in-Menteith See Gargunnock

Kippen (H) linked with Norrieston
Ellen Larson Davidson BA MDiv   2007   2015   The Manse, Main Street, Kippen, Stirling FK8 3DN   01786 871249
                                                                 [E-mail: larsondavidson@gmail.com]

Lecropt See Dunblane: St Blane's

Logie (H) (Website: sms-test.webplus.net)
R. Stuart M. Fulton BA BD   1991   2006   21 Craiglea, Causewayhead, Stirling FK9 5EE   01786 463060
                                                                 [E-mail: stuart.fulton@btinternet.com]
Anne F. Shearer BA DipEd (Aux)   2010   10 Colsnaur, Menstrie FK11 7HG   01259 769176
                                                                 [E-mail: anne.f.shearer@btinternet.com]

Menstrie (H) (Website: www.menstrieparishchurch.co.uk)
Vacant   The Manse, 7 Long Row, Menstrie FK11 7BA   01259 761461

Muckhart See Dollar
Norrieston See Kippen
Port of Menteith See Aberfoyle

Sauchie and Coalsnaughton
Margaret Shuttleworth MA BD   2013   62 Toll Road, Kincardine, Alloa FK10 4QZ   01259 731002
                                                                 [E-mail: revmshuttleworth@gmail.com]

Stirling: Allan Park South (R) (H) (Website: www.apschurch.com)
Alistair Cowper BSc BD   2011   22 Laurelhill Place, Stirling FK8 2JH   01786 358872
                                                                 [E-mail: minister@apschurch.com]   07791 524504 (Mbl)

Stirling: Church of the Holy Rude (H) (Website: http://holyrude.org) linked with Stirling: Viewfield Erskine (H)
Alan F. Miller BA MA BD   2000   2010   7 Windsor Place, Stirling FK8 2HY   01786 465166
                                                                 [E-mail: revafmiller@gmail.com]

Stirling: North (H) (01786 463376) (Website: www.northparishchurch.com)
Vacant   18 Shirras Brae Road, Stirling FK7 0BA   01786 357428

Stirling: St Columba's (H) (01786 449516) (Website: www.stcolumbasstirling.org.uk)
Alexander M. Millar MA BD MBA MCMI   1980   2010   St Columba's Manse, 5 Clifford Road, Stirling FK8 2AQ   01786 469979
[E-mail: alexmillar0406@gmail.com]

Stirling: St Mark's (Website: www.stmarksstirling.org.uk)
Stuart Davidson BD   2008   176 Drip Road, Stirling FK8 1RR   01786 473716
[E-mail: stuart_davidson1@sky.com]
Jean Porter (Mrs) BD DCS   St Mark's Church, Drip Road, Stirling FK8 1RE   07729 316321 (Mbl)
[E-mail: info@stmarksstirling.org.uk]

Stirling: St Ninians Old (H) (Website: www.stniniansold.org.uk)
Gary J. McIntyre BD DipMin   1993   1998   7 Randolph Road, Stirling FK8 2AJ   01786 474421
[E-mail: gary.mcintyre7@btinternet.com]

Stirling: Viewfield Erskine   See Stirling: Church of the Holy Rude

Strathblane (H) (Website: www.strathblanekirk.org.uk)
Richard Begg MA BD   2008   2011   2 Campsie Road, Strathblane, Glasgow G63 9AB   01360 770226
[E-mail: RBEGG711@aol.com]

Tillicoultry (H) (Website: www.tillicoultryparishchurch.co.uk)
Alison E.P. Britchfield (Mrs) MA BD   1987   2013   The Manse, 17 Dollar Road, Tillicoultry FK13 6PD   01259 750340
[E-mail: alibritchfield@gmail.com]

Tullibody: St Serf's (H)
Vacant   16 Menstrie Road, Tullibody, Alloa FK10 2RG   01259 729804

Abeledo, Benjamin J.A. BTh DipTh PTh   1991   2000   Chaplain: Army   30 Dollar Road, Tillicoultry FK13 6PD   01259 752705
[E-mail: benjamin.abeledo@btinternet.com]
Aitken, E. Douglas MA   1961   1998   (Clackmannan)   1 Dolan Grove, Saline, Dunfermline KY12 9UP   01383 852730
[E-mail: douglasaitken14@btinternet.com]

Name	Years	Charge	Address	Telephone
Allen, Valerie L. (Ms) BMus MDiv DMin	1990 2013	(Arbroath: Old and Abbey)	16 Pine Court, Doune FK16 6JE [E-mail: vl2allen@btinternet.com]	01786 842577
Barr, John BSc PhD BD	1958 1979	(Kilmacolm: Old)	6 Ferry Court, Stirling FK9 5GJ [E-mail: kilbrandon@btinternet.com]	(Mbl) 07801 291538 / 01786 472286
Boyd, Ronald M.H. BD DipTheol	1995 2010	Chaplain, Queen Victoria School	6 Victoria Green, Queen Victoria School, Dunblane FK15 0JY [E-mail:ron.boyd@qvs.org.uk]	(Mbl) 07766 004292
Brown, James H. BD	1977 2005	(Helensburgh: Park)	14 Gullipen View, Callander FK17 8HN [E-mail: revjimhbrown@yahoo.co.uk]	01877 339425
Cloggie, June (Mrs)	1997 2006	(Auxiliary Minister)	11A Tulipan Crescent, Callander FK17 8AR [E-mail: david.cloggie@hotmail.co.uk]	01877 331021
Cochrane, James P.N. LTh	1994 2012	(Tillicoultry)	12 Sandpiper Meadow, Alloa Park, Alloa FK10 1QU [E-mail: jamescochrane@pobroadband.co.uk]	01259 218883
Cook, Helen (Mrs) BD	1974 2012	Hospital Chaplain	60 Pelstream Avenue, Stirling FK7 0BG [E-mail: revhcook@btinternet.com]	01786 464128
Gaston, A. Ray C. MA BD	1969 2002	(Leuchars: St Athernase)	'Hamewith', 13 Manse Road, Dollar FK14 7AL [E-mail: gaston.arthur@yahoo.co.uk]	01259 743202
Gillespie, Irene C. (Mrs) BD	1991 2007	(Tiree)	39 King O'Muirs Drive, Tullibody, Alloa FK10 3AY [E-mail: revicg@btinternet.com]	01259 723937
Gilmour, William M. MA BD	1969 2008	(Lecropt)	14 Pine Court, Doune FK16 6JE	01786 842928
Goodison, Michael J. BSc BD	2013	Chaplain: Army	27 Hunter Crescent, Leuchars KY16 0JP [E-mail: mike.goodison@btinternet.com]	
Goring, Iain M. BSc BD	1976 2015	(Interim Minister)	4 Argyle Grove, Dunblane FK15 9DU [E-mail: imgoring@tiscali.co.uk]	01786 821688
Izett, William A.F.	1968 2000	(Law)	1 Duke Street, Clackmannan FK10 4EF [E-mail: william.izett@talktalk.net]	01259 724203
Jack, Alison M. MA BD PhD	1998 2001	Assistant Principal and Lecturer, New College, Edinburgh	5 Murdoch Terrace, Dunblane FK15 9JE [E-mail: alisonmjack809@btinternet.com]	01786 825116
MacCormick, Moira G. BA LTh	1986 2003	(Buchlyvie with Gartmore)	12 Rankine Wynd, Tullibody, Alloa FK10 2UW [E-mail: mgmaccormick@o2.co.uk]	01259 724619
McIntosh, Hamish N.M. MA	1949 1987	(Fintry)	9 Abbeyfield House, 17 Allan Park, Stirling FK8 2QG	01786 470294
McKenzie, Alan BSc BD	1988 2013	(Bellshill: Macdonald Memorial with Bellshill: Orbiston)	89 Drip Road, Stirling FK8 1RN [E-mail: rev.a.mckenzie@btopenworld.com]	01786 430450
Malloch, Philip R.M. LLB BD	1970 2009	(Killearn)	8 Michael McParland Drive, Torrance, Glasgow G64 4EE [E-mail: pmalloch@mac.com]	01360 620089
Mathew, J. Gordon MA BD	1973 2011	(Buckie: North)	45 Westhaugh Road, Stirling FK9 5GF [E-mail: jg.matthew@btinternet.com]	01786 445951
Millar, Jennifer M. (Mrs) BD DipMin	1986 1995	Teacher: Religious and Moral Education	5 Clifford Road, Stirling FK8 2AQ [E-mail: airmillar@blueyonder.co.uk]	01786 469979
Mitchell, Alexander B. BD	1981 2014	(Dunblane: St Blane's)	24 Hebridean Gardens, Crieff PH7 3BP [E-mail: alex.mitchell6@btopenworld.com]	01764 652241
Ogilvie, C. (Mrs)	1999 2015	(Cumbernauld: Old)	Seberham Flat, 1A Bridge Street, Dollar FK14 7DF [E-mail: catriona.ogilvie1@btinternet.com]	(Mbl) 07745 782785
Ovens, Samuel B. BD	1982 1993	(Slamannan)	21 Bevan Drive, Alva FK12 5PD	01259 763456
Paterson, John L. MA BD STM	1964 2003	(Linlithgow: St Michael's)	'Kirkmichael', 22 Waterfront Way, Stirling FK9 5GH [E-mail: revianpaterson@hotmail.co.uk]	01786 447165

Picken, Stuart D.B. MA BD PhD	1966	2014	(Ardoch with Blackford)	18C Kilbryde Crescent, Dunblane FK15 9BA [E-mail: picken@eikoku.demon.co.uk]	01786 825947
Pryde, W. Kenneth DA BD	1994	2012	(Foveran)	Corrie, 7 Alloa Road, Woodside, Cambus FK10 2NT [E-mail: wkpryde@hotmail.com]	01259 721562
Roderick, Maggie R. BA BD FRSA FTSI	2010	2013	(Associate: Stirling: St Ninians Old)	34 Craiglea, Stirling FK9 5EE [E-mail: revmaggieroderick@btinternet.com]	(Mbl) 07984 604205
Sangster, Ernest G. MA BD ThM	1958	1997	(Alva)	6 Lawhill Road, Dollar FK14 7BG	01259 742344
Scott, James F.	1957	1997	(Dyce)	5 Gullipen View, Callander FK17 8HN	01877 330565
Scoular, J. Marshall	1954	1996	(Kippen)	6 Buccleuch Court, Dunblane FK15 0AR	01786 825976
Sewell, Paul M.N. MA BD	1970	2010	(Berwick-upon-Tweed: St Andrew's Wallace Green and Lowick)	7 Bohun Court, Stirling FK7 7UT [E-mail: paulmsewell@btinternet.com]	01786 489969
Sherry, George T. LTh	1977	2004	(Menstrie)	4 Woodburn Way, Alva FK12 5LB [E-mail: gandms@btinternet.com]	01259 763779
Sinclair, James H. MA BD DipMin	1966	2004	(Auchencairn and Rerrick with Buittle and Kelton)	16 Delaney Court, Alloa FK10 1RB	01259 729001
Thomson, Raymond BD DipMin	1992	2013	(Slamannan)	8 Rhodders Grove, Alva FK12 5ER	01259 769083

STIRLING ADDRESSES

Allan Park South	Dumbarton Road	North	Springfield Road
Holy Rude	St John Street	St Columba's	Park Terrace
		St Mark's	Drip Road
St Ninians Old	Kirk Wynd, St Ninians		
Viewfield Erskine	Barnton Street		

(24) DUNFERMLINE

Meets at Dunfermline in St Andrew's Erskine Church, Robertson Road, on the first Thursday of each month, except January, July and August when there is no meeting, and June when it meets on the last Thursday.

Clerk:	REV. IAIN M. GREENSHIELDS BD DipRS ACMA MSc MTh	38 Garvock Hill, Dunfermline KY12 7UU [E-mail: dunfermline@churchofscotland.org.uk]	01383 741495 (Office) 01383 723955 (Home)

Aberdour: St Fillan's (H) (Website: www.stfillans.presbytery.org)

Peter S. Gerbrandy-Baird MA BD MSc FRSA FRGS	2004	St Fillan's Manse, 36 Bellhouse Road, Aberdour, Fife KY3 0TL	01383 861522

Beath and Cowdenbeath: North (H)
David W. Redmayne BSc BD   2001   10 Stuart Place, Cowdenbeath KY4 9BN   01383 511033
[E-mail: beathandnorth@dunfermlinepresbytery.org.uk]

Cairneyhill (H) (01383 882352) linked with Limekilns (H) (01383 873337)
Norman M. Grant BD   1990   The Manse, 10 Church Street, Limekilns, Dunfermline KY11 3HT   01383 872341
[E-mail: nmg57@live.com]

Carnock and Oakley (H) linked with Saline and Blairingone
Vacant   The Manse, Main Street, Carnock, Dunfermline KY12 9JG   01383 850327

Cowdenbeath: Trinity (H)
Gavin R. Boswell BTheol   1993   2 Glenfield Road, Cowdenbeath KY4 9EL   01383 510696
John Wyllie (Pastoral Assistant)   51 Seafar Street, Kelty KY4 0JX   01383 839200

Culross and Torryburn (H)
Vacant   The Manse, Culross, Dunfermline KY12 8JD   01383 880231

Dalgety (H) (01383 824092) (E-mail: office@dalgety-church.co.uk) (Website: www.dalgety-church.co.uk)
Christine Sime (Miss) BSc BD   1994   2012   9 St Colme Drive, Dalgety Bay, Dunfermline KY11 9LQ   01383 822316
[E-mail: revsime@btinternet.com]

Dunfermline: Abbey (H) (Website: www.dunfabbey.freeserve.co.uk)
MaryAnn R. Rennie (Mrs) BD MTh   1998   2012   3 Perdieus Mount, Dunfermline KY12 7XE   01383 727311
[E-mail: maryann.r.rennie@gmail.com]

Dunfermline: East (New Charge Development)
Andrew A. Morrice MA BD   1999   2010   9 Dover Drive, Dunfermline KY11 8HQ   01383 621050
[E-mail: andrew@dunfermlineeastchurch.org.uk]

Dunfermline: Gillespie Memorial (H) (01383 621253) (E-mail: gillespie.church@btopenworld.com)
Alan Greig BSc BD (Interim Minister)   1977   2015   4 Killin Court, Dunfermline KY12 7XF   01383 723329
[E-mail: agreig@churchofscotland.org.uk]

Dunfermline: North
Ian G. Thom BSc PhD BD   1990   2007   13 Barbour Grove, Dunfermline KY12 9YB   01383 733471
[E-mail: ianthom58@btinternet.com]

Dunfermline: St Andrew's Erskine (01383 841660)
Muriel F. Willoughby (Mrs) MA BD   2006   2013   71A Townhill Road, Dunfermline KY12 0BN   01383 734657
[E-mail: muriel.willoughby@btinternet.com]

Dunfermline: St Leonard's (01383 620106) (E-mail: office@stleonardsparishchurch.org.uk) (Website: www.stleonardsparishchurch.org.uk)
Monika Redman BA BD   2003   2014   12 Torvean Place, Dunfermline KY11 4YY   01383 300092
[E-mail: minister@slpc.org.uk]

Dunfermline: St Margaret's
Iain M. Greenshields   1984   2007   38 Garvock Hill, Dunfermline KY12 7UU   01383 723955
BD DipRS ACMA MSc MTh   [E-mail: revimaclg@hotmail.co.uk]

Dunfermline: St Ninian's
Elizabeth A. Fisk (Mrs) BD   1996   51 St John's Drive, Dunfermline KY12 7TL   01383 722256

Dunfermline: Townhill and Kingseat (H)
Vacant   7 Lochwood Park, Kingseat, Dunfermline KY12 0UX   01383 ~~526181~~ 723691

Inverkeithing linked with North Queensferry (R)
Colin M. Alston BMus BD BN RN   1975   2012   1 Dover Way, Dunfermline KY11 8HR   01383 621050
[E-mail: ca584400@gmail.com]

Kelty (Website: www.keltykirk.org.uk)
Hugh D. Steele LTh DipMin   1994   2013   15 Arlick Road, Kelty KY4 0BH   01383 ~~830291~~
[E-mail: hugdebra@aol.com]   831362

Limekilns See Cairneyhill

Lochgelly and Benarty: St Serf's
Vacant   82 Main Street, Lochgelly KY5 9AA   01592 780435

North Queensferry See Inverkeithing

Rosyth
Violet C.C. McKay (Mrs) BD   1988   2002   42 Woodside Avenue, Rosyth KY11 2LA   01383 412776
[E-mail: vcmckay@btinternet.com]

Morag Crawford (Miss) MSc DCS   118 Wester Drylaw Place, Edinburgh EH4 2TG   0131-332 2253
[E-mail: morag.crawford.dcs@blueyonder.co.uk]   07970 982563 (Mbl)

Saline and Blairingone See Carnock and Oakley

Tulliallan and Kincardine
Alexander Shuttleworth MA BD   2004   2013   62 Toll Road, Kincardine, Alloa FK10 4QZ   01259 731002
[E-mail: revshuttleworth@aol.com]

Boyle, Robert P. LTh   1990 2010   (Saline and Blairingone)   43 Dunipace Crescent, Dunfermline KY12 7JE   01383 740980
[E-mail: boab.boyle@btinternet.com]

Brown, Peter MA BD FRAScot   1953 1987   (Holm)   24 Inchmickery Avenue, Dalgety Bay, Dunfermline KY11 5NF   01383 822456
Chalmers, John P. BD CPS   1979 1995   Principal Clerk   10 Liggars Place, Dunfermline KY12 7XZ   01383 739130
Farquhar, William E. BA BD   1987 2006   (Dunfermline: Townhill and Kingseat)   29 Queens Drive, Middlewich, Cheshire CW10 0DG   01606 835097
Jenkins, Gordon F.C. MA BD PhD   1968 2006   (Dunfermline: North)   20 Lumsden Park, Cupar KY15 5YL   01334 652548
[E-mail: jenkinsgordon1@sky.com]

Jessamine, Alistair L. MA BD   1979 2011   (Dunfermline: Abbey)   11 Gallowhill Farm Cottages, Strathaven ML10 6BZ   01357 520934
[E-mail: chatty.1@talktalk.net]

Johnston, Thomas N. LTh   1972 2008   (Edinburgh: Priestfield)   71 Main Street, Newmills, Dunfermline KY12 8ST   01383 889240
[E-mail: tomjohnston@blueyonder.co.uk]

Kenny, Elizabeth S.S. BD RGN SCM   1989 2010   (Carnock and Oakley)   5 Cobden Court, Crossgates, Cowdenbeath KY4 8AU   (Mbl) 07831 763494
[E-mail: esskenny@btinternet.com]

Laidlaw, Victor W.N. BD   1975 2008   (Edinburgh: St Catherine's Argyle)   9 Tern Road, Dunfermline KY11 8GA   01383 620134
Leitch, D. Graham MA BD   1974 2012   (Tyne Valley Parish)   9 St Margaret Wynd, Dunfermline KY12 0UT   01383 249245
[E-mail: dgrahamleitch@gmail.com]

McLellan, Andrew R.C. CBE MA BD STM DD   1970 2002   (HM Inspector of Prisons)   4 Liggars Place, Dunfermline KY12 7XZ   01383 725959
Reid, A. Gordon BSc BD   1982 2008   (Dunfermline: Gillespie Memorial)   7 Arkleston Crescent, Paisley PA3 4TG   0141-842 1542
[E-mail: reid501@fsmail.net]   07773 300989 (Mbl)

Reid, David MSc LTh FSAScot   1961 1992   (St Monans with Largoward)   North Lethans, Saline, Dunfermline KY12 9TE   01383 733144
Stuart, Anne (Miss) DCS   (Deacon)   1 Murrell Terrace, Aberdour, Burntisland KY3 0XH   01383 860049
Sutherland, Iain A. BSc BD   1996 2014   (Dunfermline: Gillespie Memorial)   64 Beech Crescent, Rosyth KY11 2ZP   07843 089598 (Mbl)
[E-mail: RevISutherland@aol.com]

Watt, Robert J. BD   1994 2009   (Dumbarton: Riverside)   101 Birrell Drive, Dunfermline KY11 8FA   01383 735417
[E-mail: r.watt21@virginmedia.com]   07753 683717 (Mbl)

Whyte, Isabel H. (Mrs) BD   1993   (Chaplain: Queen Margaret Hospital, Dunfermline)   14 Carlingnose Point, North Queensferry, Inverkeithing KY11 1ER   01383 410732
[E-mail: iainisabel@whytes28.fsnet.co.uk]

(25) KIRKCALDY

Meets at Kirkcaldy, in the St Bryce Kirk Centre, on the first Tuesday of March, September and December, and on the last Tuesday of June. It meets also on the first Tuesday of November for Holy Communion and a conference at the church of the Moderator.

Clerk:	REV. ROSEMARY FREW (Mrs) MA BD	83 Milton Road, Kirkcaldy KY1 1TP [E-mail: kirkcaldy@churchofscotland.org.uk]	01592 260315
Depute Clerk:	MR DOUGLAS G. HAMILL BEM	41 Abbots Mill, Kirkcaldy KY2 5PE [E-mail: hamilldg@gmail.com]	01592 267500

Auchterderran Kinglassie
Vacant

7 Woodend Road, Cardenden, Lochgelly KY5 0NE   01592 720202

Auchtertool linked with Kirkcaldy: Linktown (H) (01592 641080)
Catriona M. Morrison (Mrs) MA BD   1995   2000
16 Raith Crescent, Kirkcaldy KY2 5NN [E-mail: catriona@linktown.org.uk]   01592 265536

Marc Prowe
16 Raith Crescent, Kirkcaldy KY2 5NN [E-mail: marc@linktown.org.uk]   01592 265536

Buckhaven (01592 715577) and Wemyss
Wilma Cairns (Miss) BD   1999   2004
33 Main Road, East Wemyss, Kirkcaldy KY1 4RE [E-mail: wilcairns@blueyonder.co.uk]   01592 712870

Jacqueline Thomson (Mrs) MTh DCS
16 Aitken Place, Coaltown of Wemyss, Kirkcaldy KY1 4PA [E-mail: jacqueline.thomson@churchofscotland.org.uk]   01333 301115
07806 776560 (Mbl)

Burntisland (H)
Alan Sharp BSc BD   1980   2001
21 Ramsay Crescent, Burntisland KY3 9JL [E-mail: alansharp03@aol.com]   01592 874303

Dysart: St Clair (H)
Maudeen I. MacDougall (Miss) BA BD MTh   1978   2014
1 School Brae, Dysart, Kirkcaldy KY1 2XB [E-mail: rev.maudeen@gmail.com]   01592 561967

Glenrothes: Christ's Kirk (H)
Vacant

12 The Limekilns, Glenrothes KY6 3QJ   01592 620536

Glenrothes: St Columba's (01592 752539) (Rothes Trinity Parish Grouping)
Alan Kimmitt BSc BD — 2013 — 40 Liberton Drive, Glenrothes KY6 3PB [E-mail: alan@kimmitt.org.uk] — 01592 742233

Glenrothes: St Margaret's (H) (01592 328162)
Eileen Miller BD MBACP (Snr. Accred.) DipCouns DipComEd — 2014 — 8 Alburne Park, Glenrothes KY7 5RB [Email: emiller@churchofscotland.org.uk] — 01592 752241

Glenrothes: St Ninian's (H) (01592 610560) (E-mail: office@stninians.co.uk) (Rothes Trinity Parish Grouping)
Allistair Roy BD DipSW PGDip — 2007 — 1 Cawdor Drive, Glenrothes KY6 2HN [E-mail: alli@stninians.co.uk] — 01592 611963

Kennoway, Windygates and Balgonie: St Kenneth's (01333 351372) (E-mail: stkennethsparish@gmail.com)
Richard Baxter MA BD — 1997 — 2 Fernhill Gardens, Windygates, Leven KY8 5DZ [E-mail: richard-baxter@msn.com] — 01333 352329

Kinghorn
James Reid BD — 1985 1997 — 17 Myre Crescent, Kinghorn, Burntisland KY3 9UB [E-mail: jim17reid@aol.com] — 01592 890269

Kirkcaldy: Abbotshall (H) (Website: www.abbotshallchurch.org.uk)
Rosemary Frew (Mrs) MA BD — 1988 2005 — 83 Milton Road, Kirkcaldy KY1 1TP [E-mail: rfrew@churchofscotland.org.uk] — 01592 260315

Kirkcaldy: Bennochy
Robin J. McAlpine BDS BD MTh — 1988 2011 — 25 Bennochy Avenue, Kirkcaldy KY2 5QE [E-mail: rmcalpine@churchofscotland.org.uk] — 01592 643518

Kirkcaldy: Linktown See Auchtertool

Kirkcaldy: Pathhead (H) (Tel/Fax: 01592 204635) (E-mail: pathheadchurch@btinternet.com) (Website: www.pathheadparishchurch.co.uk)
Andrew C. Donald BD DPS — 1992 2005 — 73 Loughborough Road, Kirkcaldy KY1 3DD [E-mail: andrewcdonald@blueyonder.co.uk] — 01592 652215

Kirkcaldy: St Bryce Kirk (H) (01592 640016) (E-mail: office@stbrycekirk.org.uk)
Ken Froude MA BD
1979
6 East Fergus Place, Kirkcaldy KY1 1XT
[E-mail: kenfroude@blueyonder.co.uk]
01592 264480

Kirkcaldy: Templehall (H)
Anthony J.R. Fowler BSc BD
1982   2004
35 Appin Crescent, Kirkcaldy KY2 6EJ
[E-mail: afowler@churchofscotland.org.uk]
01592 260156

Kirkcaldy: Torbain
Ian Elston BD MTh
1999
91 Sauchenbush Road, Kirkcaldy KY2 5RN
[E-mail: elston667@btinternet.com]
01592 263015

Michael Allardyce MA MPhil PGCertTHE FHEA
(Ordained Local Minister)
2014
20 Parbroath Road, Glenrothes KY7 4TH
[E-mail: m.allardice@dundee.ac.uk]
01592 772280
07936 203465 (Mbl)

Leslie: Trinity (Rothes Trinity Parish Grouping)
Guardianship of the Presbytery

Leven
Gilbert C. Nisbet CA BD
1993   2007
5 Forman Road, Leven KY8 4HH
[E-mail: gcn-leven@blueyonder.co.uk]
01333 303339

Markinch and Thornton
Vacant
7 Guthrie Crescent, Markinch, Glenrothes KY7 6AY
01592 758264

Methil: Wellesley (H)
Gillian Paterson (Mrs) BD
2010
10 Vettriano Vale, Leven KY8 4GD
[E-mail: gillianpaterson10@hotmail.co.uk]
01333 423147

Methilhill and Denbeath
Elisabeth F. Cranfield (Ms) MA BD
1988
9 Chemiss Road, Methilhill, Leven KY8 2BS
[E-mail: ecranfield@btinternet.com]
01592 713142

Adams, David G. BD	1991	2011	(Cowdenbeath: Trinity)	13 Fernhill Gardens, Windygates, Leven KY8 5DZ [E-mail: adams.69@btinternet.com]	01333 351214
Collins, Mitchell BD CPS	1996	2005	(Creich, Flisk and Kilmany with Monimail)	6 Netherby Park, Glenrothes KY6 3PL [E-mail: collinsmit@aol.com]	01592 742915
Elston, Peter K.	1963	2000	(Dalgety)	6 Cairngorm Crescent, Kirkcaldy KY2 5RF [E-mail: peterkelston@btinternet.com]	01592 205622

Name	Years	Role / Church	Address	Telephone
Ferguson, David J. MA	1966 2001	(Bellie with Speymouth)	4 Russell Gardens, Ladybank, Cupar KY15 7LT	01337 831406
Forrester, Ian L. MA	1964 1996	(Friockheim Kinnell with Inverkeilor and Lunan)		
Forsyth, Alexander R. TD BA MTh	1973 2013	(Markinch)	8 Bennochy Avenue, Kirkcaldy KY2 5QE	01592 260251
			49 Scaraben Crescent, Formonthills, Glenrothes KY6 3HL	01592 749049
			[E-mail: alex@arforsyth.com]	07756 239021 (Mbl)
Galbraith, Douglas MA BD BMus MPhil ARSCM PhD	1965 2005	Editor: *The Year Book*	34 Balbirnie Street, Markinch, Glenrothes KY7 6DA	01592 752403
			[E-mail: dgalbraith@hotmail.com]	
Gatt, David W.	1981 1995	(Thornton)	15 Beech Avenue, Thornton, Kirkcaldy KY1 4AT	01592 774328
Gibson, Ivor MA	1957 1993	(Abercorn with Dalmeny)	15 McInnes Road, Markinch, Glenrothes KY7 6BA	01592 759982
Gisbey, John E. MA BD MSc DipEd	1964 2002	(Thornhill)	Whitemyre House, 28 St Andrews Road, Largoward, Leven KY9 1HZ	01334 840540
Gordon, Ian D. LTh	1972 2001	(Markinch)	2 Somerville Way, Glenrothes KY7 5GE	01592 742487
Houghton, Christine (Mrs) BD	1997 2010	(Whitburn: South)	39 Cedar Crescent, Thornton, Kirkcaldy KY1 4BE	01592 772823
			[E-mail: c.houghton1@btinternet.com]	
McLeod, Alistair G.	1988 2005	(Glenrothes: St Columba's)	13 Greenmantle Way, Glenrothes KY6 3QG	01592 744558
			[E-mail: alistairmcleod193@gmail.com]	
McNaught, Samuel M. MA BD MTh	1968 2002	(Kirkcaldy: St John's)	6 Munro Court, Glenrothes KY7 5GD	01592 742352
			[E-mail: sjmcnaught@btinternet.com]	
Munro, Andrew MA BD PhD	1972 2000	(Glencaple with Lowther)	7 Dunvegan Avenue, Kirkcaldy KY2 5SG	01592 566129
			[E-mail: am.smm@blueyonder.co.uk]	
Nicol, George G. BD DPhil	1982 2013	(Falkland with Freuchie)	48 Fidra Avenue, Burntisland KY3 0AZ	01592 873258
			[E-mail: ggnicol@totalise.co.uk]	
Paterson, Maureen (Mrs) BSc	1992 2010	(Auxiliary Minister)	91 Dalmahoy Crescent, Kirkcaldy KY2 6TA	01592 262300
			[E-mail: m.e.paterson@blueyonder.co.uk]	
Templeton, James L. BSc BD	1975 2012	(Innerleven: East)	29 Coldstream Avenue, Leven KY8 5TN	01333 427102
			[E-mail: jamietempleton@btinternet.com]	
Thomson, John D. BD	1985 2005	(Kirkcaldy: Pathhead)	3 Tottenham Court, Hill Street, Dysart, Kirkcaldy KY1 2XY	01592 655313
			[E-mail: j.thomson10@sky.com]	07885 414979 (Mbl)
Tomlinson, Bryan L. TD	1969 2003	(Kirkcaldy: Abbotshall)	2 Duddingston Drive, Kirkcaldy KY2 6JP	01592 564843
			[E-mail: abbkirk@blueyonder.co.uk]	
Webster, Elspeth H. (Miss) DCS	1990 2012	(Deacon)	82 Broomhill Avenue, Burntisland KY3 0BP	01592 873616
Wilson, Tilly (Miss) MTh		(Dysart)	6 Citron Glebe, Kirkcaldy KY1 2NF	01592 263141
			[E-mail: tillywilson@blueyonder.co.uk]	

KIRKCALDY ADDRESSES

Abbotshall	Abbotshall Road		
Bennochy	Elgin Street	Templehall	Beauty Place
Linktown	Nicol Street x High Street	Torbain	Lindores Drive
Pathhead	Harriet Street x Church Street	Viewforth	Viewforth Street x Viewforth Terrace
St Bryce Kirk	St Brycedale Avenue x Kirk Wynd		

(26) ST ANDREWS

Meets at Cupar, in St John's Church Hall, on the first Wednesday of February, May, September, October, November and December, and on the last Wednesday of June.

Clerk:	**REV. NIGEL J. ROBB** FCP MA BD ThM MTh	Presbytery Office, The Basement, 1 Howard Place, St Andrews KY16 9HL
		01334 461300
		[E-mail: standrews@churchofscotland.org.uk]
Depute Clerk:	**MRS CATHERINE WILSON**	5 Taeping Close, Cellardyke, Anstruther KY10 3YL
		01333 310936
		[E-mail: catherine.wilson15@btinternet.com]

Abdie and Dunbog (H) linked with Newburgh (H)
Lynn Brady (Miss) BD DipMin   1996   2002
2 Guthrie Court, Cupar Road, Newburgh, Cupar KY14 6HA   01337 842228
[E-mail: revbrady1963@yahoo.co.uk]

Anstruther linked with Cellardyke (H) linked with Kilrenny
Arthur A. Christie BD   1997   2009
16 Taeping Close, Cellardyke, Anstruther KY10 3YL   01333 313917
[E-mail: revaac@btinternet.com]

Auchtermuchty (H) linked with Edenshead and Strathmiglo
James G. Redpath BD DipPTh   1988   2006
The Manse, Kirk Wynd, Strathmiglo, Cupar KY14 7QS   01337 860256
[E-mail: james.redpath2@btopenworld.com]

Balmerino (H) linked with Wormit (H)
James Connolly   1982   2004
DipTh CertMin MA(Theol) DMin
5 Westwater Place, Newport-on-Tay DD6 8NS   01382 542626
[E-mail: revconnolly@btinternet.com]

Boarhills and Dunino linked with St Andrews: Holy Trinity
Vacant

Cameron linked with St Andrews: St Leonard's (H) (01334 478702) (E-mail: stlencam@btconnect.com)
Alan D. McDonald LLB BD MTh DLitt DD   1979   1998
1 Cairnhill Gardens, St Andrews KY16 8QY   01334 472793
[E-mail: alan.d.mcdonald@talk21.com]

Carnbee linked with Pittenweem
Margaret E.S. Rose BD   2007
29 Milton Road, Pittenweem, Anstruther KY10 2LN   01333 312838
[E-mail: mgt.r@btopenworld.com]

Cellardyke See Anstruther

Ceres, Kemback and Springfield
James W. Campbell BD
1995 2010
The Manse, St Andrews Road, Ceres, Cupar KY15 5NQ
[E-mail: revjimashkirk@aol.com]
01334 829350

Crail linked with Kingsbarns (H)
Ann Allison BSc PhD BD
2000 2011
The Manse, St Andrews Road, Crail, Anstruther KY10 3UH
[E-mail: revann@sky.com]
01333 451986

Creich, Flisk and Kilmany
Vacant

Cupar: Old (H) and St Michael of Tarvit
Vacant
76 Hogarth Drive, Cupar KY15 5YH
01334 653196

Cupar: St John's and Dairsie United
Jan J. Steyn (Mr)
2011
The Manse, 23 Hogarth Drive, Cupar KY15 5YH
[E-mail: jansteyn464@btinternet.com]
01334 650751

Edenshead and Strathmiglo See Auchtermuchty

Elie (H) Kilconquhar and Colinsburgh (H)
Emma McDonald BD
2013
30 Bank Street, Elie, Leven KY9 1BW
[E-mail: lomond73@btinternet.com]
01333 330597

Falkland linked with Freuchie (H)
Vacant
1 Newton Road, Falkland, Cupar KY15 7AQ
01337 858557

Freuchie See Falkland

Howe of Fife
William F. Hunter MA BD
1986 2011
The Manse, 83 Church Street, Ladybank, Cupar KY15 7ND
[E-mail: mail@billhunter.plus.com]
01337 832717

Kilrenny See Anstruther
Kingsbarns See Crail

Largo and Newburn (H) linked with Largo: St David's
John A.H. Murdoch BA BD DPSS 1979 2006 The Manse, Church Place, Upper Largo, Leven KY8 6EH [E-mail: jm.largo@btinternet.com] 01333 360286

Largo: St David's See Largo and Newburn

Largoward (H) linked with St Monans (H)
Peter W. Mills CB BD DD CPS 1984 2013 The Manse, St Monans, Anstruther KY10 2DD [E-mail: pwmills@live.co.uk] 01333 730258

Leuchars: St Athernase
Vacant 7 David Wilson Park, Balmullo, St Andrews KY16 0NP 01334 870038

Monimail See Cupar: Old
Newburgh See Abdie and Dunbog

Newport-on-Tay (H)
Stanley A. Brook BD MTh 1977 2009 8 Gowrie Street, Newport-on-Tay DD6 8ED [E-mail: stan_brook@hotmail.com] 01382 540009

Pittenweem See Carnbee

St Andrews: Holy Trinity See Boarhills and Dunino

St Andrews: Hope Park and Martyrs' (H) linked with Strathkinness
Allan McCafferty BSc BD 1993 2011 20 Priory Gardens, St Andrews KY16 8XX [E-mail: minister@hpmchurch.org.uk] 01334 478287 (Tel/Fax)

St Andrews: St Leonard's See Cameron
St Monans See Largoward
Strathkinness See St Andrews: Hope Park and Martyrs'

Tayport
Brian H. Oxburgh BSc BD   27 Bell Street, Tayport DD6 9AP   01382 553879
[E-mail: b.oxburgh@btinternet.com]

Wornit See Balmerino

Name	Years	Position	Address	Tel.
Alexander, James S. MA BD BA PhD	1966 1973	(University of St Andrews) Principal, St Mary's College	5 Strathkinness High Road, St Andrews KY16 9RP	01334 472680
Bradley, Ian C. MA BD DPhil	1990		4 Donaldson Gardens, St Andrews KY16 9DN [E-mail: icb@st-andrews.ac.uk]	01334 475389
Brown, Harry J. LTh	1991 2009	(Dundee: Menzieshill)	6 Hall Street, Kettlebridge, Cupar KY15 7QF [E-mail: harrybrown@aol.com]	01337 830088
Cameron, John U. BA BSc PhD BD ThD	1974 2008	(Dundee: Broughty Ferry St Stephen's and West)	10 Howard Place, St Andrews KY16 9HL	01334 474474
Connolly, Daniel BD DipTheol Dip Min	1983	Army Chaplain	2 Cairngreen, Cupar KY15 2SY	(Mbl) 07951 078478
Douglas, Peter C. JP	1966 1993	(Boarhills with Dunino)	The Old Schoolhouse, Flisk, Newburgh, Cupar KY14 6HN	01337 870218
Earnshaw, Philip BA BSc BD	1986 1996	(Glasgow: Pollokshields)	22 Castle Street, St Monans, Anstruther KY10 2AP	01333 730640
Fairlie, George BD BVMS MRCVS	1971 2002	(Crail with Kingsbarns)	41 Warrack Street, St Andrews KY16 8DR	01334 475868
Fraser, Ann G. BD CertMin	1990 2007	(Auchtermuchty)	24 Irvine Crescent, St Andrews KY16 8LG [E-mail: anngilfraser@btinternet.com]	(Tel/Fax) 01334 461329
Galloway, Robert W.C. LTh	1970 1998	(Cromarty)	22 Haughgate, Leven KY8 4SG	01333 426223
Gordon, Peter M. MA BD	1958 1995	(Airdrie: West)	3 Cupar Road, Cuparmuir, Cupar KY15 5RH [E-mail: machrie@madasafish.com]	01334 652341
Hamilton, Ian W.F. BD LTh ALCM AVCM	1978 2012	(Nairn: Old)	Mossneuk, 5 Windsor Gardens, St Andrews KY16 8XL [E-mail: reviwfh@btinternet.com]	01334 477745
Harrison, Cameron	2006	(Auxiliary Minister)	Woodfield House, Priormuir, St Andrews KY16 8LP	01334 478067
Hegarty, John D. LTh ABSC	1988 2004	(Buckie: South and West with Enzie)	26 Montgomery Way, Kinross KY13 8FD [E-mail: john.hegarty@tesco.net]	01577 863829
Jeffrey, Kenneth S. BA BD PhD	2002 2014	University of Aberdeen	The North Steading, Dalgairn, Cupar KY15 4PH [E-mail: ksjeffrey@btopenworld.com]	01334 653196
MacEwan, Donald G. MA BD PhD	2001 2012	Chaplain: University of St Andrews	Chaplaincy Centre, 3A St Mary's Place, St Andrews KY16 9UY [E-mail: dgm21@st-andrews.ac.uk]	01334 462865 (Mbl) 07713 322036
McGregor, Duncan J. MIFM	1982 1996	(Channelkirk with Lauder: Old)	14 Mount Melville, St Andrews KY16 8NG	01334 478314
Mackenzie, A. Cameron MA	1955 1995	(Biggar)	Hedgerow, 5 Shiels Avenue, Freuchie, Cupar KY15 7JD	01337 857763
McLean, John P. BSc BPhil BD	1994 2013	(Glenrothes: St Margaret's)	72 Lawmill Gardens, St Andrews KY16 8QS [E-mail: john@mcleanmail.me.uk]	01334 470803
Meager, Peter MA BD CertMgmt(Open)	1971 1998	(Elie with Kilconquhar and Colinsburgh)	7 Lorraine Drive, Cupar KY15 5DY	01334 656991
Neilson, Peter MA BD MTh	1975 2006	(Mission Consultant)	Linne Bheag, 2 School Green, Anstruther KY10 3HF [E-mail: neilson.peter@btinternet.com]	01333 310477 (Mbl) 07818 418608
Petrie, Ian D. MA BD	1970 2008	(Dundee: St Andrew's)	27/111 West Savile Terrace, Edinburgh EH9 3DR [E-mail: idp-77@hotmail.com]	0131-237 2857
Reid, Alan A.S. MA BD STM	1962 1995	(Bridge of Allan: Chalmers)	Wayside Cottage, Bridgend, Ceres, Cupar KY15 5LS	01334 828509

Name	Ordained	Inducted	Charge/Position	Address	Phone
Robb, Nigel J. FCP MA BD ThM MTh	1981	2014	Presbytery Clerk	Presbytery Office, Hope Park and Martyrs' Church, 1 Howard Place, St Andrews KY16 9UY	(Mbl) 07966 286958
Roy, Alan J. BSc BD	1960	1999	(Aberuthven with Dunning)	14 Comerton Place, Drumoig, Leuchars, St Andrews KY16 0NQ [E-mail: a.roy225@btinternet.com]	01382 542225
Salters, Robert B. MA BD PhD	1966	1971	(University of St Andrews)	Vine Cottage, 119 South Street, St Andrews KY16 9UH	01334 473198
Strong, Clifford LTh	1983	1995	(Creich, Flisk and Kilmany with Monimail)		
Taylor, Ian BSc MA LTh DipEd	1983	1997	(Abdie and Dunbog with Newburgh)	60 Maryknowe, Gauldry, Newport-on-Tay DD6 8SL	01382 330445
				Lundie Cottage, Arncroach, Anstruther KY10 2RN	01333 720222
Thrower, Charles G. BSc	1965	2002	(Carnbee with Pittenweem)	Grange House, Wester Grangemuir, Pittenweem, Anstruther KY10 2RB [E-mail: charlesandsteph@btinternet.com]	01333 312631
Torrance, Alan J. (Prof.) MA BD DrTheol	1984	1999	University of St Andrews	Kincaple House, Kincaple, St Andrews KY16 9SH	(Home) 01334 850755 (Office) 01334 462843
Walker, James B. MA BD DPhil	1975	2011	(Chaplain: University of St Andrews)	5 Priestden Park, St Andrews KY16 8DL	01334 472839
Wotherspoon, Ian G. BA LTh	1967	2004	(Coatbridge: St Andrew's)	12 Cherry Lane, Cupar KY15 5DA [E-mail: wotherspoonrig@aol.com]	01334 650710
Wright, Lynda (Miss) BEd DCS			Chaplain, Cameron Hospital	Chaplain's Office, Cameron Hospital, Cameron Bridge, Windygates, Leven KY8 5RR [E-mail: lynda.keyhouse@tiscali.co.uk]	(Mbl) 07835 303395
Young, Evelyn M. (Mrs) BSc BD	1984	2003	(Kilmun (St Munn's) with Strone and Ardentinny)	2 Priestden Place, St Andrews KY16 8DP	01334 479662

(27) DUNKELD AND MEIGLE

Meets at Pitlochry on the first Tuesday of February, September and December, on the third Tuesday of April and the fourth Tuesday of October, and at the Moderator's church on the third Tuesday of June.

Clerk:	**REV. JOHN RUSSELL MA**			**Kilblaan, Gladstone Terrace, Birnam, Dunkeld PH8 0DP** [E-mail: dunkeldmeigle@churchofscotland.org.uk]	**01350 728896**
Depute Clerk:	**REV. ALISON NOTMAN BD**			**The Manse, Dundee Road, Meigle, Blairgowrie PH12 8SB**	**01828 640074**

Aberfeldy (H) linked with Dull and Weem (H)
Vacant   The Manse, Taybridge Terrace, Aberfeldy PH15 2BS

Alyth (H)
Michael J. Erskine MA BD   1985   2012   The Manse, Cambridge Street, Alyth, Blairgowrie PH11 8AW   01828 632238
[E-mail: erskinemike@gmail.com]

Amulree and Strathbraan See Aberfeldy

Ardler, Kettins and Meigle
Alison Notman BD — 2014 — The Manse, Dundee Road, Meigle, Blairgowrie PH12 8SB [E-mail: anotman@churchofscotland.org.uk] — 01828 640074

Bendochy linked with Coupar Angus: Abbey
Vacant — Caddam Road, Coupar Angus, Blairgowrie PH13 9EF — 01828 627331

Blair Atholl and Struan linked with Tenandry
Vacant — Blair Atholl, Pitlochry PH18 5SX — 01796 481213

Blairgowrie
Harry Mowbray BD CA — 2003 2008 — The Manse, Upper David Street, Blairgowrie PH10 6HB [E-mail: hmowbray@viewlands.plus.com] — 01250 872146

Braes of Rannoch linked with Foss and Rannoch (H)
Vacant — The Manse, Kinloch Rannoch, Pitlochry PH16 5QA — 01882 632381

Caputh and Clunie (H) linked with Kinclaven (H)
Peggy Ewart-Roberts BA BD — 2003 2011 — Cara Beag, Essendy Road, Blairgowrie PH10 6QU [E-mail: revpeggy.r@googlemail.com] — 01250 876897

Coupar Angus: Abbey See Bendochy
Dull and Weem See Aberfeldy

Dunkeld (H)
R. Fraser Penny BA BD — 1984 2001 — Cathedral Manse, Dunkeld PH8 0AW [E-mail: fraserpenn@aol.com] — 01350 727249

Fortingall and Glenlyon linked with Kenmore and Lawers (H)
Anne J. Brennan BSc BD MTh — 1999 — The Manse, Balnaskeag, Kenmore, Aberfeldy PH15 2HB [E-mail: annebrennan@yahoo.co.uk] — 01887 830218

Foss and Rannoch See Braes of Rannoch

Grantully, Logierait and Strathtay
Vacant — The Manse, Strathtay, Pitlochry PH9 0PG — 01887 840251

Kenmore and Lawers See Fortingall and Glenlyon
Kinclaven See Caputh and Clunie

Kirkmichael, Straloch and Glenshee linked with Rattray (H)

Linda Stewart (Mrs) BD	1996	2012	The Manse, Alyth Road, Rattray, Blairgowrie PH10 7HF [E-mail: lindacstewart@tiscali.co.uk]	01250 872462

Pitlochry (H) (01796 472160)

Mary M. Haddow (Mrs) BD	2001	2012	Manse Road, Moulin, Pitlochry PH16 5EP [E-mail: mary_haddow@btconnect.com]	01796 472774

Rattray See Kirkmichael, Straloch and Glenshee
Tenandry See Blair Atholl and Struan

Campbell, Richard S. LTh	1993	2010	(Gargunnock with Kilmadock with Kincardine-in-Menteith)	3 David Farquharson Road, Blairgowrie PH10 6FD [E-mail: revrichards@yahoo.co.uk]	01250 876386
Cassells, Alexander K. MA BD	1961	1997	(Leuchars: St Athernase and Guardbridge)	47 Burghmuir Road, Perth PH1 1JG	01738 637995
Creegan, Christine M. (Mrs) MTh	1993	2005	(Grantully, Logierait and Strathtay)	Lonag, 28 Lettoch Terrace, Pitlochry PH16 5BA	01796 472422
Duncan, James BTh FSAScot	1980	1995	(Blair Atholl and Struan)	25 Knockard Avenue, Pitlochry PH16 5JE	01796 474096
Ewart, William BSc BD	1972	2010	(Caputh and Clunie with Kinclaven)	Cara Beag, Essendy Road, Blairgowrie PH10 6QU [E-mail: ewe1@btinternet.com]	01250 876897
Knox, John W. MTheol	1992	1997	(Lochgelly: Macainsh)	Heatherlea, Main Street, Ardler, Blairgowrie PH12 8SR	01828 640731
McAlister, D.J.B. MA BD PhD	1951	1989	(North Berwick: Blackadder)	2 Duff Avenue, Moulin, Pitlochry PH16 5EN	01796 473591
McFadzean, Iain MA PhD	1989	2010	National Director: Workplace Chaplaincy (Scotland)	2 Lowfield Crescent, Luncarty, Perth PH1 3FG [E-mail: iain.mcfadzean@wpcscotland.co.uk]	01738 827338 (Mbl) 07969 227696
MacRae, Malcolm H. MA PhD	1971	2010	(Kirkmichael, Straloch and Glenshee with Rattray)	10B Victoria Place, Stirling FK8 2QU [E-mail: malcolm.macrae1@btopenworld.com]	01786 465547
MacVicar, Kenneth MBE DFC TD MA	1950	1990	(Kenmore with Lawers with Fortingall and Glenlyon)	Illeray, Kenmore, Aberfeldy PH15 2HE	01887 830514
Nelson, Robert C. BA BD	1980	2010	(Isle of Mull, Kilninian and Kilmore with Salen and Ulva with Tobermory with Torosay and Kinlochspelvie)	St Colme's, Perth Road, Birnam, Dunkeld PH8 0BH [E-mail: robertnelson@onetel.net]	01350 727455
Ormiston, Hugh C. BSc BD MPhil PhD	1969	2004	(Kirkmichael, Straloch and Glenshee with Rattray)	Cedar Lea, Main Road, Woodside, Blairgowrie PH13 9NP	01828 670539
Oswald, John BSc PhD BD	1997	2011	(Muthill with Trinity Gask and Kinkell)	1 Woodlands Meadow, Rosemount, Blairgowrie PH10 6GZ [E-mail: revdocoz@bigfoot.com]	01250 872598
Ramsay, Malcolm BA LLB DipMin	1986	2011	Overseas service in Nepal	c/o World Mission Council, 121 George Street, Edinburgh EH2 4YN [E-mail: amalcolmramsay@gmail.com]	0131-225 5722
Robertson, Matthew LTh	1968	2002	(Cawdor with Croy and Dalcross)	Inver, Strathtay, Pitlochry PH9 0PG	01887 840780

Russell, John MA	1959	2000	(Tillicoultry)	Kilblaan, Gladstone Terrace, Birnam, Dunkeld PH8 0DP	01350 728896
Shannon, W.G. MA BD	1955	1998	(Pitlochry)	19 Knockard Road, Pitlochry PH16 5HJ	01796 473533
Sloan, Robert BD	1997	2014	(Fauldhouse St Andrew's)	3 Gean Grove, Blairgowrie PH10 6TL	01250 875286
Tait, Thomas W. BD MBE	1972	1997	(Rattray)	3 Rosemount Park, Blairgowrie PH10 6TZ	01250 874833
Whyte, William B. BD	1973	2003	(Nairn: St Ninian's)	The Old Inn, Park Hill Road, Rattray, Blairgowrie PH10 7DS	01250 874401
Wilson, John M. MA BD	1965	2004	(Altnaharra and Farr)	Berbice, The Terrace, Blair Atholl, Pitlochry PH18 5SZ	01796 481619
Wilson, Mary D. (Mrs) RGN SCM DTM	1990	2004	(Auxiliary Minister)	Berbice, The Terrace, Blair Atholl, Pitlochry PH18 5SZ	01796 481619

(28) PERTH

Meets at 10am on the second Saturday of September, December, March, and June at Kinross and other venues within the bounds.

Clerk:	**REV. J. COLIN CASKIE BA BD**	
Presbytery Office:	**209 High Street, Perth PH1 5PB**	**01738 451177**
	[E-mail: perth@churchofscotland.org.uk]	

Aberdalgie (H) and Forteviot (H) linked with Aberuthven and Dunning (H)
Vacant   Aberdalgie, Perth PH2 0QD

Abernethy and Dron and Arngask
Moira Herkes BD   1985 2014   3 Manse Road, Abernethy, Perth PH2 9JP   01738 850938
[E-mail: minister@abernethydronarngaskchurch.org.uk]

Aberuthven and Dunning See Aberdalgie and Forteviot

Almondbank Tibbermore linked with Methven and Logiealmond
Philip W. Patterson BMus BD   1999 2008   The Manse, Pitcairngreen, Perth PH1 3EA   01738 583217
[E-mail: philip.patterson@btinternet.com]

Ardoch (H) linked with Blackford (H)
Vacant   01786 880217

Auchterarder (H)
Robert D. Barlow   2010 2013   22 Kirkfield Place, Auchterarder PH3 1FP   01764 662399
BA BSc MSc PhD CChem MRSC   [E-mail: rbarlow@churchofscotland.org.uk]

Auchtergaven and Moneydie linked with Redgorton and Stanley
Adrian J. Lough BD   2012   22 King Street, Stanley, Perth PH1 4ND   01738 827952
                                                                        [E-mail: alough@churchofscotland.org.uk]

Blackford See Ardoch

Cargill Burrelton linked with Collace
Vacant   The Manse, Manse Road, Woodside, Blairgowrie PH13 9NQ   01828 670352

Cleish (H) linked with Fossoway: St Serf's and Devonside
Elisabeth M. Stenhouse BD   2006   2014   Station House, Station Road, Crook of Devon, Kinross KY13 0PG   01577 842128
                                                                        [E-mail: estenhouse@churchofscotland.org.uk]

Collace See Cargill Burrelton

Comrie (H) linked with Dundurn (H)
Graham McWilliams BSc BD   2005   The Manse, Strowan Road, Comrie, Crieff PH6 2ES   01764 670076
                                                                        [E-mail: gmcwilliams@churchofscotland.org.uk]

Crieff (H)
Andrew J. Philip BSc BD   1996   2013   8 Strathearn Terrace, Crieff PH7 3AQ   01764 218976
                                                                        [E-mail: aphilip@churchofscotland.org.uk]

Dunbarney (H) and Forgandenny
Allan J. Wilson BSc MEd BD   2007   Dunbarney Manse, Manse Road, Bridge of Earn, Perth PH2 9DY   01738 812211
                                                                        [E-mail: awilson@churchofscotland.org.uk]
Susan Thorburn MTh   2014   3 Daleally Farm Cottages, St Madoes Road, Errol, Perth PH2 7TJ   01821 642681
  (Ordained Local Minister)

Dundurn See Comrie

Errol (H) linked with Kilspindie and Rait
Vacant   South Bank, Errol, Perth PH2 7PZ   01821 642279

Fossoway: St Serf's and Devonside See Cleish

Fowlis Wester, Madderty and Monzie linked with Gask (H)
Vacant   Beechview, Abercairney, Crieff PH7 3NF   01764 652116

Gask See Fowlis Wester, Madderty and Monzie
Kilspindie and Rait See Errol

Kinross (H) (Office: 01577 862570)
Alan D. Reid MA BD 1989 2009
15 Green Wood, Kinross KY13 8FG
[E-mail: areid@churchofscotland.org.uk]
01577 862952

Methven and Logiealmond See Almondbank Tibbermore

Muthill (H) linked with Trinity Gask and Kinkell
Klaus O.F. Buwert LLB BD DMin 1984 2013
The Manse, Station Road, Muthill, Crieff PH5 2AR
[E-mail: klaus@buwert.co.uk]
01764 681205

Orwell (H) and Portmoak (H) (Office: 01577 862100)
Angus Morrison MA BD PhD 1979 2011
41 Auld Mart Road, Milnathort, Kinross KY13 9FR
[E-mail: amorrison@churchofscotland.org.uk]
01577 863461

Perth: Craigie and Moncreiffe
Carolann Erskine BD 2009
The Manse, 46 Abbot Street, Perth PH2 0EE
[E-mail: cerskine@churchofscotland.org.uk]
01738 623748

Robert Wilkie 2011
(Auxiliary Minister)
24 Huntingtower Road, Perth PH1 2JS
[E-mail: rwilkie@churchofscotland.org.uk]
01738 628301

Perth: Kinnoull (H)
Vacant
The Broch, 34 Monart Road, Perth PH1 5UQ
01738 626046
Timothy E.G. Fletcher BA FCMA 1998
(Auxiliary Minister)
3 Ardchoille Park, Perth PH2 7TL
[E-mail: fletcherts495@btinternet.com]
01738 638189
07747 013985 (Mbl)

Perth: Letham St Mark's (H) (Office: 01738 446377)
James C. Stewart BD DipMin 1997
35 Rose Crescent, Perth PH1 1NT
[E-mail: diamondboy09@yahoo.com]
01738 624167

Kenneth D. McKay DCS
11F Balgowan Road, Perth PH1 2JG
[E-mail: kenneth.mckay@churchofscotland.org.uk]
01738 621169
07843 883042 (Mbl)

Perth: North (Office: 01738 622298)
Hugh O'Brien CSS MTheol 2001 2009
127 Glasgow Road, Perth PH2 0LU
[E-mail: hobrien@churchofscotland.org.uk]
01738 625728

Perth: Riverside (Office: 01738 622341)
David R. Rankin MA BD 2009 2014 44 Hay Street, Perth PH1 5HS 07810 008754 (Mbl)
[E-mail: drankin@churchofscotland.org.uk]

Perth: St John's Kirk of Perth (H) (01738 626159) linked with Perth: St Leonard's-in-the-Fields (H) (01738 632238)
Vacant   5 Strathearn Terrace, Perth PH2 0LS   01738 621709
Patricia Munro BSc DCS   4 Hewat Place, Perth PH1 2UD   01738 443088
                                                    [E-mail: pmunro@churchofscotland.org.uk]   07814 836314 (Mbl)

Perth: St Leonard's-in-the-Fields See Perth: St John's Kirk of Perth

Perth: St Matthew's (Office: 01738 636757; Vestry: 01738 630725)
Scott Burton BD DipMin 1999 2007 23 Kincarrathie Crescent, Perth PH2 7HH 01738 626828
[E-mail: minister@stmatts.org.uk]

Redgorton and Stanley See Auchtergaven and Moneydie

St Madoes and Kinfauns
Marc F. Bircham BD MTh 2000 Glencarse, Perth PH2 7NF 01738 860837
[E-mail: mbircham@churchofscotland.org.uk]

Scone and St Martins
Vacant
Alan Livingstone 2013 Meadowside, Lawmuir, Methven, Perth PH1 3SZ 01738 840682
(Ordained Local Minister) [E-mail: livingstone24@btinternet.com]

Trinity Gask and Kinkell See Muthill

Ballentine, Ann M. MA BD 1981 2007 (Kirknewton and East Calder) 17 Nellfield Road, Crieff PH7 3DU 01764 652567
[E-mail: annmballentine@gmail.com]

Name	Ord./Ind.	Charge/Position	Address	Phone
Barr, George K. ARIBA BD PhD	1967 1993	(Uddingston: Viewpark)	7 Tay Avenue, Comrie, Crieff PH6 2PF [E-mail: gbarr2@compuserve.com]	01764 670454
Barr, T. Leslie LTh	1969 1997	(Kinross)	8 Fairfield Road, Kelty KY4 0BY [E-mail: leslie_barr@yahoo.com]	01383 839330
Bertram, Thomas A.	1972 1995	(Patna Waterside)	3 Scrimgeours Corner, 29 West High Street, Crieff PH7 4AP	01764 652066
Brown, Elizabeth JP RGN	1996 2007	(Auxiliary Minister)	8 Viewlands Place, Perth PH1 1BS [E-mail: liz.brown@blueyonder.co.uk]	01738 552391
Brown, Marina D. MA BD MTh	2000 2012	(Hawick: St Mary's and Old)	Moneydie School Cottage, Luncarty, Perth PH1 3HZ [E-mail: revmdb1711@btinternet.com]	01738 582163
Buchan, William DipTheol BD	1987 2001	(Kilwinning: Abbey)	34 Bridgewater Avenue, Auchterarder PH3 1DQ [E-mail: billbuchan3@btinternet.com]	01764 660306
Cairns, Evelyn BD	2004 2012	(Chaplain: Rachel House)	15 Talla Park, Kinross KY13 8AB [E-mail: revelyn@btinternet.com]	01577 863990
Caskie, J. Colin BA BD	1977 2012	Presbytery Clerk	13 Anderson Drive, Perth PH1 1JZ [E-mail: jcolincaskie@gmail.com]	01738 445543
Coleman, Sidney H. BA BD MTh	1961 2001	(Glasgow: Merrylea)	'Blaven', 11 Clyde Place, Perth PH2 0EZ [E-mail: sidney.coleman@blueyonder.co.uk]	01738 565072
Craig, Joan H. MTheol	1986 2005	(Orkney: East Mainland)	7 Jedburgh Place, Perth PH1 1SJ [E-mail: joanhcraig@btinternet.com]	01738 580180
Donaldson, Robert B. BSocSc	1953 1997	(Kilchoman with Portnahaven)	11 Strathearn Court, Crieff PH7 3DS	01764 654976
Drummond, Alfred G. BD DMin	1991 2006	Scottish General Secretary: Evangelical Alliance	10 Errochty Court, Perth PH1 2SU [E-mail: frddrmmnd@aol.com]	01738 621305
Fleming, Hamish K. MA	1966 2001	(Banchory Ternan: East)	36 Earnmuir Road, Comrie, Crieff PH6 2EY [E-mail: hamishnan@gmail.com]	01764 679178
Graham, Sydney S. DipYL MPhil BD	1987 2009	(Iona with Kilfinichen and Kilvickeon and the Ross of Mull)	'Aspen', Milton Road, Luncarty, Perth PH1 3ES [E-mail: syd@sydgraham.plus.com]	01738 829350
Gregory, J.C. LTh	1968 1992	(Blantyre: St Andrew's)	2 Southlands Road, Auchterarder PH3 1BA	01764 664594
Gunn, Alexander M. MA BD	1967 2006	(Aberfeldy with Amulree and Strathbraan with Dull and Weem)	'Navarone', 12 Cornhill Road, Perth PH1 1LR [E-mail: sandygunn@btinternet.com]	01738 443216
Halliday, Archibald R. BD MTh	1964 1999	(Duffus, Spynie and Hopeman)	8 Turretbank Drive, Crieff PH7 4LW [E-mail: roberthalliday343@btinternet.com]	01764 656464
Kelly, T. Clifford	1973 1995	(Ferintosh)	20 Whinfield Drive, Kinross KY13 8UB	01577 864946
Lawson, James B. MA BD	1961 2002	(South Uist)	4 Cowden Way, Comrie, Crieff PH6 2NW [E-mail: james.lawson7@btopenworld.com]	01764 679180
Lawson, Ronald G. MA BD	1964 1999	(Greenock: Wellpark Mid Kirk)	6 East Brougham Street, Stanley, Perth PH1 4NJ	01738 828871
Low, J.E. Stewart MA	1957 1997	(Tarbat)	1 Cameron Court, Almond Place, Comrie PH6 2BB	01764 670461
McCormick, Alastair F.	1962 1998	(Creich with Rosehall)	14 Balmanno Park, Bridge of Earn, Perth PH2 9RJ	01738 813588
McCrum, Robert BSc BD	1982 2014	(Ayr: St James')	28 Rose Crescent, Perth PH1 1NT [E-mail: robert.mccrum@virgin.net]	01738 447906
MacDonald, James W. BD	1976 2012	(Crieff)	'Mingulay', 29 Hebridean Gardens, Crieff PH7 3BP [E-mail: rev_up@btinternet.com]	01764 654500
McGregor, William LTh	1987 2003	(Auchtergaven and Moneydie)	'Ard Choille', 7 Taypark Road, Luncarty, Perth PH1 3FE [E-mail: bill.mcgregor7@btinternet.com]	01738 827866

McIntosh, Colin G. MA BD	1976	2013	(Dunblane: Cathedral)	Drumhead Cottage, Drum, Kinross KY13 0PR [E-mail: colinmcintosh4@btinternet.com]	01577 840012
MacKenzie, Donald W. MA	1941	1983	(Auchterarder: The Barony)	81 Kingswell Terrace, Perth PH1 2DA	01738 633716
McKimmon, Eric G. BA BD MTh PhD	1983	2014	(Cargill Burrelton with Collace)	14 Marionfield Place, Cupar KY15 5JN [E-mail: ericmckimmon@gmail.com]	01334 659650
MacMillan, Riada M. BD	1991	1998	(Perth: Craigend Moncreiffe with Rhynd)	73 Muirend Gardens, Perth PH1 1JR	01738 628867
McNaughton, David J.H. BA CA	1976	1995	(Killin and Ardeonaig)	14 Rankine Court, Wormit, Newport-on-Tay DD6 8TA	
Main, Douglas M. BD	1986	2014	(Errol with Kilspindie and Rait)	14 Madoch Road, St Madoes, Perth PH2 7TT [E-mail: revdmain@sky.com]	01738 860867
Malcolm, Alistair BD DPS	1976	2012	(Inverness: Inshes)	11 Kinclaven Gardens, Murthly, Perth PH1 4EX [E-mail: amalcolm067@btinternet.com]	01738 710979
Michie, Margaret	2013		Ordained Local Minister: Loch Leven Parish Grouping	3 Loch Leven Court, Wester Balgedie, Kinross KY13 9NE [E-mail: margaretmichie@btinternet.com]	01592 840602
Millar, Archibald E. DipTh	1965	1991	(Perth: St Stephen's)	7 Maple Place, Perth PH1 1RT	01738 621813
Munro, Gillian BSc BD	1989	2003	Head of Spiritual Care, NHS Tayside	Royal Victoria Hospital, Dundee DD2 1SP	01382 423116
Paton, Iain F. BD FCIS	1980	2006	(Elie with Kilconquhar and Colinsburgh)	Muldoanich, Stirling Street, Blackford, Auchterarder PH4 1QG [E-mail: iain.f.paton@btinternet.com]	01764 682234
Patterson, Andrew R.M. MA BD	1985	2013	(Edinburgh: Portobello Old)	Hoolmyre Farm, Balbeggie, Perth PH2 6JD [E-mail: armpatterson@gmail.com]	01821 650864
Pattison, Kenneth J. MA BD STM	1967	2004	(Kilmuir and Logie Easter)	2 Castle Way, St Madoes, Glencarse, Perth PH2 7NY [E-mail: k_pattison@btinternet.com]	01738 860340
Philip, Elizabeth DCS MA BA PGCSE			Deacon	8 Strathearn Terrace, Crieff PH7 3AQ [E-mail: ephilipstitch@gmail.com]	01764 218976 (Mbl) 07970 767851
Philip, Michael R. BD	1978	2014	(Falkirk: Bainsford)	9 Muir Bank, Scone, Perth PH2 6SZ [E-mail: mrphilip@blueyonder.co.uk]	01738 564533 (Mbl) 07776 011601
Russell, Kenneth G. BD CCE	1986	2013	Prison Chaplain	158 Bannockburn Road, Stirling FK7 0EW [E-mail: kenrussell1000@hotmail.com]	01786 812680
Searle, David C. MA DipTh	1965	2003	(Warden: Rutherford House)	Stonefall Lodge, 30 Abbey Lane, Grange, Errol PH2 7GB [E-mail: dcs@davidsearle.plus.com]	01821 641004
Shirra, James MA	1945	1987	(St Martins with Scone: New)	17 Dunbarney Avenue, Bridge of Earn, Perth PH2 9BP	01738 812610
Simpson, James A. BSc BD STM DD	1960	2000	(Dornoch Cathedral)	'Dornoch', Perth Road, Bankfoot, Perth PH1 4ED [E-mail: ja@simpsondornoch.co.uk]	01738 787710
Sloan, Robert P. MA BD	1968	2007	(Braemar and Crathie)	1 Broomhill Avenue, Perth PH1 1EN [E-mail: sloan12@virginmedia.com]	01738 443904
Souter, David I. BD	1996	2015	(Perth: Kinnoull)	Duncairn, 2 Gowrie Farm, Perth PH1 4PP [E-mail: d.souter@blueyonder.co.uk]	
Stenhouse, W. Duncan MA BD	1989	2006	(Dunbarney and Forgandenny)	32 Sandport Gait, Kinross KY13 8FB	01577 866992
Stewart, Anne E. BD CertMin	1998		Prison Chaplain	35 Rose Crescent, Perth PH1 1NT [E-mail: anne.stewart2@sps.pnn.gov.uk]	01738 624167
Stewart, Gordon G. MA	1961	2000	(Perth: St Leonard's-in-the-Fields and Trinity)	'Balnoe', South Street, Rattray, Blairgowrie PH10 7BZ	01250 870626
Stewart, Robin J. MA BD STM	1959	1995	(Orwell with Portmoak)	'Oakbrae', Perth Road, Murthly, Perth PH1 4HF	01738 710220

Thomson, J. Bruce MA BD	1972	2009	(Scone: Old)	47 Elm Street, Errol, Perth PH2 7SQ [E-mail: RevBruceThomson@aol.com]	01821 641039 (Mbl) 07850 846404
Thomson, Peter D. MA BD	1968	2004	(Comrie with Dundurn)	34 Queen Street, Perth PH2 0EJ [E-mail: peterthomson208@btinternet.com]	01738 622418
Wallace, Catherine PGDipC DCS			Deacon	21 Durley Dene Crescent, Bridge of Earn PH2 9RD	
Wallace, James K. MA BD STM	1988	2015	Scotus Tours	21 Durley Dene Crescent, Bridge of Earn PH2 9RD [E-mail: jkwministry@hotmail.com]	

PERTH ADDRESSES

Craigie	Abbot Street	St John's	St John's Street
Kinnoull	Dundee Rd near Queen's Bridge	St Leonard's-in-the-Fields	Marshall Place
Letham St Mark's	Rannoch Road	St Matthew's	Tay Street
Moncreiffe	Glenbrae Crescent		
North	Mill Street near Kinnoull Street		
Riverside	Bute Drive		

(29) DUNDEE

Meets at Dundee: The Steeple, Nethergate, on the second Wednesday of February, March, May, September, November and December, and on the fourth Wednesday of June.

Clerk:	REV. JAMES L. WILSON BD CPS	[E-mail: dundee@churchofscotland.org.uk] 01382 459249 (Home) [E-mail: r3vjw@aol.com] 07885 618659 (Mobile)
Depute Clerk:	REV. JANET P. FOGGIE MA BD PhD	[E-mail: rev.foggie@btinternet.com] 01382 660152
Presbytery Office:		Whitfield Parish Church, Haddington Crescent, Dundee DD40NA 01382 503012

Abernyte linked with Inchture and Kinnaird linked with Longforgan (H)

Marjory A. MacLean LLB BD PhD RNR	1991	2011	The Manse, Longforgan, Dundee DD2 5HB [E-mail: mmaclean@churchofscotland.org.uk]	01382 360238

Auchterhouse (H) linked with Monikie and Newbigging and Murroes and Tealing (H)

David A. Collins BSc BD	1993	2006	New Kirk Manse, 25 Ballinard Gardens, Broughty Ferry, Dundee DD5 1BZ [E-mail: revdacollins@btinternet.com]	01382 778874

Dundee: Balgay (H)
Patricia Ramsay (Mrs) BD   2005   2013   150 City Road, Dundee DD2 2PW   01382 669600
[E-mail: patriciaramsay505@btinternet.com]   07813 189776 (Mbl)

Dundee: Barnhill St Margaret's (H) (01382 737294) (E-mail: church.office@btconnect.com)
Susan Sutherland (Mrs) BD   2009   2 St Margaret's Lane, Barnhill, Dundee DD5 2PQ   01382 779278
[E-mail: susan.sutherland@sky.com]

Dundee: Broughty Ferry New Kirk (H)
Catherine E.E. Collins (Mrs) MA BD   1993   2006   New Kirk Manse, 25 Ballinard Gardens, Broughty Ferry,   01382 778874
Dundee DD5 1BZ
[E-mail: revccollins@btinternet.com]

Dundee: Broughty Ferry St James' (H)
Vacant   2 Ferry Road, Monifieth, Dundee DD5 4NT   01382 534468

Dundee: Broughty Ferry St Luke's and Queen Street (01382 732094)
C. Graham D. Taylor BSc BD FIAB   2001   22 Albert Road, Broughty Ferry, Dundee DD5 1AZ   01382 779212
[E-mail: taystar.taylor@googlemail.com]

Dundee: Broughty Ferry St Stephen's and West (H) linked with Dundee (St Mary's) (H) (01382 226271)
Keith F. Hall MA BD   1980   1994   33 Strathern Road, West Ferry, Dundee DD5 1PP   01382 778808

Dundee: Camperdown (H) (01382 623958)
Vacant   Camperdown Manse, Myrekirk Road, Dundee DD2 4SF

Dundee: Chalmers-Ardler (H)
Kenneth D. Stott MA BD   1989   1997   The Manse, Turnberry Avenue, Dundee DD2 3TP   01382 827439
[E-mail: arkstotts@aol.com]

Dundee: Coldside
Anthony P. Thornthwaite MTh   1995   2011   9 Abercorn Street, Dundee DD4 7HY   01382 458314
[E-mail: tony.thornthwaite@sky.com]

Dundee: Craigiebank (H) (01382 731173) linked with Dundee: Douglas and Mid Craigie
Edith F. McMillan (Mrs) MA BD   1981   1999   19 Americanmuir Road, Dundee DD3 9AA   01382 812423
[E-mail: douglas244@tiscali.co.uk]

Dundee: Douglas and Mid Craigie See Dundee: Craigiebank

Dundee: Downfield Mains (H) (01382 810624/812166)
Vacant
9 Elgin Street, Dundee DD3 8NL
01382 827207

Dundee: Dundee (St Mary's) See Dundee: Broughty Ferry St Stephen's and West

Dundee: Fintry Parish Church
Colin M. Brough BSc BD   1998 2002   4 Clive Street, Dundee DD4 7AW
[E-mail: cbrough@churchofscotland.org.uk]
01382 458629

Dundee: Lochee (H)
Hazel Wilson (Ms) MA BD DipEd DMS   1991 2006   32 Clayhills Drive, Dundee DD2 1SX
[E-mail: hwilson704@btinternet.com]
01382 561989
Willie Strachan MBA DipY&C   2013   Ladywell House, Lucky Slap, Monikie, Dundee DD5 3QG
(Ordained Local Minister)   [E-mail: luckyslapdees@btinternet.com]
01382 370286

Dundee: Logie and St John's Cross (H) (01382 668700)
David T. Gray BArch BD   2010 2014   7 Hyndford Street, Dundee DD2 1HQ
[E-mail: minister@logies.org]
01382 668653

Dundee: Meadowside St Paul's (H) (01382 225420)
Vacant
36 Blackness Avenue, Dundee DD2 1HH
01382 668828

Dundee: Menzieshill
Robert Mallinson BD   2010   The Manse, Charleston Drive, Dundee DD2 4ED
[E-mail: bobmalli1975@hotmail.co.uk]
01382 667446
07595 249089 (Mbl)

Dundee: St Andrew's (H) (01382 224860)
Janet P. Foggie MA BD PhD   2003 2009   39 Tullideph Road, Dundee DD2 2JD
[E-mail: rev.foggie@btinternet.com]
01382 660152

Dundee: St David's High Kirk (H)
Marion J. Paton (Miss) MA BMus BD   1991 2007   6 Adelaide Place, Dundee DD3 6LF
[E-mail: sdhkrev@googlemail.com]
01382 322955

Dundee: The Steeple (H) (01382 200031) Robert A. Calvert BSc BD DMin	1983	2014	128 Arbroath Road, Dundee DD4 7HR [E-mail: robertacalvert@gmail.com]	01382 522837
Dundee: Stobswell (H) (01382 461397) William McLaren MA BD	1990	2007	23 Shamrock Street, Dundee DD4 7AH [E-mail: williammclaren63@googlemail.com]	01382 459119
Dundee: Strathmartine (H) (01382 825817) Stewart McMillan BD	1983	1990	19 Americanmuir Road, Dundee DD3 9AA [E-mail: mcmillan_strath@btinternet.com]	01382 812423
Dundee: Trinity (H) Vacant			65 Clepington Road, Dundee DD4 7BQ	01382 458764
Dundee: West Andrew T. Greaves BD	1985	2000	Manse of Dundee West Church, Wards of Keithock, by Brechin DD9 7PZ [E-mail: andrewgreaves2@btinternet.com]	01356 624479
Dundee: Whitfield (H) (01382 503012) James L. Wilson BD CPS	1986	2001	53 Old Craigie Road, Dundee DD4 7JD [E-mail: r3vjw@aol.com]	01382 459249
Fowlis and Liff linked with Lundie and Muirhead (H) Donna M. Hays (Mrs) MTheol DipEd DipTMHA	2004		149 Coupar Angus Road, Muirhead of Liff, Dundee DD2 5QN [E-mail: dmhays32@aol.com]	01382 580210
Inchture and Kinnaird See Abernyte				
Invergowrie (H) Robert J. Ramsay LLB NP BD	1986	1997	2 Boniface Place, Invergowrie, Dundee DD2 5DW [E-mail: s3rjr@tiscali.co.uk]	01382 561118
Longforgan See Abernyte **Lundie and Muirhead** See Fowlis and Liff				

Monifieth (H)

Dorothy U. Anderson (Mrs) LLB DipLP BD	2006	2009	8 Church Street, Monifieth, Dundee DD5 4JP [E-mail: dorothy@kirkyard-plus.com]	01382 532607

Monikie and Newbigging and Murroes and Tealing See Auchterhouse

Allan, Jean (Mrs) DCS			(Deacon) — 12C Hindmarsh Avenue, Dundee DD3 7LW [E-mail: jeannieallan45@googlemail.com]	01382 827299 (Mbl) 07709 959474
Barrett, Leslie M. BD FRICS	1991	2014	(Chaplain: University of Abertay, Dundee) — Dunelm Cottage, Logie, Cupar KY15 4SJ [E-mail: lesliembarrett@btinternet.com]	01334 870396
Campbell, Gordon MA BD CDipAF DipHSM MCMI MBIM AFRIN ARSGS FRGS FSAScot		2001	Auxiliary Minister: Chaplain: University of Dundee — 2 Falkland Place, Kingoodie, Invergowrie, Dundee DD2 5DY [E-mail: g.a.campbell@dundee.ac.uk]	01382 561383
Clark, David M. MA BD	1989	2013	(Dundee: Steeple) — 2 Rose Street, St Monans, Anstruther KY10 2BQ [E-mail: dmclark72@gmail.com]	01333 738034
Craik, Sheila (Mrs) BD	1989	2001	(Dundee: Camperdown) — 35 Haldane Terrace, Dundee DD3 0HT	01382 802078
Cramb, Erik M. LTh	1973	1989	(Industrial Mission Organiser) — Flat 35, Braehead, Methven Walk, Dundee DD2 3FJ [E-mail: erikcramb@aol.com]	01382 526196
Donald, Robert M. LTh BA	1969	2005	(Kilmodan and Colintraive) — 2 Blacklaw Drive, Birkhill, Dundee DD2 5RJ [E-mail: robandmoiradonald@yahoo.co.uk]	01382 581337
Douglas, Fiona C. MBE MA BD PhD	1989	1997	Chaplain: University of Dundee — 10 Springfield, Dundee DD1 4JE	01382 384157
Fraser, Donald W. MA	1958	2010	(Monifieth) — 1 Blake Avenue, Broughty Ferry, Dundee DD5 3LH [E-mail: fraserdonald37@yahoo.co.uk]	01382 477491 (Mbl) 07531 863316
Galbraith, W. James L. BSc BD MICE	1973	1996	(Kilchrenan and Dalavich with Muckairn) — 586 Brook Street, Broughty Ferry, Dundee DD5 2EA	01382 732110
Hawdon, John E. BA MTh AICS	1961	1995	(Dundee: Clepington) — 53 Hillside Road, Dundee DD2 1QT	01382 646212
Ingram, J.R.	1954	1978	(Chaplain: RAF) — 48 Marlee Road, Broughty Ferry, Dundee DD5 3EX	01382 736400
Jamieson, David B. MA BD STM	1974	2011	(Monifieth) — 8A Albert Street, Monifieth, Dundee DD5 4JS	01382 532772
Kay, Elizabeth (Miss) DipYCS	1993	2007	(Auxiliary Minister) — 1 Kintail Walk, Inchture, Perth PH14 9RY [E-mail: ekay007@btinternet.com]	01828 686029
Laidlaw, John J. MA	1964	1973	(Adviser in Religious Education) — 14 Dalhousie Road, Barnhill, Dundee DD5 2SQ	01382 477458
Laing, David J.H. BD DPS	1976	2014	(Dundee: Trinity) — 18 Kerrington Crescent, Barnhill, Dundee DD5 2TN [E-mail: david.laing@live.co.uk]	01382 739586
McLeod, David C. BSc MEng BD	1969	2001	(Dundee: Fairmuir) — 6 Carseview Gardens, Dundee DD2 1NE	01382 641371
McMillan, Charles D. LTh	1979	2004	(Elgin: High) — 11 Troon Terrace, The Orchard, Ardler, Dundee DD2 3FX	01382 831358
Mair, Michael V.A. MA BD	1967	2007	(Craigiebank with Dundee: Douglas and Mid Craigie) — 48 Panmure Street, Monifieth DD5 4EH [E-mail: mvamair@gmail.com]	01382 530538
Martin, Janie (Miss) DCS			(Deacon) — 16 Wentworth Road, Ardler, Dundee DD2 8SD	
Mitchell, Jack MA BD CTh	1987	1996	(Dundee: Menzieshill) — 29 Carrick Gardens, Ayr KA7 2RT	01382 813786
Mowat, Gilbert M. MA	1948	1986	(Dundee: Albany-Butterburn) — Abbeyfield House, 16 Grange Road, Bearsden, Glasgow G61 3PL	

Powrie, James E. LTh	1969	1995	(Dundee: Chalmers-Ardler)	3 Kirktonhill Road, Kirriemuir DD8 4HU	01575 572503
Rae, Robert LTh	1968	1983	(Chaplain: Dundee Acute Hospitals)	14 Neddertoun View, Liff, Dundee DD3 5RU	01382 581790
Reid, R. Gordon BSc BD MIET	1993	2010	(Carriden)	6 Bayview Place, Monifieth, Dundee DD5 4TN	01382 520519
					(Mbl) 07952 349884
				[E-mail: GordonReid@aol.com]	
Robertson, James H. BSc BD	1975	2014	(Culloden: The Barn)	'Far End', 35 Mains Terrace, Dundee DD4 7BZ	01382 522773
					(Mbl) 07595 465838
				[E-mail: jimrob838@gmail.com]	
Robson, George K. LTh DPS BA	1983	2011	(Dundee: Balgay)	11 Ceres Crescent, Broughty Ferry, Dundee DD5 3JN	01382 901212
				[E-mail: gkrobson@virginmedia.com]	
Rogers, James M. BA DB DCult	1955	1996	(Gibraltar)	24 Mansion Drive, Dalclaverhouse, Dundee DD4 9DD	01382 506162
Rose, Lewis (Mr) DCS			(Deacon)	6 Gauldie Crescent, Dundee DD3 0RR	01382 816580
					(Mbl) 07899 790466
				[E-mail: lewis_rose48@yahoo.co.uk]	
Scott, James MA BD	1973	2010	(Drumoak-Durris)	3 Blake Place, Broughty Ferry, Dundee DD5 3LQ	01382 739595
				[E-mail: jimscott73@yahoo.co.uk]	
Scoular, Stanley	1963	2000	(Rosyth)	31 Duns Crescent, Dundee DD4 0RY	01382 501653
Strickland, Alexander LTh	1971	2005	(Dairsie with Kemback with Strathkinness)	12 Ballumbie Braes, Dundee DD4 0UN	01382 685539
Taylor Caroline (Mrs)	1995	2014	(Leuchars: St Athernase)	The Old Dairy, 15 Forthill Road, Broughty Ferry, Dundee DD5 3DH	01382 770198
				[E-mail: caro234@btinternet.com]	

DUNDEE ADDRESSES

Balgay	200 Lochee Road
Barnhill St Margaret's	10 Invermark Terrace
Broughty Ferry	
St James'	370 Queen Street
New Kirk	5 Fort Street
St Luke's and Queen Street	5 West Queen Street
St Stephen's and West	96 Dundee Road
Camperdown	22 Brownhill Road
Chalmers-Ardler	Turnberry Avenue
Coldside	Isla Street x Main Street
Craigiebank	Craigie Avenue at Greendykes Road
Douglas and Mid Craigie	Balbeggie Place/ Longtown Terrace
Downfield Mains	Haldane Street off Strathmartine Road
Dundee (St Mary's)	Nethergate
Fintry	Fintry Road x Fintry Drive
Lochee	191 High Street, Lochee
Logie and St John's Cross	Shaftesbury Rd x Blackness Ave
Meadowside St Paul's	114 Nethergate
Menzieshill	Charleston Drive, Menzieshill
St Andrew's	2 King Street
St David's High Kirk	119A Kinghorne Road
Steeple	Nethergate
Stobswell	170 Albert Street
Strathmartine	507 Strathmartine Road
Trinity	73 Crescent Street
West	130 Perth Road
Whitfield	Haddington Crescent

(30) ANGUS

Meets at Forfar in St Margaret's Church Hall on the first Tuesday of February, March, May, September, November and December, and on the last Tuesday of June.

Clerk:	REV. MICHAEL S. GOSS BD DPS [E-mail: michaelgoss@blueyonder.co.uk]
Depute Clerk:	REV. IAN A. McLEAN BSc BD DMin [E-mail: iamclean@gmx.co.uk]
Presbytery Office:	St Margaret's Church, West High Street, Forfar DD8 1BJ [E-mail: angus@churchofscotland.org.uk] 01307 464224

Aberlemno (H) linked with Guthrie and Rescobie
Brian Ramsay BD DPS MLitt   1980   1984   The Manse, Guthrie, Forfar DD8 2TP   01241 828243
[E-mail: revdbrianr@hotmail.com]

Arbirlot linked with Carmyllie
Vacant   The Manse, Arbirlot, Arbroath DD11 2NX   01241 879800

Arbroath: Knox's (H) linked with Arbroath: St Vigeans (H)
Nelu I. Balaj BD MA ThD   2010   The Manse, St Vigeans, Arbroath DD11 4RF   01241 873206
[E-mail: nelu@gmx.co.uk]   07954 436879 (Mbl)

Arbroath: Old and Abbey (H) (Church office: 01241 877068)
Dolly Purnell BD   2003   2014   51 Cliffburn Road, Arbroath DD11 5BA   01241 872196 (Tel/Fax)
[E-mail: revdollypurnell@btinternet.com]

Arbroath: St Andrew's (H) (E-mail: office@arbroathstandrews.org.uk)
W. Martin Fair BA BD DMin   1992   92 Grampian Gardens, Arbroath DD11 4AQ   01241 873238 (Tel/Fax)
[E-mail: martin.fair@sky.com]

Stuart D. Irvin BD   2013   67 Brechin Road, Arbroath DD11 1TA   01241 872339
(Associate Minister)   [E-mail: stuart.d.irvin@googlemail.com]

Arbroath: St Vigeans See Arbroath: Knox's

Arbroath: West Kirk (H)
Alasdair G. Graham BD DipMin   1981   1986   1 Charles Avenue, Arbroath DD11 2EY   01241 872244
[E-mail: alasdairggraham@tiscali.co.uk]

Barry linked with Carnoustie
Michael S. Goss BD DPS   1991   2003   44 Terrace Road, Carnoustie DD7 7AR
[E-mail: michaelgoss@blueyonder.co.uk]
01241 410194 (Tel)
07787 141567 (Mbl)

Dougal Edwards BTh   2013   25 Mackenzie Street, Carnoustie DD7 6HD
(Ordained Local Minister)   [E-mail: dougal.edwards@blueyonder.co.uk]
01241 852666

Brechin: Cathedral (H) (Cathedral office: 01356 629360) (Website: www.brechincathedral.org.uk)
Roderick J. Grahame BD CPS   1991   2010   Chanory Wynd, Brechin DD9 6JS
[E-mail: rjgrahame@talktalk.net]
01356 624980

Brechin: Gardner Memorial (H) linked with Farnell
Jane M. Blackley MA BD   2009   15 Caldhame Gardens, Brechin DD9 7JJ
[E-mail: jmblackley6@aol.com]
01356 622034

Carmyllie See Arbirlot
Carnoustie See Barry

Carnoustie: Panbride (H)
Matthew S. Bicket BD   1989   8 Arbroath Road, Carnoustie DD7 6BL
[E-mail: matthew@bicket.freeserve.co.uk]
01241 854478 (Tel)
01241 855088 (Fax)

Colliston linked with Friockheim Kinnell linked with Inverkeilor and Lunan (H)
Peter A. Phillips BA   1995   2004   The Manse, Inverkeilor, Arbroath DD11 5SA
[E-mail: rev-p.phillips@gmail.com]
01241 830464

Dun and Hillside
Fiona C. Bullock (Mrs) MA LLB BD   2014   4 Manse Road, Hillside, Montrose DD10 9FB
[E-mail:f.c.bullock@outlook.com]
01674 830288

Dunnichen, Letham and Kirkden
Dale London BTh FSAScot   2011   2013   7 Braehead Road, Letham, Forfar DD8 2PG
[E-mail: dlondon@hotmail.com]
01307 818025

Eassie, Nevay and Newtyle
Carleen Robertson (Miss) BD   1992   2 Kirkton Road, Newtyle, Blairgowrie PH12 8TS
[E-mail: carleen.robertson120@btinternet.com]
01828 650461

Edzell Lethnot Glenesk (H) linked with Fern Careston Menmuir
Vacant
Ian Gray   2013   19 Lethnot Road, Edzell, Brechin DD9 7TG   01356 647846
(Ordained Local Minister)   'The Mallards', 15 Rossie Island Road, Montrose DD10 9NH   01674 677126
                                        [E-mail: iancelia15@aol.com]

Farnell See Brechin: Gardner Memorial
Fern Careston Menmuir See Edzell Lethnot Glenesk

Forfar: East and Old (H)
Barbara Ann Sweetin BD   2011   The Manse, Lour Road, Forfar DD8 2BB   01307 248228
                                        [E-mail: barbara.ann17@talktalk.net]

Forfar: Lowson Memorial (H)
Karen Fenwick PhD MPhil BSc BD   2006   1 Jamieson Street, Forfar DD8 2HY   01307 468585
                                        [E-mail: kmfenwick@talktalk.net]

Forfar: St Margaret's (H) (Church office: 01307 464224)
Margaret J. Hunt (Mrs) MA BD   2014   St Margaret's Manse, 15 Potters Park Crescent, Forfar DD8 1HH   01307 462044
                                        [E-mail: maggie.hunt101@gmail.com]

Friockheim Kinnell See Colliston

Glamis (H), Inverarity and Kinnettles
Guardianship of the Presbytery   (See Eassie, Nevay and Newtyle)

Guthrie and Rescobie See Aberlemno

Inchbrayock linked with Montrose: Melville South
Vacant   The Manse, Ferryden, Montrose DD10 9SD   01674 672108

Inverkeilor and Lunan See Colliston

Kirriemuir: St Andrew's (H) linked with Oathlaw Tannadice
John K. Orr BD MTh   2012   26 Quarry Park, Kirriemuir DD8 4DR   01575 572610
                                        [E-mail: minister@standrews-kirriemuir.org.uk]

Montrose: Melville South See Inchbrayock

Montrose: Old and St Andrew's

Ian A. McLean BSc BD DMin	1981	2008	2 Rosehill Road, Montrose DD10 8ST [E-mail: iamclean@gmx.co.uk]	01674 672247

Oathlaw Tannadice See Kirriemuir: St Andrew's

The Glens and Kirriemuir: Old (H) (Church office: 01575 572819) (Website: www.gkopc.co.uk)

Malcolm I.G. Rooney DPE BEd BD	1993	1999	20 Strathmore Avenue, Kirriemuir DD8 4DJ [E-mail: malcolm@gkopc.co.uk]	01575 573724 07909 993233 (Mbl)
Linda Stevens (Mrs) BSc BD PgDip (Team Minister)		2006	17 North Latch Road, Brechin DD9 6LE [E-mail: linda@gkopc.co.uk]	01356 623415 07701 052552 (Mbl)

The Isla Parishes

Brian Ian Murray BD	2002	2010	Balduff House, Kilry, Blairgowrie PH11 8HS [E-mail: bentleymurray@googlemail.com]	01575 560268

Anderson, John F. MA BD FSAScot	1966	2006	(Aberdeen: Mannofield)	8 Eider Close, Montrose DD10 9NE [E-mail: jfa941@aol.com]	01674 672029
Brodie, James BEM MA BD STM	1955	1974	(Hurlford)	25A Keptie Road, Arbroath DD11 3ED	01241 873298
Butters, David	1964	1998	(Turriff: St Ninian's and Forglen)	68A Millgate, Friockheim, Arbroath DD11 4TN	01241 828030
Dingwall, Brian BTh CQSW	1999	2013	(Upper Donside)	20 Woodend Drive, Kirriemuir DD8 4TF [E-mail: brian.d12@btinternet.com]	01575 573918 (Mbl) 07906 656847
Drysdale, James P.R.	1967	1999	(Brechin: Gardner Memorial)	51 Airlie Street, Brechin DD9 6JX	01356 625201
Duncan, Robert F. MTheol	1986	2001	(Lochgelly: St Andrew's)	25 Rowan Avenue, Kirriemuir DD8 4TB	01575 573973
Gough, Ian G. MA BD MTh DMin	1974	2009	(Arbroath: Knox's with Arbroath: St Vigeans)	23 Keptie Road, Arbroath DD11 3ED [E-mail: iangough@btinternet.com]	(Mbl) 07891 838379
Hastie, George I. MA BD	1971	2009	(Mearns Coastal)	23 Borrowfield Crescent, Montrose DD10 9BR	01674 672290
Hodge, William N.T.	1966	1995	(Longside)	19 Craigengar Park, Craigshill, Livingston EH54 5NY	01506 435813
Milton, Eric G. RD	1963	1994	(Blairdaff)	16 Bruce Court, Links Parade, Carnoustie DD7 7JE	01241 854928
Morrice, Alastair M. MA BD	1968	2002	(Rutherglen: Stonelaw)	5 Brechin Road, Kirriemuir DD8 4BX [E-mail: ambishkek@swissmail.org]	01575 574102
Norrie, Graham MA BD	1967	2007	(Forfar: East and Old)	'Novar', 14A Wyllie Street, Forfar DD8 3DN [E-mail: grahamnorrie@hotmail.com]	01307 468152
Perry, Joseph B.	1955	1989	(Farnell)	19 Guthrie Street, Letham, Forfar DD8 2PS	01307 818741
Reid, Albert B. BD BSc	1966	2001	(Ardler, Kettins and Meigle)	1 Mary Countess Way, Glamis, Forfar DD8 1RF [E-mail: abreid@btinternet.com]	01307 840213
Robertson, George R. LTh	1985	2004	(Udny and Pitmedden)	3 Slateford Gardens, Edzell, Brechin DD9 7SX [E-mail: geomag.robertson@btinternet.com]	01356 647322
Smith, Hamish G.	1965	1993	(Auchterless with Rothienorman)	11A Guthrie Street, Letham, Forfar DD8 2PS	01307 818973

Thomas, Martyn R.H. CEng MIStructE — 1987 2002 — (Fowlis and Liff with Lundie and Muirhead of Liff) (Auxiliary Minister) — 14 Kirkgait, Letham, Forfar DD8 2XQ [E-mail: martyn.thomas@mypostoffice.co.uk] — 01307 818084

Thomas, Shirley A. (Mrs) DipSocSci AMIA (Aux) — 2000 2006 — 14 Kirkgait, Letham, Forfar DD8 2XQ [E-mail: martyn.thomas@mypostoffice.co.uk] — 01307 818084

Watt, Alan G.N. MTh CQSW DipCommEd — 1996 2009 — (Edzell Lethnot Glenesk with Fern Careston Menmuir) — 128 Restenneth Drive, Forfar DD8 2DH [E-mail: watt455@btinternet.com] — 01307 461686

Webster, Allan F. MA BD — 1978 2008 — (Workplace Chaplain) — 42 McCulloch Drive, Forfar DD8 2EB [E-mail: allanfwebster@aol.com] — 01307 464252 / 07546 276725 (Mbl)

Youngson, Peter — 1961 1996 — (Kirriemuir: St Andrew's) — 'Coreen', Woodside, Northmuir, Kirriemuir DD8 4PG — 01575 572832

ANGUS ADDRESSES

Arbroath: Knox's	Howard Street	
Old and Abbey	West Abbey Street	
St Andrew's	Hamilton Green	
West Kirk	Keptie Street	
Brechin: Cathedral	Bishops Close	
Gardner Memorial	South Esk Street	
Carnoustie:	Dundee Street	
Panbride	Arbroath Road	
Forfar: East and Old	East High Street	
Lowson Memorial	Jamieson Street	
St Margaret's	West High Street	
Kirriemuir: Old	High Street	
St Andrew's	Glamis Road	
Montrose: Melville South	Castle Street	
Old and St Andrew's	High Street	

(31) ABERDEEN

Meets on the first Tuesday of February, March, May, September, October, November and December, and on the fourth Tuesday of June. The venue varies.

Clerk: REV. JOHN A. FERGUSON BD DipMin DMin
Administrator: MRS CHERYL MARWICK-WATT BA
Treasurer: MR ALAN MORRISON
Presbytery Office: Mastrick Church, Greenfern Road, Aberdeen AB16 6TR   01224 698119
[E-mail: aberdeen@churchofscotland.org.uk]

Aberdeen: Bridge of Don Oldmachar (01224 709299) (Website: www.oldmacharchurch.org)
David J. Stewart BD MTh DipMin   2000   2012   60 Newburgh Circle, Aberdeen AB22 8QZ   01224 701365
[E-mail: brigodon@clara.co.uk]

Aberdeen: Cove (New Charge Development) (Website: www.covechurch.org.uk)
David Swan BVMS BD   2005   4 Charleston Way, Cove, Aberdeen AB12 3FA   01224 899933
[E-mail: david@covechurch.org.uk]

Daniel Robertson BA BD (Associate Minister) 2009   2014   5 Bruce Walk, Nigg, Aberdeen AB12 3LX
[E-mail: dan_robertson100@hotmail.com]   01224 878418
07909 840654 (Mbl)

Aberdeen: Craigiebuckler (H) (01224 315649) (Website: www.craigiebuckler.org)
Kenneth L. Petrie MA BD   1984   1999   185 Springfield Road, Aberdeen AB15 8AA
[E-mail: patandkenneth@aol.com]   01224 315125

Aberdeen: Ferryhill (H) (01224 213093) (Website: www.ferryhillparishchurch.org)
J. Peter N. Johnston BSc BD   2001   2013   54 Polmuir Road, Aberdeen AB11 7RT
[E-mail: peter.johnston@ferryhillparishchurch.org]   01224 949192

Aberdeen: Garthdee (H) linked with Aberdeen: Ruthrieston West (H) (Website: www.ruthriestonwestchurch.org.uk)
Benjamin D.W. Byun BS MDiv MTh PhD   1992   2008   53 Springfield Avenue, Aberdeen AB15 8JJ
[E-mail: benjamin@byun1.fsnet.co.uk]   01224 312706

Aberdeen: High Hilton (H) (01224 494717) (Website: www.highhilton.zyberweb.com)
G. Hutton B. Steel MA BD   1982   2013   24 Rosehill Drive, Aberdeen AB24 4JJ
[E-mail: hsteel57@btinternet.com]   01224 493552

Aberdeen: Holburn West (H) (01224 571120) (Website: www.holburnwestchurch.org.uk)
Duncan C. Eddie MA BD   1992   1999   31 Cranford Road, Aberdeen AB10 7NJ
[E-mail: dceddies@btinternet.com]   01224 325873

Aberdeen: Mannofield (H) (01224 310087) (E-mail: office@mannofieldchurch.org.uk) (Website: www.mannofieldchurch.org.uk)
Keith T. Blackwood BD DipMin   1997   2007   21 Forest Avenue, Aberdeen AB15 4TU
[E-mail: minister@mannofieldchurch.org.uk]   01224 315748

Aberdeen: Mastrick (H) (01224 694121)
Vacant

Aberdeen: Middlefield (H)
Vacant

Aberdeen: Midstocket (01224 319519) (Website: www.midstocketchurch.org.uk)
Sarah E.C. Nicol (Mrs) BSc BD MTh   1985   2013   182 Midstocket Road, Aberdeen AB15 5HS
[E-mail: sarahmidstocket@btinternet.com]   01224 561358

Aberdeen: Northfield (01224 692332)
Scott C. Guy BD   1989   1999   28 Byron Crescent, Aberdeen AB16 7EX   01224 692332
[E-mail: scguy55@gmail.com]

Aberdeen: Queen Street (01224 643567) (Website: www.queenstreetchurch.org.uk)
Graham D.S. Deans MA BD MTh MLitt DMin   1978   2008   51 Osborne Place, Aberdeen AB25 2BX   01224 646429
[E-mail: graham.deans@btopenworld.com]

Aberdeen: Queen's Cross (H) (01224 644742) (Website: www.queenscrosschurch.org.uk)
Scott Rennie MA BD STM   1999   2009   1 St Swithin Street, Aberdeen AB10 6XH   01224 322549
[E-mail: minister@queenscrosschurch.org.uk]

Aberdeen: Rubislaw (H) (01224 645477) (Website: rubislawparishchurchofscotland.org.uk)
Robert L. Smith BS MTh PhD   2000   2013   45 Rubislaw Den South, Aberdeen AB15 4BD   01224 314773
[E-mail: rubislaw.minister@virginmedia.com]

Aberdeen: Ruthrieston West   See Aberdeen: Garthdee

Aberdeen: St Columba's Bridge of Don (H) (01224 825653) (Website: http://stcolumbaschurch.org.uk)
Louis Kinsey BD DipMin TD   1991   151 Jesmond Avenue, Aberdeen AB22 8UG   01224 705337
[E-mail: louis@stcolumbaschurch.org.uk]

Aberdeen: St George's Tillydrone (H) (01224 482204) (Website: http://tillydrone.church)
James Weir BD   1991   2003   127 Clifton Road, Aberdeen AB24 4RH   01224 483976
[E-mail: minister@saint-georges-tillydrone.org.uk]

Aberdeen: St John's Church for Deaf (H)
Use contact details for St Mark's, below.

Aberdeen: St Machar's Cathedral (H) (01224 485988) (Website: www.stmachar.com)
Barry W. Dunsmore MA BD   1982   2015   39 Woodstock Road, Aberdeen AB15 5EX   01224 314596
[E-mail: barrydunsmore@gmail.com]

Aberdeen: St Mark's (H) (01224 640672) (Website: www.stmarksaberdeen.org.uk)
Diane L. Hobson (Mrs) BA BD   2002   2010   65 Mile-end Avenue, Aberdeen AB15 5PT   01224 622470
[E-mail: dianehobson.rev@btinternet.com]

Aberdeen: St Mary's (H) (01224 487227)
Elsie J. Fortune (Mrs) BSc BD   2003   456 King Street, Aberdeen AB24 3DE   01224 633778
                                                                [E-mail: eric.fortune@lineone.net]

Aberdeen: St Nicholas Kincorth, South of (Website: www.southstnicholas.org.uk)
Edward C. McKenna BD DPS   1989   2002   The Manse, Kincorth Circle, Aberdeen AB12 5NX   01224 872820
                                                                [E-mail: eddiemckenna@uwclub.net]
Daniel Robertson BA BD   2009   2014   5 Bruce Walk, Nigg, Aberdeen AB12 3LX   01224 878418
(Associate Minister)   [E-mail: dan_robertson100@hotmail.com]   07909 840654 (Mbl)

Aberdeen: St Nicholas Uniting, Kirk of (H) (01224 643494) (Website: www.kirk-of-st-nicholas.org.uk)
B. Stephen C. Taylor BA BBS MA MDiv   1984   2005   12 Louisville Avenue, Aberdeen AB15 4TX   01224 314318
                                                                [E-mail: minister@kirk-of-st-nicholas.org.uk]   01224 649242 (Fax)

St Nicholas Uniting is a Local Ecumenical Project shared with the United Reformed Church

Aberdeen: St Stephen's (H) (01224 624443) (Website: www.st-stephens.co.uk)
Maggie Whyte BD   2010   6 Belvidere Street, Aberdeen AB25 2QS   01224 635694
                                                                [E-mail: maggiewhyte@aol.com]

Aberdeen: South Holburn (H) (01224 211730) (Website: www.southholburn.org)
George S. Cowie BSc BD   1991   2006   54 Woodstock Road, Aberdeen AB15 5JF   01224 315042
                                                                [E-mail: gscowie@aol.com]

Aberdeen: Stockethill (Website: www.stockethillchurch.org.uk)
Ian M. Aitken MA BD   1999   52 Ashgrove Road West, Aberdeen AB16 5EE   01224 686929
                                                                [E-mail: ncdstockethill@uk.uumail.com]

Aberdeen: Summerhill (H) (Website: www.summerhillchurch.org.uk)
Michael R.R. Shewan MA BD CPS   1985   2010   36 Stronsay Drive, Aberdeen AB15 6JL   01224 324669
                                                                [E-mail: michaelshewan@btinternet.com]

Aberdeen: Torry St Fittick's (H) (01224 899183) (Website: www.torrychurch.org.uk)
Edmond Gatima BEng BD MSc MPhil PhD   2013   11 Devanha Gardens East, Aberdeen AB11 7UH   01224 588245

Aberdeen: Woodside (H) (01224 277249) (Website: www.woodsidechurch.co.uk)
Markus Auffermann DipTheol   1999   2006   322 Clifton Road, Aberdeen AB24 4HQ   01224 484562
                                                                [E-mail: mauffermann@yahoo.com]

Bucksburn Stoneywood (H) (01224 712411) (Website: www.bucksburnstoneywoodchurch.com)
Nigel Parker BD MTh DMin   1994   23 Polo Park, Stoneywood, Aberdeen AB21 9JW   01224 712635
[E-mail: revdr.n.parker@btinternet.com]

Cults (H) (01224 869028) (Website: www.cultsparishchurch.co.uk)
Ewen J. Gilchrist BD DipMin DipComm   1982   2005   1 Cairnlee Terrace, Bieldside, Aberdeen AB15 9AE   01224 861692
[E-mail: ewengilchrist@btconnect.com]

Dyce (H) (01224 771295) (Website: www.dyceparishchurch.org.uk)
Manson C. Merchant BD CPS   1992   2008   100 Burnside Road, Dyce, Aberdeen AB21 7HA   01224 722380
[E-mail: mc.merchant@btinternet.com]

Kingswells (Website: www.kingswellschurch.com)
Alisa McDonald BA MDiv   2008   2013   Kingswells Manse, Lang Stracht, Aberdeen AB15 8PN   01224 740229

Newhills (H) (Tel/Fax: 01224 716161)
Hugh M. Wallace MA BD   1980   2007   Newhills Manse, Bucksburn, Aberdeen AB21 9SS   01224 710318
[E-mail: revhugh@hotmail.com]

Peterculter (H) (01224 735845) (Website: http://culterkirk.co.uk)
John A. Ferguson BD DipMin DMin   1988   1999   7 Howie Lane, Peterculter AB14 0LJ   01224 735041
[E-mail: john.ferguson525@btinternet.com]

Barron, Jane L. (Mrs) BA DipEd BD	1999	2013	(Aberdeen: St Machar's Cathedral)	Denhead Old Farm, St Andrews KY16 3PA	
Beattie, Walter G. MA BD	1956	1995	(Arbroath: Old and Abbey)	126 Seafield Road, Aberdeen AB15 7YQ	01224 329259
Cowie, Marian (Mrs) MA BD MTh	1990	2012	(Aberdeen: Midstocket)	54 Woodstock Road, Aberdeen AB15 5JF	01224 315042
				[E-mail: mcowieou@aol.com]	
Craig, Gordon T. BD DipMin	1988	2012	Chaplain to UK Oil and Gas Industry	c/o Total E and P (UK) plc, Altens Industrial Estate, Crawpeel Road, Aberdeen AB12 3FG	01224 297532
				[E-mail: gordon.craig@ukoilandgaschaplaincy.com]	
Douglas, Andrew M. MA	1957	1995	(Aberdeen: High Hilton)	219 Countesswells Road, Aberdeen AB15 7RD	01224 311932
Falconer, James B. BD	1982	1991	Hospital Chaplain	3 Brimmond Walk, Westhill AB32 6XH	01224 744621
Garden, Margaret J. (Miss) BD	1993	2009	(Cushnie and Tough)	26 Earns Heugh Circle, Cove Bay, Aberdeen AB12 3PY	
				[E-mail: mj.garden@btinternet.com]	
Goldie, George D. ALCM	1953	1995	(Aberdeen: Greyfriars)	27 Broomhill Avenue, Aberdeen AB10 6JL	01224 322503
Gordon, Laurie Y.	1960	1995	(Aberdeen: John Knox)	1 Alder Drive, Portlethen, Aberdeen AB12 4WA	01224 782703
Graham, A. David M. BA BD	1971	2005	(Aberdeen: Rosemount)	Elmhill House, 27 Shaw Crescent, Aberdeen AB25 3BT	01224 648041

Name	Ordained	Appointed	Charge / Position	Address and E-mail	Telephone
Grainger, Harvey L. LTh	1975	2004	(Kingswells)	13 St Ronan's Crescent, Peterculter, Aberdeen AB14 0RL [E-mail: harveygrainger@btinternet.com]	01224 739824
Haddow, Angus H. BSc	1963	1999	(Methlick)	25 Lerwick Road, Aberdeen AB16 6RF	07768 333216 (Mbl)
Hamilton, Helen (Miss) BD	1991	2003	(Glasgow: St James' Pollok)	The Cottage, West Tilbouries, Maryculter, Aberdeen AB12 5GD	01224 969521 / 01224 739632
Hutchison, David S. BSc BD ThM	1991	1999	(Aberdeen: Torry St Fittick's)	The Den of Keithfield, Tarves, Ellon AB41 7NU	01651 851501
Johnstone, William (Prof.) MA BD	1963	2001	(University of Aberdeen)	9/5 Mount Alvernia, Edinburgh EH16 6AW	0131-664 3140
Lundie, Ann V. DCS			(Deacon)	20 Langdykes Drive, Cove, Aberdeen AB12 3HW [E-mail: ann.lundie@btopenworld.com]	01224 898416
McCallum, Moyra (Miss) MA BD DCS			(Deacon)	176 Hilton Drive, Aberdeen AB24 4LT [E-mail: moymac@aol.com]	01224 486240 / 07986 581899 (Mbl)
Maciver, Norman MA BD DMin	1976	2006	(Newhills)	4 Mundi Crescent, Newmachar, Aberdeen AB21 0LY [E-mail: norirene@aol.com]	01651 869434
Main, Alan (Prof.) TD MA BD STM PhD DD	1963	2001	(University of Aberdeen)	Kirkfield, Barthol Chapel, Inverurie AB51 8TD [E-mail: amain@talktalk.net]	01651 806773
Montgomerie, Jean B. (Miss) MA BD	1973	2005	(Forfar: St Margaret's)	12 St Ronan's Place, Peterculter, Aberdeen AB14 0QX [E-mail: revjeanb@tiscali.co.uk]	01224 732350
Phillippo, Michael MTh BSc BVetMed MRCVS	2003		(Auxiliary Minister)	25 Deeside Crescent, Aberdeen AB15 7PT [E-mail: phillippo@btinternet.com]	01224 318317
Richardson, Thomas C. LTh ThB	1971	2004	(Cults: West)	19 Kinkell Road, Aberdeen AB15 8HR [E-mail: thomas.richardson7@btinternet.com]	01224 315328
Rodgers, D. Mark BA BD MTh	1987	2003	Head of Spiritual Care, NHS Grampian	63 Cordiner Place, Hilton, Aberdeen AB24 4SB [E-mail: mrodgers@nhs.net]	01224 379135
Sefton, Henry R. MA BD STM PhD	1957	1992	(University of Aberdeen)	25 Albury Place, Aberdeen AB11 6TQ	01224 572305
Sheret, Brian S. MA BD DPhil	1982	2009	(Glasgow: Drumchapel Drumry St Mary's)	59 Airyhall Crescent, Aberdeen AB15 7QS	01224 323032
Stewart, James C. MA BD STM	1960	2000	(Aberdeen: Kirk of St Nicholas)	54 Murray Terrace, Aberdeen AB11 7SB	01224 587071
Swinton, John (Prof.) BD PhD	1999		University of Aberdeen	51 Newburgh Circle, Bridge of Don, Aberdeen AB22 8XA [E-mail: j.swinton@abdn.ac.uk]	01224 825637
Torrance, Iain R. (Prof.) TD DPhil DD DTheol LHD FRSE	1982	2012	(President: Princeton Theological Seminary)	25 The Causeway, Duddingston Village, Edinburgh EH15 3QA [E-mail: irt@ptsem.edu]	0131-661 3092
Wilkie, William E. LTh	1978	2001	(Aberdeen: St Nicholas Kincorth, South of)	32 Broomfield Park, Portlethen, Aberdeen AB12 4XT	01224 782052
Wilson, Thomas F. BD	1984	1996	Education	55 Allison Close, Cove, Aberdeen AB12 3WG	01224 873501
Youngson, Elizabeth J.B. BD	1996	2015	(Aberdeen: Mastrick)	47 Corse Drive, The Links, Dubford, Aberdeen AB23 8NL [E-mail: elizabeth.youngson@btinternet.com]	07788 294745 (Mbl)

ABERDEEN ADDRESSES

Bridge of Don Oldmachar	Ashwood Park
Cove	Loirston Primary School, Loirston Avenue
Craigiebuckler	Springfield Road
Cults	Quarry Road, Cults
Dyce	Victoria Street, Dyce
Ferryhill	Fonthill Road x Polmuir Road
Garthdee	Ramsay Gardens
High Hilton	Hilton Drive
Holburn West	Great Western Road
Kingswells	Old Skene Road, Kingswells

Mannofield	Great Western Road x Craigton Road
Mastrick	Greenfern Road
Middlefield	Manor Avenue
Midstocket	Mid Stocket Road
New Stockethill	
Northfield	Byron Crescent
Peterculter	Craigton Crescent
Queen Street	Queen Street
Queen's Cross	Albyn Place
Rubislaw	Queen's Gardens
Ruthrieston West	Broomhill Road
St Columba's	Brachead Way, Bridge of Don
St George's	Hayton Road, Tillydrone
St John's for the Deaf	at St Mark's
St Machar's	The Chanonry
St Mark's	Rosemount Viaduct
St Mary's	King Street
St Nicholas Kincorth, South of	Kincorth Circle
St Nicholas Uniting, Kirk of	Union Street
St Stephen's	Powis Place
South Holburn	Holburn Street
Summerhill	Stronsay Drive
Torry St Fittick's	Walker Road
Woodside	Church Street, Woodside

(32) KINCARDINE AND DEESIDE

Meets in various locations as arranged on the first Tuesday of September, October, November, December, March and May, and on the last Tuesday of June at 7pm.

Clerk: REV. HUGH CONKEY BSc BD   39 St Ternans Road, Newtonhill, Stonehaven AB39 3PF   01569 739297
[E-mail: kincardinedeeside@churchofscotland.org.uk]

Aberluthnott linked with Laurencekirk (H)
Ronald Gall BSc BD   1985 2001   Aberdeen Road, Laurencekirk AB30 1AJ   01561 378838
[E-mail: ronniegall@live.com]

Aboyne-Dinnet (H) (01339 886989) linked with Cromar (E-mail: aboynedinnet.cos@virgin.net)
Frank Ribbons MA BD DipEd   1985 2011   49 Charlton Crescent, Aboyne AB34 5GN   01339 887267
[E-mail: frankribs@gmail.com]

Arbuthnott, Bervie and Kinneff
Dennis S. Rose LTh   1996 2010   10 Kirkburn, Inverbervie, Montrose DD10 0RT   01561 362560
[E-mail: dennis2327@aol.co.uk]

Banchory-Ternan: East (H) (01330 820380) (E-mail: banchoryeastchurchoffice@btconnect.com)
Alan J.S. Murray BSc BD PhD   2003 2013   East Manse, Station Road, Banchory AB31 5YP   01330 822481
[E-mail: alanjsm54@btopenworld.com]

Banchory-Ternan: West (H) Antony Stephen MA BD	2001	2011	The Manse, 2 Wilson Road, Banchory AB31 5UY [E-mail: tony@banchorywestchurch.com]	01330 822811
Birse and Feughside (H) Anita van der Wal	2008	2013	The Manse, Finzean, Banchory AB31 6PB [E-mail: vanderwal@btinternet.com]	01330 850776
Braemar and Crathie Kenneth I. Mackenzie DL BD CPS	1990	2005	The Manse, Crathie, Ballater AB35 5UL [E-mail: crathiemanse@tiscali.co.uk]	01339 742208
Cromar See Aboyne-Dinnet				
Drumoak (H)-Durris (H) Vacant			26 Sunnyside Drive, Drumoak, Banchory AB31 3EW	01330 811031
Glenmuick (Ballater) (H) Vacant			The Manse, Craigendarroch Walk, Ballater AB35 5ZB	01339 754014
Laurencekirk See Aberluthnott				
Maryculter Trinity (01224 735983) (E-mail: thechurchoffice@tiscali.co.uk) Melvyn J. Griffiths BTh DipTheol DMin	1978	2014	The Manse, Kirkton of Maryculter, Aberdeen AB12 5FS [E-mail: thehavyn@btinternet.com]	01224 730150
Mearns Coastal Colin J. Dempster BD CertMin	1990	2010	The Manse, Kirkton, St Cyrus, Montrose DD10 0BW [E-mail: coldcoast@btinternet.com]	01674 850880
Mid Deeside Alexander C. Wark MA BD STM	1982	2012	The Manse, Torphins, Banchory AB31 4GQ [E-mail: alecwark@yahoo.co.uk]	01339 882276
Newtonhill Hugh Conkey BSc BD	1987	2001	39 St Ternans Road, Newtonhill, Stonehaven AB39 3PF [E-mail: hugh@conkey.plus.com]	01569 730143

Portlethen (H) (01224 782883)
Flora J. Munro (Mrs) BD DMin — 1993 2004 — 18 Rowanbank Road, Portlethen, Aberdeen AB12 4NX [E-mail: floramunro@aol.co.uk] — 01224 780211

Stonehaven: Dunnottar (H) linked with Stonehaven: South (H)
Rosslyn P. Duncan BD MTh — 2007 — Dunnottar Manse, Stonehaven AB39 3XL [E-mail: rosslynpduncan@gmail.com] — 01569 762166

Stonehaven: Fetteresso (H) (01569 767689) (E-mail: fetteresso.office@btinternet.com)
Fyfe Blair BA BD DMin — 1989 2009 — 11 South Lodge Drive, Stonehaven AB39 2PN [E-mail: fyfeblair@talktalk.net] — 01569 762876

Stonehaven: South See Stonehaven: Dunnottar

West Mearns
Vacant — West Mearns Parish Church Manse, Fettercairn, Laurencekirk AB30 1UE — 01561 340203

Broadley, Linda J. (Mrs) LTh DipEd	1996	2013	(Dun and Hillside)	Snaefell, Lochside Road, St Cyrus, Montrose DD10 0DB [E-mail: lindabroadley@btinternet.com]	01674 850141
Brown, J.W.S. BTh	1960	1995	(Cromar)	10 Forestside Road, Banchory AB31 5ZH [E-mail: iainisobel@aol.com]	01330 824353
Cameron, Ann J. (Mrs) CertCS DCE TEFL	2005		Auxiliary Minister	Currently resident in Qatar [E-mail: anncameron2@googlemail.com]	
Christie, Andrew C. LTh	1975	2000	(Banchory-Devenick and Maryculter/Cookney)	17 Broadstraik Close, Elrick, Aberdeen AB32 6JP	01224 746888
Forbes, John W.A. BD	1973	1999	(Edzell Lethnot with Fern, Careston and Menmuir with Glenesk)	Little Ennochie Steading, Finzean, Banchory AB31 6LX [E-mail: jrbbbb@icloud.com]	01330 850785
Kinninburgh, Elizabeth B.F. (Miss) MA BD	1970	1986	(Birse with Finzean with Strachan)	21 Glen Tanar, Allachburn, Low Road, Aboyne AB34 5GW	01339 886757
Lamb, A. Douglas MA	1964	2002	(Dalry: St Margaret's)	9 Luther Drive, Laurencekirk AB30 1FE [E-mail: lamb.edzell@talk21.com]	01561 376816
Smith, Albert E. BD	1983	2006	(Methlick)	42 Haulkerton Crescent, Laurencekirk AB30 1FB [E-mail: aesmith42@googlemail.com]	01561 376111
Wallace, William F. BDS BD	1968	2008	(Wick: Pulteneytown and Thrumster)	Lachan Cottage, 29 Station Road, Banchory AB31 5XX [E-mail: williamwallace39@talktalk.net]	01330 822259
Watt, William D. LTh	1978	1996	(Aboyne-Dinnet)	2 West Toll Crescent, Aboyne AB34 5GB [E-mail: wdwatt22@tiscali.co.uk]	01339 886943
Watts, Anthony BD DipTechEd JP	1999	2013	(Glenmuick (Ballater))	7 Cumiskie Crescent, Forres IV36 2QB [E-mail: tony.watts6@btinternet.com]	

| Wilson, Andrew G.N. MA BD DMin | 1977 2012 | (Aberdeen: Rubislaw) | Auchintarph, Coull, Tarland, Aboyne AB34 4TT [E-mail: agn.wilson@gmail.com] | 01339 880918 |

(33) GORDON

Meets at various locations on the first Tuesday of February, March, April, May, September, October, November and December, and on the last Tuesday of June.

| Clerk: | REV. G. EUAN D. GLEN BSc BD | The Manse, 26 St Ninians, Monymusk, Inverurie AB51 7HF [E-mail: gordon@churchofscotland.org.uk] | 01467 651470 |

Barthol Chapel linked with Tarves
Vacant | 8 Murray Avenue, Tarves, Ellon AB41 7LZ | 01651 851250

Belhelvie (H)
Paul McKeown BSc PhD BD | 2000 2005 | Belhelvie Manse, Balmedie, Aberdeen AB23 8YR [E-mail: pmckeown1@btconnect.com] | 01358 742227

Blairdaff and Chapel of Garioch
Vacant | The Manse, Chapel of Garioch, Inverurie AB51 5HE | 01467 681619

Cluny (H) linked with Monymusk (H)
G. Euan D. Glen BSc BD | 1992 | The Manse, 26 St Ninians, Monymusk, Inverurie AB51 7HF [E-mail: euan.glen_1@btinternet.com] | 01467 651470

Culsalmond and Rayne linked with Daviot (H)
Mary M. Cranfield MA BD DMin | 1989 | The Manse, Daviot, Inverurie AB51 0HY [E-mail: marymc@ukgateway.net] | 01467 671241

Cushnie and Tough (R) (H)
Rosemary Legge (Mrs) BSc BD MTh | 1992 2010 | The Manse, Muir of Fowlis, Alford AB33 8JU [E-mail: cushnietough@aol.com] | 01975 581239

Daviot See Culsalmond and Rayne

Echt linked with Midmar (H)
Elspeth M. McKay (Mrs)
LLB LLM PGCert BD
2014 — The Manse, Echt, Westhill AB32 7AB
[E-mail: elspethmckay@me.com]
01330 860004

Ellon
Alastair J. Bruce BD MTh PGCE
2015 — The Manse, 12 Union Street, Ellon AB41 9BA
[E-mail: alastair.j.bruce@btinternet.com]
01358 723787

Fintray Kinellar Keithhall
Vacant
20 Kinmohr Rise, Blackburn, Aberdeen AB21 0LJ
01224 791350

Foveran
Richard Reid BSc BD MTh
1991 2013 — The Manse, Foveran, Ellon AB41 6AP
[E-mail: reidricky8@hotmail.com]
01358 789288

Howe Trinity
John A. Cook MA BD
1986 2000 — The Manse, 110 Main Street, Alford AB33 8AD
[E-mail: john.cook2@homecall.co.uk]
01975 562282

Huntly Cairnie Glass
Thomas R. Calder LLB BD WS
1994 — The Manse, Queen Street, Huntly AB54 8EB
[E-mail: cairniechurch@aol.com]
01466 792630

Insch-Leslie-Premnay-Oyne (H)
Kay Gauld BD STM PhD
1999 2015 — 66 Denwell Road, Insch AB52 6LH
[E-mail: kaygauld@gmail.com]
01464 820404

Inverurie: St Andrew's (Website: standrewschurchinverurie.org.uk)
James M. Davies BSc BD (Interim Minister)
1982 2014 — 27 Buchan Drive, Newmachar, Aberdeen AB21 0NR
[E-mail: daviesjim@btinternet.com]
01651 862281
07921 023144 (Mbl)

Inverurie: West
Ian B. Groves BD CPS
1989 — West Manse, 1 Westburn Place, Inverurie AB51 5QS
[E-mail: i.groves@inveruriewestchurch.org]
01467 620285

Kennay
Vacant
Kennay, Inverurie AB51 9ND
01467 642219 (Tel/Fax)

Kintore (H) Neil W. Meyer BD MTh	2000	2014	28 Oakhill Road, Kintore, Inverurie AB51 0FH [E-mail: kintorekirk.minister@gmail.com]	01467 632219
Meldrum and Bourtie Alison Jaffrey (Mrs) MA BD FSAScot	1990	2010	The Manse, Urquhart Road, Oldmeldrum, Inverurie AB51 0EX [E-mail: alison@revjaffrey.com]	01651 872250
Methlick Will Stalder BA MDiv MLitt PhD	2014		The Manse, Manse Road, Methlick, Ellon AB41 7DG [E-mail: bostowill@gmail.com]	01651 806264
Midmar See Echt **Monymusk** See Cluny				
New Machar Douglas G. McNab BA BD	1999	2010	The New Manse, Newmachar, Aberdeen AB21 0RD [E-mail: dougie.mcnab@btinternet.com]	01651 862278
Noth Regine U. Cheyne (Mrs) MA BSc BD	1988	2010	Manse of Noth, Kennethmont, Huntly AB54 4NP	01464 831690
Skene (H) Stella Campbell MA (Oxon) BD	2012		The Manse, Manse Road, Kirkton of Skene, Westhill AB32 6LX [E-mail: minister.skeneparish@mail.com]	01224 745955
Marion G. Stewart (Miss) DCS			Kirk Cottage, Kirkton of Skene, Westhill AB32 6XE [E-mail: m313stewart@btinternet.com]	01224 743407
Strathbogie Drumblade Neil I.M. MacGregor BD	1995		49 Deveron Park, Huntly AB54 8UZ	01466 792702
Tarves See Barthol Chapel				
Udny and Pitmedden Gillean P. Maclean (Ms) BA BD	1994	2013	The Manse, Manse Road, Udny Green, Ellon AB41 7RS [E-mail: minister@uppc.org.uk]	01651 843794

Upper Donside (H) (E-mail: upperdonsideparishchurch@btinternet.com)
Vacant
The Manse, Lumsden, Huntly AB54 4GQ   01464 861757

Craggs, Sheila (Mrs)	2001 2008	(Auxiliary Minister)	7 Morar Court, Ellon AB41 9GG	01358 723055
Craig, Anthony J.D. BD	1987 2009	(Glasgow: Maryhill)	4 Hightown, Collieston, Ellon AB41 8RS	01358 751247
			[E-mail: craig.glasgow@gmx.net]	
Dryden, Ian MA DipEd	1988 2001	(New Machar)	16 Glenhome Gardens, Dyce, Aberdeen AB21 7FG	01224 722820
			[E-mail: ian@idryden.freeserve.co.uk]	
Hawthorn, Daniel MA BD DMin	1965 2004	(Belhelvie)	7 Crimond Drive, Ellon AB41 8BT	01358 723981
			[E-mail: donhawthorn@compuserve.com]	
Jones, Robert A. LTh CA	1966 1997	(Marnoch)	13 Gordon Terrace, Inverurie AB51 4GT	01467 622691
Lyon, Andrew LTh	1971 2007	(Fraserburgh West with Rathen West)	20 Barnview, Culloden, Inverness IV2 7EX	
			[E-mail: andrewlyon70@hotmail.co.uk]	
Macalister, Eleanor	1994 2006	(Ellon)	Quarryview, Ythan Bank, Ellon AB41 7TH	01358 761402
			[E-mail: macal1ster@aol.com]	
Mack, John C. JP	1985 2008	(Auxiliary Minister)	The Willows, Auchleven, Insch AB52 6QB	01464 820387
McLeish, Robert S.	1970 2000	(Insch-Leslie-Premnay-Oyne)	19 Western Road, Insch AB52 6JR	01464 820749
Renton, John P. BA LTh	1976 2014	(Kennay)	2 Fettermear Way, Kennay, Inverurie AB51 5JH	01467 642403
			[E-mail: j.m.renton@btinternet.com]	
Rodger, Matthew A. BD	1978 1999	(Ellon)	15 Meadowlands Drive, Westhill AB32 6EJ	01224 743184
Scott, Allan D. BD	1977 1989	(Culsalmond with Daviot with Rayne)	Hilbury View, Hill Farm Lane, Duns Tew, Bicester OX25 6JH	
Stoddart, A. Grainger	1975 2001	(Meldrum and Bourtie)	6 Mayfield Gardens, Insch AB52 6XL	01464 821124
Taylor, Jane C. (Miss) BD DipMin	1990 2013	(Insch-Leslie-Premnay-Oyne)	1/2, 72 St Vincent Crescent, Glasgow G3 8NQ	0141-204 3022
			[E-mail: jane.c.taylor@btinternet.com]	
Thomson, Iain U. MA BD	1970 2011	(Skene)	4 Keirhill Gardens, Westhill AB32 6AZ	01224 746743
			[E-mail: iainuthomson@googlemail.com]	

(34) BUCHAN

Meets at St Kane's Centre, New Deer, Turriff on the first Tuesday of February, March, May, September, October, November and December, and on the third Tuesday of June.

Clerk: **REV. SHEILA M. KIRK BA LLB BD**   **The Manse, Old Deer, Peterhead AB42 5JB**   **01771 623582**
[E-mail: buchan@churchofscotland.org.uk]

Aberdour linked with Pitsligo

Auchaber United linked with Auchterless
Stephen J. Potts BA | 2012 | The Manse, Auchterless, Turriff AB53 8BA [E-mail: stevejpotts@hotmail.co.uk] | 01888 511058

Auchterless See Auchaber United

Banff linked with King Edward
David I.W. Locke MA MSc BD | 2000 | 2012 | 7 Colleonard Road, Banff AB45 1DZ [E-mail: davidlockerev@yahoo.co.uk] | 01261 812107 / 07776 448301 (Mbl)

Crimond linked with Lonmay
Vacant | The Manse, Crimond, Fraserburgh AB43 8QJ | 01346 532431

Cruden (H)
Vacant | The Manse, Hatton, Peterhead AB42 0QQ | 01779 841229

Deer (H)
Sheila M. Kirk BA LLB BD | 2007 | 2010 | The Manse, Old Deer, Peterhead AB42 5JB [E-mail: skirk@churchofscotland.org.uk] | 01771 623582

Fraserburgh: Old
Vacant | 4 Robbies Road, Fraserburgh AB43 7AF | 01346 515332

Fraserburgh: South (H) linked with Inverallochy and Rathen: East
Ronald F. Yule | 1982 | 15 Victoria Street, Fraserburgh AB43 9PJ | 01346 518244

Fraserburgh: West (H) linked with Rathen: West
Vacant | 4 Kirkton Gardens, Fraserburgh AB43 8TU | 01346 513303

Fyvie linked with Rothienorman
Robert J. Thorburn BD | 1978 | 2004 | The Manse, Fyvie, Turriff AB53 8RD [E-mail: rjthorburn@aol.com] | 01651 891230

Inverallochy and Rathen: East See Fraserburgh: South
King Edward See Banff

Longside
Robert A. Fowlie BD | 2007 | The Manse, Old Deer, Peterhead AB42 5JB [E-mail: bob.fowlie@googlemail.com] | 01771 622228

Lonmay See Crimond

Macduff
Calum Stark LLB BD | 2011 | 10 Ross Street, Macduff AB44 1NS [E-mail: revcstark@gmail.com] | 01261 832316

Marnoch
Alan Macgregor BA BD PhD | 1992   2013 | Marnoch Manse, 53 South Street, Aberchirder, Huntly AB54 7TS [E-mail: marnochkirk@btconnect.com] | 01466 781143

Maud and Savoch linked with New Deer: St Kane's
Vacant | The Manse, New Deer, Turriff AB53 6TD | 01771 644216

Monquhitter and New Byth linked with Turriff: St Andrew's
James Cook MA MDiv | 1999   2002 | St Andrew's Manse, Balmellie Road, Turriff AB53 4SP [E-mail: jmscook9@aol.com] | 01888 560304

New Deer: St Kane's See Maud and Savoch

New Pitsligo linked with Strichen and Tyrie
Andrew Fothergill BA | 2012 | Kingsville, Strichen, Fraserburgh AB43 6SQ [E-mail: andrewfothergill@btinternet.com] | 01771 637365

Ordiquhill and Cornhill (H) linked with Whitehills
W. Myburgh Verster BA BTh LTh MTh | 1981   2011 | 6 Craigneen Place, Whitehills, Banff AB45 2NE [E-mail: wverster8910@btinternet.com] | 01261 861317

Peterhead: Old
Vacant | 1 Hawthorn Road, Peterhead AB42 2DW

Peterhead: St Andrew's (H)
Vacant
1 Landale Road, Peterhead AB42 1QN
01779 238200

Peterhead: Trinity
Vacant
18 Landale Road, Peterhead AB42 1QP

Pitsligo See Aberdour

Portsoy
Norman Nicoll BD   2003   2010
The Manse, 4 Seafield Terrace, Portsoy, Banff AB45 2QB
[E-mail: minister.portsoychurch@gmail.com]
01261 842272

Rathen: West See Fraserburgh: West
Rothienorman See Fyvie

St Fergus
Jeffrey Tippner BA MDiv MCS PhD   1991   2012
26 Newton Road, St Fergus, Peterhead AB42 3DD
[E-mail: revjeff@btconnect.com]
01779 838287

Sandhaven
Vacant

Strichen and Tyrie See New Pitsligo
Turriff: St Andrew's See Monquhitter and New Byth

Turriff: St Ninian's and Forglen (H) (L)
Kevin R. Gruer BSc BA   2011
4 Deveronside Drive, Turriff AB53 4SP
[E-mail: kgruer@churchofscotland]
01888 563850

Whitehills See Ordiquhill and Cornhill

Coutts, Fred MA BD	1973	1989	(Hospital Chaplain)	Ladebank, 1 Manse Place, Hatton, Peterhead AB42 0UQ [E-mail: fred.coutts@btinternet.com]	01779 841320
Fawkes, G.M. Allan BA BSc JP	1979	2000	(Lonmay with Rathen: West)	3 Northfield Gardens, Hatton, Peterhead AB42 0SW [E-mail: afawkes@aol.com]	01779 841814

Gehrke, Robert B. BSc BD CEng MIEE	1994 2013	(Blackridge with Harthill: St Andrew's)	140 The Green, Gardenstown, Banff AB45 3BD [E-mail: bob.gehrke@gmail.com]	01261 839129
McMillan, William J. CA LTh BD	1969 2004	(Sandsting and Aithsting with Walls and Sandness)	7 Ardinn Drive, Turriff AB53 4PR [E-mail: revbillymcmillan@aol.com]	01888 560727
Macnee, Iain LTh BD MA PhD	1975 2011	(New Pitsligo with Strichen and Tyrie)	Wardend Cottage, Alvah, Banff AB45 3TR [E-mail: macneeiain4@googlemail.com]	01261 815647
Noble, George S. DipTh	1972 2000	(Carfin with Newarthill)	Craigowan, 3 Main Street, Inverallochy, Fraserburgh AB43 8XX	01346 582749
Ross, David S. MSc PhD BD	1978 2013	(Prison Chaplain Service)	3–5 Abbey Street, Old Deer, Peterhead AB42 5LN [E-mail: padsross@btinternet.com]	01771 623994
Stewart, William	2015	Ordained Local Minister	Denend, Strichen, Fraserburgh AB43 6RN [E-mail: billandjunes@live.co.uk]	01771 637256
van Sittert, Paul BA BD	1997 2011	Chaplain: Army	4Bn The Royal Regiment of Scotland, Bourlon Barracks, Plumer Road, Catterick Garrison DL9 3AD [E-mail: padre.pvs@gmail.com]	

(35) MORAY

Meets at St Andrew's-Lhanbryd and Urquhart on the first Tuesday of February, March, May, September, October, November and December, and at the Moderator's church on the fourth Tuesday of June.

| Clerk: | REV. GRAHAM W. CRAWFORD BSc BD STM | The Manse, Prospect Terrace, Lossiemouth IV31 6JS [E-mail: moray@churchofscotland.org.uk] | 07944 287777 (Mbl) |

Aberlour (H)

| Shuna M. Dicks BSc BD | 2010 | The Manse, Mary Avenue, Aberlour AB38 9QU [E-mail: revshuna@btinternet.com] | 01340 871687 |

Alves and Burghead linked with Kinloss and Findhorn

| Louis C. Bezuidenhout BA MA BD DD | 1978 2014 | The Manse, 4 Manse Road, Kinloss, Forres IV36 3GH [E-mail: macbez@gmail.com] | 01309 690474 |

Bellie and Speymouth

| Alison C. Mehigan BD DPS | 2003 | 11 The Square, Fochabers IV32 7DG [E-mail: alison@mehigan.org] | 01343 820256 |

Birnie and Pluscarden linked with Elgin: High

| Stuart M. Duff BA | 1997 2014 | The Manse, Daisy Bank, 5 Forteath Avenue, Elgin IV30 1TQ [E-mail: stuart.duff@gmail.com] | 01343 545703 |

Buckie: North (H) linked with Rathven
Isabel C. Buchan (Mrs) BSc BD RE(PgCE)   1975   2013   The Manse, 14 St Peter's Road, Buckie   AB56 1DL   01542 832118
[E-mail: revicbuchan@bluebucket.org]

Buckie: South and West (H) linked with Enzie
Vacant   Craigendarroch, 14 Cliff Terrace, Buckie   AB56 1LX   01542 833775

Cullen and Deskford (Website: www.cullen-deskford-church.org.uk)
Douglas F. Stevenson BD DipMin   1991   2010   3 Seafield Place, Cullen, Buckie   AB56 4UU   01542 841963
[E-mail: dstevenson655@btinternet.com]

Dallas linked with Forres: St Leonard's (H) linked with Rafford
Donald K. Prentice BSc BD   1989   2010   St Leonard's Manse, Nelson Road, Forres IV36 1DR   01309 672380
[E-mail: donald.prentice@tesco.net]
Anne Attenburrow BSc MB ChB   2006   2013   4 Jock Inksons Brae, Elgin IV30 1QE   01343 552330
(Auxiliary Minister)   [E-mail: AAttenburrow@aol.com]
John Morrison BSc BA PGCE   2013   35 Kirkton Place, Elgin IV30 6JR   01343 550199
(Ordained Local Minister)   [E-mail: shalla57@aol.com]

Duffus, Spynie and Hopeman (H) (Website: www.duffusparish.co.uk)
Jennifer Adams BEng BD   2013   The Manse, Duffus, Elgin IV30 5QP   01343 830276
[E-mail: jennyadamsbd@gmail.com]

Dyke linked with Edinkillie
Vacant   Manse of Dyke, Brodie, Forres IV36 2TD   01309 641239

Edinkillie See Dyke
Elgin: High See Birnie and Pluscarden

Elgin: St Giles' (H) and St Columba's South (01343 551501) (Office: Williamson Hall, Duff Avenue, Elgin IV30 1QS)
Steven Thomson BSc BD   2001   2013   18 Reidhaven Street, Elgin IV30 1QH   01343 545729
[E-mail: stevie.thomson284@btinternet.com]   07841 368797 (Mbl)

Enzie See Buckie: South and West

Findochty linked with Portknockie
Hilary W. Smith BD DipMin MTh PhD   1999   2014   20 Netherton Terrace, Findochty, Buckie   AB56 4QD   01542 833484
[E-mail: hilaryoxfordsmith1@gmail.com]

Forres: St Laurence (H)
Barry J. Boyd LTh DPS — 1993 — 12 Mackenzie Drive, Forres IV36 2JP — 01309 672260 / 07778 731018 (Mbl)
[E-mail: barryj.boydstlaurence@btinternet.com]

Forres: St Leonard's See Dallas
Keith: North, Newmill, Boharm and Rothiemay (H) (01542 886390)
Vacant — North Manse, Church Road, Keith AB55 5BR — 01542 882559

Keith: St Rufus, Botriphnie and Grange (H)
Vacant — Church Road, Keith AB55 5BR — 01542 882799

Kinloss and Findhorn See Alves and Burghead

Knockando, Elchies and Archiestown (H) linked with Rothes (Website: www.moraykirk.co.uk)
Robert J.M. Anderson BD FInstLM — 1993 — 2000 — The Manse, Rothes, Aberlour AB38 7AF — 01340 831381
[E-mail: robert@carmanse.freeserve.co.uk]

Lossiemouth: St Gerardine's High (H)
Geoffrey D. McKee BA — 1997 — 2014 — The Manse, St Gerardine's Road, Lossiemouth IV31 6RA — 01343 813146
[E-mail: geoff.mckee@btinternet.com]

Lossiemouth: St James'
Graham W. Crawford BSc BD STM — 1991 — 2003 — The Manse, Prospect Terrace, Lossiemouth IV31 6JS — 07817 504042 (Mbl)
[E-mail: pictishreiver@aol.com]

Mortlach and Cabrach (H)
Vacant — Mortlach Manse, Dufftown, Keith AB55 4AR — 01340 820380

Portknockie See Findochty
Rafford See Dallas
Rathven See Buckie: North
Rothes See Knockando, Elchies and Archiestown

St Andrew's-Lhanbryd (H) and Urquhart
Andrew J. Robertson BD — 2008 — 2010 — 39 St Andrews Road, Lhanbryde, Elgin IV30 8PU — 01343 843765
[E-mail: ajr247@btinternet.com]

Speymouth See Bellie

Name	Ord.	Ind.	Charge	Address	Tel.
Bain, Brian LTh	1980	2007	(Gask with Methven and Logiealmond)	Bayview, 13 Stewart Street, Portgordon, Buckie AB56 5QT [E-mail: brian.bain4@btinternet.com]	01542 831215
Buchan, Alexander MA BD PGCE	1975	1992	(North Ronaldsay with Sanday)	The Manse, 14 St Peter's Road, Buckie AB56 1DL [E-mail: revabuchan@bluebucket.org]	01542 832118
Davidson, A.A.B. MA BD	1960	1997	(Grange with Rothiemay)	11 Sutors Rise, Nairn IV12 5BU	01343 820937
King, Margaret MA DCS			(Deacon in Presbytery)	56 Murrayfield, Fochabers IV32 7EZ	01309 671719
Morton, Alasdair J. MA BD DipEd FEIS	1960	2000	(Bowden with Newtown)	16 St Leonard's Road, Forres IV36 1DW [E-mail: alasgilmor@hotmail.co.uk]	01309 671719
Morton, Gillian M. (Mrs) MA BD PGCE	1983	1996	(Hospital Chaplain)	16 St Leonard's Road, Forres IV36 1DW [E-mail: gillianmorton@hotmail.co.uk]	
Oliver, G. BD	1979	2015		129 Knockomie Rise, Forres IV36 2HE	01309 641046
Poole, Ann McColl (Mrs) DipEd ACE LTh	1983	2003	(Dyke with Edinkillie)	Kirkside Cottage, Dyke, Forres IV36 2TF	01309 676769
Robertson, Peter BSc BD	1988	1998	(Dallas with Forres: St Leonard's with Rafford)	17 Ferryhill Road, Forres IV36 2GY [E-mail: peterrobertsonforres@talktalk.net]	01343 835226
Rollo, George B. BD	1974	2010	(Elgin: St Giles' and St Columba's South)	'Struan', 13 Meadow View, Hopeman, Elgin IV30 5PL [E-mail: rollos@gmail.com]	
Shaw, Duncan LTh CPS	1984	2011	(Alves and Burghead with Kinloss and Findhorn)	73 Woodside Drive, Forres IV36 0UF	
Smith, Hugh M.C. LTh	1973	2013	(Mortlach and Cabrach)	6 Concraig Walk, Kingswells, Aberdeen AB15 8DU	01224 745275
Smith, Morris BD	1988	2013	(Cromdale and Advie with Dulnain Bridge with Grantown-on-Spey)	1 Urquhart Grove, New Elgin IV30 8TB [E-mail: mosmith.themanse@btinternet.com]	01343 545019
Thomson, James M. BA	1952	2000	(Elgin: St Giles' and St Columba's South: Associate)	48 Mayne Road, Elgin IV30 1PD	01343 547664
Whittaker, Mary	2011		Auxiliary Minister	11 Templand Road, Lhanbryde, Elgin IV30 8BR	
Whyte, David LTh	1993	2011	(Boat of Garten, Duthil and Kincardine)	1 Lemanfield Crescent, Garmouth, Fochabers IV32 7LS [E-mail: whytedj@btinternet.com]	01343 870667
Wright, David L. MA BD	1957	1998	(Stornoway: St Columba)	84 Wyvis Drive, Nairn IV12 4TP	01667 451613

(36) ABERNETHY

Meets at Boat of Garten on the first Tuesday of February, March, May, September, October, November and December, and on the last Tuesday of June.

Clerk: REV. CATHERINE A. BUCHAN MA MDiv   The Manse, Fort William Road, Newtonmore PH20 1DG   01540 673238
[E-mail: abernethy@churchofscotland.org.uk]

Abernethy (H) linked with Boat of Garten (H), Duthil (H) and Kincardine
Donald K. Walker BD   1979   2013   The Manse, Deshar Road, Boat of Garten PH24 3BN   01479 831252
[E-mail: donaldabdk@gmail.com]

Alvie and Insh (R) (H) linked with Rothiemurchus and Aviemore (H)
Vacant
The Manse, 8 Dalfaber Park, Aviemore PH22 1QF   01479 810280

Boat of Garten, Duthil and Kincardine See Abernethy

Cromdale (H) and Advie linked with Dulnain Bridge (H) linked with Grantown-on-Spey (H)
Gordon Strang   2014
The Manse, Golf Course Road, Grantown-on-Spey PH26 3HY   01479 872084
[E-mail: gstrang@churchofscotland.org.uk]

Dulnain Bridge See Cromdale and Advie
Grantown-on-Spey See Cromdale and Advie

Kingussie (H)
Alison H. Burnside (Mrs) MA BD   1991   2013
The Manse, 18 Hillside Avenue, Kingussie PH21 1PA   01540 662327
[E-mail: alisonskyona@btinternet.com]

Laggan (H) linked with Newtonmore: St Bride's (H)
Catherine A. Buchan (Mrs) MA MDiv   2002   2009
The Manse, Fort William Road, Newtonmore PH20 1DG   01540 673238
[E-mail: catherinebuchan567@btinternet.com]

Newtonmore: St Bride's See Laggan
Rothiemurchus and Aviemore See Alvie and Insh

Tomintoul (H), Glenlivet and Inveraven
Christopher Wallace BD DipMin   1988   2014
The Manse, Tomintoul, Ballindalloch AB37 9HA   01807 580254
[E-mail: cw@churchofscotland.onmicrosoft.com]

Burnside, William A.M. MA BD PGCE	1990	2013	(Stromness)	The Manse, 18 Hillside Avenue, Kingussie PH21 1PA [E-mail: bburnside@btinternet.com]	01540 662327
Duncanson, Mary (Ms) BTh	2013		Ordained Local Minister: Presbytery Pastoral Support	3 Balmenach Road, Cromdale, Grantown-on-Spey PH26 3LJ [E-mail: mary1105@hotmail.co.uk]	01479 872165
MacEwan, James A.I. MA BD	1973	2012	(Abernethy with Cromdale and Advie)	Rapness, Station Road, Nethy Bridge PH25 3DN [E-mail: wurrus@hotmail.co.uk]	01479 821116
Ritchie, Christine A.Y. (Mrs) BD DipMin	2002	2012	(Braes of Rannoch with Foss and Rannoch)	25 Beachen Court, Grantown-on-Spey PH26 3JD [E-mail: cayritchie@btinternet.com]	01479 873419
Thomson, Mary Ellen (Mrs)	2013		Ordained Local Minister	Riverside Flat, Gynack Street, Kingussie PH21 1EL [E-mail: marythomson835@btinternet.com]	01540 661772

Wallace, Sheila (Mrs) DCS BA BD   Deacon   Beannach Cottage, Spey Avenue, Boat of Garten PH24 3BE   01479 831548
[E-mail: sheilad.wallace53@gmail.com]

(37) INVERNESS

Meets at Inverness, in Inverness; Trinity, on the first Tuesday of February, March, May, September, October, November and December, and at the Moderator's church on the fourth Tuesday of June.

Clerk: REV. TREVOR G. HUNT BA BD   7 Woodville Court, Culduthel Avenue, Inverness IV2 6BX   01463 250355
[E-mail: inverness@churchofscotland.org.uk]   07753 423333 (Mbl)

Ardersier (H) linked with Petty
Robert Cleland   1997   2014   The Manse, Ardersier, Inverness IV2 7SX   01667 462224
[E-mail: cleland810@btinternet.com]

Auldearn and Dalmore linked with Nairn: St Ninian's (H)
Thomas M. Bryson BD   1997   2015   The Manse, Auldearn, Nairn IV12 5SX   01667 451675
[E-mail: thomas@bryson3.wanadoo.co.uk]

Cawdor (H) linked with Croy and Dalcross (H)
Janet S. Mathieson MA BD   2003   The Manse, Croy, Inverness IV2 5PH   01667 493217
[E-mail: mathieson173@btinternet.com]

Croy and Dalcross See Cawdor

Culloden: The Barn (H)
Michael Robertson BA   2014   45 Oakdene Court, Culloden IV2 7XL   01463 239785
07740 984395 (Mbl)

Daviot and Dunlichity linked with Moy, Dalarossie and Tomatin
Vacant   The Manse, Daviot, Inverness IV2 5XL   01463 772242

Dores and Boleskine
Vacant

Inverness: Crown (H) (01463 231140) Peter H. Donald MA PhD BD	1991	1998	39 Southside Road, Inverness IV2 4XA [E-mail: peter.donald7@btinternet.com]	01463 230537
Inverness: Dalneigh and Bona (GD) (H) Vacant			9 St Mungo Road, Inverness IV3 5AS	01463 232339
Inverness: East (H) Andrew T.B. McGowan (Prof.) BD STM PhD	1979	2009	2 Victoria Drive, Inverness IV2 3QD [E-mail: atbmcgowan@invernesseast.com]	01463 238770
Inverness: Hilton Duncan MacPherson LLB BD	1994		66 Culduthel Mains Crescent, Inverness IV2 6RG [E-mail: duncan@hiltonchurch.org.uk]	01463 231417
Inverness: Inshes (H) David S. Scott MA BD	1987	2013	48 Redwood Crescent, Milton of Leys, Inverness IV2 6HB [E-mail: david@insheschurch.org]	01463 772402
Inverness: Kinmylies (H) Andrew Barrie BD	2013		2 Balnafettack Place, Inverness IV3 8TQ [E-mail: andrewabarrie@hotmail.co.uk]	01463 224307
Inverness: Ness Bank (R) (H) Fiona E. Smith (Mrs) LLB BD	2010		15 Ballifeary Road, Inverness IV3 5PJ [E-mail: fiona.denhead@btopenworld.com]	01463 234653
Inverness: Old High St Stephen's Peter W. Nimmo BD ThM	1996	2004	24 Damfield Road, Inverness IV2 3HU [E-mail: peter.nimmo7@btinternet.com]	01463 250802
Inverness: St Columba (New Charge Development) (H) Scott A. McRoberts BD MTh	2012		20 Bramble Close, Inverness IV2 6BS [E-mail: scottmcroberts@stcolumbainverness.org]	01463 230308 07535 290092 (Mbl)
Inverness: Trinity (H) Alistair Murray BD	1984	2004	60 Kenneth Street, Inverness IV3 5PZ [E-mail: a.murray111@btinternet.com]	01463 234756

Kilmorack and Erchless
Vacant   'Roselynn', Croyard Road, Beauly IV4 7DJ   01463 782260

Kiltarlity linked with Kirkhill
Jonathan W. Humphrey BSc BD PhD   2015   Wardlaw Manse, Wardlaw Road, Kirkhill, Inverness IV5 7NZ   01463 831662
                                                                                          [E-mail: jonkateh588@tiscali.co.uk]

Kirkhill See Kiltarlity
Moy, Dalarossie and Tomatin See Daviot and Dunlichity

Nairn: Old (H)
Vacant

Nairn: St Ninian's See Auldearn and Dalmore
Petty See Ardersier

Urquhart and Glenmoriston (H)
Hugh F. Watt BD DPS DMin   1986   1996   Blairbeg, Drumnadrochit, Inverness IV3 6UG   01456 450231
                                                                                          [E-mail: hugh.watt2@btinternet.com]

Archer, Morven (Mrs)	2013		Ordained Local Minister	42 Firthview Drive, Inverness IV3 8QE	01463 237840
				[E-mail: morvarch@btinternet.com]	
Black, Archibald T. BSc	1964	1997	(Inverness: Ness Bank)	16 Elm Park, Inverness IV2 4WN	01463 230588
Brown, Derek G. BD DipMin DMin	1989	1994	Lead Chaplain: NHS Highland	Cathedral Manse, Cnoc-an-Lobht, Dornoch IV25 3HN	01862 810296
				[E-mail: derek.brown1@nhs.net]	
Buell, F. Bart BA MDiv	1980	1995	(Urquhart and Glenmoriston)	6 Towerhill Place, Cradlehall, Inverness IV2 5FN	01463 794634
				[E-mail: bartbuell@talktalk.net]	
Campbell, Reginald F.	1979	2015	(Urquhart and Glenmoriston)	12 Alloway Drive, Kirkcaldy KY2 6DX	
				[E-mail: campbell578@talktalk.net]	
Chisholm, Archibald F. MA	1957	1997	(Braes of Rannoch with Foss and Rannoch)	32 Seabank Road, Nairn IV12 4EU	01667 452001
Christie, James LTh	1993	2003	(Dores and Boleskine)	20 Wester Inshes Crescent, Inverness IV2 5HL	01463 710534
Duncan, John C. BD MPhil	1987	2001	Chaplain: Army	3 Bn The Black Watch, The Royal Regiment of Scotland,	(Mbl) 07825 119227
				Fort George, Ardersier, Inverness IV1 2TD	
				[E-mail: john.duncan831@mod.uk]	
Fraser, Jonathan MA(Div) MTh ThM	2012		Associate: Inverness: Hilton	20 Moy Terrace, Inverness IV2 4EL	(Home) 01463 711609
				[E-mail: jonathan@hiltonchurch.org.uk]	(Work) 01463 233310
Frizzell, R. Stewart BD	1961	2000	(Wick: Old)	98 Boswell Road, Inverness IV2 3EW	01463 231907
Hunt, Trevor G. BA BD	1986	2011	(Evie with Firth with Rendall)	7 Woodville Court, Culduthel Avenue, Inverness IV2 6BX	01463 250355
				[E-mail: trevorhunt@gmail.com]	(Mbl) 07753 423333

Name		Dates	Role	Address / E-mail	Telephone
Jeffrey, Stewart D.	BSc BD	1962 1997	(Banff with King Edward)	10 Grigor Drive, Inverness IV2 4LP [E-mail: stewart.jeffrey@talktalk.net]	01463 230085
Livesley, Anthony	LTh	1979 1997	(Kiltearn)	87 Beech Avenue, Nairn IV12 4ST [E-mail: tonylivesley@googlemail.com]	01667 455126
Mackenzie, Seoras L.	BD	1996 1998	Chaplain: Army	Carver Barracks, Wimbish, Saffron Walden, Essex CB10 2YA	
MacQuarrie, Donald A.	BSc BD	1979 2012	(Fort William: Duncansburgh MacIntosh with Kilmonivaig)	Birch Cottage, 4 Craigrorie, North Kessock, Inverness IV1 3XH [E-mail: pdmacq@ukgateway.net]	01463 731050
McRoberts, T. Douglas	BD CPS FRSA	1975 2014	(Malta)	24 Redwood Avenue, Inverness IV2 6HA [E-mail: doug.mcroberts@btinternet.com]	01463 772594
Mitchell, Joyce (Mrs)	DCS	1994	(Deacon)	Sunnybank, Farr, Inverness IV2 6XG [E-mail: joyce@mitchell71.freeserve.co.uk]	01808 521285
Morrison, Hector	BSc BD MTh	1981 1994	Principal: Highland Theological College	24 Oak Avenue, Inverness IV2 4NX	01463 238561
Rettie, James A.	BTh	1981 1999	(Melness and Eriboll with Tongue)	2 Trantham Drive, Westhill, Inverness IV2 5QT	01463 798896
Ritchie, Bruce	BSc BD PhD	1977 2014	(Dingwall: Castle Street)	16 Brinckman Terrace, Westhill, Inverness IV2 5BL [E-mail: brucezomba@hotmail.com]	01463 791389
Robb, Rodney P.T.		1995 2004	(Stirling: St Mark's)	2A Mayfield Road, Inverness IV2 4AE	01463 230831
Robertson, Fergus A.	MA BD	1971 2010	(Inverness: Dalneigh and Bona)	16 Druid Temple Way, Inverness IV2 6UQ [E-mail: faavrobertson@yahoo.co.uk]	01463 718462
Stirling, G. Alan S.	MA	1960 1999	(Leochel Cushnie and Lynturk with Tough)	97 Lochlann Road, Culloden, Inverness IV2 7HJ	01463 798313
Turner, Fraser K.	LTh	1994 2007	(Kiltarlity with Kirkhill)	20 Caulfield Avenue, Inverness IV2 5GA [E-mail: fraseratq@yahoo.co.uk]	01463 794004
Warwick, Ivan C.	MA BD TD	1980	Army Chaplain	Ardcruidh Croft, Heights of Dochcarty, Dingwall, IV15 9UF [E-mail: L70rev@btinternet.com]	01349 861464 (Mbl) 07787 535083
Waugh, John L.	LTh	1973 2002	(Ardclach with Auldearn and Dalmore)	58 Wyvis Drive, Nairn IV12 4TP [E-mail: jwaugh334@btinternet.com]	01667 456397 (Tel/Fax)
Younger, Alastair S.	BScEcon ASCC	1969 2008	(Inverness: St Columba High)	33 Duke's View, Slackbuie, Inverness IV2 6BB [E-mail: younger873@btinternet.com]	01463 242873

INVERNESS ADDRESSES

Inverness

Crown	Kingsmills Road x Midmills Road
Dalneigh and Bona	St Mary's Avenue
East	Academy Street x Margaret Street
Hilton	Druid Road x Tomatin Road
Inshes	Inshes Retail Park
Kinmylies	Kinmylies Way
Ness Bank	Ness Bank x Castle Road
St Stephen's	Old Edinburgh Road x Southside Road
The Old High	Church Street x Church Lane
Trinity	Huntly Place x Upper Kessock Street

Nairn

Old	Academy Street x Seabank Road
St Ninian's	High Street x Queen Street

(38) LOCHABER

Meets at Caol, Fort William, in Kilmallie Church Hall at 6pm, on the first Tuesday of September and December, on the last Tuesday of October and on the fourth Tuesday of March. The June meeting is held at 6pm on the first Tuesday in the church of the incoming Moderator.

Clerk:	MRS ELLA GILL	5 Camus Inas, Acharacle PH36 4JQ [E-mail: lochaber@churchofscotland.org.uk]	01967 431834
Treasurer:	MRS CONNIE ANDERSON	Darach, Duror, PA38 4BS [E-mail : faoconnie@gmail.com]	01631 740334

Acharacle (H) linked with Ardnamurchan
Fiona Ogg (Mrs) BA BD   2012   The Manse, Acharacle PH36 4JU   01967 431654
                                                           [E-mail: fiona.ogg@churchofscotland.org.uk]

Ardgour and Kingairloch linked with Morvern linked with Strontian
Donald G.B. McCorkindale BD DipMin   1992   2011   The Manse, 2 The Meadows, Strontian, Acharacle PH36 4HZ   01967 402234
                                                        [E-mail: donald.mccorkindale@sky.com]
                                                        [E-mail: donald@aksm.org.uk]

Ardnamurchan See Acharacle

Duror (H) linked with Glencoe: St Munda's (H) (R)
Vacant

Fort Augustus linked with Glengarry
Tabea Baader   2012   The Manse, Fort Augustus PH32 4BH   01320 366210
                                                        [E-mail: tbaader@churchofscotland.org.uk]

Fort William: Duncansburgh MacIntosh (H) linked with Kilmonivaig
Vacant   The Manse of Duncansburgh, The Parade, Fort William PH33 6BA   01397 703635

Glencoe: St Munda's See Duror
Glengarry See Fort Augustus

Kilmallie
Richard T. Corbett BSc MSc PhD BD   1992   2005   Kilmallie Manse, Corpach, Fort William PH33 7JS   01397 772736
                                                        [E-mail: rcorbett@churchofscotland.org.uk]

Kilmonivaig See Fort William: Duncansburgh MacIntosh

Kinlochleven (H) linked with Nether Lochaber (H)   2010
Malcolm A. Kinnear MA BD PhD

The Manse, Lochaber Road, Kinlochleven PH50 4QW   01855 831227
[E-mail: mkinnear@churchofscotland.org.uk]

Morvern See Ardgour
Nether Lochaber See Kinlochleven

North West Lochaber
Edgar J. Ogston BSc BD   1976   2013

Church of Scotland Manse, Annie's Brae, Mallaig PH41 4RG   01687 460042
[E-mail: eogston@churchofscotland.org.uk]

Strontian See Ardgour

Anderson, David M. MSc FCOptom	1984	2012	(Ordained Local Minister)	'Mirlos', 1 Dumfries Place, Fort William PH33 6UQ [E-mail: david.anderson@churchofscotland.org.uk]	01397 702091
Lamb, Alan H.W. BA MTh	1959	2005	(Associate Minister)	Smiddy House, Arisaig PH39 4NH [E-mail: h.a.lamb@handalamb.plus.com]	01687 450227
Millar, John L. MA BD	1981	1990	(Fort William: Duncansburgh with Kilmonivaig)	Flat 0/1, 12 Chesterfield Gardens, Glasgow G12 0BF [E-mail: johnmillar123@btinternet.com]	0141-339 4098
Muirhead, Morag (Mrs)	2013		Ordained Local Minister	6 Dumbarton Road, Fort William PH33 6UU [E-mail: mmuirhead@churchofscotland.org.uk]	01397 703643
Perkins, Mairi	2012		Ordained Local Minister	Ashlea, Cuil Road, Duror, Appin PA38 4DA [E-mail: mperkins@churchofscotland.org.uk]	01631 740313
Rae, Peter C. BSc BD	1968	2000	(Beath and Cowdenbeath: North)	8 Wether Road, Great Cambourne, Cambridgeshire CB23 5DT [E-mail: rae.fairview@btinternet.com]	01954 710079
Varwell, Adrian P.J. BA BD PhD	1983	2011	(Fort Augustus with Glengarry)	19 Enrick Crescent, Kilmore, Drumnadrochit, Inverness IV63 6TP [E-mail: adrian.varwell@btinternet.com]	01456 459352
Winning, A. Ann MA DipEd BD	1984	2006	(Morvern)	'Westering', 13C Carnoch, Glencoe, Ballachulish PH49 4HQ [E-mail: awinning009@btinternet.com]	01855 811929

LOCHABER Communion Sundays Please consult the Presbytery website: www.cofslochaber.co.uk

(39) ROSS

Meets on the first Tuesday of September in the church of the incoming Moderator, and in Dingwall: Castle Street Church on the first Tuesday of October, November, December, February, March and May, and on the last Tuesday of June.

Clerk: MR RONALD W. GUNSTONE BSc   20 Bellfield Road, North Kessock, Inverness IV1 3XU   01463 731337
[E-mail: ross@churchofscotland.org.uk]

Alness
Vacant
Michael Macdonald   2004   2014   27 Darroch Brae, Alness IV17 0SD   01349 882238
(Auxiliary Minister)   73 Firhill, Alness IV17 0RT   01349 884268
                                           [E-mail: mike_mary@hotmail.co.uk]

Avoch linked with Fortrose and Rosemarkie
Alan T. McKean BD CertMin   1982   2010   5 Ness Way, Fortrose IV10 8SS   01381 621433
                                           [E-mail: a.mckean2345@btinternet.com]

Contin (H) linked with Fodderty and Strathpeffer (H)
Fanus Erasmus MA LTh MTh ThD 1978 2013 The Manse, Contin, Strathpeffer IV14 9ES 01997 421028
                                           [E-mail: fanuserasmus@yahoo.com]

Cromarty linked with Resolis and Urquhart
Vacant   The Manse, Culbokie, Dingwall IV7 8JN   01349 877452

Dingwall: Castle Street (H)
Stephen Macdonald BD MTh   2008   2014   16 Achany Road, Dingwall IV15 9JB   01349 866792
                                           [E-mail: sm.2@hotmail.co.uk]   07570 804193   (Mbl)

Dingwall: St Clement's (H)
Bruce Dempsey BD   1997   2014   8 Castlehill Road, Dingwall IV15 9PB   01349 292055
                                           [E-mail: revbrucedempsey@gmail.com]

Fearn Abbey and Nigg linked with Tarbat
Robert G.D.W. Pickles   2003   2015   Church of Scotland Manse, Fearn, Tain IV20 1WN   01862 832282
BD MPhil ThD   [E-mail: robert.pickles@btopenworld.com]

Ferintosh Andrew F. Graham BTh DPS	2001	2006	Ferintosh Manse, Leanaig Road, Conon Bridge, Dingwall IV7 8BE [E-mail: afg1960@tiscali.co.uk]	01349 861275
Fodderty and Strathpeffer See Contin **Fortrose and Rosemarkie** See Avoch				
Invergordon Kenneth Donald Macleod BD CPS	1989	2000	The Manse, Cromlet Drive, Invergordon IV18 0BA [E-mail: kd-macleod@tiscali.co.uk]	01349 852273
Killearnan (H) linked with Knockbain (H) Vacant			The Church of Scotland Manse, Coldwell Road, Artafallie, North Kessock, Inverness IV1 3ZE	01463 731333
Kilmuir and Logie Easter Fraser M.C. Stewart BSc BD	1980	2011	The Manse, Delny, Invergordon IV18 0NW [E-mail: fraserstewart1955@hotmail.com]	01862 842280
Kiltearn (H) Donald A. MacSween BD	1991	1998	The Manse, Swordale Road, Evanton, Dingwall IV16 9UZ [E-mail: donaldmacsween@hotmail.com]	01349 830472
Knockbain See Killearnan				
Lochbroom and Ullapool (GD) Vacant			The New Manse, Garve Road, Ullapool IV26 2SX	01854 613146
Resolis and Urquhart See Cromarty				
Rosskeen Robert Jones BSc BD	1990		Rosskeen Manse, Perrins Road, Alness IV17 0XG [E-mail: rob2jones@btinternet.com]	01349 882265
Tain Vacant			14 Kingsway Avenue, Tain IV19 1NJ	01862 894140
Tarbat See Fearn Abbey and Nigg				

Urray and Kilchrist

Scott Polworth LLB BD	2009		The Manse, Corrie Road, Muir of Ord IV6 7TL [E-mail: scottpolworth@btinternet.com]	01463 870259

Name	Ordained/Inducted	Former Charge	Address	Tel
Archer, Nicholas D.C. BA BD	1971 1992	(Dores and Boleskine)	2 Aldie Cottages, Tain IV19 1LZ [E-mail: na.2ac777@btinternet.com]	01862 821494
Dupar, Kenneth W. BA BD PhD	1965 1993	(Christ's College, Aberdeen)	The Old Manse, The Causeway, Cromarty IV11 8XJ	01381 600428
Forsyth, James LTh	1970 2000	(Fearn Abbey with Nigg Chapelhill)	Rhives Lodge, Golspie, Sutherland KW10 6DD	
Glass, Alexander OBE MA	1998 2009	(Auxiliary Minister)	Craigton, Tulloch Avenue, Dingwall IV15 9TU	01349 863258
Horne, Douglas A. BD	1977 2009	(Tain)	151 Holm Farm Road, Culduthel, Inverness IV2 6BF [E-mail: douglas.horne@talktalk.net]	01463 712677
Liddell, Margaret (Miss) BD DipTh	1987 1997	(Contin)	20 Wyvis Crescent, Conon Bridge, Dingwall IV7 8BZ [E-mail: margaretliddell@talktalk.net]	01349 865997
Lincoln, John MPhil BD	1986 2014	(Balquhidder with Killin and Ardeonaig)	59 Obsdale Park, Alness IV17 0TR [E-mail: johnlincoln@minister.com]	01349 882791
Mackinnon, R.M. LTh	1968 1995	(Kilmuir and Logie Easter)	27 Riverford Crescent, Conon Bridge, Dingwall IV7 8HL	01349 866293
MacLennan, Alasdair J. BD DCE	1978 2001	(Resolis and Urquhart)	Airdale, Seaforth Road, Muir of Ord IV6 7TA	01463 870704
Macleod, John MA	1959 1993	(Resolis and Urquhart)	'Benview', 19 Balvaird, Muir of Ord IV6 7RG [E-mail: sheilaandjohn@yahoo.co.uk]	01463 871286
Munro, James A. BA BD DMS	1979 2013	(Port Glasgow: Hamilton Bardrainney)	1 Wyvis Crescent, Conon Bridge, Dingwall IV7 8BZ [E-mail: james781munro@btinternet.com]	01349 865752
Niven, William W. BTh	1982 1995	(Alness)	4 Obsdale Park, Alness IV17 0TP	
Scott, David V. BTh	1994 2014	(Fearn Abbey and Nigg with Tarbat)	29 Sunnyside, Culloden Moor, Inverness IV2 5ES	01349 882427 / 01463 795802
Smith, Russel BD	1994 2013	(Dingwall: St Clement's)	1 School Road, Conon Bridge, Dingwall IV7 8AE [E-mail: russanmtwo@btinternet.com]	01349 861011
Tallach, John MA MLitt	1970 2010	(Cromarty)	29 Firthview Drive, Inverness IV3 8NS [E-mail: j.tallach@tiscali.co.uk]	01463 418721

(40) SUTHERLAND

Meets at Lairg on the first Tuesday of March, May, September, November and December, and on the first Tuesday of June at the Moderator's church.

Clerk:	REV. STEWART GOUDIE BSc BD	St Andrew's Manse, Tongue, Lairg IV27 4XL [E-mail: sutherland@churchofscotland.org.uk]	01847 611230 (Tel/Fax) 07957 237757 (Mbl)

Altnaharra and Farr

Vacant	The Manse, Bettyhill, Thurso KW14 7SS	01641 521208

Assynt and Stoer
Vacant
Canisp Road, Lochinver, Lairg IV27 4LH
01571 844342

Clyne (H) linked with Kildonan and Loth Helmsdale (H)
John Macgregor BD   2001   2013
Golf Road, Brora KW9 6QS
[E-mail: john_macg@hotmail.com]
01408 621239

Creich See Kincardine Croick and Edderton

Dornoch Cathedral (H)
Susan M. Brown (Mrs) BD DipMin   1985   1998
Cathedral Manse, Croc-an-Lobht, Dornoch IV25 3HN
[E-mail: revsbrown@aol.com]
01862 810296

Durness and Kinlochbervie
John T. Mann BSc BD   1990   1998
Manse Road, Kinlochbervie, Lairg IV27 4RG
[E-mail: jimklb@aol.com]
01971 521287

Eddrachillis
John MacPherson BSc BD   1993
Church of Scotland Manse, Scourie, Lairg IV27 4TQ
01971 502431

Golspie
John B. Sterrett BA BD PhD   2007
The Manse, Fountain Road, Golspie KW10 6TH
[E-mail: johnsterrett659@btinternet.com]
01408 633295 (Tel/Fax)

Kildonan and Loth Helmsdale See Clyne

Kincardine Croick and Edderton linked with Creich linked with Rosehall
Anthony M. Jones
BD DPS DipTheol CertMin FRSA   1994   2010
The Manse, Ardgay IV24 3BG
[E-mail: revanthonyjones@yahoo.com]
01863 766285
Hilary Gardner (Miss) (Aux)   2010   2012
Cayman Lodge, Kincardine Hill, Ardgay IV24 3DJ
[E-mail: gardnerhilary@hotmail.com]
01863 766107

Lairg (H) linked with Rogart (H)
Vacant
The Manse, Lairg IV27 4EH

Melness and Tongue (H)
Stewart Goudie BSc BD 2010 St Andrew's Manse, Tongue, Lairg IV27 4XL 01847 611230 (Tel/Fax)
[E-mail: stewart@goudie.me.uk] 07957 237757 (Mbl)

Rogart See Lairg
Rosehall See Kincardine Croick and Edderton

Chambers, John OBE BSc	1972	2009	(Inverness: Ness Bank)	Barnlagan Lodge, 4 Earls Cross Gardens, Dornoch IV25 3NR [E-mail: chambersdornoch@btinternet.com]	01862 811520
Goskirk, J.L. LTh	1968	2010	(Lairg with Rogart)	Rathvilly, Lairgmuir, Lairg IV27 4ED [E-mail: leslie_goskirk@sky.com]	01549 402569
McCree, Ian W. BD	1971	2011	(Clyne with Kildonan and Loth Helmsdale)	Tigh Ardachu, Mosshill, Brora KW9 6NG [E-mail: ian@mccree.f9.co.uk]	01408 621185
Stobo, Mary J. (Mrs)		2013	Ordained Local Minister; Community Healthcare Chaplain	Druim-an-Sgairmich, Ardgay IV24 3BG [E-mail: sutherland@churchofscotland.org.uk]	01863 766868

(41) CAITHNESS

Meets alternately at Wick and Thurso on the first Tuesday of February, March, May, September, November and December, and the third Tuesday of June.

Clerk: **REV. RONALD JOHNSTONE BD**   **2 Comlifoot Drive, Halkirk KW12 6ZA**   **01847 839033**
[E-mail: caithness@churchofscotland.org.uk]

Bower linked with Halkirk Westerdale linked with Watten
Alastair H. Gray MA BD   1978   2005   The Manse, Station Road, Watten, Wick KW1 5YN   01955 621220
[E-mail: alastair.h.gray@btinternet.com]

Canisbay linked with Dunnet linked with Keiss linked with Olrig
Vacant   The Manse, Canisbay, Wick KW1 4YH   01955 611756

Dunnet See Canisbay
Halkirk Westerdale See Bower
Keiss See Canisbay
Olrig See Canisbay

The North Coast Parish
Vacant — Church of Scotland Manse, Reay, Thurso KW14 7RE — 01847 811441

The Parish of Latheron
Vacant — Central Manse, Main Street, Lybster KW3 6BN [E-mail: parish-of-latheron@btconnect.com] — 01593 721706

Thurso: St Peter's and St Andrew's (H)
David S.M. Malcolm BD — 2011 2014 — The Manse, 46 Rose Street, Thurso KW14 8RF [E-mail: DavidSMMalcolm@aol.com] — 01847 895186

Thurso: West (H)
Vacant — Thorkel Road, Thurso KW14 7LW — 01847 892663

Watten See Bower

Wick: Pulteneytown (H) and Thrumster
Vacant — The Manse, Coronation Street, Wick KW1 5LS — 01955 603166

Wick: St Fergus
John Nugent — 1999 2011 — Mansefield, Miller Avenue, Wick KW1 4DF [E-mail: johnmugentis@mail2web.com] — 01955 602167

Craw, John DCS — (Deacon) — Liabost, 8 Proudfoot Road, Wick KW1 4PQ [E-mail: johncraw607@btinternet.com] — 01955 603805 (Mbl) 07544 761653

Duncan, Esme (Miss) — 2013 — Ordained Local Minister — Avalon, Upper Warse, Canisbay, Wick KW1 4YD [E-mail: esmeduncan@btinternet.com] — 01955 611455

Johnstone, Ronald BD — 1977 2011 — (Thurso: West) — 2 Comlifoot Drive, Halkirk KW12 6ZA [E-mail: ronaldjohnstone@btinternet.com] — 01847 839033

Nicol, Robert — 2013 — Ordained Local Minister — 3 Castlegreen Road, Thurso KW14 7DN [E-mail: robert.nicol1@btinternet.com]

Rennie, Lyall — 2013 — Ordained Local Minister — Ruachmarra, Lower Warse, Canisbay, Wick KW1 4YB [E-mail: lyall.rennie@btinternet.com] — 01955 611756

Stewart, Heather (Mrs) — 2013 — Ordained Local Minister — Burnthill, Thrumster, Wick KW1 5TR [E-mail: heatherburnthill@btopenworld.com] — 01955 651717

Warner, Kenneth BD — 1981 2008 — (Halkirk and Westerdale) — Kilearnan, Clayock, Halkirk KW12 6UZ [E-mail: wrnrkenn@btinternet.com] — (Work) 01955 603333 01847 831825

CAITHNESS Communion Sundays

Bower	1st Jul, Dec	
Canisbay	1st Jun, Nov	
Dunnet	last May, Nov	
Halkirk Westerdale	Apr, Jul, Oct	
Keiss	1st May, 3rd Nov	
Latheron	Apr, Jul, Sep, Nov	
North Coast	Mar, Easter, Jun, Sep, Dec	
Olrig	last May, Nov	
Thurso: St Peter's and St Andrew's	Mar, Jun, Sep, Dec	
Watten	4th Mar, Jun, Nov	
Wick: Pulteneytown and Thrumster	1st Jul, Dec / 1st Mar, Jun, Sep, Dec	
St Fergus	Apr, Oct	

(42) LOCHCARRON – SKYE

Meets in Kyle on the first Tuesday of each month, except January, May, July and August.

Clerk: REV. JOHN W. MURRAY LLB BA   1 Totescore, Kilmuir, Portree, Isle of Skye IV51 9YN   **01470 542297**
[E-mail: lochcarronskye@churchofscotland.org.uk]

Applecross, Lochcarron and Torridon (GD)
Vacant   The Manse, Colonel's Road, Lochcarron, Strathcarron IV54 8YG   01520 722829

Bracadale and Duirinish (GD)
Vacant   Duirinish Manse, Dunvegan, Isle of Skye IV55 8WQ   01470 521457

Gairloch and Dundonnell (GD)
Vacant   Church of Scotland Manse, The Glebe, Gairloch IV21 2BT   01445 712053 (Tel/Fax)

Glenelg Kintail and Lochalsh
Vacant   Church of Scotland Manse, Inverinate, Kyle IV40 8HE   01599 511245
New change formed by the union of Glenelg and Kintail and Lochalsh

Kilmuir and Stenscholl (GD)
John W. Murray LLB BA   2003   2015   1 Totescore, Kilmuir, Isle of Skye IV51 9YN   01470 542297
[E-mail: jwm7@hotmail.co.uk]

Portree (GD)
Sandor Fazakas BD MTh   1976   2007   Viewfield Road, Portree, Isle of Skye IV51 9ES   01478 611868
[E-mail: fazakass52@yahoo.com]

Snizort (H) (GD)
Vacant   The Manse, Kensaleyre, Snizort, Portree, Isle of Skye IV51 9XE   01470 532453

Strath and Sleat (GD)

| Rory A.R. MacLeod BA MBA BD DMin | 1994 | 2015 | The Manse, 6 Upper Breakish, Isle of Skye IV42 8PY [E-mail: rorymofg@gmail.com] | 01471 822416 |

Anderson, Janet (Miss) DCS			(Deaconess)	Creagard, 31 Lower Breakish, Isle of Skye IV42 8QA [E-mail: jaskye@hotmail.co.uk]	01471 822403
Beaton, Donald MA BD MTh	1961	2002	(Glenelg and Kintail)	Budhmore Home, Portree, Isle of Skye IV51 9DJ	
Kellas, David J. MA BD	1966	2004	(Kilfinan with Kyles)	Buarblach, Glenelg, Kyle IV40 8LA [E-mail: davidkellas@btinternet.com]	01599 522257 (Mbl) 07909 577764
Macarthur, Allan I. BD	1973	1998	(Applecross, Lochcarron and Torridon)	High Barn, Croft Road, Lochcarron, Strathcarron IV54 8YA [E-mail: a.macarthur@btinternet.com]	(Tel) 01520 722278 (Fax) 01520 722674
McCulloch, Alen J.R. MA BD	1990	2012	(Chaplain: Royal Navy)	Aros, 6 Gifford Terrace Road, Plymouth PL3 4JE [E-mail: aviljoen90@hotmail.com]	01752 657290
Mackenzie, Hector M.	2008		Chaplain: Army	3 Bn The Parachute Regiment, Merville Barracks, Colchester CO2 7UT [E-mail: mackenziehector@hotmail.com]	
Martin, George M. MA BD	1987	2005	(Applecross, Lochcarron and Torridon)	8(1) Buckingham Terrace, Edinburgh EH4 3AA	0131-343 3937
Morrison, Derek	1995	2013	(Gairloch and Dundonnell)	2 Cliffton Place, Poolewe, Achnasheen IV22 2JU [E-mail: derekmorrison1@aol.com]	01445 781333

LOCHCARRON – SKYE Communion Sundays

Applecross	1st Sep	Glenshiel	1st Jul
Arnisort	3rd Mar, Sep	Kilmuir	1st Mar, Sep
Bracadale	Last Feb	Kintail	3rd Apr, Jul
Broadford	3rd Jan, Easter, 3rd Sep	Kyleakin	Last Sep
Duirinish	4th Jun	Lochalsh and Stromeferry	4th Jan, Jun, Sep, Christmas, Easter
Dundonnell	1st Aug	Lochcarron and Shieldaig	Easter; communion held on a revolving basis when there is a fifth Sunday in the month
Elgol	3rd Jun, Nov		
Gairloch	2nd Jun, Nov		
Glenelg			

Plockton and Kyle	2nd May, 1st Oct	Sleat	Last May
Portree	Easter, Pentecost, Christmas, 2nd Mar, Aug, 1st Nov	Snizort	1st Jan, 4th Mar
		Stenscholl	1st Jun, Dec
		Strath	4th Jan
		Torridon and Kinlochewe	

In the Parish of Strath and Sleat, Easter communion is held on a revolving basis.

(43) UIST

Meets on the first Tuesday of February, March, September and November in Lochmaddy, and on the third Tuesday of June in Leverburgh.

Clerk:	MR WILSON McKINLAY	Heatherburn Cottage, Rhughasnish, Isle of South Uist HS8 5PE [E-mail: uist@churchofscotland.org.uk]	01870 610393

Benbecula (GD) (H) linked with Carinish
Vacant
Church of Scotland Manse, Griminish, Isle of Benbecula HS7 5QA   01870 602180

Berneray and Lochmaddy (GD) (H)
Vacant
Church of Scotland Manse, Lochmaddy, Isle of North Uist HS6 5AA   01876 500414

Carinish (GD) (H) See Benbecula
Church of Scotland Manse, Clachan, Locheport, Lochmaddy, Isle of North Uist HS6 5HD   01876 580219

Kilmuir and Paible (GE)
Vacant
Paible, Isle of North Uist HS6 5ED   01876 510310

Manish-Scarista (GD) (H)
David Donaldson MA BD DMin   1969   2015
Church of Scotland Manse, Scarista, Isle of Harris HS3 3HX   01859 550200
[E-mail: davidandjeandonaldson@gmail.com]

Tarbert (GD) (H)
Ian Murdo M. Macdonald DPA BD   2001   2015
The Manse, Manse Road, Tarbert, Isle of Harris HS3 3DF   01859 502231
[E-mail: ian.macdonald@churchofscotland.org.uk]

Elliott, Gavin J. MA BD	1976	2015	(Ministries Council)	5a Aird, Isle of Benbecula HS7 5LT [E-mail: gavkondwani@gmail.com]	
MacDonald, Angus J. BSc BD	1995	2001	(Lochmaddy and Trumisgarry)	7 Memorial Avenue, Stornoway, Isle of Lewis HS1 2QR	01851 706634
Macdonald, Ishabel		2011	Ordained Local Minister	'Cleat Afe Ora', 18 Carinish, Isle of North Uist HS6 5HN	01876 580367
MacInnes, David MA BD	1966	1999	(Kilmuir and Paible)	9 Golf View Road, Kinmylies, Inverness IV3 8SZ	01463 717377
MacIver, Norman BD	1976	2011	(Tarbert)	57 Boswell Road, Wester Inshes, Inverness IV2 3EW [E-mail: norman@n-cmaciver.freeserve.co.uk]	

Macpherson, Kenneth J. BD	1988	2002	(Benbecula)	70 Baile na Cille, Balivanich, Isle of Benbecula HS7 5ND	01870 602751
Morrison, Donald John	2001		Auxiliary Minister	22 Kyles, Tarbert, Isle of Harris HS3 3BS	01859 502341
Petrie, Jackie G.	1989	2011	(South Uist)	7B Malaclete, Isle of North Uist HS6 5BX	01876 560804
				[E-mail: jackiegpetrie@yahoo.com]	
Smith, John M.	1956	1992	(Lochmaddy)	Hamersay, Clachan, Locheport, Lochmaddy, Isle of North Uist HS6 5HD	
Smith, Murdo MA BD	1988	2011	(Manish-Scarista)	Aisgeir, 15A Upper Shader, Isle of Lewis HS3 3MX	01876 580332

UIST Communion Sundays

Benbecula	2nd Mar, Sep	Carinish	4th Mar, Aug
Berneray and Lochmaddy	4th Jun, last Oct	Kilmuir and Paible	1st Jun, 3rd Nov
		Manish-Scarista	3rd Apr, 1st Oct
		Tarbert	2nd Mar, 3rd Sep

(44) LEWIS

Meets at Stornoway, in St Columba's Church Hall, on the second Tuesday of February, March, September and November. It also meets if required in April, June and December on dates to be decided.

| Clerk: | MR JOHN CUNNINGHAM | 1 Raven's Lane, Stornoway, Isle of Lewis HS2 0EG | 01851 709977 |
| | | [E-mail: lewis@churchofscotland.org.uk] | 07789 878840 (Mbl) |

Barvas (GD) (H)
Vacant

Barvas, Isle of Lewis HS2 0QY   01851 840218

Carloway (GD) (H) (Office: 01851 643211)
Vacant

Church of Scotland Manse, Knock, Carloway, Isle of Lewis HS2 9AU 01851 643255

Cross Ness (GE) (H)
Vacant

Cross Manse, Swainbost, Ness, Isle of Lewis HS2 0TB   01851 810375

Kinloch (GE) (H)
Iain M. Campbell BD   2004 2008

Laxay, Lochs, Isle of Lewis HS2 9LA   01851 830218
[E-mail: i455@btinternet.com]

Knock (GE) (H)
Guardianship of the Presbytery

Lochs-Crossbost (GD) (H)
Guardianship of the Presbytery

Lochs-in-Bernera (GD) (H) linked with Uig (GE) (H)   2008
Hugh Maurice Stewart DPA BD
4 Seaview, Knock, Point, Isle of Lewis HS2 0PD   01851 870379
(Temporary Manse)
[E-mail: berneralwuig@btinternet.com]

Stornoway: High (GD) (H)
A. S. Wayne Pearce MA PhD
High Manse, 1 Goathill Road, Stornoway, Isle of Lewis HS1 2NJ   01851 703106
[E-mail: wayne.pearce66@btinternet.com]

Stornoway: Martin's Memorial (H) (Church office: 01851 700820)   2002 2006
Thomas MacNeil MA BD
Matheson Road, Stornoway, Isle of Lewis HS1 2LR   01851 704238
[E-mail: tommymacneil@hotmail.com]

Stornoway: St Columba (GD) (H) (Church office: 01851 701546)   2012
William J. Heenan BA MTh
St Columba's Manse, Lewis Street, Stornoway, Isle of Lewis HS1 2JF   01851 705933
[E-mail: wmheenan@hotmail.co.uk]   07837 770589 (Mbl)

Uig See Lochs-in-Bernera

Amed, Paul LTh DPS	1992	2015	(Barvas)	6 Scotland Street, Stornoway, Isle of Lewis HS1 2JQ	01851 706450
Jamieson, Esther M.M. (Mrs) BD	1984	2002	(Glasgow: Penilee St Andrew)	1 Redburn, Bayview, Stornoway, Isle of Lewis HS1 2UU	01851 704789
				[E-mail: iandejamieson@btinternet.com]	07867 602963 (Mbl)
Johnstone, Ben MA BD DMin	1973	2013	(Strath and Sleat)	Loch Alainn, 5 Breaclete, Great Bernera, Isle of Lewis HS2 9LT	01851 612445
				[E-mail: benonbernera@gmail.com]	
Macdonald, James LTh CPS	1984	2001	(Knock)	Elim, 8A Lower Bayble, Point, Isle of Lewis HS2 0QA	01851 870173
				[E-mail: elim8a@hotmail.co.uk]	
Maclean, Donald A. DCS			(Deacon)	8 Upper Barvas, Isle of Lewis HS2 0QX	01851 840454
MacLennan, Donald Angus	1975	2006	(Kinloch)	4 Kestrel Place, Inverness IV2 3YH	01463 243750
				[E-mail: maclennankinloch@btinternet.com]	07799 668270 (Mbl)
Macleod, William	1957	2006	(Uig)	54 Lower Barvas, Isle of Lewis HS2 0QY	01851 840217
Shadakshari, T.K. BTh BD MTh	1998	2006	Healthcare Chaplain	23D Benside, Newmarket, Stornoway, Isle of Lewis HS2 0DZ	(Home) 01851 701727
					(Office) 01851 704704
				[E-mail: tk.shadakshari@nhs.net]	(Mbl) 07403 697138

LEWIS Communion Sundays

Barvas	3rd Mar, Sep	Knock	3rd Apr, 1st Nov	Stornoway: High	3rd Feb, last Aug
Carloway	1st Mar, last Sep	Lochs-Crossbost	4th Mar, Sep	Martin's Memorial	3rd Feb, last Aug, 1st Dec, Easter
Cross Ness	2nd Mar, Oct	Lochs-in-Bernera	1st Apr, 2nd Sep	Stornoway: St Columba	3rd Feb, last Aug
Kinloch	3rd Mar, 2nd Jun, 2nd Sep			Uig	3rd Jun, 4th Oct

(45) ORKNEY

Normally meets at Kirkwall, in the St Magnus Centre, on the second Tuesday of February, May, September and November. One meeting is usually held outwith the St Magnus Centre.

Clerk: MR DAVID BAKER MSc MCIOB   59 Albert Street, Kirkwall, Orkney KW15 1HQ   **01856 878381**
[E-mail: orkney@churchofscotland.org.uk]   **07500 050855 (Mbl)**

Birsay, Harray and Sandwick
David G. McNeish MB ChB BSc BD   2015   The Manse, North Biggings Road, Dounby, Orkney KW17 2HZ   01856 771599
[E-mail:dmcneish@churchofscotland.org.uk]

East Mainland
Wilma A. Johnston MTheol MTh   2006   2014   The Manse, Holm, Orkney KW17 2SB   01856 781772
[E-mail: rev.wilmajohnston@btinternet.com]

Eday linked with Stronsay: Moncur Memorial (H)
Vacant   The Manse, Stronsay, Orkney KW17 2AF   01857 616311

Evie (H) linked with Firth (H) (01856 761117) linked with Rendall linked with Rousay
Roy Cordukes BSc BD   2014   The Manse, Finstown, Orkney KW17 2EG   01856 761328
[E-mail: minister@cordukes.plus.com]

Firth See Evie

Flotta linked with Hoy and Walls linked with Orphir (H) and Stenness (H)
Vacant   Stenness Manse, Stenness, Stromness, Orkney KW16 3HH

Hoy and Walls See Flotta

Name	Ordained/Inducted	Address	Telephone
Kirkwall: East (H) linked with Shapinsay Julia Meason MTh	2013	East Church Manse, Thoms Street, Kirkwall, Orkney KW15 1PF [E-mail: julia.meason@hotmail.com]	01856 874789
Kirkwall: St Magnus Cathedral (H) G. Fraser H. Macnaughton MA BD	1982 2002	Berstane Road, Kirkwall, Orkney KW15 1NA [E-mail: macnaughton187@btinternet.com]	01856 873312
North Ronaldsay linked with Sanday (H) Vacant		The Manse, Sanday, Orkney KW17 2BW	01857 600429

Orphir and Stenness See Flotta

Name	Ordained/Inducted	Address	Telephone
Papa Westray linked with Westray Iain D. MacDonald BD	1993	The Manse, Hilldavale, Westray, Orkney KW17 2DW [E-mail: idmacdonald@btinternet.com]	01857 677357 (Tel/Fax) 07710 443780 (Mbl)

Rendall See Evie
Rousay (Church centre: 01856 821271) See Evie
Sanday See North Ronaldsay
Shapinsay See Kirkwall: East

Name	Ordained/Inducted	Address	Telephone
South Ronaldsay and Burray Stephen Manners MA BD (Assoc)	1989 2012	St Margaret's Manse, Church Road, St Margaret's Hope, Orkney KW17 2SR [E-mail: sk.manners@me.com]	01856 831670 07747 821458 (Mbl)
Stromness (H) Magdaléna Trgalová	2013	5 Manse Lane, Stromness, Orkney KW16 3AP	01856 850203

Stronsay: Moncur Memorial See Eday
Westray See Papa Westray

Brown, R. Graeme BA BD	1961 1998	(Birsay with Rousay)	Bring Deeps, Orphir, Orkney KW17 2LX [E-mail: graeme_sibyl@btinternet.com]	(Tel/Fax) 01856 811707

Clark, Thomas L. BD	1985	2008	(Orphir with Stenness)	7 Headland Rise, Burghead, Elgin IV30 5HA [E-mail: toml.clark@btinternet.com]
				01343 830144
Fidler, David G.		2013	Ordained Local Minister	34 Guardhouse Park, Stromness, Orkney KW16 3DP [E-mail: dvdfid@yahoo.co.uk]
				01856 850575 (Mbl) 07900 386473
Prentice, Martin		2013	Ordained Local Minister	Cott of Howe, Cairston, Stromness, Orkney KW16 3JU [E-mail: mwm.prentice@virgin.net]
				01856 851139 (Mbl) 07795 817213
Tait, Alexander	1967	1995	(Glasgow: St Enoch's Hogganfield)	Ingermas, Evie, Orkney KW17 2PH [E-mail: jen1957@hotmail.co.uk]
				01856 751477
Whitson, William S. MA	1959	1999	(Cumbernauld: St Mungo's)	2 Chapman's Brae, Bathgate EH48 4LH [E-mail: william_whitson@tiscali.co.uk]
				01506 650027
Wishart, James BD	1986	2009	(Deer)	Upper Westshore, Burray, Orkney KW17 2TE [E-mail: jwishart06@btinternet.com]
				01856 731672

(46) SHETLAND

Meets at Lerwick on the first Tuesday of February, April, June, September, November and December.

Clerk:	REV. CHARLES H.M. GREIG MA BD		6 Hayhoull Place, Bigton, Shetland ZE2 9GA [E-mail: shetland@churchofscotland.org.uk]	**01950 422468**

Burra Isle linked with Tingwall

Deborah Dobby (Mrs) BA BD PGCE RGN RSCN	2014	The Manse, 25 Hogalee, East Voe, Scalloway, Shetland ZE1 0UU [E-mail: deborahdobby@gmail.com]	01595 881157

Delting linked with Northmavine

Vacant		The Manse, Grindwell, Brae, Shetland ZE2 9QJ	01806 522219
Robert M. MacGregor (Aux) CMIOSH DipOSH RSP	2004	Olna Cottage, Brae, Shetland ZE2 9QS [E-mail: revbobdelting@mypostoffice.co.uk]	01806 522604

Dunrossness and St Ninian's inc. Fair Isle linked with Sandwick, Cunningsburgh and Quarff

Charles H.M. Greig MA BD	1976	1997	6 Hayhoull Place, Bigton, Shetland ZE2 9GA [E-mail: chm.greig@btinternet.com]	01950 422468

Lerwick and Bressay

Caroline R. Lockerbie BA MDiv DMin (Transition Minister)	2007	2013	The Manse, 82 St Olaf Street, Lerwick, Shetland ZE1 0ES [E-mail: caroline.lockerbie@btinternet.com]	01595 692125

Nesting and Lunnasting linked with Whalsay and Skerries
Irene A. Charlton (Mrs) BTh   1994 1997   The Manse, Marrister, Symbister, Whalsay, Shetland ZE2 9AE   01806 566767
[E-mail: icharlton@churchofscotland.org.uk]

Northmavine See Delting

Sandsting and Aithsting linked with Walls and Sandness
D. Brian Dobby MA BA   1999 2014   The Manse, 25 Hogalee, East Voe, Scalloway, Shetland ZE1 0UU   01595 881184
[E-mail: briandobby@googlemail.com]

Sandwick, Cunningsburgh and Quarff See Dunrossness and St Ninian's

Tingwall See Burra Isle

Unst and Fetlar linked with Yell
David Cooper BA MPhil   1975   2008   North Isles Manse, Gutcher, Yell, Shetland ZE2 9DF   01957 744258
[E-mail: reverenddavidcooper@googlemail.com]
(David Cooper is a minister of the Methodist Church)

Walls and Sandness See Sandsting and Aithsting
Whalsay and Skerries See Nesting and Lunnasting
Yell See Unst and Fetlar

Kirkpatrick, Alice H. (Miss) MA BD FSAScot	1987	2000	(Northmavine)	1 Daisy Park, Baltasound, Unst, Shetland ZE2 9EA	
Knox, R. Alan MA LTh AInstAM	1965	2004	(Fetlar with Unst with Yell)	27 Killyvalley Road, Garvagh, Co. Londonderry, Northern Ireland BT51 5LX	02829 558925 / 01950 477549
Macintyre, Thomas MA BD	1972	2011	(Sandsting and Aithsting with Walls and Sandness)	Lappideks, South Voxter, Cunningsburgh, Shetland ZE2 9HF [E-mail: the2macs.macintyre@btinternet.com]	
Smith, Catherine (Mrs) DCS			(Presbytery Assistant)	21 Lingaro, Bixter, Shetland ZE2 9NN	01595 810207
Williamson, Magnus J.C.	1982	1999	(Fetlar with Yell)	Creekhaven, Houl Road, Scalloway, Shetland ZE1 0XA	01595 880023

(47) ENGLAND

Meets at London, in Crown Court Church, on the second Tuesday of February, and at St Columba's, Pont Street, on the second Tuesday of June and the second Saturday of October.

Clerk: REV. ALISTAIR CUMMING MSc CCS FInstLM   64 Prince George's Avenue, London SW20 8BH   07534 943986 (Mbl)
[E-mail: england@churchofscotland.org.uk]

Corby: St Andrew's (H)
Vacant   43 Hempland Close, Corby, Northants NN18 8LR   01536 746429

Corby: St Ninian's (H) (01536 265245)
Kleber Machado BTh MA MTh — 1998 — 2012 — The Manse, 46 Glyndebourne Gardens, Corby, Northants NN18 0PZ — 01536 669478
[E-mail: klebermachado@ymail.com]

Guernsey: St Andrew's in the Grange (H)
Graeme W. Beebee BD — 1993 — 2003 — The Manse, Le Villocq, Castel, Guernsey GY5 7SB — 01481 257345
[E-mail: beehive@cwgsy.net]

Jersey: St Columba's (H)
David Logan MStJ BD MA CF(V) FRSA — 2009 — 2014 — 18 Claremont Avenue, St Saviour, Jersey JE2 7SF — 01534 730659 / 07797 742012 (Mbl)
[E-mail: minister@castleroy.org]

Liverpool: St Andrew's
Guardianship of the Presbytery
Session Clerk: Mr Robert Cottle — 0151-524 1915

London: Crown Court (H) (020 7836 5643)
Philip L. Majcher BD — 1982 — 2007 — 53 Sidmouth Street, London WC1H 8JX — 020 7278 5022
[E-mail: minister@crowncourtchurch.org.uk]

London: St Columba's (H) (020 7584 2321) linked with Newcastle: St Andrew's (H)
C. Angus MacLeod MA BD — 1996 — 2012 — 29 Hollywood Road, Chelsea, London SW10 9HT — 020 7584 2321 (Office)
[E-mail: minister@stcolumbas.org.uk]
Andrea E. Price (Mrs) (Associate Minister) — 1997 — 2014 — St Columba's, Pont Street, London SW1X 0BD — 020 7610 6994 (Home) / 020 7584 2321 (Office)
[E-mail: associateminister@stcolumbas.org.uk]
Dorothy Lunn (Auxiliary Minister) — 2002 — 2002 — 14 Bellerby Drive, Ouston, Co. Durham DH2 1TW — 0191-492 0647
[E-mail: dorothylunn@hotmail.com]

Newcastle: St Andrew's   See London: St Columba's

Anderson, Andrew F. MA BD — 1981 2011 — (Edinburgh: Greenside) — 58 Reliance Way, Oxford OX4 2FG — 01865 778397
[E-mail: andrew.relianceway@gmail.com]

Binks, Mike — 2007 — Auxiliary Minister — Hollybank, 10 Kingsbrook, Corby NN18 9HY — (Mbl) 07590 507917
[E-mail: mike@hollybank.net]

Bowie, A. Glen CBE BA BSc — 1954 1984 — (Principal Chaplain: RAF) — 16 Weir Road, Hemingford Grey, Huntingdon PE18 9EH — 01480 381425
Brown, Scott J. CBE QHC BD — 1993 2015 — (Chaplain of the Fleet: Royal Navy) — [E-mail: scott3568@gmail.com] — (Mbl) 07769 847876

Name	Dates	Position	Address / Contact
Cairns, W. Alexander BD	1978 2006	(Corby: St Andrew's)	Kirkton House, Kirkton of Craig, Montrose DD10 9TB — [E-mail: sandy.cairns@btinternet.com] — (Mbl) 07808 588045
Cameron, R. Neil	1975 1981	(Chaplain: Community)	6 Upper Abbey Road, Belvedere, Kent DA17 5AJ — [E-mail: neilandminacameron@yahoo.co.uk] — 01322 402818
Cherry, Alastair J. BA BD FPLD	1982 2009	(Glasgow: Penilee St Andrew's)	8 Ashdown Terrace, Tidworth, Wilts SP9 7SQ — [E-mail: alastair.j.cherry@btinternet.com] — 01980 842175
Coulter, David G. QHC BA BD MDA PhD CF	1989 1994	Chaplain General, HM Land Forces	64 Prince George's Avenue, London SW20 8BH — [E-mail: padredgcoulter@yahoo.co.uk] — 020 8540 7365
Cumming, Alistair MSc CCS FInstLM	2010	Auxiliary Minister: London: St Columba's	Mill House, High Street, Staplehurst, Tonbridge, Kent TN12 0AU — [E-mail: afcumming@hotmail.com] — (Mbl) 07534 943986 / 01580 891271
Dowswell, James A.M.	1991 2001	(Lerwick and Bressay)	The Bungalow, The Ridgeway, Mill Hill, London NW7 1QX — [E-mail: jdowswell@btinternet.com] — 020 8201 1397
Fields, James MA BD STM	1988 1997	School Chaplain	37 Milburn Road, Coleraine BT52 1QT — 02870 353869
Francis, James BD PhD	2002 2009	Chaplain: Army	
Langlands, Cameron H. BD MTh ThM PhD MInstLM	1995 2012	Chaplain South London and Maudsley NHS Foundation Trust	Maudsley Hospital, Denmark Road, London SE5 8EZ — (Mbl) 07989 642544
Lovett, Mairi F. BSc BA DipPS MTh	2005 2013	Hospital Chaplain	Royal Brompton Hospital, Sydney Street, London SW3 6NP — [E-mail: m.lovett@rbht.nhs.uk] — 020 7352 8121 ext. 4736
Lugton, George L. MA BD	1955 1997	(Guernsey: St Andrew's in the Grange)	6 Clos de Beauvoir, Rue Cohu, Guernsey GY5 7TE — (Tel/Fax) 01481 254285
Macfarlane, Peter T. BA LTh	1970 1994	(Chaplain: Army)	4 rue de Rives, 37160 Abilly, France
McIndoe, John H. MA BD STM DD	1966 2000	(London: St Columba's with Newcastle: St Andrew's)	5 Dunlin, Westerlands Park, Glasgow G12 0FE — [E-mail: johnandeve@mcindoe555.fsnet.co.uk] — 0141-579 1366
MacLeod, Rory N. BA BD	1986 1992	Chaplain: Army	21 Engr Regt, Clara Barracks, Chatham Road, Ripon HG4 2RD
McMahon, John K.S. MA BD	1998 2012	Head of Spiritual and Pastoral Care, West London Mental Health Trust	Broadmoor Hospital, Crowthorne, Berkshire RG45 7EG — [E-mail: john.mcmahonrev@wlmht.nhs.uk] — 01344 754098
Mather, James BA DipArch MA MBA	2010	Auxiliary Minister: University Chaplain	24 Ellison Road, Barnes, London SW13 0AD — [E-mail: jsm.johnstonmather@btinternet.com] — (Home) 020 8876 6540 / (Work) 020 7361 1670 / (Mbl) 07836 715655
Middleton, Paul BMus BD ThM PhD	2000	University Lecturer	97B Whipcord Lane, Chester CH1 4DG
Munro, Alexander W. MA BD	1978	Chaplain and Teacher of Religious Studies	Columba House, 12 Alexandra Road, Southport PR9 0NB — [E-mail: sheila.munro781@halton.raf.mod.uk] — 01704 543044
Munro, Sheila BD	1995 2003	Chaplain: RAF	
Trevorrow, James A. LTh	1971 2003	(Glasgow: Cranhill)	12 Test Green, Corby, Northants NN17 2HA — [E-mail: jimtrevorrow@compuserve.com] — 01536 264018
Walker, R. Forbes BSc BD ThM	1987 2013	School Chaplain	Flat 5, 18 Northside Wandsworth Common, London SW18 2SL — [E-mail: revrfw@gmail.com] — 020 8870 0953
Wallace, Donald S.	1950 1980	(Chaplain: RAF)	7 Dellfield Close, Watford, Herts WD1 3BL — 01923 223289
Ward, Michael J. BSc BD PhD MA PGCE	1983 2009	Training and Development Officer: Presbyterian Church of Wales	Apt 6, Bryn Hedd, Conwy Road, Penmaen-mawr, Gwynedd LL34 6BS — [E-mail: revmw@btopenworld.com] — (Mbl) 07765 598816
Wood, Peter J. MA BD	1993	(College Lecturer)	97 Broad Street, Cambourne, Cambridgeshire CB23 6DH — [E-mail: pejowood@tiscali.co.uk] — 01954 715558

Wylie, Jonathan	2000 2014	Chaplain: RAF	

Staff Chaplain PJHQ, Northwood HQ, Sandy Lane, Northwood HA6 3HP   (Mbl) 07818 401402
[E-mail: jonathan.wylie922@mod.uk]

ENGLAND – Church Addresses

Corby: St Andrew's St Ninian's	Occupation Road Beanfield Avenue	**Liverpool:**	

London: Crown Court   Crown Court WC2
St Columba's   Pont Street SW1

Newcastle: Sandyford Road

The Western Rooms,
Anglican Cathedral

(48) EUROPE

Meets over the weekend of the second Sunday of March and October, hosted by congregations in mainland Europe.

Clerk: REV. JAMES SHARP   **102 Rue des Eaux-Vives, CH-1207 Geneva, Switzerland**   **0041 22 786 4847**
[E-mail: europe@cofscotland.org.uk]

Depute Clerk: REV. DEREK G. LAWSON   **2 Rue Joseph Guillemot, 87210 Oradour St Genest, France**   **0033 555 68 53 03**
[E-mail: deputeclerk@europepresbytery.net]

Amsterdam: English Reformed Church   2014   Jan Willem Brouwersstraat 9, NL–1071 LH Amsterdam,   0031 20 672 2288
Lance Stone BD MTh PhD   The Netherlands
[E-mail: minister@ercadam.nl]
Church address: Begijnhof 48, 1012WV Amsterdam

Bermuda: Christ Church, Warwick (H) (001 441 236 1882)
Vacant   The Manse, 6 Manse Road, Paget PG 01, Bermuda   001 441 236 0400
Church address: Christ Church, Middle Road, Warwick, Bermuda
Mailing address: PO Box PG88, Paget PG BX, Bermuda
[E-mail: christchurch@logic.bm; Website: www.christchurch.bm]

Bochum (Associated congregation)
James M. Brown MA BD   1982   Neustrasse 15, D-44787 Bochum, Germany   0049 234 133 65
[E-mail: j.brown56@gmx.de]
Church address: Pauluskircke, Grabenstrasse 9, 44787 Bochum

Brussels St Andrew's (H) (0032 2 649 02 19) Andrew Gardner BSc BD PhD	1997	2004	23 Square des Nations, B-1000 Brussels, Belgium [E-mail: minister@churchofscotland.be] Church address: Chaussée de Vieurgat 181, 1050 Brussels [E-mail: secretary@churchofscotland.be]	0032 2 672 40 56
Budapest St Columba's (0036 1 373 0725) Aaron Stevens BA MDiv MACE	2010		Stefánia út 32, H-1143, Budapest, Hungary [E-mail: revastevens@yahoo.co.uk] Church address: Vörösmarty utca 51, 1064 Budapest	(Mbl) 0036 70 615 5394
Colombo, Sri Lanka: St Andrew's Scots Kirk (0094 112 323 765) Roderick D.M. Campbell OStJ TD BD DMin FSAScot	1975	2014	73 Galle Road, Colpetty, Colombo 3, Sri Lanka [E-mail: minister@standrewsscotskirk.org]	0094 112 386 774
Costa del Sol Vacant			Avenida Jesus Santos Rein, 24 Edf. Lindamar 4 – 3Q, Fuengirola, 29640 Malaga. Spain Church address: Lux Mundi Ecumenical Centre, Calle Nueva 3, 29460 Fuengirola	0034 951 260 982
Geneva (0041 22 788 08 31) Ian A. Manson BA BD	1989	2001	6 chemin Taverney, 1218 Geneva, Switzerland [E-mail: cofsg@pingnet.ch] Church address: Auditoire de Calvin, 1 Place de la Taconnerie, Geneva	0041 22 788 08 31
Gibraltar St Andrew's Ewen MacLean BA BD	1995	2009	St Andrew's Manse, 29 Scud Hill, Gibraltar [E-mail: scotskirk@gibraltar.gi] Church address: Governor's Parade, Gibraltar	00350 200 77040
Lausanne: The Scots Kirk (H) Ian J.M. McDonald MA BD	1984	2010	26 Avenue de Rumine, CH-1005 Lausanne, Switzerland [E-mail: minister@scotskirklausanne.ch]	0041 21 323 98 28

Lisbon St Andrew's
Vacant

Rua Coelho da Rocha, N°75 - 1°
Campa de Ourique, 1350-073 Lisbon, Portugal
[E-mail: cofslx@netcabo.pt]
Church address: Rua da Arriaga, Lisbon

00351 213 951 165

Malta St Andrew's Scots Church (H)
Kim Hurst   2014

La Romagnola, 15 Triq is-Seiqia, Misrah Kola, Attard
ATD 1713, Malta
[E-mail: minister@saintandrewsmalta.com]
Church address: 210 Old Bakery Street, Valletta, Malta

(Tel/Fax) 00356 214 15465

Paris: The Scots Kirk
James M. Cowie BD   1977   2011

10 Rue Thimmonier, F-75009 Paris, France
[E-mail: jimcowie@europe.com]
Church address: 17 Rue Bayard, 75009 Paris

0033 1 48 78 47 94

Regensburg (University) (Associated congregation)
Rhona Dunphy (Mrs) BD DPTheol   2005

Liskircherstrasse 9, D-93049 Regensburg, Germany
[E-mail: r@dunphy.de]

(Mbl) 0049 941 3813 6933

Rome: St Andrew's
William B. McCulloch BD   1997   2002

Via XX Settembre 7, 00187 Rome, Italy
[E-mail: revwbmcculloch@hotmail.com]

(Tel) 0039 06 482 7627
(Fax) 0039 06 487 4370

Rotterdam: Scots International Church (0031 10 412 4779)
Vacant

Church address: Schiedamse Vest 121, 3013H
Rotterdam, The Netherlands
Meeuwenstraat 4A, NL-3071 PE Rotterdam, The Netherlands
[E-mail: info@scotsintchurch.com]

0031 10 220 4199

Trinidad: Greyfriars St Ann's, Port of Spain l/w Arouca and Sangre Grande
Vacant

50 Frederick Street, Port of Spain, Trinidad

001 868 623 6684

Turin (Associated Congregation)
Vacant

Via S. Pio V 17, 10125 Torino, Italy
[E-mail: esc.torino@alice.it]
Church address: Via Sant Anselmo 6, 10125 Turin, Italy

0039 011 650 5770
0039 011 650 9467

Name	Dates	Position	Address	Phone
Born, Irene	2008	Ordained Local Minister-worship resourcing	Bergpolderstraat 53A, NL–3038 KB Rotterdam, The Netherlands [E-mail: ibsalem@xs4all.nl]	0031 10 265 1703
Burns, Terry BA MA	2014	Nicosia Community Church, Cyprus	63-65 Vyronos, Flat 501, 1096 Nicosia, Cyprus [E-mail: terrance.burns1955@yahoo.com]	00357 22 783 101
Dick, James S. MA BTh	1988 1997	(Glasgow: Ruchazie)	Rua da Liberdade, Bloco A, 1°Dto, 9760-031 Areiras Benavente, Portugal [E-mail: jim.s.dick@gmail.com]	
Lawson, Derek G. LLB BD	1998 2011	(Redgorton and Stanley)	2 Rue Joseph Guillemot, 87210 Oradour St Genest, France [E-mail: derek.lawson@sfr.fr]	0033 555 68 53 03
McLay, Neil BA BD	2006 2012	Chaplain: Army (Brussels)	Barker Barracks, Paderborn, BFPO 22	
Pitkeathly, Thomas C. MA CA BD	1984 2004		77 St Thomas Road, Lytham St. Anne's FY8 1JP [E-mail: tpitkeathly@yahoo.co.uk]	01253 789634
Pot Joost BSc	1992 2004	(Rotterdam – Aux.)	[E-mail: joostpot@gmail.com]	
Sharp, James	2005	(OLM, Presbytery Clerk)	102 Rue des Eaux-Vives, 1207 Geneva, Switzerland [E-mail: jimsharp@bluewin.ch]	0041 22 786 4847

(49) JERUSALEM

Clerk:	**JOANNA OAKLEY-LEVSTEIN**	**St Andrew's, Galilee, PO Box 104, Tiberias 14100, Israel**	**00972 50 5842517**

Jerusalem: St Andrew's

Paraic Reamonn BA BD	1982 2014	St Andrew's Scots Memorial Church, 1 David Remez Street, PO Box 8619, Jerusalem 91086, Israel [E-mail: stachjer@netvision.net.il]	00972 2 673 2401

Tiberias: St Andrew's

Name	Dates	Address	Phone
Katharine S. Reynolds BA MSc BD MLitt (Scottish Episcopal Church)	2012 2015	St Andrew's, Galilee, 1 Gdud Barak Street, PO Box 104, Tiberias 14100, Israel [E-mail: kreynolds@churchofscotland.org.uk]	00972 4 671 0759
Johnston, Colin D. MA BD	1986 2015	(Tiberias: St Andrews's) c/o World Mission Council, 121 George Street, Edinburgh EH2 4YN [E-mail: revcdj60@gmail.com]	0131-225 5722

SECTION 6

Additional Lists of Personnel

LIST A – ORDAINED LOCAL MINISTERS

NAME	ORD	ADDRESS	TEL	PR
Allardice, Michael MA MPhil PGCertTHE FHEA	2014	20 Parbroath Road, Glenrothes KY7 4TH [E-mail: m.allardice@dundee.ac.uk] (Mbl)	01592 772280 / 07936 203465	15
Archer, Morven (Mrs)	2013	42 Firthview Drive, Inverness IV3 8QE	01463 237840	37
Bellis, Pamela A. BA	2013	Maughold, Low Killantrae, Port William, Newton Stewart DG8 9QR	01988 700590	9
Black, Sandra (Mrs)	2013	5 Doon Place, Troon KA10 7EQ	01292 220075	10
Bom, Irene	2008	Bergpolderstraat 53A, NL-3038 KB Rotterdam, The Netherlands	0031 10 265 1703	48
Breingan, Mhairi	2011	6 Park Road, Inchinnan, Renfrew PA4 4QJ	0141-812 1425	14
Brown, Kathryn (Mrs)	2014	1 Callendar Park Walk, Callendar Grange, Falkirk FK1 1TA	01324 617352	22
Crossan, William	2014	Gowanbank, Kilkerran Road, Campbeltown PA28 6JL	01586 553453	19
Dee, Oonagh	2014	'Kendoon', Merse Way, Kippford, Dalbeattie DG5 4LL	01556 620001	8
Don, Andrew MBA	2006	5 Eskdale Court, Penicuik EH26 8HT	01968 675766	3
Duncan, Esme (Miss)	2013	Avalon, Upper Warse, Canisbay, Wick KW1 4YD	01955 611455	41
Duncanson, Mary (Ms)	2013	3 Balmenach Road, Cromdale, Grantown-on-Spey PH26 3LJ	01479 872165	36
Edwards, Dougal BTh	2013	25 Mackenzie Street, Carnoustie DD7 6HD	01241 852666	30
Fidler, David G.	2013	34 Guardhouse Park, Stromness, Orkney KW16 3DP	01856 850575	45
Fulcher, Christine	2012	St Blaan's Manse, Southend, Campbeltown PA28 6RQ	01586 830504	19
Geddes, Elizabeth (Mrs)	2013	9 Shillingworth Place, Bridge of Weir PA11 3DY	01505 612639	14
Gray, Ian	2013	'The Mallards', 15 Rossie Island Road, Montrose DD10 9NH	01674 677126	30
Hardman Moore, Susan (Prof.) BA PGCE MA PhD	2013	c/o New College, Mound Place, Edinburgh EH1 2LX	0131-650 8908	1
Harrison, Frederick	2013	33 Castle Avenue, Gorebridge EH23 4TH	01875 820908	3
Harvey, Joyce (Mrs)	2013	4A Allanfield Place, Newton Stewart DG8 6BS	01671 403693	9
Hickman, Mandy R. RGN	2013	Lagnaleon, 4 Wilson Street, Largs KA30 9AQ	01475 675347	12
Hughes, Barry MA	2011	Dunslair, Cardrona Way, Cardrona, Peebles EH45 9LD	01896 831197	4
Johnston, June E. BSc MEd BD	2013	Tarmachan, Main Street, Killin FK21 8TN (Mbl) [E-mail: johnstone330@btinternet.com]	07754 448889	23
Livingstone, Alan	2013	Meadowside, Lawmuir, Methven, Perth PH1 3SZ	01738 840682	28
McAllister, Anne C. (Mrs) BSc DipEd CCS	2013	39 Bowes Rigg, Stewarton, Kilmarnock KA3 5EN	01560 483191	11
McCutcheon, John	2014	Flat 2/6 Parkview, Milton Brae, Milton, Dumbarton G82 2TT	01389 739034	18
Macdonald, Ishabel	2011	'Cleat Afe Ora', 18 Carinish, Isle of North Uist HS6 5HN	01876 580367	43
MacDonald, Monica (Mrs)	2014	32 Reilly Gardens, High Bonnybridge, Bonnybridge FK4 2BB	01324 874807	22
Mack, Lynne (Mrs)	2013	36 Middleton, Menstrie FK11 7HD	01259 761465	23
McLaughlin, Cathie H. (Mrs)	2014	8 Lamlash Place, Glasgow G33 3XH	0141-774 2483	16
MacLeod, Iain A.	2012	6 Hallydown Drive, Glasgow G13 1UF (Mbl)	07795 014889	16
McLeod, Tom	2014	3 Martnaham Drive, Coylton KA6 6JE [E-mail: tamlin410@btinternet.com]	01292 570100	10
Maxwell, David	2014	248 Old Castle Road, Glasgow G44 5EZ	0141-569 6379	16
Michie, Margaret (Mrs)	2013	3 Loch Leven Court, Wester Balgedie, Kinross KY13 9NE	01592 840602	28
Morrison, John BSc BA PGCE	2013	35 Kirkton Place, Elgin IV30 6JR	01343 550199	35
Muirhead, Morag (Mrs)	2013	6 Dumbarton Place, Fort William PH33 6UU	01397 703643	38

NAME	ORD	ADDRESS	TEL	PR
Murphy, Jim	2014	10 Hillview Crescent, Bellshill ML4 1N [E-mail: jim.murphy5@btopenworld.com]	01698 740189	17
Nicol, Robert	2013	3 Castlegreen Road, Thurso KW14 7DN		41
Noonan, Pam (Mrs)	2013	Kilmorich, 14 Balloch Road, Balloch, Alexandria G83 8SR	01389 754505 (Work)	18
Nutter, Margaret	2014	Ashlea, Cuil Road, Duror, Appin PA38 3DA	01631 740313	38
Perkins, Mairi (Mrs)	2012	Cott of Howe, Cairston, Stromness, Orkney KW16 3JU	01856 851139	45
Prentice, Martin	2013	Ruachmarra, Lower Warse, Canisbay, Wick KW1 4YB	01955 611756	41
Rennie, Lyall	2013	Oakdene, 81 Bonhill Road, Dumbarton G82 2DU	01389 763436	18
Robertson, Ishbel A.R. MA BD	2013	26 Wood Avenue, Annan DG12 6DA	07830 697976 (Mbl)	7
Sanders, Martyn S. BA CertEd MA	2013	114 High Station Road, Falkirk FK1 5LN	01324 621648	22
Sarle, Andrew BSc BD	2005	102 Rue des Eaux-Vives, CH-1207 Geneva, Switzerland	0041 22 786 4847	48
Sharp, James	2011	143 Springfield Park, Johnstone PA5 8JT	0141-886 2131	14
Stevenson, Stuart	2013	Burnthill, Thrumster, Wick KW1 5TR	01955 651717	41
Stewart, Heather (Mrs)	2013	Druim-an-Sgairnich, Ardgay IV24 3BG	01863 766868	40
Stobo, Mary J. (Mrs)	2015	Glenhighton, Broughton, Biggar ML12 6JF	01899 830423	4
Strachan, Pamela D. (Lady) MA (Cantab)		[E-mail: pamelastrachan@btinternet.com]	07837 873688 (Mbl)	
Strachan, Willie MBA DipY&C	2013	Ladywell House, Lucky Slap, Monikie, Dundee DD5 3QG	01382 370286	29
Stuart, Alex P.	2014	107 Baldorran Crescent, Cumbernauld, Glasgow G68 9EX	01236 727710	16
Sturrock, Roger (Prof.) BD MD FCRP	2014	36 Thomson Drive, Bearsden, Glasgow G61 3PA	0141-942 7412	16
Thomson, Mary Ellen (Mrs)	2013	Riverside Flat, Gynack Street, Kingussie PH21 1EL	01540 661772	36
Thorburn, Susan (Mrs) MTh	2014	3 Daleally Cottages, St Madoes Road, Errol, Perth PH2 7JH	01821 642681	28
Tweedie, Fiona BSc PhD	2011	121 George Street, Edinburgh EH2 4YN	0131-225 5722	1
Wallace, Mhairi (Mrs)	2013	5 Dee Road, Kirkcudbright DG6 4HQ [E-mail: mhairiwallace54@gmail.com]	07701 375064 (Mbl)	8
Watson, Michael D.	2013	47 Crichton Terrace, Pathhead EH37 5QZ	01875 320043	3

ORDAINED LOCAL MINISTERS (Retired List)

NAME	ORD	ADDRESS	TEL	PR
Anderson, David M. MSc FCOptom	1984	'Mirlos', 1 Dumfries Place, Fort William PH33 6UQ	01397 702091	38

LIST B – AUXILIARY MINISTERS

NAME	ORD	ADDRESS	TEL	PR
Attenburrow, Anne BSc MB ChB	2006	4 Jock Inksons Brae, Elgin IV30 1QE	01343 552330	35
Binks, Mike	2007	Hollybank, 12 Kingsbrook, Corby NN18 9HY [E-mail: mike@hollybank.net]	07590 507917 (Mbl)	47

Name	Year	Address	Telephone	Page
Buck, Maxine	2007	Brownlee House, Mauldslie Road, Carluke ML8 5HW	01555 759063	17
Cameron, Ann J. (Mrs) CertCS DCE TEFL	2005	Currently resident in Qatar		32
Campbell, Gordon MA BD CDipAF DipHSM MCMI MIHM AFRIN ARSGS FRGS FSAScot	2001	2 Falkland Place, Kingoodie, Invergowrie, Dundee DD2 5DY	01382 561383	29
Cumming, Alistair MSc CCS FInstLM	2010	64 Prince George's Avenue, London SW20 8BH	(Mbl) 07534 943986	47
Dick, Roddy S.	2010	27 Easter Crescent, Wishaw ML2 8XB	01698 383453	17
Fletcher, Timothy E.G. BA FCMA	1998	3 Ardchoille Park, Perth PH2 7TL	01738 638189 (Mbl) 07747 013985	28
Forrest, Kenneth P. CBE BSc PhD	2006	5 Carruth Road, Bridge of Weir PA11 3HQ	01505 612651	14
Gardner, Hilary (Miss)	2010	Cayman Lodge, Kincardine Hill, Ardgay IV24 3DJ	01863 766107	40
Griffiths, Ruth I. (Mrs)	2004	Kirkwood, Mathieson Lane, Innellan, Dunoon PA23 7TA	01369 830145	19
Hood, Catriona A.	2006	'Elyside', Dalintober, Campbeltown PA28 6EB	01586 551490	19
Howie, Marion L.K. (Mrs) MA ARCS	1992	51 High Road, Stevenston KA20 3DY	01294 466571	12
Jackson, Nancy	2009	35 Auchentrae Crescent, Ayr KA7 4BD [E-mail: nancyjaxon@btinternet.com]	01292 262034	10
Kemp, Tina MA	2005	12 Oaktree Gardens, Dumbarton G82 1EU	01389 730477	18
Landale, William S.	2005	Green Hope Guest House, Green Hope, Duns TD11 3SG	01361 890242	5
Lunn, Dorothy	2002	14 Bellerby Drive, Ouston, Co. Durham DH2 1TW	0191-492 0647	47
Macdonald, Michael	2004	73 Firhill, Alness IV17 0RT	01349 884268	39
MacDougall, Lorna I. (Miss) MA DipGC	2003	34 Millar Place, Carron, Falkirk FK2 8QB	01324 552739	22
MacGregor, Robert M. CMIOSH DipOSH RSP	2004	Olna Cottage, Brae, Shetland ZE2 9QS	01806 522604	46
Manson, Eileen (Mrs) DipCE	1994	1 Cambridge Avenue, Gourock PA19 1XT	01475 632401	14
Mather, James	2010	24 Ellison Road, Barnes, London SW13 0AD	(Home) 020 8876 6540 (Work) 020 7361 1670 (Mbl) 07836 715655	47
Moore, Douglas T.	2003	9 Milton Avenue, Prestwick KA9 1PU [E-mail: douglastmoore@hotmail.com]	01292 671352	10
Morrison, Donald John	2001	22 Kyles, Tarbert, Isle of Harris HS3 3BS	01859 502341	43
O'Donnell, Barbara BD PGSE	2007	Ashbank, 258 Main Street, Alexandria G83 0NU	01389 752356	18
Paterson, Andrew E. JP	1994	6 The Willows, Kelty KY4 0FQ	01383 830998	24
Perry, Marion (Mrs)	2009	17a Tarbolton Road, Cumbernauld, Glasgow G67 2AJ	01236 898519 (Mbl) 07563 180662	22
Riddell, Thomas S. BSc CEng FIChemE	1993	4 The Maltings, Linlithgow EH49 6DS	01506 843251	2
Robson, Brenda (Dr)	2005	2 Baird Road, Ratho, Newbridge EH28 8RA	0131-333 2746	2
Shearer, Anne F. BA DipEd	2010	10 Colsnaur, Menstrie FK11 7HG	01259 769176	23
Sutherland, David A.	2001	3/1, 145 Broomhill Drive, Glasgow G11 7ND	0141-357 2058	16
Vivers, Katherine A.	2004	Blacket House, Eaglesfield, Lockerbie DG11 3AA	01461 500412	7
Walker, Linda	2008	18 Valeview Terrace, Glasgow G42 9LA	0141-649 1340	16
Wallace, Kristian (Mrs) BA BD CertTheol DRM PhD	2007	Lorne and Lowland Manse, Castlehill, Campbeltown PA28 6AN	01586 552468	19
Wandrum, David	1993	5 Cawder View, Carrickstone Meadows, Cumbernauld, Glasgow G68 0BN		22
Whittaker, Mary	2011	11 Templand Road, Lhanbryde, Elgin IV30 8BR	01236 723288	35
Wilkie, Robert	2011	24 Huntingtower Road, Perth PH1 2JS	01738 628301	28
Zambonini, James LIADip	1997	100 Old Manse Road, Netherton, Wishaw ML2 0EP	01698 350889	17

AUXILIARY MINISTERS (Retired List)

NAME	ORD	ADDRESS	TEL	PR
Birch, James PgDip FRSA FIOC	2001	1 Kirkhill Grove, Cambuslang, Glasgow G72 8EH	0141-583 1722	16
Brown, Elizabeth (Mrs) JP RGN	1996	8 Viewlands Place, Perth PH1 1BS	01738 552391	28
Cloggie, June (Mrs)	1997	11A Tulipan Crescent, Callander FK17 8AR	01877 331021	23
Craggs, Sheila (Mrs)	2001	7 Morar Court, Ellon AB41 9GG	01358 723055	33
Ferguson, Archibald M. MSc PhD CEng FRINA	1989	The Whins, 2 Barrowfield, Station Road, Cardross, Dumbarton G82 5NL	01389 841517	18
Glass, Alexander OBE MA	1998	Craigton, Tulloch Avenue, Dingwall IV15 9TU	01349 863258	39
Harrison, Cameron	2006	Woodfield House, Priormuir, St Andrews KY16 8LP	01334 478067	26
Jenkinson, John J. JP LTCL ALCM DipEd DipSen	1991	8 Rosehall Terrace, Falkirk FK1 1PY	01324 625498	22
Kay, Elizabeth (Miss) DipYCS	1993	1 Kintail Walk, Inchture, Perth PH14 9RY	01828 686029	29
McAlpine, John BSc	1988	Braeside, 201 Bonkle Road, Newmains, Wishaw ML2 9AA	01698 384610	17
MacDonald, Kenneth MA BA	2001	5 Henderland Road, Bearsden, Glasgow G61 1AH	0141-943 1103	16
MacFadyen, Anne M. (Mrs) BSc BD FSAScot	1995	295 Mearns Road, Glasgow G77 5LT	0141-639 3605	16
Mack, Elizabeth A. (Miss) DipPEd	1994	24 Roberts Crescent, Dumfries DG2 7RS	01387 264847	8
Mailer, John C. JP	1985	The Willows, Auchleven, Insch AB52 6QB	01464 820387	33
Mailer, Colin	1996	Innis Chonain, Back Row, Polmont, Falkirk FK2 0RD	01324 712401	22
Munro, Mary (Mrs) BA	1993	14 Auchneel Crescent, Stranraer DG9 0JH	01776 702305	9
Paterson, Maureen (Mrs) BSc	1992	91 Dalmahoy Crescent, Kirkcaldy KY2 6TA	01592 262300	25
Phillippo, Michael MTh BSc BVetMed MRCVS	2003	25 Deeside Crescent, Aberdeen AB15 7PT	01224 318317	31
Pot, Joost BSc	1992	[E-mail: joostpot@gmail.com]		48
Ramage, Alastair E. MA BA ADB CertEd	1996	16 Claremont Gardens, Milngavie, Glasgow G62 6PG	0141-956 2897	18
Shaw, Catherine A.M. MA	1998	40 Merrygreen Place, Stewarton, Kilmarnock KA3 5EP	01560 483352	11
Thomas, Shirley A. (Mrs) DipSocSci AMIA	2000	14 Kirkgait, Letham, Forfar DD8 2XQ	01307 818084	30
Wilson, Mary D. (Mrs) RGN SCM DTM	1990	Berbice, The Terrace, Bridge of Tilt, Blair Atholl, Pitlochry PH18 5SZ	01796 481619	27

LIST C – THE DIACONATE

NAME	COM	APP	ADDRESS	TEL	PRES
Beaton, Margaret (Miss) DCS	1989	1988	64 Gardenside Grove, Carmyle, Glasgow G32 8EZ [E-mail: margaret@churchhouse.plus.com]	0141-646 2297 (Mbl) 07796 642382	16
Beck, Isobel DCS	2014	2014	16 Patrick Avenue, Stevenston KA20 4AW [E-mail: deaconcastlemilk@aol.co.uk]	(Mbl) 07919 193425	16

Black, Linda (Miss) BSc DCS	1993	2004	148 Rowan Road, Abronhill, Cumbernauld, Glasgow G67 3DA [E-mail: lnan@blueyonder.co.uk]	01236 786265	22
Blair, Fiona (Miss) DCS	1994	2010	Mure Church Manse, 9 West Road, Irvine KA12 8RE [E-mail: fblair@churchofscotland.org.uk]	(Mbl) 07977 235168	11
Buchanan, Marion (Mrs) MA DCS	1983	2006	16 Almond Drive, East Kilbride, Glasgow G74 2HX [E-mail: marion.buchanan@btinternet.com]	(Mbl) 07999 889817	16
Brydson, Angela (Mrs) DCS	2015		52 Victoria Park, Lockerbie DG11 2AY	07543 796820 01383 873131	7
Carson, Christine (Miss) MA DCS	2006		36 Upper Wellhead, Limekilns, Dunfermline KY11 3JQ	07919 137294	24
Cathcart, John Paul (Mr) DCS	2000		9 Glen More, East Kilbride, Glasgow G74 2AP [E-mail: paulcathcart@msn.com]	(Mbl) 01355 243970 07708 396074	16
Corrie, Margaret (Miss) DCS	1989	2013	44 Sunnyside Street, Camelon, Falkirk FK1 4BH [E-mail: deakcorr@virginmedia.com]	01324 670656 (Mbl) 07955 633969	2
Crawford, Morag (Miss) MSc DCS	1977	1998	118 Wester Drylaw Place, Edinburgh EH4 2TG [E-mail: morag.crawford.dcs@blueyonder.co.uk]	(Tel/Fax) 0131-332 2253 (Mbl) 07970 982563	24
Crocker, Liz (Mrs) DipComEd DCS	1985	2003	77C Craigcrook Road, Edinburgh EH4 3PH	0131-332 0227	1
Cunningham, Ian (Mr) DCS	1994	2002	110 Nelson Terrace, Keith AB55 5FD [E-mail: icunninghamdcs@btinternet.com]		35
Cuthbertson, Valerie (Miss) DipTMus DCS	2003		105 Bellshill Road, Motherwell ML1 3SJ [E-mail: v.cuthbertson333@btinternet.com]	01698 259001	22
Deans, Raymond (Mr) DCS	1994	2003	60 Ardmory Road, Rothesay, Isle of Bute PA20 0PG [E-mail: r.deans93@btinternet.com]	01700 504893	19
Dunnett, Linda (Mrs) BA DCS	1976	2000	5 Fincastle Place, Cowie, Stirling FK7 7DS [E-mail: lindadunnett@sky.com]	01786 818413 (Mbl) 07838 041683	23
Evans, Mark (Mr) BSc MSc DCS	1988	2006	13 Easter Drylaw Drive, Edinburgh EH4 2QA [E-mail: mark.evans59@nhs.net]	0131-343 3089 (Office) 01383 674136	1
Gargrave, Mary (Mrs) DCS	1989	2002	12 Parkholm Quad, Glasgow G63 7ZH [E-mail: mary.gargrave@btinternet.com]	0141-880 5532 (Mbl) 07896 866618	16
Getliffe, Dot (Mrs) DCS BA BD DipEd	2006	2013	3 Woodview Terrace, Hamilton ML3 9DP [E-mail: dgetliffe@aol.co.uk]	01698 423504 (Mbl) 07766 910171	16
Hamilton, James (Mr) DCS	1997	2000	6 Beckfield Gate, Glasgow G33 1SW [E-mail: j.hamilton111@btinternet.com]	0141-558 3195 07584 137314	16
Hamilton, Karen (Mrs) DCS	1995	2009	6 Beckfield Gate, Glasgow G33 1SW [E-mail: k.hamilton6@btinternet.com]	0141-558 3195 (Mbl) 07514 402612	16
Love, Joanna (Ms) BSc DCS	1992	2009	92 Everard Drive, Glasgow G21 1XQ [E-mail: jo@iona.org.uk]	0141-772 0149 (Office) 0141-332 6343	16
Lyall, Ann (Miss) DCS	1980	2013	24 Pennywell Road, Edinburgh EH4 4HD [E-mail: ann.lyall@btinternet.com]	0131-332 4354	1
MacDonald, Anne (Miss) BA DCS	1980	2002	502 Castle Gait, Paisley PA1 2PA [E-mail: anne.macdonald2@ggc.scot.nhs.uk]	0141-840 1875 (Mbl) 07976 786174	16
McIntosh, Kay (Mrs) DCS	2008	2013	4 Jacklin Green, Livingston EH54 8PZ [E-mail: kay@backedge.co.uk]	01506 440543	2
McKay, Kenneth D. (Mr) DCS	1996	1998	11F Balgowan Road, Letham, Perth PH1 2IG [E-mail: deakendan@gmail.com]	01738 621169 (Mbl) 07843 883042	28
McLellan, Margaret DCS	1986	2014	18 Broom Road East, Newton Mearns, Glasgow G77 5SD [E-mail: margaretmclellan@rocketmail.com]	0141-639 6853	16

NAME			ADDRESS	TEL.	PRES
McPheat, Elspeth (Miss) DCS	1985	2001	11/5 New Orchardfield, Edinburgh EH6 5ET	0131-554 4143	1
Munro, Patricia (Ms) BSc DCS	1986	2012	4 Hewat Place, Perth PH1 2UD [E-mail: pat.munrodcs@gmail.com]	01738 443088 (Mbl) 07814 836314	28
Nicholson, David (Mr) DCS	1994	1993	2D Doonside, Kildrum, Cumbernauld, Glasgow G67 2HX [E-mail: deacdave@btinternet.com]	01236 732260	22
Ogilvie, Colin (Mr) DCS	1998		32 Upper Bourtree Court, Rutherglen, Glasgow G73 4HT [E-mail: colinogilvie2@gmail.com]	0141-569 2725 (Mbl) 07837 287804	11
Pennykid, Gordon J. BD DCS	2015		8 Glenfield, Livingston EH54 7BG [E-mail: gpennykid@churchofscotland.org.uk]	07747 652652 (Mbl)	2
Philip, Elizabeth (Mrs) DCS MA BA PGCSE	2007		8 Strathearn Terrace, Crieff PH7 3AQ [E-mail: ephilipstitch@gmail.com]	01764 218976 (Mbl) 07970 767851	28
Porter, Jean (Mrs) BD DCS	2006	2008	St Mark's Church, Drip Road, Stirling FK8 1RE [E-mail: info@stmarksstirling.org.uk]	07729 316321 (Mbl)	23
Robertson, Pauline (Mrs) DCS BA CertTheol	2003	2006	6 Ashville Terrace, Edinburgh EH6 8DD [E-mail: pauline70@rocketmail.com]	0131-554 6564	1
Ross, Duncan (Mr) DCS	1996	2006	1 John Neilson Avenue, Paisley PA1 2SX [E-mail: duncan@saintninians.co.uk]	0141-887 2801	14
Stewart, Marion G. (Miss) DCS	1991	1994	Kirk Cottage, Kirkton of Skene, Westhill, Skene AB32 6XE [E-mail: m313stewart@btinternet.com]	01224 743407	33
Thomson, Jacqueline (Mrs) MTh DCS	2004	2004	16 Aitken Place, Coaltown of Wemyss, Kirkcaldy KY1 4PA [E-mail: jacqueline.thomson@churchofscotland.org.uk]	07806 776560 (Mbl)	25
Urquhart, Barbara (Mrs) DCS	1986	2006	9 Standalane, Kilmaurs, Kilmarnock KA3 2NB [E-mail: barbaraurquhart1@gmail.com]	01563 538289	11
Wallace, Catherine (Mrs) PGDipC DCS	1987		21 Durley Dene Crescent, Bridge of Earn PH2 9RD [E-mail: samesky2407@aol.com]	01738 621709	28
Wallace, Sheila (Mrs) DCS BA BD	2009	2011	Beannach Cottage, Spey Avenue, Boat of Garten PH24 3BE [E-mail: sheilad.wallace53@gmail.com]	01479 831548 (Mbl) 07733 243046	36
Wilson, Glenda (Mrs) DCS	1990	2006	5 Allan Terrace, Sandbank, Dunoon PA23 8PR [E-mail: deacglendamwilson@gmail.com]	01369 704168	19
Wright, Lynda (Miss) BEd DCS	1979	1992	Key Cottage, High Street, Falkland, Cupar KY15 7BU [E-mail: lynda.keyhouse@tiscali.co.uk]	01337 857705 (Mbl) 07835 303395	26

THE DIACONATE (Retired List)

NAME	COM	ADDRESS	TEL.	PRES
Allan, Jean (Mrs) DCS	1989	12C Hindmarsh Avenue, Dundee DD3 7LW [E-mail: jeanmieallan45@googlemail.com]	01382 827299 (Mbl) 07709 959474	29
Anderson, Janet (Miss) DCS	1979	Creagard, 31 Lower Breakish, Isle of Skye IV42 8QA [E-mail: jaskye@hotmail.co.uk]	01471 822403	42
Bayes, Muriel C. (Mrs) DCS	1963	Flat 6, Carleton Court, 10 Fenwick Road, Glasgow G46 4AN	0141-633 0865	16
Bell, Sandra (Mrs) DCS	2001	62 Loganswell Road, Thornliebank, Glasgow G46 8AX	0141-638 5884	16

Buchanan, John (Mr) DCS	2010	19 Gillespie Crescent, Edinburgh EH10 4HZ	0131-229 0794	3
Burns, Marjory (Mrs) DCS	1997	22 Kirklee Road, Mossend, Bellshill ML4 2QN [E-mail: mburns8070@aol.co.uk]	01698 292685 (Mbl) 07792 843922	17
Cameron, Margaret (Miss) DCS	1961	2 Rowans Gate, Paisley PA2 6RD	0141-840 2479	14
Craw, John (Mr) DCS	1998	Liabost, 8 Proudfoot Road, Wick KW1 4PQ [E-mail: johncraw607@btinternet.com]	01955 603805 (Mbl) 07544 761653	41
Drummond, Rhoda (Miss) DCS	1960	Flat K, 23 Grange Loan, Edinburgh EH9 2ER	0131-668 3631	1
Erskine, Morag (Miss) DCS	1979	111 Mains Drive, Park Mains, Erskine PA8 7JJ	0141-812 6096	14
Flockhart, Andrew (Mr) DCS	1988	Flat 0/1, 8 Hardie Avenue, Rutherglen, Glasgow G73 3AS	0141-569 0716	16
Forrest, Janice (Mrs)	1990	4/1, 7 Blochairn Place, Glasgow G21 2EB	0141-552 1132	16
Gordon, Fiona S. (Mrs) MA DCS	1958	Machrie, 3 Cupar Road, Cuparmuir, Cupar KY15 5RH [E-mail: machrie@madasafish.com]	01334 652341	26
Gordon, Margaret (Mrs) DCS	1998	92 Lanark Road West, Currie EH14 5LA	0131-449 2554	1
Gray, Catherine (Miss) DCS	1969	10C Eastern View, Gourock PA19 1RJ [E-mail: gray_catherine2@sky.com]	01475 637479	14
Gray, Christine M. (Mrs) DCS	1969	11 Woodside Avenue, Thornliebank, Glasgow G46 7HR	0141-571 1008	16
Gray, Greta (Miss) DCS	1992	67 Crags Avenue, Paisley PA2 6SG [E-mail: greta.gray@ntlworld.com]	0141-884 6178	14
Hughes, Helen (Miss) DCS	1977	2/2, 43 Burnbank Terrace, Glasgow G20 6UQ [E-mail: helhug35@gmail.com]	0141-333 9459 (Mbl) 07752 604817	16
Hutchison, Alan E.W. (Mr) DCS	1988	132 Lochbridge Road, North Berwick EH39 4DR	01620 894077	3
Johnston, Mary (Miss) DCS	1988	19 Lounsdale Drive, Paisley PA2 9ED	0141-849 1615	14
King, Chris (Mrs) DCS	2002	28 Kinford Drive, Dundonald, Kilmarnock KA2 9ET [E-mail: chrisking99@tiscali.co.uk]	01563 851197	10
King, Margaret MA DCS	2002	56 Murrayfield, Fochabers IV32 7EZ	01343 820937	35
Lundie, Ann V. (Miss) DCS	1972	20 Langdykes Drive, Cove, Aberdeen AB12 3HW	01224 898416	31
McBain, Margaret (Miss) DCS	1974	33 Quarry Road, Paisley PA2 7RD	0141-884 2920	14
McCallum, Moyra (Miss) MA BD DCS	1965	176 Hilton Drive, Aberdeen AB24 4LT [E-mail: moymac@aol.com]	01224 486240 (Mbl) 07986 581899	31
McCully, M. Isobel (Miss) DCS	1974	10 Broadstone Avenue, Port Glasgow PA14 5BB [E-mail: mi.mccully@btinternet.com]	01475 742240	14
MacKinnon, Ronald (Mr) DCS	1996	12 Mossywood Court, McGregor Avenue, Airdrie ML6 7DY [E-mail: ronnie@ronniemac.plus.com]	01236 763389 (Mbl) 07594 427960	22
MacLean, Donald A. (Mr) DCS	1988	8 Upper Barvas, Isle of Lewis HS2 0QX	01851 840454	44
McNaughton, Janette (Miss) DCS	1982	4 Dunellan Avenue, Moodiesburn, Glasgow G69 0GB	01236 870180	22
MacPherson, James B. (Mr) DCS	1988	0/1, 104 Cartside Street, Glasgow G42 9TQ	0141-616 6468	16
MacQuien, Duncan (Mr) DCS	1988	35 Criffel Road, Mount Vernon, Glasgow G32 9JE	0141-575 1137	14
Martin, Janie (Miss) DCS	1979	16 Wentworth Road, Dundee DD2 3SD [E-mail: janimar@aol.com]	01382 813786	29
Merrilees, Ann (Miss) DCS	1994	23 Cuthill Brae, Willow Wood Residential Park, West Calder EH55 8QE [E-mail: ann@merrilees.freeserve.co.uk]	01501 762909	2
Miller, Elsie M. (Miss) DCS	1974	30 Swinton Avenue, Rowanbank, Baillieston, Glasgow G69 6JR	0141-771 0857	22
Mitchell, Joyce (Mrs) DCS	1994	Sunnybank, Farr, Inverness IV2 6XG [E-mail: joyce@mitchell71.freeserve.co.uk]	01808 521285	37
Morrison, Jean (Dr) DCS	1964	45 Corslet Road, Currie EH14 5LZ [E-mail: jean.morrison@blueyonder.co.uk]	0131-449 6859	1
Moyes, Sheila (Miss) DCS	1957	158 Pilton Avenue, Edinburgh EH5 2JZ [E-mail: sheilamoyes@btinternet.com]	0131-551 1731	1

Name	Year	Address	Telephone	No.
Mulligan, Anne MA DCS	1974	27A Craigour Avenue, Edinburgh EH17 7NH [E-mail: mulliganne@aol.com]	0131-664 3426	1
Nicol, Joyce (Mrs) BA DCS	1974	93 Brisbane Street, Greenock PA16 8NY [E-mail: joycenicol@hotmail.co.uk]	01475 723235 (Mbl) 07957 642709	14
Palmer, Christine (Ms) DCS	2003	Flat 4, Carissima Court, 99 Elmer Road, Elmer, Bognor Regis PO22 6LH	01243 858641	28
Rennie, Agnes M. (Miss) DCS	1974	3/1 Craigmillar Court, Edinburgh EH16 4AD	0131-661 8475	1
Rose, Lewis (Mr) DCS	1993	6 Gauldie Crescent, Dundee DD3 0RR [E-mail: lewis_rose48@yahoo.co.uk]	01382 816580 (Mbl) 07899 790466	29
Smith, Catherine (Mrs) DCS	1964	21 Lingaro, Bixter, Shetland ZE2 9NN	01595 810207	46
Steele, Marilynn J. (Mrs) BD DCS	1999	2 Northfield Gardens, Prestonpans EH32 9LQ	01875 811497	1
Steven, Gordon R. BD DCS	1997	51 Nantwich Drive, Edinburgh EH7 6RB [E-mail: grsteven@btinternet.com]	0131-669 2054	3
Stuart, Anne (Miss) DCS	1966	1 Murrell Terrace, Aberdour, Burntisland KY3 0XH	07904 385256 (Mbl) 01383 860049	24
Tait, Agnes (Mrs) DCS	1995	10 Carnoustie Crescent, Greenhills, East Kilbride, Glasgow G75 8TE	01389 873196	17
Teague, Yvonne (Mrs) DCS	1965	46 Craigcrook Avenue, Edinburgh EH4 3PX [E-mail: y.teague.1@blueyonder.co.uk]	0131-336 3113	1
Thom, Helen (Miss) BA DipEd MA DCS	1959	84 Great King Street, Edinburgh EH3 6QU	0131-556 5687	1
Thomson, Phyllis (Miss) DCS	2003	63 Caroline Park, Mid Calder, Livingston EH53 0SJ	01506 883207	2
Trimble, Robert DCS	1988	5 Templar Rise, Livingston EH54 6PJ	01506 412504	2
Webster, Elspeth H. (Miss) DCS	1950	82 Broomhill Avenue, Burntisland KY3 0BP	01592 873616	25
Wilson, Muriel (Miss) MA BD DCS	1997	28 Bellevue Crescent, Ayr KA7 2DR [E-mail: muriel.wilson4@btinternet.com]	01292 264939	10
Wishart, William (Mr) DCS	1994	1 Brunstane Road North, Edinburgh EH15 2DL [E-mail: bill@wishartfamily.co.uk]	(Mbl) 07846 555654	1

THE DIACONATE (Supplementary List)

Name	Year	Address	Telephone
Gilroy, Lorraine (Mrs) DCS	1988	5 Bluebell Drive, Cheverel Court, Bedward CO12 0GE	02476 366031
Guthrie, Jennifer M. (Miss) DCS	1993	14 Eskview Terrace, Ferryden, Montrose DD10 9RD	01674 674413
Harris, Judith (Mrs) DCS	1988	243 Western Avenue, Sandfields, Port Talbot, West Glamorgan SA12 7NF	01639 884855
Hood, Katrina (Mrs) DCS	1982	67C Farquhar Road, Edgbaston, Birmingham B18 2QP	
Hudson, Sandra (Mrs) DCS	1969	10 Albany Drive, Rutherglen, Glasgow G73 3QN	
Muir, Alison M. (Mrs) DCS	1978	77 Arthur Street, Dunfermline KY12 0JJ	
Ramsden, Christine (Miss) DCS	1970	2 Wykeham Close, Bassett, Southampton SO16 7LZ	
Walker, Wikje (Mrs) DCS		24 Brodie's Yard, Queen Street, Coupar Angus PH13 9RA	01828 628251

LIST D – MINISTERS WHO HOLD PRACTISING CERTIFICATES (in accordance with Act II (2000), but who are not members of a Presbytery)

NAME	ORD	ADDRESS	TEL	PRES
Adamson, Hugh M. BD	1976	38F Maybole Road, Ayr KA7 4SF [E-mail: hmadamson768@btinternet.com]	01292 440958	11
Aitken, Ewan R. BA BD	1992	159 Restalrig Avenue, Edinburgh EH7 6PJ	0131-467 1660	1
Alexander, William M. BD	1971	110 Fairview Circle, Danestone, Aberdeen AB22 8YR	01224 703752	31
Anderson, David MA BD	1975	Rowan Cottage, Aberlour Gardens, Aberlour AB38 9LD	01340 871906	35
Anderson, Kenneth G. MA BD	1967	8 School Road, Arbroath DD11 2LT	01241 874825	30
Anderson, Susan M. (Mrs) BD	1997	32 Murrayfield, Bishopbriggs, Glasgow G64 3DS [E-mail: susanbbriggs32@gmail.com]	0141-772 6338	11
Barclay, Neil W. BSc BEd BD	1986	4 Gibsongray Street, Falkirk FK2 7LN	01324 874681	22
Bardgett, Frank D. MA BD PhD	1987	Tigh an Iasgair, Street of Kincardine, Boat of Garten PH24 3BY [E-mail: tigh@bardgett.plus.com]	01479 831751	36
Bartholomew, Julia (Mrs) BSc BD	2002	Kippenhill, Dunning, Perth PH2 0RA	01764 684929	28
Beattie, Warren R. BSc BD MSc PhD	1991	Director for Mission Research, OMF International, 2 Cluny Road, Singapore 259570	0065 6319 4550	1
Biddle, Lindsay (Ms)	1991	30 Ralston Avenue, Glasgow G52 3NA [E-mail: beattiewarren@omf.net]	0141-883 7405	
Birrell, John M. MA LLB BD	1974	'Hiddlehame', 5 Hewat Place, Perth PH1 2UD [E-mail: lindsaybiddle@hotmail.com]	01738 443335	28
Bjarnason, Sven S. CandTheol	1975	14 Edward Street, Dunfermline KY12 0JW [E-mail: john.birrell@nhs.net]	01383 724625	36
Black, James S. BD DPS	1976	7 Breck Terrace, Penicuik EH26 0RJ [E-mail: sven@bjarnason.org.uk]	01968 677559	3
Boyd, Ian R. MA BD PhD	1989	33 Castleton Drive, Newton Mearns, Glasgow G77 3LE [E-mail: jsb.black@btopenworld.com]		
Bradley, Andrew W. BD	1975	Flat 1/1, 38 Cairnhill View, Bearsden, Glasgow G61 1RP	0141-931 5344	16
Brown, Robert F. MA BD ThM	1971	55 Hilton Drive, Aberdeen AB24 4NJ	01224 491451	31
Caie, Albert LTh	1983	34 Ringwell Gardens, Stonehouse, Larkhall ML9 3QW [E-mail: Bjacob546@aol.com]	01698 792187	17
Coogan, J. Melvyn LTh	1992	19 Glen Grove, Largs KA30 8QQ		12
Cowieson, Roy J. BD	1979	2160-15 Hawk Drive, Courtenay, BC V9N 9B2, Canada [E-mail: arjay1232@gmail.com]		13
Davidson, John F. BSc DipEdTech	1970	49 Craigmill Gardens, Carnoustie DD7 6HX [E-mail: davidson900@btinternet.com]	01241 854566	30
Davidson, Mark R. MA BD STM PhD RN	2005	20 Kinmohr Rise, Blackburn, Aberdeen AB21 0LJ [E-mail: mark.davidson122@mod.uk]	01224 791350	33
Dick, John H.A. MA MSc BD	1982	18 Fairfield Road, Kelty KY4 0BY	01506 237597	31
Dickson, Graham T. MA BD	1985	43 Hope Park Gardens, Bathgate EH48 2QT [E-mail: gtd194@googlemail.com]		2
Donaldson, Colin V.	1982	3A Playfair Terrace, St Andrews KY16 9HX	01334 472889	3

Name	Year	Address	Telephone	No.
Drake, Wendy F. (Mrs) BD	1978	21 William Black Place, South Queensferry EH30 9QR [E-mail: revwdrake@hotmail.co.uk]	0131-331 1520	1
Drummond, Norman W. (Prof.) CBE MA BD DUniv FRSE	1976	c/o Columba 1400 Ltd, Staffin, Isle of Skye IV51 9JY	01478 611400	42
Ellis, David W. GIMechE GIProdE	1962	4 Wester Tarsappie, Rhynd Road, Perth PH2 8PT	01738 449618	16
Espie, Howard	2011	1 Sprucebank Avenue, Langbank, Port Glasgow PA14 6YX [E-mail: howardespie.me.com]	01475 540391	1
Ferguson, Ronald MA BD ThM DUniv	1972	Vinbreck, Orphir, Orkney KW17 2RE [E-mail: ronbluebrazil@aol.com]	01856 811353	45
Fowler, Richard C.A. BSc MSc BD	1978	4 Gardentown, Whalsay, Shetland ZE2 9AB	01806 566538	46
Fraser, Ian M. MA BD PhD	1946	Ferndale, Gargunnock, Stirling FK8 3BW	01786 860612	23
Frew, John M. MA BD	1946	17 The Furrows, Walton-on-Thames KT12 3JQ		16
Gammack, George BD	1985	13A Hill Street, Broughty Ferry, Dundee DD5 2JP	01382 778636	29
Gardner, Bruce K. MA BD PhD	1988	21 Hopetown Crescent, Bucksburn, Aberdeen AB21 9QY [E-mail: drbrucegardner@aol.com]	(Mbl) 07891 186724	31
Gauld, Beverly G.D.D. MA BD	1972	7 Rowan View, Lanark ML11 9FQ	01555 665765	13
Gillies, Janet E. BD	1998	18 McIntyre Lane, Macmerry, Tranent EH33 1QL	01875 824607	3
Gordon, Elinor J. (Miss) BD	1988	6 Balgibbon Drive, Callander FK17 8EU [E-mail: elinorgordon@btinternet.com]	01877 331049	22
Grainger, Alison J. BD	1995	2 Hareburn Avenue, Avonbridge, Falkirk FK1 2NR [E-mail: revajgrainger@btinternet.com]	01324 861632	2
Grubb, George D.W. BA BD BPhil DMin	1962	10 Wellhead Close, South Queensferry EH30 9WA	0131-331 2072	1
Harper, Anne J.M. (Miss) BD STM MTh CertSocPsych	1979	122 Greenock Road, Bishopton PA7 5AS	01505 862466	16
Haslett, Howard J. BA BD	1972	26 The Maltings, Haddington EH41 4EF [E-mail: howard.haslett@btinternet.com]	01620 820292	3
Hendrie, Yvonne (Mrs) MA BD	1995	The Manse, 16 McAdam Way, Maybole KA19 8FD	01655 883710	10
Hibbert, Frederick W. BD	1986	4 Cemydd Terrace, Senghemydd, Caerphilly, Mid Glamorgan CF83 4HL	02920 831653	47
Homewood, Ivor Maxwell MSc BD	1997	An der Fließwiese 26, D-14052 Berlin, Germany [E-mail: maxhomewood@me.com]	0049 30 3048722	48
Hosie, James MA BD MTh	1959	Hilbre, Baycrofts, Strachur, Cairndow PA27 8BY	01369 860634	19
Hutcheson, Norman M. MA BD	1973	66 Maxwell Park, Dalbeattie DG5 4LS [E-mail: norman.hutcheson@gmail.com]		8
Hutchison, Alison M. (Mrs) BD DipMin	1988	Ashfield, Drumoak, Banchory AB31 5AG [E-mail: amhutch62@aol.com]	01330 811309	31
Jenkinson, John J. JP LTCL ALCM DipEd DipSen (Aux)	1991	8 Rosehall Terrace, Falkirk FK1 1PY	01324 625498	22
Kenny, Celia G. BA MTh MPhil PhD	1995	37 Grosvenor Road, Rathgar, Dublin 6, Ireland [E-mail: cgkenny@tcd.ie]		5
Kerr, Hugh F. MA BD	1968	134C Great Western Road, Aberdeen AB10 6QE	01224 580091	31
Lamont, Stewart J. BSc BD	1972	13/1 Grosvenor Crescent, Edinburgh EH12 5EL [E-mail: lamontsj@gmail.com]	(Mbl) 07557 532012	30
Lawrie, Robert M. BD MSc DipMin LLCM(TD) MCMI	1994	18/1 John's Place, Edinburgh EH6 7EN [E-mail: robert.lawrie@ed.ac.uk]	0131-554 9765	1

Name	Year	Address / E-mail	Tel	No.
Ledgard, J. Christopher BA	1969	Streonshalh, 8 David Hume View, Chirnside, Duns TD11 3SX [E-mail: ledgard07@btinternet.com]	01890 817124	5
Leishman, James S. LTh BD MA	1969	11 Hunter Avenue, Heathhall, Dumfries DG1 3UX	01387 249241	8
Liddiard, F.G.B. MA	1957	34 Trinity Fields Crescent, Brechin DD9 6YF	01356 622966	30
Lindsay, W. Douglas BD CPS	1978	3 Drummond Place, Calderwood, East Kilbride, Glasgow G74 3AD	01355 234169	16
Lithgow, Anne R. (Mrs) MA BD	1992	14 Thorntonloch Holdings, Dunbar EH42 1QT [E-mail: anne.lithgow@btinternet.com]		3
Logan, Thomas M. LTh	1971	3 Duncan Court, Kilmarnock KA3 7TF	01563 524398	11
Lyall, David BSc BD STM PhD	1965	16 Brian Crescent, Tunbridge Wells, Kent TN4 0AP [E-mail: lyall3@gmail.com]	01892 670323	47
McAdam, David J. BSc BD (Assoc)	1990	12 Dunellan Crescent, Moodiesburn, Glasgow G69 0GA [E-mail: dmca29@hotmail.co.uk]	01236 870472	16
McDonald, Ross J. BA BD ThM RNR	1998	HMS Dalriada, Navy Buildings, Eldon Street, Greenock PA16 7SL [E-mail: rossjmcdonald@tiscali.co.uk]	0141-883 7545 (Mbl) 07952 558767	16
McFadyen, Gavin BEng BD	2006	20 Tennyson Avenue, Bridlington YO15 2EP [E-mail: mcfadyen.gavin@gmail.com]	01262 608659 (Mbl) 07503 971068	18
McGillivray, A. Gordon MA BD STM	1951	36 Larchfield Neuk, Balerno EH14 7NL		1
Maciver, Iain BD	2007	5 MacLeod Road, Stornoway, Isle of Lewis HS1 2HJ [E-mail: iain.maciver@hebrides.net]		44
MacKay, Alan H. BD	1974	Flat 1/1, 18 Newburgh Street, Glasgow G43 2XR [E-mail: alanhmackay@aol.com]	0141-632 0527	
McKay, Johnston R. MA BA PhD	1969	15 Montgomerie Avenue, Fairlie, Largs KA29 0EE [E-mail: johnston.mckay@btopenworld.com]	01475 568802	16
McKay, Margaret MA BD MTh	1991	19 Richmond Road, Huntly AB54 8BH [E-mail: elricksmithy@yahoo.co.uk]	01466 793937	34
McKean, Martin J. BD DipMin	1984	56 Kingsknowe Drive, Edinburgh EH14 2JX	0131-466 1157	1
McLean, Gordon LTh	1972	Beinn Dhorain, Kinnettas Square, Strathpeffer IV14 9BD [E-mail: gmaclean@hotmail.co.uk]	01997 421380	39
MacPherson, Gordon C.	1963	203 Capelrig Road, Patterton, Newton Mearns, Glasgow G77 6ND	0141-616 2107	16
McPherson, William BD DipEd	1993	83 Laburnum Avenue, Port Seton, Prestonpans EH32 0UD	01875 812252	22
McWilliam, Thomas M. MA BD	1964	Flat 3, 13 Culduthel Road, Inverness IV2 4AG [E-mail: tommcwilliam@btconnect.com]	01463 718981	39
Mailer, Colin (Aux)	1996	Innis Chonain, Back Row, Polmont, Falkirk FK2 0RD	01324 712401	22
Main, Arthur W.A. BD	1954	13/3 Eildon Terrace, Edinburgh EH3 5NL	0131-556 1344	16
Masson, John D. MA BD PhD BSc	1984	2 Beechgrove, Craw Hall, Brampton CA8 1TS [E-mail: jmasson96@btinternet.com]	ex-directory	7
Melville, David D. BD	1989	28 Porterfield, Comrie, Dunfermline KY12 9HJ	01383 850075	24
Millar, Peter W. MA BD PhD	1971	6/5 Ettrickdale Place, Edinburgh EH3 5JN [E-mail: ionacottage@hotmail.com]	0131-557 0517	1
Minto, Joan E. (Mrs) MA BD	1993	139/1 New Street, Musselburgh EH21 6DH	0131-665 6736	3
Moodie, Alastair R. MA BD	1978	4 Burnbrae Road, Auchinloch, Glasgow G66 5DQ		16
Morton, Andrew Q. MA BSc BD FRSE	1949	Sunnyside, 4A Manse Street, Aberdour, Burntisland KY3 0TY		18

Name	Year	Address	Phone	No.
Muckart, Graeme W.M. MTh MSc FSAScot MTheol DipPTheol	1983	Kildale, Clashmore, Dornoch IV25 3RG [E-mail: gw2m.kildale@gmail.com]	01862 881715	40
Muir, Eleanor D. (Miss)	1986	[E-mail: eleanordmuir@tiscali.co.uk]		28
Muir, Margaret A. (Miss) MA LLB BD	1989	59/4 South Beechwood, Edinburgh EH12 5YS	0131-313 3240	13
Neilson, Rodger BSc BD	1972	4 Waulkmill Steading, Charlestown, Dunfermline KY12 8ZS	01383 873336	34
Newell, Alison M. (Mrs) BD	1986	1A Inverleith Terrace, Edinburgh EH3 5NS [E-mail: alinewell@aol.com]	0131-556 3505	1
Newell, J. Philip MA BD PhD	1982	1A Inverleith Terrace, Edinburgh EH3 5NS	0131-556 3505	1
Newlands, George M. (Prof.) MA BD PhD DLitt FRSA FRSE	1970	12 Jamaica Street North Lane, Edinburgh EH3 6HQ		16
Nicolson, John Murdo	1997	731 16th Street North, Lethbridge, Alberta, Canada T1H 3B3		42
Notman, John R. BSc BD	1990	5 Dovecote Road, Bromsgrove, Worcs B61 7BN		47
Ostler, John H. MA LTh	1975	5 Osborne Terrace, Port Seton, Prestonpans EH32 0BZ	01875 814358	3
Owen, Catherine W. MTh	1984	10 Waverley Park, Kirkintilloch, Glasgow G66 2BP	0141-776 0407	16
Paterson, Andrew E. JP	1994	6 The Willows, Kelty KY4 0FQ	01383 830998	24
Penman, Iain D. BD	1977	33/5 Carnbee Avenue, Edinburgh EH16 6GA [E-mail: iainpenmanklm@aol.com]	0131-664 0673 (Mbl) 07931 993427	1
Pieterse, Ben BA BTh LTh	2001	15 Bakeoven Close, Seaforth Sound, Simon's Town 7975, South Africa		25
Provan, Iain W. MA BA PhD	1991	Regent College, 5800 University Boulevard, Vancouver BC V6T 2E4, Canada	001 604 224 3245	1
Risby, Lesley P. (Mrs) BD	1994	Tigh an Achaidh, 21 Fernoch Crescent, Lochgilphead PA31 8AE [E-mail: mrsrisby@hotmail.com]	01546 600464	19
Rosener, Alexandra M (Mrs)	2007	Lüttenglehn 3, 41352 Korschenbroich, Germany	0049 2182 833 9535	25
Roy, Alistair A. MA BD	1955	1 Broaddykes Close, Kingswells, Aberdeen AB15 8UF	01224 743310	31
Saunders, Keith BD	1983	Western Infirmary, Dumbarton Road, Glasgow G11 6NT	0141-211 2000	16
Sawers, Hugh BA	1968	2 Rosemount Meadows, Castlepark, Bothwell, Glasgow G71 8EL	01698 853960	17
Scotland, Ronald J. BD	1993	7A Rose Avenue, Elgin IV30 1NX [E-mail: ronnieandjill@thescotlands.co.uk]	01343 543086	35
Scouller, Hugh BSc BD	1985	11 Kirk View, Haddington EH41 4AN [E-mail: h.scouller@btinternet.com]		3
Shaw, D.W.D. BA BD LLB WS DD	1960	4/13 Succoth Court, Edinburgh EH12 6BZ	0131-337 2130	26
Smith, Ronald W. BA BEd BD	1979	1F1, 2 Middlefield, Edinburgh EH7 4PF	0131-553 1174 (Mbl) 07900 896954	23
Stewart, Margaret L. (Mrs) BSc MB ChB BD	1985	28 Inch Crescent, Bathgate EH48 1EU [E-mail: famstewart@ormail.co.uk]	01506 653428	2
Stewart, Una B. (Ms) BD DipEd	1995	10 Inch Park, Kelso TD5 7BQ [E-mail: rev.ubs@virgin.net]	01573 219231	13
Storrar, William F. (Prof.) MA BD PhD	1984	Director, Center of Theological Inquiry, 50 Stockton Street, Princeton, NJ 08540, USA		1
Strachan, Alexander E. MA BD	1974	2 Leafield Road, Dumfries DG1 2DS [E-mail: aestrachan@aol.com]	01387 279460	8
Strachan, David G. BD DPS	1978	1 Deeside Park, Aberdeen AB15 7PQ	01224 324101	31
Strachan, Ian M. MA BD	1959	'Cardenwell', Glen Drive, Dyce, Aberdeen AB21 7EN	01224 772028	31
Tamas, Bertalan		Pozsonyi út 34, Budapest H-1137, Hungary [E-mail: bertalantamas@hotmail.com]	0036 1 239 6315 (Mbl) 0036 30 638 6647	48

NAME	ORD	ADDRESS	TEL	PRES
Thomas, W. Colville ChLJ BTh BPhil DPS DSc	1964	11 Muirfield Crescent, Gullane EH31 2HN	01620 842415	3
Tollick, Frank BSc DipEd	1958	3 Bellhouse Road, Aberdour, Burntisland KY3 0TL	01383 860559	24
Turnbull, John LTh	1994	4 Rathmor Road, Biggar ML12 6QG	01899 221502	13
Turnbull, Julian S.	1980	39 Suthern Yett, Prestonpans EH32 9GL [E-mail: jules@turnbull25.plus.com]	01875 818305	3
Watson, John M. LTh BSc BD MSc CEng MBCS	1989	20 Greystone Place, Newtonhill, Stonehaven AB39 3UL [E-mail: watson-john18@sky.com]	01569 730604 (Mbl) 07733 334380	31
Weatherhead, James L. CBE MA LLB DD	1960	59 Brechin Road, Kirriemuir DD8 4DE	01575 572237	30
Webster, Brian G. BSc BD CEng MIET	1998	3/1 Cloch Court, 57 Albert Road, Gourock PA19 1NJ [E-mail: revwebby@aol.com]	01475 638332	23
Whitton, John P.	1977	115 Sycamore Road, Farnborough, Hants GU14 6RE	01252 674488	47
Whyte, Ron C. BD CPS	1990	13 Hillside Avenue, Kingussie PH21 1PA [E-mail: ron4xst@btinternet.com]	01540 661101 (Mbl) 07979 026973	36
Wilkie, James L. MA BD	1959	7 Comely Bank Avenue, Edinburgh EH4 1EW [E-mail: jl.wilkie@btinternet.com]	0131-343 1552	1
Wood, James L.K.	1967	1 Glen Drive, Dyce, Aberdeen AB21 7EN	01224 722543	31

LIST E – MINISTERS WHO ARE NOT MEMBERS OF A PRESBYTERY AND WHO DO NOT CURRENTLY HOLD A PRACTISING CERTIFICATE (in terms of Act II (2000))

NAME	ORD	ADDRESS	TEL	PRES
Aitchison, James W. BD	1993	84 Wakefords Park, Church Crookham, Fleet, Hampshire GU52 8EZ		31
Beck, John C. BD	1975	31 The Woodlands, Stirling FK8 2LB	01738 443335	35
Birrell, Isobel (Mrs) BD	1994	'Hiddlehame', 5 Hewat Place, Perth PH1 2UD [E-mail: isobel@ibmail.org.uk]	(Mbl) 07540 797945	17
Black, W. Graham MA BD	1983	72 Linksview, Linksfield Road, Aberdeen AB24 5RG [E-mail: graham.black@virgin.net]	01224 492491	31
Bonar, Alexander F. LTh LRIC	1988	7 Westbank Court, Westbank Terrace, Macmerry, Tranent EH33 1QS [E-mail: sandybonar@tiscali.co.uk]	01875 615165	3
Breakey, Judith (Ms) LizTheol MTh DipEd	2010	52 Henderson Drive, Kintore, Inverurie AB51 0FB [E-mail: judith.breakey@gmail.com]		16
Brown, Alastair BD	1986	The Orchard, Hermitage Lane, Shedden Park Road, Kelso TD5 7AN	01467 632787	32
Brown, Joseph MA	1954	Springvale, Halket Road, Lugton, Kilmarnock KA3 4EE	01573 223481	6
Burgess, Paul C.J. MA	1968	[E-mail: paulandcathie@gmail.com]	01505 850254	2
Campbell, J. Ewen R. MA BD	1967	85/15 High Street, North Berwick EH39 4HD	01620 894839	25
Cooper, George MA BD	1943	8 Leighton Square, Alyth, Blairgowrie PH11 8AQ	01828 633746	1
Craig, Eric MA BD BA	1959	5 West Relugas Road, Edinburgh EH9 2PW	0131-667 8210	1

Name	Ord.	Address	Tel.	No.
Craig, Gordon W. MBE MA BD	1972	1 Beley Bridge, Dunino, St Andrews KY16 8LT	01334 880285	26
Crawford, Michael S.M. LTh	1966	Brownside of Strichen, New Pitsligo, Fraserburgh AB43 6NY		31
Cumming, David P.L. MA	1957	Shillong, Tarbat Ness Road, Portmahomack, Tain IV20 1YA	01862 871794	19
Currie, Gordon C.M. MA BD	1975	43 Deanburn Park, Linlithgow EH49 6HA	01506 842759	2
Davies, Gareth W. BA BD	1979	Pitadro House, Fordell Gardens, Dunfermline KY11 7EY	01383 417634	24
Dean, Roger A.F. LTh	1983	0/2, 20 Ballogie Road, Glasgow G44 4TA [E-mail: roger.dean4@btopenworld.com]		16
Dodman, R.	1983	8 Malthouse Drive, Belper DE56 1RU		
Duncan, G.A. BEd BD	1977	56 Daphne Drive, Maroelana, 0081 Pretoria, SA		
Dutton, David W. BA	1973	13 Acredales, Haddington EH41 4NT [E-mail: duttondw@gmail.com]	01620 825999	9
Finlay, Quintin BA BD	1975	Ivy Cottage, Greenlees Farm, Kelso TD5 8BT	(Mbl) 07901 981171	6
Flockhart, D. Ross OBE BA BD DUniv	1956	Longwood, Humbie EH36 5PN [E-mail: rossflock@btinternet.com]	01875 833208	3
Foggitt, Eric W. MA BSc BD	1991	Christiaan de Wet Straat 19/2, 1091 NG Amsterdam, The Netherlands [E-mail: ericleric3@btinternet.com]		1
Forrester, Duncan B. (Prof.) MA BD DPhil DD FRSE	1962	25 Kingsburgh Road, Edinburgh EH12 6DZ [E-mail: dbforrester@rosskeen.org.uk]	0131-337 5646	1
Gardner, Frank J. MA	1966	1 Levanne Place, Gourock PA16 1AX [E-mail: fjg@clyde-mail.co.uk]	01475 630187	14
Gow, Neil BSc MEd BD	1996	Hillhead Lodge, Portknockie, Buckie AB56 4PB [E-mail: n.gow334@btinternet.com]	01542 840625	35
Greig, James C.G. MA BD STM	1955	Block 2, Flat 2, Station Lofts, Strathblane, Glasgow G63 9BD [E-mail: james.greig12@btinternet.com]	01360 771915	16
Hamilton, David S.M. MA BD STM	1958	63 Pendreich Avenue, Bonnyrigg EH19 2EE [E-mail: dandmhamilton@gmail.com]	0131-654 2604	47
Homewood, I.M. MSc BD	1997	Ander Fließwiese 26, D-14052 Berlin, Germany [E-mail: maxhomewood@me.com]		48
Howie, William MA BD STM	1964	26 Morgan Road, Aberdeen AB16 5JY	01224 483669	31
Huie, David F. MA BD	1962	17 St Mary's Mead, Witney OX28 4EZ	01993 778310	48
Hurst, Frederick R. MA	1965	Flat 6, 21 Bulldale Place, Glasgow G14 0NE	0141-959 2604	40
Inglis, Donald B.C. MA MEd BD	1975	39 Thomson Drive, Bearsden, Glasgow G61 3PA	0141-942 1387	18
Logan, Robert J.V. MA BD	1962	Lindores, 1 Murray Place, Smithton, Inverness, IV2 7PX [E-mail: rjvlogan@btinternet.com]	01463 790226	
Lynn, Joyce (Mrs) MIPM BD	1995	Flat 8, 131 St Vincent Street, Broughty Ferry, Dundee DD5 2DA	01382 690556	29
Macaskill, Donald MA BD PhD	1994	4 Glendale Gardens, Randalstown, Co. Antrim BT41 3EJ [E-mail: paul.mcclenaghan@gmail.com]		16
McClenaghan, L. Paul BA	1973		02894 478545	34
McCreadie, David W.	1961	23 Willoughby Place, Callander PH17 8DG	01877 330785	23
Macdonald, Murdo C. MA BD	2002	36 Graham Court, Blackburn, Bathgate EH47 7BT [E-mail: murdocmacdonald@gmail.com]	(Mbl) 07714 016805	2
McDonald, William J.G. DD	1953	7 Blacket Place, Edinburgh EH9 1RN	0131-667 2100	1
Macfarlane, Alwyn J.C. MA	1951	Flat 12, Homeburn House, 177 Fenwick Road, Giffnock, Glasgow G46 6JD	0141-620 3235	1
Macfarlane, Thomas G. BSc PhD BD	1956	12 Elphinstone Court, Lochwinnoch Road, Kilmacolm PA13 4DW [E-mail: sandimac376@gmail.com]	01505 874962	14
McGill, Sandi (Ms) BD	2002			2
McGill, Thomas W.	1972	Flat 75, J M Barry House, George Street, Dumfries DG1 1EA		9
McKenzie, Mary O. (Miss)	1976	4 Dunellan Avenue, Moodiesburn, Glasgow G69 0GB	01236 870180	16
McKenzie, W.M.	1958	41 Kingholm Drive, Dumfries DG1 4SR		8

Name	Ord.	Address	Tel	No.
Mackie, John F. BD	1979	1A Halls Close, Weldon, Corby, Northants NN17 3HH		40
Mackinnon, Thomas J.R. LTh DipMin	1996	4 Flashadder, Arnisort, Portree, Isle of Skye IV51 9PT	01470 582377	39
McLean, John MA BD	1967	16 Eastside Drive, Westhill AB32 6QN	01224 747701	33
Mair, John BSc	1965	21 Kenilworth Avenue, Helensburgh G84 7JR	01436 671744	18
Miller, Irene B. (Mrs) MA BD	1984	5 Braeside Park, Aberfeldy PH15 2DT	01887 829396	27
Murray, Douglas R. MA BD	1965	32 Forth Park, Bridge of Allan, Stirling FK9 5NT [E-mail: d-smurray@supanet.com]	01786 831081	23
O'Leary, Thomas BD	1983	1 Carter's Place, Irvine KA12 0BU	01294 313274	11
Osbeck, John R. BD	1979	15 Deeside Crescent, Aberdeen AB15 7PT	01224 315595	31
Park, Christopher BSc BD	1977	65 Moubray Road, Dalgety Bay, Dunfermline KY11 9JP [E-mail: chrispark8649@hotmail.com]	01383 821111	24
Patterson, James BSc BD	2003	c/o 9 Oakview, Balmedie, Aberdeen AB23 8SR		1
Peacock, Heather M. BSc PhD BD	2009	9 Frankscroft, Peebles EH45 9DX [E-mail: hmpeacock@btinternet.com]		32
Petrie, Ian D. MA BD	1970	136 Colinton Mains Drive, Edinburgh EH13 9BN	0131-366 0520	29
Pryce, Stuart F.A.	1963	36 Forth Park, Bridge of Allan, Stirling FK9 5NT	01786 831026	23
Purves, John P.S. MBE BSc BD	1978	37 Hollywood, Largs KA30 8SR	01475 676180	48
Ramsay, Alan MA	1967	12 Riverside Grove, Lochyside, Fort William PH33 7RD	01397 702054	38
Reid, Janette G. (Miss) BD	1991	c/o Glasgow Presbytery Office, 260 Bath Street, Glasgow G2 4JP		16
Reid, William M. MA BD	1966	10 Rue Rossini, F-75009 Paris, France		48
Ritchie, Garden W.M.	1961	23 Croft Road, Kelso TD5 7EP	01573 224419	6
Robertson, John M. BSc BD	1975	8 North Green Drive, The Wilderness, Airth, Falkirk FK2 8RA	01324 832244	16
Robertson, Thomas G.M. LTh	1971	23 Muirend Avenue, Perth PH1 1JL	01738 624432	28
Roy, James A. MA BD	1965	'Beechwood', 7 Northview Terrace, Wormit, Newport-on-Tay DD6 8PP [E-mail: jim.roy@dundeepresbytery.org.uk]	01382 543578	29
Duncan Shaw of Chapelverna Bundesverdienstkreuz PhD ThDr Drhc	1951	4 Sydney Terrace, Edinburgh EH7 6SL		19
Smith, Ralph C.P. MA STM	1960	2A Waverley Road, Eskbank, Dalkeith EH22 3DJ [E-mail: rcpsmith@waitrose.com]	0131-663 1234	1
Spowart, Mary G. (Mrs) BD	1978	Aldersyde, St Abbs Road, Coldingham, Eyemouth TD14 5NR	01890 771697	26
Stone, W. Vernon MA BD	1949	36 Woodrow Court, Port Glasgow Road, Kilmacolm PA13 4QA [E-mail: stone@kilmacolm.fsnet.co.uk]	01505 872644	14
Sutcliffe, Clare B. BSc BD	2000	4 Dalmailing Avenue, Dreghorn, Irvine KA11 4HX		11
Taylor, David J. MA BD	1982	32 Croft an Righ, Inverkeithing KY11 1PF	01383 413227	24
Thomson, Alexander BSc BD MPhil PhD	1973	4 Munro Street, Dornoch IV25 3RA [E-mail: alexander.thomson6@btinternet.com]	01862 811650	40
Thomson, Gilbert L. BA	1965	3 Fortharfield, Freuchie, Cupar KY15 7JJ	01337 857431	25
Watson, James B. BSc	1968	3 Royal Terrace, Hutton, Berwick-upon-Tweed TD15 1TP [E-mail: jimwatson007@hotmail.com]	01289 386282	5
Webster, John G. BSc	1964	Plane Tree, King's Cross, Brodick, Isle of Arran KA27 8RG	01770 700747	16
Wedderburn, A.J.M. (Prof.) MA BA PhD	1975	Therese-Danner-Platz 3, D-80636 Munich, Germany [E-mail: ajmw42@gmx.de]	0049 89 1200 3726	
Weir, Mary K. BD PhD	1968	1249 Millar Road RRI, SITEH-46, BC V0N 1G0, Canada	001 604 947 0636	1

Westmarland, Colin A.	PO Box 5, Cospicua, CSPO1, Malta	00356 216 923552	1971	48
Wilkie, George D. OBE BL	2/37 Barnton Avenue West, Edinburgh EH4 6EB	0131-339 3973	1948	1
Wilkie, William E. LTh	32 Broomfield Park, Portlethen, Aberdeen AB12 4XT	01224 782052	1978	31
Wilson, M.	37 King's Avenue, Longniddry EH32 0QN		1988	

LIST F – HEALTH AND SOCIAL CARE CHAPLAINS (NHS)

LOTHIAN

Head of Service, Spiritual Care and Bereavement Alexander (Sandy) W. Young
[E-mail: sandy.young@nhslothian.scot.nhs.uk]

Lead Chaplain Caroline Applegath
[E-mail: carrie.applegath@nhslothian.scot.nhs.uk]

Spiritual Care Office: 0131-242 1990

The Royal Infirmary of Edinburgh
51 Little France Crescent, Edinburgh EH16 4SA (0131-536 1000)

Full details of chaplains and contacts in all hospitals: www.nhslothian.scot.nhs.uk > Services > Health Services A-Z > Spiritual Care

BORDERS

Rev. Anna Garvie [E-mail: annagarvie@borders.scot.nhs.uk]   Chaplaincy Centre, Borders General Hospital, Melrose TD6 9BS 01896 826564
Further information: www.nhsborders.scot.nhs.uk > Patients and Visitors > Our services > Chaplaincy Centre

DUMFRIES AND GALLOWAY

Spiritual Care Lead Rev. Dr Ewan R. Kelly   Room 3, Logan West, Crichton Hall, Dumfries DG1 4TG (Mbl) 07795 120965
[E-mail: ewankelly@nhs.net]   01387 246246 ext. 36601

Further information: www.nhsdg.scot.nhs.uk > Focus on > Search > Chaplaincy

AYRSHIRE AND ARRAN

Service Lead for Chaplaincy and Staff Care   Rev. Judith A. Huggett   Crosshouse Hospital, Kilmarnock KA2 0BE   01563 827301
[E-mail: judith.huggett@aaaht.scotnhs.uk]

Further information: www.nhsaaa.net > Services A-Z > Chaplaincy services

LANARKSHIRE

Head of Spiritual Care   Rev. Robert P. Devenny   Law House, Airdrie Road, Carluke ML8 5EP   01698 377637
[E-mail: bob.devenny@lanarkshire.scot.nhs.uk]

Further information: www.nhslanarkshire.org.uk > Our services A-Z > Palliative care > Palliative care support > Spiritual care

GREATER GLASGOW AND CLYDE

Head of Chaplaincy and Spiritual Care   Rev. Blair Robertson   Chaplaincy Centre, South Glasgow University Hospital,   0141-201 2156
1345 Govan Road, Glasgow G51 4TF
[E-mail: blair.robertson@ggc.scot.nhs.uk]

Further information: www.nhsggc.org.uk > Services > Spiritual Care

FORTH VALLEY

Head of Spiritual Care   Rev. Margery Collin   Forth Valley Royal Hospital, Larbert FK5 4WR   01324 566072
[E-mail: margery.collin@nhs.net]   (Mbl) 07824 460882

Further information: www.nhsforthvalley.com > Services > Spiritual Care

FIFE

Head of Spiritual Care   Mr Mark Evans DCS   Department of Spiritual Care, Queen Margaret Hospital,   01383 674136
Whitefield Road, Dunfermline KY12 0SU
[E-mail: mark.evans59@nhs.net]

Victoria Hospital, Kirkcaldy   Chaplain's Office   01592 648158
Queen Margaret Hospital, Dunfermline   Chaplain's Office   01383 674136
Community Chaplaincy Listening (Scotland):   Miss Lynda Wright DCS   [E-mail: lynda.wright1@nhs.net]   (Mbl) 07835 303395
National Coordinator

Further information: www.nhsfife.org > Your Health > Support Services > Spiritual Care

TAYSIDE

Head of Spiritual Care	Rev. Gillian Munro	The Spiritual Care Centre, Ninewells Hospital, Dundee DD1 9SY [E-mail: lynne.downie@nhs.net]	01382 423110

Further information: www.nhstayside.scot.nhs.uk > Your Health/Wellbeing > Our Services A-Z > Spiritual Care

GRAMPIAN

Head of Spiritual Care	Rev. Mark Rodgers	Chaplains' Office, Aberdeen Royal Infirmary, Foresterhill, Aberdeen AB25 2ZN [E-mail: mrodgers@nhs.net]	01224 553166

Further information: www.nhsgrampian.co.uk > Home > Local Services and Clinics > Spiritual Care

HIGHLAND

Lead Chaplain	Rev. Dr Derek Brown	Raigmore Hospital, Old Perth Road, Inverness IV2 3UJ [E-mail: derek.brown1@nhs.net]	01463 704463
Community Healthcare Chaplain (East Sutherland)	Rev. Mary Stobo	Druim-an-Sgairnich, Ardgay IV24 3BG	01863 766868

Further information: www.nhshighland.scot.nhs.uk > Services > All Services A-Z > NHS Chaplaincy

WESTERN ISLES HEALTH BOARD

Lead Chaplain	Rev T. K. Shadakshari	23D Benside, Newmarket, Stornoway, Isle of Lewis HS2 0DZ [E-mail: tk.shadakshari@nhs.net]	(Home) 01851 701727 (Office) 01851 704704 (Mbl) 07403 697138

NHS SCOTLAND

Programme Director for Health & Social Care Chaplaincy & Spiritual Care	Rev Sheila Mitchell	NHS Education for Scotland, 3rd Floor, 2 Central Quay, 89 Hydepark Street, Glasgow G3 8BW [E-mail: sheila.mitchell@nes.scot.nhs.uk]	0131-656 3372

LIST G – CHAPLAINS TO HM FORCES

The three columns give dates of ordination and commissioning, and branch where the chaplain is serving: Royal Navy, Army, Royal Air Force, Royal Naval Reserve, Army Reserve, Army Cadet Force, or where the person named is an Officiating Chaplain to the Military.

NAME	ORD	COM	BCH	ADDRESS
Abeledo, Benjamin J.A. BTh DipTh PTh	1991	1999	A	HQ 42 Infantry Brigade, Fulwood Barracks, Preston PR2 8AB
Anderson, David P. BSc BD	2002	2007	A	HQ 102 LOG Bde, Prince William of Gloucester Barracks, Grantham NG31 7TG
Begg, Richard MA BD	2008		ACF	Argyll and Sutherland Highlanders BN, ACF, Harfield House, Bonhill Road, Dumbarton G82 2DG
Berry, Geoff T. BD BSc	2009	2012	OCM	JSSU Cyprus, Mercury Barracks, Ayios Nikolaos, BFPO 59
Blackwood, Keith T. BD DipMin	1997		ACF	Shetland Independent Battery, ACF, TA Centre, Fort Charlotte, Lerwick, Shetland ZE1 0JN
Blakey, Stephen A. BSc BD	1977	1977	AR	6 Bn The Royal Regiment of Scotland, Walcheran Barracks, 122 Hotspur Street, Glasgow G20 8LQ
Blakey, Stephen A. BSc BD	1977	1977	ACF	Lothian & Borders Bn ACF, Drumshoreland House, Broxburn EH52 5PF
Bryson, Thomas M. BD	1977	1977	OCM	HQ 51 Infantry Brigade & 2 SCOTS, Glencorse Barracks, Penicuik EH26 0QH
Bryson, Thomas M. BD	1997		OCM	2 Bn The Highlanders, ACF, Cadet Training Centre, Rocksley Drive, Boddam, Peterhead AB42 3BA
Campbell, Karen K. BD MTh DMin	1997		AR	51 Infantry Brigade, Forthside, Stirling FK7 7RR
Cobain, Alan R. BD	2000		AR	Personnel Recovery Centre, Edinburgh
Connolly, Daniel BD DipTheol DipMin	1983		AR	71 Engineer Regiment, RAF Leuchars, Fife KY16 0JX; Scottish and North Irish Yeomanry, Redford Barracks, Colinton Road, Edinburgh EH13 0PP
Coulter, David G. QHC BA BD MDA PhD	1989	1994	A	Chaplain General, MoD Chaplains (Army), HQ Land Forces, 2nd Floor Zone 6, Ramillies Building, Marlborough Lines, Andover, Hants SP11 8HJ
Dalton, Mark BD DipMin RN	2002		RN	HM Naval Base Clyde, Faslane, Helensburgh G84 8HL
Davidson, Mark R. MA BD STM PhD RN	2005		RN	The Chaplaincy, 45 Commando RM, RM Condor, Arbroath DD11 3SP
Dicks, Shuna M. BSc BD	2010		ACF	2 Bn The Highlanders, ACF, Cadet Training Centre, Rocksley Drive, Boddam, Peterhead AB42 3BA
Duncan, John C. BD MPhil	1987	2001	A	3 Bn, The Royal Regiment of Scotland, Fort George, Ardersier, Inverness IV1 2TD
Frail, Nicola BLE MBA MDiv	2000	2012	A	32 Engineer Regiment, Marne Barracks, Catterick Garrison, DL10 7NP
Francis, James BD PhD	2002	2009	A	2 (Training) Regiment Army Air Corps, Middle Wallop, Stockbridge, SO20 8DY
Gardner, Neil N. MA BD RNR	1991		OCM	Edinburgh Universities Officers' Training Corps
Gardner, Neil N. MA BD RNR	1991	2015	RNR	Honorary Chaplain, Royal Navy
Goodison, Michael J. BSc BD	2013		A	Royal Scots Dragoon Guards, Leuchars Station, Leuchars KY16 0JX
Kellock, Chris N. MA BD	1998	2012	A	1 Bn The Royal Regiment of Fusiliers, Mooltan Barracks, Tidworth SP9 7SJ
Kennon, Stanley BA BD RN	1992	2000	RN	HMS *Raleigh*, Torpoint, Cornwall PL11 2PD
Kinsey, Louis BD DipMin TD	1991		AR	205 (Scottish) Field Hospital (V), Graham House, Whitefield Road, Glasgow G51 6JU
Lancaster, Craig MA BD	2004	2011	RAF	RAF Brize Norton, Carterton OX18 3LX

Name	Year	Cat.	Year	Posting
Logan, David MStJ BD MA FRSA	2009	ACF		Jersey Militia ACF, La Quesne TA Centre, Mount Bingham, Havre des Pas, St Helier, Jersey JE2 4EA
McCulloch, Alen J.R. MA BD	1990	ACF		Cornwall ACF, 7 Castle Canyke Road, Bodmin PL31 1DX
MacDonald, Roderick I.T. BD CertMin	1992	ACF		West Lowland Bn, ACF, Fusilier House, Seaforth Road, Ayr KA8 9HX
MacKay, Stewart A.	2009	A	2009	Infantry Training Battalion, Helles Barracks, Catterick Garrison, DL9 4HH
Mackenzie, Cameron BD	1997	ACF	2011	Lothian and Borders Bn, ACF, Drumshoreland House, Broxburn EH52 5PF
Mackenzie, Hector M.	2008	A	2008	HQ Military Corrective Training Centre, Berechurch Hall Camp, Berechurch Hall Road, Colchester CO2 9NU
Mackenzie, Seoras L. BD	1996	A	1998	39 Engr Regt (Air Support), Kinloss Barracks, Kinloss, Forres IV36 3XL
McLaren, William MA BD	1990	ACF		Angus and Dundee Bn, ACF, Barry Buddon, Carnoustie DD7 7RY
McLaren, William MA BD	1990	OCM		225 GS Med Regt (V), Oliver Barracks, Dalkeith Road, Dundee DD4 7DL
McLay, Neil BA BD	2006	A	2012	1 Bn Princess of Wales's Royal Regiment, Barker Barracks, Sennelager, Paderborn BFPO 22
MacLean, Marjory A. LLB BD PhD RNR	1991	RNR		HMS Scotia, MoD Caledonia, Hilton Road, Rosyth, Dunfermline KY11 2XH
MacLeod, Rory N. MA BD	1986	A	1992	21 Engineer Regt, Claro Barracks, Chatham Road, Ripon HG4 2RD
MacPherson, Duncan J. BSc BD	1993	A	2002	DACG ARTD (North), Infantry Training Centre, Vimy Barracks, Scotton Road, Catterick DL9 3PS
Mathieson, Angus R. MA BD	1988	OCM		Edinburgh Garrison & the Personnel Recovery Unit (PRU)
Milliken, Jamie BD	2005	RNR		HMS Dalriada, Govan, Glasgow G51 3JH
Munro, Sheila BD	1995	RAF	2003	RAF Leeming, Northallerton DL7 9NJ
Patterson, Philip BMus BD	1999	AR	2014	7 Bn Royal Regiment of Scotland, Queen's Barracks, 131 Dunkeld Road, Perth PH1 5BT
Prentice, Donald K. BSc BD	1989	OCM		205 (Scottish) Field Hospital (V), Graham House, Whitefield Road, Glasgow G51 6JU
Rankin, Lisa-Jane BD CPS	2003	OCM		2 Bn Royal Regiment of Scotland, Glencorse Barracks, Penicuik EH26 0QH
Rowe, Christopher J. BA BD	2008	AR	2008	32 (Scottish) Signal Regiment, 21 Jardine Street, Glasgow G20 6JU
Selemani, Ecilo LTh MTh	1993	ACF	2011	Glasgow and Lanark Bn, ACF, Gilbertfield Road, Cambuslang, Glasgow G72 8YP
Selemani, Ecilo LTh MTh	1993	OCM	2011	51 Infantry Brigade, Forthside, Stirling FK7 7RR
Shackleton, Scott J.S. QCVS BA RN BD PhD	1993	RN	2010	Chaplaincy Team Leader, Commando Training Centre, Royal Marines, Exmouth EX8 5AR
Stewart, Fraser M.C. BSc BD	1980	ACF		1 Bn The Highlanders, ACF, Gordonville Road, Inverness IV2 4SU
Stewart, Fraser M.C. BSc BD	1980	OCM		51 Infantry Brigade, Forthside, Stirling FK7 7RR
Taylor, Gayle J.A. MA BD	1999	OCM		3 Bn The Rifles, Redford Barracks, Colinton Road, Edinburgh EH13 0PP
Thom, David J. BD DipMin	1999	A	2015	1 Bn Scots Guards, Mons Barracks, Prince's Avenue, Aldershot GU11 2LF
van Sittert, Paul BA BD	1997	A	2011	4 Bn The Royal Regiment of Scotland, Bourton Barracks, Plumer Road, Catterick Garrison DL9 3AD
Warwick, Ivan C. MA BD TD	1980	ACF		1 Bn The Highlanders, ACF, Gordonville Road, Inverness IV2 4SU
Warwick, Ivan C. MA BD TD	1980	ACF		Orkney Independent Battery, ACF, Territorial Army Centre, Weyland Park, Kirkwall KW1 5LP
Warwick, Ivan C. MA BD TD	1980	OCM		Fort George and Cameron Barracks, Inverness
Wilson, Fiona A. BD	2008	ACF		West Lowland Battalion, ACF, Fusilier House, Seaforth Road, Ayr KA8 9HX
Wylie, Jonathan	2000	RAF	2014	Staff Chaplain PJHQ, Northwood HQ, Sandy Lane, Northwood, Middlesex HA6 3HP

LIST H – READERS

1. EDINBURGH

Brown, Ivan	4 St Cuthberts Court, Edinburgh EH13 0LG	0131-441 1245
	[E-mail: j.ivanb@btinternet.com]	(Mbl) 07730 702860
Christie, Gillian L. (Mrs)	32 Allan Park Road, Edinburgh EH14 1LJ	0131-443 4472
	[E-mail: mrsglchristie@aol.com]	(Mbl) 07914 883354
Davies, Ruth (Ms) (attached to Liberton)	4 Hawkhead Grove, Edinburgh EH16 6LS	0131-664 3608
	[E-mail: ruth@mdavies.me.uk]	
Farrant, Yvonne (Ms)	Flat 7, 14 Duddingston Mills, Edinburgh EH8 7NF	0131-661 0672
	[E-mail: yvonne.farrant@crossreach.org.uk]	(Mbl) 07747 766405
Farrell, William J.	50 Ulster Crescent, Edinburgh EH8 7JS	0131-661 1026
	[E-mail: w.farrell154@btinternet.com]	
Farrow, Edmund	14 Brunswick Terrace, Edinburgh EH7 5PG	0131-558 8210
	[E-mail: edmundfarrow@blueyonder.co.uk]	
Johnston, Alan	8/19 Constitution Street, Edinburgh EH6 7BT	0131-554 1326
	[E-mail: alanacj@cairnassoc.wanadoo.co.uk]	(Mbl) 07901 510819
Kerrigan, Herbert A. (Prof.) MA LLB QC	Airdene, 20 Edinburgh Road, Dalkeith EH22 1JY	0131-660 3007
	[E-mail: kerrigan@kerriganqc.com]	07725 953772
McKenzie, Janet (Mrs)	80C Colinton Road, Edinburgh EH14 1DD	0131-444 2054
	[E-mail: jintymck@talktalk.net]	
McPherson, Alistair	77 Bonaly Wester, Edinburgh EH13 0RQ	0131-478 5384
	[E-mail: amjhmcpherson@blueyonder.co.uk]	
Pearce, Martin	4 Corbiehill Avenue, Edinburgh EH4 5DR	0131-336 4864
	[E-mail: martin.j.pearce@blueyonder.co.uk]	07801 717222
Sherriffs, Irene (Mrs)	22/2 West Mill Bank, Edinburgh EH13 0QT	(Mbl) 0131-466 9530
	[E-mail: reenie.sherriffs@blueyonder.co.uk]	
Tew, Helen (Mrs)	318 Lanark Road, Edinburgh EH14 2LJ	0131-478 1268
	[E-mail: helentew9@gmail.com]	(Mbl) 07986 170802
Wyllie, Anne (Miss)	2F3, 46 Jordan Lane, Edinburgh EH10 4QX	0131-447 9035
	[E-mail: anne.wyllie@tiscali.co.uk]	

2. WEST LOTHIAN

Coyle, Charlotte (Mrs)	28 The Avenue, Whitburn EH47 0DA	01501 740687
	[E-mail: paulcharlotte@talktalk.net]	
Elliott, Sarah (Miss)	105 Seafield Rows, Seafield, Bathgate EH47 7AW	01506 654950
	[E-mail: sarah.elliott6@btopenworld.com]	
Galloway, Brenda (Dr)	Lochend, 58 St Ninians Road, Linlithgow EH49 7BN	01506 842028
	[E-mail: bhgallo@yahoo.co.uk]	
Holder, Louise (Mrs)	Am Batnach, Easter Breich, West Calder EH55 8PP	01506 873030
	[E-mail: louise.holden@btinternet.com]	

Middleton, Alex — 19 Cramond Place, Dalgety Bay KY11 9LS [E-mail: alex.middleton@btinternet.com] — 01383 820800

Orr, Elizabeth (Mrs) — 64a Marjoribanks Street, Bathgate EH48 1AL [E-mail: liz-orr@hotmail.co.uk] — 01506 653116

Paxton, James — 5 Main Street, Longridge, Bathgate EH47 8AE [E-mail: jim_paxton@btinternet.com] — 01501 772192

Salmon, Jeanie (Mrs) — 81 Croftfoot Drive, Fauldhouse, Bathgate EH47 9EH [E-mail: jeaniesalmon@aol.com] — (Work) 01501 772468 / 01501 828509

Scoular, Iain W. — 15 Bonnyside Road, Bonnybridge FK4 2AD [E-mail: iain@iwsconsultants.com] — 01324 812395 / (Mbl) 07717 131596

Wilkie, David — 53 Goschen Place, Broxburn EH52 5JH [E-mail: david-fmu_09@tiscali.co.uk] — 01506 854777

3. LOTHIAN

Evans, W. John IEng MIIE(Elec) — Waterlily Cottage, 10 Fenton Steading, North Berwick EH39 5AF [E-mail: jevans7is@hotmail.com] — 01620 842990

Hogg, David MA — 82 Eskhill, Penicuik EH26 8DQ [E-mail: hogg-d2@sky.com] — 01968 676350 / (Mbl) 07821 693946

Millan, Mary (Mrs) — 33 Polton Vale, Loanhead EH20 9DF [E-mail: marymillan@fsmail.net] — 0131-440 1624 / (Mbl) 07814 466104

Trevor, A. Hugh MA MTh — 29A Fidra Road, North Berwick EH39 4NE [E-mail: htrevor@talktalk.net] — 01620 894924

Yeoman, Edward T.N. FSAScot — 75 Newhailes Crescent, Musselburgh EH21 6EF [E-mail: edwardyeoman6@aol.com] — 0131-653 2291 / (Mbl) 07896 517666

4. MELROSE AND PEEBLES

Cashman, Margaret D. (Mrs) — 38 Abbotsford Road, Galashiels TD1 3HR [E-mail: mcashman@tiscali.co.uk] — 01896 752711

Selkirk, Frances (Mrs) — 2 The Glebe, Ashkirk, Selkirk TD7 4PJ [E-mail: f.selkirk@btinternet.com] — 01750 32204

5. DUNS

Landale, Alison (Mrs) — Green Hope Guest House, Ellemford, Duns TD11 3SG [E-mail: alison@greenhope.co.uk] — 01361 890242

Taylor, Christine (Mrs) — Rowardennan, Main Street, Gavinton, Duns TD11 3QT [E-mail: christine2751@btinternet.com] — 01361 882994

6. JEDBURGH

Findlay, Elizabeth (Mrs) — 2 Hendersons Court, Kelso TD5 7BG [E-mail: elizabeth@findlay8124.fsworld.co.uk] — 01573 226641

Knox, Dagmar (Mrs)
3 Stichill Road, Ednam, Kelso TD5 7QQ
[E-mail: dagmar.knox.riding@btinternet.com]
01573 224883

7. ANNANDALE AND ESKDALE

Boncey, David
Redbrae, Beattock, Moffat DG10 9RF
[E-mail: david.boncey613@btinternet.com]
01683 300613

Brown, Martin J.
Lochhouse Farm, Beattock, Moffat DG10 9SG
[E-mail: martin@lochhousefarm.com]
01683 300451

Brown, S. Jeffrey BA
Skara Brae, 8 Ballplay Road, Moffat DG10 9JU
[E-mail: sjbrown@btinternet.com]
01683 220475

Chisholm, Dennis A.G. MA BSc
Moss-side, Hightae, Lockerbie DG11 1JR
[E-mail: dchis@talktalk.net]
01387 811803

Dodds, Alan
Trinco, Battlehill, Annan DG12 6SN
[E-mail: alanandjen46@talktalk.net]
01461 201235

Jackson, Susan (Mrs)
48 Springbells Road, Annan DG12 6LQ
[E-mail: peter-jackson24@sky.com]
01461 204159

Morton, Andrew A. BSc
19 Sherwood Park, Lockerbie DG11 2DX
[E-mail: andrew.a.morton@btinternet.com]
[E-mail: andrew_morton@mac.com]
01576 203164

Saville, Hilda A. (Mrs)
32 Crosslaw Burn, Moffat DG10 9LP
[E-mail: saville.c@sky.com]
01683 222854

8. DUMFRIES AND KIRKCUDBRIGHT

Corson, Gwen (Mrs)
7 Sunnybrae, Borgue, Kirkcudbright DG6 4SJ
01557 870328

Matheson, David
44 Auchenkeld Avenue, Heathhall, Dumfries DG1 3QY

Ogilvie, D. Wilson MA FSAScot
Lingerwood, 2 Nelson Street, Dumfries DG2 9AY
01387 264267

Paterson, Ronald M. (Dr)
Mirkwood, Ringford, Castle Douglas DG7 2AL
[E-mail: mirkwoodtyke@aol.com]
01557 820202

Smith, Nicola (Mrs)
Brightwater Lodge, Kelton, Castle Douglas DG7 1SZ
[E-mail: nickysasmith@btinternet.com]
01556 680453

9. WIGTOWN AND STRANRAER

McQuistan, Robert
Old Schoolhouse, Carsluith, Newton Stewart DG8 7DT
[E-mail: mcquistan@mcquistan.plus.com]
01671 820327

Williams, Roy
120 Belmont Road, Stranraer DG9 7BG
[E-mail: roywilliams84@hotmail.com]
01776 705762

10. AYR

Anderson, James (Dr)
BVMS PhD DVM FRCPath FIBiol MRCVS
67 Henrietta Street, Girvan KA26 9AN
[E-mail: jc.anderson@tesco.net]
01465 710059
(Mbl) 07952 512720

Gowans, James — 2 Cochrane Avenue, Dundonald, Kilmarnock KA2 9EJ [E-mail: jim@luker42.freeserve.co.uk] — 01563 850904 (Mbl) 07985 916814

Jamieson, Ian A. — 2 Whinfield Avenue, Prestwick KA9 2BH [E-mail: ian@jamieson4189.freeserve.co.uk] — 01242 476898

Morrison, James — 27 Monkton Road, Prestwick KA9 1AP [E-mail: jim.morrison@talktalk.net] — 01292 479313 (Mbl) 07773 287852

Murphy, Ian — 56 Lamont Crescent, Netherthird, Cumnock KA18 3DU [E-mail: iann_cumnock@yahoo.co.uk] — 01290 423675

Riome, Elizabeth (Mrs) — Monkwood Mains, Minishant, Maybole KA19 8EY [E-mail: aj.riome@btinternet.com] — 01292 443440

Stewart, Christine (Mrs) — 52 Kilnford Drive, Dundonald KA2 9ET [E-mail: christistewart@btinternet.com] — 01563 850486

11. IRVINE AND KILMARNOCK

Bircham, James F. — 8 Holmlea Place, Kilmarnock KA1 1UU [E-mail:james.bircham@sky.com] — 01563 532287

Cooper, Fraser — 5 Balgray Way, Irvine KA11 1RP [E-mail: frasercooper@wightcablenorth.net] — 01294 211235

Crosbie, Shona (Mrs) — 4 Campbell Street, Darvel KA17 0DA [E-mail: fawltytowersdarvel@yahoo.co.uk] — 01560 322229

Dempster, Ann (Mrs) — 20 Graham Place, Kilmarnock KA3 7JN [E-mail: ademp99320@aol.com] — 01563 529361 (Work) 01563 534080 (Mbl) 07729 152945

Gillespie, Janice (Miss) — 12 Jeffrey Street, Kilmarnock KA1 4EB [E-mail: janice.gillespie@tiscali.co.uk] — 01563 540009

Hamilton, Margaret A. (Mrs) — 59 South Hamilton Street, Kilmarnock KA1 2DT [E-mail: tomhnltn@sky.com] — 01563 534431

Jamieson, John H. BSc DEP AFBPSS — 22 Moorfield Avenue, Kilmarnock KA1 1TS [E-mail: johnhjamieson@tiscali.co.uk] — 01563 534065

McGeever, Gerard — 23 Kinloch Avenue, Stewarton, Kilmarnock KA3 3HQ [E-mail: gerard@gmcgeever.freeserve.co.uk] — 01560 484331 (Work) 0141-847 5717

MacLean, Donald — 1 Four Acres Drive, Kilmaurs, Kilmarnock KA3 2ND [E-mail: donannmac@yahoo.co.uk] — 01563 538475

Mills, Catherine (Mrs) — 59 Crossdene Road, Crosshouse, Kilmarnock KA2 0IU [E-mail: cfmills5lib@hotmail.com] — 01563 535305

Raleigh, Gavin — 21 Landsborough Drive, Kilmarnock KA3 1RY [E-mail: gavin.raleigh@lineone.net] — 01563 539377

Robertson, William — 1 Archers Avenue, Irvine KA11 2GB [E-mail: willie.robert@yahoo.co.uk] — 01294 203577

Whitelaw, David — 9 Kirkhill, Kilwinning KA13 6NB [E-mail: whitelawfam@talktalk.net] — 01294 551695

12. ARDROSSAN

Barclay, Elizabeth (Mrs)
2 Jacks Road, Saltcoats KA21 5NT
[E-mail: mfiz98@dsl.pipex.com] — 01294 471855

Clarke, Elizabeth (Mrs)
Swallowbrae, Torbeg, Isle of Arran KA27 8HE
[E-mail: lizahclarke@gmail.com] — 01770 860219, (Mbl) 07780 574367

Currie, Archie BD
55 Central Avenue, Kilbirnie KA25 6JP
[E-mail: archiecurrie@yahoo.co.uk] — 01505 681474, (Mbl) 07881 452115

Hunter, Jean C.Q. (Mrs) BD
Church of Scotland Manse, Shiskine, Isle of Arran KA27 3EP
[E-mail: j.hunter744@btinternet.com] — 01770 860380

McCool, Robert
17 McGregor Avenue, Stevenston KA20 4BA — 01294 466548

Mackay, Brenda H. (Mrs)
19 Eglinton Square, Ardrossan KA22 8LN
[E-mail: bremac82@aol.com] — 01294 464491

Macleod, Sharon (Mrs)
Creag Dhubh, Golf Course Road, Whiting Bay, Isle of Arran KA27 8QT
[E-mail: macleodsharon@hotmail.com] — 01770 700353

Nimmo, Margaret (Mrs)
12 Muirfield Place, Kilwinning KA13 6NL
[E-mail: margtmcmn@aol.com] — 01294 553718, 01292 220336

Ross, Magnus BA MEd
39 Beachway, Largs KA30 8QH
[E-mail: m.b.ross@btinternet.com] — (Work) 01475 689572

13. LANARK

Grant, Alan
25 Moss-side Avenue, Carluke ML8 5UG
[E-mail: amgrant25@aol.com] — 01555 771419

Love, William
30 Barmore Avenue, Carluke ML8 4PE
[E-mail: janbill30@tiscali.co.uk] — 01555 751243

14. GREENOCK AND PAISLEY

Allan, Douglas

Banks, Russell
18 Aboyne Drive, Paisley PA2 7SJ
[E-mail: margaret.banks2@ntlworld.com] — 0141-884 6925

Bird, Mary Jane

Boag, Jennifer (Miss)
11 Madeira Street, Greenock PA16 7UJ
[E-mail: jenniferboag@hotmail.com] — 01475 720125

Campbell, Tom BA DipCPC
3 Grahamston Place, Paisley PA2 7BY
[E-mail: tomcam38@googlemail.com] — 0141-840 2273

Davey, Charles L.
16 Divert Road, Gourock PA19 1DT
[E-mail: charles.davey@talktalk.net] — 01475 631544

Glenny, John C.
49 Cloch Road, Gourock PA19 1AT
[E-mail: jacklizg@aol.com] — 01475 636415

Hood, Eleanor (Mrs)
12 Clochoderick Avenue, Kilbarchan, Johnstone PA10 2AY
[E-mail: eleanor.hood.kilbarchan@ntlworld.com] — 01505 704208

MacDonald, Christine (Ms)
33 Collier Street, Johnstone PA5 8AG
[E-mail: christine.macdonald10@ntlworld.com] — 01505 355779

Name	Address	Telephone
McFarlan, Elizabeth (Miss)	20 Fauldswood Crescent, Paisley PA2 9PA [E-mail: elizabeth.mcfarlan@ntlworld.com]	01505 358411
McHugh, Jack	'Earlshaugh', Earl Place, Bridge of Weir PA11 3HA [E-mail: jackmchugh@tiscali.co.uk]	01505 612789
Marshall, Leon M.	'Glenisla', Gryffe Road, Kilmacolm PA13 4BA [E-mail: lm@stevenson-kyles.co.uk]	01505 872417
Maxwell, Sandra A. (Mrs) BD	2 Grants Avenue, Paisley PA2 6AZ [E-mail: sandra1.maxwell@virgin.net]	0141-884 3710
Munro, Irene (Mrs)	80 Bardrainney Avenue, Port Glasgow PA14 6HA [E-mail: irenemunro906@hotmail.com]	01475 701213
Orry, Geoff	'Rhu Eilan', 4 Seaforth Crescent, Barrhead, Glasgow G78 1PL [E-mail: geoff.orry@googlemail.com]	0141-881 9748

16. GLASGOW

Name	Address	Telephone
Birchall, Edwin		
Bremner, David	Greenhill Lodge, 1 Old Humbie Road, Glasgow G77 5DF [E-mail: david.bremner@tiscali.co.uk]	0141-639 1742
Campbell, Jack T. BD BEd	40 Kenmure Avenue, Bishopbriggs, Glasgow G64 2DE [E-mail: jack.campbell@ntlworld.com]	0141-563 5837
Dickson, Hector M.K.	'Gwito', 61 Whitton Drive, Giffnock, Glasgow G46 6EF [E-mail: hectordickson@hotmail.com]	0141-637 0080
Fullarton, Andrew		0141-883 9518
Grant, George	8 Erskine Street, Stirling FK7 0QN [E-mail: georgegrant@gmail.com]	01786 609594 07921 168057 (Mbl)
Grieve, Leslie	23 Hertford Avenue, Glasgow G12 0LG [E-mail: leslie.grieve@gmail.com]	0141-576 1376
Horner, David J.	20 Ledi Road, Glasgow G43 2AJ [E-mail: djhorner@btinternet.com]	0141-637 7369
Hunt, Roland BSc PhD CertEd	4 Flora Gardens, Bishopbriggs, Glasgow G64 1DS [E-mail: roland.hunt@ntlworld.com]	0141-563 3257 0141-563 3257 (Evenings and weekends)
Joansson, Tordur	1/2, 18 Eglinton Court, Glasgow G5 9NE [E-mail: to41jo@yahoo.co.uk]	0141-429 6733
Kilpatrick, Mrs Joan	39 Brent Road, Regent's Park, Glasgow G46 8JG [E-mail: je-kilpatrick@sky.com]	0141-621 1809
McChlery, Stuart	62 Grenville Drive, Cambuslang, Glasgow G72 8DP [E-mail: s.mcchlery@gcu.ac.uk]	0141-643 9730
McColl, John	2FL, 53 Aberfoyle Street, Glasgow G31 3RP [E-mail: solfolly11@gmail.com]	0141-554 9881 07757 303195 (Mbl)
McFarlane, Robert	25 Avenel Road, Glasgow G13 2PB [E-mail: robertmcfrln@yahoo.co.uk]	0141-954 5540
McInally, Gordon	10 Melville Gardens, Bishopbriggs, Glasgow G64 3DF [E-mail: gmcinally@sky.com]	0141-563 2685

Mackenzie, Norman — Flat 3/2, 41 Kilmailing Road, Glasgow G44 5UH [E-mail: mackenzie799@btinternet.com] — (Mbl) 07780 733710

MacLeod, John — 2 Shuna Place, Newton Mearns, Glasgow G77 6TN [E-mail: jmacleod2@sky.com] — 0141-639 6862

Millar, Kathleen (Mrs) — 9 Glenbank Court, Thornliebank, Glasgow G46 7EJ [E-mail: kathleen.millar@tesco.net] — 0141-638 6250 / (Mbl) 07793 203045

Montgomery, Hamish — 13 Avon Avenue, Bearsden, Glasgow G61 2PS — 0141-942 3640

Nairne, Elizabeth — 229 Southbrae Drive, Glasgow G13 1TT — 0141-959 5066

Nicolson, John — 2 Lindsaybeg Court, Chryston, Glasgow G69 9DD [E-mail: john.c.nicolson@btinternet.com] — 0141-779 2447

Phillips, John B. — 2/3, 30 Handel Place, Glasgow G5 0TP [E-mail: johnphillips@fish.co.uk] — 0141-429 7716

Robertson, Adam — 423 Amulree Street, Glasgow G32 7SS — 0141-573 6662

Roy, Mrs Shona — 81 Busby Road, Clarkston, Glasgow G76 8BD [E-mail: theroyfamily@yahoo.co.uk] — 0141-644 3713

Smith, Ann — 52 Robslee Road, Thornliebank, Glasgow G46 7BX — 0141-621 0638

Stead, Mrs Mary — 9A Carrick Drive, Mount Vernon, Glasgow G32 0RW [E-mail: maystead@hotmail.co.uk] — 0141-764 1016

Stewart, James — 45 Airthrey Avenue, Glasgow G14 9LY [E-mail: jmstewart325@btinternet.com] — 0141-959 5814

Tindall, Margaret (Mrs) — 23 Ashcroft Avenue, Lennoxtown, Glasgow G65 7EN [E-mail: margarettindall@aol.com] — 01360 310911

Wilson, George A. — 46 Maxwell Drive, Garrowhill, Baillieston, Glasgow G69 6LS [E-mail: healthandsafety@talk21.com] — 0141-771 3862

17. HAMILTON

Allan, Angus J. — Blackburn Mill, Chapelton, Strathaven ML10 6RR [E-mail: angus.allan@hotmail.com] — 01357 528548

Beattie, Richard — 4 Bent Road, Hamilton ML3 6QB [E-mail: richardbeattie1958@hotmail.com] — 01698 420086

Bell, Sheena — 2 Langdale, East Kilbride, Glasgow G74 4RP [E-mail: belljsheena@hotmail.co.uk] — 01355 248217

Chirnside, Peter — 141 Kyle Park Drive, Uddingston, Glasgow G71 7DB — 01698 813769

Codona, Joy (Mrs) — Dykehead Farm, 300 Dykehead Road, Airdrie ML6 7SR [E-mail: jcodona772@btinternet.com] — 01236 767063 / (Mbl) 07810 770609

Hastings, William Paul — 186 Glen More, East Kilbride, Glasgow G74 2AN [E-mail: wphastings@hotmail.co.uk] — 01355 521228

Hislop, Eric — 1 Castlegait, Strathaven ML10 6FF [E-mail: eric.hislop@tiscali.co.uk] — 01357 520003

Jardine, Lynette — 32 Powburn Crescent, Uddingston, Glasgow G71 7SS [E-mail: lpjardine@blueyonder.co.uk] — 01698 812404

Keir, Dickson — 46 Brackenhill Drive, Hamilton ML3 8AY — 01698 457351

McCleary, Isaac
[E-mail: dickson.keir@btinternet.com]
719 Coatbridge Road, Baillieston, Glasgow G69 7PH — 01236 421073

Preston, J. Steven
24 Glen Prosen, East Kilbride, Glasgow G74 3TA — 01355 237359
[E-mail: steven.preston1@btinternet.com]

Robertson, Rowan
68 Townhead Road, Coatbridge ML5 2HU — 01236 425703

Stevenson, Thomas
34 Castle Wynd, Quarter, Hamilton ML3 7XD — 01698 282263

White, Ian T.
21 Muirhead, Stonehouse, Larkhall ML9 3HG — 01698 792772
[E-mail: iantwhite@aol.com]

18. DUMBARTON

Foster, Peter
Flat 3 Templeton, 51 John Street, Helensburgh G84 8XN — 01436 678226
[E-mail: peterfostera39@btinternet.com]

Galbraith, Iain B. MA MPhil MTh ThD FTCL
Beechwood, Overton Road, Alexandria G83 0LJ — 01389 753563

Giles, Donald (Dr)
Levern House, Stuckenduff, Shandon, Helensburgh G84 8NW — 01436 820565
[E-mail: don.giles@btopenworld.com]

Harold, Sandy
The Laurels, Risk Street, Clydebank G81 3LW — 0141-952 3673
[E-mail: harold996@btinternet.com]

Hart, R.J.M. BSc
7 Kidston Drive, Helensburgh G84 8QA — 01436 672039
[E-mail: rjm7k@yahoo.com]

Morgan, Richard
Annandale, School Road, Rhu, Helensburgh G84 8RS — 01436 821269
[E-mail: themorgans@hotmail.co.uk]

Rettie, Sara (Mrs)
86 Dennistoun Crescent, Helensburgh G84 7JF — 01436 677984
[E-mail: sarajayne.rettie@btinternet.com]

19. ARGYLL

Alexander, John
11 Cullipool Village, Isle of Luing, Oban PA34 4UB — 01852 314242
[E-mail: j.alexander42@btinternet.com]

Binner, Aileen (Mrs)
'Ailand', North Connel, Oban PA37 1QX — 01631 710264
[E-mail: binners@ailand.plus.com]

Logue, David
3 Braeface, Tayvallich, Lochgilphead PA31 8PN — 01546 870647
[E-mail: david@loguenet.co.uk]

MacKellar, Janet BSc
Laurel Bank, 23 George Street, Dunoon PA23 8JT — 01369 705549
[E-mail: jkmackellar@aol.com]

McLelan, James A.
West Drimvore, Lochgilphead PA31 8SU — 01546 606403
[E-mail: james.mclellan8@btinternet.com]

Mills, Peter
Northton, Ganavan, Oban PA34 5TU
[E-mail: Pmillspij@aol.com]

Morrison, John L.
Tigh na Barnashaig, Tayvallich, Lochgilphead PA31 8PN — 01546 870637
[E-mail: jolomo@thejolomostudio.com]

Ramsay, Mathew M.
Portnastorm, Carradale, Campbeltown PA28 6SB — 01583 431381
[E-mail: portnastorm@tiscali.co.uk]

Sinclair, Margaret (Mrs)
2 Quarry Place, Furnace, Inveraray PA32 8XW
[E-mail: margaret_sinclair@btinternet.com]
01499 500633

Stather, Angela (Mrs)
9 Gartness Cottages, Ballygrant, Isle of Islay PA45 7QN
[E-mail: angel.stather@virgin.net]
01496 840527

Thornhill, Christopher R.
4 Ardfern Cottages, Ardfern, Lochgilphead PA31 9QN
[E-mail: c.thornhill@btinternet.com]
01852 500674

Waddell, Martin
2 Kilbrandon Cottages, Balvicar, Isle of Seil, Oban PA34 4RA
[E-mail: waddell715@btinternet.com]
01852 300395

Zielinski, Jennifer C. (Mrs)
26 Cromwell Street, Dunoon PA23 7AX
[E-mail: jczyefo@aol.com]
01369 706136

22. FALKIRK

Duncan, Lorna M. (Mrs) BA
Richmond, 28 Solway Drive, Head of Muir, Denny FK6 5NS
[E-mail: ell.dee@blueyonder.co.uk]
01324 813020

Mathers, Sandra (Mrs)
10 Ercall Road, Brightons, Falkirk FK2 0RS
[E-mail: alexena@btinternet.com]
01324 872253

Stewart, Arthur MA
51 Bonnymuir Crescent, Bonnybridge FK4 1GD
[E-mail: arthur.stewart1@btinternet.com]
01324 812667

Struthers, Ivar B.
7 McVean Place, Bonnybridge FK4 1QZ
[E-mail: ivar.struthers@btinternet.com]
01324 841145
(Mbl) 07921 778208

23. STIRLING

Durie, Alastair (Dr)
25 Forth Place, Stirling FK8 1UD
[E-mail: acdurie@btinternet.com]
01786 451029

Grier, Hunter
17 Station Road, Bannockburn, Stirling FK7 8LG
[E-mail: hunter@xaltmail.com]
01786 815192

Tilly, Patricia (Mrs)
25 Meiklejohn Street, Stirling FK9 5HQ
[E-mail: Trishatilly@aol.com]
01786 446401
(Mbl) 07428 559554

Weir, Andrew (Dr)
16 The Oaks, Killearn, Glasgow G63 9SF
[E-mail: andrewweir@btinternet.com]
01360 550779
(Mbl) 07534 506075

24. DUNFERMLINE

Brown, Gordon
Nowell, Fossoway, Kinross KY13 0UW
[E-mail: brown.nowell@hotmail.co.uk]
01577 840248

Conway, Bernard
4 Centre Street, Kelty KY4 0EQ
01383 830442

Grant, Allan
6 Normandy Place, Rosyth KY11 2HJ
[E-mail: allan75@btinternet.com]
01383 428760

McCafferty, Joyce (Mrs)
53 Foulford Street, Cowdenbeath KY4 9AS
01383 515775

McDonald, Elizabeth (Mrs)
Parleyhill, Culross, Dunfermline KY12 8JD
01383 880231

Meiklejohn, Barry
40 Lilac Grove, Dunfermline KY11 8AP
[E-mail: barry.meiklejohn@btinternet.com]
01383 731550

Mitchell, Ian G. QC — 17 Carlingnose Point, North Queensferry, Inverkeithing KY11 1ER
[E-mail: jgmitchell@easynet.co.uk] — 01383 416240

25. KIRKCALDY

Biernat, Ian — 2 Formonthills Road, Glenrothes KY6 3EF
[E-mail: ian.biernat@btinternet.com] — 01592 655565

26. ST ANDREWS

Elder, Morag Anne (Ms) — 5 Provost Road, Tayport DD6 9JE
[E-mail: benuardin@tiscali.co.uk] — 01382 552218

King, C.M. (Mrs) — 8 Bankwell Road, Anstruther KY10 3DA — 01333 310017

Porteous, Brian — Kirkdene, Westfield Road, Cupar KY15 5DS
[E-mail: brian@porteousleisure.co.uk] — 01334 653561

Smith, Elspeth (Mrs) — Whinstead, Dalgairn, Cupar KY15 4PH
[E-mail: elspeth.smith@btopenworld.com] — 01334 653269

27. DUNKELD AND MEIGLE

Howat, David — Lilybank Cottage, Newton Street, Blairgowrie PH10 6HZ
[E-mail: david@thehowats.net] — 01250 874715

Steele, Grace (Ms) — 12A Farragon Drive, Aberfeldy PH15 2BQ
[E-mail: gmfsteele@tiscali.co.uk] — 01887 820025

Theaker, Phillip — 5 Altamount Road, Blairgowrie PH10 6QL
[E-mail: ptheaker@talktalk.net] — 01250 871162

28. PERTH

Archibald, Michael — Wychwood, Culdeesland Road, Methven, Perth PH1 3QE
[E-mail: michael.archibald@gmail.com] — 01738 840995

Begg, James — 8 Park Village, Turretbank Road, Crieff PH7 4JN
[E-mail: Bjimmy37@aol.com] — 01764 655907

Benneworth, Michael — 7 Hamilton Place, Perth PH1 1BB
[E-mail: mbenneworth@hotmail.com] — 01738 628093

Davidson, Andrew — 95 Needless Road, Perth PH2 0LD
[E-mail: a.r.davidson.91@cantab.net] — 01738 620839

Laing, John — 10 Graybank Road, Perth PH2 0GZ
[E-mail: johnandmarylaing@hotmail.co.uk] — 01738 623888

Ogilvie, Brian — 67 Whitecraigs, Kinnesswood, Kinross KY13 9JN
[E-mail: brianj.ogilvie1@btopenworld.com] — 01592 840823
(Mbl) 07815 759864

Stewart, Anne — Ballcraine, Murthly Road, Stanley, Perth PH1 4PN
[E-mail: anne.stewart13@btinternet.com] — 01738 828637

Yellowlees, Deirdre (Mrs) — Ringmill House, Gannochy Farm, Perth PH2 7JH
[E-mail: d.yellowlees@btinternet.com] — 01738 633773
(Mbl) 07920 805399

29. DUNDEE

Brown, Isobel (Mrs)
10 School Wynd, Muirhead, Dundee DD2 5LW
[E-mail: isobel73@btinternet.com]
01382 580545

Brown, Janet (Miss)
G2, 6 Baxter Park Terrace, Dundee DD4 6NL
[E-mail: j.herries.brown@blueyonder.co.uk]
01382 453066

Sharp, Gordon
6 Kelso Street, Dundee DD2 1SJ
01382 643002
01382 630355

Xenophontos-Hellen, Tim
Aspro Spiti, 23 Ancrum Drive, Dundee DD2 2JG
[E-mail: tim.xsf@btinternet.com]
(Work) 01382 567756

30. ANGUS

Beedie, Alexander W.
62 Newton Crescent, Arbroath DD11 3JZ
[E-mail: bill.beedie@hotmail.co.uk]
01241 875001

Davidson, Peter I.
24 Kinnaird Place, Brechin DD9 7HF
[E-mail: mail@idavidson.co.uk]

Gray, Linda (Mrs)
8 Inchgarth Street, Forfar DD8 3LY
[E-mail: lindamgray@sky.com]
01307 464039

Nicoll, Douglas
16 New Road, Forfar DD8 2AE
01307 463264

31. ABERDEEN

Cooper, Gordon
4 Springfield Place, Aberdeen AB15 7SF
[E-mail: ga_cooper@hotmail.co.uk]
01224 316667

Gray, Peter (Prof.)
165 Countesswells Road, Aberdeen AB15 7RA
[E-mail: pmdgray165@btinternet.com]
01224 318172

32. KINCARDINE AND DEESIDE

Bell, Robert
27 Mearns Drive, Stonehaven AB39 2DZ
[E-mail: r.bell282@btinternet.com]
01569 767173
(Mbl) 07733 014826

Broere, Teresa (Mrs)
3 Balnastraid Cottages, Dinnet, Aboyne AB34 5NE
[E-mail: broere@btinternet.com]
01339 880058

Coles, Stephen
43 Mearns Walk, Laurencekirk AB30 1FA
[E-mail: steve@sbcco.com]
01561 378400

McCafferty, W. John
Lynwood, Cammachmore, Stonehaven AB39 3NR
[E-mail: wjmccafferty@yahoo.co.uk]
01569 730281

McLuckie, John
7 Monaltrie Close, Ballater AB35 5PT
[E-mail: johnemcluckie@btinternet.com]
01339 755489

Middleton, Robin B. (Capt.)
7 St Ternan's Road, Newtonhill, Stonehaven AB39 3PF
[E-mail: robbiemiddleton7@hotmail.co.uk]
01569 730852

Platt, David
2 St Michael's Road, Newtonhill, Stonehaven AB39 3RW
[E-mail: daveplatt01@btinternet.com]
01569 730465

Simpson, Elizabeth (Mrs)
Connemara, 33 Golf Road, Ballater AB35 5RS
[E-mail: connemara33@yahoo.com]
01339 755597

33. GORDON

Bichard, Susanna (Mrs) — Beechlee, Haddo Lane, Tarves, Ellon AB41 7JZ
[E-mail: smbichard@aol.com]
01651 851345

Doak, Alan B. — 17 Chievres Place, Ellon AB41 9WH
[E-mail: alanbdoak@aol.com]
01358 721819

Findlay, Patricia (Mrs) — Douglas View, Tullynessle, Alford AB33 8QR
[E-mail: p.a.findlay@btopenworld.com]
01975 562379

Mitchell, Jean (Mrs) — 6 Cowgate, Oldmeldrum, Inverurie AB51 0EN
[E-mail: j.g.mitchell@btinternet.com]
01651 872745

Robb, Margaret (Mrs) — Chrislouan, Keithhall, Inverurie AB51 0LN
[E-mail: Robbminister1@aol.com]
01651 882310

Robertson, James Y. MA — 1 Nicol Road, Kintore, Inverurie AB51 0QA
[E-mail: j.robertson833@btinternet.com]
01467 633001

34. BUCHAN

Armitage, Rosaline (Mrs) — Whitecairn, Blackhills, Peterhead AB42 3LR
[E-mail: r.r.armitage@btinternet.com]
01779 477267

Barker, Tim — South Silverford Croft, Longmanhill, Banff AB45 3SB
[E-mail: tbarker05@aol.com]
01261 851839

Brown, Lillian (Mrs) — 45 Main Street, Aberchirder, Huntly AB54 7ST
01466 780330

Forsyth, Alicia (Mrs) — Rothie Inn Farm, Forgue Road, Rothienorman, Inverurie AB51 8YH
[E-mail: a.forsyth@btinternet.com]
01651 821359

Givan, James — Zimra, Longmanhill, Banff AB45 3RP
[E-mail: jim.givan@btinternet.com]
01261 833318
(Mbl) 07753 458664

Grant, Margaret (Mrs) — 22 Elphin Street, New Aberdour, Fraserburgh AB43 6LH
[E-mail: margaret@wilmar.demon.co.uk]
01346 561341

Higgins, Scott — St Ninian's, Manse Terrace, Turriff AB53 4BA
[E-mail: mhairiandscott@btinternet.com]
01888 569103

Lumsden, Vera (Mrs) — 8 Queen's Crescent, Portsoy, Banff AB45 2PX
[E-mail: ivsd@lumsden77.freeserve.co.uk]
01261 842712

McColl, John — East Cairmchina, Lonmay, Fraserburgh AB43 8RH
[E-mail: solfolly11@gmail.com]
01346 532558
(Mbl) 07757 303195

MacLeod, Ali (Ms) — 11 Pitfour Crescent, Fetterangus, Peterhead AB42 4EL
[E-mail: aliow1@hotmail.com]
01771 622992
(Mbl) 07821 670705

Macnee, Anthea (Mrs) — Wardend Cottage, Alvah, Banff AB45 3TR
[E-mail: macneeiain4@googlemail.com]
01261 815647

Mair, Dorothy L.T. (Miss) — Flat F, 15 The Quay, Newburgh, Ellon AB41 6DA
[E-mail: dorothymair2@aol.com]
01358 788832
(Mbl) 07505 051305

Noble, John M. — 44 Henderson Park, Peterhead AB42 2WR
[E-mail: john_m_noble@hotmail.co.uk]
01779 472522

Ogston, Norman — Rowandale, 6 Rectory Road, Turriff AB53 4SU
[E-mail: norman.ogston@gmail.com]
01888 560342

Simpson, Andrew C.
10 Wood Street, Banff AB45 1JX
[E-mail: andy.louise1@btinternet.com]
01261 812538

Smith, Ian M.G.
2 Hill Street, Cruden Bay, Peterhead AB42 0HF
01779 812698

Sneddon, Richard
100 West Road, Peterhead AB42 2AQ
[E-mail: richard.sneddon@btinternet.com]
01779 480803

Taylor, Elaine (Mrs)
101 Cairnrodlie, Peterhead AB42 2AY
[E-mail: elaine.taylor60@btinternet.com]
01779 472978

35. MORAY

Forbes, Jean (Mrs)
Greenmoss, Drybridge, Buckie AB56 2JB
[E-mail: dancingfeet@tinyworld.co.uk]
01542 831646
(Mbl) 07974 760337

36. ABERNETHY

Bardgett, Alison (Mrs)
Tigh an Iasgair, Street of Kincardine, Boat of Garten PH24 3BY
[E-mail: tigh@bardgett.plus.com]
01479 831751

37. INVERNESS

Appleby, Jonathan
91 Cradlehall Park, Inverness IV2 5DB
[E-mail: jon.wyvis@gmail.com]
01463 791470

Cazaly, Leonard
9 Moray Park Gardens, Culloden, Inverness IV2 7FY
[E-mail: len_cazaly@lineone.net]
01463 794469

Cook, Arnett D.
66 Millerton Avenue, Inverness IV3 8RY
[E-mail: arnett.cook@btinternet.com]
01463 224795

Dennis, Barry
50 Holm Park, Inverness IV2 4XU
[E-mail: barry.dennis@tiscali.co.uk]
01463 225883
(Work) 01463 663448

Innes, Derek
Allanswell, Cawdor Road, Auldearn, Nairn IV12 5TQ
[E-mail: dereklinnes@btinternet.com]

MacInnes, Ailsa (Mrs)
Kilmartin, 17 Southside Road, Inverness IV2 3BG
[E-mail: ailsa.macinnes@btopenworld.com]
01463 230321
(Mbl) 07704 485055

Robertson, Hendry
Park House, 51 Glenurquhart Road, Inverness IV3 5PB
[E-mail: hendry.robertson@connectfree.co.uk]
01463 231858
(Mbl) 07929 766102

Robertson, Stewart J.H.
21 Towerhill Drive, Cradlehall, Inverness IV2 5FD
01463 793144

Roden, Vivian (Mrs)
15 Old Mill Road, Tomatin, Inverness IV13 7YW
[E-mail: vroden@btinternet.com]
01808 511355
(Mbl) 07887 704915

Todd, Iain
9 Leanach Gardens, Inverness IV2 5DD
[E-mail: itoddyo@aol.com]
01463 791161

38. LOCHABER

Chalkley, Andrew BSc
41 Hillside Road, Campbeltown PA28 6NE
[E-mail: andrewjoan@googlemail.com]

Ogston, Jean (Mrs) — Church of Scotland Manse, Annie's Brae, Mallaig PH41 4RG [E-mail: jeanogston@googlemail.com] — 01687 460042

Walker, Eric — Tigh a' Chlann, Inverroy, Roy Bridge PH31 4AQ [E-mail: line15@btinternet.com] — 01397 712028

Walker, Pat (Mrs) — Tigh a' Chlann, Inverroy, Roy Bridge PH31 4AQ [E-mail: pat.line15@btinternet.com] — 01397 712028

39. ROSS

Finlayson, Michael R. — Amberlea, Glenskiach, Evanton, Dingwall IV16 9UU [E-mail: finlayson935@btinternet.com] — 01349 830598

Greer, Kathleen (Mrs) MEd — 17 Duthac Wynd, Tain IV19 1LP [E-mail: greer2@talktalk.net] — 01862 892065

Gunstone, Ronald W. — 20 Bellfield Road, North Kessock, Inverness IV1 3XU [E-mail: ronald.gunstone@virgin.net] — 01463 731337 / (Mbl) 07974 443948

Jamieson, Patricia A. (Mrs) — 9 Craig Avenue, Tain IV19 1JP [E-mail: hapjam179@yahoo.co.uk] — 01862 893154

McAlpine, James — 5 Cromlet Park, Invergordon IV18 0RN [E-mail: jmca1@tinyworld.co.uk] — 01349 852801

McCreadie, Frederick — 7 Castle Gardens, Dingwall IV15 9HY [E-mail: fredmccreadie@tesco.net] — 01349 862171

Munro, Irene (Mrs) — 1 Wyvis Crescent, Conon Bridge, Dingwall IV15 9HY [E-mail: irenemunro@rocketmail.com] — 01349 865752

Riddell, Keith — 2 Station Cottages, Fearn, Tain IV20 1RR [E-mail: keithriddell@hotmail.co.uk] — 01862 832867 / (Mbl) 07719 645995

40. SUTHERLAND

Baxter, A. Rosie (Dr) — Daylesford, Invershin, Lairg IV27 4ET [E-mail: drrosiereid@yahoo.co.uk] — 01549 421326 / (Mbl) 07748 761694

Roberts, Irene (Mrs) — Flat 4, Harbour Buildings, Main Street, Portmahomack, Tain IV20 1YG [E-mail: ireneroberts43@hotmail.com] — 01862 871166

Weidner, Karl — 6 St Vincent Road, Tain IV19 1JR [E-mail: kweidner@btinternet.com] — (Mbl) 07854 436854 / 01862 894202

41. CAITHNESS

42. LOCHCARRON – SKYE

Lamont, John H. BD — 6 Tigh na Filine, Aultbea, Achnasheen IV22 2JE [E-mail: jhlamont@btinternet.com] — (Mbl) 07714 720753

MacRae, Donald E. — Nethania, 52 Strath, Gairloch IV21 2DB [E-mail: Dmgair@aol.com] — 01445 712235

Ross, R. Ian — St Conal's, Inverinate, Kyle IV40 8HB — 01599 511371

43. UIST

Browning, Margaret (Miss) — 1 Middlequarter, Sollas, Lochmaddy, Isle of North Uist HS6 5BU [E-mail: margaretckb@tiscali.co.uk] — 01876 560392

Lines, Charles M.D. — Flat 1/02, 8 Queen Margaret Road, Glasgow G20 6DP

MacAulay, John — Fernhaven, 1 Flodabay, Isle of Harris HS3 3HA — 01859 530340

MacNab, Ann (Mrs) — Druim Skiivat, Scolpaig, Lochmaddy, Isle of North Uist HS6 5DH [E-mail: annabhan@hotmail.com] — 01876 510701

44. LEWIS

Macleod, Donald — 14 Balmerino Drive, Stornoway, Isle of Lewis HS1 2TD [E-mail: donaldmacleod25@btinternet.com] — 01851 704516

Macmillan, Iain — 34 Scotland Street, Stornoway, Isle of Lewis HS1 2JR [E-mail: macmillan@brocair.fsnet.co.uk] — 01851 704826 / (Mbl) 07775 027987

Murray, Angus — 4 Ceann Chilleagraidh, Stornoway, Isle of Lewis HS1 2UJ [E-mail: angydmurray@btinternet.com] — 01851 703550

45. ORKNEY

Dicken, Marion (Mrs) — 6 Claymore Brae, Kirkwall, Orkney KW15 1UQ [E-mail: mj44@hotmail.co.uk] — 01856 879509

Robertson, Johan (Mrs) — Old Manse, Eday, Orkney KW17 2AA — 01857 622251

46. SHETLAND

Greig, Diane (Mrs) MA — 6 Hayhoull Place, Bigton, Shetland ZE2 9GA [E-mail: mrschm.greig@btinternet.com] — 01950 422468

Harrison, Christine (Mrs) BA — Gerdavatn, Baltasound, Unst, Shetland ZE2 9DY [E-mail: chris4242@btinternet.com] — 01957 711578

Smith, M. Beryl (Mrs) DCE MSc — Vakterlee, Cumliewick. Sandwick, Shetland ZE2 9HH [E-mail: beryl@brooniestaing.co.uk] — 01950 431280

47. ENGLAND

Houghton, Mark (Dr) — Kentcliffe, Charney Road, Grange-over-Sands, Cumbria LA11 6BP [E-mail: mark@chaplain.me.uk] — 01539 525048 / (Work) 01629 813505

Menzies, Rena (Mrs) — 49 Elizabeth Avenue, St Brelade's, Jersey JE3 8GR [E-mail: menzfamily@jerseymail.co.uk] — 01534 741095

Milligan, Elaine (Mrs) — 16 Surrey Close, Corby, Northants NN17 2TG — 01536 205259

Munro, William

[E-mail: elainemilligan@ntlworld.com]
35 Stour Road, Corby, Northants NN17 2HX

01536 504864

48. EUROPE
Ross, David

Urb. El Campanario, EDF Granada, Esc. 14, Baja B, Ctra Cadiz N-340,
Km 168, 29680 Estepona, Malaga, Spain
[E-mail: rosselcampanario@yahoo.co.uk]

(Tel/Fax) 0034 952 88 26 34

49. JERUSALEM
Oakley-Levstein, Joanna

ASSOCIATE (Ireland)
Binnie, Jean (Miss)

2 Ailesbury Lawn, Dundrum, Dublin 16, Ireland
[E-mail: jeanbinnie@eircom.net]

00353 1 298 7229

LIST I – MINISTRIES DEVELOPMENT STAFF

Ministries Development Staff support local congregations, parish groupings and presbyteries in a wide variety of ways, bringing expertise or experience to pastoral work, development, and outreach in congregation and community. Some of these may be ministers and deacons undertaking specialist roles; these are not listed below but are found in Section 5 (Presbyteries), with deacons also in List C of the present section. However, these are included in a fuller list, with further information related to those listed below, at:

www.churchofscotland.org.uk/yearbook > Section 6-I

NAME	APPOINTMENT AND PRESBYTERY	CONTACT
Adam, Pamela BD	Ellon (Gordon)	pbaker@churchofscotland.org.uk
Amanaland, John	Aberdeen: Garthdee l/w Ruthrieston West	jiamanaland@churchofscotland.org.uk
Anderson, Christopher	Newton and Loanhead (Lothian)	
Archibald, Trish BD PGCE	North Ayr Family Development Worker (Ayr)	trishdalmilling@gmail.com
Baker, Paula (Mrs)	Birnie and Pluscarden l/w Elgin: High – Parish Assistant (Moray)	paulabakerknow@yahoo.co.uk
Bloomfield, Frances (Rev)	Glasgow: St Christopher's Priesthill and Nitshill (Glasgow)	fbloomfield@churchofscotland.org.uk
Binnie, Michelle	Possilpark (Glasgow)	0141-336 8028
Boland, Susan (Mrs) DipHE(Theol)	Cumbernauld: Abronhill (Falkirk)	sboland@churchofscotland.org.uk
Broere, Paula (Mrs)	Aberdeen: Mastrick – Parish Assistant (Aberdeen)	pbroere@churchofscotland.org.uk

Name	Role / Parish	Contact
Bruce, Stuart	Glasgow: Queen's Park Govanhill – Parish Assistant (Glasgow)	alasdair.campbell@churchofscotland.org.uk
Campbell, Alasdair D. BA	Annan and Gretna churches – Parish Assistant (Annandale and Eskdale)	0141-944 3758
Campbell, Julie	Drumchapel: St Andrew's (Glasgow)	
Campbell, Neil MA	Dundee: Craigiebank l/w Douglas and Mid Craigie – Youth and Young Adult Development Worker (Dundee)	01382 731173
Crawford, Fiona	Presbytery Strategy Officer (Glasgow)	07801 855314
Crossan, Morag BA	Dalmellington l/w Patna Waterside – Youth and Childen's Worker (Ayr)	mcrossan@churchofscotland.org.uk
Crumlin, Melodie BA PGMgt DipBusMgt	PEEK (Possibilities for Each and Every Kid) – Project Development Manager (Glasgow)	chiefexecutive@peekproject.co.uk
Currie, Archie	Ardrossan Park – Outreach and Family Worker (Ardrossan)	archie.currie@churchofscotland.org.uk
Douglas, Ian	Motherwell Crosshill l/w St Margaret's – Parish Assistant (Hamilton)	01698 263604
Duncan, Emma	Montrose churches (Angus)	emacdonald@churchofscotland.org.uk
Dungavel, Marie Claire	Dumbarton: Riverside l/w West, Development Worker (Dumbarton)	01389 742551
Finch, John BA	Gorbals Parish Church – Community Development Worker (Glasgow)	jfinch@churchofscotland.org.uk
Fraser, Kate	Torry, Aberdeen – Parish Assistant (Aberdeen)	kfraser@churchofscotland.org.uk
Gray, Ian	Esk Parish Grouping – Pastoral Assistant (Angus)	iancelia15@aol.com
Gunn, Philip BSc	Aberdeen: Mannofield – Parish Assistant (Aberdeen)	pgunn@churchofscotland.org.uk
Guy, Helen J. (Miss)	Edinburgh: Tron Kirk (Edinburgh)	hguy@churchofscotland.org.uk
Haringman, Paul MSc	Culloden: The Barn – Community Worker (Inverness)	01463 798946
Harper, Kirsty (Mrs) BA	Edinburgh: Granton (Edinburgh)	kharper@churchofscotland.org.uk
Hislop, Donna	Youth Worker (Annandale and Eskdale)	dhislop@churchofscotland.org.uk
Hunter, Jean (Mrs)	Brodick and linked parishes – Parish Assistant (Ardrossan)	01770 303517
Hutchison, John BA	Rothes Trinity Parish Grouping (Kirkcaldy)	01592 752539
Hyndman, Graham	Church House, Bridgeton – Youth Worker (Glasgow)	0141-554 8045
Johnston, Ashley (Miss)	Abercorn with Pardovan, Kinscavil and Winchburgh – Family Development Worker (West Lothian)	07711 272996
Keenan, Deborah	Glasgow: Easterhouse St George's and St Peter's (Glasgow)	dkeenan@churchofscotland.org.uk
Kennedy, Sarah	Kilmarnock New Laigh l/w Onthank – Community Development (Irvine/Kilmarnock)	
Knights, Chris (Rev Dr)	Musselburgh churches (Lothian)	revchrisknights@gmail.com
Lightbody, Philip (Rev)	Credo Centre – Mission Development (Aberdeen)	pgunn@churchofscotland.org.uk
McDougall, Hilary	Presbytery Congregational Facilitator (Glasgow)	0141-332 6066
McGreechin, Anne	Glasgow: Cranhill, Ruchazie and Garthamlock and Craigend East Parish Grouping (Glasgow)	annemcgreechin@hotmail.com
McIlreavy, Gillian	Glasgow: Govan and Linthouse (Glasgow)	glpcglasgow@googlemail.com
McKay, Angus	Glasgow Lodging House Mission (Glasgow)	0141-552 0285
McLaren, Gordon	Thurso: St Peter's and St. Andrew's – Pastoral Assistant (Caithness)	

Name	Role	Contact
McLarty, Margaret	Glasgow: Castlemilk – Community Arts Worker (Glasgow)	0141-634 1480
MacLeod, Penny	Glasgow: Queen's Park Govanhill – Community Research Worker (Glasgow)	0141-423 3654
McMillan, Esther	Glasgow: Cranhill, Ruchazie, Garthamlock and Craigend East Parish Grouping (Glasgow)	mcmillan@live.co.uk
McQuaid, Ruth Clements	Glasgow: Castlemilk – Community Arts Worker (Glasgow)	0141-634 1480
Middlemass, Deborah	Tranent Cluster (Lothian)	dmiddlemass@churchofscotland.org.uk
Miller, Susan	Glasgow: Shettleston New – Youth and Children's Worker (Glasgow)	0141-778 0857
Morrison, Iain	Glasgow: Colston Milton – Community Arts Worker	0141-772 1922
Morrocco, Ellie	Glenrothes: Christ's Kirk and St Margaret's (Kirkcaldy)	elliemorrocco@gmail.com
Moyo, Fabulous BD MTh PhD	North Ayr Family Development Worker (Ayr)	fmoyo@churchofscotland.org.uk
Orr, Gillian	Presbytery Youth Worker (Abernethy)	gorr@churchofscotland.org.uk
Philip, Darren BSc	Livingston United – Youth and Children's Worker (West Lothian)	dphilip@churchofscotland.org.uk
Pryde, Erica	Newbattle Parish Church – Mission and Outreach Co-ordinator (Lothian)	0131-663 3245
Reynolds, Jessica (Mrs)	Inverness Trinity – Children's and Family Worker (Inverness)	07445 491132
Robertson, Douglas BEng BA MTh	Kaimes Lockhart Memorial – Team Leader, Project Worker (Edinburgh)	07825 397018
Robertson, Douglas	Baillieston – Children, Young People and Family Worker (Glasgow)	0141-773 1216/771 6629
Robinson, Katy	Edinburgh: Richmond Craigmillar (Edinburgh)	0131-661 6561
Safrani, Zoltan (Rev.)	Bathgate: St John's – Parish Development Worker (West Lothian)	07411 444743
Smith, David	Dundee: Lochee – Children and Young Persons Development Worker (Dundee)	01382 612549
Smith, Rebecca	Edinburgh: Richmond Craigmillar – Community Project Worker (Edinburgh)	rebecca.smith@churchofscotland.org.uk
Stark, Alastair BA	Glenrothes and Leslie: Youth and Children's Worker (Kirkcaldy)	01592 366009
Stark, Jennifer MA MATheol	Glenrothes and Leslie – Families and Projects (Kirkcaldy)	jstark@churchofscotland.org.uk
Stirling, Diane (Miss) BSc DipCPC BTh	Dundee: Craigiebank l/w Douglas and Mid Craigie – Parish Assistant (Dundee)	parish.assistant@yahoo.co.uk
Taylor, Valerie AssocCIPD PGDip	Aberdeen: Torry St Fittick's – Ministry Assistant (Aberdeen)	vtaylor@churchofscotland.org.uk
Thomas, Jay MA BA	Glasgow: St James' (Pollok) (Glasgow)	jthomas@churchofscotland.org.uk
Usher, Eileen	Glasgow: Cranhill, Ruchazie, Garthamlock and Craigend East Parish Grouping (Glasgow)	eusher@churchofscotland.org.uk
Wellstood, Keith PGDip MICG	Perth: Riverside – Community Worker (Perth)	keithw2011@btinternet.com
Wilson, Jeanette L.	Parish Assistant (Annandale and Eskdale, Dumfries and Kircudbright)	jlisa@tiscali.co.uk
Willis, Mags	Dundee: Chalmers-Ardler (Dundee)	mwillis@churchofscotland.org.uk
Young, Neil James	Glasgow: St Paul's – Youth Worker (Glasgow)	0141-770 8559

LIST J – OVERSEAS LOCATIONS

AFRICA
MALAWI

Church of Central Africa Presbyterian
Synod of Blantyre
Dr Ruth Shakespeare (2011)

Mulanje Mission Hospital, PO Box 45, Mulanje, Malawi
[E-mail: shakespeareruth@gmail.com]

(Tel) 00265 9922 61569
(Fax) 00265 1 467 022

Synod of Livingstonia

CCAP Girls' Secondary School, PO Box 2, Ekwendeni, Malawi
[E-mail: helenms1960@yahoo.co.uk]

(Tel) 00265 1929 1932

Synod of Nkhoma
Dr David Morton (2009)

Nkhoma Hospital, PO Box 48, Nkhoma, Malawi
[E-mail: kuluva2@gmail.com]

(Tel) 00265 9940 74022

Mr Rob Jones (2010)

Nkhoma Hospital, PO Box 48, Nkhoma, Malawi
[E-mail: robert@thejonesfamily.org.uk]

(Tel) 00265 998 951500

ZAMBIA

United Church of Zambia
Mr Keith and Mrs Ida Waddell (Ecum) (2008)

Mwandi UCZ Mission, PO Box 60693, Livingstonia, Zambia
[E-mail: keithida2014@gmail.com]

(Tel) 00260 977 328 767

Ms Jenny Featherstone (Ecum) (2007)

c/o Chodort Training Centre, PO Box 630451, Choma, Zambia
[E-mail: jenny.featherstone@googlemail.com]

(Tel) 00260 979 703 130

Mr Glen Lund (2010)

UCZ Theological College, PO Box 20429, Kitwe, Zambia
[E-mail: redhair.community@googlemail.com]

(Tel) 00260 978 363 400

ASIA
BANGLADESH

Church of Bangladesh
Miss Pat Jamieson (Ecum) (2010)

Flat 5N, Quamroon Noor Apartments, 9/1 Sir Sayed Ahmed Road, Block A Mohammadpur, Dhaka 1207, Bangladesh
[E-mail: patjamieson30@gmail.com]

NEPAL   Mr Joel Githinji (2010)   c/o United Mission to Nepal, PO Box 126, Kathmandu, Nepal
(Tel: 00 977 1 4228 118)
[E-mail: joelkavari2003@gmail.com]

Rev. Malcolm and Mrs Cati Ramsay (Ecum) (2011)   Address and telephone as above
[E-mail: amalcolmramsay@gmail.com]

Mr Joel Hasvenstein and Mrs Fiona Hasvenstein (2015)Address and telephone as above

For European, Middle Eastern and other locations, see the Presbyteries of Europe and Jerusalem (Section 5; 48 and 49, above)

LIST K – OVERSEAS RESIGNED AND RETIRED MISSION PARTNERS (ten or more years' service)

For a full list see: www.churchofscotland.org.uk/yearbook > Section 6-K

LIST L – FULL-TIME WORKPLACE CHAPLAINS

CHIEF EXECUTIVE OFFICER   Rev. Iain McFadzean   iain.mcfadzean@wpcscotland.co.uk   (Mbl) 07969 227696
For a full list of Regional Organisers, Team Leaders and Chaplaincy Locations see: www.churchofscotland.org.uk/yearbook > Section 6-L

LIST M – PRISON CHAPLAINS

ADVISER TO SCOTTISH PRISON SERVICE   Rev. William R. Taylor   SPS HQ, Calton House, 5 Redheughs Rigg, South Gyle,   0131-244 8640
(NATIONAL)   Edinburgh EH12 9DQ
[E-mail: bill.taylor@sps.pnn.gov.uk]

For a list of Prisons and Chaplains see: www.churchofscotland.org.uk/yearbook > Section 6-M

LIST N – UNIVERSITY CHAPLAINS

For a list of Universities and Chaplains see: www.churchofscotland.org.uk/yearbook > Section 6-N

LIST O – REPRESENTATIVES ON COUNCIL EDUCATION COMMITTEES

For a full list see: www.churchofscotland.org.uk/yearbook > Section 6-O

LIST P – RETIRED LAY AGENTS

See further: www.churchofscotland.org.uk/yearbook > Section 6-P

LIST Q – MINISTERS ORDAINED FOR SIXTY YEARS AND UPWARDS

For a full list see: www.churchofscotland.org.uk/yearbook > Section 6-Q

LIST R – DECEASED MINISTERS

The Editor has been made aware of the following ministers who have died since the publication of the previous volume of the *Year Book*.

Barbour, Robert Alexander Stewart DD	(University of Aberdeen)
Blaikie, James	(Berwick-on-Tweed: St Andrew's Wallace Green and Lowick)
Brown, Lawson Richard	(Cameron with St Andrews: St Leonard's)

Campbell, William Murdoch Maclean	(Hospital Chaplain)
Cooper, George	(Kenya and Tanzania)
Cranston, George	(Rutherglen: Wardlawhill)
Crawford, Samuel Gerald Victor	(Glasgow: Calton Parkhead)
Duncan, Louise Jane	(Balerno)
Fox, George Hunter	(Coalsnaughton)
Gibson, Henry Montgomery	(Dundee: The High Kirk)
Hay, Bruce John Laird	(Makerstoun and Smailholm l.w. Stichill, Hume and Nenthron)
Henderson, Charles Malcolm	(Campbeltown: Highland)
Henderson, John Donald	(Cluny l/w Monymusk)
Hepburn, Catherine Anne	West Mearns
Laing, William Frederick	(Selkirk: St Mary's West)
Leishman, Robert Murray	(Hospital Chaplain)
McCabe, William Alexander Beck	(Glasgow: Eastbank)
Macdonell, Alasdair William	(Haddington: St Mary's)
Mackenzie, Murdoch	(Glenrothes: St Ninian's)
McLay, Alastair David	(Glasgow: Shawlands)
Philpot, David Howard	(Kenya, Switzerland)
Reid, David Tindal	(Cleish l/w Fossoway: St Serf's and Devonside)
Stone, Walter Vernon	(Langbank) Tell Pauline 1st April
Taylor, Peter Reynolds	(Torphins)
Tierney, John Paul	(Peterhead: West, Associate Minister)
Smith, Rosemary Ann	(Dunfermline: Townhill and Kingseat)
Wilkinson, John	(Kikuyu, Kenya)

SECTION 7

Legal Names and Scottish Charity Numbers for Individual Congregations

(All congregations in Scotland, and congregations furth of Scotland which are registered with OSCR, the Office of the Scottish Charity Regulator)

For a complete list of legal names see:
www.churchofscotland.org.uk/yearbook
('Section 7')

Further information

All documents, as defined in the Charities References in Documents (Scotland) Regulations 2007, must specify the Charity Number, Legal Name of the congregation, any other name by which the congregation is commonly known and the fact that it is a Charity. For more information, please refer to the Law Department circular on the Regulations on the Church of Scotland website.

www.churchofscotland.org.uk > Resources > Subjects > Law Department Circulars
('Charity Law')

SECTION 8

Church Buildings: Ordnance Survey
National Grid References

Please go to: www.churchofscotland.org.uk/yearbook > Section 8

SECTION 9

Discontinued Parish
and Congregational Names

The purpose of this list is to assist those who are trying to identify the present-day successor of some former parish or congregation whose name is now wholly out of use and which can therefore no longer be easily traced. Where the former name has not disappeared completely, and the whereabouts of the former parish or congregation may therefore be easily established by reference to the name of some existing parish, the former name has not been included in this list. Present-day names, in the right-hand column of this list, may be found in the 'Index of Parishes and Places' in the print edition of the Year Book.

The full list, with further explanatory notes, may be found at:

www.churchofscotland.org.uk/yearbook > Section 9

SECTION 10

Congregational
Statistics
2014

CHURCH OF SCOTLAND
Comparative Statistics: 1974–2014

	2014	2004	1994	1984	1974
Communicants	396,422	535,834	715,571	887,165	1,061,706
Elders	31,146	41,621	46,091	46,223	48,560

NOTES ON CONGREGATIONAL STATISTICS

Com   Number of communicants at 31 December 2014.

Eld   Number of elders at 31 December 2014.

G   Membership of the Guild including Young Woman's Group and others as recorded on the 2014 annual return submitted to the Guild Office.

In 14   Ordinary General Income for 2014. Ordinary General Income consists of members' offerings, contributions from congregational organisations, regular fund-raising events, income from investments, deposits and so on. This figure does not include extraordinary or special income, or income from special collections and fund-raising for other charities.

M&M   Final amount allocated to congregations after allowing for Presbytery-approved amendments up to 31 December 2014, but before deducting stipend endowments and normal allowances given for stipend purposes in a vacancy.

–18   This figure shows 'the number of children and young people aged 17 years and under who are involved in the life of the congregation'.

(NB: Figures may not be available for new charges created or for congregations which have entered into readjustment late in 2014 or during 2015. Figures might also not be available for congregations which failed to submit the appropriate schedule.)

Congregation	Com	Eld	G	In 14	M&M	–18
1. Edinburgh						
Albany Deaf Church of Edinburgh	71	3	-	-	-	-
Balerno	594	76	33	135,013	71,585	66
Barclay Viewforth	323	32	-	173,577	116,285	52
Blackhall St Columba's	764	70	30	195,809	102,792	34
Bristo Memorial Craigmillar	73	8	-	58,534	27,324	46
Broughton St Mary's	209	26	-	68,516	49,031	31
Canongate	358	45	-	111,450	69,846	14
Carrick Knowe	393	48	73	61,889	36,011	323
Colinton	888	67	-	199,392	125,606	102
Corstorphine: Craigsbank	495	27	-	94,248	62,745	74
Corstorphine: Old	424	50	51	109,013	70,521	61
Corstorphine: St Anne's	360	51	74	99,963	61,647	48
Corstorphine: St Ninian's	739	82	54	157,089	93,972	55
Craigentinny St Christopher's	87	11	-	24,746	20,367	-
Craiglockhart	441	44	29	149,359	76,720	100
Craigmillar Park	221	19	22	84,199	51,158	5
Cramond	1,039	90	-	255,178	155,821	91
Currie	549	39	68	-	93,557	70
Dalmeny	104	9	-	26,136	19,427	9
Queensferry	541	43	60	-	60,875	144
Davidson's Mains	496	53	39	-	111,102	67
Dean	140	21	-	55,715	37,568	8
Drylaw	93	10	-	18,463	3,536	7
Duddingston	542	45	35	-	68,745	259
Fairmilehead	556	60	35	101,347	70,201	58
Gorgie Dalry	222	25	-	96,414	56,683	30
Granton	199	18	-	-	22,714	32
Greenbank	760	81	32	-	140,819	83
Greenside	143	30	-	-	32,125	18
Greyfriars Kirk	305	39	-	156,000	85,497	22
High (St Giles')	503	35	-	297,277	171,776	10
Holyrood Abbey	36	1	-	-	84,388	-
Holy Trinity	223	-	-	-	79,109	67
Inverleith St Serf's	375	40	22	107,291	90,975	170
Juniper Green	323	21	-	97,902	64,625	40
Kaimes Lockhart Memorial	45	6	-	-	1,850	6
Liberton	720	77	44	223,114	113,211	85
Kirkliston	264	32	49	98,038	61,928	39
Leith: North	232	27	-	80,283	48,236	37
Leith: St Andrew's	246	33	-	78,369	53,834	60
Leith: South	364	65	-	141,862	76,973	105
Leith: Wardie	533	58	39	171,944	83,535	136
Liberton Northfield	208	8	19	47,357	32,341	40
London Road	183	30	28	64,082	36,212	9
Marchmont St Giles'	226	34	29	107,564	69,600	54
Mayfield Salisbury	526	51	-	251,909	134,933	35
Morningside	454	63	16	218,317	110,622	90
Morningside United	223	40	-	84,206	52,838	24

Congregation	Com	Eld	G	In 14	M&M	–18
Murrayfield	542	76	-	-	92,780	73
Newhaven	162	15	37	84,075	56,663	117
New Restalrig	67	3	-	31,239	89,733	-
Old Kirk and Muihouse	132	14	-	33,687	13,732	35
Palmerston Place	383	38	-	172,630	101,948	86
Pilrig St Paul's	228	19	25	41,321	32,395	25
Polwarth	200	24	13	65,759	53,692	22
Portobello and Joppa	979	97	112	192,586	175,556	198
Priestfield	127	19	22	86,387	40,919	54
Ratho	193	18	-	48,850	24,657	8
Reid Memorial	300	18	-	97,498	68,640	14
Richmond Craigmillar	90	11	-	-	3,992	14
St Andrew's and St George's West	313	46	-	230,847	182,078	25
St Andrew's Clermiston	221	13	-	-	35,724	11
St Catherine's Argyle	351	-	-	-	95,633	-
St Cuthbert's	336	50	-	144,347	92,353	16
St David's Broomhouse	130	13	-	34,714	17,349	84
St John's Colinton Mains	222	19	-	60,435	38,685	42
St Margaret's	351	32	19	52,496	33,462	53
St Martin's	89	10	-	17,747	5,520	12
St Michael's	347	28	32	66,089	46,470	13
St Nicholas' Sighthill	343	25	16	43,496	26,555	15
St Stephen's Comely Bank	207	16	-	103,171	84,049	54
Slateford Longstone	220	16	40	49,571	30,578	36
Stenhouse St Aidan's	66	7	-	23,693	18,324	3
Stockbridge	206	22	-	71,710	56,413	33
Tron Kirk (Gilmerton and Moredun)	91	10	-	27,486	4,696	132

2. West Lothian

Abercorn	75	9	-	14,139	10,174	2
Pardovan, Kingscavil and Winchburgh	272	29	11	-	39,320	127
Armadale	534	45	31	88,547	46,054	210
Avonbridge	82	-	-	15,626	7,046	-
Torphichen	232	15	-	-	31,606	84
Bathgate: Boghall	246	27	24	82,000	44,285	167
Bathgate: High	512	36	32	87,993	56,907	31
Bathgate: St John's	357	25	35	50,950	37,107	100
Blackburn and Seafield	403	36	-	72,939	45,111	101
Blackridge	68	5	-	19,093	11,310	-
Harthill: St Andrew's	185	8	31	53,574	35,804	74
Breich Valley	193	11	25	29,035	23,050	12
Broxburn	355	33	44	84,843	47,379	148
Fauldhouse: St Andrew's	201	14	-	53,791	32,440	11
Kirknewton and East Calder	337	36	27	102,292	66,886	80
Kirk of Calder	558	43	18	81,032	48,891	61
Linlithgow: St Michael's	1,359	112	56	324,835	166,658	96
Linlithgow: St Ninian's Craigmailen	417	40	65	69,546	43,286	86
Livingston Ecumenical Parish	344	27	-	78,656	30,322	180
Livingston: Old	357	37	20	90,650	55,804	45
Polbeth Harwood	173	24	-	20,731	16,678	6

Congregation	Com	Eld	G	In 14	M&M	–18
West Kirk of Calder	260	18	18	56,281	40,025	25
Strathbrock	300	29	18	107,214	68,534	90
Uphall South	209	24	-	70,402	38,022	56
Whitburn: Brucefield	231	19	18	78,233	46,424	160
Whitburn: South	357	27	25	76,992	45,032	107

3. Lothian

Congregation	Com	Eld	G	In 14	M&M	–18
Aberlady	214	21	-	36,185	20,092	6
Gullane	367	26	20	56,851	38,849	26
Athelstaneford	204	13	-	29,011	15,345	12
Whitekirk and Tyninghame	136	14	-	-	20,975	15
Belhaven	662	40	61	78,737	49,471	27
Spott	106	7	-	11,990	9,099	4
Bilston	91	3	15	12,417	4,179	-
Glencorse	301	13	1	29,150	15,461	5
Roslin	233	8	-	27,363	18,126	11
Bolton and Saltoun	139	17	-	30,783	17,230	11
Humbie	71	9	-	21,571	12,949	12
Yester	169	16	18	25,943	15,363	12
Bonnyrigg	665	60	44	100,252	65,644	25
Cockenzie and Port Seton: Chalmers M'rl	204	29	30	-	31,700	80
Cockenzie and Port Seton: Old	237	21	18	-	28,362	18
Cockpen and Carrington	205	23	42	28,520	17,884	42
Lasswade and Rosewell	292	21	-	29,394	21,517	8
Dalkeith: St John's and King's Park	455	39	25	161,242	56,133	65
Dalkeith: St Nicholas' Buccleuch	386	20	-	65,481	35,992	11
Dirleton	234	17	-	-	34,154	12
North Berwick: Abbey	284	30	44	89,035	50,653	18
Dunbar	403	18	32	108,939	65,222	83
Dunglass	295	13	14	32,627	19,345	-
Garvald and Morham	43	10	-	-	6,531	15
Haddington: West	229	22	30	59,105	41,519	27
Gladsmuir	181	12	-	-	17,164	24
Longniddry	356	44	39	79,787	49,131	20
Gorebridge	102	14	-	115,278	56,408	71
Haddington: St Mary's	535	41	-	-	62,596	69
Howgate	40	6	-	24,046	9,285	9
Penicuik: South	127	14	-	-	40,228	20
Loanhead	317	25	35	-	29,899	42
Musselburgh: Northesk	326	26	42	68,085	41,603	86
Musselburgh: St Andrew's High	304	28	24	70,675	39,767	8
Musselburgh: St Clement's & St Ninian's	209	13	-	24,595	16,969	-
Musselburgh: St Michael's Inveresk	399	41	-	82,592	46,751	12
Newbattle	455	34	18	83,241	44,265	210
Newton	116	9	13	15,452	12,698	15
North Berwick: St Andrew Blackadder	613	37	39	142,675	87,640	95
Ormiston	174	8	24	42,737	24,749	20
Pencaitland	176	7	-	-	23,816	31
Penicuik: North	500	32	-	75,733	45,844	71
Penicuik: St Mungo's	342	21	21	59,702	44,372	5

Congregation	Com	Eld	G	In 14	M&M	–18
Prestonpans: Prestongrange	302	26	18	53,655	33,741	12
Tranent	223	14	30	-	34,672	15
Traprain	436	31	35	70,387	46,552	56
Tyne Valley Parish	343	25	-	70,997	53,691	35

4. Melrose and Peebles

Congregation	Com	Eld	G	In 14	M&M	–18
Ashkirk	40	5	-	9,161	4,744	1
Selkirk	481	20	-	70,945	37,200	20
Bowden and Melrose	882	69	39	117,572	76,674	51
Broughton, Glenholm and Kilbucho	145	10	26	18,782	10,822	-
Skirling	65	6	-	8,355	5,545	-
Stobo and Drumelzier	89	8	-	15,595	11,174	3
Tweedsmuir	-	-	-	-	4,820	-
Caddonfoot	-	-	-	19,004	9,738	-
Galashiels: Trinity	436	42	36	59,574	42,930	6
Carlops	63	13	-	-	8,673	22
Kirkurd and Newlands	90	13	14	25,165	14,652	12
West Linton: St Andrew's	216	20	-	42,119	22,984	-
Channelkirk & Lauder	412	25	23	61,158	39,506	22
Earlston	394	23	12	51,098	30,062	34
Eddleston	108	-	6	12,846	8,289	-
Peebles: Old	485	41	-	101,726	66,845	23
Ettrick and Yarrow	195	-	-	43,508	30,065	-
Galashiels: Old and St Paul's	264	26	25	57,184	39,869	23
Galashiels: St John's	200	-	-	40,239	27,680	-
Innerleithen, Traquair and Walkerburn	384	28	37	54,508	32,638	60
Lyne and Manor	108	7	-	-	17,467	16
Peebles: St Andrew's Leckie	561	34	-	102,220	59,764	112
Maxton and Mertoun	129	-	-	16,601	11,610	-
Newtown	137	10	-	15,854	8,195	1
St Boswells	200	24	26	34,211	23,837	-
Stow: St Mary of Wedale and Heriot	182	14	-	33,366	18,084	15

5. Duns

Congregation	Com	Eld	G	In 14	M&M	–18
Ayton and Burnmouth	160	10	-	-	10,773	-
Foulden and Mordington	70	6	-	7,066	7,179	-
Grantshouse and Houndwood and Reston	96	7	14	10,610	10,117	3
Berwick-upon-Tweed: St Andrew's Wallace Green & Lowick	365	23	23	56,683	30,003	16
Bonkyl and Edrom	125	11	-	15,015	10,093	-
Duns	500	25	35	-	26,353	45
Chirnside	102	6	19	14,086	14,472	-
Hutton and Fishwick and Paxton	65	9	11	20,095	10,115	-
Coldingham and St Abb's	78	10	-	38,660	22,662	17
Eyemouth	170	19	32	45,073	23,389	40
Coldstream	352	26	-	49,586	31,653	24
Eccles	75	11	16	13,955	7,523	3
Fogo and Swinton	96	6	-	9,206	9,348	5
Ladykirk and Whitsome	-	-	-	-	11,785	-
Leitholm	70	7	-	12,140	6,673	1

Congregation	Com	Eld	G	In 14	M&M	–18
Gordon: St Michael's	64	9	-	7,041	5,662	4
Greenlaw	93	9	10	19,875	11,597	1
Legerwood	60	6	-	8,389	5,187	7
Westruther	45	8	13	4,770	4,572	29
Langton and Lammermuir Kirk	147	13	20	35,276	32,067	3

6. Jedburgh

Congregation	Com	Eld	G	In 14	M&M	–18
Ale and Teviot United	417	26	16	56,753	38,908	22
Cavers and Kirkton	118	8	-	10,774	9,447	-
Hawick: Trinity	743	28	50	50,275	29,530	68
Hawick: Burnfoot	94	15	12	25,919	19,673	96
Hawick: St Mary's and Old	424	22	22	40,501	26,224	74
Hawick: Teviot and Roberton	288	8	12	49,761	35,695	2
Hawick: Wilton	354	25	-	49,812	21,915	56
Teviothead	72	4	-	6,024	2,658	1
Hobkirk and Southdean	167	14	16	17,736	17,439	12
Ruberslaw	255	19	19	38,627	18,830	18
Jedburgh: Old and Trinity	661	98	30	78,771	52,175	2
Kelso Country Churches	214	17	16	29,022	32,608	13
Kelso: Old and Sprouston	498	33	-	42,717	38,125	8
Kelso: North and Ednam	1,159	69	30	141,873	84,815	30
Linton, Morebattle, Hownam & Yetholm	370	25	34	66,390	50,792	50
Oxnam	129	11	-	12,997	5,888	25

7. Annandale and Eskdale

Congregation	Com	Eld	G	In 14	M&M	–18
Annan: Old	377	43	40	65,436	44,931	24
Dornock	114	10	-	-	7,129	4
Annan: St Andrew's	639	44	52	73,059	36,424	90
Brydekirk	55	6	-	11,528	4,319	-
Applegarth, Sibbaldbie and Johnstone	158	8	8	9,556	9,746	-
Lochmaben	417	20	42	68,564	34,936	6
Canonbie United	100	15	-	31,767	17,690	16
Liddesdale	127	8	22	27,626	25,048	2
Dalton	105	9	-	14,486	6,709	3
Hightae	82	3	11	-	1,282	-
St Mungo	87	11	13	15,258	8,264	5
Gretna: Old, Gretna: St Andrew's Half Morton & Kirkpatrick Fleming	331	30	30	-	13,134	91
Hoddom, Kirtle-Eaglesfield and Middlebie	208	20	36	17,571	16,781	26
Kirkpatrick Juxta	109	7	-	11,229	8,013	1
Moffat: St Andrew's	376	32	24	65,213	45,502	70
Wamphray	55	6	-	8,513	3,631	2
Langholm Eskdalemuir Ewes and Westerkirk	452	34	16	68,813	39,006	37
Lockerbie: Dryfesdale, Hutton and Corrie	758	41	31	71,456	43,664	29
The Border Kirk	314	45	38	65,081	38,985	42
Tundergarth	34	8	-	12,386	4,460	-

8. Dumfries and Kirkcudbright

Congregation	Com	Eld	G	In 14	M&M	–18
Balmaclellan and Kells	69	7	12	16,013	16,011	7
Carsphairn	95	12	-	8,911	6,612	5

Congregation	Com	Eld	G	In 14	M&M	–18
Dalry	80	13	16	23,315	10,403	2
Balmaghie	69	8	5	14,050	8,488	-
Tarff and Twynholm	145	13	22	24,292	18,220	30
Bengairn	-	-	-	30,652	23,186	-
Borgue	45	2	-	3,677	4,756	-
Gatehouse of Fleet	260	16	15	53,132	29,224	7
Caerlaverock	109	7	-	11,960	6,942	2
Dumfries: St Mary's-Greyfriars	444	32	33	70,859	45,475	7
Castle Douglas	382	23	11	63,072	41,215	9
Closeburn	194	12	-	26,239	17,669	9
Colvend, Southwick and Kirkbean	224	18	20	84,811	55,038	-
Corsock and Kirkpatrick Durham	89	14	19	17,204	15,050	14
Crossmichael and Parton	156	8	13	22,031	14,682	4
Cummertrees, Mouswald and Ruthwell	198	18	14	-	18,121	-
Dalbeattie and Kirkgunzeon	-	-	38	62,928	35,912	-
Urr	185	9	-	-	12,755	-
Dumfries: Maxwelltown West	606	44	40	92,322	64,687	127
Dumfries: Northwest	375	13	-	36,646	27,034	12
Dumfries: St George's	512	46	36	129,544	69,000	105
Dumfries: St Michael's and South	766	45	35	100,314	59,729	103
Dumfries: Troqueer	269	24	33	102,965	59,948	63
Dunscore	202	19	8	34,918	27,371	-
Glencairn and Moniaive	171	14	-	45,094	28,067	8
Durisdeer	149	6	-	25,395	12,430	9
Penpont, Keir and Tynron	163	10	-	-	16,767	10
Thornhill	154	9	12	26,419	24,902	-
Irongray, Lochrutton and Terregles	209	24	13	-	25,795	-
Kirkconnel	276	10	-	-	7,787	21
Kirkcudbright	519	23	-	95,832	54,227	28
Lochend and New Abbey	201	16	12	30,661	18,042	3
Kirkmahoe	298	14	12	22,519	20,428	5
Kirkmichael, Tinwald & Torthorwald	442	41	34	-	43,857	9
Sanquhar: St Bride's	409	24	18	44,690	28,102	36

9. Wigtown and Stranraer

Congregation	Com	Eld	G	In 14	M&M	–18
Ervie Kirkcolm	203	14	-	21,199	14,998	29
Leswalt	302	15	-	29,541	16,787	13
Glasserton and Isle of Whithorn	100	6	-	-	9,172	-
Whithorn: St Ninian's Priory	318	9	23	40,878	26,169	25
Inch	217	14	10	16,631	14,054	10
Portpatrick	220	9	23	23,834	15,810	-
Stranraer: Trinty	547	41	40	89,193	74,595	61
Kirkcowan	117	10	-	34,738	18,838	7
Wigtown	171	14	10	34,412	22,452	40
Kirkinner	129	8	12	18,429	9,091	-
Mochrum	245	20	27	25,983	19,747	30
Sorbie	120	9	-	-	12,141	-
Kirkmabreck	131	12	21	18,266	11,556	-
Monigaff	240	17	-	27,593	25,149	20
Kirkmaiden	209	18	10	30,322	21,159	17

Congregation	Com	Eld	G	In 14	M&M	–18
Stoneykirk	300	23	14	32,115	25,685	6
New Luce	88	6	-	7,505	6,910	8
Old Luce	122	17	27	49,192	25,151	20
Penninghame	417	24	19	82,766	49,758	19
Stranraer: High Kirk	558	43	29	82,470	49,134	127
10. Ayr						
Alloway	1,102	97	-	226,932	116,394	440
Annbank	267	17	15	33,128	23,404	6
Tarbolton	326	28	22	55,093	32,750	13
Auchinleck	314	18	23	-	29,841	24
Catrine	117	11	18	24,216	17,442	-
Ayr: Auld Kirk of Ayr	508	60	36	79,676	53,286	-
Ayr: Castlehill	597	37	47	99,388	65,970	175
Ayr: Newton Wallacetown	402	48	52	119,780	73,757	20
Ayr: St Andrew's	312	-	12	87,067	41,158	-
Ayr: St Columba	1,316	-	79	290,721	128,414	-
Ayr: St James'	397	44	48	77,189	46,186	169
Ayr: St Leonard's	513	51	33	78,754	45,723	10
Dalrymple	126	12	-	26,891	16,820	-
Ayr: St Quivox	239	25	13	48,581	31,559	7
Ballantrae	226	16	22	34,051	25,204	11
St Colmon (Arnsheen Barrhill and Colmonell)	226	9	-	29,763	17,887	6
Barr	66	-	-	2,265	3,397	-
Dailly	135	9	11	21,251	11,074	-
Girvan: South	308	-	28	33,572	23,795	-
Coylton	323	-	-	41,370	27,043	-
Drongan: The Schaw Kirk	180	17	20	35,965	20,721	82
Craigie and Symington	394	26	20	51,528	43,872	3
Crosshill	170	12	20	17,572	10,977	-
Maybole	340	30	31	77,578	33,069	12
Dalmellington	214	19	30	32,566	32,203	50
Patna: Waterside	134	17	-	-	15,845	15
Dundonald	433	46	54	-	53,723	97
Fisherton	110	10	10	12,182	8,642	-
Kirkoswald	219	14	20	29,614	21,570	4
Girvan: North (Old and St Andrew's)	648	43	-	70,318	41,837	14
Kirkmichael	202	18	16	23,633	16,064	5
Straiton: St Cuthbert's	170	9	15	17,620	13,736	10
Lugar	158	9	16	20,350	8,503	6
Old Cumnock: Old	350	15	29	59,638	46,444	38
Mauchline	435	24	44	70,358	48,713	44
Sorn	144	11	15	16,861	14,175	12
Monkton and Prestwick: North	322	34	38	-	59,829	20
Muirkirk	181	-	-	20,888	15,161	-
Old Cumnock: Trinity	344	18	35	62,299	39,647	16
New Cumnock	477	32	31	72,715	45,424	135
Ochiltree	244	20	19	36,399	23,516	27
Stair	218	16	17	29,333	24,776	40
Prestwick: Kingcase	651	85	82	128,977	76,629	170

Congregation	Com	Eld	G	In 14	M&M	–18
Prestwick: St Nicholas'	621	71	64	117,935	72,454	201
Prestwick: South	281	37	28	86,151	53,922	85
Troon: Old	899	60	-	141,238	84,802	170
Troon: Portland	527	47	33	133,965	75,050	25
Troon: St Meddan's	845	89	43	-	69,825	113

11. Irvine and Kilmarnock

Congregation	Com	Eld	G	In 14	M&M	–18
Caldwell	233	17	-	66,886	42,524	15
Dunlop	395	37	26	86,708	38,549	48
Crosshouse	287	-	16	52,048	35,387	-
Darvel	337	27	35	58,947	26,888	45
Dreghorn and Springside	484	44	30	90,689	49,773	51
Fenwick	324	23	28	58,406	36,271	26
Galston	640	53	60	95,341	68,155	51
Hurlford	354	26	33	62,749	40,138	10
Irvine: Fullarton	376	43	53	100,937	56,215	194
Irvine: Girdle Toll	156	17	24	-	18,173	89
Irvine: Mure	320	23	19	70,531	44,406	48
Irvine: Old	399	-	20	83,734	63,325	-
Irvine: Relief Bourtreehill	235	23	31	47,834	26,671	20
Irvine: St Andrew's	275	-	32	65,958	34,365	-
Kilmarnock: Kay Park	562	78	41	132,282	86,273	17
Kilmarnock: New Laigh Kirk	866	84	70	211,364	113,866	151
Kilmarnock: Riccarton	248	27	20	65,035	44,553	55
Kilmarnock: St Andrew's & St Marnock's	841	97	44	170,290	100,428	460
Kilmarnock: St John's Onthank	251	22	23	39,678	30,202	100
Kilmarnock: St Kentigern's	273	24	-	53,356	31,780	90
Kilmarnock: South	267	12	23	39,940	24,867	30
Kilmaurs: St Maur's Glencairn	295	16	23	51,205	31,661	15
Newmilns: Loudoun	220	12	-	40,028	42,131	5
Stewarton: John Knox	277	28	19	94,563	48,788	70
Stewarton: St Columba's	413	38	44	69,574	49,864	114

12. Ardrossan

Congregation	Com	Eld	G	In 14	M&M	–18
Ardrossan: Park	410	30	48	69,131	43,764	28
Ardrossan and Saltcoats Kirkgate	-	-	36	93,674	60,795	-
Beith	778	58	35	106,275	67,464	34
Brodick	138	17	-	59,921	33,094	85
Corrie	44	5	-	22,121	10,133	2
Lochranza and Pirnmill	66	14	10	22,109	10,689	3
Shiskine	70	8	17	-	19,564	12
Cumbrae	244	21	42	52,020	37,004	58
Largs: St John's	731	45	50	139,844	82,764	29
Dalry: St Margaret's	619	58	33	-	83,586	88
Dalry: Trinity	204	18	-	81,477	52,820	18
Fairlie	234	31	51	-	46,472	17
Largs: St Columba's	380	43	70	96,882	57,702	22
Kilbirnie: Auld Kirk	315	32	-	64,965	36,452	10
Kilbirnie: St Columba's	535	29	20	65,457	36,654	75
Kilmory	36	7	-	12,115	6,668	-

Congregation	Com	Eld	G	In 14	M&M	–18
Lamlash	88	12	26	-	21,675	20
Kilwinning: Mansefield Trinity	242	12	25	61,408	29,079	20
Kilwinning: Old	574	49	44	113,604	67,564	20
Largs: Clark Memorial	795	96	65	130,187	85,039	31
Saltcoats: North	288	23	28	52,189	30,340	42
Saltcoats: St Cuthbert's	272	32	14	82,050	52,176	154
Stevenston: Ardeer	243	27	28	44,087	26,709	135
Stevenston: Livingstone	285	35	28	52,133	34,170	12
Stevenston: High	244	18	20	79,442	55,921	41
West Kilbride	488	46	31	111,141	76,848	44
Whiting Bay and Kildonan	90	10	-	42,416	25,653	10

13. Lanark

Congregation	Com	Eld	G	In 14	M&M	–18
Biggar	555	25	30	-	51,057	30
Black Mount	66	7	15	-	9,781	-
Cairngryffe	165	15	13	25,591	20,591	20
Libberton and Quothquan	85	14	-	16,020	7,149	13
Symington	189	19	22	33,584	19,290	7
Carluke: Kirkton	761	51	27	120,831	69,162	355
Carluke: St Andrew's	208	12	18	49,748	31,490	30
Carluke: St John's	656	44	40	88,178	57,167	80
Carnwath	139	12	17	-	24,040	-
Carstairs and Carstairs Junction	211	20	17	44,985	32,597	120
Coalburn	122	8	17	18,622	11,269	4
Lesmahagow: Old	413	22	17	76,583	49,703	35
Crossford	169	6	-	34,843	16,025	64
Kirkfieldbank	81	7	20	17,765	9,226	-
Forth: St Paul's	343	24	43	54,431	37,300	80
Kirkmuirhill	144	12	57	73,504	57,642	22
Lanark: Greyfriars	559	50	36	104,619	50,837	180
Lanark: St Nicholas'	508	43	25	100,667	66,439	76
Law	178	11	28	-	29,178	131
Lesmahagow: Abbeygreen	173	16	-	78,281	55,261	160
The Douglas Valley Church	318	24	35	57,124	31,538	6
The Upper Clyde	206	12	16	26,939	20,527	10

14. Greenock and Paisley

Congregation	Com	Eld	G	In 14	M&M	–18
Barrhead: Bourock	447	40	45	91,932	58,173	206
Barrhead: St Andrew's	467	47	40	147,403	87,066	258
Bishopton	632	46	-	102,722	57,976	80
Bridge of Weir: Freeland	395	-	-	-	72,014	-
Bridge of Weir: St Machar's Ranfurly	361	34	31	95,695	57,070	81
Erskine Kirk	477	45	50	106,187	71,546	161
Erskine	342	31	42	93,311	62,360	285
Gourock: Old Gourock and Ashton	686	58	33	-	74,168	208
Gourock: St John's	563	67	16	117,972	55,902	353
Greenock: East End	56	-	-	13,556	4,500	-
Greenock: Mount Kirk	310	-	-	61,026	42,008	-
Greenock: Lyle Kirk	796	53	21	-	103,865	133
Greenock: St Margaret's	159	24	-	32,607	14,135	18

Congregation	Com	Eld	G	In 14	M&M	–18
Greenock: St Ninian's	228	18	-	-	16,956	48
Greenock: Wellpark Mid Kirk	533	42	13	-	57,704	78
Greenock: Westburn	686	98	30	133,311	77,719	104
Houston and Killellan	669	57	74	145,225	88,661	150
Howwood	146	10	16	41,393	30,222	10
Lochwinnoch	107	14	-	36,632	25,797	138
Inchinnan	328	28	25	-	44,631	28
Inverkip	381	33	30	59,540	35,832	23
Skelmorlie and Wemyss Bay	263	35	-	75,615	52,418	10
Johnstone: High	238	35	28	96,408	55,088	151
Johnstone: St Andrew's Trinity	217	28	26	42,635	31,387	89
Johnstone: St Paul's	411	62	-	75,762	47,747	154
Kilbarchan: East	343	40	26	71,311	44,340	60
Kilbarchan: West	400	44	27	81,396	61,009	28
Kilmacolm: Old	409	43	-	147,755	70,773	20
Kilmacolm: St Columba	190	29	-	87,852	35,000	49
Langbank	137	13	-	-	17,643	14
Port Glasgow: St Andrew's	493	68	33	79,907	49,497	338
Linwood	216	20	19	52,121	34,708	14
Neilston	493	30	16	113,882	64,163	195
Paisley: Abbey	709	44	-	174,086	101,243	98
Paisley: Glenburn	231	19	-	46,493	30,343	8
Paisley: Lylesland	326	46	23	93,320	58,421	33
Paisley: Martyrs' Sandyford	526	65	24	119,018	70,751	92
Paisley: Oakshaw Trinity	494	62	34	-	55,917	44
Paisley: St Columba Foxbar	162	20	-	30,381	21,095	112
Paisley: St James'	204	29	-	66,139	41,086	50
Paisley: St Luke's	212	27	-	61,594	34,646	14
Paisley: St Mark's Oldhall	476	55	63	116,452	62,831	41
Paisley: St Ninian's Ferguslie	56	-	-	9,063	4,000	6
Paisley: Sherwood Greenlaw	593	75	34	115,236	71,214	173
Paisley: Stow Brae Kirk	363	68	58	102,532	62,856	94
Paisley: Wallneuk North	386	31	-	67,723	44,880	25
Port Glasgow: Hamilton Bardrainney	238	15	14	49,401	23,324	20
Port Glasgow: St Martin's	156	9	-	-	13,783	12
Renfrew: North	708	65	36	-	67,479	138
Renfrew: Trinity	377	29	52	92,751	58,682	54

16. Glasgow

Banton	68	11	-	16,129	7,784	10
Twechar	72	-	-	20,809	10,564	-
Bishopbriggs: Kenmure	267	21	35	94,126	63,049	146
Bishopbriggs: Springfield Cambridge	648	46	88	122,363	70,543	143
Broom	537	52	30	119,687	91,184	420
Burnside Blairbeth	593	36	98	264,117	148,010	259
Busby	239	34	26	80,390	45,128	35
Cadder	754	77	45	-	93,181	128
Cambuslang: Flemington Hallside	297	26	23	52,785	32,241	60
Cambuslang Parish Church	679	68	40	139,466	95,927	142
Campsie	148	15	21	63,030	36,199	64

Congregation	Com	Eld	G	In 14	M&M	–18
Chryston	620	30	18	221,037	116,613	94
Eaglesham	552	-	50	-	83,694	-
Fernhill and Cathkin	260	26	19	58,300	36,675	78
Gartcosh	144	14	-	32,924	10,937	84
Glenboig	115	9	11	-	6,970	11
Giffnock: Orchardhill	429	46	18	-	82,751	228
Giffnock: South	619	80	40	195,017	103,450	106
Giffnock: The Park	252	27	-	82,146	42,370	163
Greenbank	885	78	69	254,304	123,915	240
Kilsyth: Anderson	312	22	56	75,376	47,502	132
Kilsyth: Burns and Old	381	29	45	89,157	50,690	63
Kirkintilloch: Hillhead	104	9	12	15,126	8,300	22
Kirkintilloch: St Columba's	437	36	40	89,546	56,682	6
Kirkintilloch: St David's Memorial Park	578	44	36	-	45,103	112
Kirkintilloch: St Mary's	732	-	38	110,979	47,637	-
Lenzie: Old	440	44	-	114,343	71,890	15
Lenzie: Union	604	61	84	192,645	103,225	287
Maxwell Mearns Castle	303	-	-	167,236	90,537	-
Mearns	837	52	-	-	117,711	56
Milton of Campsie	339	31	45	69,609	47,090	102
Netherlee	633	62	30	201,937	117,245	279
Newton Mearns	418	41	22	114,577	80,200	127
Rutherglen: Old	302	30	-	65,375	37,453	5
Rutherglen: Stonelaw	322	42	-	198,103	82,040	32
Rutherglen: West and Wardlawhill	476	-	54	81,295	62,385	-
Stamperland	347	34	23	73,913	44,370	220
Stepps	304	22	-	-	31,711	195
Thornliebank	106	10	31	38,182	29,309	10
Torrance	315	13	-	99,035	63,182	164
Williamwood	427	69	35	-	76,237	665
Glasgow: Anderston Kelvingrove	50	7	8	-	19,860	9
Glasgow: Baillieston Mure Memorial	415	38	85	87,707	56,351	168
Glasgow: Baillieston St Andrew's	272	24	36	58,954	38,312	154
Glasgow: Balshagray Victoria Park	182	26	17	100,276	61,500	38
Glasgow: Barlanark Greyfriars	90	-	12	-	21,154	-
Glasgow: Blawarthill	172	30	20	-	15,096	54
Glasgow: Bridgeton St Francis in the East	81	14	15	32,802	21,361	6
Glasgow: Broomhill	419	59	50	141,369	84,365	210
Glasgow: Hyndland	233	40	22	85,907	56,561	50
Glasgow: Calton Parkhead	86	-	-	-	9,597	-
Glasgow: Cardonald	354	37	50	-	71,304	247
Glasgow: Carmunnock	301	-	22	53,801	33,082	-
Glasgow: Carmyle	91	5	16	23,312	11,246	21
Glasgow: Kenmuir Mount Vernon	122	10	24	61,262	35,414	60
Glasgow: Carnwadric	148	16	-	36,841	22,801	30
Glasgow: Castlemilk	147	-	11	26,245	8,791	-
Glasgow: Cathcart Old	269	43	38	89,131	61,380	347
Glasgow: Cathcart Trinity	439	52	56	214,094	109,760	130
Glasgow: Cathedral (High or St Mungo's)	402	-	-	93,891	66,065	-
Glasgow: Clincarthill	260	33	46	97,984	67,567	134

Congregation .... Com	Eld	G	In 14	M&M	–18
Glasgow: Colston Milton..64	-	-	25,863	12,415	-
Glasgow: Colston Wellpark 100	12	-	22,966	13,732	52
Glasgow: Cranhill...44	8	-	-	1,971	51
Glasgow: Croftfoot 270	39	43	78,293	48,071	25
Glasgow: Dennistoun New 189	37	22	87,164	60,636	83
Glasgow: Drumchapel St Andrew's...................................194	-	-	50,201	42,212	-
Glasgow: Drumchapel St Mark's...69	-	-	15,151	2,480	-
Glasgow: Easterhouse St George's and St Peter's 48	5	-	-	237	39
Glasgow: Eastwood 225	45	20	89,561	59,368	94
Glasgow: Gairbraid..128	-	17	36,694	23,526	-
Glasgow: Gallowgate...50	15	-	27,797	10,708	6
Glasgow: Garthamlock and Craigend East..........................87	-	-	-	4,180	-
Glasgow: Gorbals..90	-	-	27,626	18,285	-
Glasgow: Govan and Linthouse..201	47	48	-	49,052	338
Glasgow: High Carntyne 262	22	39	70,117	36,888	118
Glasgow: Hillington Park 288	23	35	71,034	44,008	100
Glasgow: Ibrox..130	20	21	48,672	32,611	61
Glasgow: John Ross Memorial (For Deaf People)..53	3	-	-	-	-
Glasgow: Jordanhill...392	66	27	173,026	106,166	154
Glasgow: Kelvinbridge 189	-	10	39,153	39,301	-
Glasgow: Kelvinside Hillhead 157	26	-	-	48,751	97
Glasgow: King's Park 585	69	41	143,145	89,497	42
Glasgow: Kinning Park 131	11	-	30,339	23,766	-
Glasgow: Knightswood St Margaret's................................204	26	26	-	28,406	108
Glasgow: Langside...204	51	19	86,237	48,803	112
Glasgow: Lochwood 61	6	8	-	8,043	65
Glasgow: Maryhill 139	15	13	-	24,883	97
Glasgow: Merrylea...306	-	26	77,520	50,116	-
Glasgow: Mosspark 118	24	35	46,110	31,705	55
Glasgow: Newlands South 474	62	22	150,507	60,000	28
Glasgow: Partick South..140	24	-	-	39,864	15
Glasgow: Partick Trinity 167	-	-	87,872	51,317	-
Glasgow: Penilee St Andrew's..100	13	-	43,038	23,176	100
Glasgow: Pollokshaws..124	21	-	42,295	24,884	25
Glasgow: Pollokshields...193	30	24	90,595	58,546	100
Glasgow: Possilpark...115	-	12	27,338	18,012	-
Glasgow: Queen's Park Govanhill.....................................263	46	38	120,668	79,908	27
Glasgow: Renfield St Stephen's..142	20	29	-	39,008	15
Glasgow: Robroyston...39	-	-	32,991	3,000	-
Glasgow: Ruchazie 26	-	-	-	1,925	-
Glasgow: Ruchill Kelvinside 79	23	-	41,874	46,521	20
Glasgow: St Andrew's East...70	12	14	38,352	22,252	35
Glasgow: St Christopher's Priesthill and Nitshill...............228	-	-	-	30,982	-
Glasgow: St Columba 140	-	16	-	12,012	-
Glasgow: St David's Knightswood.....................................266	22	29	77,037	54,564	32
Glasgow: St Enoch's Hogganfield 135	17	30	-	25,278	8
Glasgow: St George's Tron...380	-	-	7,483	1,350	-
Glasgow: St James' (Pollok) 164	25	30	53,992	12,624	94

Congregation	Com	Eld	G	In 14	M&M	–18
Glasgow: St John's Renfield	315	41	-	139,985	90,144	211
Glasgow: St Margaret's Tollcross Park	132	-	-	-	9,829	-
Glasgow: St Nicholas' Cardonald	242	21	11	51,514	34,508	355
Glasgow: St Paul's	62	6	-	10,369	5,579	189
Glasgow: St Rollox	76	8	-	36,069	24,436	25
Glasgow: Sandyford Henderson Memorial	261	-	14	174,217	102,599	-
Glasgow: Sandyhills	272	28	50	78,261	48,036	27
Glasgow: Scotstoun	127	6	-	57,300	41,191	15
Glasgow: Shawlands	240	19	27	80,075	57,032	42
Glasgow: South Shawlands	157	26	-	58,197	46,085	80
Glasgow: Sherbrooke St Gilbert's	251	-	-	-	81,734	-
Glasgow: Shettleston New	226	34	30	-	49,725	84
Glasgow: Shettleston Old	221	27	20	49,995	33,921	80
Glasgow: South Carntyne	48	7	-	-	18,520	50
Glasgow: Springburn	208	32	28	54,327	41,821	75
Glasgow: Temple Anniesland	293	24	56	88,698	59,083	114
Glasgow: Toryglen	97	12	-	16,131	8,852	5
Glasgow: Trinity Possil and Henry Drummond	66	7	-	58,917	36,511	2
Glasgow: Tron St Mary's	106	16	-	-	27,957	45
Glasgow: Victoria Tollcross	88	-	18	26,525	15,168	-
Glasgow: Wallacewell	126	-	-	-	-	-
Glasgow: Wellington	169	19	-	96,857	71,501	17
Glasgow: Whiteinch	41	4	-	-	33,304	21
Glasgow: Yoker	97	-	-	26,737	15,760	-

17. Hamilton

Congregation	Com	Eld	G	In 14	M&M	–18
Airdrie: Broomknoll	234	29	27	64,923	27,932	81
Calderbank	112	9	12	20,066	10,092	-
Airdrie: Clarkston	357	39	26	66,577	41,774	135
Airdrie: Flowerhill	555	37	-	-	76,508	188
Airdrie: High	299	33	-	72,140	40,847	138
Airdrie: Jackson	335	49	20	81,308	51,518	188
Airdrie: New Monkland	295	30	18	55,794	34,748	149
Greengairs	122	9	-	22,355	13,143	5
Airdrie: St Columba's	228	7	-	25,899	10,012	53
Airdrie: The New Wellwynd	744	87	-	151,691	81,781	57
Bargeddie	105	-	-	-	37,886	-
Bellshill: Central	401	31	35	54,928	31,554	22
Bellshill: West	491	40	24	70,420	45,203	28
Blantyre: Livingstone Memorial	213	22	19	57,902	33,907	160
Blantyre: St Andrew's	212	22	-	54,457	36,813	24
Blantyre: Old	263	15	27	62,095	44,872	35
Bothwell	480	55	31	-	67,270	79
Caldercruix and Longriggend	196	-	-	70,752	27,524	-
Chapelhall	219	23	38	41,984	27,987	68
Kirk o' Shotts	169	9	9	-	21,279	19
Chapelton	160	17	18	26,139	14,021	31
Strathaven: Rankin	539	54	25	84,082	50,400	189
Cleland	170	11	-	24,022	18,051	12
Wishaw: St Mark's	320	29	46	72,589	47,841	112

Congregation	Com	Eld	G	In 14	M&M	–18
Coatbridge: Blairhill Dundyvan	267	23	22	55,310	34,669	116
Coatbridge: Middle	351	39	33	54,516	37,950	169
Coatbridge: Calder	341	-	30	53,119	31,440	-
Coatbridge: Old Monkland	220	22	21	54,084	32,787	60
Coatbridge: New St Andrew's	738	79	24	126,298	68,068	215
Coatbridge: Townhead	126	18	-	41,527	29,071	64
Dalserf	210	19	29	77,962	55,813	75
East Kilbride: Claremont	594	49	-	112,367	70,094	253
East Kilbride: Greenhills	175	14	20	41,075	17,398	15
East Kilbride: Moncrieff	651	67	55	120,553	70,170	313
East Kilbride: Mossneuk	258	13	-	28,258	21,340	169
East Kilbride: Old	684	61	41	-	69,943	37
East Kilbride: South	279	32	22	58,175	53,809	83
East Kilbride: Stewartfield	-	-	-	13,387	5,500	11
East Kilbride: West	378	30	38	54,534	43,582	60
East Kilbride: Westwood	509	40	-	86,536	51,548	87
Glasford	121	7	15	22,767	11,063	-
Strathaven: East	301	30	36	60,516	36,436	31
Hamilton: Cadzow	442	61	44	128,386	80,927	140
Hamilton: Gilmour and Whitehill	156	26	-	40,383	34,408	87
Hamilton: West	267	27	-	62,462	46,166	20
Hamilton: Hillhouse	378	48	30	91,565	47,804	212
Hamilton: Old	532	76	28	-	82,636	63
Hamilton: St Andrew's	-	-	-	-	430	-
Hamilton: St John's	526	51	60	-	69,565	200
Hamilton: South	204	27	23	60,642	35,495	26
Quarter	94	13	19	26,531	16,821	9
Hamilton: Trinity	298	24	-	48,534	34,955	125
Holytown	176	18	28	52,529	29,617	62
New Stevenston: Wrangholm Kirk	94	12	17	35,712	26,580	22
Larkhall: Chalmers	112	12	26	36,527	14,963	18
Larkhall: St Machan's	433	44	43	96,001	63,724	75
Larkhall: Trinity	185	19	28	47,418	31,990	199
Motherwell: Crosshill	350	-	55	100,489	50,888	-
Motherwell: St Margaret's	357	-	11	44,175	21,023	-
Motherwell: Dalziel St Andrew's	510	71	39	134,064	77,660	200
Motherwell: North	131	18	35	57,358	34,148	107
Motherwell: St Mary's	764	107	70	145,168	75,401	309
Motherwell: South	399	63	56	103,633	71,833	260
Newarthill and Carfin	368	28	23	68,471	36,436	148
Newmains: Bonkle	129	18	-	34,610	24,815	14
Newmains: Coltness Memorial	201	21	19	-	34,632	73
Overtown	265	38	52	50,363	29,606	153
Shotts: Calderhead Erskine	458	36	24	89,331	52,477	13
Stonehouse: St Ninian's	359	-	30	88,938	41,925	-
Strathaven: Avendale Old and Drumclog	666	59	51	147,124	83,678	57
Uddingston: Burnhead	256	24	10	55,770	23,321	71
Uddingston: Old	555	65	48	115,705	75,515	18
Uddingston: Viewpark	433	71	30	100,875	58,495	250
Wishaw: Cambusnethan North	450	36	-	70,396	48,484	125

Congregation	Com	Eld	G	In 14	M&M	–18
Wishaw: Cambusnethan Old & Morningside	408	32	25	82,517	47,057	200
Wishaw: Craigneuk and Belhaven	146	28	18	49,576	31,980	16
Wishaw: Old	216	29	-	36,175	28,225	68
Wishaw: South Wishaw	438	31	38	82,329	59,202	40

18. Dumbarton

Alexandria	292	39	22	72,284	48,856	30
Arrochar	62	9	14	-	13,389	16
Luss	101	20	29	73,698	24,386	-
Baldernock	181	19	-	40,437	22,548	16
Bearsden: Baljaffray	359	29	41	90,585	45,909	80
Bearsden: Cross	852	96	38	178,335	103,865	45
Bearsden: Killermont	631	56	40	158,688	85,485	60
Bearsden: New Kilpatrick	1,408	127	127	311,321	159,669	183
Bearsden: Westerton Fairlie Memorial	376	43	47	-	51,092	7
Bonhill	835	63	-	62,097	50,355	85
Renton: Trinity	245	19	-	33,529	19,597	2
Cardross	387	38	30	82,736	51,281	15
Clydebank: Abbotsford	148	14	-	47,771	31,326	36
Dalmuir: Barclay	202	16	-	45,421	28,097	28
Clydebank: Faifley	174	16	34	45,484	25,589	-
Clydebank: Kilbowie St Andrew's	263	22	17	46,481	30,882	156
Clydebank: Radnor Park	157	26	20	47,142	29,968	4
Clydebank: St Cuthbert's	119	12	16	15,529	10,659	2
Duntocher	224	23	41	37,910	31,633	1
Craigrownie	149	18	27	38,774	26,857	5
Garelochhead	179	16	-	66,865	38,043	48
Rosneath: St Modan's	115	11	19	22,920	16,770	4
Dumbarton: Riverside	509	62	48	116,914	68,090	240
Dumbarton: West Kirk	281	31	-	-	27,033	9
Dumbarton: St Andrew's	111	22	-	33,562	18,571	-
Old Kilpatrick Bowling	242	26	20	49,188	37,230	94
Helensburgh: Park	339	33	13	54,962	44,825	4
Helensburgh: St Andrew's Kirk	874	63	45	199,604	126,549	30
Rhu and Shandon	270	21	33	64,237	43,289	17
Jamestown	345	21	18	-	29,910	7
Kilmaronock Gartocharn	215	13	-	28,320	16,514	11
Milngavie: Cairns	448	39	-	146,204	76,523	20
Milngavie: St Luke's	387	28	30	106,734	47,684	40
Milngavie: St Paul's	901	89	93	207,912	117,008	180

19 Argyll

Appin	102	12	22	23,042	12,676	12
Lismore	42	6	15	12,617	8,701	14
Ardchattan	110	-	7	32,061	14,968	-
Ardrishaig	134	20	30	36,404	21,752	14
South Knapdale	34	6	-	10,952	4,325	1
Barra	45	4	-	-	8,355	54
South Uist	51	-	-	22,727	15,098	8
Campbeltown: Highland	400	34	-	47,716	36,616	-

Congregation	Com	Eld	G	In 14	M&M	–18
Campbeltown: Lorne and Lowland	794	51	40	87,824	52,377	83
Coll	15	3	-	3,985	1,561	-
Connel	123	15	14	39,844	27,753	15
Colonsay and Oronsay	13	2	-	-	6,960	-
Craignish	47	4	-	7,979	2,243	-
Kilbrandon and Kilchattan	96	19	-	-	17,456	23
Kilninver and Kilmelford	60	6	-	-	8,081	12
Cumlodden, Lochfyneside and Lochgair	89	16	12	23,478	14,107	-
Glenaray and Inveraray	104	19	-	25,361	18,358	1
Dunoon: St John's	174	23	39	39,686	31,603	4
Kirn	283	30	-	54,547	46,572	15
Sandbank	102	9	-	-	9,054	-
Dunoon: The High Kirk	318	33	37	-	44,269	23
Innellan	58	9	-	19,117	12,220	2
Toward	66	11	-	21,081	11,895	13
Gigha and Cara	33	7	-	11,334	3,921	8
Kilcalmonell	47	12	14	11,545	4,402	5
Killean and Kilchenzie	123	13	17	19,640	15,621	4
Glassary, Kilmartin and Ford	99	13	-	-	16,762	15
North Knapdale	53	6	-	28,299	22,611	4
Glenorchy and Innishael	59	6	-	-	5,602	2
Strathfillan	45	-	-	10,580	5,914	-
Iona	13	6	-	6,050	6,977	5
Kilfinichen & Kilvickeon & the Ross of Mull	34	7	-	11,161	3,342	4
Jura	24	5	-	-	4,192	-
Kilarrow	49	12	-	32,585	17,048	6
Kildalton and Oa	87	16	-	41,314	24,869	-
Kilchoman	81	8	-	14,035	16,377	14
Kilmeny	34	5	-	11,081	6,111	-
Portnahaven	25	5	10	-	1,866	2
Kilchrenan and Dalavich	23	7	8	11,892	8,831	-
Muckairn	137	17	8	28,435	18,106	-
Kilfinan	29	5	-	8,021	3,003	-
Kilmodan and Colintraive	77	10	-	17,657	13,438	12
Kyles	104	18	18	27,130	848	6
Kilmore and Oban	495	47	35	92,213	57,649	51
Kilmun (St Munn's)	78	7	15	14,998	11,469	-
Strone and Ardentinny	111	15	16	34,588	21,479	5
Kilninian and Kilmore	26	5	-	11,476	4,138	-
Salen and Ulva	37	5	-	-	7,308	-
Tobermory	55	12	-	20,681	15,289	6
Torosay and Kinlochspelvie	24	3	-	8,750	3,640	1
Lochgilphead	217	-	20	-	18,871	-
Lochgoilhead and Kilmorich	63	9	-	30,052	16,874	-
Strachur and Strachlachlan	121	14	17	27,187	23,470	1
Rothesay: Trinity	376	42	28	67,140	41,001	48
Saddell and Carradale	196	15	21	-	13,105	12
Southend	222	13	13	31,347	20,310	14
Skipness	18	6	-	9,901	3,854	3
Tarbert, Loch Fyne and Kilberry	50	17	23	-	12,023	3

Congregation	Com	Eld	G	In 14	M&M	–18
The United Church of Bute	529	33	45	77,358	47,107	60
Tiree	82	9	18	-	18,364	2

22. Falkirk

Congregation	Com	Eld	G	In 14	M&M	–18
Airth	152	6	18	-	29,362	40
Blackbraes and Shieldhill	167	23	20	32,845	17,408	9
Muiravonside	200	23	-	38,701	24,933	4
Bo'ness: Old	358	28	9	56,890	43,052	30
Bo'ness: St Andrew's	504	25	-	85,343	33,550	250
Bonnybridge: St Helen's	343	20	-	60,083	39,441	10
Bothkennar and Carronshore	218	22	-	33,290	21,481	15
Brightons	638	42	59	-	40,698	212
Carriden	446	46	25	64,401	36,728	5
Cumbernauld: Abronhill	217	21	27	63,285	36,896	113
Cumbernauld: Condorrat	325	24	38	67,693	45,099	104
Cumbernauld: Kildrum	277	40	-	54,036	37,612	145
Cumbernauld: Old	325	40	-	-	52,826	111
Cumbernauld: St Mungo's	195	35	-	65,631	25,972	21
Denny: Old	353	44	26	-	46,473	50
Denny: Westpark	478	31	38	87,193	60,624	120
Dunipace	345	27	-	54,742	37,836	55
Falkirk: Bainsford	137	12	-	37,383	24,589	100
Falkirk: Camelon	294	22	-	-	52,413	14
Falkirk: Grahamston United	330	42	36	-	-	18
Falkirk: Laurieston	217	20	27	38,552	22,530	15
Redding and Westquarter	158	13	22	25,307	17,356	6
Falkirk: St Andrew's West	444	33	-	85,074	63,344	40
Falkirk: St James'	231	25	-	31,188	21,290	-
Falkirk: Trinity	819	80	9	165,244	146,944	107
Grangemouth: Abbotsgrange	396	54	26	65,605	47,231	59
Grangemouth: Kirk of the Holy Rood	390	37	-	61,636	33,889	42
Grangemouth: Zetland	744	59	66	-	72,061	109
Haggs	256	28	16	38,799	22,282	58
Larbert: East	652	53	50	123,509	69,577	193
Larbert: Old	327	24	-	76,899	52,520	123
Larbert: West	380	39	37	83,709	47,044	112
Polmont: Old	359	27	45	76,255	50,007	94
Slamannan	210	8	-	-	22,191	11
Stenhouse and Carron	366	34	16	-	44,344	15

23. Stirling

Congregation	Com	Eld	G	In 14	M&M	–18
Aberfoyle	99	7	20	21,862	13,888	6
Port of Menteith	57	7	-	17,452	7,683	-
Alloa: Ludgate	310	24	22	82,014	46,596	14
Alloa: St Mungo's	361	43	54	-	47,676	19
Alva	486	53	23	77,369	46,471	80
Balfron	142	16	18	50,898	33,964	15
Fintry	121	10	18	19,138	14,743	9
Balquhidder	63	2	-	14,896	13,644	3
Killin and Ardeonaig	95	6	6	24,348	13,521	8

Congregation	Com	Eld	G	In 14	M&M	–18
Bannockburn: Allan	381	31	-	55,129	35,911	5
Bannockburn: Ladywell	397	17	-	-	16,585	18
Bridge of Allan	723	56	68	122,788	81,210	235
Buchanan	97	8	-	39,320	10,029	7
Drymen	252	25	-	72,559	40,561	30
Buchlyvie	210	12	16	26,621	21,549	10
Gartmore	71	10	-	19,103	14,208	2
Callander	551	23	35	97,500	72,021	60
Cambusbarron: The Bruce Memorial	319	20	-	66,216	32,400	41
Clackmannan	408	25	30	78,813	49,131	18
Cowie and Plean	181	9	6	18,972	11,195	2
Fallin	247	7	-	34,026	17,841	65
Dollar	248	30	65	97,790	55,378	20
Glendevon	44	-	-	6,741	3,265	-
Muckhart	112	1	-	22,594	13,065	11
Dunblane: Cathedral	837	75	58	211,112	123,788	344
Dunblane: St Blane's	320	34	37	96,276	60,982	27
Lecropt	158	16	-	43,094	31,506	13
Gargunnock	150	13	-	27,322	19,403	19
Kilmadock	94	11	-	16,734	11,198	1
Kincardine-in-Menteith	80	7	-	18,608	9,858	8
Killearn	389	28	39	103,040	59,721	182
Kippen	205	17	21	27,551	20,097	-
Norrieston	113	10	9	20,061	13,418	2
Logie	528	60	32	98,126	60,617	27
Menstrie	364	20	24	66,136	45,385	25
Sauchie and Coalsnaughton	596	28	17	55,261	35,899	9
Stirling: Allan Park South	179	23	-	41,996	25,963	63
Stirling: Church of The Holy Rude	152	21	-	-	7,991	12
Stirling: Viewfield Erskine	281	22	30	41,682	25,486	13
Stirling: North	370	29	24	89,312	53,299	85
Stirling: St Columba's	485	60	-	112,999	61,236	20
Stirling: St Mark's	187	7	-	-	18,085	65
Stirling: St Ninian's Old	708	61	-	94,836	54,352	47
Strathblane	201	-	43	-	45,886	-
Tillicoultry	632	65	40	79,693	57,971	110
Tullibody: St Serf's	376	17	24	61,684	35,037	60

24. Dunfermline

Aberdour: St Fillan's	370	18	-	74,711	47,728	114
Beath and Cowdenbeath: North	213	21	14	61,092	35,825	38
Cairneyhill	113	-	-	28,983	15,352	-
Limekilns	251	45	-	76,827	41,297	8
Carnock and Oakley	180	23	22	60,743	33,084	38
Saline and Blairingone	157	14	15	41,569	26,104	28
Cowdenbeath: Trinity	311	27	15	71,661	40,795	14
Culross and Torryburn	99	22	-	50,730	35,201	25
Dalgety	518	48	26	125,919	66,876	81
Dunfermline: Abbey	671	72	-	131,840	83,021	160
Dunfermline: East	56	-	-	36,764	7,979	60

Congregation	Com	Eld	G	In 14	M&M	–18
Dunfermline: Gillespie Memorial	225	29	19	50,892	55,562	22
Dunfermline: North	167	14	-	41,252	22,167	9
Dunfermline: St Andrew's Erskine	189	25	18	51,471	27,074	25
Dunfermline: St Leonard's	325	28	32	79,425	45,556	38
Dunfermline: St Margaret's	243	29	19	75,142	44,337	46
Dunfermline: St Ninian's	183	25	29	-	23,115	78
Dunfermline: Townhill and Kingseat	327	26	26	-	42,754	27
Inverkeithing	309	26	-	62,967	38,464	39
North Queensferry	59	7	-	18,944	9,799	5
Kelty	282	13	55	68,039	45,863	18
Lochgelly and Benarty: St Serf's	411	50	-	64,039	40,264	22
Rosyth	237	30	-	36,473	18,881	50
Tulliallan and Kincardine	306	20	35	-	32,970	16

25. Kirkcaldy

Congregation	Com	Eld	G	In 14	M&M	–18
Auchterderran Kinglassie	331	29	13	53,762	38,120	10
Auchtertool	64	7	-	10,448	5,048	6
Kirkcaldy: Linktown	252	35	35	57,708	36,905	46
Buckhaven and Wemyss	253	21	30	52,227	33,956	8
Burntisland	319	36	16	76,820	46,901	19
Dysart: St Clair	471	33	20	-	42,374	12
Glenrothes: Christ's Kirk	208	17	39	40,476	24,605	10
Glenrothes: St Columba's	464	41	8	56,316	36,768	63
Glenrothes: St Margaret's	306	30	37	59,512	32,888	70
Glenrothes: St Ninian's	244	36	13	70,322	42,066	78
Kennoway, Windygates and Balgonie St Kenneth's	640	44	66	96,938	56,889	30
Kinghorn	329	19	-	79,679	45,950	35
Kirkcaldy: Abbotshall	508	44	-	80,321	47,563	13
Kirkcaldy: Bennochy	469	43	41	86,794	59,303	10
Kirkcaldy: Pathhead	356	35	38	76,426	49,615	122
Kirkcaldy: St Bryce Kirk	396	25	37	83,461	73,623	55
Kirkcaldy: Templehall	174	11	14	38,029	26,332	-
Kirkcaldy: Torbain	225	33	17	53,786	25,832	83
Leslie: Trinity	182	16	14	27,891	23,601	4
Leven	490	32	39	111,976	68,115	5
Markinch and Thornton	632	48	-	85,546	56,999	8
Methil: Wellesley	322	24	20	53,841	20,060	130
Methilhill and Denbeath	199	19	38	36,882	20,657	15

26. St Andrews

Congregation	Com	Eld	G	In 14	M&M	–18
Abdie and Dunbog	160	18	-	19,304	14,831	14
Newburgh	229	13	-	20,311	15,429	12
Anstruther	209	23	-	38,229	29,849	5
Cellardyke	251	22	46	50,643	29,682	9
Kilrenny	118	15	-	29,544	19,253	10
Auchtermuchty	268	19	22	42,179	25,129	-
Edenshead and Strathmiglo	162	12	-	-	13,642	-
Balmerino	123	13	16	-	16,326	-
Wormit	240	16	27	39,867	25,204	17

Congregation	Com	Eld	G	In 14	M&M	–18
Boarhills and Dunino	140	9	-	20,304	16,243	-
Cameron	95	13	14	24,925	12,264	14
St Andrews: St Leonard's	574	47	29	136,337	77,733	40
Carnbee	91	14	20	16,205	11,782	-
Pittenweem	246	14	14	24,832	17,823	10
Ceres, Kemback and Springfield	402	37	23	59,996	68,121	20
Crail	365	23	39	46,910	35,426	-
Kingsbarns	72	8	-	15,927	10,195	-
Creich, Flisk and Kilmany	105	11	11	21,330	14,419	3
Cupar: Old and St Michael of Tarvit	580	-	27	154,999	74,955	-
Monimail	100	14	-	19,704	16,762	3
Cupar: St John's and Dairsie United	703	-	41	-	65,606	18
Elie Kilconquhar and Colinsburgh	432	33	72	68,055	61,447	22
Falkland	154	15	-	36,099	19,168	5
Freuchie	137	16	14	23,856	11,844	10
Howe of Fife	494	28	-	60,948	36,554	28
Largo and Newburn	263	17	-	54,435	33,717	8
Largo: St David's	135	17	28	37,090	23,075	3
Largoward	71	7	-	11,904	6,223	-
St Monans	268	15	32	-	43,159	20
Leuchars: St Athernase	319	27	34	50,370	41,657	-
Newport-on-Tay	377	42	-	73,408	45,224	13
St Andrews: Holy Trinity	441	35	51	-	80,199	86
St Andrews: Hope Park and Martyrs'	619	57	27	161,541	87,047	2
Strathkinness	92	11	-	17,483	11,635	-
Tayport	347	24	20	39,515	37,788	-

27. Dunkeld and Meigle

Congregation	Com	Eld	G	In 14	M&M	–18
Aberfeldy	192	12	15	-	30,123	170
Dull and Weem	105	14	15	24,474	14,733	6
Alyth	682	33	26	94,424	41,244	18
Ardler, Kettins and Meigle	401	21	36	40,712	34,790	20
Bendochy	83	12	-	26,293	15,015	2
Coupar Angus: Abbey	294	20	-	44,519	24,820	98
Blair Atholl and Struan	130	16	10	16,087	18,827	-
Tenandry	54	9	-	21,964	16,817	1
Blairgowrie	890	47	30	123,071	68,565	101
Braes of Rannoch	26	7	-	13,014	8,386	-
Foss and Rannoch	88	11	12	17,531	13,587	12
Caputh and Clunie	153	15	18	24,616	17,474	-
Kinclaven	144	15	18	20,358	17,097	-
Dunkeld	377	27	15	-	56,180	65
Fortingall and Glenlyon	49	9	-	16,490	15,488	-
Kenmore and Lawers	68	6	24	-	23,939	-
Grantully, Logierait and Strathtay	138	11	9	26,747	26,948	13
Kirkmichael, Straloch and Glenshee	103	5	-	12,590	9,484	5
Rattray	355	17	18	40,015	16,321	1
Pitlochry	378	28	25	85,231	57,078	44

Congregation	Com	Eld	G	In 14	M&M	–18
28. Perth						
Aberdalgie and Forteviot	177	13	-	-	30,855	18
Aberuthven and Dunning	193	13	-	42,218	30,855	43
Abernethy & Dron & Arngask	311	26	-	37,747	35,495	19
Almondbank Tibbermore	273	17	33	-	26,783	11
Methven and Logiealmond	257	17	15	-	21,397	-
Ardoch	169	16	25	37,340	16,810	26
Blackford	110	15	-	30,178	11,007	42
Auchterarder	590	29	42	125,465	58,750	42
Auchtergaven and Moneydie	497	20	31	-	34,044	83
Redgorton and Stanley	344	19	33	42,702	27,353	21
Cargill Burrelton	266	12	28	-	23,683	8
Collace	116	8	17	15,773	11,353	-
Cleish	218	14	19	45,700	29,960	8
Fossoway St Serf's and Devonside	228	19	-	45,964	26,892	17
Comrie	426	24	23	119,163	57,842	12
Dundurn	55	8	-	16,146	11,233	3
Crieff	728	42	33	-	67,635	50
Dunbarney and Forgandenny	559	31	12	87,973	51,441	12
Errol	265	22	19	42,306	32,275	22
Kilspindie and Rait	67	6	-	10,000	7,933	-
Fowlis Wester, Madderty & Monzie	296	20	12	46,297	31,946	10
Gask	86	9	12	22,583	19,852	1
Kinross	670	32	48	106,398	63,372	165
Muthill	267	24	15	40,277	26,441	14
Trinity Gask and Kinkell	53	-	-	10,870	4,771	-
Orwell and Portmoak	439	36	39	71,942	47,446	18
Perth: Craigie and Moncrieffe	710	47	37	-	44,581	86
Perth: Kinnoull	427	43	23	-	45,754	36
Perth: Letham St Mark's	499	10	23	-	64,356	80
Perth: North	1,033	64	39	225,886	108,038	93
Perth: Riverside	59	5	-	-	14,748	26
Perth: St John's Kirk of Perth	485	32	-	94,157	59,438	-
Perth: St Leonard's-in-the-Fields	464	34	-	70,952	57,230	6
Perth: St Matthew's	793	30	19	91,002	65,938	160
St Madoes and Kinfauns	295	30	20	-	32,584	61
Scone and St Martins	-	-	61	130,560	73,608	-
29. Dundee						
Abernyte	91	8	-	17,432	11,909	10
Inchture and Kinnaird	163	23	-	42,223	18,596	10
Longforgan	183	22	24	-	20,354	15
Auchterhouse	143	13	14	23,676	15,948	9
Monikie & Newbigging and Murroes & Tealing	548	28	27	53,189	39,581	24
Dundee: Balgay	376	34	18	80,839	47,864	24
Dundee: Barnhill St Margaret's	785	55	67	168,983	91,040	70
Dundee: Broughty Ferry New Kirk	759	50	52	115,813	67,738	18
Dundee: Broughty Ferry St James'	139	4	12	-	38,108	63

Congregation	Com	Eld	G	In 14	M&M	–18
Dundee: Broughty Ferry St Luke's and Queen Street	427	51	31	-	48,508	3
Dundee: Broughty Ferry St Stephen's and West	319	25	-	-	29,636	23
Dundee: Dundee (St Mary's)	541	44	24	91,881	62,308	10
Dundee: Camperdown	137	10	11	-	21,399	10
Dundee: Chalmers Ardler	222	22	32	81,149	50,170	113
Dundee: Coldside	283	20	-	-	31,850	37
Dundee: Craigiebank	180	14	-	26,753	25,957	40
Dundee: Douglas and Mid Craigie	125	13	17	29,185	17,958	70
Dundee: Downfield Mains	394	32	31	84,157	61,944	142
Dundee: Fintry Parish Church	93	7	-	50,360	34,935	25
Dundee: Lochee	539	33	29	78,666	43,669	214
Dundee: Logie and St John's Cross	221	11 *	21	61,883	66,609	10
Dundee: Meadowside St Paul's	481	27	20	63,323	38,785	38
Dundee: Menzieshill	265	18	-	-	450	170
Dundee: St Andrew's	476	57	32	124,547	61,899	38
Dundee: St David's High Kirk	271	46	25	-	32,524	42
Dundee: Steeple	245	28	-	118,977	76,663	16
Dundee: Stobswell	427	41	-	69,764	43,277	13
Dundee: Strathmartine	272	23	26	49,180	32,020	-
Dundee: Trinity	454	36	34	-	31,785	44
Dundee: West	301	28	24	84,750	48,704	-
Dundee: Whitfield	44	7	-	-	5,848	56
Fowlis and Liff	149	14	12	25,724	26,465	17
Lundie and Muirhead	316	25	-	48,450	25,048	27
Invergowrie	413	54	48	67,809	40,301	-
Monifieth	1,129	59	42	169,921	78,171	112
30. Angus						
Aberlemno	195	11	-	22,947	12,597	9
Guthrie and Rescobie	224	10	12	22,462	12,526	14
Arbirlot	163	11	-	-	17,761	2
Carmyllie	125	12	-	21,619	16,124	-
Arbroath: Knox's	301	22	26	43,703	26,463	18
Arbroath: St Vigeans	549	40	26	66,783	44,825	58
Arbroath: Old and Abbey	510	40	28	-	69,861	30
Arbroath: St Andrew's	610	44	40	157,506	87,854	70
Arbroath: West Kirk	759	73	45	104,625	56,884	47
Barry	206	13	10	28,317	15,921	-
Carnoustie	351	25	26	-	46,740	16
Brechin: Cathedral	523	35	18	-	42,523	18
Brechin: Gardner Memorial	483	24	-	55,969	38,973	30
Farnell	111	11	-	9,069	9,986	11
Carnoustie: Panbride	685	33	-	68,981	39,199	40
Colliston	171	-	9	17,310	11,455	3
Friockheim Kinnell	144	14	21	18,267	12,203	-
Inverkeilor and Lunan	121	9	22	23,388	16,766	5
Dun and Hillside	416	48	32	-	39,396	200
Dunnichen, Letham and Kirkden	269	16	25	42,109	24,691	3
Eassie, Nevay and Newtyle	221	17	22	26,039	23,963	28

Congregation	Com	Eld	G	In 14	M&M	–18
Edzell Lethnot Glenesk	333	24	28	35,567	34,241	10
Fern Careston Menmuir	102	6	-	13,799	14,750	9
Forfar: East and Old	829	57	44	92,280	61,403	34
Forfar: Lowson Memorial	901	40	30	88,063	53,817	254
Forfar: St Margaret's	514	30	17	-	47,344	116
Glamis, Inverarity and Kinettles	372	26	17	38,735	37,606	17
Inchbrayock	189	10	-	26,989	26,324	18
Montrose: Melville South	288	-	-	30,633	21,676	-
Kirriemuir: St Andrew's	288	21	29	47,191	34,966	20
Oathlaw Tannadice	157	9	-	17,650	17,779	8
Montrose: Old and St Andrew's	698	47	27	87,826	63,352	47
The Glens and Kirriemuir Old	992	69	40	-	78,206	1,009
The Isla Parishes	158	20	-	35,020	29,595	10

31. Aberdeen

Congregation	Com	Eld	G	In 14	M&M	–18
Aberdeen: Bridge of Don Oldmachar	205	10	-	55,942	36,803	17
Aberdeen: Cove	72	-	-	27,568	6,000	17
Aberdeen: Craigiebuckler	781	75	44	-	69,590	110
Aberdeen: Ferryhill	363	50	25	79,886	58,412	90
Aberdeen: Garthdee	208	14	8	-	462	10
Aberdeen: Ruthrieston West	356	-	16	-	40,969	-
Aberdeen: Gilcomston South	-	-	-	-	-	-
Aberdeen: High Hilton	349	26	30	51,314	27,500	90
Aberdeen: Holburn West	424	41	26	108,887	68,067	16
Aberdeen: Mannofield	1,138	121	55	170,426	94,583	179
Aberdeen: Mastrick	250	16	9	46,802	30,650	30
Aberdeen: Middlefield	113	7	-	14,627	2,208	10
Aberdeen: Midstocket	495	48	43	97,401	78,575	26
Aberdeen: Northfield	163	12	15	28,306	16,861	10
Aberdeen: Queen Street	394	42	36	88,223	59,303	35
Aberdeen: Queen's Cross	430	42	28	169,957	82,419	160
Aberdeen: Rubislaw	472	70	35	143,018	86,101	30
Aberdeen: St Columba's Bridge of Don	256	15	-	-	55,476	120
Aberdeen: St George's Tillydrone	98	12	12	14,407	715	5
Aberdeen: St John's Church for Deaf People	91	1	-	-	-	-
Aberdeen: St Machar's Cathedral	524	-	-	149,870	61,725	-
Aberdeen: St Mark's	336	35	32	109,780	62,324	27
Aberdeen: St Mary's	332	33	-	80,255	39,896	68
Aberdeen: St Nicholas Kincorth, South of	338	32	29	70,986	44,183	38
Aberdeen: St Nicholas Uniting, Kirk of	358	33	15	-	8,704	6
Aberdeen: St Stephen's	168	23	13	-	40,154	47
Aberdeen: South Holburn	503	50	43	90,410	65,014	25
Aberdeen: Stockethill	96	7	-	30,508	621	15
Aberdeen: Summerhill	133	19	-	30,043	18,277	5
Aberdeen: Torry St Fittick's	352	19	23	64,997	39,542	1
Aberdeen: Woodside	269	35	31	44,015	30,393	40
Bucksburn: Stoneywood	426	16	9	-	28,989	4
Cults	764	69	47	165,341	89,889	40
Dyce	1,004	51	34	-	57,480	255
Kingswells	386	24	22	55,646	32,403	22

Congregation	Com	Eld	G	In 14	M&M	–18
Newhills	447	41	45	-	75,400	25
Peterculter	606	47	-	111,752	61,923	247

32. Kincardine and Deeside

Aberluthnott	188	8	11	15,842	11,260	8
Laurencekirk	406	10	32	38,902	23,287	40
Aboyne and Dinnet	325	7	26	51,597	32,621	45
Cromar	223	13	-	32,795	23,014	-
Arbuthnott, Bervie and Kinneff	670	33	32	82,734	52,902	28
Banchory-Devenick and Maryculter/Cookney	177	10	10	35,340	27,360	61
Banchory-Ternan East	570	32	27	116,387	72,186	125
Banchory-Ternan West	581	27	28	137,983	69,259	130
Birse and Feughside	232	18	18	33,856	33,916	36
Braemar and Crathie	210	33	11	61,658	40,943	12
Drumoak – Durris	392	19	23	55,523	46,948	42
Glenmuick (Ballater)	274	20	29	39,959	24,733	8
Mearns Coastal	254	11	15	22,846	14,025	6
Mid Deeside	647	42	19	57,396	51,912	14
Newtonhill	348	11	13	27,923	20,835	74
Portlethen	306	21	-	61,004	43,935	85
Stonehaven: Dunnottar	598	28	26	73,318	55,775	12
Stonehaven: South	249	14	-	-	25,247	15
Stonehaven: Fetteresso	780	30	25	148,399	106,645	131
West Mearns	504	-	31	-	33,072	-

33. Gordon

Barthol Chapel	93	10	10	9,470	4,430	11
Tarves	398	18	33	36,263	23,603	-
Belhelvie	375	35	21	-	50,974	40
Blairdaff and Chapel of Garioch	358	34	11	-	29,460	10
Cluny	200	9	-	30,851	18,889	28
Monymusk	110	5	-	23,932	11,452	19
Culsalmond and Rayne	174	9	-	15,792	9,725	22
Daviot	141	7	-	13,940	10,071	15
Cushnie and Tough	259	14	9	29,139	19,441	1
Echt	220	11	-	23,024	14,317	6
Midmar	140	7	-	-	8,984	3
Ellon	1,468	93	-	176,818	98,680	166
Fintray Kinellar Keithhall	191	-	14	-	25,766	-
Foveran	314	15	-	55,148	28,933	25
Howe Trinity	572	21	24	74,486	41,286	31
Huntly: Cairnie Glass	633	9	15	-	34,898	-
Insch-Leslie-Premnay-Oyne	328	-	18	29,123	24,333	-
Inverurie: St Andrew's	984	32	-	-	68,514	5
Inverurie: West	660	47	29	100,439	56,347	37
Kemnay	509	35	-	68,215	48,698	135
Kintore	697	45	-	69,563	62,315	-
Meldrum and Bourtie	441	29	36	71,066	45,855	26
Methlick	355	24	21	54,869	35,509	13

Congregation	Com	Eld	G	In 14	M&M	–18
New Machar	433	20	16	60,008	53,973	35
Noth	247	13	-	21,170	22,338	6
Skene	1,264	84	61	140,896	83,710	191
Strathbogie Drumblade	514	36	34	70,126	45,169	76
Udny and Pitmedden	271	28	18	68,899	37,957	53
Upper Donside	377	22	-	34,291	28,813	33
34. Buchan						
Aberdour	108	8	8	10,131	7,823	6
Pitsligo	97	-	-	19,931	11,528	-
Auchaber United	149	13	11	13,556	13,256	6
Auchterless	185	19	11	21,915	15,066	10
Banff	599	32	15	65,464	48,678	136
King Edward	145	17	12	-	11,745	10
Crimond	191	11	-	-	13,339	15
Lonmay	106	11	13	12,660	9,604	-
Cruden	394	24	27	51,786	34,061	40
Deer	707	22	24	54,500	38,031	10
Fraserburgh: Old	541	56	62	110,395	76,708	187
Fraserburgh: South	276	19	-	-	30,141	3
Inverallochy and Rathen: East	86	10	-	18,081	7,620	11
Fraserburgh: West	497	42	-	74,901	46,918	104
Rathen: West	103	-	-	13,428	5,683	-
Fyvie	268	-	14	44,124	25,493	-
Rothienorman	130	-	8	15,096	8,008	-
Gardenstown	2	9	24	-	30,908	46
Longside	484	28	-	65,260	42,795	68
Macduff	634	29	42	96,722	55,189	126
Marnoch	393	-	14	28,614	21,880	-
Maud and Savoch	191	-	-	26,646	19,384	-
New Deer: St Kane's	353	-	19	49,158	39,529	-
Monquhitter and New Byth	318	-	12	22,908	23,304	-
Turriff: St Andrew's	545	30	15	-	31,174	59
New Pitsligo	270	6	-	28,470	17,046	25
Strichen and Tyrie	451	17	30	51,814	29,667	62
Ordiquihill and Cornhill	136	-	12	10,672	7,344	-
Whitehills	281	19	21	43,420	28,282	6
Peterhead: Old	385	-	30	58,872	38,902	-
Peterhead: St Andrew's	461	32	35	57,908	37,084	28
Peterhead: Trinity	270	19	20	93,446	72,570	1
Fordyce	347	15	27	-	30,765	-
St Fergus	174	-	14	14,788	7,857	-
Sandhaven	69	-	-	6,376	4,033	-
Turriff: St Ninian's and Forglen	787	-	29	78,537	49,991	-
35. Moray						
Aberlour	285	20	25	52,168	32,559	35
Alves and Burghead	152	17	40	44,458	19,127	10
Kinloss and Findhorn	91	15	12	26,636	17,148	-
Bellie and Speymouth	357	33	36	67,211	49,138	163

Congregation	Com	Eld	G	In 14	M&M	–18
Birnie and Pluscarden	255	23	29	41,393	30,112	1
Elgin: High	510	40	-	68,517	48,528	25
Buckie: North	391	34	59	60,530	40,019	15
Rathven	85	17	19	19,934	16,894	4
Buckie: South and West	230	22	36	34,383	28,691	-
Enzie	68	6	10	9,990	11,042	-
Cullen and Deskford	304	24	21	-	39,530	-
Dallas	47	6	10	13,308	8,365	1
Forres: St Leonard's	184	10	35	50,923	34,312	40
Rafford	67	8	-	13,702	8,005	26
Duffus, Spynie and Hopeman	246	27	22	52,166	28,714	60
Dyke	123	11	11	-	16,052	12
Edinkillie	78	9	-	15,149	13,074	9
Elgin: St Giles' & St Columba's South	384	60	45	126,748	81,881	19
Findochty	44	8	8	-	8,860	4
Portknockie	60	11	14	20,178	12,410	30
Forres: St Laurence	399	-	32	71,484	52,148	-
Keith: North, Newmill, Boharm and Rothiemay	526	33	27	47,295	76,004	30
Keith: St Rufus, Botriphnie and Grange	943	72	34	86,786	65,075	120
Knockando, Elchies and Archiestown	234	12	11	39,055	27,684	4
Rothes	300	18	14	42,070	28,455	-
Lossiemouth: St Gerardine's High	266	14	23	45,758	33,442	1
Lossiemouth: St James'	302	17	33	54,006	34,055	23
Mortlach and Cabrach	332	13	14	29,155	24,382	1
St Andrew's-Lhanbryd and Urquhart	372	41	30	65,293	45,442	50

36. Abernethy

Abernethy	146	-	-	45,510	23,503	-
Boat of Garten, Duthil and Kincardine	140	-	33	38,963	20,586	-
Alvie and Insh	70	-	-	28,906	17,059	-
Rothiemurchus and Aviemore	-	-	-	15,300	10,318	-
Cromdale and Advie	60	-	-	13,433	16,074	-
Dulnain Bridge	34	-	-	12,158	8,658	-
Grantown-on-Spey	160	-	13	39,446	27,765	-
Kingussie	93	-	-	-	19,513	-
Laggan	37	-	-	18,777	8,829	-
Newtonmore	79	-	-	34,783	17,528	-
Tomintoul, Glenlivet and Inveraven	138	-	-	26,128	21,293	-

37. Inverness

Ardersier	51	8	-	15,291	10,595	12
Petty	68	10	10	16,408	9,986	-
Auldearn and Dalmore	56	4	-	17,607	9,065	-
Nairn: St Ninian's	198	14	27	48,894	27,300	8
Cawdor	149	11	-	31,362	22,321	6
Croy and Dalcross	56	8	13	16,084	9,050	6
Culloden: The Barn	242	-	27	89,216	54,895	-
Daviot and Dunlichity	59	5	9	18,352	11,149	5
Moy, Dalarossie and Tomatin	29	5	14	11,093	8,584	10

Congregation	Com	Eld	G	In 14	M&M	–18
Dores and Boleskine	71	9	-	14,597	11,349	-
Inverness: Crown	565	-	40	-	79,020	-
Inverness: Dalneigh and Bona	224	19	20	81,323	52,899	90
Inverness: East	255	30	-	115,906	66,240	101
Inverness: Hilton	243	10	-	76,096	37,784	54
Inverness: Inshes	224	18	-	-	79,507	81
Inverness: Kinmylies	98	9	-	42,156	24,135	65
Inverness: Ness Bank	561	66	31	169,134	77,255	210
Inverness: Old High St Stephen's	415	38	-	119,226	74,592	23
Inverness: St Columba	47	-	-	47,153	3,000	22
Inverness: Trinity	221	29	18	66,257	49,840	50
Kilmorack and Erchless	102	-	15	42,912	32,640	-
Kiltarlity	47	6	-	17,171	12,702	17
Kirkhill	73	9	8	25,248	9,283	-
Nairn: Old	517	43	21	104,778	65,892	34
Urquhart and Glenmoriston	110	6	-	55,448	35,336	30

38. Lochaber

Congregation	Com	Eld	G	In 14	M&M	–18
Acharacle	37	6	-	17,417	9,300	8
Ardnamurchan	17	5	-	9,266	4,956	13
Ardgour and Kingairloch	51	6	20	13,215	6,866	1
Morvern	43	6	9	11,536	7,811	15
Strontian	26	4	-	10,937	4,823	15
Duror	36	6	12	12,473	6,887	18
Glencoe: St Munda's	44	9	-	20,869	7,716	-
Fort Augustus	70	9	6	23,052	16,822	26
Glengarry	29	5	9	-	8,560	12
Fort William: Duncansburgh MacIntosh	363	26	23	78,807	60,289	45
Kilmonivaig	63	5	13	15,776	17,859	12
Kilmallie	111	14	25	45,766	26,677	12
Kinlochleven	54	5	16	18,103	12,461	8
Nether Lochaber	46	9	-	16,626	12,782	3
North West Lochaber	96	15	19	35,494	20,017	20

39. Ross

Congregation	Com	Eld	G	In 14	M&M	–18
Alness	75	7	-	29,743	19,437	21
Avoch	17	4	-	16,932	10,212	10
Fortrose and Rosemarkie	83	9	-	41,314	29,811	8
Contin	52	11	-	16,090	15,373	-
Fodderty and Strathpeffer	104	16	-	30,490	16,807	32
Cromarty	40	5	-	13,582	3,751	3
Resolis and Urquhart	72	7	-	34,312	23,851	12
Dingwall: Castle Street	142	20	27	51,049	34,775	18
Dingwall: St Clement's	200	27	29	59,376	32,958	16
Fearn Abbey and Nigg	53	8	-	-	17,467	-
Tarbat	43	6	-	13,862	9,351	-
Ferintosh	139	23	13	46,811	30,690	16
Invergordon	142	10	-	60,947	33,707	10
Killearnan	116	17	-	26,181	35,480	6
Knockbain	52	10	-	-	14,984	-

Congregation	Com	Eld	G	In 14	M&M	–18
Kilmuir and Logie Easter	75	9	20	30,118	21,255	9
Kiltearn	59	8	-	29,623	20,152	8
Lochbroom and Ullapool	38	6	11	-	20,285	11
Rosskeen	119	9	20	60,465	38,485	70
Tain	105	7	20	-	33,871	14
Urray and Kilchrist	80	13	13	52,060	28,633	100

40. Sutherland

Congregation	Com	Eld	G	In 14	M&M	–18
Altnaharra and Farr	20	1	-	-	8,945	-
Assynt and Stoer	13	2	-	9,443	5,861	2
Clyne	62	11	-	-	1,889	2
Kildonan and Loth Helmsdale	35	5	-	-	6,885	6
Creich	18	7	-	10,775	15,503	3
Kincardine Croick and Edderton	44	10	-	21,684	17,059	10
Rosehall	19	2	-	12,037	6,014	8
Dornoch: Cathedral	336	35	48	-	73,513	89
Durness and Kinlochbervie	17	3	-	-	12,819	-
Eddrachillis	8	2	-	14,878	7,968	2
Golspie	71	15	12	43,442	26,419	25
Lairg	47	3	14	25,403	15,214	-
Rogart	15	3	-	-	10,418	1
Melness and Tongue	47	5	-	-	12,678	12

41. Caithness

Congregation	Com	Eld	G	In 14	M&M	–18
Bower	36	-	12	10,365	6,673	-
Halkirk Westerdale	59	-	12	14,206	11,950	-
Watten	40	-	-	12,164	8,459	-
Canisbay	30	4	14	17,454	8,035	21
Dunnet	17	-	5	6,653	4,301	-
Keiss	27	-	9	8,667	5,029	-
Olrig	51	-	10	9,743	5,491	-
Thurso: St Peter's and St Andrew's	119	14	22	50,093	39,356	10
The North Coast Parish	46	-	24	19,955	15,561	-
The Parish of Latheron	71	-	12	23,370	16,655	-
Thurso: West	218	-	20	53,628	28,953	-
Wick: Pultneytown and Thrumster	241	-	28	44,960	35,240	-
Wick: St Fergus	261	34	28	55,882	41,993	6

42. Lochcarron-Skye

Congregation	Com	Eld	G	In 14	M&M	–18
Applecross, Lochcarron and Torridon	84	4	15	41,665	33,649	30
Bracadale and Duirinish	54	7	25	-	22,465	1
Gairloch and Dundonnell	71	3	-	-	44,488	37
Glenelg and Kintail	50	6	-	-	19,574	14
Kilmuir and Stenscholl	44	5	-	-	24,915	12
Lochalsh	78	4	11	-	23,580	6
Portree	91	9	-	59,775	38,235	18
Snizort	38	3	-	-	25,146	3
Strath and Sleat	130	6	17	-	64,613	50

Congregation	Com	Eld	G	In 14	M&M	–18
43. Uist						
Benbecula	63	-	9	35,592	23,479	-
Carinish	69	-	15	46,268	31,302	-
Berneray and Lochmaddy	46	-	14	16,374	20,765	-
Kilmuir and Paible	28	4	-	28,596	20,288	10
Manish-Scarista	26	3	-	37,102	25,809	14
Tarbert	138	-	-	53,853	47,512	-
44. Lewis						
Barvas	80	11	-	65,757	49,124	30
Carloway	46	2	-	19,657	21,047	20
Cross Ness	62	3	-	50,755	34,374	54
Kinloch	37	9	-	36,604	24,860	14
Knock	52	2	-	-	24,697	10
Lochs-Crossbost	11	1	-	20,526	17,163	4
Lochs-in-Bernera	25	1	-	-	12,670	6
Uig	28	4	-	24,558	18,108	2
Stornoway: High	78	4	-	-	77,631	12
Stornoway: Martin's Memorial	270	-	-	149,441	54,552	-
Stornoway: St Columba	137	14	49	102,575	50,146	180
45. Orkney						
Birsay, Harray and Sandwick	329	-	33	29,587	26,029	-
East Mainland	240	-	15	22,245	18,577	-
Eday	10	-	-	3,368	1,586	-
Stronsay: Moncur Memorial	81	-	-	18,593	9,166	-
Evie	23	-	-	6,086	9,506	-
Firth	94	-	-	-	17,135	-
Rendall	51	-	-	14,149	5,994	-
Rousay	17	-	-	1,720	3,304	-
Flotta	25	-	-	-	2,295	-
Hoy and Walls	55	-	15	7,000	2,967	-
Orphir and Stenness	154	-	16	24,491	13,292	-
Kirkwall: East	378	-	34	66,664	44,740	-
Shapinsay	47	-	-	9,378	4,772	-
Kirkwall: St Magnus Cathedral	560	-	27	73,651	43,876	-
North Ronaldsay	12	-	-	-	1,308	-
Sanday	64	-	9	7,561	6,925	-
Papa Westray	5	-	-	4,990	3,168	-
Westray	78	-	27	22,635	17,138	-
South Ronaldsay and Burray	147	-	14	18,938	10,655	-
Stromness	312	-	24	48,698	28,463	-
46. Shetland						
Burra Isle	36	6	20	11,007	4,831	12
Tingwall	123	14	12	29,499	20,053	-
Delting	73	7	13	-	10,289	12
Northmavine	65	8	-	-	6,268	9
Dunrossness and St Ninian's	50	-	-	15,967	12,715	-

Congregation	Com	Eld	G	In 14	M&M	–18
Sandwick, Cunningsburgh & Quarff	70	10	6	25,377	14,386	20
Fetlar	14	3	-	-	796	-
Unst	111	7	21	25,749	11,321	-
Yell	46	11	23	14,795	8,400	-
Lerwick and Bressay	361	29	-	78,344	50,793	37
Nesting and Lunnasting	31	6	15	7,288	6,121	-
Whalsay and Skerries	183	14	15	24,273	13,560	18
Sandsting and Aithsting	41	9	-	6,416	4,122	20
Walls and Sandness	31	10	-	6,215	4,712	2

47. England

Congregation	Com	Eld	G	In 14	M&M	–18
Corby: St Andrew's	249	12	37	48,554	31,697	3
Corby: St Ninian's	191	16	-	39,730	29,520	-
Guernsey: St Andrew's in the Grange	184	21	-	72,409	42,230	28
Jersey: St Columba's	118	13	-	57,765	42,697	14
Liverpool: St Andrew's	24	4	-	24,112	12,204	5
London: Crown Court	224	31	5	-	59,250	14
London: St Columba's	922	55	-	-	195,607	30
Newcastle: St Andrew's	102	17	-	-	7,525	25

INDEX OF ADVERTISERS

INDEX OF MINISTERS

NOTE: Ministers who are members of a Presbytery are designated 'A' if holding a parochial appointment in that Presbytery, or 'B' if otherwise qualifying for membership. 'A-1, A-2' etc. indicate the numerical order of congregations in the Presbyteries of Edinburgh, Glasgow, and Hamilton.

Also included are ministers listed in Section 6:

(1) Ministers who have resigned their seat in Presbytery and hold a Practising Certificate (List 6-D)

(2) Ministers who have resigned their seat in Presbytery but who do not hold a Practising Certificate (List 6-E)

(3) Ministers serving overseas (List 6-J) – see also Presbyteries 48 and 49

(4) Ordained Local Ministers and Auxiliary Ministers, who are listed both in Presbyteries and in List 6-A and List 6-B respectively

(5) Ministers who have died since the publication of the last *Year Book* (List 6-R)

NB *For a list of the Diaconate, see List 6-C.*

INDEX OF PARISHES AND PLACES

NOTE: Numbers on the right of the column refer to the Presbytery in which the district lies. Names in brackets are given for ease of identification. They may refer to the name of the parish, which may be different from that of the district, or they distinguish places with the same name, or they indicate the first named charge in a union.

INDEX OF SUBJECTS

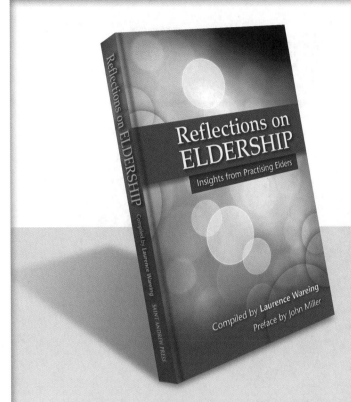

REFLECTIONS ON ELDERSHIP
INSIGHTS FROM PRACTISING ELDERS

Compiled by Laurence Wareing
Preface by John Miller

ISBN: 978-0-86153-821-8 ● paperback

Please see our website for details of this and
many other useful resources.
www.standrewpress.com

SAINT ANDREW PRESS

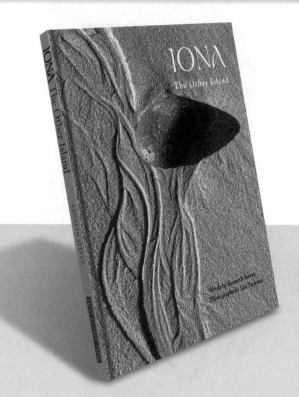

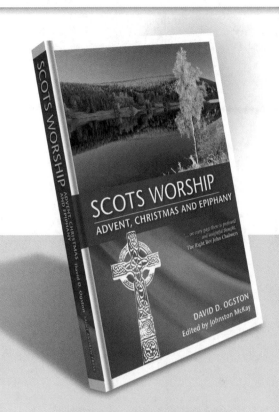